PRESSING TOWA ̶ ̶ ̶ ̶ *MARK*

J. Gresham Machen, 1881–1937

PRESSING TOWARD THE MARK

Essays Commemorating Fifty Years of the Orthodox Presbyterian Church

Edited by

Charles G. Dennison & Richard C. Gamble

The Committee for the Historian of the
Orthodox Presbyterian Church
Philadelphia · 1986

Copyright © 1986 by
The Committee for the Historian of
the Orthodox Presbyterian Church
7401 Old York Rd.
Philadelphia, Pennsylvania

Library of Congress Cataloging in Publication Data

Dennison, Charles G., ed.
Gamble, Richard C., ed.
PRESSING TOWARD THE MARK.
Essays Commemorating Fifty Years of the Orthodox Presbyterian Church.
    Includes Bibliography of J. Gresham Machen
    1. Church History— Presbyterianism
    2. American Denominations— The Orthodox Presbyterian Church
    I. Title   II. Presbyterian Church
ISBN 0-934688-36-2

Book designed by Eric D. Bristley
Olive Tree Graphics
Set in Goudy Old Style
Printed in the United States of America

Contents

Introduction   1

PART I FOUNDATIONS FOR HISTORIC PRESBYTERIANISM

1   Thoughts on the Covenant   7
     Charles G. Dennison

2   Two Offices and Two Orders of Elders   23
     George W. Knight, III

3   A Sabbath Rest Still Awaits the People of God   33
     Richard B. Gaffin, Jr.

4   Presbyterianism and the Ancient Church   53
     Richard C. Gamble

5   The Reformers' Rediscovery of Presbyterian Polity   63
     Peter A. Lillback

6   The Westminster Assembly's
     Directory for Church Government   83
     Wayne R. Spear

7   Distinctive Emphases in Presbyterian Church Polity   99
     Edmund P. Clowney

PART II THE AMERICAN PRESBYTERIAN EXPERIENCE

8   Transition to the New World   113
     Samuel T. Logan, Jr.

9   Background and Significance of the Adopting Act of 1729   131
     James R. Payton, Jr.

10   Jonathan Edwards and the New Divinity, 1758–1858   147
     Allen C. Guelzo

11   The New School Heritage and Presbyterian Fundamentalism   169
     George M. Marsden

12   Henry B. Smith: Theologian of New School Presbyterianism   183
     John R. Wiers

13   Chicago Presbyterians and the Businessman's Religion   201
     Paul H. Heidebrecht

14   John McNaugher and the Confessional Revision of 1925   221
     James T. Dennison, Jr.

PART III PERSPECTIVES ON THE ORTHODOX PRESBYTERIAN CHURCH

15   The Spirit of Old Princeton and the Spirit of the OPC   235
     Mark A. Noll

16   Machen and Liberalism   247
     D. Clair Davis

17   Machen, Van Til, and the
     Apologetical Tradition of the OPC   259
     Greg L. Bahnsen

18   Perspective on the Division of 1937   295
     George M. Marsden

19   The Battle over the Ordination of Gordon H. Clark   329
     Michael A. Hakkenberg

20   Apologetics before and after Butler   351
     Thomas M. Gregory

21   The Life and Death of a Dakota Church   369
     David W. Kiester

PART IV THE MISSION OF THE ORTHODOX PRESBYTERIAN CHURCH

22   Current Issues in Missions   391
     Laurence N. Vail

23   Taiwan and the Cross-Cultural Challenge   397
     Lendall H. Smith

24   Where Are We Going in Missions?   405
     Victor B. Atallah

25   The Ecumenical Vision of the OPC   411
     John P. Galbraith

26   The Discussion of the Theology of the Diaconate   427
     Leonard J. Coppes

27   Reflections on Professor John Murray   435
     Lawrence Eyres

28   Wheaton College and the OPC   445
     Edward L. Kellogg

29   The Church and the Harvest   449
     James D. Phillips

30   A Backward Look with a Forward Perspective   453
     David L. Neilands

PART V THE WRITINGS OF J. GRESHAM MACHEN, 1881–1937

31   A Bibliography of the Writings of J. Gresham Machen   461
     James T. Dennison, Jr., and Grace Mullen

     Contributors   487

Introduction

PRESSING TOWARD THE MARK is an offering of thanksgiving to God for the Orthodox Presbyterian Church on her fiftieth birthday. Contributors include lay persons, ruling elders, scholars, missionaries, and pastors who belong to a variety of Presbyterian and Reformed churches: the Presbyterian Church in America, the Reformed Presbyterian Church of North America, the Reformed Episcopal Church, the Christian Reformed Church, and of course the Orthodox Presbyterian Church. Despite the diversity of background, opinion, and role in the church, each writer has seasoned his "offering" with zeal for the body of Christ and has added his voice to the celebration of the Orthodox Presbyterian Church's stand for twentieth-century Protestant orthodoxy.

The spirit of such a tribute should be kept in mind as we read the different essays. I say this because we may disagree, even violently, with some of the viewpoints expressed. My objective in gathering these articles, however, has not been the presentation of a single slant on things. Instead, in keeping with the importance of the celebration, I intended this book to touch the broad strokes of Presbyterianism and reflect something of its convictions and struggles, especially as they have relevance to the OPC.

Still, the range of the various opinions may leave you bewildered. The significance of the covenant, the number of ecclesiastical offices, the meaning of the Sabbath, Calvin's doctrine of the church, Presbyterian vs. Reformed polity, the nature of subscription, the worth of Edwards and the Great Awakening, the virtues and failures of the Old School and New School Presbyterians — all these matters and others are reviewed. Added to them are questions of special interest to the OPC — questions like, what really happened in '36? what were Machen's essential theological convictions? why the division of '37 and the severe strains of the forties? what is the long-termed place of Van Tillian apologetics in the church? how unique is the Orthodox Presbyterian Church as a Presbyterian body?

With the number of issues and the disagreement about them, we ask if there has not been, *in pressing toward the mark* over the years, some progress for Presbyterians. Has no clarity or consensus appeared, or are we left with continual confusion and debate? Of course, unanimity on every issue is neither possible nor desired. Nevertheless, to use Paul's words, a good work has begun in us that is still at work until the day of Jesus Christ (Phil 1:6). In fact the Orthodox Presbyterian Church, like the church of Christ as a whole, need not hesitate to say that there is a point to which "we have already attained" (Phil 3:16). In working out her salvation with fear

1

and trembling, she gives glory to him who is at work in her to will and do of his good pleasure (Phil 2:12–13).

Specifically, God has been pleased for the OPC to stand as a statement against the twentieth-century "boast in the flesh," the cancer of liberalism. He has also made plain once more that other threats exist that attack from within the company of the biblically committed. Paul in Philippians mentions "envy and strife" (1:15), the lack of like-mindedness (2:2; 4:2); he also mentions with tears those whom he describes as "enemies of the cross" because of their earthly-mindedness (3:18–19). Opposite such things is the mind of Christ (2:5ff) and a life definable only in terms of Christ himself: "For me to live is Christ, and to die is gain" (1:21).

It is actually the latter part of Philippians 1:21 that intimates the mark at which we aim; that is, the "gain" for us in death provides the light by which we presently live. Our Christ-mindedness is impossible apart from clear sight of "the prize of the high calling of God in Christ Jesus" (3:14), apart from our desire to be "made conformable unto [Christ's] death; if by any means [we] might attain unto the resurrection of the dead" (3:10–11), apart from our hope that "our vile bodies . . . may be fashioned like unto [Christ's] glorious body" (3:21). Our citizenship is in heaven and for its sake and the sake of him whom we eagerly await (3:20), we presently suffer (1:29–30) and endure the loss of all things (3:8). We also joyfully (4:4) and wisely assess our privation and prosperity (4:12–13) and live as servants patterned after Jesus Christ (2:5ff). As such we shine as lights in the world (2:15).

But do the confusion and debate, the lack of clarity and consensus which we noted earlier extinguish the light of Presbyterianism generally and dim the light of the OPC? As I have said, the Orthodox Presbyterian Church signals a positive gain. If there is to be progress, however, if a nudge (maybe a shove) is appropriate, it must be in terms of the "mark" to which our Savior would have us press. In fact, this mark, measured by its heavenly character, may well expose one of the flaws of our heritage, the establishmentarian nature of Presbyterianism. Certain essays presented here hint at this. More fully developed it might provide as profitable a line as any for the study of the OPC and the Presbyterian movement at large.

Have we, for example, thought of ourselves a bit vainly as "world-shapers"? Have we functioned within society as a religious aristocracy and as "king-makers"? Were the Old School and New School to varying degrees establishmentarian and their theologies finally overruled by establishmentarian concerns? Was Machen blessed by the finest attainments of cultural Presbyterianism but stripped of its prestige and privilege when defrocked? Is there a scriptural censure pronounced as much upon the Presbyterian enterprise generally as upon the apostasy of the old church by the events of the thirties? In this regard, did the Orthodox Presbyterian

Church constitute a Presbyterian anomaly, her uniqueness as much a matter of her disenfranchisement as her aggressive Calvinism? Was her disenfranchisement, after all, the rock of offense over which even some of those closest to her stumbled?

And, in a different direction, is there something at the base of the OPC that suggests great promise? Can a Presbyterian church, freed of an establishment identity, better declare God's word? advise friends? warn foes? manifest a true catholicity? be a servant in the world for the sake of the Savior whose kingdom in not of this world? If it can, we dare not shrink from such a liberation but embrace it and encourage others to embrace it with us.

This book, then, is offered in the interest of *pressing toward the mark.* It rehearses the journey already past and honors present gains. I also hope it will serve as a prod to better attainments in keeping with that incomparable attainment; i.e., that we might win Christ and be found in him not having our own righteousness, which is of the law, but that which is through the faith of Christ, the righteousness which is of God by faith (Phil 3:8–9).

I wish to thank many whose contributions to this book were indispensible. Robert Tuten greatly helped me with copy editing, Eric and Kathleen Bristley with book design, manuscript preparation, and production, Alvera Billingsley with typing and proofreading, and Grace Mullen with research. John Deliyannides and Ray Gilliland provided wise counsel, and Roger Schmurr and the Committee on Christian Education of the Orthodox Presbyterian Church provided much-needed support. I also wish to thank co-editor, Dr. Richard C. Gamble. May the Lord supply all your need according to his riches in glory by Christ Jesus (Phil 4:19).

Charles G. Dennison

God is always gracious. He has been particularly gracious to us in the Orthodox Presbyterian Church. By the power of his might we have been conformed more and more to his image. This volume will hopefully help us to understand more fully who we are and where we have come from.

I wish to thank all the contributors for their time and efforts in making this volume possible. Besides the names mentioned in Mr. Dennison's introduction, and a host of thanks to him for his tireless efforts, I would like to thank especially the Rev. James Bordwine for aiding me in research and editing.

Richard C. Gamble

*Other works dealing with the history
of the Orthodox Presbyterian Church:*

Robert K. Churchill, *Lest We Forget: A Personal Reflection on the Formation of the Orthodox Presbyterian Church* (Philadelphia: The Committee for the Historian of the Orthodox Presbyterian Church, 1986).

Charles G. Dennison, ed., *The Orthodox Presbyterian Church, 1936–1986* (Philadelphia: The Committee for the Historian of the Orthodox Presbyterian Church, 1986).

Edwin H. Rian, *The Presbyterian Conflict* (Grand Rapids: Eerdmans, 1940).

Ned B. Stonehouse, *J. Gresham Machen: A Biographical Memoir* (Grand Rapids: Eerdmans, 1954).

The First Ten Years (Philadelphia: The Committee on Home Missions and Church Extension of the Orthodox Presbyterian Church, 1946).

Part I

Foundations for Historic Presbyterianism

Calvin and other Reformers

Charles G. Dennison

1 Thoughts on the Covenant

THAT THE COVENANT is important to divine revelation seems obvious enough.[1] Just how central it is, together with its meaning, significance, and goal, remains a subject of intense debate.[2] A dominant tendency has been to convert the covenant into an idea, or *principium* for either biblical or dogmatic theology rather than to see it as a dynamic and historical reality.

While written along the biblical theological line, this study wishes its readers to be drawn into the Scriptures and closer to the covenant's vital redemptive-historical center. God's people after all are not spectators but *participants* in the drama of salvation, and what follows is written by one who does not hesitate to acknowledge with deepest gratitude to his Savior his own participation in that drama.

At the same time, it should be evident that participation in the covenant is anything but solitary. Therefore God's covenant is essentially corporate or ecclesiastical. This study, while it may appear somewhat random, moves upon that assumption and concludes on a note about the structure of the church.

The covenant is pinpointed historically by its concrete appearance at specific junctures in the divine economy: e.g., the flood, Abraham's call, the exodus, the enthronement of David, the appearance and work of the Christ. These events are divine acts that uniformly call attention to God's incomparable power. They preach a unitive purpose and at the same time a transitional diversity that is meant to instruct those in the covenant about their eschatological end. In short, the covenant comes to light as an administration of the mighty King; his enemies are subdued while his people are constituted (i.e., created)[3] in blessing.

7

Concentration upon the mighty acts of God draws even the creation of the world within range of the covenant. From the beginning creation itself had an eschatological end beyond any idyllic setting of this world. This point cannot be stressed too much since many, even in Reformed circles, continue to deny a radical distinction between the eternal state of glory and man's original estate of innocence.[4] It was the eschatological end that was threatened by sin's intrusion but reasserted in the promise of a new work of God. Ultimately in view are the new heavens and earth (Isa 65:17; 66:22) in which a new song will be sung (Ps 33:3; 40:3; 96:1; 98:1; 149:9; Isa 42:10; cf. Rev 5:9) and a new everlasting covenant will be in place (Jer 31:31–34; cf. Jer 32:40; Ezek 37:26; 2 Cor 3:6; Heb 8:8 –12). Despite maintaining a grip on a basic continuity between this world and the next, the biblical language bursts the bonds of the conceivable in a vision of transcendent consummate blessing.[5]

Covenant Frame: Time and Place

The temporal-historical quality of the covenant is as fundamental as any. It is expressed by the rehearsal of God's great deeds and in the attention paid to various calculations of time (e.g., the days of creation, the Sabbath, "today," "the day of the Lord," "the days are coming," "those days," "the last days," the covenant qualifiers, "everlasting," and "forever," etc.). An era is marked by its inaugural event. In the similarities of these events there is exhibited a correspondence and an inner coherence. Each era as well possesses an inner development by which it promotes, in concert with the successive stages of redemptive development, that age beyond which there are no more.

This interplay between the inner coherence and development creates the tension of continuity and discontinuity. To be sure, we are reminded of the singularity of God's intention and the remarkable structural harmony of the covenant despite its diverse expression. Still, when the new comes, the old must give place to it or be judged in the words of 2 Corinthinans 3 as having no glory at all.[6]

God himself expresses this dynamic in his very person. On the one hand, God is one (Deut 6:4); he never changes. On the other hand, he subjects himself to the progression of his covenant by his gracious condescension. For example, he reveals himself by his new name to Moses (Exod 6:2–3), and in the Exodus he *becomes* his people's salvation (Exod 15:2). There is no proper reading of his previous covenantal dealings except in light of his new name and work. At the same time, those in each covenant era reach out to grasp the yet future fulness of God. Here the tension can be described as the "already-not yet"[7] as the people by way of the blessings of the "already" long for the fulness of the blessings and those "not yet" theirs. The patriarchs, who own no land, reach out to grasp the time when they will possess the inheritance; unsettled tribes of Israel hear about the time of permanence; the people of the exile are treated with a message about unthreatened security.

But the nature of the covenant is by no means exhausted by the historical consideration. It is also what we might call environmental and atmospheric. In a certain sense the historical is foundational and takes precedence; nevertheless, the topological sets before us the covenant's spatial descriptions.[8] Here we span the comprehensiveness of the heavens and the earth and the particularity of the land, garden, vineyard, house, throne, city, tabernacle, and temple, etc. Important in this regard is the architectural imagery of the Old Testament together with the theme of wisdom and its relationship to the building enterprise.[9]

Again, as with the temporal quality, continuity and discontinuity are very much evident. While all bear the stamp of the final dwelling place of God and his people, one dwelling contrasts and compares with another.[10] Through this process the people are taught that they are the true habitation of God and that God himself is their reward (Gen 15:1; Ps 16:5; 73:25–28) and ultimate resting place (Ps 91:1).[11] Thus, the covenantal objective is that the people of the covenant dwell (topological) with God forever (temporal).

Covenant Pulse: God With Man

Gaining clarity now are the dynamics of the covenant. To some extent, however, a bald concentration upon time and place leaves us at a distance from the covenant's heartbeat. If we say that the covenantal objective is God's people dwelling with him forever, then consideration of the people *with God* interests us here. In the context of time and place, God meets his people.[12] This meeting is due to the free act of God; he graciously condescends to establish a bond of union and communion with his own. Foundational, therefore, to the covenant is the message, "You shall be my people and I will be your God" (Lev 26:12; cf. Jer 31:1,33).

Underscored is the relational character of God's covenant. Its intimacy is the occasion of God's self-revelation which is according to his sovereign electing love. The bond between him and his people is cemented by his resolute faithfulness (i.e., it endures to all generations; Ps 119:90). Of value in this light are the various relationships among his creatures that carry witness to his devotion: the husband and wife,[13] father and son,[14] and even the image of shepherd and flock.[15] God's loving faithfulness stands in the foreground. Corollary to it is the certain curse upon those who profane and abuse his magnificent benevolence.

Seeing God's covenantal love and faithfulness drives us to consider what response his covenant produces in his people. Essential to the covenant is the reflection of God in those he has called. We are reminded of the connection in creation as man was created in God's image. Within the fallen order God sets about to restore what was defaced and marred and to grant the eschatological hope of man. When he sovereignly calls his own into covenant by his redemptive act, he binds them to be conformed to him. They are to be holy as he is holy (Lev 11:44; 19:2; note also 1 Pet 1:16).[16] Conformity means that the loving faithfulness observed in him comes to expression in them. In fact, the obligatory dimension of the covenant impresses the people with the understanding that their future in the covenant (while not the covenant itself) depends upon their obedience and conformity to their covenant Lord.

Two matters are of importance at this juncture: first the thorny problem of the covenant's conditional character, and second the controversial question about the covenant as legal arrangement.[17] Dealing with the covenant's conditional nature has been difficult because of the affront it is thought to present to the covenant's essential graciousness. Still, a denial of the conditional dimension flies in the face of what is read throughout the Old and New Testaments.[18] But what then of grace? Obviously the covenant must be considered in two directions. As unconditional it originates in God, and man's position in it can be on no other basis than God's grace.

This becomes particularly clear in the New Testament. Ultimately the covenant and the kingdom are viewed redemptive-historically; just as the works and merits of men cannot inaugurate the kingdom, neither can they establish the covenant. Furthermore, whatever "righteousness" appears to commend man in Scripture is only born of the bond with God and evidenced in a trust in which God's grace and power provide hope.[19]

Nevertheless, while such righteousness is finally the eschatological gift of God in Christ, nowhere in Scripture is the believer led to think he is without obligation to maintain or reflect it. Ironically, he "gains" what is originally given. So ironic is this arrangement that James is able to say ". . . by works is a man justified, and not by faith only" (2:24).[20]

As far as the legal arrangement is concerned, it is obvious that the covenant is wider than the company of those finally saved. Therefore, some in the covenant (as a legal arrangement) reject it; for them it is not effectual. But the covenant must also be viewed as a vital communion between God and his people in keeping with his electing and regenerating purposes. In fact this latter understanding overshadows the former. The entirety of the covenantal administration is understood from the perspective of a living fellowship. Therefore all in the covenant legally speaking are beckoned and judged by the covenant "communionally" speaking.

At issue here is not just an accounting for covenant desertion but more positively an approach to covenant children. They are in the covenant and at the same time beckoned and scrutinized by the covenant in its ideal form. The sign and seal by which they are included in the covenant is a testimony to the radical character of sin and God's grace. Far from a witness to their superiority, it evidences a common heritage in sinful humanity from which they have been separated by a gracious covenant for fellowship with God.[21]

Covenant Life: God's Word

Conformity and obedience to God call to mind the special place of the covenantal word, law, and commandment. Too often, at this point, we concentrate exclusively on the Word's directive and prescriptive aspects. We must not forget, however, its creative and constitutive role. It establishes; and in "ethical" considerations it establishes the indicative upon which the imperative is meaningful. God's Word brings into being; it gives life, and by it God acts.[22]

Furthermore, there is a comprehensiveness to the Word of God that unfortunately is truncated or denied by much modern theology.[23] It may even precede his act as if his act were the consequence or fulfillment of his Word. The Word also follows God's act in order to declare and interpret it. This comprehensiveness is observed particularly when the Word functions after the event of redemption and in its interpretive role. Here we are struck not only with its foundation-laying ability but by its architectonic character. Having made his people by his Word, God now instructs them how to live. An image at work here is that of the progression from God's triumph over his enemies and creation of his people to the building of his house and his people living in it. The covenantal word creates the atmosphere in which the blueprints (laws) are meaningful, but also delivers that explication of wisdom and pattern of praise that serve as norm for all who would dwell with God.[24]

Equally important for an understanding of the Word is its mediatorial role and its relationship to eschatology. With regard to its mediatorial connection, God reveals himself and acts by his Word. His truth and presence are communicated in his Word so that he is inseparable if not indistinguishable from it. But he sends out his mediatorial Word by his elect messengers who embody that Word and extend it into creation. Therefore, God's truth and presence are not only conveyed in the Word *per se*, but in the person of the messenger. Human messengers may fill various offices such as prophet, priest, and ruler. Heavenly beings also appear as messengers (especially the Angel of the Lord). In either case these messengers, in their proximity to God, are placed on the side of God who sends his Word to his people.[25]

Consideration of eschatology and the Word deserves a special note. First of all, the Word is an eschatological reality. It carries with it both judgment and blessing; it opens present (already) access to God as eschatological reward (not yet). In the Word the future is made present.

Furthermore, the manner in which the Word is given bears an eschatological significance. With regard to the messenger of the Word, the people are instructed in their own eschatological hope. The messenger is a picture of the future state of the redeemed. Therefore, the prophet who has access to the heavenly council of Yahweh not only announces hope but, in his person, is hope.[26] Likewise, the priest is the people's hope because they long to participate in the direct communion with God in the sanctuary that he enjoys. The king is called the son of God and as such exhibits the exaltation the people of God anticipate.

The medium of the Word also relates to eschatology. Inscripturation marks the Word with a permanence and constancy that reflects eternity. In fact, the transition from the oral to the written Word proclaims the transition from this age to the age to come. In this regard it would be well to take exception to the "historicistic" claim for the primacy of the oral tradition. Not that the Scripture itself ever divides the speaking and writing of God's Word in the manner some critics do. Still, the written Word bears a distinct eschatological stamp that grants it an elevated and even incomparable position for the people of God.

Covenant Mind: Devotion and Identity

Against the background of these considerations much can be said about the inner disposition of the covenant people. We might think, first of all, of the summary of covenantal obedience: to love the Lord God with the whole heart, soul, and might (Deut 6:5). This love is joined in Israel to a regard for one's neighbor. Therefore, Israel, no less than the New Testament church, is created unto good works; she must demonstrate mercy and kindness to the stranger, widow, and orphan (Isa 1:17,23; Jer 5:28; Ezek 22:7; Zech 7:10). Such displays of grace have their origin in God (cf. Ps 10:14; 68:5; 146:9). Again we touch the issue of imitation or conformity (cf. Deut 10:17–19).

The covenant mind is also thoroughly conscious of the divine election by which God has separated a people to himself (Exod 19:4–6; Deut 7:6 –8). Israel is set apart from the world, a treasure people for God. The ground of her uniqueness is not her own merit or attractiveness, but God's seemingly inexplicable choice. He offers no other explanation than his love. As a result, Israel's attitude can never be haughtiness or presumption. Her separation from the world must find its expression in her humble service before her creator. She must be what she is by her call (election): a holy nation to God.

Three things are important in this regard. First, Israel's separation from the world should not be read along the lines of a sacred/secular distinction. The thought is not that Israel must live in two realms, but that as a holy nation her life is understood as wholly consecrated to God. At no point can she disassociate herself from the one to whom she belongs. Therefore, she is called upon to understand that the distinction is made between her and the nations in the totality of her existence.

Secondly, Israel is not to forsake the Lord in order to be conformed to the other nations. While this is understood clearly enough, the matter is clouded by what appear to be borrowings from other cultures. To name just a few areas, we think of the ancient suzerain treaties, the wisdom literature, and the Babylonian mythical poems. Many believe that in each of these areas Israel was guilty of direct pilfering of pagan formats. This whole question is a study in its own right but sufficiently complex as to shortcut the supposition that Israel naively incorporated these structures.

Undoubtedly in each of these areas the objective was in large measure didactic. Covenant forms were not invented by Hittites or any other civilization. Scripture grounds covenant in the person and work of God. What is called covenant is part and parcel of the structure of reality. If there are similarities between the structure of God's dealing with Israel and the treaties of nations, it is because of common origin. The nations are degenerative, while God's relationship with Israel is remedial. When God makes covenant with Israel, he not only sanctifies a people but a "form."

The same can also be said about the wisdom literature and the similarities in Scripture to Mesopotamian mythology. Regarding the latter and taking as an example Habakkuk 3, we are not witnessing an unholy and unimaginative dependence upon pagan material. Instead the prophet has wrestled glory from gods who are no gods and affirmed that the glory the Chaldean wishes to ascribe to his deities can only be rightly ascribed to the true God. In this way the prophet employs his own program of "demythologizing" which leaves the myth no reality and his own testimony no myth. As a result, the Scripture is not evidence for the compromise of the covenant mind but just the opposite. A bold antithetical perspective is rigorously and consistently at work.

Finally, it must be emphasized that Israelite uniqueness was never an end in itself. Neither was the land of Canaan. Nevertheless the law actually became viewed as in the service of both. Eventually, contention erupted with the later prophets reacting strenuously against the mistaken notions abroad in the people. Those described as false prophets hid in the law and especially in its ritualistic expression. At the same time, they preached a better tomorrow in the land and the message of Jewish invincibility and world domination. Such misconstructions brought to light the sharpest definition of suffering service and messianic humiliation.[27] They also prepared the way for a more thorough presentation of the qualitative view of the law in place of the merely quantitative view held by much of Judaism.[28]

Before leaving our discussion of the covenant mind, we want to think more about the Messiah and the corporate character of his relationship with his people. We recognize that the Messianic servant and those whom he serves are intrinsically united (Isa 53:4–8, 10–12). In fact, we note that the representative heads of the people are more than individuals. They have a corporate dimension; they reach beyond themselves and embody whole groups and peoples.[29]

One place this is particularly clear is with Jacob and Esau. Rebekah is told she has two nations in her womb (Gen 25:23). Later we read, "Esau is Edom" (36:8), while Jacob is called Israel (32:28). The life of their descendants is bound up in them, and before their people live their life, that life, as it were, is played out in each of the tribal heads.

Abraham's life is quite comprehensive. His life can be interpreted as a survey of Israel's history. He comes out of Ur to Canaan, descends into Egypt, returns through the Negev, separates from Lot, witnesses invasion by "Babylon" and the restoration of the tribe.[30]

This corporate dimension is likewise observed during the days of the monarchy. We hear repeatedly of how the nation was determined by the life of its rulers for good or ill. Also, the psalmist speaks for the covenant people and the prophets are bound up in those who share in common faith the same expectation, i.e., their disciples (cf. Isa 8:18).

Such a perspective is of great significance for each Israelite. Not only is he tied up in the various figure of headship but he is also enabled to overcome great gaps in time. It matters little, for instance, how many generations removed he is from Jacob; Jacob is still his father (Deut 26:5). By the same token, it does not matter that the original Exodus generation has died out in the wilderness; Moses is able to speak to the next generation as if it were the congregation at Sinai (Deut 5:1ff.; esp. v 3-4). Nor does it matter how far removed one is from the initial Passover, he is always able to say, "This is what the Lord did for *me* when *I* came out of Egypt" (Exod 13:8; Deut 6:20–25). And we must not forget, Israel's vision cannot be restricted to the past. The vistas of the future are also opened. The people in the plains of Moab are addressed as if they cover the full range of Israel's history from Horeb through the exile (Deut 4:15–31).

By way of the extension of personality, therefore, an immediacy of involvement is preserved with both persons and events determinative for the people as a whole. We might also say the people as a whole are as one man with a single history. Life and individuality within Israel find their orientation within this context.

Moving from the historical to the personal, even the distance between the Israelite and his neighbor is overcome. To love one's neighbor as oneself (Lev 19:18) is to see the whole people as a single person and an extension of one's self. As a result, when one is blessed, all are blessed; when one suffers, all suffer.

Of course, all of these considerations come to rest in the Messiah and his people. He has an incomparable position in the history of salvation in which he parallels but supercedes Adam (cf. Romans 5 and 1 Corinthians 15). In him, his people have died and been raised (Romans 6). They are even ascended with him in glory (Ephesians 1); and from there, hid as they are in him, they participate in his appearance in glory (Colossians 3). The New Testament addresses its audience as if it spans the entire age from Christ's coming to his return. Therefore, it does not matter how far removed in time any particular generation of believers is from the New Testament events or where they live with respect to the end; they are addressed as dwelling in the same redemptive-historical epoch. As Vos says, "[W]e know full well that we ourselves live just as much in the New Testament as did Peter and Paul and John."[31] We are also that final generation upon which the end of the ages has come (1 Cor 11:11); it is the last hour (1 John 2:18).

Covenant Development: Type and Topic

The question of covenant development is hotly debated. This is true not simply because of disagreements over the relationship between the testaments but because of the difficulty in assessing the inner testamental progress. Obviously, we are drawn at first to the pivotal transitional events (i.e., the flood, the exodus, the establishment of the monarchy, the exile). Passing through the periods marked out by these events, we witness the progress of God's revelation of himself in his relationship with his people.

But as that development peaks we observe Israel overshadowed by the pressures of the eternal. Land and sanctuary fall under judgment and are lost and destroyed. The prophets, while announcing God's covenantal justice, also bring hope of an estate that will never be lost nor diminished. Actually, their call for moral and ritual renovation became perfunctory. Needed was not repair to the old; not the refurbishing of the Mosaic theocracy, but the revelation of the transcendent kingdom of God.[32] Repentance, therefore, is not to preserve the people's place in the land but to prepare them for God's eternal presence in glory. Faith is always that by which God's ultimate intention is grasped, and God's gift of himself as refuge and reward is perceived (Hab 2:4; note also Heb 11:1,6).

At a closer look, the development of the covenant can be explicated even more finely. Comparative study of the different periods of covenantal history brings to light the typological structure of revelation. Besides demonstrating an awareness of the boundaries for this provocative discipline, the exegete must have firmly in mind the definitive character of the biblical type. Here his sensitivity to the historical will be tested. The temptation is to allow typology to live at the level of the symbolic and representational. Such a tendency is more pagan than scriptural. Not only does it dehistoricize the type, but it suggests that the type, on the one hand, is disassociated from the reality to which it points; or on the other, lost in it. For the pagan the symbol stood in the place of the reality or became strictly identified with it.[33] Properly handled, however, typology accents the historical dimension of revelation, insists upon the historicalness of the biblical figures and events, and emphasizes that these figures and events in their historicity are means of divine revelation and grace.[34]

The covenant's development can be studied from many perspectives.[34] One perspective of great importance for an essay in honor of the Orthodox Presbyterian Church is that of the movement toward the establishment of "God's kingdom-house" and its polity.[35] Following Meredith G. Kline, we note that the house of God was constituted under divine law. This law then addresses itself to three distinct stages.[36] First comes the period of actual constitution: the covenant is made through the one mediator and preliminary steps are taken toward the covenant's goal. This is the time of the wilderness wanderings and Transjordan conquests. The people move with their tents with the God who lives in his.

The second stage sees the people under the charismatic leadership of Joshua and the Judges settle in the land and displace their enemies. But this period remains one of flux. Enemies still survive. Disorder and individualism are rampant. Also, there is that disjunction between God and the people in that they live in houses and he lives in a tent. The period cries out for something more.

It is the third stage which has the stamp of permanence. God, through his chosen servant, has subdued the enemies within the land, and now his victory house is built. The temple testifies to the covenant's goal — the permanent dwelling of God with his people. It also speaks of the maturity of covenantal order and zeal as prescription for both praise and wisdom adorn the abode of God with man. (The significance of the Psalter and wisdom literature once more surfaces.) These prescriptions amplify the original covenant bond and give expression to the norms for conduct in God's household. Still, as the prophets make clear, even this stage which bears the stamp of permanence, was only relative.[37] It, together with all of the stages of covenant development, anticipates the full revelation of God in Christ and the final eternal dwelling of God with his people in the Spirit.

When we turn to the New Testament, we immediately perceive the parallels. What was extended over more than a thousand years in the Old Testament is now condensed into less than one hundred in the New. Yet the New Testament's comprehensiveness matches that of the previous administration. Therefore, we identify the period of constitution and covenant-making with the New Testament gospels. They are "foundation to the building of the house of God over which Jesus was set as a Son."[38] Stage two is that of transition and community expansion.[39] At the heart of this period is the charismatic leadership of the church. To continue the imagery of the building enterprise, the house of God is *being* built during this time. Finally, there appears "the stable, permanent stage of church order."[40] The house is viewed as built, and now it must be occupied and managed.

This appears to be a very profitable line to pursue in many regards, but especially as it affords a better grasp of ecclesiastic structure and office. For example, Kline's suggestion has monumental importance for the much-maligned pastoral epistles. Their difference in style and content is predictable on the basis of an intra-covenantal progression comparable to that of the Old Testament. They are to be viewed against the background of God's establishment of the Old Testament "kingdom-house"; e.g., the temple and its order (1 Tim 3:15). The familial references should be understood more along these lines than as strictly domestic; e.g., the so-called Greco-Roman *Haustafel*[41] and the house church model.[42] The repeated call to godliness arises from consideration of behavior fit for those who live in God's new temple. The controversial question of who should teach in the church finds its orientation here. Therefore, even though all God's people[43] — not simply the priests as in the Old Testament — have access to the presence of the Lord, not all are capable (1 Tim 1:6–7; 3:2) or endowed (1 Tim 4:14) or permitted (2:10ff.) to teach.

Another profitable line to pursue concerns Presbyterians specifically. Over the last century Presbyterians have lost their grip on former commitments that inspired their forefathers to maintain an Old Testament foundation for New Testament offices. The tendency has been to imagine church offices as "dropping down out of heaven," more a product of the Spirit's ingenuity, or of convenience and organizational pressure than of reflection upon or pressures from the *whole* of revelation. The "three (plus) office" view and such practices as reserving for the minister the right of preaching of the Word, the administration of the sacraments, and pronouncing the benediction were not testimony of a residual Catholicism but of study of the Scriptures in their entirety. The suggestion that the New Testament church, like the temple before it, rises under the sign "God's kingdom-house," provides entrance to forgotten doors and access to a deeper appreciation of the church's covenantal and traditional Presbyterian structure.

NOTES

1. Reformed orthodoxy has been generally looked upon as espousing covenant theology. Its hermeneutic has endeavored to do justice to the covenantal structure of the whole of revelation in such a way as to exhibit the underlying unity of the plan of salvation; cf. John Calvin, *Institutes of the Christian Religion*, ed. Ford L. Battles, Volume 1 (Philadelphia: Westminster Press, 1960), 42ff.; *Westminster Confession of Faith*, VII; Geerhardus Vos, "The Doctrine of the Covenant in Reformed Theology," *Redemptive History and Biblical Interpretation: The Shorter Writings of Geerhardus Vos*, ed. Richard B. Gaffin, Jr. (Nutley, N.J.: Presbyterian and Reformed, 1980), 234–67; John Murray, *The Covenant of Grace* (London: Tyndale, 1954); cf. Meredith G. Kline, *By Oath Consigned* (Grand Rapids: Eerdmans, 1968), esp. pp. 13–38; C. K. Campbell, *God's Covenant* (n.p.: Presbyterian and Reformed, 1974); O. Palmer Robertson, *The Christ of the Covenants* (Grand Rapids: Baker, 1980); Mark W. Karlberg, "Reformed Interpretation of the Mosaic Covenant," *Westminster Theological Journal* 43 (1980):1–57. For a recent discussion of the covenant as it has been understood in the

Christian Reformed Church, see Anthony A. Hoekema's "The Christian Reformed Church and the Covenant," *Perspectives on the Christian Reformed Church: Studies in its History, Theology and Ecumenicity*, ed. Peter De Klerk and Richard R. De Ridder (Grand Rapids: Baker, 1983), 185–201.

2. Those familiar with the literature listed in note 1 know that, even within Reformed orthodoxy, discussion of the covenant is anything but a "peaceful kingdom." In critical circles the debate focuses on the work of Walter Eichrodt [*Theology of the Old Testament* (Philadelphia: Westminster Press, 1961, 65] who contends that the theological center of the Old Testament is found in the covenant. Reaction to Eichrodt has been severe; cf. the discussions in Herbert F. Hahn, *The Old Testament in Modern Research* (Philadelphia: Fortress, 1966), 233ff.; Gerhard Hasel, *Old Testament Theology: Basic Issues in the Current Debate* (Grand Rapids: Eerdmans, 1972), 49–63; Ronald E. Clements, *One Hundred Years of Old Testament Interpretation* (Philadelphia: Westminster Press, 1976), 128ff. Compounding the debate for both Reformed orthodoxy and the critical schools has been the archeological discoveries relating to ancient Near Eastern treaties; cf. George E. Mendenhall, *Law and Covenant in Israel and the Ancient Near East* (Pittsburgh: The Biblical Colloquium, 1955); Meredith G. Kline, *The Treaty of the Great King* (Grand Rapids, Eerdmans, 1963); D. J. McCarthy, *Treaty and Covenant* (Rome: Pontifical Biblical Institute, 1963); Delbert R. Hillers, *Covenant: The History of a Biblical Idea* (Baltimore: Johns Hopkins, 1969); D. J. McCarthy, *Old Testament Covenant* (Atlanta: John Knox, 1972).

3. Cf. Ps 100:3; Mal 2:10; the New Testament doctrine of the new creation in Christ is germane, 2 Cor 5:17.

4. This is apparent in S. G. De Graaf's *Promise and Deliverance* volumes [cf. my review of Volume 3, *Westminster Theological Journal* 43 (1980)1:208–11]. Note also John H. White, who says, "The Bible tells us how God is moving to restore man to the garden of Eden and to his place as vicegerent in God's world" [Found in "Approaching the Bible for Study," *The Book of Books: Essays on the Scripture in Honor of Johannes G. Vos*, ed. John H. White (n.p.: Presbyterian and Reformed, 1978), 14]. Interestingly Geerhardus Vos, the father of the man to whom White dedicates his article, expounded so magnificently a contrary view; cf. Vos's *The Pauline Eschatology* (Princeton: published by the author, 1930) and the overlooked, if not misunderstood chapter, "The Content of Pre-redemptive Special Revelation," *Biblical Theology* (Grand Rapids: Eerdmans, [1975]), 27–40.

5. The "realistic" language of the Bible prophecy, in its particularity provides the grist for postmillenarian as well as premillenarian mills; cf. note 7. In a sardonic way it also does the same for liberals.

6. Nothing less than this is coming to expression in Jesus' understanding of his ministry (cf. Mark 2:18–22).

7. As the final goal is in view, especially for the prophets, the "not yet" is read through the figures and images of the current period.

8. An analysis of Genesis 1–4 can be instructive at this point. These chapters are divided into two sections: 1:1–2:3 and 2:4–4:26 taking the characteristic phrase, "These are the generations of . . ." as pivotal. The dominant feature of the first section is its generality with regard to place and its *specific* concentration on the temporal in the succession of days. Even the inaugural, "In the beginning," asserts a temporal dominance and context for the heavens and the earth. But what was dominant in Gen 1:1-2:3 becomes subordinate in Gen 2:3–4:26. Concentration is now upon the spatial and descriptions of time become non-specific.

This structure may well determine an axiomatic hermeneutic principle. Far from historicism's tendency of absolutizing the historical, the Bible, nevertheless, lays the foundation of revelation in its fundamental temporal quality so that the spatial consideration of intimate fellowship and exchange (language) must be appreciated from this base. Stated even more tersely the language of revelation and the experience of communion with God have an historical setting which is denied and ignored only to the detriment of a proper hermeneutic.

9. God by wisdom builds the worlds (Prov 8:22–31); Moses is blessed with Bezalel and Oholiab, men filled with wisdom, for building the tabernacle (Exod 35:30–35); Solomon in his wisdom builds the temple in Jerusalem (2 Chr 1,2).

10. Cf. Edmund P. Clowney, "The Final Temple," *Westminster Theological Journal* 35 (1973):156–89. Important here as well is the juxtaposition of pilgrim and citizen imagery in the Bible; there is a tension between the movement of God's people and their permanence.

11. The Levites who had no inheritance but God are a picture of the peoples' eschatological end (Num 18:20; Deut 18:2; Josh 13:33; Ezek 44:28).

12. The tabernacle is even called the tent of meeting (Exod 30:32). Note also the centrality of this theme in Gen 2:4–4:26. So central is it that the fall itself is portrayed as a breach and thus the poignancy of the "call" in 4:26.

The repair of the breach in the time of Moses focuses on sacrifice and atonement. The meeting of God with his people, therefore, is sealed with blood. So fundamental is this that later we are told, "Without the shedding of blood there is no remission" (Heb 9:22). Jesus likewise summarizes his entire ministry from the vantage point of his atoning death: ". . . the Son of man came not to be ministered unto, but to minister, and to give his life a ransom for many" (Mark 10:45).

13. Isa 54:5; Jer 3:1,6–10,14; 31:32; Hos 1:2; 3:1.

14. Exod 4:22; Deut 1:31; 8:5; Isa 1:2; 63:16; 64:8; Jer 31:9; Ezek 16:1–14; Hos 11:1.

15. Ps 23:1; 77:20; 78:52; 80:1; 95:7; 100:3; Isa 40:11; Jer 31:10; Ezek 34:11–13,30,31.

16. Cf. Calvin's arguments for the motivations for Christian life, "From what foundation may righteousness better arise than from the Scriptural warning that we must be made holy because our God is holy?" *Institutes*, Volume 1, 685.

17. Cf. the discussion of Vos's view of the covenant in Hoekema, 186–89.

18. For example, reading the fifth petition of the Lord's Prayer, or the warnings of Hebrews as somehow "hypothetical" is exegetically irresponsible.

19. Such has been the clear-headed perspective of Reformed people. Their adamant rejection of Pelagianism and Arminianism has been expressed in classic form by Benjamin B. Warfield in *The Plan of Salvation* (Grand Rapids: Eerdmans [1966]); cf. R. B. Kuiper *To Be or Not to Be Reformed* (Grand Rapids: Zondervan, 1959), especially his statement, "Whatever contribution man makes to his salvation, he makes by the grace of God" (p. 180).

Confirmation of this viewpoint even comes from what might be considered surprising sources; e.g., in treating the very knotty exegetical issue of the "Psalmist's boast" in Ps 18:20–24, J. W. Rogerson and J. W. McKay say, "The Lord delights in his servant because he is faithful. This is not an arrogant statement of self-righteousness, nor a claim to sinlessness, for the psalmist knows that both his strength and his blamelessness come from God himself (v 32). His theme is God's unfailing loyalty to those who are loyal to him (v 25) and in this section he pleads his own fidelity. Nor is this a matter of boasting, for he is completely aware of his own weakness and of the need for humility (v 27). His only boast is in God who saved him when he was utterly helpless." *Psalms 1–50: The Cambridge Commentary* (Cambridge: Cambridge University, 1977), 79–80.

20. Charges that James and Paul contradict each other must be dismissed because of passages where Paul says virtually the same thing as James. Of importance here is Gal 5:6 and the so-called "indicative and imperative" of the Pauline doctrine of the Christian life, most noticeably expressed in his discussions of the "new man" in Ephesians and Colossians, cf. the section below, "Covenant Mind: Devotion and Identity."

21. Cf. the treatment of circumcision by Geerhardus Vos in *Biblical Theology*, 88–90.

22. We cannot overlook at this point the importance of the Holy Spirit. After all, it is of the Spirit that Jesus says, "It is the Spirit who gives life" (John 6:63). Not that the Spirit is to be separated from the Word since that very passage drives on to Peter's confession, "Lord . . . thou hast the words of eternal life" (v 68). Neither are we permitted to employ Paul's distinctions of "letter" and "Spirit" in 2 Corinthians 3 for the purposes of denigrating

the Word. Indeed, "the ministry of the Spirit" (v 8) and "of righteousness [exceeding] in glory" (v 9) is the apostolic ministry which does not "corrupt the Word of God" and *speaks* in Christ in the sight of God (2:17). Such a ministry, contends the apostle, comes in "plainness of speech" (3:12), with proper handling of the Word of God (4:2), and by the preaching of Christ (4:5).

23. Such a view of the Word is in keeping with the most sound orthodoxy. Properly expounded, this position exposes the myopic and anemic view of neo-orthodoxy which in its preoccupation with dynamism makes word and event synonymous. For a fierce and penetrating critique of neo-orthodoxy, see Cornelius Van Til's *The New Modernism* (Philadelphia: Presbyterian and Reformed, 1946).

24. Cf. the Psalter and wisdom literature of the Old Testament. One of the difficulties in arguing the covenantal perspective on the Old Testament has been the place the Old Testament wisdom literature is to have. Can it be related at all? Many have charged that the redemptive-historical approach to Scripture must fail since the Scriptures possess many types of material, only some of which has anything to do with the development of redemptive history.

25. This observation is as applicable to the New Testament as it is to the Old; it offers an avenue of criticism against the redaction criticism method which has made the Word more the product of the community than that of the transcendent God of the Scriptures.

26. Consider the prophet's access to the heavenly counsel of the Lord; cf. Jer 23:18; note also Isaiah's vision in Isaiah 6.

27. Given the situation of Jerusalem at the end of the eighth century, it seems unrealistic to deny its genuine prophets a well-developed understanding of the "suffering servant." The false shepherds of Isaiah's and Micah's day lacked the ability to lead the people through humiliation. Expectation, says Micah, must be trained so as to recognize the Judge who undergoes suffering before glory arises from obscurity (4:14–5:3). Micah himself speaks vicariously in his famous "I" passages (1:8; 3:8; 6:6–8; 7:7) and Israel (the northern tribes) is seen as the one who bears the reproach of God's people (6:16).

28. See Herman Ridderbos's discussion in *When the Time Had Fully Come* (Grand Rapids: Eerdmans, 1957), 62–66.

29. Cf. A. R. Johnson, *The One and the Many in the Israelite Conception of God* (Cardiff: University of Wales, 1942); also his *The Vitality of the Individual in the Thought of Ancient Israel* (Cardiff: University of Wales, 1949). Cf. the bibliography in H. Wheeler Robinson's *Corporate Personality in Ancient Israel* (Philadelphia: Fortress Press, [1980]), 63–64.

30. In the hands of a Christian exegete, Abraham encompasses the entire history of redemption, demonstrating in his person the transition from the era of Israel to the era of faith; cf. Paul's treatment of Abraham in Galatians 3.

31. Vos, *Biblical Theology*, 303; cf. also the diagram by Vos in *The Pauline Eschatology*, 38.

Vos's fundamental insight continues to be ignored or denied in much of modern biblical interpretation. Bultmann is the most ruthlessly consistent in this regard. His hermeneutic assumes as axiomatic the qualitative difference between the New Testament age and our own. The distance is overcome only by an "event" of self-understanding, called a *Krisis*, in which twentieth-century man is linked with man in the first century in a common humanness. The New Testament is made relevant through a radical program of demythologizing.

Oddly enough modern evangelicalism in large measure has a similar hermeneutic. It as well as Bultmann operates on the axiom of the qualitative difference between our time and the New Testament. The route by which it overcomes the distance is that of "application." This method has distinct advantages. It appeals to modern man in his setting; and putting it in the very best light , it does this out of love for those in need of the gospel. It has a popular ring which lends to it a relevance and appeal.

Unfortunately this approach is essentially lethal because of its rejection of the basic structure of divine revelation. In its worst expressions it is hopelessly faddish. Even among those who are more sane in its exposition we find an endless preoccupation with the trivial.

There is even a propensity for a new form of legalism. The "how-to" mania within contemporary evangelicalism has no biblical counterpart except by way of the most skewed exegesis if any exegesis is thought necessary at all. Attempts to gain respect for such silliness through appeals to psychology and sociology or even the sophisticated "science" of ethics merely accent the banality to those with a discerning eye.

It is no secret that our times have witnessed the triumph of the practical and practical theology. Neither is it a secret that on this very ground liberalism and evangelicalism joined hands earlier in this century. As a result "anthropology" displaced "theology"; the well-managed programs of men displaced the "methods" of the gospel; and the church was tragically ripped apart.

Over against this agenda stands Vos's observation. Its simple truth is a door to an entire world of Christian maturity in keeping with the best of Reformed and covenantal reflection.

32. Vos, *Biblical Theology*, 189.

33. The same difficulty arises in connection with the biblical use of the word "sign." It is easy to see that more than an approach to type and sign is in the balance. Directly related is an understanding of the sacraments. Reformed theology, therefore, sees the sacraments neither as mere representation nor strict identity while Catholics have held to strict identity and many Baptists to representation.

34. Biblical theologians have organized the Old Testament around various foci; e.g., Edmond Jacob around the names of God in *Theology of the Old Testament* (New York: Harper & Row, 1958); Ernest Sellin around the theme of holiness in *Theologie des Alten Testaments* (Leipzig: Teubner, 1933); Ludwig Kohler around God's kingship in *Old Testament Theology* (Philadelphia: Westminster Press, 1957); John Bright around the kingdom itself in *The Kingdom of God* (Nashville: Abingdon, 1953); O. Palmer Robertson around messianic expectation in *The Christ of the Covenant*.

35. Meredith G. Kline, *The Structure of Biblical Authority* (Grand Rapids: Eerdmans, 1972), 103.

36. Ibid., 103ff.

37. Ibid., 103.

38. Ibid., 106.

39. Ibid.

40. Ibid.

41. Cf. David C. Verner, *The Household of God: The Social World of the Pastoral Epistles* (Decatur, GA: Scholars Press, 1983).

42. Cf. Robert Banks, *Paul's Idea of Community: The Early House Churches in their Historical Setting* (Grand Rapids: Eerdmans, 1980). A most disturbing feature of this book (and there are many) is its failure throughout to do justice to the Old Testament background of the church.

43. Here seems to be the force of 1 Tim 2:1–7 and its repeated use of the inclusive "all" (vv 1,4,6); note Paul's specific reference to his ministry to the Gentiles (v 7); e.g., even the Gentiles enter God's new temple.

George W. Knight, III

2 Two Offices and Two Orders of Elders

JESUS CHRIST IS LORD AND HEAD of the church which is his body. He rules over the church by his Word and Spirit. Through the work of the Spirit he gives to his church men as officers to equip believers for service in order that the church may more faithfully serve Christ in maturity and love (Eph 4:11ff.). Through his Word, the Bible, he specifies the qualifications and duties of those men so that his people may recognize, elect, and appoint such men and acknowledge Christ's rule in and through them (1 Tim 3; Titus 1). In this way the Scriptures provide the description of the offices (or officers) that Christ gives to his church. They also serve as the only infallible guide for the church in recognizing those offices and those who serve in them.

The Word, therefore, lays down the qualifications of such servants and gives them descriptive titles or designations that indicate the functions they are to fulfill in the church. In so designating these offices by specific titles and differentiated functions, Scripture provides the church the answer to the question: What offices does Christ continue to give to the church and how many are there?

Answers to this question have varied in the history of the Christian church and particularly in the Presbyterian church. Among Presbyterians, the answer has tended toward one of two conclusions: (1) a three-office view in which the clergy (teaching offices) are distinguished from lay ruling officers (elders) and deacons (lay serving officers); and (2) a two-office view in which elders (teaching and ruling, clergy and lay officers) are distinguished from deacons (lay serving officers).

Proponents of each view have been vigorous in their advocacy and have produced extreme polarizations. Some three-office advocates have gone so

23

far as to state that the references to elders or bishops in the New Testament apply only to ministers and not to ruling elders. Reference to ruling elders is restricted to "helps" and/or "administrations" (or "governments") as in 1 Cor 12:28. Responsibility here is limited to ruling or administration and does not include any form of teaching. On the other hand, some two-office advocates have stated that there is no distinction within the office of elder at all, such as is commonly designated by teaching elder and ruling elder, or by minister and ruling elder.

The basis for these two positions in not hard to find. The New Testament uses only two titles for church officers (cf. Phil 1:1; 1 Tim 3:1-2,8,12). But it also describes these officers by way of three functions; that is, teaching, ruling, and serving (cf. 1 Tim 3:2 [teaching], 5 [ruling or caring], 13 [serving]). The two-office advocates have emphasized the fact that the offices may be designated by two titles only, elders (or bishops) and deacons. Three-office advocates have capitalized on the three functions and insisted that the offices should correspond to them; namely, teaching (ministers), ruling (ruling elders) and serving (deacons).

The thesis of this study is that the solution to this apparent dilemma is found in the fact that there are indeed two titles for church officers, elders (or bishops) and deacons; but also that within the offices of elder there are two functions. Furthermore, the teaching function may be given in a heightened way or as a special gift to some but not to all the elders. Therefore, a distinction may be made within the office of elder, designating some as teachers (or ministers) as the New Testament does.

The study that follows examines the biblical texts and seeks to demonstrate that the thesis proposed is indeed true. The first portion studies the two offices in Scripture. It emphasizes that the term "elders" (or "bishops") is used in the plural and embraces all the governors or rulers in the church. The second half of the study directs attention to the distinction within the one office of elder and indicates that there are some who labor in the Word and teaching.

Before going any further, however, it would be well to say a word about the continuation of the offices of apostle and prophet. Christ does not continually give to the church those special and extraordinary offices. The apostles of Jesus Christ are those personally and directly chosen by him (Mark 3:14; Luke 6:13; Gal 1:1), who were eyewitnesses of his resurrection (Acts 1:22; 1 Cor 15:8–10). With the prophets they are the special recipients of revelation (Eph 3:5) and thus form the non-repeatable foundation of the church (Eph 2:20). These two offices, since they have accomplished their unique and non-repeatable functions and tasks, occur only during the foundation days of the church, the New Testament age. They are not now found in the growing and continuing superstructure of the church (cf. 1 Pet 2:15ff.). What offices then do continue?

TWO OFFICES

Moving beyond the apostles and prophets, we find that the offices which Christ continues to give his church are sometimes referred to without a specific name or title but simply by their function and activity (cf. Heb 13:7,17; 1 Thess 5:12–13). Sometimes different words (elders, pastors and teachers, bishops [or overseers]) are used to describe the ministry in view. In the midst of this variegated usage, two terms (elders or bishops) are used throughout the New Testament, in Acts (11:30; 14:23; 15:2,4,6,22 –23; 16:4; 20:17,28) and by Paul (Phil 1:1; 1 Tim 3:1-2; 5:17; Titus 1:5,7), Peter (1 Pet 5:1), and James (5:14). These include the other terms and the descriptions of functions that relate to oversight.

On two occasions we find a third term, deacons, used alongside of this pervasive use of elders/bishops (Phil 1:1; 1 Tim 3:12). We thus find three terms used in a more or less technical sense to describe offices. They are elders (*presbyteroi*), bishops (*episkopoi*), and deacons (*diakonoi*). The first two refer to the same group of men and thus are different words for the same office. We can therefore speak of the New Testament as referring to elders or bishops on the one hand and deacons on the other, and thereby grouping the offices into these two categories.[1]

Elders or Bishops

That two words, elders and bishops, refer to the same office is clear from the following passages: Acts 20:17,28; Titus 1:5,7; and a comparison of 1 Tim 3:1ff. and 1 Tim 5:17. In Acts 20:17 the elders are called from Ephesus to meet with Paul. In Acts 20:28 Paul designates that same group as bishops or overseers (*episkopoi*). He later directs Titus to appoint elders in every city (Titus 1:5) and then goes on to describe those same officers as bishops or overseers (Titus 1:7). In 1 Tim 3:2 he uses the term bishop to speak of the office of those who teach and rule the church (1 Tim 3:2,5). When he returns to the question of the remuneration for those who rule and spend their full time in the occupation of teaching the church, he calls them elders or presbyters (1 Tim 5:17).

In light of this evidence, we see that the terms, elders and bishops, designate the same office in the church. Elder or presbyter reflects particularly the Old Testament background and usage and refers to the maturity and authority of the person in view. Bishop or overseer, a term common to the Greek-speaking world, designates the office in its particular responsibility for oversight and care of the church.

These terms encompass the other designations found in the New Testament for the same activities or functions. This is most evident in 1 Pet 5:1 where even the Apostle Peter speaks of himself as a fellow elder since he shares with the elders responsibility for the oversight of the people of God. This is also apparent in Acts 15 where the decision rendered comes from the apostles and elders acting together and sharing the oversight

(15:2,4,6,22–23; 16:4). Elsewhere, ordination or laying on of hands is by the presbytery (1 Tim 4:14), that is, the elders considered as a group. The presbytery included the Apostle Paul (2 Tim 1:6). In Acts 13:1–3 the men who lay on hands are specifically designated as prophets and teachers.

Furthermore, we should note that the officers in the church at Ephesus are called elders or bishops in Acts 20:17,28, 1 Tim 3:1, and 5:17, and evangelists and pastors and teachers in Eph 4:11. Since apostles are fellow elders, and prophets and teachers perform the action of presbytery by laying on of hands, and since Acts, 1 Timothy, and Ephesians refer to the same church and the same officers, we may properly infer as a "good and necessary consequence" that evangelists, pastors, and teachers are elders. Certainly the Ephesians passage regards them as leaders who equip the church, a ministry recognized elsewhere as the particular responsibility of elders (cf. among others, Acts 20:28; 1 Tim 3:4–5; 5:17).

Also borne out by the New Testament is the fact that the elders/bishops are always considered as a group of men who share the two responsibilities involved in oversight, namely, teaching and ruling. References to a plurality of elders in various churches preclude only those whom we call ministers or preachers today and clearly include those whom we call ruling, as well as teaching elders. For instance, the churches established by Paul on his first missionary journey have a plurality of elders appointed for them (Acts 14:23, "appointed elders for them in every church").

Later elders (plural) are summoned from Ephesus to Miletus. All of them are called overseers (*episkopoi*) and are given the task of shepherding (*poimainein*, Acts 20:28) and defending the church of God (Acts 20:30–31). Like the church at Ephesus, the church at Philippi has a plurality of elders/bishops (Phil 1:1). So also the new congregations on the island of Crete have a plurality of elders in every city (Titus 1:5). And, again, like the elders at Ephesus, these elders have their unified oversight function described in the two tasks of teaching and ruling (Titus 1:9–11,13).

Others agree with Paul's usage. James speaks of a group of men called elders who minister to a particular need in a congregation (Jas 5:14). Peter refers to elders in the plural (1 Pet 5:1; notice also all the plural references in vv 2–4) in each of the congregations addressed by his letter (cf. 1 Pet 1:1). He also speaks of them as shepherding (*poimanate*) the particular flock among them (1 Pet 5:2). In 1 Thessalonians 5 and in Hebrews 13 the officers are not referred to by the designations elders or bishops but in both cases as a group that has the unified and shared responsibility of teaching and ruling (1 Thess 5:12–13; Heb 13:7,17).

In all these references the elders share the responsibility of teaching and ruling, of shepherding and exercising oversight. Thus a uniform picture emerges from the New Testament. From the earliest days of the New Testament church to the last letter written by Paul (from Acts 11:30 and 14:23 to 1 Tim 3:1ff., 5:17, and Titus 1:9) to the unified testimony of the various writers (Luke in Acts, Paul, Peter, James, the writer of Hebrews), there is agreement that one group of men, called elders or bishops, has oversight and that this oversight includes both teaching and ruling.

Deacons

The New Testament adds to the terms elders and bishops the term deacon which is a technical designation for the task of service in the church. Therefore the New Testament refers to the offices in the church under only these two heads or two offices. When the Apostle Paul addresses the officers of the church of Philippi, he uses two terms. Addressing two groups of officers he writes, ". . . the bishops (overseers) and deacons" (Phil 1:1). In his first letter to Timothy the apostle again speaks of only two groups, bishops and deacons (1 Tim 3:1–2,12). Similarly, when divisions of labor were assigned in the early church at Jerusalem (Acts 6:1–6), we find the same two-fold division. The apostles (fellow elders) continue in the oversight functions of ruling and teaching (Acts 6:2,4), while the seven are given the responsibility of service (*diakonein*) at tables (Acts 6:2–3).

When we inquire about the difference between these two offices, we find that the terms themselves describe that difference. The elders/bishops (overseers) are those who have the spiritual oversight (cf. 1 Pet 5:2, *episkopountes*), which is specifically said to be ruling and teaching (1 Tim 3:2,5; 5:17; Titus 1:9ff.). Such ruling and teaching is not specified for the deacons in 1 Timothy 3 by the list which in other ways is almost parallel to that for the bishops (see 1 Tim 3:8ff.). Furthermore, we deduce from Acts 6:1–6 that the deacons should continue the practice of those first deacons, which was to care for the poor and needy and to perform other service ministries for the church under the oversight of the elders (cf. Acts 11:30). From the example in Acts, it seems permissible for a congregation, when first formed, to omit deacons from the offices elected. The diaconal work may be carried on by the elders until it is too heavy. Then men may be chosen for such service (Acts 14:23; Titus 1:5ff.; cf. Acts 6:1–6).

TWO ORDERS OF ELDERS

Joined to the evidence for the two offices should be the emphasis upon the function of teaching.

1 Timothy 5:17

Let the elders who rule well be considered worthy of double honor, especially those who work hard at preaching and teaching.

1 Tim 5:17 introduces this function among those who serve in the office of elder. This passage causes us to focus on the two functions found in the one office of elder; namely, ruling and teaching. Sometimes, as here, teaching receives particular emphasis.

All elders should be able to teach (1 Tim 3:2) and thus to instruct the people of God and to communicate with those who oppose biblical teaching (Titus 1:9ff.). Nevertheless, 1 Tim 5:17 recognizes that, among the elders, there are those uniquely gifted by God with the calling to teach the Word and as such deserve remuneration for their ministry. We can say that any elder who devotes his time to the ruling of the church so that it becomes his calling and occupation is worthy of respect and the "double honor" of a wage. Still, the one designated the teaching elder or the teacher among the elders is particularly in view in 1 Tim 5:17 because the text says "especially those who work hard at preaching and teaching" (NASB). Because such responsibility demands full-time service, this calling demands a wage.[2]

Once it is recognized that within the office of elder there is a specialized function of teaching and preaching the Word, insight is provided for integrating other passages into our study, especially those that refer to teachers. We have already seen teachers acting as elders in Acts 13:1–3 in laying hands on Paul and Barnabas (cf. 1 Tim 4:14). Paul in two passages distinguishes the functions which he fulfilled as a minister of Jesus Christ by using the words preacher, apostle, and teacher (1 Tim 2:7; 2 Tim 1:11). These verses do not describe separate and distinct offices but rather various functions. Thus Paul authoritatively announces the good news (preacher or herald), authoritatively testifies as an eyewitness and spokesman (apostle), and authoritatively instructs in the truth (teacher). By distinguishing the functions which he fulfills as a minister of Jesus Christ, he highlights each aspect of his unified ministry and calling.

1 Corinthians 12:28

And God has appointed in the church, first apostles, second prophets, third teachers, then miracles, then gifts of healings, helps, administrations, various kinds of tongues.

Similarly, when the apostle considers the manifold gifts of the Holy Spirit in 1 Corinthians 12, he distinguishes various gifts relating to church offices alongside and intermingled with other gifts which have no office in the church in view (1 Cor 12:28–31; cf. vv 4ff., esp. v 7). Apostles and prophets are at one end of the spectrum and refer to offices. Tongues are at the other end of the spectrum and are regarded as a gift without reference to office. In this list we find two gifts mentioned which relate to the office of elder; namely, teachers, and administrations (*kuberneiseis*, "governments" KJV; cf. 1 Cor 12:28, NASB). The reference to "helps" (*antileimpseis*) probably is to be related primarily to the deacons whom we see in Acts 6 performing helpful deeds in serving and caring for widows Acts 6:1–6). Here the two-fold functions of teaching and ruling are now distinguished and emphasized. The distinction is given emphasis by referring to the one gift as teachers rather than as teaching and by ranking it as third, thus putting it immediately after apostles and prophets. As to the gift of administrations (NIV renders as "those with gifts of administration"), the Greek lexicon of Bauer-Arndt-Gingrich-Danker states that "the plural indicates proofs of ability to hold a leading position in the church."[3]

These observations should not be surprising because they are quite in accord with 1 Tim 5:17. There we noticed that among the elders, all of whom are to rule, some "work hard at preaching and teaching" (NASB). In 1 Corinthians Paul acknowledges the need for the gift of administrations or governments for the rule and oversight of the church. Alongside this gift he recognizes some who also labor in the Word and teaching (again cf. 1 Tim 5:17).

The teachers of 1 Corinthians 12 must not be regarded as exclusive of those with the gift of administrations because we have already seen that Paul can refer to himself as being not only an apostle but also a preacher and teacher. Since at least two of the gifts in the list in 1 Cor 12:28–31 can refer to one person, we must not let the distinction between gifts of teachers and administrations lead us to think of them as separate offices.

Ephesians 4:11

And he gave some as apostles, and some as prophets, and some as evangelists, and some as pastors and teachers.

Eph 4:11 provides in principle further insights into the proper correlation of the two orders of elders. The statement "and some as pastors and teachers" (*tous de poimenas kai didaskalous*) is better understood when we recognize that the pastors and teachers in the church at Ephesus are referred to in three other places in the New Testament; namely, Acts 20:17–35, 1 Tim 3:1–7, and 5:17. This triple perspective throws light on the two terms.

The first term, pastors, literally means "shepherd" and is used in this literal sense in the New Testament of the shepherds in the Lucan birth narrative. Because the people of God are figuratively regarded as sheep, the one who tends, feeds, and exercises oversight over them is called the shepherd. This usage was already evident in the Old Testament (cf. Jer 2:8; 3:15; Ezek 34:2). It is found in the New Testament letters only in Eph 4:11. Heb 13:20, 1 Pet 2:25, and the Gospels use it figuratively of Jesus.

The question as to what group is in view under this term is answered by recognizing that the pastoring responsibility is given to all the elders in Acts 20:28: "Be on guard for yourselves and for all the flock (*poimnio*), among which the Holy Spirit has made you overseers, to shepherd [to feed, KJV] (*poimainein*) the church of God which he purchased with his own blood" (NASB). The verb used in Acts 20:28 "to shepherd," "to pastor" (*poimainein*, also translated "to feed") is the verbal form of the

term we are considering in Eph 4:11. The Acts passage indicates by its
usage that all elders have a pastoral responsibility.

When we ask who are the pastors of Eph 4:11, we answer from Acts
20:28 and context that they are the elders. This answer also is borne out
by 1 Pet 5:1–4. Here again the task of elders in their collective capacity
is described in shepherding or pastoring terms: "shepherd (*poimanate*) the
flock (*poimnion*) among you" (1 Pet 5:2, cf. v 3, "the flock"). So we may
deduce from the Apostle Peter as well as from the Apostle Paul in Luke's
account in Acts that pastors equal elders.

Confirmation of this insight comes by way of the other references to
elders in Ephesus in 1 Tim 3:1–7 and 5:17. Taking care of (1 Tim 3:5)
and ruling the church (1 Tim 5:17) is another way of speaking about the
shepherd or pastor of the church. Since the tasks in these passages are the
task of elders as a whole, we may conclude that the pastors in view in Eph
4:11 are all the elders.

We must now turn our attention to the "teachers" in Eph 4:11 and their
relationship to the pastors. Of grammatical interest is the fact that each
of the positions named in Eph 4:11 has the definite article *the* before it,
except for the term teachers. The list would read in a literal translation as
follows: "And he gave *the* apostles, and *the* prophets, and *the* evangelists,
and *the* pastors and teachers." The effect of omitting the definite article
before teachers is that it groups pastors and teachers together in one class.
(In Greek grammars this is called the *Granville Sharp Rule.*) In effect, we
may say that the apostle regards the teachers as belonging to the category
of pastors. At the same time, and especially in the light of 1 Cor 12:28–
31, the teachers are a specialized order within that larger class.

This is exactly how Paul spoke of elders in 1 Tim 5:17, which states
that among that larger group of elders, all of whom rule, there are those
who labor in the Word and teaching. What is said in 1 Tim 5:17 is now
said in Eph 4:11 by the expression "the pastors and teachers." All elders
are pastors. Among the elders, all of whom have a pastoral or shepherding
responsibility, there are some called teachers who labor in the Word.
Elsewhere in the New Testament these teachers are identified as those
who preach. The teacher is thus a preaching or teaching pastor/elder.

To use Dabney's terms, we have two orders within the one office.[4] The
one office is that of pastor/elder/bishop. The two orders within that one
office are teaching or preaching pastors/elders on the one hand and ruling
pastors/elders on the other hand. The non-repeated definite article tightly
joins the two orders together in one class or office. The word "teachers"
added to that of "pastors" indicates a specialized ministry among that of
the pastors/elders.[5]

The evidence of the New Testament seems conclusive; there are two
offices, elder and deacon. The New Testament also teaches the unity of

the office of elder and the double function of that office. We must give adequate weight to the fact that these functions can be distinguished and emphasized. This is what we found in 1 Tim 5:17, 1 Cor 12:28–31, and Eph 4:11. To do justice to such distinction and emphasis we may say, as R. L. Dabney has already done, that within the one office or class of elders there are embraced two orders, that of the preaching or teaching elders and that of the ruling elders.

The church, in order to be faithful to the New Testament, must reflect this perspective. Specifically, it must seek to keep in balance the unity of the office of elders and also the distinguishing function given to some among the elders by means of a particular gift of teaching. This will mean that all the elders rule together and are together responsible for the teaching of the church. It will also mean that, within the plurality, some will be more gifted by God to teach and therefore will make the teaching ministry their vocation.[6] The other elders, possessing the same authority, will remain in their several vocations and share in the oversight.

The unity and parity among the elders help to foster mutual submission, which in turn helps to preserve the servant quality of the eldership and the unique Lordship of Christ. The recognition of differing manifestations of gifts within the unified eldership exalts Christ's sovereignty. He gives gifts as he will for the good of his church and ensures that the most needed gift of teaching will have full emphasis and free course among his people. By his Word of instruction and the enabling of his Spirit, he orders and edifies his flock as the elder without equal.

NOTES

This is an edited and extensively revised edition of an aricle that appeared in *Presbyterion* 11 (1985):1–12.

1. The office of evangelist may be regarded as a specialized manifestation of the office of elder. It is referred to only three times in the New Testament. In addition to its occurrence in Eph 4:11, Philip, one of the seven of Acts 6, is designated an evangelist (Acts 21:8), and Timothy is urged to do the work of an evangelist (2 Tim 4:5). The term itself provides the best definition of the task in view, namely, that of proclaiming the evangel, the gospel. This is a function which may be distinguished from that of the pastors and teachers (Eph 4:11). It is a specialized ministry (cf. Philip, Acts 21:8), but at the same time it is also a function which should mark the ministry and proclamation of all those who, like Timothy, are called to preach the Word (cf. 1 Tim 4:15). Since the gift of proclaiming the gospel and planting churches is necessary in the church until the end of the age, this ministry is permanent and not confined to the apostolic period. Also because evangelists in Eph 4:11 are in the list of offices which are distinguished from the saints or believers in general (Eph 4:12), we may properly regard them as a specialized manifestation of the office of elder.

2. If we render the Greek word *malista*, which is commonly translated "especially," by the phrase "that is" in 1 Tim 5:17, our understanding of the passage would not be changed but it would be more focused. With the translation "especially," those who work hard at preaching and teaching are the particular group among the elders who should be considered worthy of double honor but not necessarily the only group. With the translation "that is" the text reads: "let the elders who rule well be considered worthy of double honor, *that is,*

those who work hard at preaching and teaching." With the translation "that is," those who work hard at preaching and teaching are explicitly specified as the group which should be considered worthy of double honor. The suggestion of "that is" as the meaning for *malista* in a few, but not all passages where it occurs in the New Testament has been made and fairly well demonstrated by T. C. Skeat in the *Journal of the Theological Studies*, new series, 30 (1979):173–77. He shows that this meaning is found elsewhere in Greek literature and that it is a legitimate, indeed perhaps preferable meaning for several places in the New Testament (cf., for example, the great significance this would have in 1 Tim 4:10). The designation of some among the elders as "those who work hard at preaching and teaching" as a distinguishable group among the elders still remains the teaching of the passage on either understanding of *malista*.

3. Bauer-Arndt-Gingrich-Danker, *A Greek-English Lexicon of the New Testament*, 2d ed (Chicago: University of Chicago, 1979), 456.

4. See Robert L. Dabney, "Theories of the Eldership," *Discussions: Evangelical and Theological*, Volume 2 (London: The Banner of Truth [1967]), 133.

5. Why then was the term "evangelist" separated from that of pastors and teachers? Because evangelists, unlike teachers, as important as they are to the work of the church and the eldership, are not so intrinsically a part of the eldership in terms of the role of pastor that they should be mentioned as an aspect of pastoring. To be an elder in reference to the flock is by definition to be one of the pastors of the flock. And pastoring the flock involves of necessity some in the labor of the Word as teachers. But pastoring the flock does not intrinsically include evangelists. Evangelists are gaining lost sheep, not caring for saved and gathered ones. So the apostle has placed the evangelists in a separate category.

6. Further inquiry about the duties and responsibilities of those among the elders who labor in the Word and teach leads us not only to the passages about elders and bishops in general but also those passages that refer to Timothy and to Paul as teaching or preaching elders (cf. 1 Cor 9; 2 Cor 3–5; 1 Tim 4:6–16; 6:11–16; 2 Tim 1:3–14; 2; 3:10–4:8).

Richard B. Gaffin, Jr.

3 A Sabbath Rest Still Awaits the People of God

FROM ITS BEGINNING the Orthodox Presbyterian Church has had a concern for the sanctity of the Lord's Day as the Christian Sabbath, a concern which is not merely traditional but an element in its confessional commitment (*Westminster Confession of Faith*, XXI:7,8). I hope in this chapter to help maintain the vitality of that concern, in the face of signs that it is weakening and at a time when it is being challenged as never before.

In the perennial Sabbath-Sunday debate, *From Sabbath to Lord's Day*[1] unquestionably represents a significant milestone. In the words of its editor (D. A. Carson), "it is not merely a symposium but a unified, cooperative effort" (p. 11, see also p. 18), an effort calculated above all to convince the reader that the Lord's Day is not the Christian Sabbath. Even those, like myself, who remain unconvinced are bound to value the care, balance and, for the most part, the thoroughness with which this project has been planned and carried out. A cooperative response of similar magnitude would appear to be demanded of those who disagree with its major conclusion. My remarks here are limited to just one link, albeit a crucial and substantial one, in the argumentation for that conclusion.

Central in the design of the volume, particularly its exegetical parts, is the chapter by Andrew T. Lincoln, "Sabbath, Rest, and Eschatology in the New Testament" (pp. 197–220). The pivotal place of this chapter can be seen by the prominence of its principal conclusions in the final, integrating chapter ("From Sabbath to Lord's Day: a Biblical and Theological Perspective," pp. 343–412), also written by Lincoln. Within the former chapter the greatest amount of attention is given to Hebrews 3:7

–4:13, "the passage," as Lincoln says, "that contributes most to our investigation" (p. 205). In what follows I will comment briefly on the eschatological structure of Hebrews, discuss the interpretation of 3:7ff., assess Lincoln's treatment of this passage, and make several concluding observations.

Eschatological Structure of Hebrews[2]

The opening words of Hebrews give a pronounced eschatological, re-demptive-historical orientation to the entire document: God's former speech through the prophets, "partial and piecemeal," not only contrasts with but culminates in his final speech in his Son "in these last days" (1:1–2). The present character of this "last days," eschatological revela-tion, embodied in the Son, is even more explicit in 9:26: in making sacrifice for sin Christ "has appeared once for all at the end of the ages"; in terms of the fundamental historical-eschatological distinction between the two ages, Christ's death and exaltation inaugurate the coming escha-tological age. Accordingly, through God's word and the Holy Spirit the church already experiences ("tastes") nothing less than "the powers of the age to come" (6:5). Similarly, "salvation" is a present reality resulting from God's eschatological speech "through the Lord" (2:3; cf. 1:1–2: 6:9). Again, believers have already come to "the city of the living God, the heavenly Jerusalem" (12:22) and are present in what is fairly described as the eschatological assembly gathered there (12:22–24). "Realized es-chatology," then, undoubtedly has an integral place in the message of Hebrews.

At the same time, eschatological reality is seen to be still future. Christ, having "appeared" eschatologically, "once for all"[3] (9:26), "will appear a second time" (9:28). For believers that future, second appearance will be "for salvation" (9:28, cf. 1:14; 6:9). A "lasting city" is what they are still seeking; it is "the city to come" (13:14; cf. the "homeland" as well as the "city" in 11:10, 13–16). The "appearance" of the Son, salvation, the heavenly city (homeland), then, all eschatological in character, are both present and future in the view of the writer.

Two comments on this present-future pattern are in order here. First, the bond between believers and Christ, the high priest in heaven (e.g., 4:14; 6:20; 7:26; 8:1), explains how they presently enjoy eschatological blessings. They are "partakers of Christ," "those who share in (with) Christ" (*metochoi tou Christou*, 3:14). Even though this expression may not answer fully to Paul's teaching on union with Christ, it does accent a relationship of fellowship and solidarity (cf. the correlative expressions in 1:9; 2:11; 3:6).[4] In the mode of this union with Christ, the exalted high priest, they, while still on earth, have already entered the heavenly city-sanctuary, where he, their "author-leader" (*archēgos*, 2:10; cf. 12:2) and "forerunner" (6:20), has gone before them; they are there, and already share in attendant eschatological benefits, because he is there.

Secondly, the still future, unrealized side of the writer's eschatology provides the scope for his considerable parenesis (exhortation). Hebrews is essentially parenetic; most likely, "this word of exhortation" (13:22) is intended to characterize the whole document. A careful survey reveals just how appropriate this label is. Not only are there numerous exhortations dealing with specific matters in chapter 13 and 12:12–14, but the well-known chapter 11 ("the roll call of faith") in its entirety is hortatory in effect. Beyond that, exhortations occur frequently throughout the entire book, not simply as the consequence or derivative of didactic portions, but as they themselves shape and determine the doctrinal discussion.[5]

It is misleading to view Hebrews basically as an apologetic-polemic treatment of the person and work of Christ and the superiority of the new covenant to the old, to which various imperatives have been appended in a secondary fashion. On this view doctrine (e.g., the high priestly ministry of Christ) would be intelligible apart from considering the exhortation. Hebrews does provide profound and extensive teaching, especially in the areas of Christology and soteriology, but it does that only "in solution" with application, only as the parenetic element is pervasive and shapes the course of the argument as a whole.

In this respect, Hebrews is an exceptionally instructive example of the integration of doctrine and exhortation (life) that in various ways characterizes the entire New Testament. The author is sustained by "a firm belief in the efficacy of doctrine as a means of grace."[6] At the same time the hortatory materials serve to disclose an important dimension of the present circumstances of the readers (the church); the imperatives connote the indicative situation of the church. To be more specific, looking at the primary, more sweeping exhortation, the situation of the church is characterized by "holding fast" (3:6,14; 4:14; 10:23) and "pressing on" (6:1); all in all a key ingredient is the need for endurance and perseverance (*hupomonē;* 10:36; 12:1; cf. 10:32 12:2,7). Further, plainly at work on believers are forces which threaten to break their "hold," stresses which make endurance and diligence especially necessary and central. Much of the exhortation has a decidedly negative cast. It takes the form of warning: against, for example, "drifting away" (2:1), "neglecting salvation" (2:3), "falling away" (3:12), "being hardened" (3:13), "coming short" (4:1), "refusing him who is speaking" (12:25); in three passages warnings against apostasy occur with unusual gravity: 6:4–6; 10:26–31; 12:15–17. The situation of the readers, then, is one where testing and temptation are present in a quite fundamental way.

To sum up these remarks on eschatological structure, two factors constitute the situation of believers: triumph and testing. The present time is defined both by the eschatological triumph of Christ, their high priest in heaven, and the severe testing of the church. These two factors are always kept together; the one is never allowed to tone down or eclipse the other.

Interpretation of Hebrews 3:7–4:13

At a first glance this section may seem parenthetical and therefore secondary in the writer's overall argument. It appears to interrupt his discussion of Christ as high priest, introduced on the one side in 2:17,18 (as the climax of much of the argument to that point), continued in 3:1–6, and picked up again on the other side at 4:14ff. It is not, however, a parenthesis or digression in any material sense, for it introduces considerations basic to the entire book. Primarily it serves to bring into sharper focus the situation of the church, for which Christ is high priest; it sets out a concrete model for viewing their experience.

(1) 3:1–6, making use of Num 12:7, elaborates the fundamental contrast already expressed at the outset in 1:1–2, now in terms of Moses (*the* Old Testament prophet, cf. Deut 18:15,18) and the Son ("Jesus, the apostle and high priest," v 1; "Christ," v 6). Anticipated implicitly, as in 1:1–2, is the contrast, made explicit in chapters 7–10, between the covenants, the old, "first" and the "new."

Underlying this contrast, however, is a more basic continuity. Both Moses and the Son are involved in the construction of "God's house," the redemptive, covenantal edifice built by God; both are faithful to the building commission each has received (v 2). Where they differ is as the house and its builder (vv 3–4), as a servant in the house and the Son over the house (vv 5–6). The intent is to highlight, by contrast, the finality of the building activity of Christ and so of his sonship over the house (cf. 1:3–4). The work of Moses was anticipatory and pre-eschatological ("testifying to what would be spoken in the future," v 5; note the link with God's eschatological "speech" (*lalein*) in 1:2 and 2:3); Christ's work is final, eschatological.

(2) In v 6b ("whose house we are, if we hold fast our confidence and the boast of our hope"[7]) the discussion takes an unexpected turn. What up to this point has been a broad, sweeping treatment of the greater part of the whole history of redemption, involving general distinctions, is suddenly focused, in zoom-lenslike fashion, on the readers: [1] they have a place in the house, that is, they share in the great end-time salvation revealed in Christ (cf. "partakers of Christ," v 14; "partakers of the heavenly calling," v 1); [2] they have this share only if they hold fast until the end (cf. v 14).

It is fair to observe that v 6b brings to a focus the two basic, constitutive factors, noted above, in the situation of the readers, namely the *final and definitive,* yet *conditional* character of the church's present experience of salvation. The tension inherent in this experience comes out strikingly in the syntax of v 6b: the consequent contains a sweeping present indicative ("we are his house"; cf. the perfect indicative ["we have become partakers of Christ"] in the parallel construction in v 14), capturing the writer's sustained Christological-eschatological emphasis. But this indicative is conditioned on believers "holding fast"; in back of this conditional clause lies the entire hortatory element of the book.[8] A *present* place in the eschatological house is contingent on persevering into the *future* (cf. v 14).

As v 6b pinpoints this tension, the conditional clause in particular triggers what is said in 3:7–4:13, a unity which is more or less self-contained but is by no means isolated or subordinate. It performs the integral function of amplifying the situation of new covenant believers. It seeks to make clear and graphic the nature of the tension they are experiencing by means of a concrete model: the church as a wilderness community, a pilgrim people. This model provides, by way of historical analogy, a rationale especially for the exhortations that permeate the letter.

(3) The *mode* of argumentation in this passage is frequently experienced as baffling and has attracted a fair amount of scholarly discussion.[9] Without entering here into how closely it conforms to Jewish exegesis, especially the *pesher* method present in the Qumran materials, its midrash-like character is plain. Difficulties are created by the presumption that the writer is developing an argument that has its integrity and logical coherence apart from his use of Scripture, so that the Old Testament citations only have an auxiliary, corroborating ("proof-texting") role. Just the reverse is the case: in terms of basic structure, the Scriptures cited are the major, the writer's comments, the minor element. This passage is fairly seen as an annotated, interpretive handling of Scripture (apparently some form of the Septuagint), applied to the readers' situation. In particular it is an applied exposition of Ps 95:7–11, along with Gen 2:2, the only treatment of either passage in the New Testament.

(4) The writer makes Ps 95:7b–11 (LXX, Psalm 94) his point of departure for amplifying the conditional clause at the end of v 6. In that Psalm portion with its reference to Israel in the desert— specifically Israel between Egypt (3:16, "all those Moses led out of Egypt") and Canaan (4:8, "if Joshua had given them rest")— he finds those factors that bear directly on the situation of his readers and serves to define it: the voice of God speaking both promises and threats, the promise of imminently entering his rest held out to those who believe, the wrath of God eventually poured out on the wilderness generation and their failure to enter that rest because of unbelief. In short, pivotal are the factors of God's promise and warning, with their correlatives of faith and unbelief.

It is essential to grasp, then, that the entire passage rests on an assumption which is never spelled out; Israel in the wilderness and believers under the new covenant are in analogous situations. Christians receive the same promise of rest (3:11; 4:1); they are exposed to similar trials and the same danger of unbelief and apostasy (3:12,19; 4:6); they are exhorted to the same perseverance in faith (3:8,14; 4:1,11). In New Testament as well as Old Testament times God's people are pilgrims and travelers; now, as then, they are a people "on the way." Believers have already experienced deliverance from the power of sin, pictured by the Exodus from bondage in Egypt; but they have not yet attained to that experience of salvation which is unthreatened and unchallenged, represented by the rest and peace of Canaan (see, e.g., Deut 12:9,10; Josh 1:13,15). The New Testament church is a wilderness community; it is a company of "aliens and strangers on earth" (11:13; cf. 1 Pet 1:1; 2:11). Without at all suggesting that the church as a congregation of wilderness-aliens is the basic theme of Hebrews, that notion is certainly central and all-controlling in this passage. It is as well the model that serves to clarify graphically the fundamental need for exhortation, not only here but in the rest of the document.[10]

(5) Two words or expressions in the Psalm citation are picked up by the writer and become focal in his own comments: "today" and "my [God's] rest." They appear several times, either alone or with the clauses where they occur. Note how they bracket the quotation; this is hardly mere coincidence but highlights their key function.

What, more exactly, is the reference of each? Despite numerous attempts to show the contrary and others who don't face the issue squarely,[11] their time reference is not identical or even overlapping.

(a) "Today" is plainly applied to the *present* situation of the readers. It refers to the time, any time,[12] in which "good news," "the word of hearing" is being proclaimed (4:2), in which "the promise of entering his rest remains" (4:1). It is the time of summons to faith and obedience, when, correlatively, unbelief and apostasy are present and very real threats (3:12,13,15; 4:6–7). It is the time, consequently, in which final judgment and the consummation associated with it are still future (cf. 9:28; 12:25–29). In short, "today" is the time of wilderness sojourn, when God's people "walk by faith, not by sight" (2 Cor 5:7; cf. the entirety of Hebrews 11).

(b) "My rest," as *rest*, stands in pointed contrast to the believer's present circumstances; it is the antithesis of exposure to hardship and temptation, to the *toil* which the present involves. Believers are presently *at work* (cf. 6:10; 10:24); they are not at rest, but are strenuously seeking it (*spoudazōmen*, 4:11).

"My rest," in distinction, is the particular focus of faith and hope; it is a matter of "promise" (4:1). It stands before the church as Canaan before Israel in the desert (4:8), as the land about to be inherited (cf. 1:14; note the identification of the land as rest, resting-place [and inheritance] in Deut 12:9,10; 25;19; Josh 1:13,15; 11:23; 22:4). Accordingly, it has an unmistakably *local* character; it is a place of rest.[13] Repeatedly it is what believers *enter into* (e.g., 4:1,11). It appears to be identical to the "heavenly homeland" (11:16) and correlative with "the city with foundations" (11:10), "the lasting city to come" (13:14); note that "homeland" and "city" are natural counterparts, by opposition, to the wilderness.[14] It is correlate with "salvation" (1:14; 9:28) and "the eternal inheritance" (9:15; cf. 1:14), as still future.

All told, "my rest" is the eschatological order in the future, yet-to-be realized sense. Throughout the passage it is on the horizon; it refers to what is still future "as long as it is called today" (3:13). This exclusively future understanding of "my rest" is not merely based on explicit statements of the writer but flows out of the basic thrust of his argument, controlled by the notion of the church as wilderness-community. Objections to this conclusion will be taken up below in considering Lincoln's position.

(6) In 4:4 the writer adds to the scriptural base of his argument almost all the second main clause in Gen 2:2 (the only citation of, or apparently, allusion to this verse in the New Testament). This has the effect, along with v 9, of bringing the Sabbath into view, inasmuch as this is the only way Gen 2:2 is used elsewhere in the Old Testament (Exod 20:11; 31:17).[15] Here it is cited to support the last part of v 3 ("although his works were finished from the foundation of the world"). Together vv 3c and 4 serve to identify more precisely the origin and nature of "my rest" in 3b. This, in turn, is in the interests of establishing the unqualified nature of the antithesis: faith-unbelief, which is central to the entire passage.

The central thrust of vv 3–5 is that the wilderness generation failed to enter God's rest, not because of its nonavailability (it has been there "from the foundation of the world"), but solely on account of unbelief. Conversely, believers may be certain of entering it (v 3a). From Gen 2:2 in combination with Ps 95:11 the writer derives, respectively, the two premises expressed by the compound subordinate clause in v 6: [1] by God's design ("it remains"), some are to enter his rest, and [2] disobedience (lack of faith, cf. 3:18–19) bars entrance.

We must appreciate, then, what broad perspectives the writer opens up by introducing Gen 2:2. The rest of God, the consummation of redemption mentioned in Ps 95:11, of which the eventual possession of Canaan was only a shadow or type,[16] and which the new covenant people of God are presently seeking to enter — this rest is none other than the rest of God at creation. Eschatological redemption-rest is not merely an analogue of God's creation-rest; the latter is not simply the model for the former. Rather, the writer knows of only one rest, "my rest," entered by God at creation and by believers at the consummation.

Further, it appears that in Gen 2:2b (in its context) he finds not only a reference to the existence of God's rest, but the *design* and *mandate* that others should enter and share it; Gen 2:2 is prescriptive as well as descriptive. If this were not the case, the first premise in v 6 ("it remains for some to enter it") would be without foundation.

The way in which Psalm 95 and Genesis 2 are brought together here indicates the scope of the promised rest in the writer's view. The fulfillment of the church's hope represents nothing less than the fulfillment of the original purpose of God in creation, or more accurately, the realization of his purposes of redemption is the means to the end of realizing his purposes of creation.[17]

A similar pattern of thought, apparently, is present in 1 Cor 15:42–49, where Paul anchors the believer's hope of bodily resurrection in the parallel between Adam and Christ. In the flow of his argument the contrast between the pre-eschatological body, subject to decay and death, and the eschatological, resurrection body (vv 42–44a) is expanded to include the persons of Adam and Christ, "the last Adam" (v 48); not only do they exemplify, respectively, these two bodies, but at the same time they are representatives of nothing less than two ages or creations, the original, "psychical"[18] creation, subject to death because of Adam's sin (cf. Rom 5:12ff.), and the new, "spiritual" creation. That this broadening is actually the trend of the argument appears from the generalizing expressions in v 46 (after which it would be a mistake to read "body"), as well as the shift to explicitly cosmological, spatial terminology in vv 47–49 (the contrast "heaven"–"earth" and correlative adjectives).

Particularly noteworthy for our interests is the fact that on the one side of the contrast in v 45, Gen 2:7 is cited to introduce Adam, not as fallen and hence mortal, but as he is by virtue of creation.[19] Further, as in Hebrews 4, the Genesis 2 narrative is also prescriptive: v 45c is syntactically dependent on "it is written" (45a), which introduces the Gen 2:7 quote; "the last Adam became life-giving Spirit" answers to God's design in the creation of Adam. For Paul, like the writer of Hebrews, eschatology and protology are related; the new, resurrection, "spiritual" creation order, brought about de facto, in view of Adam's fall, by the work of Christ, the last Adam, will be the realization of the purposes of the original, "psychical" creation. Note further that the eschatological order in view here is the order commensurate with and appropriate to the resurrection *body* (cf. esp. Rom 8:18–25), and so that order as it will *first* arrive at the return of Christ (v 49: "we shall also bear the image of the heavenly man";[20] cf. Phil 3:20–21).

(7) In 4:9, where we expect another occurrence of "my rest," the writer instead has "Sabbath-rest" (*sabbatismos*). This substitution is not only striking; it appears quite deliberate. Very likely he has coined the word on the basis of the Septuagint usage of *sabbatizō* (e.g., Exod 16:30; Lev 23:32; 2 Chr 36:21) and the Old Testament occurrences of *sabbaton* (e.g., Exod 16:23; 35:2; Lev 16:31), both of which describe Sabbath observance.[21]

The reference, then, is not so much to the Sabbath day itself as to its use or celebration, "Sabbath-resting," "Sabbath-keeping."

What motivated the writer to introduce this word is difficult to determine fully.[22] Certain effects, however, are unmistakable, or at least difficult to deny. [1] "My rest" (in its local character, see above) is a place of Sabbath-rest. In explicit fashion, reinforced by the use of Gen 2:2 in v 4, v 9 ties God's rest, in its sweeping, eschatological scope, to the institution of the Sabbath and its observance. [2] There is an inner connection between ongoing Sabbath observance and eschatological (Sabbath-) rest; this ostensibly is the tie between anticipatory sign and reality. Although the writer does not say so explicitly, the clear implication is that recurring Sabbath observance has its significance as a sign or type of eschatological rest.[23] [3] In view of the use of Gen 2:2 in v 4, it would appear to be the seventh *day* sign specifically, the typology of the *weekly* Sabbath, that the writer has in view, at least primarily.

(8) *Conclusion.* Our discussion of Hebrews 3:7ff has highlighted the following considerations: [1] In terms of composition or structure, this passage is biblical exposition, based on Ps 95 (LXX:94):7b–11, with the inclusion of Gen 2:2b. [2] The controlling motif, drawn from the Psalm and developed in the exposition, is the church as wilderness-congregation; the church is a gathering of the tempted and tested, and so of those who need to be exhorted (cf. Paul's use of the same motif in 1 Cor 10:1–13). [3] In relation to the present situation of the church ("today"), entrance into "God's rest" lies entirely in the future; in terms of the controlling model, this rest is the *non*-wilderness situation, the absence of exposure to trial and temptation. [4] This future rest is related to the institution of the Sabbath and is itself called "Sabbath-rest."

(For the sake of clarity it may be worth noting what so far I have *not* tried to argue. I have not suggested that the writer is concerned explicitly with the issue of Sabbath-keeping under the new covenant, or that 4:9, for instance, should be read: "it remains for God's people to keep the fourth commandment." The bearing of his statements on the notion of a Christian Sabbath have yet to be spelled out.)

Lincoln's Treatment of Hebrews 3:7ff

A large measure of agreement exists between Lincoln's treatment of this passage and my own, not only on individual points but also on a number of emphases. Where we differ is over "my rest" — on when believers enter it and, to a certain extent, on what it is. From this difference largely follows the decisively different conclusions each of us draws from this passage for the whole Sabbath-Sunday issue.

While Lincoln holds that "my rest" is future, he rejects the position, argued above, that it is entirely future. "This," he writes, "would not only be to ignore the evidence of this passage but to miss the structure of the

writer's thought throughout" (p. 210). Accordingly, his arguments that
the rest is already present are of two sorts, from the passage itself and from
the rest of the book (pp. 210–213). To these we now turn, though not
necessarily in the order he presents them.

(1) The substance of Lincoln's appeal to the wider context in Hebrews
is that the writer holds to a realized eschatology. As believers are said to
have already come to the heavenly Jerusalem of the future, as they already
have access to the heavenly sanctuary, as "faith makes real in the present
that which is future, unseen, or heavenly" (p. 211), as believers are
partakers of Christ, their great high priest who has already passed through
the heavens and entered the heavenly rest — so, too, they have already
entered God's rest; "this rest has already become a reality for those who
believe" (p. 210).

That "the eschatological benefits of salvation are already present" (p.
210) is beyond question. Certainly that is not the issue here; I myself
have already drawn attention to the realized side of the writer's eschatology
above (under "Eschatological Structure"). Nor should we question that
the writer *could* have spoken of eschatological rest as already present for
believers; a statement like that of Jesus in Matt 11:28–30 ("Come to me,
all who are weary and burdened, and I will give you rest.") is thoroughly
in harmony with the eschatology of Hebrews. The sole issue here is
whether in fact 3:7ff. teach, either expressly or by implication, that God's
rest is already present for the church. How does the notion of rest function
in these verses? The fact that realized eschatological elements are undeniable elsewhere in Hebrews has no decisive bearing on answering that
question.

(2) Looking within the passage itself, Lincoln attempts to undercut the
prominence of the wilderness or pilgrimage-motif. He faults the title of
Ernst Käsemann's influential study on Hebrews, *The Wandering People of
God,*[24] as misleading, and he appeals to the work of Hofius, who has argued
in great detail that in his exegesis of Psalm 95 (94) the writer has in view,
not the experience of the wilderness generation in general, but specifically
the events of Numbers 14, at Kadesh, where the people are at the end of
their travels (not *wandering* but *waiting*), about to enter the promised land,
but rebel at the report of the returning spies.[25] From this Lincoln maintains that the writer's point of comparison with believers is that they
"have arrived at the goal of their pilgrimage," and that the church is
"confronted by this direct availability of the entry to heavenly rest" (p.
211).

I find this not only unconvincing but puzzling as an argument for the
presence of the rest. Israel at Kadesh is not Israel in Canaan; the people
"on the verge of entry into the promised land" (p. 211) are not the people
in any sense entered into the land. Close proximity is not arrival. Granting
that the writer is thinking, primarily at least, of Numbers 14 and in this

respect differs from the Psalmist himself, who likely has in view an earlier incident at Rephidim (Exod 17:1–7),[26] this difference is no more than one of emphasis. Both events exemplify basic elements in the writer's hortatory concern: (a) rebellion and rejection of God's promise, (b) under desert conditions, (c) short of the promised destination. The wilderness generation has its identity for the writer as "all those Moses led out of Egypt" (3:16). This is a clear indication that he has in view the structure and theological significance of their desert experience as a whole (from the outset), or at least that he sees continuity between Kadesh and their prior experience. (It is worth noting here that 3:16 is also a clear indication that deliverance from Egyptian bondage, *not* present rest, provides the element of realized eschatology in this passage; cf. 1 Cor 10:1–4).

The title of Käsemann's book is misleading only if "wandering" carries the connotation "wandering aimlessly," or is associated, as Käsemann does, with Gnostic speculation about the migratory return of alienated divine "sparks" to the heavenly world. Otherwise it is helpful, like the book itself despite substantial flaws in its overall argument, in drawing attention to one of the principal motifs in Hebrews. Darnell is right in observing that on this point we do not have to take sides in the debate between Käsemann and Hofius: in Hebrews 3–4 the people of God are both "on the way" and "waiting."[27] But they have not yet arrived.

(3) The present tense in 4:3, "we enter (*eiserchometha*) that rest," is often taken as an emphatic, undeniable indication that the rest has become a present reality for believers. Lincoln holds this to be a true present on the basis of the "general considerations" (p. 211) he has already mentioned. But we have just found that these considerations do not show that the rest is already present.

Of itself the present tense-form gives no more than a presumption of a present sense. In view of the various forces the present indicative can have, considerations from the immediate context are decisive. Here a true present is excluded because, as I have tried to show, it would violate the way the wilderness-model is being used. In terms of that model either of two translations fits: "we will enter," the use of the present tense giving a note of certainty,[28] or perhaps a progressive sense ("we are entering"), actually underway but not yet there.[29]

The closest parallel to 4:3 in the New Testament, as far as I can discover, is Acts 14:22. Though not an exact parallel syntactically, it is instructive on more than one count. There the substance, in part, of Paul's words to believers in Pisidia is that "through many tribulations we must enter (*dei hēmas eiselthein*) the Kingdom of God." [1] "Entering the Kingdom of God" corresponds materially to "entering God's rest." The Kingdom, more obviously than God's rest, is a comprehensive eschatological category. Elsewhere in Luke-Acts it is present (e.g., Luke 7:28; 11:20; 17:21). Yet, to my knowledge, none of the commentators find a present meaning here;

an entirely future sense is obvious. [2] "Through many tribulations" answers to the desert situation of Hebrews 3–4. These tribulations are not
the conditions under which the kingdom is now being realized, but through
which believers must presently pass to reach the kingdom beyond. [3] The
correlate of entering the kingdom is "continuing in the faith." Here
perseverance (faith) does not possess the kingdom already come but reaches
out toward the kingdom yet to come. [4] The whole of what Paul says is
exhortation/encouragement (*parakalountes;* cf. the pervasively parenetic
character of Hebrews, especially the writer's own assessment in 13:22).

(4) Lincoln holds that the use of "today" throughout the passage shows
the rest to be present as well as future: " 'Today' brackets the period of
'already' and 'not yet' as regards God's rest for those who live during the
period when the ages overlap" (p. 212). But is this the case? Certainly
"today" can't be detached from the writer's announced eschatological
point of departure (1:1–2) or his stress throughout on the eschatological
nature of Christ's work (e.g., 9:26). But that Hebrews has a realized
eschatology is not the issue here. *Within* the passage (3:15,17), "today,"
picked up from Ps 95 (94):7, is plainly the wilderness-time, as the time
when faith in God's promise of eventual entry into the land/rest ("if you
hear his voice") is continually tempted to unbelief ("do not harden your
hearts"). In the remaining occurrence, 4:7 ("God, through David, has set
a certain day, 'today' "; cf. v 8b), the point is that "today" has its fulfillment or ultimate realization, not as the church's "time for entry into rest"
(p. 212), but in the church as the new and final wilderness-congregation.

Lincoln at this point quotes approvingly C. K. Barrett to the effect that
paradoxically the rest is both present and future, a paradox shared with all
New Testament eschatology.[30] Undoubtedly, in keeping with his eschatology as a whole, the writer *could* have spoken of rest as present. But *does*
he, in this passage or elsewhere, either expressly or by implication? That
he has a realized eschatology does not mean that the rest in chapters 3–4
must somehow be present, no more than Jesus' statements that the kingdom is present mean that he cannot also, in other places, only speak of it
as future.

(5) Lincoln holds that eschatological "Sabbath-rest" in 4:9 is not entirely future, not only for the reasons just considered, which he finds in
the preceding verses, but also because of the way he understands v 10.
This reading, in my judgment, brings to light a basic flaw in his understanding of rest throughout the passage; in fact, a proper understanding of
3:7ff as a whole pivots on rightly interpreting 4:10.

Verse 10 reads: "The one who enters his [God's] rest has himself rested
from his [own] works, just as God did from his." At least two things are
immediately apparent. [1] Through the introduction of Gen 2:2 in v 4
and the term 'Sabbath-rest' in v 9, God's rest at creation again comes into

view. [2] A parallel is drawn, with some deliberateness, between believers[31] and God: their resting is to their works, as God's resting is to his works.

What does it mean for believers to (enter) rest from their works? Lincoln understands these works to be what the writer elsewhere (6:1; 9:14) calls "dead works" (p. 213). Rest, then, means "cessation from reliance on one's own works" (p. 215; cf. p. 213), "cessation from evil works" (p. 397). In other words, the point of v 10 (and the present rest he finds elsewhere in the passage) is justification by faith (cf. p. 214). This exegetical decision, it should be noted, becomes a controlling assumption in the argumentation of the concluding chapter (pp. 365, 378, 396–97).

This interpretation has a venerable tradition, extending back at least to Calvin,[32] but it is hardly correct. For one thing it loses sight of the local character of "my rest" (as a resting-place) throughout the passage and fails to do justice to the writer's use of the wilderness-motif. Even more telling, it does not seem to perceive the jarring incongruity of drawing a direct (and therefore *positive*) parallel between man's sinful works and God's works.[33] Where elsewhere does the New Testament even remotely approach the notion that "repentance from dead works" is analogous to God's resting from his labors at creation? Does it really overstate to say that such a synthetic association is a glaring impossibility for any New Testament writer?

Correct interpretation of v 10 depends on seeing that the believer's works are being viewed positively. They are not "dead works," but their "love and good works" (10:24), their "work and love" (6:10). Both contexts further identify these works. "God is not unjust so as to forget" them (looking foward final judgment, cf. 9:28), "as you see the Day approaching" (10:25). These are works toward which believers are to "spur one another on" (10:24), for which they are to maintain the "diligence" (cf. 4:11) they have already shown, "to the very end" (6:11; cf. 3:14). They are works bound up with "holding fast," "without wavering," to the promised hope (6:11–12; 10:23), and with not being "lazy" but "patient/persevering" (6:12).

In a word, the works of 4:10 are *desert*-works, the works of believers in the present wilderness, that is, *non*-rest situation, looking toward the future, hoped-for, promised rest. They are the wilderness-works of the church on the way between exodus from Egypt/redemption (cf. 3:16; *here* in this passage, and in terms of its controlling model, is justification by faith) and Canaan/rest. The main verb in v 10a, then, the aorist "has rested" (*katepausen*), has a generalizing or gnomic force.[34] And the clause as a whole describes a future state of rest with the wilderness left behind, that rest toward which the writer immediately goes on to exhort his readers to *exert* themselves (v 11).

As far as I can see, it is necessary to hold Lincoln's view of v 10, or some variant thereof (the works are sinful, self-justifying works; the rest is the forgiveness of sins, justification by faith), if present "spiritual" rest elsewhere in 3:7ff. is to be demonstrated convincingly. But this view cannot be maintained. Beyond the difficulties already noted, it breaks down the writer's basic distinction throughout the passage, the distinction which his choice of the wilderness/rest motif makes graphic, and on which the need for the parenesis permeating the entire book is based: the distinction between the present necessity for perseverance (wilderness) and the future when there will be no need to persevere (rest). The opposite of rest, wilderness, is not sin but tested faith. The view which finds present rest in v 10 confuses the goal (rest) with what appropriates the goal (persevering faith), hoping with the object of hope (cf. Rom 8:24–25). It trys to *include* in the notion of rest precisely what (the present life of faith), in its wilderness character, the writer wishes, throughout this passage, to *contrast* with rest.

It is important to recognize that the wilderness in 3:7ff, while essentially a place of testing and temptation, is also a place of *redemption;* those in the desert are "all those Moses led out of Egypt" (3:16). The presupposition of temptation to apostasy (3:12), is salvation. Put another way, realized eschatology creates the wilderness-congregation (the church as *new* and *final* wilderness-community). Throughout the passage, not rest but the wilderness contrasted with rest is the index of present eschatological reality. This points up that the wilderness-works of v 10 are not dead, sinful works but that persevering faith and obedience, commanded elsewhere in the passage, which compare positively with God's works at creation.

The closest, though not exact, New Testament parallel to v 10a seems to be Rev 14:13. (In view are "the dead who die in the Lord," while rest in Hebrews 3–4 begins at the Parousia [cf. 9:28]. But the viewpoints are complementary; according to Hebrews the present assembly in the heavenly Jerusalem includes "the spirits of righteous men made perfect," 12:23.) Believers, the Spirit says in Revelation, "will rest from their labor, for their works will follow them." Or, as Hebrews says, "God is not unjust so as to forget" their works (6:10).

I conclude, then, that the rest of v 10 is not present but future and so, too, the eschatological Sabbath-resting in v 9, which v 10 functions to explain.

(6) *Conclusion:* Lincoln's interpretation of Heb 3:7ff. is faulty because he does not recognize that virtually every detail is determined by the model of the church as a pilgrim people or wilderness community. Because he misses the controlling significance of this motif, other factors from outside the passage, primarily of a realized eschatological sort, enter and dispose him to conclude that "my rest" is present as well as future. In fact, to try to read the concept of rest in Hebrews 3–4, determined *univocally* throughout as it is by its contrast to the wilderness, as *both* cessation from

unbelief (present rest) *and* cessation of (tempted and persevering) *faith* (future rest) is more than paradoxical; such a reading of the passage amounts to a semantic overload that distorts much of its argumentation and blurs its main point.

Concluding Observations

(1) It would be perverse to suggest that the Sabbath-Sunday issue can be settled solely on the basis of Heb 3:7ff., and there is always the danger of reading into the passage what is not there. But it would be equally remiss to overlook or minimize relevant exegetical givens, whether explicit or implied.

Rest for the church in Hebrews 3–4, in gist, is:

> [a] eschatological,
> [b] entirely future,
> [c] called Sabbath-resting and
> [d] grounded in God's rest at creation.

1. In view of [a] and [c] the (weekly) Sabbath, whatever else may be its significance(s) and function(s), is an eschatological sign or type, a pointer to eschatological rest. To deny this is to suppose that the writer, as we have seen, not only apparently coined the term 'Sabbath-resting' for eschatological rest himself but also connected that rest with Gen 2:2–3 (which elsewhere in Scripture is only used for instituting the weekly Sabbath), yet that he did so without any thought of the weekly ordinance— a rather unlikely supposition.

2. In view of [b] the weekly Sabbath continues in force under the new covenant. To deny this is to suppose that for the writer the weekly sign has ceased, even though the reality to which it points is still future— again, an unlikely supposition. What rationale could explain such a severing, by cessation, of sign and unfulfilled reality?

3. In view of [d] the weekly Sabbath is a "creation ordinance." To deny this is to disagree with the writer's own interpretive treatment of Gen 2:2. He finds there not only a description of God's rest at creation but the (eschatological) design and mandate that mankind enter and share it (4:3b–4,6a). Accordingly, the sign pointing to the reality mandated at creation is itself grounded in that mandate. As eschatology is the goal of protology, so the eschatological sign has a protological basis. There are no offsetting considerations to this inference in the context.[35]

4. *Sum:* For the writer the weekly Sabbath is an eschatological sign, grounded in creation and continuing under the new covenant until the consummation. He does not support the view that because of the "spiritual rest" already brought by Christ weekly Sabbath-keeping is no longer necessary or even appropriate. The notion of an evangelical

or Christian Sabbath is entirely in harmony with the teaching of Hebrews 3–4.

(2) One of Lincoln's reasons for denying that the weekly Sabbath is a continuing creation mandate is that the rest of Gen 2:2–3, whose eschatological orientation the writer of Hebrews makes clear, has been fulfilled and transformed, at least in part, by the (eschatological) salvation already revealed in Christ (e.g., pp. 215, 395–96). Here we come upon an important crux in the Sabbath-Sunday debate, one with far-reaching consequences.

In fact, the eschatological rest of Genesis 2 has not yet been realized. *As that rest is in view in Genesis 2* it is still entirely future. The finished work of Christ has secured it and guarantees it, but it will not arrive until his return. This the writer of Hebrews confirms by referring, without exception, to rest as future for the church.

In Genesis 2 eschatological rest is in view without respect to the fall and its consequences; it is a consummation order where sin and death are not relevant or conditioning factors. Genesis 2 teaches, and Hebrews 4 confirms, that "the eschatological is an older strand in revelation than the soteric."[36] But realized eschatology, the new creation already present in Christ (2 Cor 5:17), including the spiritual rest brought by him (Matt 11:28), is always eschatology in the context of, or in tension with, sin and its consequences; it is always a matter, to cite several biblical descriptions, of being "alive from the dead . . . in the mortal body" (Rom 6:12–13), of "having this treasure in clay jars" (2 Cor 4:7), of "walking by faith, not by sight" (2 Cor 5:7), of redemption into the wilderness (Heb 3:7ff.). In contrast, sin and death are irrelevant and no longer present for the eschatological order of Hebrews 3–4 (to which the weekly Sabbath sign points with continuing relevance). It is the order where sight will replace tested faith, it is the rest beyond the wilderness.

In the Introduction to *From Sabbath to Lord's Day*, D. A. Carson observes that the Sabbath-Sunday question "touches many areas of theological study"; among these he mentions "the proper understanding of salvation history" and "biblical patterns of eschatology" (p. 17). This is in fact the case. The Sabbath-theology of Hebrews, rightly understood, is an important corrective against the tendency for the "already"— "not yet" pattern of New Testament eschatology to be expressed as a dialectic of paradoxical, virtually undifferentiated statements.

We have already noted the similarity between the pattern of argument in Heb 3:7ff. and 1 Cor 15:42–49. Here I would further observe that to argue that eschatological rest is in some sense present in the Hebrews passage is akin to arguing that Paul views the believer's *bodily* resurrection, and the eschatological "sight" inseparable from it (cf. Rom 8:18–25), as somehow already present. Lincoln is sensitive to this danger of a spiritualizing overemphasis on realized eschatology and seeks to dispel the notion that the basic viewpoint of the book is "gnostic" (p. 403; cf. p. 215). Certainly his own position is not, but the tendency is there. In fact, the weekly Sabbath, grounded in the outlook on eschatological rest in Hebrews 3–4, is an important safeguard against the overreaching "enthusiasm" that constantly threatens Christian faith; it is a protection against tendencies to blur or even lose sight of the differences between the eschatological "already" and "not yet." The Sabbath is a sure sign to the church, the eschatological community, that it is still "on the way."[37]

(3) *From Sabbath to Lord's Day* finds significant support in Heb 3:7ff for its basic position that the Lord's Day is not the Christian Sabbath. Upon examination, however, that passage proves to be a significant loose end, one for which this position has yet to give an adequate accounting. As far as I can see, it cannot.

NOTES

1. ed. D. A. Carson (Grand Rapids: Zondervan, 1982).

2. Helpful treatments of the eschatology of Hebrews are C. K. Barrett, "The Eschatology of the Epistle to the Hebrews," in ed. W. D. Davies and D. Daube, *The Background of the New Testament and Its Eschatology* (Cambridge: University Press, 1956), 363–93; B. Klappert, *Die Eschatologie des Hebräerbriefs* (Munchen: Chr. Kaiser, 1969); G. Vos, *The Teaching of the Epistle to the Hebrews* (Grand Rapids: Eerdmans, 1956), 49–87.

3. The force of *hapax* is eschatological in the light of the following prepositional phrase *epi sunteleia tōn aionōn*.

4. ". . . not that of participation in Him (as in the Pauline expression 'in Christ'), but rather that of participation with Him . . ." (F. F. Bruce, *The Epistle to the Hebrews* (Grand Rapids: Eerdmans, 1964), 68).

5. Among fundamental, "first order" parenesis are the following: 2:1,3; 3:1,12–14; 4:1,14,16; 6:1,4–6; 10:26–27,35–36; 12:1,5 –6,15,25.

6. Vos, *Teaching*, 69.

7. Even if the variant "until the end" (*mechri telous*) is not to be read, that is the virtual sense; cf. 3:14.

8. Note that this reverses the syntactical pattern in Paul, where the indicative is in the protasis, the hortatory element in the apodosis; e.g., Gal 5:25; Col 3:1.

9. Cf. e.g., D. Darnell, *Rebellion, Rest, and the Word of God* (Ann Arbor: University Microfilms, 1973), 15–25, 54; S. Kistemaker, *The Psalm Citations in the Epistle to the Hebrews* (Amsterdam: Wed. G. Van Soest, 1961), 71–75, 85–86.

10. E. Käsemann, *The Wandering People of God* (trans. R. A. Harrisville and I. L. Irving [Minneapolis: Augsburg, 1984], German original, 2d ed., 1957), especially, has argued that wilderness wandering is the principal motif of the letter. Lincoln's objection to this assessment will be considered below.

11. Cf. the commentaries.

12. The writer no doubt intends that "today" has its fulfillment or ultimate realization in the present gospel-day of the church, but it is also relevant to the generation of the Psalmist and so to anytime where God's promise is heard; cf. Darnell, *Rebellion*, 162–63.

13. Cf. esp. O. Hofius, *Katapausis. Die Vorstellung vom endzeitlichen Ruheort im Hebräerbrief* (Tübingen: J. C. B. Mohr, 1970), 51–53.

14. Hofius's arguments that the rest is not the heavenly land or city, but specifically the Holy of Holies of the heavenly sanctuary (*Katapausis*, 53–54), are not convincing.

15. Cf. N. A. Andreasen, *The Old Testament Sabbath: A Traditional-Historical Investigation* (Missoula, Mont.: The Society of Biblical Literature, 1972), 197–203.

16. Typology is no doubt subject to abuse, but to deny that in 4:8 the writer intends a typological (sign-reality) connection between Canaan and eschatological rest, as Hofius (*Katapausis*, 180, n. 351) and Darnell (*Rebellion*, 257f.) hold, is unduly cautious and in fact restricts the writer's outlook.

17. Cf. P. Fairbairn, *The Typology of Scripture*, Vol. I (Grand Rapids: Zondervan, n.d.), 420. Note also the backhanded support of this conclusion by G. Von Rad, who says that the writer "has welded together" "proof-texts . . . which have absolutely nothing whatever in common" (*The Problem of the Hexateuch* [Edinburgh and London: Oliver and Boyd, 1966], 101f.). It would have been fairer to the writer to have spoken of his making explicit in the light of Christ's work a connection that was latent in the Old Testament; close to Von Rad's assessment of the writer's hermeneutics is that of H. Strathmann, *Der Brief an die Hebräer* (*Das Neue Testament Deutsch*, 9; Göttingen: Vandenhoeck & Ruprecht, 1963), 95f.

18. The usual translation "natural" for *psychikon* in vv 44,46, as does the translation "soul" for *psychē* in v 45, masks the connection between the Greek adjective and noun; cf. "spiritual" (*pneumatikon*)-"Spirit" (*pneuma*) on the other side of the contrast.

19. This, apparently, happens already in v 44b, where Paul argues *directly, not concessively*, from the existence of the psychical body to the spiritual body; cf. G. Vos, *The Pauline Eschatology* (Grand Rapids: Baker, 1979 [1930]), 169f., n. 19 and R. B. Gaffin, Jr., *The Centrality of the Resurrection* (Grand Rapids: Baker, 1978), 81–83.

20. Despite its weaker attestation, the future indicative is more likely on contextual grounds. In favor of the aorist subjunctive ("let us bear"), see A. Lincoln, *Paradise Now and Not Yet* (Cambridge: University Press, 1981), 50f.

21. For detailed argumentation, see Darnell, *Rebellion*, 262-66; Hofius, *Katapausis*, 102 –110.

22. Cf. Darnell, *Rebellion*, 266, 270f.

23. Cf. G. Vos, *Biblical Theology* (Grand Rapids: Eerdmans, 1959), 156–58.

24. See above, n. 10.

25. *Katapausis*, 117–39.

26. Ibid., 117.

27. *Rebellion*, 93f., 163, 308.

28. See N. Turner, *A Grammar of New Testament Greek*, Vol. III, *Syntax* (Edinburgh, T. & T. Clark, 1963), 63 (These presents differ from the future "mainly in the tone of assurance which is imported," quoting Moulton); A. T. Robertson, *A Grammar of the Greek New Testament in the Light of Historical Research* (Nashville: Broadman Press, 1934), 869– 70 ("It affirms and not merely predicts. It gives a sense of certainty."); cf. E. D. Burton, *Syntax of the Moods and Tenses in New Testament Greek* (Edinburgh: T. & T. Clark, 1898), 9f.

29. See R. Funk, *A Greek Grammar of the New Testament* (The University of Chicago Press, 1961), 168 ("Verbs of going [coming] however also have the meaning of 'to be in the process of going [coming]' for which reaching the destination still lies in the future.") By the way, this, not as Lincoln quotes him (p. 212), seems to be the view of H. Montefiore, *A Commentary on the Epistle to the Hebrews* (New York: Harper and Row, 1964), 83. A few lines below the sentence Lincoln quotes in favor of a true present, Montefiore adds, "The text does not mean that Christians have actually entered, but that they are entering that rest," and that "there is no realized eschatology" in Hebrews (not even in 12:22!, see pp. 229f.)

30. See Barrett, "Eschatology," 372.

31. To refer "the one who enters" to Christ [e.g., J. Owen, *An Exposition of Hebrews*, Vol. 2 (Evansville, Ind.: Sovereign Grace Publishers, 1960 [1674]), 331–36], is not exegetically credible.

32. *Commentaries on the Epistle of Paul the Apostle to the Hebrews* (Grand Rapids: Baker, 1979), 98f.

33. R. Jewett [*Letter to Pilgrims* (New York: Pilgrim Press, 1981), 68] suggests that the point of comparison is "simply in the term rest and not that from which they rest." If that were true the writer would not likely have added *apo tōn idiōn* to describe God's rest.

34. Cf. Burton, *Moods*, 21; a proleptic use of the aorist also fits well here, see M. Zerwick, *Biblical Greek* (Rome: Pontifical Biblical Institute, 1963), 84.

35. In rejecting the Sabbath as a creation ordinance, Lincoln concludes: "The writer's quotation of Genesis 2:2 in Hebrews 4:3–4 is not in order to ground the Sabbath in creation but rather to ground the eschatological salvation rest, which God has for His people, in the divine rest at creation"; in Scripture "the notion of God's rest in Genesis 2 was treated eschatologically" but "was not held . . . to be a 'creation ordinance' " (p. 351). Why the disjunction? Why not both?, especially since the writer himself draws a connection between the Sabbath institution and the rest of Gen 2:2–3.

36. Vos, *Biblical Theology*, 157. Eminently valuable for a theology of rest and the Sabbath is his entire discussion of the fourth commandment (pp. 155–59).

37. It would be beyond the scope of the present study but the concern of an overall biblical theology of the Sabbath to show (1) that the protological origin of the Sabbath is without prejudice as to when a weekly Sabbath actually began to be observed (that is, the question of a patriarchal, pre-Mosaic Sabbath is not decisive for the issue of the weekly Sabbath as a continuing creation mandate); and (2) that the shift of the weekly Sabbath from the seventh to the first day reflects the present eschatological situation of the church (the *change* to the *first* day is an index of eschatology already realized, of the eschatological, new-creation rest inaugurated by Christ, especially by his resurrection; the *continuation* of a weekly rest-day is a sign of eschatology still future, a pointer to the eschatological rest to come at Christ's return).

Richard C. Gamble

4 Presbyterianism and the Ancient Church

IN A BOOK CELEBRATING the Presbyterian church in general and the Orthodox Presbyterian Church in particular, an examination of the historical roots of Presbyterianism is certainly in order. However, we must be careful not to proceed out of blind adoration. Instead, we are compelled to investigate Christian history critically and to ask important questions about the relation of Presbyterianism to the overall development of the body of Christ. In this essay we are specifically concerned with Presbyterianism and the ancient church and the question, was Presbyterianism known in the earliest period of church history?

As we begin it would be beneficial to remind ourselves of some orienting factors. First, our commitment to Scripture is such that we cannot allow historical arguments to run away with us. In the end observations of the development of the church play a secondary role to the prescriptive message of the Bible. Therefore, it is perfectly conceivable for Presbyterianism to be correct biblically and yet lack much precedence in any particular period of church history.

This leads us to a second consideration. It is undeniably true that, regardless of what we think about the early church, the medieval church was governed by the papal system or what we call more broadly "monarchical episcopacy." This system has exerted such an influence that to it belongs natural "bragging rights" over what has been often thought of as a sixteenth-century innovation, i.e., Presbyterianism. Its roots are believed to run quite deep and thus provide a foundation for a continuous heritage in the development of church government. But despite its entrenchment, are its claims correct? or is it predated by Presbyterianism?

53

When Did the Papacy Arise?

In answering the question about the origin of the papacy[1], we might do well to remind ourselves of how the Roman Church defines its relationship to the pope. Representative of the position is the *Baltimore Catechism* which asserts Peter's authoritative jurisdiction over the church by Christ's ordination, and the same authority by apostolic succession for the men who follow Peter as bishop of Rome.[2]

A few Patristic texts have been thought to support these two propositions. Tertullian, for instance, is quoted as saying, "Was anything hidden from Peter, who was called the rock on which the Church was to be built, who obtained the keys of the kingdom of heaven and the power of loosing and binding, in heaven and earth?"[3] Cullmann, however, warns us that careful analysis of the historical circumstances surrounding Tertullian is essential. He notes in his work on Peter[4] what role church politics played in the exegesis of Matt 16:18–19. Tertullian himself was engaged in a battle with Callistus, the bishop of Rome, over the extension of penance, and both he and Callistus attempted to use these verses to their own advantage.[5] Tertullian claimed the authority of Matt 16:18–19 for Peter personally and in the church for "spiritual men," not for the bishop "near to Peter." Therefore, in the quote above, Tertullian, while exalting Peter, in no sense similarly exalts the bishop of Rome.

Another passage which is often cited as support for the papacy comes from Origen, who is quoted as saying, "When the supreme authority as regards the sheep was delivered to Peter, and upon him, as upon a rock, was founded the Church, the confession of no other virtue than charity was required of him."[6] But again, we must understand the full weight of Origen's position. In his comments on Matt 16:17ff, he contrasts the letter with the Spirit. He applies the letter ("the rock is Peter") to Peter, but the Spirit he applies to all who were like Peter (e.g. ". . . rock means every disciple of Christ"). It is difficult, to say the least, to claim Origen in maintaining the primacy of the bishop of Rome.[7]

But what shall we do with Cyprian? In his tract *On the Unity of the Catholic Church*, it appears that Peter not only has primacy but that his chair provides a sign of unity for the Christian church. To make things more problematic, there are two text traditions of the important paragraph that comes under discussion. One of the texts asserts the primacy of Peter and the other is not as clear in that regard. It is helpful to look at the two versions:

> No doubt the others were all that Peter was, but a primacy is given to Peter and it is (thus) made clear that there is but one church and one chair. . . . If a man does not hold fast to this oneness of Peter, does he imagine that he still holds

the faith? If he deserts the chair of Peter . . . has he still confidence that he is in the church?

The other text reads,

> No doubt the other Apostles were all that Peter was, endowed with equal dignity and power, but the start comes from him alone, in order to show that the church of Christ is unique. Indeed, this oneness of the church is figured in the canticle of Canticles. . . . If a man does not hold fast to this oneness of the church, does he imagine that he still holds the faith? If he resists and withstands the church, has he still confidence that he is in the church . . . ?[8]

What are we to do with these two strikingly different passages? Is the first text in fact a forgery written to shore up the pope's defenses? Perhaps both texts were written by Cyprian with the first passage later revised because of a political situation involving the church in Rome. Or was the first version written by Cyprian who then wrote the second, but not for the purpose of counteracting the former? We are not surprised to find a number of apologists for Rome holding to the exclusive authenticity of the first text.[9]

Whatever option scholars may wish to choose, at least this much is clear. A power struggle had developed in Rome, not completely unlike the one mentioned in connection with Tertullian. The text of Matt 16:18 was used against Cyprian by Stephen, bishop of Rome, in a dispute about baptism. Cyprian's remarks, it can be admitted, recognize a primacy for Peter *as a sign of unity*, but hardly a derivative primacy for the bishop of Rome. In fact a thorough study of Cyprian confirms what William Shaw Kerr says about the debated text,

> In it there is not a trace of consciousness that the Bishop of Rome is the centre of unity, the true Vicar of Christ. To Cyprian he was the bishop of the 'principle Church', but had no more authority than any other bishop.[10]

Our investigation so far leads us to believe that the Catholic doctrine of Petrine supremacy and a corresponding supremacy for the bishopric of Rome had not been established by the period of Cyprian, even though there were pressures in that direction. But in addition to what we have reviewed, we can remind ourselves that in the earliest Patristic literature Paul is venerated as often as Peter, a fact admitted by Roman Catholic scholars.[11] We could cite I Clement, for example,[12] or Irenaeus who specifically mentions the founding of the church of Rome by Peter *and* Paul in his work *Against Heresies*.[13] Making things even more difficult for Catholic claims is the startling conclusion of the Roman Catholic apologist, H. Burn-murdoch, who writes, "None of the writings of the first two centuries describes St. Peter as a bishop of Rome."[14]

After Cyprian, a number of church fathers address the issue of whether Matt 16:18 supports the notion of Petrine supremacy. John Chrysostom, a Greek church leader, maintains that it is the confession made by Peter to which Christ referred and that the confession of faith in Christ is the foundation of the church. Augustine, as we would imagine, says that the rock of which Jesus was speaking is actually Jesus himself. (Augustine's exegesis was later adopted by Luther.) Cyril, bishop of Alexandria (in Egypt) argues along the lines of Chrysostom and Augustine.[15]

When, then, did the papacy gain a foothold? When did it take on its unmistakable shape? In my opinion, 380 is the earliest possible date for the ascendency of the Roman Catholic system of church government, although a date in the early fifth century would be more likely.

The move to supremacy of the Roman bishop with his claims over the other bishops was primarily a result of political and cultural factors. Even the texts of Scripture that were thought to support a Petrine supremacy did not play as important a role as these cultural events. The church was, of course, just coming out of the tailspin of the Arian problem[16] and other theological struggles. Just as important, however, were administrative problems. A spirit of anarchy seemed to have overrun things, and proper discipline of heretics, such as the Arians, was lacking. Between the turbulent years of 325 and 381 (the time of two great councils of the church) especially, there were many local synods called throughout the empire, some to counteract previous synods. In the western sector the rulings of synods were not enjoying high popularity and authority in matters of doctrine. The burning question of the day was where the proper interpretation of the Scriptures was to come from if it could not be found in local synods.

Toward the end of the fourth century the answer became apparent. Administratively, the church began to collect various acts of synods and councils in order that a body of ecclesiastical legislation be available to solve problems. Geographically, Rome was perhaps the most important city in the empire. It was the only western city whose church laid claim to apostolic origin. Since Peter was thought to be the founder of the church, and since Rome was the capital of the western empire (and given the situation), Damasus, then bishop (366–384), developed further than any before him the notion that his bishopric was the most important in the western world. As different bishops requested information or advice from him, he began to answer with letters in the same epistulary form as that used by the emperor.

Leo I's papacy marks a period when Rome stood as the complete authority in the west. During his time (440–461) the western emperor, Valentinian III, decreed that all bishops in the western part of the empire were to submit to the authority of the pope upon pain of punishment. Leo also assumed heroic stature. He was instrumental as the ambassador of Rome in his plea for the city against Attila the Hun. The helpless city was sacked and stripped of its wealth, but many lives were spared by his appeal. Furthermore, he was responsible for the saying that has such importance for the papacy: "the dignity of St. Peter is not lacking even in an unworthy heir."

How Was the Early Church Governed?

It seems obvious enough that episcopacy or the papacy was not the earliest form of church government. How, then, was the early church governed? To answer this question we turn again to the literature of the first three Christian centuries.

Clement of Rome's (bishop from 92–101) *Epistle to the Corinthians* confirms the fact that the apostles appointed bishops and deacons in the church. The appointment was done with the consent of the whole church. It is scarcely disputed that the bishops were synonymous with the presbyters. Therefore, we find in Clement's letter the same pattern as that of the New Testament, i.e., the apostles appointed two orders of normal office-bearers in the church, one called bishops or presbyters and the other called deacons.[17] And this is exactly what we would expect since Clement's epistle appears in the same time and cultural frame as the New Testament itself.

Going on to Polycarp's *Epistle to the Philippians* (ca. 110), we find basic agreement with Clement. The main point learned from this epistle is that the church in Philippi had two groups of officers, bishops and deacons. Of further note is the fact that there does not appear to have been any other type of higher office. This particular epistle is also important in establishing continuity between the New Testament and later history. We remember that some fifty or sixty years earlier, Paul had written to this same church and to its bishops and deacons (Phil 1:1). Thus, the common form of government in this particular church is plain.[18]

From this harmonious testimony we turn to the writings of Ignatius (who died sometime between 107 and 116). Here we meet problems. The epistles of Ignatius speak of three classes of office-bearers: bishops, presbyters, and deacons.[19] However, there are various interpretations of this fact. First, we could conclude that these writings are falsified, or, second, that they are genuine and can be interpreted from a Presbyterian standpoint. A third conclusion is that they support monarchical episcopacy and are expressive of the system of government found at that time.

The first viewpoint came to light at the time of the Reformation. Calvin mentions in the *Institutes* (I.13,29) that there is nothing more senseless than the material collected under the name of this martyr. His point of view was maintained without question by most non-episcopal Protestants until the nineteenth century. However, at the end of the last century and the beginning of this, there have been numerous defenses of the authenticity of Ignatius' writings by Protestants such as Harnack, Zahn, Lightfoot, and Funck.

What conclusions might we draw from the debate? In my opinion the best approach is a blend of the two perspectives. Ignatius either wrote or at least dictated parts of the epistles; they are not complete forgeries. Therefore, they are worthy of a qualified confidence. This means, however, that there remains strong historical argument for a limited confidence. Some time ago it was stated this way,

> No other writer of the first and second centuries, inspired or uninspired, has uniformly used the words bishop and presbyter as descriptive of two distinct classes of functionaries, the one higher and the other lower; this distinction is uniformly and systematically made in the epistles of Ignatius: and therefore these epistles, or at least these parts of them, were not written by one who lived in the beginning of the second century.[20]

But, as was mentioned, there is a second method of interpreting these epistles. This method perceives in them a system consistent with Presbyterianism. It is argued that in Ignatius' epistles, the bishop functioned as the pastor of a single congregation. Furthermore, so it is said, there is no decisive evidence that the presbyters functioned as pastors or preachers. Those who wish to argue in this manner maintain that the bishops are the pastors, and the presbyters are the equivalent of our ruling elders. However, there are difficulties with this position, since other sources of the same time period hold that the presbyters were also pastors.

The third interpretation sees Ignatius propounding a position of monarchical episcopacy. If, however, it is granted that monarchical episcopacy is in view, certain qualifying statements are obvious from the text itself. Schaff points them out when he says,

> The peculiarity in this Ignatian view is that the bishop appears in it as the head and centre of a single congregation, and not as equally the representative of the whole church; also, that . . . he is the vicar of Christ, and not . . . merely the successor of the apostles, — the presbyters and deacons around him being represented as those successors; and finally, that there are no distinctions of order among the bishops, no trace of a primacy; all are fully coordinate vicars of Christ, who provides for himself in them, as it were, a sensible, perceptible, omnipresence in the church. The Ignatian episcopacy, in short, is congregational, not diocesan; a new and growing institution, not a settled policy of apostolic origin.[21]

Ignatius' writing is without a doubt difficult to interpret. Nevertheless, it seems that a few conclusions are possible. The literature is not entirely a forgery as was maintained in earlier centuries and should probably be understood within the context of supporting three different offices of ministry. This could be interpreted as a first step toward monarchical episcopacy. However, we find no evidence that monarchical episcopacy was elsewhere present at this time in the church. Neither would it be in accord with the evidence to assert that a Presbyterian form of government is implied. Is this, then, the beginning of a new system, a system developing in a limited geographical area?

Moving on historically, we take up evidence from the later second century through the middle of the third. Immediately we observe during this period a tendency toward indiscriminate use of different classes for the offices of bishop and presbyter. Sometimes bishop and presbyter appear to be different classes of office-bearers. Certain references clearly distinguish three offices, some maintain two offices; at times it is difficult to tell exactly what is being maintained. To be sure, the writings of Irenaeus, Tertullian, Clement of Alexandria, and Origen distinguish between bishops, presbyters, and deacons. However, these distinctions are not very great in and of themselves, nor are they constantly observed.

As has been noted in early post-apostolic Christianity, there were only two classes of church officers, bishops and deacons, with the bishops serving as pastors of the churches. It seems that through the middle of the third century, when pastors from one area assembled into what may be called a presbytery, the president of that group came gradually to be called the bishop while the pastors maintained the title of presbyter. Bishop and presbyter were at one time synonymous, but later bishop became the technical term for the president of the presbytery. While the writers of this period at times use the words bishop and presbyter indiscriminately, they certainly do not conceive of the bishops as a superior order above the presbyters. Also a bishop was selected by both the presbytery and the people.

Moving on to Cyprian and the middle of the third century, we take stock of a new development. There is little question that Cyprian maintained a distinction between bishops and presbyters. In a certain sense, he also maintained a priority of the bishops over the presbyters and advanced their "technical" superiority. We have already seen that he argued for a certain primacy of Peter over the other disciples; from here, one could conceivably argue by way of Peter's relationship to Rome for a certain primacy of the bishop of Rome over the other bishops. However, Cyprian never did.[22]

At any rate, the time of Cyprian witnessed a fixed president of the presbytery, called the bishop. With regard to Cyprian himself, there is no evidence he maintained that the bishops were blessed by a superiority to the presbyters because of a divine appointment or that they were privileged to perform ministerial functions reserved for them alone. Cyprian himself tells us that he did nothing without the consent of his presbytery, and when certain grave matters were decided he acted with the consent of the people as well. Therefore, despite the outline of future ecclesiastical structures, monarchical episcopacy or the papacy are hardly in place.

How then was the church governed in its early history? It is difficult if not impossible to say that the earliest system of government is exactly like what we enjoy in twentieth-century Presbyterianism. In my opinion, however, the general pattern was something like this: in each separate congregation there was a board of presbyters and a board of deacons. The deacons performed the acts of mercy necessary for the congregation. The board of presbyters ruled and supervised the activities of the church. Within that board of presbyters was the pastor of the church. The pastor, who held the title of presbyter, also held the title of bishop. It is possible that the other presbyters (the equivalent of our ruling elders) would at times hold the title of bishop as well, functioning as shepherds for their sheep.

Within a certain locale, the presbyters from different congregations gathered for deliberations. In that group, as in modern-day presbyteries, one pastor was elected as moderator or president. Whether there were annual elections of the moderator, as presently practiced in Presbyterianism or whether they were elected for life, as Calvin was in Geneva, is difficult to determine.

In rough outline, I believe that this was the earliest system. However, apologists for both monarchical episcopacy and Presbyterianism agree that there were a number of changes in church government after the first few centuries. That is about all we agree on, however! Presbyterians view the changes as a degeneration and non-Presbyterians see the development as solidification of earlier (i.e., non-Presbyterian) systems.

A few citations help to confirm a Presbyterian reading. Ambrose of Milan (376) wrote in one of his commentaries,

After churches were planted in all places, and officers ordained, matters were settled otherwise than they were in the beginning. And hence it is that the Apostles' writings do not, in all things, agree with the present constitution of the Church; because they were written under the first rise of the Church; for he calls Timothy, who was created a Presbyter by him, a Bishop, for so, at first, the Presbyters were called.

Jerome, at about the same time is equally clear in his comments,

Among the ancients, Presbyters and Bishops were the same. But by little and little, that all the seeds of dissension might be plucked up, the whole care was devolved on one. As, therefore, the Presbyters know, that by the custom of the Church, they are subject to him who is their president, so let Bishops know, that they are above Presbyters more by the custom of the Church, than by the true dispensation of Jesus Christ!

Augustine, writing to Jerome, states,

I entreat you to correct me faithfully when you see I need it; for, although, according to the names of honour which the custom of the Church has now brought into use, the office of Bishop is greater than that of Presbyter, nevertheless, in many respects, Augustine is inferior to Jerome.[23]

Here concludes our short study of Presbyterianism in the ancient church. Unfortunately, the evidence is sufficiently controversial to require many volumes to analyze the original state of affairs. Admittedly, much that I have presented is hotly disputed. Nevertheless, I am convinced that during the first few centuries of the church at least, Presbyterianism as a general system was employed by the church, and that system of government approximated what we find in the New Testament. Again the issue should be put as clearly as possible; the Bible and Bible alone is our standard, even in matters of church government. The early church attempted to remain true to the Scriptures. Because she did, she governed herself in a Presbyterian manner. The church today should do likewise.

NOTES

1. Cf. William Cunningham, *Historical Theology*, I (Edinburgh: Banner of Truth, [1979]), 253.

2. The *Baltimore Catechism* reads: "Christ gave special powers in His Church to St. Peter by making him the head of the Apostles and the chief teacher and ruler of the entire Church. Christ did not intend that the special power of chief teacher and ruler of the entire Church should be exercised by St. Peter alone, but intended that this power should be passed down to his successor, the Pope, the Bishop of Rome, who is the Vicar of Christ on earth and the visible head of the Church," [taken from John A. O'Brien, *Understanding the Catholic Faith* (Notre Dame: Ave Maria, 1955), 112]. This two-pronged structure is apparent from many other sources as well; for example, Henry T. Hudson, *Papal Power* (Welwyn, England: Evangelical Press, 1981), 10f.

3. Cited by J. N. Murphy, *The Chair of Peter* (London: Burns and Oats, 1886), 27.

4. Oscar Cullmann, *Peter: Disciple-Apostle-Martyr* (Philadelphia: Westminster, 1953).

5. Ibid., 159–61; cf. 121.

6. Cited by Murphy, *The Chair*, 28.

7. Cf. Cullmann, *Peter*, 159.

8. As cited by Michael M. Winter, *Saint Peter and the Popes* (Baltimore: Helicon, 1960), 40.

9. A few supporters may be mentioned: Colin Lindsay, *The Evidence for the Papacy* (London: Longmans, 1870), 29; J. N. Murphy, *The Chair*, 29; H. Burn-murdoch, *The Development of the Papacy* (London: Faber & Faber, 1954), 130f.

10. William Shaw Kerr, *A Handbook on the Papacy* (Toronto: Evangelical Publishers, 1950), 99.

11. An example is Burn-murdoch, *The Development*, 27.

12. Cullmann gives extensive analysis of this piece of literature; see *Peter*, 89–109; cf. 235.

13. *Adv. haer.* III, 3,2. This interpretation is not accepted by all scholars. P. Batiffol, *Cathedra Petri* (Paris: Les Éditions du Cerf, 1938) attempts to interpret the text to assert Petrine supremacy, p. 14.

14. Burn-murdoch, *The Development*, 66.

15. Cf. Cullmann, *Peter*, 162.

16. Cf. the author's *Augustinus Contra Maximinum: An Analysis of Augustine's Anti-Arian Writings* (Ann Arbor: MacNaughton and Gunn, 1985).

17. Concerning this important piece of literature, see Cunningham, *Historical*, 246. Cunningham is emphatic in asserting the continuity between the New Testament and Clement and that this continuity precludes the conception of monarchical episcopacy. Philip Schaff, writing at about the same time period although not a strong defender of Presbyteri-

anism, says: "Clement knows nothing of an episcopate above the presbyterate; and his epistle itself is written, not in his own name, but in that of the church of Rome" [*History of the Christian Church*, II (New York: Scribners, 1910), 646].

18. Cf. the discussion in Cunningham, *Historical*, 247 and Schaff, *History*, 666.

19. *Epistle to the Magnesians*, 6,1.

20. Cunningham, *Historical*, 114f.

21. Schaff, *History*, 148. The opinion of Schaff is not strongly disputed to this day. In a more recent work supporting episcopacy, *The Apostolic Ministry: Essays on the History and Doctrine of Episcopacy*, edited by K. Kirk (London: Hodder & Stoughton, 1946), Dix tells us that Ignatius "makes no reference to any sort of 'succession' in the episcopate." Although Dix does not want to give much weight to this silence, he also asserts that Ignatius "does not directly connect the two offices (episcopacy and apostolate)" (p. 251). Dix does go too far, however, in his attempts to see the threefold ministry as existing before this time, an argument that would be important to Dix's thesis but not able to be substantiated by the literature of the time. This would, of course, be where he would disagree with Schaff's statement that this is a "new and growing institution."

22. On Cyprian's supposed inconsistency, see Cullmann, *Peter*, 161, note 11.

23. Citations from Ambrose, Jerome, and Augustine are from Samuel Miller, "Presbyterianism the truly Primitive and Apostolical Constitution of the Church of Christ," *Presbyterian Tracts* (Philadelphia: Presbyterian Board of Publications, 1842), 15f.

Peter A. Lillback

5 The Reformers' Rediscovery of Presbyterian Polity

A MONG THE MANY INGREDIENTS that blended together to produce the Protestant Reformation, two stand out as foundational and worthy of emphasis. The *first* is the fact that the Reformation was from its very onset a reformation of the church. It was the attempt of all the reformers of the sixteenth century to purify the medieval church from its manifold corruptions, whether these corruptions took the form of the sale of indulgences, the purchasing of church offices, or the superstitions affixed to the sacramental administrations. The *second* ingredient is the standard by which the church was to be reformed, namely, the Word of God. The Scriptures were the benchmark by which all doctrine and practice were to be examined. In other words, *sola scriptura* had very direct implications for the doctrine and practice of the church, indeed, even for its government.[1]

This is illustrated in Beza's *Life of Calvin*. Beza relates the events of Calvin's return to Geneva after Calvin's short exile to Strasburg as follows,

Calvin being thus restored at the urgent entreaty of his Church, proceeded to set it in order. Seeing that the city stood greatly in need of a curb, he declared, in the first place, that he could not properly fulfil his ministry, unless, along with Christian doctrine, a regular presbytery with full ecclesiastical authority were established. At that time, therefore, . . . laws for the election of a presbytery, and for the due maintenance of that order, were passed, agreeably to the Word of God, and with the consent of the citizens themselves.[2]

A few pages later, Beza continues,

To resume our narrative, as soon as he returned to the city, calling to mind the saying, (Matth. vi.33,) "Seek ye first the kingdom of God, and his righteousness; and all other things will be added unto you," the first thing he did was to obtain the consent of the Senate to a form of ecclesiastical polity, which was agreeable to the Word of God, and from which neither ministers nor people should afterwards be permitted to depart. . . . He demonstrated that not only doctrines, but also the form of Church government, must be sought for in Scripture, and appealed, in support of his views, to the expressed opinion of the most distinguished men of the age, as OEcolampadius, Zuinglius, Zuichius, Philip, Bucer, Capito, and Myconius; still not condemning as antichristian those Churches which had not proceeded the same length, or those pastors who thought that their flocks did not require to be so curbed.[3]

From Calvin's conviction that the Scriptures prescribe a form of church government, there arose what has come to be known as the *jure divino* doctrine of the church. This view has been especially connected with Andrew Melville, the great architect of the government of the Scottish Presbyterian church.[4] In essence, the *jure divino* position maintains that the Scriptures contain a true form of church government. Since this form of government possesses the authority of the divine law, any other governmental form is unlawful inasmuch as it is opposed to the Scriptures. This view had much influence on the Westminster divines of the following century.[5]

The true significance of this question of the *jus divinum* for the form of church government for the English-speaking world is seen in the fact that churches still designate themselves by the form of government that they practice: Episcopalian, Presbyterian, Congregational, and Independent. During the years 1640 to 1660, it is said that some 30,000 British pamphlets were produced on the subject of church government![6]

What then was the form of church government discovered in the Scriptures by the Protestant reformers? The answer to this question cannot be given in any short statement. This is because there never was one unified system of government gleaned from the Scriptures. The aftermath of the attempt to codify the scriptural form is well described by Richard Baxter as he attempted to form a church union in the late 1600s in England. He writes,

> The ministers of the churches were then (as is usual) of divers opinions about Church Government; (1) Some were for our Diocesane Episcopacy as stated by the Reformation. (2) Some were for a more Reformed Episcopacy, described by Bucer, . . . Usher, etc. (3) Some were for Diocesans in a higher strain, as subject to a foreign Jurisdiction . . . the pope being *principium Unitatis.* (4) Some were for National and Classical Government by Presbyters only, without Bishops. (5) And some were for a parity of Ministers and Churches, without any superior Bishops, or Synods, or Governeurs; but to have every Congregation to have all governing power in their proper pastors. (6) And some were for each Congregation to be governed by the major vote of the people; the Pastor being but to gather and declare their vote; Among all these the 3rd sort, the Foreigners, were utterly unreconcileable; and of the 6th we had no great hopes. But

with the other four we attempted such a measure of agreement as might be useful in a loose, unsettled time. . . . The most laborious ministers took the hint, and seconded us in many counties: first and chiefly in Westmoreland and Cumberland, and then in Dorsetshire, Wiltshire, Hampshire, and Essex. . . . But when it came to closest practice, As the Foreigners (Prelatists) and Popular *called* Brownists, kept off, so but few of the rigid Presbyterians or Independents joyned with us; (and indeed Worcestershire and the adjoining Counties had but few of either sort). But the main body of our Association were men that thought the Episcopal, Presbyterian, and Independent, had each of them some good in which they excelled the other two parties, and each of them some mistakes; and that to select out of all three the best part, and leave the worst, was the most desirable (and ancient) Form of Government.[7]

Although such divergent views ultimately developed among Protestants, it is nevertheless true that among the followers of the Genevan reformer John Calvin, a fairly homogeneous view of ecclesiastical government emerged. That this view would ultimately be called Presbyterianism is not surprising when one considers the frequency with which this term arises in Beza's biography of Calvin.[8]

Through his students, Calvin's ecclesiology was carried to wherever the Reformed faith was taught. Presbyterian Scotland was influenced mightily by two of Calvin's students, John Knox and Andrew Melville. Knox called Calvin's Geneva, "the maist perfyt schoole of Chryst since the dayis of the Apostilis."[9] Melville was not only a student at Geneva, but he had been asked by Calvin to serve as a Greek instructor. He declined to do this in favor of searching for Greek and Hebrew manuscripts under the patronage of the Augsburg banker, Ulrich Fugger. He later served at Geneva by accepting the chair of civil law. When Melville returned to Scotland, Beza wrote to the general assembly, "The graitest token of affection the Kirk of Geneva could schaw to Scotland is that they suffered themselves to be spuiled of Mr. Andro Melville, whereby the Kirk of Scotland might be enritched."[10]

Melville's influence on Scotland in favor of a strict Presbyterianism is perhaps best seen in his work in preparing *The Second Book of Discipline*. Knox had consented to the idea of a modified bishop called a *superintendent* after the model of the French Reformed Church.[11] Consequently, *The First Book of Discipline* provided for ten superintendents for the Church of Scotland. The superintendents, however, were clearly under the oversight of the general assembly. The *First Book* states,

These men must not be suffered to live as your idle bishops have done heretofore, neither must they remain where gladly they would; but they must be preachers themselves, and such as may not make long residence in any place till their kirkes be planted and provided of ministers, or at the least readers, ... If the superintendent be found negligent in any of the chiefe points of his office, and specially if he be noted negligent in preaching of the Word, and visitation of the kirkes; or if he be convicted of such crimes which in common members are damned, he must be deposed without respect of his person or office. [12]

Moreover, that Knox did not have in mind the bishop of the prelatical variety is seen by his own refusal to accept the office of bishop of Rochester in 1552. [13] This is confirmed by Miller,

> It may be supposed by some, however, that Knox opposed prelacy because a participation in its honour was not within his reach. But, the truth is, a bishopric was offered him, which he refused, because he considered prelacy as unlawful. Accordingly when John Douglas was made tulchan (or nominal) bishop of St. Andrews, Knox utterly refused to induct or instal him. And when this refusal was imputed to unworthy motives, he publicly declared from the pulpit, on the next sabbath, "I have refused a greater bishopric than ever it was; and might have had it with the favour of greater men than he hath this: but I did and do repine for the discharge of my conscience, that the church of Scotland be not subject to that order." [14]

In view of the death of Knox in 1572, and the reintroduction of episcopacy into Scotland in the same year by the then regent of Scotland, the Earl of Morton, it is hardly surprising that the general assembly was willing to follow the lead of Melville toward a stricter Presbyterian polity. The assembly had seen their hoped-for superintendents turned into *tulchan bishops*. The Gaelic word, *tulchan*, means a stuffed calf-skin used to induce the mother cow to yield her milk. [15] This term was expressive of the Scots' distaste not simply for episcopacy, but for the many abuses that accompanied the preferment of prelates. For example, John Douglas who had not been installed by Knox was finally inducted into his office by the backing of the Earl of Morton. Douglas had secured the archbishopric through a bargain that had given the Earl most of the revenue generated by the position. This was not the superintendent that Knox had in mind. Such a bishop was a "superintendent" stuffed with a "prelate" to "milk" the Scottish church. They were in fact tulchan bishops.

Melville's leadership toward a church government founded only upon the Scriptures, or a *jure divino* Presbyterianism, was to be completed in 1580 with the adoption of *The Second Book of Discipline*. Melville had returned to Scotland in 1574 from Geneva, two years after Knox's death. At his urging, the general assembly in 1576 declared, "The name of bishop is common to all who are appointed to take charge of a particular flock." Following the teaching of Calvin, the *Second Book* states that *bishops, pastors*, and *ministers* are equivalent terms. [16] The complete demise of episcopacy for the Scottish church is evident not only in the significant absence of the "superintendent" in the *Second Book*, but also in the resolution adopted by the general assembly in 1580 which denies the legitimacy of episcopacy on the *jus divinum* basis:

Forsuameikle as the office of ane bischope, as it is now usit, and commonlie taken within this realme, hes no sure warrant, auctoritie, or good ground, out of the Scripture of God, but is brought in by the folie and corruptione, to the great overthrow of the Kirk of God; the haill Assemblie of the Kirk, in ane voyce, efter libertie give to all men to reasone in the matter, nane opposing himself in defending the said pretended office — Finds and declares the said pretended office, usit and termit as is above said, unlawful in the self, as haveing naither foundament, ground, nor warrant, within the Word of God.[17]

The British Kingdom to the south was deeply involved in the dispute over the biblical form of church government. The issue had been raised by the "morning star of the Reformation," John Wiclif. He had written,

One thing I boldly assert, that in the primitive church, or in the time of the apostle Paul, two orders of clergy were thought sufficient, viz. *priest* and *deacon*; and I do also say, that in the time of Paul, *fuit idem presbyter atque episcopus*, i.e., a priest and a bishop were one and the same; for, in those times, the distinct orders of Pope, Cardinals, Patriarchs, Archbishops, Bishops, arch-deacons, officials, and deans, were not invented.[18]

Wiclif's assertion was sounded again at the beginning of the English Reformation by no less a person than Archbishop Cranmer. In 1537 during Henry VIII's reign a book was published entitled *The Institution of a Christian Man*. This was dubbed the "Bishop's Book" because of Cranmer's joint authorship with other prelates. It was recommended and subscribed by the two archbishops and nineteen bishops, and published under the king's authority. It states,

. . . although the fathers of the succeeding church, after the apostles, instituted certain inferior degrees of ministry; yet the truth is, that in the New Testament there is no mention made of any other degree or distinction in orders, but only of deacons or ministers, and of presbyters or bishops.[19]

The early English Reformation's recognition of the Presbyterian principle of the identity of the bishop and presbyter was to be joined eventually to the Genevan views imported by Knox. Knox's refusal of preferment to the bishopric of Rochester in 1552 certainly helped fan the flames of nonconformity in England. Thus in 1554 Archdeacon Philpot of Winchester said to his examiners before his martyrdom,

I allow the church of Geneva, and the doctrine of the same; for it is catholic and apostolic, and follows the doctrine which the apostles preached; and the doctrine taught and preached in king Edward's days, was also according to the same. And are you not ashamed to persecute me and others for your church's sake, which is Babylonian, and contrary to the true catholic church?[20]

Was Philpot correct in asserting that King Edward had the doctrine of the Church of Geneva proclaimed during his rule? This would appear to be the case if one is to receive the testimony of John à Lasco. Writing in his dedication of a book printed in 1555 in honor of Sigismund, king of Poland, he relates,

> When I was called by that king, (Edward VI,) and when certain laws of the country stood in the way, so that the public rites of divine worship used under popery could not immediately be purged out; (which the king himself desired;) and when I was earnest for the foreign churches, it was at length his pleasure, that the public rites of the English churches should be reformed by degrees, as far as could be got done by the laws of the country; but that strangers, who were not strictly bound to these laws in this matter, should have churches granted unto them, in which they should freely regulate all things, *wholly according to apostolical doctrine and practice*, without any regard to the rites of the country; that by this means the English churches also might be excited to embrace the apostolical purity, by the unanimous consent of all the estates of the kingdom. Of the project, the king himself, from his great piety, was both the chief author and the defender.[21]

Although à Lasco does not mention the church of Geneva here, the key phrase in italics indicates that the Genevan principle of finding the church's government in Scripture was intended. M'Crie makes it manifest that à Lasco's views of the church were nearly identical with those of Scotland. This corroborates the idea that Edward was moving strongly in the direction of the Genevan church:

> à Lasco published an account of the form of government and worship used in these congregations, which greatly resembled that which was introduced into Scotland at the establishment of the reformation. The affairs of each congregation were managed by a minister, ruling elders, and deacons; and each of these offices was considered as of divine institution. . . . The inspection of the different congregations was committed to a superintendent, 'who was greater only in respect of his greater trouble and care, not having more authority than the other elders, either as to the ministry of the word and sacraments, or as to the exercise of ecclesiastical discipline, to which he was subject equally with the rest. . . . '[22]

By 1570 the Puritan program for reforming the government of the church had become fully delineated. In this year, Thomas Cartwright, Professor of Divinity at Cambridge wrote,

> (1) That the names and functions of archbishops and archdeacons ought to be abolished. (2) That the offices of the lawful ministers of the Church, viz., bishops and deacons, ought to be reduced to their apostolical institution: bishops to preach the word of God, and pray, and deacons to be employed in taking care of the poor. (3) That the government of the Church ought not to be intrusted to bishop's chancellors, or the officials of archdeacons; but every church ought to be governed by its own ministers and presbyters. (4) That ministers ought not to be at large, but every one should have the charge of a particular congregation. (5) That no man ought to solicit, or to stand as a candidate for the ministry. (6) That ministers ought not to be created by the sole authority of the bishop, but to be openly and fairly chosen by the people.[23]

Cartwright's affinity to Scottish Presbyterianism is evident. In fact, he was invited to a Scottish chair of theology.[24] Archbishop Bancroft on February 9, 1588, finally claimed for the episcopal theory the *jus divinum* that had become the nemesis of the establishment in the hands of non-conforming Presbyterians. To bolster his counter-attack on the Puritan ecclesiology, he charged the Scottish Presbyterians with "Genevating" and the English Puritans with "Scottizing."[25] Again, it was quite clear to the opponents of Presbyterian polity that the Genevan reformer was behind the despised system of ecclesiastical government.

In 1574 the first book of discipline produced by the English Puritans of Presbyterian conviction was published. This work was entitled, *The Sacred Discipline of the Church, Described in the Word of God*, written by Thomas Cartwright and Walter Travers. By 1590 it had been signed by as many as five hundred ministers in all parts of England. The second edition was published in Geneva as the episcopal party sought to destroy it wherever possible.[26] The first paragraph surveys the entire scope of Presbyterian polity and discipline and offers the *jus divinum* principle. The second and fourth paragraphs challenge the basis of prelacy:

> The discipline of Christ's Church that is necessary for all times is delivered by Christ, and set downe in the holy Scriptures. Therefore the true and lawfull Discipline is to be fetched from thence, and from thence alone. And that which resteth upon any other foundation ought to be esteemed unlawfull and counterfeit.
>
> Of all particular Churches there is one and the same right order and forme: Therefore also no one may challenge to itselfe any power over others; nor any right which doth not alike agree to others.
>
> The Ministers of publique charges in every particular Church ought to be called and appointed to their charges by a lawfull Ecclesiasticall calling, such as hereafter is set downe.
>
> All these for the divers regard of their severall kinds are of equall power amongst themselves.[27]

What is remarkable about this *Sacred Discipline of the Church* is that it does not even mention the office of bishop! It simply states the offices of the church as pastors, teachers, elders, and deacons. It never even bothers to say that the term bishop is equal to presbyter. Such silence in the face of the established ecclesiastical system reveals the disdain that the primitive English Presbyterians had for episcopacy. Under the guidance of the Westminster Assembly, Presbyterianism was to become the supplanter of episcopacy in England for a brief period of some twenty years.

The impact of Calvin's biblically-based Presbyterianism was not only felt in the British Isles. His students also took his system into the European countries on the continent. The entrance of Reformed polity into France is an amazing story of suffering, perseverance, secrecy, and success.[28] The observers of the Gallican Reformed Church's growth saw the imprint of the Genevan reformer everywhere. Thus the Venetian Ambassador in France in 1561 reports,

> Unless it otherwise pleases the Almighty, religious affairs will soon be in an evil case in France, because there is not one single province uncontaminated. Indeed in some provinces, such as Normandy, almost the whole of Brittany, Touraine, Poitou, Gascony, and a great part of Languedoc, of Dauphiny, and of Provence, comprising three-fourths of the kingdom, congregations and meetings, which they call assemblies, are held; and in these assemblies they read and preach, according to the rites and usages of Geneva, without any respect either for the ministers of the king or the commandments of the king himself. This contagion has penetrated so deeply that it affects every class of persons, and, what appears more strange, even the ecclesiastical body itself. I do not mean only priests, friars, and nuns, for there are but few monasteries that are not corrupted, but even bishops and many of the principal prelates, who hitherto had not shown any such disposition; and it is only on account of the rigorous execution of the law that other persons besides the populace have not disclosed themselves, because they have restrained themselves for the time being, from fear of the loss of their property and lives. . . . more than fifty others, who are called ministers, were summoned from various parts of France to travel, and teach and preach the 'Word,' for thus they term the Gospels, and their own doctrine. Your Serenity will hardly believe the influence and the great power which the principal minister of Geneva, by name Calvin, a Frenchman, and a native of Picardy, possesses in this kingdom; he is a man of extraordinary authority, who by his mode of life, his doctrines, and his writings, rises superior to all the rest; and it is almost impossible to believe the enormous sums of money which are secretly sent to him from France to maintain his power.[29]

While the Venetian Ambassador was aware of fifty ministers proclaiming the doctrines of Calvin in France in 1561, the research of Robert Kingdon has indicated that some 142 men were involved in 151 separate missions during 1561 alone.[30] The great success of these missionary efforts emanating from Geneva can be deduced from the official count taken of the Huguenot churches in 1562 by order of the Queen Mother Catherine de Medici. The count revealed that there were 2,150 churches! Emile Doumergue has estimated that nearly three million of the twenty million population of France had at this time espoused the Huguenot faith.[31] The growth of the church's structure is equally phenomenal. In 1555 the first regularly organized church was found in Paris. The congregation elected its own pastor, and had a board of elders and deacons. Four years later in 1559 the First National Synod was held. This was accompanied, following Calvin's advice, by the organization of appellate courts.[32]

The First National Synod was held in secrecy in order to protect the lives of the commissioners. The synod adopted the *Gallican Confession*, the work of Calvin's pupil Antione de la Roche Chandieu, and *La Discipline Ecclésiastique*.[33] Consequently, the French church was the first national church to be organized fully along the lines of the Calvinist city of

Geneva. This short list of the articles from the *Confession* dealing with the doctrine of church government presents Calvin's main line of thought:

XXV The Church is established by Christ's authority. In it He has established pastors for the preaching of the Word and administering the sacraments. Hence the Church cannot exist without pastors.

XXVI No one may separate himself from the true order of the Church, even if magistrates are opposed to it.

XXVII The true Church is the company of the faithful who agree to follow the Word of God.

XXVIII There is no Church where the Word of God is not received with submission and the use of the sacraments. The papal assemblies are therefore condemned, although some trace of the true Church is left there. Thus those with Roman baptism do not need a second baptism.

XXIX (Quoted in full) As to the true Church, we believe that it should be governed according to the order established by our Lord Jesus Christ. That there should be pastors, overseers, and deacons, so that true doctrine may have its course, that errors may be corrected and suppressed, and the poor and all who are in affliction may be helped in their necessities; and that assemblies may be held in the name of God, so that great and small may be edified.

XXX (Quoted in full) We believe that all true pastors, wherever they may be, have the same authority and equal power under one head, one only sovereign and universal bishop, Jesus Christ; and that consequently no Church shall claim any authority or dominion over any other.

XXXI The authority to govern in the Church comes by election. All pastors, overseers, and deacons should have evidence of being called to their office.

XXXII (Quoted in full) We believe, also, that it is desirable and useful that those elected to be superintendents devise among themselves what means should be adopted for the government of the whole body, and yet that they should never depart from that which was ordained by our Lord Jesus Christ. Which does not prevent there being some special ordinances in each place, as convenience may require.

XXXIII No human invention may be used in the service of God. The Christian conscience cannot be bound by such laws. Yet all are bound by God's laws. This includes the practice of excommunication taught by Christ.[34]

One can evidently recognize the sum of Presbyterian polity in these articles: (1) Christ is the sole Head of the church (XXX), (2) He has delegated authority to men who hold the offices of pastors, overseers (elders), and deacons (XXV, XXIX, XXXI), (3) These officers are elected by the people (XXXI). (4) All pastors possess equal power (XXX). (5) The officers of the church are responsible for doctrine, the correction of errors, and mercy to the poor (XXIX), (6) Discipline is a practice of the church as seen in excommunication (XXXIII). The only distinctive not mentioned in the *Confession* is the idea of the ascending courts from session or consistory to the general assembly. This lack, however, is amply accounted for by the very thorough treatment of this matter in *La Discipline*.[35]

Moreover, the *jure divino* concept of church government appears in the *Confession* in articles XXIX and XXXII. Article XXIX says that the "true church . . . should be governed according to the order established by our Lord Jesus Christ." Article XXXII states that those elected as superintendents should devise means "for the government of the whole body, and yet that they should never depart from that which was ordained by our Lord Jesus Christ." The *Confession* therefore insists that Christ has given an order for government for his church in the Scriptures.

However, the *Confession* raises the matter of the superintendent which has been considered already in the *First Book of Discipline* of the Scottish church and the foreigner's church of John à Lasco in England. It is clear from article XXXII that superintendents were to be elected. But what exactly was to be their function and power? Again, *La Discipline Ecclesiastique* provides the answers. In articles II and III, it is said,

> . . . a president, in each colloquy (or classis) or synod shall be chosen, with a common consent, to preside in the colloquy or synod, and to do every thing that belongs to it; and the said office shall end with each colloquy or synod and council.[36]

In order to prevent any misunderstanding, the national synod also determined, "that the word superintendent in the . . . article, is not to be understood of any superiority of one pastor above another, but only in general of such as have office and charge in the church."[37] From these statements, it would appear that the Gallican superintendent would be tantamount to the moderator of a presbytery or general assembly in terms of modern presbyterian polity. In the final portion of this study, consideration will be given to Calvin's own conception of the office of the superintendent.

The French Reformed Church's polity had a great deal of influence upon Scottish and English Presbyterianism.[38] This is seen in an incidental way through various French ecclesiastical terms that have been anglicized. Examples of these are: minister, pastor (*pasteur*), probationer (*proposants*), moderator (*moderateur*), consistory (*consistoire*), overture (*oeuveture*). The *First Book of Discipline* of Scotland followed *La Discipline* by making the eldership a term office. The *Second Book*, however, broke from the French model and ordained the ruling elder for life. (It is interesting to note that the Orthodox Presbyterian Church has allowed both term and life service for its elders according to the convictions of the individual congregation.) On the other hand, *The First Book* had considered the imposition of hands at ordination to be "nott necessarie," while the *Second Book* followed the French example of laying on of hands.

Perhaps another influence from Gallican church life on the British scene is the struggle with independency. Under the profound duress of the ruling Valois-Angouléme family, the highly organized national system of the French church found that it could not always function. Persecution, limited numbers of trained pastors, the struggle to retain secrecy, all contributed to the halting steps of the church's progress.

In order to deal with the beleaguered consistories and the non-existent discipline in many areas, a member of the Paris church named Jean Morély proposed a congregational-type organization. In 1562 he published a book entitled *Traicte* which contained his views and arguments on the subject of church polity. The official reply to the work was released anonymously with the title *The Confirmation of the Ecclesiastical Discipline Observed in the Reformed Churches of the Kingdom of France; with the Answer to Objections Proposed Against It.* It was published in 1566 in an edition from Geneva and another from La Rochelle.

Morély was initially discredited due to public disclosure of some of his personal letters in which he slandered Beza with such epithets as, "this Jupiter of the Lake of Geneva, this new Antichrist." Ultimately, Morély died in the St. Bartholomew's Massacre of 1572.[39] That Morély might in some measure have prodded the development of English independency that was such a challenge to the Presbyterians at the Westminster Assembly is seen by the many who wrote against his ideas. Gray writes,

> By the Synod of La Rochelle in 1571 the power of Morély's threat was pretty well dissipated. However, fear that similar challenges might arise continued to disturb Beza and the Genevans as well as leaders like Jean Taffin and Thomas van Til in the Low Countries, Thomas Cartwright and Walter Travers in England, Caspar Olevianus in the Palatinate. These men vigorously defended Calvinistic discipline and became unbending in the necessity of Calvinistic synodical polity. The entire international community became committed to strict discipline and presbyterian polity in tight unity for spreading the gospel.[40]

Before leaving this analysis of the French church, one last item of interest should be mentioned. One of the recurring questions for Reformed ecclesiastical discussion is whether the synods and national assemblies are "higher" courts or "broader" courts.[41] Presbyterians generally conceive of the regional gatherings and national gatherings of their church as a "higher judicatory," while the Reformed tend to think of them as having primarily advisory power. Such a distinction, of course, is by no means universally accurate. What is significant at this juncture is the unmistakable commitment of the French church to the concept of a "higher judicatory." This is seen in the terms of the commission with which the provincial synods of France were obliged to furnish their deputies to the national synod:

> We promise before God to submit ourselves unto all that shall be concluded and determined in your holy assembly, to obey and execute it to the utmost of our

power, being persuaded that God will preside among you and lead you by his Holy Spirit into all truth and equity by the rule of his word, for the good and edification of his Church, to the glory of his great name, which we humbly beg of his divine Majesty in our daily prayers.[42]

The French church established its unity with the churches of the Netherlands in 1583 when the French National Synod subscribed the *Belgic Confession* and the body of church discipline practiced in the Netherlands.[43] It has been said that the early reformers of the Dutch provinces were Huguenots.[44] The affinity of the Dutch churches for the Genevan model of polity is manifest in the action of the Synod of Emden in October of 1571. At that time, a polity on the Genevan model was adopted as one that was best suited for "churches under the cross."[45]

Thus far a survey of the spread of Genevan Presbyterianism to various Calvinistic churches has been presented. Yet relatively little has been offered from Calvin's own thought. In concluding this study, then, it would seem fitting to offer some of Calvin's own insights into the polity that he fashioned from the Scriptures and taught to his students.

One question that is significant for this study is Calvin's understanding of the superintendent. Did Calvin hold to a modified episcopalism that blended together a system of bishops and presbyters? Such a claim was made at least as early as 1708 by Benedict Pictet, the Swiss theologian. In a letter Pictet writes,

> If Mr. Calvin had entertained any prejudices against the episcopal order, or if he had had any thoughts of propagating the polity of the Genevan church among other countrys, or if he had thought that that would best conduce to keep up good order in the church, how comes it that in that long letter which he wrote to the Duke of Somerset concerning the Reformation of the Church of England, he does not speak one word against the dignity of Bishops? For then he had a very fair occasion of breaking his mind upon this head, and deserving well of the church. How comes it to pass that when he wrote to A. Bp. Cranmer he gives him all the honorable titles which are paid to that character? Nay, be pleased to hear what he says in his book of the necessity of a Reformation in the Church, *Talem nobis*, etc. Let them give us such an Hierarchy in which Bishops may be so advanced that they may not refuse to be subject to Christ and may depend upon him as their only head and refer themselves to him and so cultivate a brotherly fellowship among themselves, that they be not bound together with any other knott than that of the Gospel truth; then we shall confess them to deserve ye heaviest curse who shall not reverence it; and pay a willing obedience to it. And writing to his friend, Mr. Farell, he observes that there ought to be among Christians such a hatred of schism, that they must, upon all occasions, to the utmost of their power, avoid it.[46]

Pictet's sentiments would have pleased the orthodox Calvinist and outstanding Huguenot Pierre du Moulin. He declared in 1639, "The French Church never unbishopped any prelate; it was necessitie, not any theological decision that made them frame a Church without Bishops."[47] In more recent times, Dr. Pannier has compiled evidence that he believes proves Calvin had no objection to Bishops, provided that their function was merely administrative.[48] We have already seen that the Scottish church, à Lasco's congregation, and the Gallican church all at one time had superintendents. To these facts can be added Beza's response to Hadrian Saravia's work in defense of the hierarchy. Alluding to his own tract entitled "De Triplici Episcopatu" Beza says,

> Let those who will go now and wonder, that a triple episcopate should be constituted by us; one, namely, that which is evidently *divine*, constituted by the apostles, and which we desire to be restored, another human, by which an order (or matter of arrangement) was imperceptibly changed into a grade, (or distinct rank,) which may truly be enjoyed by those who are persuaded, that the right use of it can be renewed and maintained; a third, oligarchical and tyrannical, nay, even satanic, which is both to be abominated in the manifestly anti-christian despotism of Rome, and to be reformed from the word of God, in the still remaining oligarchical domination of episcopacy.[49]

From this it would seem clear that Beza would allow for a bishop that was of "human" invention if it could be renewed and maintained. Yet he himself desired that which was "divine" in origin to be restored. This, of course, was the biblical office of pastor.

Two things must be said of Calvin's view. First, he did desire to have a government drawn only from the Scriptures. Second, he too allowed for the position of a superintendent yet insisting that there is no difference between *pastor* and *bishop* in the Scriptures. Was Calvin inconsistent at this point? Perhaps a couple of quotations from his commentaries will elucidate Calvin's position. Commenting on Philippians 1:1 he states,

> *Bishops.* He names the *pastors* separately, for the sake of honour. We may, however, infer from this that the name of *bishop* is common to all the ministers of the Word, inasmuch as he assigns several bishops to one Church. The titles, therefore, of *bishop* and *pastor*, are synonymous. And this is one of the passages which Jerome quotes for proving this in his epistle to Evagrius, and in his exposition of the Epistle to Titus. Afterwards there crept in the custom of applying the name of *bishop* exclusively to the person whom the presbyters in each church appointed over their company. It originated, however, in a human custom, and rests on no Scripture authority. I acknowledge, indeed, that, as the minds and manners of men are, there cannot be order maintained among the ministers of the word, without one presiding over the others. I speak of particular bodies, not of whole provinces, much less of the whole world. Now, although we must not contend for words, it were at the same time better for us in speaking to follow the Holy Spirit, the author of tongues, than to change for the worse forms of speech which are dictated to us by Him. For from the corrupted signification of the word this evil has resulted, that, as if all the presbyters were not colleagues, called to the same office, one of them, under the pretext of a new appellation, usurped dominion over the others.[50]

In this remark, Calvin affirms the necessity of "Scripture authority" for church offices. Further, he affirms the equality of the terms *bishop* and *pastor* in the Scriptures, and that the office of bishop in distinction from that of the presbyter is contrary to the Holy Spirit's words given in Scripture. This, of course, is clearly Presbyterianism. Yet, he also adds that in "particular bodies" one must preside to maintain order. This would be Calvin's idea of the superintendent. It is also manifest that the person who "presides" at the meetings is *not* a prelate. This would make Calvin contradict himself in the very same paragraph. In fact, Calvin avers that the idea of a prelate has resulted in the "evil" of "usurped dominion over others." Calvin's alleged episcopalism is not obvious here![51]

But can Calvin offer any scriptural proof for the office of the superintendent? This would seem most necessary on his own terms of Scripture support for church polity. If the superintendent is simply a matter of good order and hence expedience, would not such an argument support the office of a bishop also? Calvin's interpretation of Titus 1:5, where Paul instructs Titus to "ordain elders in every city," gives insight into Calvin's scriptural support for the office of the superintendent. He writes,

> But it may be thought that he gives too much power to Titus, when he bids him appoint ministers for all the churches. That would be almost royal power. Besides, this method takes away from each church the right of choosing, and from the College of Pastors the power of judging; and thus the sacred administration of the Church would be almost wholly profaned. The answer is easy. He does not give permission to Titus, that he alone may do everything in this matter, and may place over the churches those whom he thinks fit to appoint to be bishops; but only bids him preside, as moderator, at the elections, which is quite necessary. This mode of expression is very common. In the same manner, a consul, or regent, or dictator is said to have created consuls, on account of having presided over the public assembly in electing them. Thus also Luke relates that Paul and Barnabas ordained elders in every church (Acts xiv.23). Not that they alone, in an authoritative manner, appointed pastors which the churches had neither approved nor known; but that they ordained fit men, who had been chosen or desired by the people. From this passage we do indeed learn, that there was not at that time such equality among the ministers of Christ but that some one had authority and deliberative voice above others; but this has nothing to do with the tyrannical and profane custom which prevails in Popery as to Collations. The apostles had a widely different mode of procedure.[52]

In sum, Calvin here declares that Paul had appointed Titus to "preside as moderator." While Calvin emphatically denies that any individual can have "royal power" in the church by going over the wishes of the local assembly and the judgments of the "College of pastors," he nevertheless insists that there was not absolute equality among the pastors. "There was not," he insists, "at that time such equality among the ministers of Christ but that some one had authority and deliberative voice above others." In these words, Calvin declares his antagonism to the royal power of prelacy, and his belief in the biblical warrant for a superintendent or moderator to preside over other pastors. Calvin's Presbyterianism is patent: the people choose, the pastors judge, the moderator presides over the elections.

Why then did Calvin not speak out against the prelacy of Britain in his letter to Archbishop Cranmer? The answer is found in Calvin's priorities of reform and his desire to maintain a unified front in the face of Rome. In this very letter these concerns are evident. The first goal of the Reformation, namely the *sola scriptura* principle, had not yet been reached. Calvin explains to the Archbishop,

> Now, seeing that a serious and properly adjusted agreement between men of learning upon the rule of Scripture is still a desideratum, by means of which Churches, though divided on other questions, might be made to unite, I think it right for me, at whatever cost of toil and trouble, to seek to obtain this project [i.e., a general meeting of the leaders of the reformation, proposed by Cranmer].[53]

Since an agreement upon "the rule of Scripture" was still a "desideratum" between the English and Genevan churches, Calvin hardly found himself in a position to press for a fully biblical form of church polity with his co-laborer in the gospel. For Calvin there was a priority in the principle of *sola scriptura*. Consequently, he was able to proceed patiently in logical sequence toward the goal of a fully scriptural reformation. To echo Beza's words, Calvin was "still not condemning as antichristian those Churches which had not proceeded the same length, or those pastors who thought that their flocks did not require to be so curbed."[54] Calvin was obviously confident that the archbishop was an instrument of God for the Reformation. Accordingly, Calvin could wait for the Spirit's work to be accomplished. Thus Calvin concludes, "Adieu, very distinguished Archbishop, deserving of my hearty reverence. May the Lord continue to guide you by his Spirit, and to bless your holy labours!"[55]

Further, Calvin in this very letter was affirming the need for unity in spite of the fact that the two churches were "divided on other questions." Calvin did not desire to increase the division between the two. Thus he laments to Cranmer, "Thus it is that the members of the Church being severed, the body lies bleeding."[56] In the common struggle for the gospel against Rome, Calvin could subordinate other issues of disagreement.

In the same manner the letter of Calvin to the Duke of Sommerset can be explained. It is true that this letter in calling for a complete reformation of the Church of England fails to mention the matter of church polity in terms of prelacy. Yet the inference that is drawn from this to the effect that Calvin therefore had "no prejudices against the episcopal order" is not true. Such "prejudices" have already been noted elsewhere. Moreover, Calvin in this very letter lays down the principle of the *jus divinum* for church government, even though he does not draw any direct conclusion against episcopacy. He says,

> In worldly matters, that may be quite bearable, wherein it is allowable to yield one to another, and to forego one's right for the sake of peace; but it is not altogether the same thing in regard to the spiritual governance of the Church, which ought to be according to the ordinance of the word of God.[57]

Further Calvin enjoins upon the spiritual leaders of the church the duties of discipline that would have ultimately issued in a polity similar to Geneva's had it been executed. Writing to Sommerset Calvin affirms,

> For as doctrine is the soul of the Church for quickening, so discipline and the correction of vices are like the nerves to sustain the body in a state of health and vigour. The duty of bishops and curates is to keep watch over that, to the end that the Supper of our Lord may not be polluted by people of scandalous lives.[58]

Since Sommerset was the regent in the minority of Edward VI, and Edward had strong desires to reform the Church along Genevan lines as was seen above, it would appear safe to conclude that Sommerset had not learned an indifference to the question of episcopacy from Calvin. Rather, Calvin's patient insistence upon the Scriptures as the basis of church government influenced Edward to the point of allowing à Lasco's Presbyterianism to exist so that "the English churches also might be excited to embrace the apostolical purity, by the unanimous consent of all the estates of the kingdom."[59]

Calvin's willingness to secure reformation by a sequence of priorities is best illustrated in a letter to Bullinger concerning Bishop Hooper of England. Hooper had left Europe for England in 1550 and was appointed bishop of Gloucester through the patronage of Cranmer. Hooper, however, refused to wear at the time of his consecration the vestments then used in the Anglican Church. As a result he was imprisoned for a few days. Calvin's statements concerning this situation are quite revealing of his reformational priorities.

> Meanwhile, we have heard the sad news of Hooper's imprisonment. I was somewhat apprehensive of this long ago. I am now afraid that the bishops, as if victorious, will become much more ferociously insolent. While, therefore, I admire his firmness in refusing the anointing, I had rather he had not carried his opposition so far with respect to the cap and the linen vestment, even although I do not approve of these: I recently recommended this. He has many and powerful adversaries, and I doubt not but they will set themselves violently to crush him. But I trust that the Lord will be with him, especially because, as I am informed, some treacherously oppose him, who in other respects pretend to be favourable to the Gospel.[60]

Calvin was willing to allow something he opposed to occur so that a greater good could result. This was not only true in the case of having a Reformed bishop like Hooper in office in England even if he had to wear the vestments. But it was also true in the greater case of having the gospel preached in truth in the English church even if it had to be ruled by bishops.

These considerations would seem to answer the arguments raised by the letter of Benedict Pictet relative to Calvin's view of the episcopal order. If the opportunity in Britain had been ripe, there is no question that Calvin would have counseled the British church to end the "royal power" of the prelate and establish Presbyterianism. This Calvin's students nearly a century later did in fact accomplish. It should never be forgotten that the Westminster Assembly was composed of *Anglicans* as well as Scottish Presbyterians.

The reformation of the church according to the Word of God was the cry of the reformers. As that reformation went forward, it was soon evident that there would be no full agreement on the subject of the Bible's requirements for the government of the church. Nevertheless, the polity of the church as taught by Calvin was destined to make an enduring mark upon the structure of Protestantism. Calvin believed that the form of government he advocated was declared by the Word of God to be the true form of ecclesiastical polity. It is no accident, then, that wherever Calvinistic theology has gone, Presbyterian polity has accompanied it. This was true in Scotland, England, France, the Netherlands, as well as the Swiss cantons in league with Geneva.[61]

For Calvin and his allies, the Scriptures as the *jus divinum* gave the true church government. There were differences of application of this principle. This is seen in Knox's refusal of a bishopric and his refusal to install John Douglas, and Calvin's willingness to work with the system for the greater good of the gospel in the cases of Archbishop Cranmer and Bishop Hooper. These differences cannot be denied. In fact, it is quite possible that the different attitudes seen in Knox and Calvin toward working within the episcopal order helped to give rise to the distinctive subgroups of Puritans in England.[62] Yet this fact in no way weakens the basic agreement of all of Calvin's followers with the principle that the Scriptures teach the form of government that is to be practiced by the church of Christ. Consequently, for those of Calvinist persuasion, the rediscovery of the principle of *sola Scriptura* included the rediscovery of Presbyterian polity.[63]

NOTES

1. Cf. John Calvin, "The Necessity of Reforming the Church," *Selected Works of John Calvin*, Volume I (Grand Rapids: Baker, 1983), 140–45, 170–76, 197–221; Martin Luther, "The Pagan Servitude of the Church," *Martin Luther: Selections from His Writings*, ed. John Dillenberger (New York: Anchor Books, 1961), 249–359.

2. Theodore Beza, "The Life of John Calvin," *Selected Works of John Calvin*, ed. and trans. Henry Beveridge, xxxviii.

3. Ibid., xl–xli.

4. Cf. Charles A. Briggs, *American Presbyterianism* (New York: Charles Scribner's Sons, 1885), 45.

5. Cf. John R. De Witt, *Jus Divinum: The Westminster Assembly and the Divine Right of Church Government* (Kampen: J. H. Kok, 1969).

6. Cf. Thomas Smyth, *Presbytery and Not Prelacy the Scriptural and Primitive Polity,* Volume II (Boston: Crocker and Brewster, 1843), 561 note.

7. Richard Baxter, *Church Concord* (London, 1691), Preface.

8. Beza, "presbytery" occurs on xxix, xxxviii, xxxix, li, lxii, lxiii, lxxiv; "consistory" occurs on xxxii, xxxvi, xlix.

9. J. T. McNeill, *The History and Character of Calvinism* (New York: Oxford University Press, 1954), 295.

10. A. L. Drummond, *The Kirk and the Continent* (Edinburgh: Saint Andrews Press, 1956), 3–5.

11. The subject of the superintendent in Calvin's view and the French church will be discussed below.

12. Cited in Briggs, 41.

13. Cf. T. M. Lindsay, *History of the Reformation,* Volume II (Edinburgh: T. & T. Clark, 1964), 286–87.

14. Samuel Miller, *The Primative and Apostolical Order of the Church of Christ Vindicated* (Philadelphia: Presbyterian Board of Publication, 1840), 290.

15. Cf. McNeill, 304–305.

16. The passage in Calvin's *Institutes* is IV. iii. 8.

17. Alexander Peterkin, *Booke of the Universall Kirk of Scotland* (Edinburgh: Blackwood, 1839), 194.

18. Cited in Miller, 272.

19. Ibid., 276.

20. Smyth, 434–35.

21. Ibid., 434.

22. Thomas M'Crie, *Life of John Knox,* Volume I (Philadelphia: Presbyterian Board of Publication, 1845), 405.

23. Benjamin Brook, *Memoir of the Life and Writings of Thomas Cartwright* (London: J. Snow, 1845), 69.

24. John Macleod, *Scottish Theology in Relation to Church History Since the Reformation* (Edinburgh: Banner of Truth, 1974), 35.

25. Briggs, 45.

26. This book of discipline is offered in Briggs as an appendix.

27. Ibid., ii.

28. Cf. Janet Glenn Gray, *The French Huguenots: Anatomy of Courage* (Grand Rapids: Baker, 1981), 55–83.

29. B. J. Kidd, *Documents Illustrative of the Continental Reformation* (Oxford: Clarendon Press, 1911), 679–80.

30. Robert M. Kingdon, *Geneva and the Coming of the Wars of Religion in France, 1555–1563* (Geneva: Librairie E. Droz, 1956), 79.

31. Ibid.

32. George P. Hays, *Presbyterians* (New York: J. A. Hill & Co., 1892), 42.

33. *The Gallican Confession* is found in Philip Schaff, *The Creeds of Christendom,* Volume III (Grand Rapids: Baker, 1977), 356ff.; *La Discipline* is found in Kidd, 673ff.

34. Schaff, 374–78.

35. Cf. articles 2–7, Kidd, 673–74.

36. This translation is found in Smyth, 427.

37. Ibid.

38. Drummond, 15–17.

39. Cf. Gray, 78–83.

40. Ibid., 83.
41. Cf. Herman Hoeksema, *Reformed Dogmatics* (Grand Rapids: Reformed Free Publishing Assoc., 1976), 625–27.
42. Cf. Wm. P. Breed, *Presbyterianism Three Hundred Years Ago* (Philadelphia: Presbyterian Board of Publication, 1872), 19.
43. Ibid., 19–20.
44. Ibid.
45. Kidd, 682. The unity between Reformed France and Reformed Holland can be seen by a cursory comparison of the *Belgic Confession* of 1561 with the *Gallican Confession* of 1559. It is obvious that Guy de Brés, the author of the former, modeled his confession after the *Gallican Confession* written by Calvin's pupil De Chandieu; Cf. Schaff, 383ff.
46. Briggs, 40.
47. Drummond, 14.
48. J. Pannier, "Calvin et l'episcopat," *Revue d'Histoire et de Philosophie religieuse* 6 (1926):434–70.
49. Smyth, Volume I, 24.
50. John Calvin, *Calvin's Commentaries*, ed. and trans. John Pringle, Volume XXI (Grand Rapids: Baker, 1979), 23–24.
51. Cf. Calvin's remark in "Remarks on the Letter of Pope Paul III," *Selected Works*, Volume I, 269, "When bishops assume to themselves the sole right of passing judgment on priests, they endeavour, after the manner of the giants, to push God from his seat."
52. *Commentaries*, Volume XXI, 290–91.
53. *Selected Works*, Volume V, 348.
54. Quoted above from *Selected Works*, Volume I, xli.
55. Ibid.
56. Ibid.
57. Ibid., Volume V, 195.
58. Ibid., 197.
59. Cited above from Smyth, Volume II, 434.
60. *Selected Works*, Volume V, 307.
61. Beza mentions in his quotation above the many reformers that Calvin appealed to for support of the idea that the Scriptures supply the church with a form of government. One Swiss named was Zwingli. Zwingli's successor, Heinrich Bullinger, states his views very succinctly in his *Second Helvetic Confession* of 1566; Cf. Schaff, *Creeds*, 875–84, Article XVIII.
62. For a discussion of the different types of Puritans in the English church that roughly parallel the differences in attitude toward the episcopal order reflected in Knox and Calvin, cf. Leonard J. Trinterud, *Elizabethan Puritanism* (New York: Oxford University Press, 1971), 9–14.
63. Due to space limitations, this study has not sought to develop the question of the relationship between Lutheran and Presbyterian polity. For those who might wish to consider this important question of the Reformation, the following works will be helpful: Miller, 294–302; Breed, 20–23; Charles Hodge, *Discussions in Church Polity* (New York: Charles Scribner's Sons, 1878), 106–116; Heinrich Schmid, *Doctrinal Theology of the Evangelical Lutheran Church* (Minneapolis: Augsburg Publishing House, 1961), 608–610; Werner Elert, *The Structure of Lutheranism* (St. Louis: Concordia, 1962), 367–85.

Wayne R. Spear

6 *The Westminster Assembly's Directory for Church Government*

THE DOCUMENTS PRODUCED by the Westminster Assembly in the seventeenth century have been a formative influence in the life and teaching of the Orthodox Presbyterian Church, as the name of the seminary most closely associated with the denomination attests. The *Westminster Confession of Faith* and *Shorter Catechism* (and, to a lesser degree, the *Larger Catechism*) shaped the theology of American Presbyterianism through more than two centuries, and the Orthodox Presbyterian Church has sought to carry on that theological heritage with integrity.

The formulation of confessional statements, however, was not the primary task for which the Westminster Assembly was called together. The Assembly was not a regular ecclesiastical body, but an advisory commission for the English Parliament, called by the Parliament in a time of national crisis for advice concerning a "further and more perfect reformation" of the government and worship of the Church of England.[1] The Long Parliament, which had begun meeting in 1640, was under the control of Puritans, especially in the House of Commons. They were resisting what they perceived to be a movement toward Rome by Archbishop Laud and the hierarchy, and growing tyranny in the state under the personal rule of Charles I. For doctrinal reasons, but also because the bishops were among the strongest supporters of the divine right monarchy of the Stuart kings, the majority in Parliament took measures to end the rule of bishops in the Church of England. In 1643 they called together an assembly of ministers and members of both Houses, to assist in the formulation of the legislation which would provide a new structure of government for the national church.

As originally constituted, the Westminster Assembly was strictly an English body. However, when Scotland came into the war being waged between Charles and the Parliament, Scottish commissioners were sent as consultative members of the Assembly. Under the terms of the Solemn League and Covenant, there was a commitment on the part of both nations to seek "the nearest conjunction and uniformity in religion, confession of faith, form of church-government, directory for worship and catechising."[2] As things turned out, the Puritan movement in its political aspects first splintered under Cromwell, and then was suppressed ruthlessly by Charles II. The documents of the Westminster Assembly, however, found a permanent reception in Scotland, and from there were carried to the New World.

Although it would be the doctrinal statements which would later have the greatest influence, the production of documents dealing with church government and worship occupied the Westminster Assembly during the first two years of its meetings. The discussions of church government took a long time because there was considerable diversity of opinion among the approximately sixty members who regularly attended the sessions being held in the Jerusalem Chamber of Westminster Abbey. Speaking generally, four points of view were represented. There was a substantial number of "divine-right Presbyterians," who held that the basic structure (and many details) of church government had been prescribed by Jesus Christ in the New Testament, and that it was obligatory upon the church to follow this pattern. This group had strong allies in the Scottish commissioners.[3] Another sizeable group in the Assembly were "pragmatic Presbyterians," opposed to episcopacy in the form in which they had experienced it, but reluctant to assert scriptural authority for presbyterian distinctives. The "independents" were a small but very influential minority, opposed to any church authority beyond the local eldership, though they were willing for wider consultative associations. They argued interminably in the Assembly that their form of church government was the only one having scriptural warrant. Having powerful support from many in Parliament were the so-called "Erastians" who believed that the civil magistrate had the God-given right to determine the form and functions of church government.

After long debates, and with considerable use of the art of accommodation, the Westminster Assembly produced the three documents which embodied their advice for the government and worship of the church. The *Directory for Worship* and the *Form of Church Government* were both completed in December of 1644. Both documents are fairly well-known, because they have been published repeatedly in the Scottish editions of the Confession of Faith.[4]

The third document, A *Directory for Church-Government, Church-Censures, and Ordination of Ministers*, was completed on July 4, 1645.[5] It was the basis for legislation passed three years later by the English Parliament setting up presbyteries in London and in counties where the Parliament had military control. Shortly thereafter, Oliver Cromwell purged the Parliament of its Presbyterian members, and the experiment in England with Presbyterian church government came to an end.

The *Directory for Church Government* was presented to the General Assembly of the Church of Scotland in 1647, and was ordered to be printed for study by the presbyteries. The rise of Cromwell in England brought about the collapse of the effort to achieve agreement in religion between Scotland and England, and no further action on the Directory was taken. The document was reprinted a number of times during the seventeenth and eighteenth centuries in Scotland, but not in the last 200 years, and never in America.[6] Today this product of the deliberations of the Westminster Assembly has been almost entirely forgotten.

This "lost" document of the Westminster Assembly, however, deserves to be better known. While it contains much material that is also in the better-known *Form of Church Government*, it is a much more polished document. In my doctoral dissertation, I asserted that the *Form of Church Government* is "a virtual mosaic, whose bits and pieces are the sentences debated and approved by the Assembly over a period of many months, and subsequently rearranged by two different editorial committees."[7] It was put together in haste, as a kind of progress report. The *Directory for Government* clears up some of the confusion in the language of the earlier document. More importantly, it contains the results of the Assembly's deliberations on the subject of church discipline. It also adds practical details about the operation of church government. In his Baird Lectures, A. F. Mitchell said of the *Directory for Church Government*,

> It is practical and comprehensive, a storehouse of valuable counsels as to many things in government, and still more in discipline, not touched on in the propositions [i.e., Form of Church Government], and is well worthy of being studied by Presbyterian ministers still, who wish to do full justice to the system of government the Westminster Assembly sanctioned.[8]

It seems appropriate, then, to include in this commemorative volume a re-printing of the Westminster *Directory for Government*. It will be of interest to the historians who will be attracted to the book. It will help to illuminate the degree to which not only the doctrinal stance, but also the practical working of the Orthodox Presbyterian Church have been shaped, even though indirectly, by the deliberations of the great Assembly which met at Westminster Abbey three centuries ago.

The text which follows is reprinted from a volume of Scottish ecclesiastical documents, including the *Westminster Confession*, published in Glasgow in 1771. A copy is owned by the library of the Reformed Presbyterian Theological Seminary in Pittsburgh, Pennsylvania.[9]

A DIRECTORY

For Church-Government, for Church-Censures,
and Ordination of Ministers;
Agreed upon by the
Assembly of Divines at Westminster, &c.

The Preface

JESUS CHRIST, *upon whose shoulder the government is, whose name is called Wonderful, Counsellor, the Mighty God, the Everlasting Father, the Prince of Peace; of the increase of whose government and peace there shall be no end; who sits upon the throne of David, and upon his kingdom, to order it, and establish it with judgment and justice, from henceforth even for ever; having all power given unto him in heaven and earth by the Father, who raised him from the dead, and set him at his own right hand, far above all principality and power, and might, and dominion, and every name that is named, not only in this world, but also in that which is to come: and put all things under his feet, and gave him to be head over all things to the church, which is his body, the fulness of him that filleth all in all: he being ascended up far above all heavens, that he might fill all things, received gifts for his church, and gave all officers necessary for the edification of his church, and perfecting of his saints.*

Of the Church

THERE is one general church visible held forth in the New Testament; unto which general church visible, the ministry, oracles and ordinances of the New Testament, are given by Jesus Christ, for the gathering and perfecting of the saints in this life, until his second coming.

Particular visible churches, members of the general church, are also held forth in the New Testament: which particular churches, in the primitive times, were made up of visible saints, viz. of such as, being of age, professed faith in Christ, and obedience unto Christ (according to the rules of faith and life taught by him and his apostles) and of their children.

Of the Officers of the Church

APOSTLES, prophets and evangelists, were extraordinary officers in the church, and are ceased.

The pastor is an ordinary and perpetual officer in the church; to whose office it belongeth to pray for and with his flock, to read the scriptures publicly in the congregation, which is an holy ordinance in God's church, although there follow no immediate explication of what is read; to preach the word, to be instant in season, and out of season; to reprove, correct, instruct, rebuke, exhort, convince and comfort: one special way of discharging which work of preaching, is by a plain laying down the first principles of the oracles of God, which is commonly called catechising;

to administer the sacraments; in the name of God to bless the people; to take care for the poor; and he hath also a ruling power over the flock as pastor.

In the scripture, we have also the name and title of teacher, who is a minister of the word, and hath power of administration of the sacraments and discipline, as well as the pastor.

The Lord hath given different gifts, and divers exercises according to those gifts in the ministers of the word; though these different gifts may meet in, and accordingly be exercised by one and the same minister, yet, where there be several ministers in the same congregation, they may be designed to several employments, according to the different gifts wherein each of them doth excel: and he who doth more excel in exposition of scripture, in teaching sound doctrine, and in convincing gainsayers, than he doth in application, and is accordingly employed therein, may be called a teacher or doctor. Nevertheless, where there is but one minister in a particular congregation, he is to perform so far as he is able, the whole work of the ministry.

A teacher or doctor is of most excellent use in schools and universities, as of old in the schools of the prophets, and at Jerusalem, where Gamaliel and others taught as doctors.

It is likewise agreeable to, and warranted by the word of God, that some others, besides the minister of the word, be church governors, to join with the ministers in the government of the church; which officers, reformed churches commonly call elders.

These elders ought to be such as are men of good understanding in matters of religion, sound in the faith, prudent, grave, and of unblameable conversation. Deacons also are distinct officers in the church, to whose office it belongeth not to preach the word, or administer the sacraments, but to take special care for the necessities of the poor, by collecting for, and distributing to them, with direction of the eldership, that none amongst the people of God be constrained to be beggars.

The deacons must be wise, sober, grave, of honest report, and not greedy of filthy lucre.

Of Church-Government,
and the Several Sorts of Assemblies for the Same

CHRIST hath instituted a government, and governors ecclesiastical in the church; and, to that end, the Apostles did immediately receive the keys from the hand of Jesus Christ, and did use and exercise them, in all the churches of the world, upon all occasions, and Christ hath, from time to time, furnished some in his church, with gifts for government, and with commission to exercise the same, when called thereunto.

It is agreeable to, and warranted by the word of God, that some others, besides the ministers of the word, be church governors, as was mentioned before.

It is lawful, and agreeable to the word of God, that the church be governed by several sorts of assemblies, which are presbyteries and synods; or assemblies congregational, classical and synodical.

The scripture doth hold out a presbytery in a church, which presbytery consisteth of ministers of the word, and those other church officers who are to join with the ministers in the government of the church.

The scripture doth hold out another sort of assemblies for the government of the church, besides classical and congregational, which we call synodical.

Of the Power in Common of All These Assemblies, and the Order to be Observed in Them

IT is lawful, and agreeable to the word of God, that the several assemblies before mentioned do convent and call before them any person within their several bounds, whom the ecclesiastical business, which is before them shall concern, either as a party, or a witness, or otherwise, and to examine them according to the nature of the business; and that they do hear and determine such causes and differences as shall orderly come before them, and accordingly dispense church censures.

It is most expedient, that in these meetings, one, whose office is to labor in the word and doctrine, do moderate in their proceedings, who is to vote as well as the rest of the members; to begin and end every meeting with prayer; to propose questions, gather the votes, pronounce the resolves; but not to do any act of government, unless in and jointly with the assembly whereof he is moderator.

All the members of these assemblies, respectively, are to attend on the appointed days of their meetings, or to send the reason of their absence, to be judged by the assembly where they ought to meet.

The final resolutions shall be by the major part of the votes of those members who are present.

Of particular Congregations

IT is expedient, that particular congregations be fixed, both in their officers and members, which are to meet in the same assembly ordinarily for public worship.

When their number is great, that they cannot conveniently meet in one place, it is expedient that they be divided according to the respective bounds of their dwellings into distinct and fixed congregations for the better administration of such ordinances as belong unto them, and the discharge of mutual duties; wherein all, according to their several places and callings, are to labour to promote whatever appertains to the power of godliness and credit of religion, that the whole land, in the full extent of it, may become the kingdom of the Lord and of his Christ.

Parochial congregations in this kingdom, consisting of ministers and people, who profess faith in Christ, and obedience unto Christ, according to the rules of faith and life taught by him and his apostles, and join together in the public worship of hearing, praying, and administration of the sacraments, are churches truly constituted.

If any person or persons, in the congregation, do not answer his or their profession, but by open sin and wickedness cross and deny it; or if there be a want of some officers, or a sinful neglect of officers in the due execution of discipline; yet this doth not make that congregation cease to be a church, but requires that there should be a supply of officers which are wanting, and a careful endeavor for the reformation of the offending person or persons, and of negligent officers, by just censures, according to the nature of the cause.

Communion and membership in congregations thus constituted, notwithstanding the forementioned defects, is not unlawful. And to refuse or renounce membership and church communion, or to separate from church-communion with congregations thus constituted, as unlawful to be joined with, in regard of their constitution, is not warranted by the word of God.

Separation from a church thus constituted, where the government is lawful, upon an opinion that it is unlawful, and that therefore all the godly are also bound to separate from all such churches so constituted and governed, and to join themselves to another church of another constitution and government, is not warranted by the word of God, but contrary to it.

To gather churches into an independent form of government out of churches of a presbyterial form of government, upon an opinion that the presbyterial government is unlawful, is not lawful and warranted by the word of God; nor is it lawful for any member of a parochial congregation, if the ordinances be there administered in purity, to go and seek them elsewhere ordinarily.

Of Ordinances of a particular Congregation

ORDINANCES in a particular congregation are prayer, thanksgiving, singing of psalms, reading the word, preaching and catechising, administering the sacraments, blessing people in the name of God, and collection for the poor. As for discipline, we refer ourselves to what we have elsewhere expressed.

Of the Officers of a particular Congregation

IN the congregation there must be some who are set apart to bear office: one at the least to labor in the word and doctrine, and to rule; and let others be chosen ruling elders to join with him in the government.

When any ruling elder is to be chosen, where an eldership is constituted, let it be done by them, with the consent and approbation of the people of that congregation, and that not for a limited time; yet the exercise of their office may be so ordered by the eldership, as that their civil employ-ments be least hindered thereby.

Where there are many ruling officers in a particular congregation, let some of them more especially attend the inspection of one part, some of another, as may be most convenient; and let them at fit times visit the several families for their spiritual good.

Let there be deacons also to take special care for the relief of the poor; who are likewise to be chosen by the eldership, with the consent of the people of that congregation; and the continuance of them in that office is to be determined by the eldership, with consent of the congregation, so as may least hinder their civil employments.

These officers are to meet together, at convenient and set times, for the well ordering of the affairs of that congregation, each according to his office.

The number of elders and deacons, in each congregation, is to be proportioned according to the condition of the congregation.

Of Congregational Elderships, or Assemblies for Governing in a particular Congregation

THE congregational eldership, consisting of the minister, or ministers, and the other ruling officers of that congregation, hath power, as they shall see just occasion, to enquire into the knowledge and spiritual estate of any member of the congregation; to admonish and rebuke; to suspend from the Lord's table, though the person be not yet cast out of the church: all which is agreeable to the word of God. Although the truth of conver-sion and regeneration be necessary to every worthy communicant, for his own comfort and benefit; yet those only are to be by the eldership excluded, or suspended from the Lord's table, who are found by them to be ignorant or scandalous.

Where there are more fixed ministers than one in a congregation, it is expedient that they moderate by course in that eldership.

Of Classical Assemblies

WHEN congregations are divided and fixed, they need all mutual help one from another, both in regard of their intrinsical weakness, and mutual dependence; as also in regard of enemies from without.

The scripture doth hold forth, that many particular congregations may be under one presbyterial government.

A classical presbytery is an assembly made up of ministers of the word, and other ruling officers belonging unto several neighboring congregations, and doth ordinarily consist of all the pastors and teachers belonging to the several congregations so associated, and of one of the other ruling officers, at the least, from every of these congregations, to be sent by their respective presbyteries.

Let them meet once every month, or oftner, as occasion shall require, in such place as they shall judge most convenient. And, before they sit about other business, let there be a sermon or exposition of scripture, made by some minister of that classis, or expectant, as they shall agree amongst themselves.

For the more orderly managing of such affairs as come before them, let there be one moderator chosen by the classis at every meeting out of the ministers of the word, who shall continue until the next meeting.

To the enabling them to perform any classical act of government or ordination, there shall be present a major part, at least, of the ministers of the whole classis.

It Belongeth unto Classical Presbyteries,

TO consider of, to debate, and to resolve, according to God's word, such cases of conscience, and other difficulties in doctrine, as are brought unto them out of their association, according as they shall find needful for the good of the churches.

To examine and censure, according to the word any erroneous doctrines, which have been either publicly, or privately, vented within their association, to the corrupting of the judgments of men; and to endeavour the converting of recusants, or any others in error or schism.

To order all ecclesiastical matters of common concernment within the bounds of their association.

To take cognizance of causes omitted or neglected in particular congregations, and to receive appeals from them.

To dispense censures in cases within their cognizance by admonition, suspension, or excommunication.

To admonish, or further to censure scandalous ministers, whether in life or doctrine, according to the nature of the offence; and that not only for such offences, for which any other member of the congregation shall incur any censure of the church (in which case he is to be censured by the classis with the like censure for the like offence) but likewise particularly for simony, entering into any ministerial charge without allowance of authority, false doctrine, affected lightness and vanity in preaching, wilful neglect of preaching, or slight performance of it, wilful non-residence from his charge without call or cause approved by the classis, neglect of administration of the sacraments, or other ministerial duties required of him in the directory of worship, depraving and speaking reproachfully against the wholesome orders by authority settled in the church, casting reproach upon the power of godliness, which he by his office ought chiefly to promote: yet so as that no minister be deposed, but by the resolution of a synod.

To examine, ordain, and admit ministers for the congregations respectively therein associated, according to the advice formerly sent up to the honourable houses of parliament.

Of Synodical Assemblies

SYNODICAL assemblies do consist of pastors, teachers, church governors, and other fit persons (when it shall be deemed expedient) where they have a lawful calling thereunto.

These assemblies have ecclesiastical power and authority to judge and determine controversies of faith, and cases of conscience, according to the word.

They may also lawfully excommunicate, and dispense other church censures.

Synodical assemblies are of several sorts, *viz.*, provincial, national, oecumenical.

Of Provincial Assemblies

LET provincial assemblies generally be bounded according to the civil division of the kingdom into counties: and, where any very great counties are divided within themselves, let the provincial assemblies follow these divisions, as in the ridings of Yorkshire.

Provincial assemblies consist of delegates sent from several classes within that province, whose number shall exceed the number of any one classical presbytery within that province: and, to that end, there shall be at the least two ministers and two ruling elders out of every classis; and where it shall appear necessary to increase the number, let it not exceed six of each from any one classis. Let these assemblies meet twice every year; and, for enabling them unto any act of government, let there be a major part at the least of the ministers delegated from the several classes.

Of the National Assembly

THE national assembly consists of ministers and ruling elders, delegated from each provincial assembly: the number of which delegates shall be three ministers and three ruling elders out of every province, and five learned and godly persons from each university.

Let this assembly meet once every year, and oftner if there shall be cause.

The first time to be appointed by the honourable houses of parliament.

Of the Subordination of These Assemblies

IT is lawful and agreeable to the word of God, that there be a subordination of congregational, classical, provincial, and national assemblies for the government of the church, that so appeals may be made from the inferior to the superior respectively.

The provincial and national assemblies are to have the same power in all points of government and censures brought before them within their several bounds respectively, as is before expressed, to belong to classical presbyteries within their several associations.

The Directory for Church Censures

CHURCH *censures and discipline, for judging and removing of offences, being of great use and necessity in the church, that the name of God, by reason of ungodly and wicked persons living in the church, be not blasphemed, nor his wrath provoked against his people; that the godly be not leavened with, but preserved from the contagion, and stricken with fear; and that the sinners who are to be censured may be ashamed, to the destruction of the flesh, and saving of the spirit in the day of the Lord Jesus; we judge this course of proceeding therein to be requisite.*

The Order of Proceeding with Offenders, Who before Excommunication Manifest Repentance

WHEN the offence is private, the order of admonition, prescribed by our Lord, Mat. xviii, 15. is in all wisdom and love to be observed, that the offender may either be recovered by repentance, or, if he add obstinancy or contempt to his fault, he may be cut off by excommunication.

If the sin be publicly scandalous, and the sinner, being examined, be judged to have the si[g]ns of unfeigned repentance, and nothing justly objected against it, when made known to the people; let him be admitted to public confession of his sin, and manifestation of his repentance before the congregation.

When the penitent is brought before the congregation, the minister is to declare his sin, whereby he hath provoked God's wrath, and offended his people; his confession of it, and profession of unfeigned repentance for it, and of his resolution (through the strength of Christ) to sin no more: and his desire of their prayers for mercy and grace to be kept from falling again into that or any the like sin; of all which the penitent also is to make a full and free expression, according to his ability.

Which being done, the minister, after prayer to God for the penitent, is to admonish him to walk circumspectly, and the people to make a right use of this fall and rising again; and so to declare that the congregation resteth satisfied.

The Order of Proceeding to Excommunication

EXCOMMUNICATION being a shutting out of a person from the communion of the church (and therefore the greatest and last censure

of the church) ought not to be inflicted without great and mature deliberation, nor till all other good means have been essayed.

Such errors as subvert the faith, or any other errors which overthrow
the power of godliness, if the party who holds them spread them, seeking
to draw others after him; and such sins in practice, as cause the name and
truth of God to be blasphemed, and cannot stand with the power of
godliness; and such practices, as in their own nature manifestly subvert
that order, unity and peace, which Christ hath established in his church:
those being publicly known, to the just scandal of the church, the sentence
of excommunication shall proceed according to the directory.

But the persons who hold other errors in judgment about points, wherein
learned and godly men possibly may or do differ, and which subvert not
the faith, nor are destructive to godliness; or that be guilty of such sins of
infirmity, as are commonly found in the children of God; or, being otherwise sound in the faith, and holy in life (and so not falling under censure
by the former rules) endeavour to keep the unity of the Spirit in the bond
of peace, and do yet out of conscience not come up to the observation of
all those rules, which are or shall be established by authority for regulating
the outward worship of God and government of his church: We do not
discern to be such against whom the sentence of excommunication for
these causes should be denounced.

When the sin becomes public and justly scandalous, the offender is to
be dealt with by the eldership, to bring him to repentance, and to such a
manifestation thereof, as that his repentance may be as public as the
scandal: but, if he remain obstinate, he is at last to be excommunicated,
and, in the mean time, to be suspended from the Lord's supper.

And whereas there be divers and various judgments, touching the power
of excommunication, whether concerning doctrine or conversation, the
classical presbytery, upon the knowledge thereof, may examine the person,
consider the nature of the offence, with the aggravations thereof, and as
they shall see just cause, may declare and decern that he is to be excommunicated; which shall be done by the eldership of that congregation
whereof he is a member, with the consent of the congregation, in this or
the like manner.

As there shall be cause, several public admonitions shall be given to the
offender (if he appears) and prayers made for him.

When the offence is so hainous, that it cries to heaven for vengeance,
wasteth the conscience, and is generally scandalous; the censures of the
church may proceed with more expedition.

In the admonitions, let the fact be charged upon the offender, with the
clear evidence of his guilt thereof: then let the nature of his sin, the
particular aggravations of it, the punishments and curses threatened against
it, the danger of impenitency, especially after such means used, the woful
condition of them cast out from the favour of God and communion of the

saints, the great mercy of God in Christ to the penitent, how ready and willing Christ is to forgive, and the church to accept him upon his serious repentance. Let these, or the like particulars, be urged upon him out of some suitable places of the holy scriptures.

The same particulars may be mentioned in prayer, wherein the Lord is to be intreated to bless this admonition to him, and to affect his heart with the consideration of these things, thereby to bring him unto true repentance.

If, upon the last admonition and prayer, there be no evidence nor sign of his repentance, let the dreadful sentence of excommunication be pronounced, with calling upon the name of God, in these or the like expressions.

'Whereas thou N. (Speak this in the third person, if the party be absent.) hast been by sufficient proof convicted of (here mention the sin) and after due admonition and prayer remain obstinate, without any evidence or sign of repentance, therefore, in the name of the Lord Jesus Christ, and before this congregation, I pronounce and declare thee N. excommunicated, and shut out from communion of the faithful,'

Let the prayer accompanying sentence be to this effect. 'That God, who hath appointed this terrible sentence for removing offences, and reducing of obstinate sinners, would be present with this his ordinance, to make it effectual to all these holy ends for which he hath appointed it; that this retaining of the offender's sin, and shutting him out of the church, may fill him with fear and shame, break his obstinate heart, and be a means to destroy the flesh, and to recover him from the power of the Devil, that his spirit may yet be saved: that others also may be stricken with fear, and not dare to sin presumptuously: and that all such corrupt leaven being purged out of the church (which is the house of God) Jesus Christ may delight to dwell in the midst of them.'

After the denunciation of this sentence the people are to be warned, that they hold him to be cast out of the communion of the church, and to shun all communion with him. Nevertheless, excommunication dissolveth not the bonds of civil or natural relations, nor exempt from the duties belonging to them.

This sentence is likewise to be made known, not only to that, but to any other classis or congregation, as occasion shall require, by reason of his abode or conversing with them.

The Order of Proceeding to Absolution

IF, after excommunication, the signs of repentance appear in the excommunicated person, such as, godly sorrow for sin, as having thereby incurred God's heavy displeasure, occasioned grief to his brethren, and justly provoked them to cast him out of their communion; together with a full purpose of heart to turn from his sin unto God, and to reform what hath been amiss in him; with a humble desire of recovering his peace with

God and his people, and to be restored to the light of God's countenance, and the communion of the church; he is to be brought before the congregation, and there also to make free confession of his sin with sorrow for it, to call upon God for mercy in Christ, to seek to be restored to the communion of the church; promising to God new obedience, and to them more holy and circumspect walking, as becometh the gospel; he is to be pronounced in the name of Christ absolved and free from the censures of the church, and declared to have right to all the ordinances of Christ, with praising of God for his grace, and prayer that he may be fully accepted to his favour, and hear joy and gladness, to this effect.

'To praise God who delighteth not in the death of a sinner, but that he may repent and live, for blessing the ordinance of excommunication, and making it effectual by his Spirit to the recovering of this offender; to magnify the mercy of God, through Jesus Christ, in pardoning and receiving to his favour the most grievous offenders, whensoever they unfeignedly repent and forsake their sins.'

'To pray for assurance of mercy and forgiveness to this penitent, and so to bless this ordinance of absolution, that he may find himself loosed thereby; and that the Lord would henceforth so uphold and strengthen him by his Spirit, that, being sound in the faith, and holy in all manner of conversation, God may be honored, the church edified, and himself saved in the day of the Lord Jesus.'

Then shall follow the sentence of absolution in these or the like words.

'Whereas thou N. hast for thy sin been shut out from the communion of the faithful, and hast now manifested thy repentance, wherein the church resteth satisfied: in the name of Jesus Christ, before this congregation, I pronounce and declare thee absolved from the sentence of excommunication formerly denounced against thee; and do receive thee to the ordinances of Christ, that thou mayest be partaker of all his benefits, to thy eternal salvation.'

After this sentence of absolution, the minister speaketh to him as a brother, exhorting him to watch and pray, or comforting him if there be need; the elders embrace him, and the whole congregation holdeth communion with him as one of their own.

Although it be the duty of pastors and other ruling officers to use all diligence and vigilancy, both by doctrine and discipline, respectively, for the preventing and purging out such errors, heresies, schisms, and scandals, as tend to the detriment and disturbance of the church: yet, because it may fall out, through the pride and stubbornness of offenders, that these means alone will not be effectual to that purpose; it is therefore necessary, after all this, to implore the aid of the civil magistrate, who ought to use his coercive power for the suppressing of all such offences, and vindicating the discipline of the church from contempt.

Of Ordination of Ministers

BECAUSE no man ought to take upon him the office of a minister of the word without a lawful call, therefore ordination, which is the solemn setting apart of a person unto some public church office, is always to be continued in the church.

When he who is to be ordained minister, hath been first duly examined touching his fitness, both for life and ministerial abilities, according to the rules of the apostle, by those who are to ordain him, and hath been by them approved; he is then to be ordained, by imposition of hands and prayer with fasting. But, if any person be found unfit, he is not to be ordained.

It is agreeable to the word, and very expedient, that such as are to be ordained ministers be designed to some particular church, or other ministerial charge.

Ordination is the act of a presbytery, unto which the power of ordering the whole work belongs: yet so as that the preaching presbyters, orderly associated, either in cities, or in neighboring villages, are those to whom the imposition of hands doth appertain, for those congregations within their bounds respectively. And therefore it is very requisite, that no single congregation, which can conveniently associate, do assume to itself all and sole power in ordination.

No person or persons may or ought to nominate, appoint, or choose any man to be a minister for a congregation, who is not fit and able for that work: and, if any unfit man be nominated to the classical presbytery, they are to refuse to admit him.

When any minister is to be ordained for a particular congregation, or translated from one place to another, the people of that congregation, to which he is to be ordained or admitted, shall have notice of it; and, if they shew just cause of exception against him, he is not to be ordained or admitted. And the mean time, till one be admitted, the presbytery shall provide for the supply of the congregation.

The congregation, if they conceive themselves wronged by an act of the presbytery, shall have liberty to appeal to the next synod, which, upon hearing of the matter, shall judge as the cause shall require.

Here followed the Directory for Ordination of Ministers, word for word, as found in the Form of Church Government.[10]

NOTES

1. Alexander F. Mitchell, *The Westminster Assembly: Its History and Standards* (Philadelphia: Presbyterian Board of Publication, 1884), ix.

2. "The Solemn League and Covenant," in *The Confession of Faith; The Larger and Shorter Catechisms*, &c. (Inverness: Free Presbyterian Publications, [1983]), 359.

3. J. R. DeWitt, *Jus Divinum: The Westminster Assembly and the Divine Right of Church Government* (Kampen: J. H. Kok, 1969), 229–34.

4. See also Iain Murray, *The Reformation of the Church* (London: Banner of Truth Trust, 1965), 203–230.

5. Mitchell, 257ff.

6. Ibid., 264. See also my unpublished dissertation, "Covenanted Uniformity in Religion: The Influence of the Scottish Commissioners upon the Ecclesiology of the Westminster Assembly" (University of Pittsburgh, 1976), 327 note.

7. "Covenanted Uniformity in Religion," 257.

8. Mitchell, 264.

9. *The Confessions of Faith, Catechisms, Directories, Form of Church-Government, Discipline, &c. of Public Authority in the Church of Scotland* . . . (Glasgow: Robert and Thomas Duncan, 1771).

10. *The Confession of Faith;* (Inverness, 1983), 412–16; Murray, *Reformation of the Church,* 226–30.

Edmund P. Clowney

7 Distinctive Emphases in Presbyterian Church Polity

THE PURPOSE OF THIS STUDY is to identify emphases in Presbyterian polity that are central rather than peripheral and that contrast with continental Reformed polity. In view, broadly speaking, is the "genius" of Reformed polity on the continent and the "genius" of Presbyterian polity in Britain.

However, demonstrating the differences between these polities is an enterprise in which in some sense I would hope not to succeed. I am sanguine in the expectation of failure for a number of reasons. First, in both geographical areas the Reformed churches sought to order their government under the authority of Scripture. Renouncing "human inventions" in doctrine, worship, and polity, they sought to reform the church under Christ the King by obeying his rule in Scripture. It was not their common esteem for Calvin or their common experience in the work of reformation that produced their agreement in doctrine and order. It was their submission to the Word of God. Second, the leaders of the Reformation movement enjoyed many opportunities for communication through literature, correspondence, and consultation. "Enjoyed" might not be an adequate term; some of the best contacts were developed by men who were fellow-exiles at different periods in Geneva, London, or Amsterdam. Finally, both the direct contacts and the similarities of situations tended to produce not only common agreements but also common disagreements. Differences on particulars of polity did not come into existence along geographical lines, in spite of political pressures toward national uniformity.

In the conservative Reformed and Presbyterian tradition we recognize that our common convictions are central and extensive, and that they offer a firm basis for approaching our differences. We also recognize that each of the churches represented could muster a variety of opinions on issues of church polity. Some of these differences might be labeled as Scotch or Dutch "genius"; other differences may reveal how far we have progressed beyond our fathers, or perhaps how far we have fallen behind them.

We ought not to assume, therefore, that differences that now exist between, let us say, the Christian Reformed Church and the Orthodox Presbyterian Church may be laid to substantial differences that must obtain between continental and British polity. Certainly Presbyterianism in the United States is heir to the continent as well as to Scotland and Ireland.[1] Individuals and congregations from Holland, France, and Germany (to mention three main streams) have brought their convictions and practice into the life of American Presbyterianism.

Nevertheless reflection on possible differences between church polity in the Dutch and Scotch traditions can be useful, particularly if we focus on the issues rather than the continuity or discontinuity of tradition. Let me propose two emphases of British or Scottish Presbyterianism that may be regarded as both central and distinctive. The first is often called the *regulative principle*. The second I will call the *organic principle*.

The Regulative Principle

The regulative principle is stated in these words in the *Westminster Confession of Faith* (Chapter XX:2): "God alone is Lord of the conscience, and hath left it free from the doctrines and commandments of men, which are, in any thing, contrary to His Word; or beside it, if matters of faith, or worship. So that, to believe such doctrines, or to obey such commands, out of conscience, is to betray true liberty of conscience: and the requiring of an implicit faith, and an absolute and blind obedience, is to destroy liberty of conscience, and reason also."

The key words here are "or beside it, if matters of faith, or worship." Of course the Christian conscience cannot be bound in anything to do what God's Word forbids. Yet it may be bound to do what God's Word does not expressly require. This is commonly the case in obeying the authority of the state for conscience sake. But the confession marks out an area where the conscience cannot be bound by any addition to the Word. That is the area of matters of faith or worship. For the church to go beyond Scripture in requiring religious belief or observance is to destroy the liberty of the Christian conscience.

What is stated generally in this chapter is applied with particular force to worship in the next (Chapter XXI:1): "But the acceptable way of worshipping the true God is instituted by Himself, and so limited by His own revealed will, that He may not be worshipped according to the imaginations and devices of men, or the suggestions of Satan, under any visible representation, or any other way not prescribed in the holy Scripture." Any way of worship not commanded in the Bible is therefore forbidden. This principle is established not merely from the divine institution of worship, but from the divine limitation of worship in scriptural revelation. "Will-worship," the arbitrary worship of God in ways chosen by men rather than God is excluded.

The general principle limiting the requirements of the church to the requirements of Scripture is, in the confession, closely related to the principle of the sufficiency of Scripture. In the first chapter (I:6) where the sufficiency and finality of Scripture are asserted, the following qualification is added: "Nevertheless, we acknowledge . . . that there are some circumstances concerning the worship of God, and government of the Church, common to human actions and societies, which are to be ordered by the light of nature, and Christian prudence, according to the general rules of the Word, which are always to be observed."

Leaving aside for the moment the question of the boundaries of "circumstances," we find this qualification makes a sweeping claim. Only in some circumstances of worship and church government does Christian prudence operate or the light of nature prove determinative. Even in this area the general rules of the Word are to be observed.[2] Note that these are circumstances, not a substantial part of government or worship. When the Book of Common Prayer pleads religious value for ceremonies not contained in Scripture ("to stir up the dull mind of man to the remembrance of his duty to God by some notable and special signification whereby he might be edified"), that very plea shatters the argument that these are only circumstances of worship. If the ceremony has a purported value, it is no mere circumstance but a significant observance.

Further, only *some* circumstances are in this class of things to be determined by prudence. This is true because Scripture prescribes, by precept or normative example, many circumstances of government and worship.

Finally, these circumstances are described as "common to human actions and societies." Not the circumstances that are distinctive for the order of church government or worship can be determined apart from the Word, but only those that are common. In debating the propriety of the use of instrumental music in worship, this question would require discussion. Is the use of such accompaniment to group singing only a circumstance common in our particular culture? Or is the instrument distinctively religious and therefore its use an observance rather than a circumstance?

Of course some circumstances may entail much more regulation than others. The reaching of a decision by majority vote may be considered a circumstance of church government common to human societies. Yet the elaboration of such a circumstance for the direction of the church may require numerous stipulations.

We must further note that in this first chapter of the confession government is linked with worship in reference to the regulative principle. Church government, too, has been instituted by Christ: "The Lord Jesus, as King and Head of His Church, hath therein appointed a government, in the hand of Church officers, distinct from the civil magistrate" (Chapter XXX:1). Church ordinances respecting government could also presume to bind the conscience if they went beyond Scripture. In government, therefore, as in faith and worship generally, what is not commanded is forbidden, with the exception of some circumstances. Also, the important Presbyterian manifesto, the *Jus Divinum Regiminus Ecclesiastici* (London: 1646), construes the divine right of Presbyterian government as including the light of nature on such important circumstances as the need of a society for distinct government, majority rule, and the right of appeal from lower to higher judicatories (Chapter III).

The regulative principle is not a distinctive principle of English as over against continental Reformed leadership. It is clearly stated in Article Thirty-two of the *Belgic Confession* (1561). Rulers of the church may institute and establish ordinances "yet they ought studiously to take care that they do not depart from those things which Christ, our only master, hath instituted. And, therefore, (*c'est pourquoi*) we reject all human inventions, and all laws which man would introduce into the worship of God, thereby to bind and compel the conscience in any manner whatsoever."

Nevertheless the regulative principle has become a more distinctive emphasis in British and Scottish Presbyterianism. The reason is not far to seek. It lies in the century-long Puritan struggle against state-imposed forms of government and worship. From the time of the Elizabethan settlement particularly, the Puritan struggle for a truly Reformed church was directed against those compromising survivals of extra-scriptural ordinances that seemed so politically expedient to the Queen. It was the campaign to the death against vestments and bishops that burned the regulative principle into the consciousness of British Presbyterianism.

Does this emphasis mark a real departure from Reformed polity on the continent? Dr. James I. Packer holds that it does. "The idea that direct biblical warrant, in the form of precept or precedent, is required to sanction every item included in the public worship of God was in fact a Puritan innovation, which crystallised out in the course of the prolonged debates that followed the Elizabethan settlement."[3] Packer further argues that the Puritans were mistaken in thinking that this principle is a necessary implication of the authority and sufficiency of Scripture. The disagreement relates, he says "to the interpretation and contents of Holy Scripture rather than to the formal principle of the nature and extent of its authority."[4]

Both of Packer's contentions merit careful consideration. In the second, I think he is certainly right, although I suppose he would agree that the confusion could arise only because certain of the teachings of Scripture seemed so evident to the Puritans. From an abstract standpoint it is true that our having an inspired and authoritative revelation from God does not necessarily mean that the revelation must contain commandments or prohibitions sufficiently specific to determine the form of church worship and government. Some Puritan reasoning, particularly that grounded in a "light of nature" starting-point seemed to find it inconceivable that a revelation given by Christ to his church could fail to provide an order for the church. "Every society needs a distinct government: the church is a society and this need must be met in the revelation of the King to his church."

The difficulty for this line of reasoning is the dramatic contrast between the New Testament and the Old with respect to the ordering of government and worship. The New Testament has no Book of Leviticus, and for that matter, no Manual of Discipline like that of the Qumran Community. This contrast gives some plausibility to the contention that no form of government is instituted in the New Testament. Those who hold this do not deny that various officers and organizational forms are evident in the New Testament. But they hold that these are not normative for subsequent ages. They only represent the early history of organizational variation (or perhaps improvement) that has continued in the church.

The cure for this unfocused view of the New Testament doctrine of the church is a strong dose of biblical theology. The form as well as the content of the New Testament is significant, but it does not signify the dissolving of the normative in the historically descriptive. The New Testament does not have the form of a dictionary of theology, a legal code, a directory for worship, or a form of government but it abounds in normative direction for all of these concerns. The *Form of Government* drawn up by the Westminster Assembly follows a wise course in stressing first the kingship of Christ and his absolute authority over his church, and then in proceeding to describe the officers appointed by Christ for rule in his church. Biblical theology may not be given its due, but neither is it omitted. The distinction between the office of the apostles and prophets on the one hand and that of pastors, teachers, governors, and deacons on the other can be made only with an eye on the progress of redemptive history in the New Testament. In doctrine, ethics, worship, and order the development of New Testament biblical theology is not open-ended and goalless. Rather it traces the way in which Christ, who is the Alpha and Omega of all revelation showed to his apostles the fullness of the "all things" he commanded to be taught to the nations. Really, we are in a far better position than our Puritan forefathers to discern the positive riches of biblical theology with respect to the order of the church. For example, it should be clearer to us that the Gospel of Luke is no less significant for church order than the Book of Acts which completes it.

Now if, as a matter of fact, there is authoritative revelation from Christ, the King of the church, respecting the order of his kingdom; if the keys of the kingdom are his to give and are to be used by church governors meeting in his name; then the problem of conscience that the Puritans faced in fact as well as in theory cannot be evaded. It is a necessary corollary of the ministerial character of rule in the church. No man or court can rule in his own name or in collective human authority. Rule must be in Christ's name, in his authority. Only Christ's Word has that authority; the authority of his ministers is therefore declarative, not legislative. All of which brings us to perceive what the Puritans perceived, but which Calvin surely perceived before them.[5] The church cannot make new laws, it can only enforce by spiritual means the laws of Christ. It cannot plead the general directives of Scripture (that all be done to the glory of God, 1 Cor 10:31; Rom 14:7–8; decently and in order, 1 Cor 14:40; to edification, 1 Cor 13:26; and without creating a stumblingblock, Rom 14:21; 1 Cor 10:23) as warrant for specific requirements in worship or order that bind the conscience with substantive observances and duties.

Here there appears to be an important difference, for example, in the formulations of the Christian Reformed Church and the Orthodox Presbyterian Church. It may be pointedly phrased in the substitute language proposed by a committee of the Orthodox Presbyterian Church for Article 29 of the church order adopted by the Synod of 1965. The key sentence is:

> The decisions of the assemblies shall be considered settled and binding, unless it is proved that they conflict with the Word of God or the Church Order.

The Committee on Revisions to the Form of Government of the Orthodox Presbyterian Church suggested the following revision which would in the opinion of the committee make the article conformable to the standards of that church:

> The decisions of the assemblies shall be considered settled and binding unless it is proved that they are without warrant in the Word of God or conflict with the Church Order.

According to the regulative principle as set forth in the *Westminster Confession,* to require obedience to any decision of an assembly that cannot be proved to conflict with the Word of God is to violate the liberty of the Christian conscience which is free from the commandments of men which are beside the Word in matters of faith or worship.

This difficulty cannot be overcome from the standpoint of the *Westminster Confession* by pleading the voluntary subscription of the churches to the church order. It has been urged that the authority of ecclesiastical assemblies does not finally bind the conscience apart from the Word since the binding force rests upon an initial mutual agreement to be governed according to the provisions of the church order. But surely this reduces the church from its position as a divine institution to that of an arbitrary social organization. The church cannot define its authority in terms of social contract. The sentence of excommunication does not deliver a man to the Baptists but to the devil. The government of the church must be exercised in Christ's name; it must bind men's consciences, declaring that what is bound on earth is bound in heaven. For that very reason the church cannot bind beyond the Word.

Differences of judgment may exist as to defining the circumstances of government and worship.[6] Allowance needs to be made for varying circumstances, and indeed for changes in what may properly be regarded as circumstances (does a *Geneva* gown now mean what a surplice meant in Elizabethan England?). But precisely at the point of binding the conscience the church must preserve that liberty in which Christ has set his people free from the traditions of men.

The Organic Principle

The second central principle, that seems to convey a distinction of emphasis between British and Dutch Reformed polity is what we may call the organic principle in the Presbyterian tradition. In Britain Presbyterians had to struggle not only against the Elizabethan settlement but also against their Independent brethren who had shared the Puritan cause with them. Independents were among the members of the Westminster Assembly. The *Jus Divinum* declaration of Presbyterian divines may reflect some of the answers given by the assembly to queries from parliament about the "divine right" of a church government distinct from the state. The comparison of the Presbyterian and Independent positions on church government in *Jus Divinum* may not do justice to the actual position of the Independents, but it shows how a vigorous rejection of Independency led to a stress on the organic elements of Presbyterian government.[7]

In contrast to Roman Catholic prelacy and Episcopalian hierarchy the Presbyterian "genius" was the rule of the church presbyters. Three distinguishable points are included in "presbyterial" government in this context: (1) No permanent office in the church is higher than that of the preaching presbyter. (2) Government in the church is not exclusively clerical. Calvinistic "church governors" share with pastors the ruling function. (3) Church rule is joint, not merely individual.

In contrast to Independency the emphasis on presbyterial government was somewhat different. As against the congregationalism of Independency, the Presbyterians stressed the authority of church governors: "The church-governors act immediately as the servants of Christ, and as appointed by him."[8] They are not mere deputies of the congregation, nor are their decisions subject to review or determination by the congregation.

As against the principle of Independency the emphasis fell not on the "Parochiall Presbyteries"[9] but on the "greater" or "Classical" presbyteries.[10] "Jesus Christ our Mediator hath laid down in his Word a pattern of a Presbyterial government in common over divers single Congregations in one Church, for a rule to his Church in all after ages."

The *Form of Presbyterial Church Government* of the Westminster Assembly identifies the "Classical Assembly" as the presbytery: "The scripture doth hold out a presbytery in a church. A presbytery consisteth of ministers of the word and such other public officers as are agreeable to and warranted by the word of God to be church-governors to join with the ministers in the government of the church. The scripture doth hold forth, that many particular congregations may be under one presbyterian government."[11]

The significance of this position is far-reaching. The scriptural model in view is the "city-church" of Jerusalem and of Ephesus. These are seen as unified churches under one presbyterial government but including a number of congregations. There is therefore manifest the unity of the church in the fullest sense beyond the local congregation. The membership of preaching presbyters in the presbytery is therefore in no sense artificial. They are members of the church of the city; the scope of their teaching gifts makes it entirely natural that the gathering in which they take counsel be that of the city rather than that of a "house-church." In this broader unity they are in subjection to their brethren, including those of similar gifts who will be best prepared to encourage and admonish them in the discharge of their office. The Westminster *Form of Government* does not even think it essential to demonstrate that the membership of the local congregations in the city was fixed. The unity of the church comes to expression on the local level and at the metropolitan level. We can even say, if a local church is dissolved, the names of the members may be carried on the rolls of Presbytery.

In the *Jus Divinum* contrast between Independency and Presbyterianism, the following is the first antithesis:

> In the Independent government no other visible Church of Christ is acknowledged but only a single congregation meeting in one place to partake of all ordinances. In the Presbyterial government one general visible church of Christ on earth is acknowledged, and all particular churches, and single congregations are but as similar parts of that whole.[12]

The analysis of presbytery in the Westminster *Form of Government* actually points beyond the "parts of the whole" scheme. The unity of the church is fully recognized at both the local (parish) and the area (city) level. The New Testament presents a church that shows unity at local, regional, and ecumenical levels (Rom 16:5; 1 Cor 16:19; 2 Cor 11:8;

12:13; Acts 8:1; 11:22,26; 13:1; Acts 9:31; 1 Cor 10:32; 12:28; Gal 1:13; Eph 1:22; Col 1:18).

Underlying this flexibility is the heavenly reality of the church of Christ which is manifested in the world. The doctrine of the church in Scripture is centered upon the Lord of the covenant, the Savior. It is in its structure theological through and through. Many of the problems that plague polity discussions are false problems because they are not theologically grounded. If the church is approached from a sociological rather than theological standpoint the individual will be sundered from the community, and authority will become magisterial rather than ministerial. The confusion about the relation of the aspects of visibility and invisibility of the church can only grow until it is again recognized that the church as invisible is not some abstract ideal, but simply the church as God sees it, in contrast with the church as we see it. So also the church cannot be initially defined in terms either of the local congregation or of the church universal.

In the theological approach of Scripture the church is the people of God, the kingdom and body of Christ, and the fellowship of the Spirit. The history of the scholarly discussions of the term *ecclesia* is revealing.[13] Before Harnack and Sohm the term was referred to the local assembly by many scholars. The "assembling" of local believers was regarded as accounting for the term *ecclesia*. A shift in opinion linked the Greek term with its Old Testament equivalent *ēdhah* and understood *ecclesia* as describing the congregation of the new people of God whether assembled or not. Neither explanation does justice to the use of *ēdhah* and *ecclesia* in Scripture. The terms are active in force, describing an actual assembling. The active force, however, establishes the theological meaning. The "assembly" of God is not any gathering of the people of God. It is their gathering before the face of the Lord in the definitive assembly at Sinai, in "the day of the assembly" (Deut 4:10 LXX; 9:10; 10:4; 18:16).

In the subsequent assemblies of covenant renewal and in the festival assemblies before the Lord in Jerusalem the people of God are repeatedly manifested as those who stand before him. In the New Testament realization of the people of God the mount of the Lord to which the people come is not Sinai nor even the earthly Zion, but the heavenly Zion (Hebrews 12). Here the festival assembly of the holy ones is gathered, and the saints and angels are assembled where Christ is and where the mercy seat is sprinkled with his blood. The immediacy with which the New Testament grasps the reality of the heavenly assembly gives a different perspective to the concept of "the church of God which is at Corinth." Corinth is one place of manifestation, for God has "much people" in that city, but the church is not the church of Stephanas (16:15), or of Paul, Peter, or Apollos (1:12), or of Corinth. It is the church of God; therefore it includes those who are called to be saints and they are addressed with "all that call upon the name of our Lord Jesus in every place" (1:2).

The organic concept of the church that appears in the New Testament has made a particularly deep mark upon the Presbyterian mind. Presbyterian polity does not stand against the centralized catholicism of Rome and the decentralized independency of congregationalism as a mediating way. Rather it presents a more theological, Christ-centered, spiritual view of the church as defined not by one earthly hierarchical center nor by many earthly congregational centers, but by a heavenly center that requires multiform earthly manifestation. Earthly assemblies do not define but manifest the nature and the center of the church.

This insight is characteristic of all the Reformed communions. W. Heyns, for example, may describe the Reformed polity by saying "Only in the local church does the concept, the significance, the task of the church come to its rights."[14] But he then goes on to balance this statement with a recognition of the organic unity of the church beyond the congregational limits.

Again, however, there seems to be a significant difference in emphasis. The authors of the Westminster *Form of Government* could not have written Heyns' first statement, and Presbyterians in general would feel called to dispute it. Some aspects of Reformed order, as distinct from Presbyterian polity, reflect the place of primacy given to the local church and its consistory. Ministers of the gospel are members of the local church and are subject to the discipline of the consistory. This is tempered, however, by the requirement that the concurring judgment of the consistory of the nearest neighboring church of the classis must be secured for the suspension of a minister. For the deposition of a minister the approval of classis and the concurrence of the synodical deputies is necessary.

Consistency with this position requires that even ministers called to foreign missionary service be subject to the discipline of the consistory of a local church. This practice is maintained although the direction of missionary work has been placed in the hands of the synod.

A further reflection of emphasis on the primacy of the congregation is the representative character of the classes. There are no permanent members of the classis and those who meet in classical assemblies are delegated as representatives of the consistories. Since the minister of each church is regularly made a delegate to classis, the practical difference in the membership of any meeting is small. There does appear to be a difference, however, in understanding the function of the classis. In the Reformed churches an associate understanding of the classis contrasts with a more integral conception of the presbytery.

To the Presbyterian it may appear that the associative view had produced a surprisingly high estimate of the powers of classical and especially of synodical assemblies. Indeed, at times the associative character of these bodies is made the ground of what appears to the Presbyterian to be their arbitrary authority. The churches have bound themselves to associate according to a certain order and therefore must be bound by the decisions produced in the operation of the order.

In the Presbyterian view the character of office in the church is intimately related to the organic unity of the church. Early British Independency regarded a minister's ordination as ceasing when he left a pastoral charge. Since office was in the local congregation he must be re-ordained to the pastoral office in another congregation when a new call was issued. Presbyterians saw this practice as a misunderstanding of the character of office in Christ's church. The gifts by which a man is endued for office are gifts of Christ to his church as one body (Eph 4:7–12). Good order requires that the gift for rule be recognized by those among whom it is exercised, but the whole body of Christ, not simply its manifestation in one congregation is the fellowship of the saints for whose edification the gifts of Christ are given.

Do these differences, then, indicate another "genius" requiring separate development of two irreconcilable traditions? The very modifications that each tradition has undergone and the variations of conviction that each shelters would indicate that this is not the case. For both historical traditions the authority of Scripture is regulative of all faith and practice, for both the unity of the church comes to expression beyond the level of the local congregation, for both office in the church derives from the gift of Christ and is to be discharged as a stewardship to him. No "genius" can be isolated as distinctive that compares with the "genius" that is in common. What is needed rather is a deeper appreciation of the Reformed faith in its understanding of the sovereign rule of Christ in the church as his body. Even in the differences of emphasis that we have the solution is not a simple obliteration of one or the other, or a simple synthesis of the two, but rather a new appreciation of the controlling theological principles from which our understanding of polity springs.

Particularly in the doctrine of the church as Christ's body and as the fellowship of the Spirit there are refreshing springs of truth from which we can draw together. No church government can operate apart from the power of the Spirit and no improvements in understanding polity can be made apart from an illumined understanding of what the Spirit says to the churches.

NOTES

1. Leonard J. Trinterud shows this in *The Forming of an American Tradition: A Re-examination of Colonial Presbyterianism* (Philadelphia: Westminster Press, 1949), 15–52. Charles Hodge, *The Constitutional History of the Presbyterian Church* (Philadelphia: Presbyterian Board of Publication, 1851) also shows this, though rightly stressing Scotch-Irish leadership.

2. On the following section see James Bannerman, *The Church of Christ*, Volume 1 (Edinburgh: T. & T. Clark, 1868), 340–75, and especially the citations from George Gillespie.

3. "The Puritan Approach to Worship" in *Diversity in Unity* (Papers read at the Puritan and Reformed Studies Conference, December 1963), 4–5.

4. Ibid.

5. John Calvin, *Tracts and Treatises on the Doctrine and Worship of the Church*, Volume 2 (Edinburgh: Calvin Translation Society, 1849; reprinted by Eerdmans, 1958), 118: "First, whatever is not commanded, we are not free to choose." See also p. 122.

6. Sometimes debates about the extent of "circumstantials" may unfortunately be cast as debates about the regulative principle. Charles Hodge hotly protests against Thornwell: "There is as much difference between this extreme doctrine of divine right, this idea that everything is forbidden which is not commanded, as there is between this free, exultant Church of ours, and the mummified forms of medieval Christianity. . . . The doctrine need only be clearly propounded to be rejected" *Discussions in Church Polity* (New York: Scribner's, 1878), 133. But the discussion was about the propriety of church boards. Thornwell opposed them on the ground that they were no part of scriptural church government. Hodge defended them on the ground that the form of government prescribed in the New Testament includes only general principles or features and that the church is free to arrange matters of detail. The debate misconceives the issue. One may question, on Hodge's ground, whether the structure of boards is a detail. Further, some of the form of government that Hodge must admit to be prescribed in Scripture consists of "details." It is the meaning of the proposed innovation in terms of scriptural polity that must be determined. Does it bind the consciences of God's people by introducing a new authority structure to which they must submit? Or does it merely arrange the circumstances or organization to allow for the full operation of scriptural government in the particular situation?

7. This section of *Jus Divinum* is reprinted in Iain Murray, ed., *The Reformation of the Church* (London: Banner of Truth Trust, 1965), 294–96.

8. Ibid., 295.

9. *Jus Divinum* (London, 1647, Second ed.), 205.

10. Ibid., 211, 213.

11. Iain Murray, 218–19.

12. Iain Murray, 294.

13. See Krister Stendahl, "Kirche im Urchristentum," in *Die Religion in Geschichte und Gegenwart*, Volume 3 (Tubingen: J. C. B. Mohr, 1959), Cols. 1297–1304.

14. W. Heyns, *Kybernetiek* (Grand Rapids, 1910 mimeo.), 157.

Part II

The American
Presbyterian Experience

Princeton Theological Seminary

Samuel T. Logan, Jr.

8 Transition to the New World

THE TRANSITION OF PRESBYTERIANISM from the old world to the new is a difficult matter to discuss. As Charles Hodge pointed out, "It is admitted that the early history of the Presbyterian Church in the United States is involved in great obscurity."[1] Hodge continues,

> The reason of this fact is obvious. Presbyterians did not at first emigrate in large bodies, or occupy by themselves extensive districts of country. In New England the early settlers were Congregationalists. The history of that portion of our country is, therefore, in a great measure, the history of that denomination. The same remark, to a certain extent, is applicable to the Dutch in New York, the Quakers in Pennsylvania, the Catholics in Maryland. The case was very different with regard to the Presbyterians. They came, as a general rule, as individuals, or in small companies, and settled in the midst of people of other denominations. It was, therefore, in most instances, only gradually that they became as sufficiently numerous in any one place to form congregations, or to associate in a presbyterial capacity.[2]

In light of this difficulty, we might well ask, "Who was the first American Presbyterian?" Answering this question may help us understand some elements in the transition of the Presbyterian Church from the old world to the new. However, we must first take one further step back and seek a commonly accepted definition of Presbyterianism. On the strictly theological side, we might say that Presbyterianism is Calvinistic in doctrine. The *Westminster Confession of Faith* defines thoroughly the Presbyterian's theological perspective. But, of course, the theological thrust of the *Westminster Confession* is basically shared by numerous other groups.

113

Therefore, the focus of our attention must move from theology to ecclesiology. Here distinctions among various early settlers in America become clearer. The most important distinction to be drawn among the early settlers is that between Congregational Calvinists and Presbyterian Calvinists. Leonard Trinterud summarizes the important difference between these two groups:

> The issues upon which Puritanism in England had finally divided into Congregationalists and Presbyterians grew out of two seemingly irreconcilable concepts of the Church. To those of the Congregationalist persuasion, the Church of Christ on earth existed only in its individual congregations. The Church Universal was but the totality of these congregations. To the Presbyterian wing of Puritanism, the Church Universal transcended all its local manifestations, being an entity greater even than the sum of its parts. It was the one body of Christ. From these two starting points, each group went on to differ with the other on a number of crucial issues.[3]

Trinterud goes on to trace the various implications of these differing concepts of the church. Among the most important were an understanding of church membership, the nature of ordination, and the office of ministry.[4] Behind all of these specific differences lay contrary concepts of the extent of the church; at least, so it has seemed to many historians for the past three centuries.

In order to answer, therefore, our original question about the identity of the first American Presbyterian, we need to reconsider carefully the degree to which the distinction outlined by Trinterud was maintained in early New England. If it can be demonstrated that the religious establishment of Massachusetts Bay actually operated on the basis of a more or less regional church concept, then the question of transition from old world to new will be greatly clarified.

As Charles Hodge reminds us, Presbyterianism, separatism, and the "middle way" of non-separating Congregationalism all originated in dissatisfaction with the extent of the Reformation under the auspices of the Church of England.[5] The original break with Rome occurred for other than doctrinal reasons, and the subsequent history of the Anglican Church was, to say the very least, checkered. The regents of Edward moved the church in a more thoroughly Reformed direction, Mary had sought to return it to the Roman Catholic fold, and Elizabeth, who ruled from 1558 to 1603, had taken a politically pragmatic attitude toward the church. Those who sought genuine reformation had experienced various forms of persecution under Elizabeth and, even more so, under her successors James I and Charles I.[6]

What is fairly well known about this situation is that those who opposed the Anglican establishment became known as "Puritans" because they wanted to purify further the Church of England. What is perhaps not so well known is the degree to which Presbyterianism dominated the early

Puritan movement. Once again, Hodge described the situation accurately when he says that ". . . the great majority of Puritans in England were Presbyterians."[7] They were Presbyterians because intrinsic to their ecclesiology was the conviction that the fate of the church in England, rather than the fate of the various individual churches in England, was of paramount importance. This corporate sense continued to dominate Puritan thinking when individual Puritans moved from England to New England.

The only non-conformists who genuinely rejected the entire Presbyterian way of understanding the church were the separatists. Represented best by such individuals as Robert Browne, John Smyth, and John Robinson, the separatists despaired of achieving adequate purification of the Anglican establishment. They were determined to bring about, in Browne's own words, "Reformation without tarying for anie" by forming their own separate congregations in which the appropriate purity was much more achievable.[8] This was the first Anglo-American rending of the previously seamless regional church garment. Its impact has been felt by all Christians, even by those who today regard themselves as Presbyterians.

The Presbyterians and the non-separating Congregationalists among the Puritans rejected the separatists' way. They both believed that the biblical teaching about the church required them to see it as an institution in need of reformation, to be sure, but one church nevertheless. The fascinating story is how the difference between Presbyterian Puritans and non-separating Congregational Puritans began and how it developed during this period.

Basically, the difference beween these two latter groups of Puritans arose out of pragmatic considerations that led the separatists to renounce completely any notion of the church universal. Both Presbyterians and non-separating Congregationalists recognized that the struggle to reform the Anglican establishment was a difficult one. Ecclesiological differences developed around the question of how difficult the task was perceived to be. To simplify but not oversimplify, those who remained Presbyterian in orientation had more confidence in the possibility of reforming the entire Anglican establishment than did those who became non-separating Congregationalists. Events in Scotland, particularly under John Knox's leadership in 1560 and after, encouraged many of the Puritans to believe that the ongoing Reformation of the entire national church was possible. The single-minded resistance by Elizabeth and her two sucessors to such thorough reformation convinced others among the Puritans that while purification of the church as a whole in England was the ultimate goal (because the church was whole), real progress would only be made as individual parts of that whole conformed more completely to the Word of God. Those who took this line were not fully Presbyterian, but neither were they separatists.

Another way to approach the distinctions among these various groups in Britain in the late sixteenth and early seventeenth centuries is to focus on the selection of church officers and the degree to which church and state are co-extensive. Both Presbyterians and non-separating Congregationalists believed that the Anglican way of choosing church officers was unbiblical. Rather than appointing local church officials from the lofty reaches of an ecclesiastical hierarchy, both Puritan groups believed they were most appropriately chosen by church members. But the Presbyterians among the Puritans were actually closer to the Anglicans than they were to the non-separating Congregationalists in their understanding of the co-extensiveness of church and state. Following the model that was being developed in Scotland, Presbyterians identified church and state quite closely — not in terms of jurisdiction or authority, but in terms of membership. For both Anglicans and Presbyterians, citizenship and church membership were correlative if not synonymous. Presbyterians determined to achieve what they regarded as necessary reformation by changing the method of choosing clergy and by taking the presbytery out from under the direct control of the political Sovereign.

The non-separating Congregationalists, in essence, did not believe that the Presbyterian method would work. They were convinced that as long as those who elected elders were themselves potentially un-Reformed, the officers they chose to lead them might very well continue to be un-Reformed. Therefore, the non-separating Congregationalists earned their Puritan appellation by focusing initial attention on the purification of local congregations. They did not, however, in any way abandon the goal of reforming the regional church. Since they continued to concentrate so much energy on that ultimate goal, it is quite proper to regard them as having very strong Presbyterian leanings.

Obviously, the process by which non-separating Congregationalism came to focus its purifying attention on local church membership was a very long and complicated one. What has just been suggested is a summary of ecclesiological developments over a half century and across three thousand miles of salt water. The details of this shift have been told thoroughly and quite well before.[9] The objective here has been simply to summarize this development for the purposes of comparing Puritan non-separating Congregationalism to Puritan Presbyterianism. From this comparison, both differences and significant similarities between the two groups can be seen.

As a matter of fact, this comparison suggests in simplified form a point which cannot be stressed too strongly: Presbyterianism in early seventeenth-century Britain was a very different thing from Presbyterianism today. Likewise, the non-separating Congregationalism of that same period should not be regarded as identical with Congregationalism in the United States at the present time. As a matter of fact, it may well be that twentieth-century American Presbyterianism has more in common with seventeenth-century non-separating Congregationalism than it does with seventeenth-century Presbyterianism. This is just one of the reasons why identifying the first American Presbyterian becomes so inordinately difficult.

As we move into the second quarter of the seventeenth century, the differences both between earlier and modern Presbyterianism and between earlier and modern Congregationalism become even clearer. A close examination, for example, of the political nature of the *National Covenant* signed at Greyfriars Kirk in Edinburgh in 1638 and the affirmation of the *Solemn League and Covenant* in 1643 reveal a concept of the co-extensiveness of church and state that has no place in modern Presbyterianism. Perhaps even more to the point of this essay is the degree to which non-separating Congregationalism represented both a corporate sense and a view of church membership with which modern Presbyterians would be both familiar and comfortable.

A central question, therefore, might very well be, "Why did English Puritans (of the non-separating Congregationalist variety) come to America in such large numbers at the beginning of the second quarter of the seventeenth century?" Answering this question will illumine the degree to which they had Presbyterian leanings and address more directly the matter of the transition of Presbyterianism from the Anglo-European to the American situation.

John Winthrop was a layman but he was also an extremely influential leader among the Puritans who migrated from England to Massachusetts Bay. A native of East Anglia (within which was located both Cambridge University and the greatest concentration of Puritan sentiment), Winthrop represents very well the classical non-separating Congregationalist mindset. Deeply distressed over the failure of the English church to complete the Reformation, he felt mandated by Scripture to deal with the results of that failure in corporate terms. Like most other Puritans, he believed that God related not just to individuals but also to corporate units of which various individuals were parts. Specifically, Winthrop shared the Puritan understanding of a national covenant. This meant he believed that a nation that lived in disobedience to God could expect to be judged by God.

While on business in London on May 15, 1629, Winthrop wrote the following letter to his wife.

> My good wife, I prayse the Lorde for the wished newes of thy well-fare and of the rest of our companye, and for the continuance of ours heer: It is a great favour, that we may enioye so much comfort and peace in these so euill and declininge tymes and when the increasinge of our sinnes giues vs so great cause to looke for some heauye Scquorge and Judgment to be comminge vpon us: the Lorde hath admonished, threatened, corrected and astonished vs, yet we growe worse and worse, so as his spirit will not allwayes striue with vs, he must needs giue waye to his furye at last: he hath smitten all the other Churches before our

eyes, and hath made them to drinke of the bitter cuppe of tribulation, euen vnto death; we sawe this, and humbled not ourselues, to turne from our euill wayes, but haue prouoked him more than all the nationals rounde about vs: therefore he is turninge the cuppe towars vs also, and because we are the last, our portion must be to drinke the verye dreggs which remain: my deare wife, I am veryly perswaded, God will bringe some heauye Affliction vpon this lande, and that speedylye: but be of good Comfort, the hardest that come shall be a meanes to mortifie this bodye of Corruption which is a thousand tymes more dangerous to vs than any outward tribulation, and to bringe vs into neerer communion with our Lo: Jes: Christ, and more Assurance of his kingdome. If the Lord seeth it wilbe good for vs, he will prouide a shelter and a hidinge place for vs and ours. . . . [10]

To Winthrop the individual was primary, but he was very conscious of the degree to which the group was also real before God. This affected his understanding of the church and the state and led to his decision to travel three thousand miles to try to set up a holy commonwealth in which both church and state would live in obedience to the Word of God. Paramount among the many reasons for the transition by the Puritans from England to New England was this corporate sense. This notion is in basic agreement with the Presbyterian understanding of the church and was at the very heart of the great migration.

It must also be remembered that the group of Puritans that came to Massachusetts Bay was different in some crucial ways from the group which settled at Plymouth. The Plymouth group (known to later generations as the "Pilgrims") was comprised primarily of separatists. As one reads William Bradford's journal, *History of Plimoth Plantation,* and contrasts it with Winthrop's *History of New England,* one is struck continually with the degree to which the former breathes a spirit of individualism (both in personal and church life), while the latter is much more conscious of corporate realities. Therefore, when we speak of the movement of this Presbyterian-like corporate sense from England to New England, we must be very clear that we are referring, not to the settlers at Plymouth, but to the much larger colony established some ten years later around Boston, Massachusetts. It is this latter group that influenced in a major way the development of American Presbyterianism.

But if Winthrop and those who came with him felt that the body of which they were part in England was increasingly corrupt, and that the sickness of that body threatened their own spiritual health, what exactly did they do after arriving in Massachusetts to achieve a healthy body? In a word, they sought to safeguard membership in both church and state in order to protect and provide for biblical holiness in both. The Puritans *never* confused church and state. To their way of thinking, each had its own distinct function and stood in a corporate relationship (in covenant) with God. Both church and state were required to be obedient to God's

Word. As reflected in Winthrop's letter to his wife, both church and state should expect the favor of God if they obeyed his Word. His judgment was certain if they disobeyed it.

The actual structure of church and state in New England in the early 1630s is described in great detail in Edmund Morgan's brilliant volume, *The Puritan Dilemma: The Story of John Winthrop.*[11] To summarize that structure briefly, the franchise was restricted to male members of Puritan churches. Furthermore, membership in those churches was limited to those individuals who demonstrated doctrinal orthodoxy, lived sanctified lives, and perhaps most important, were able to describe their experience of grace.

Several things need to be said about this structure at the very beginning. First of all, only those who could vote could hold political office. The Puritans hoped thereby to make significant progress toward building a society that genuinely held the glory of God as its first priority. From the beginning, however, ministers were prohibited from holding political office. The official lines between church and state were drawn clearly for all to see. Winthrop's journal traces in great detail the relationships between elected political officers and church officers. While frequent disagreements between the two groups arose, there was no confusion between them regarding their respective roles, rights, and responsibilities.

The second point focuses on the question of "fairness." Many modern scholars question the restriction of the franchise to church members. They accuse the Puritans of narrow-minded bigotry. In response to such a charge, it must be stated that political liberty was not the highest priority for the Puritans. The highest priority was the glory of God. If achieving the glory of God required the sacrifice of other legitimate values, the Puritans were willing to make that sacrifice. Modern America, however, with its near deification of individual freedom cannot understand a mindset which genuinely sought to worship the Creator rather than the creature.

Having said this, nevertheless, it is necessary to understand the degree to which the Puritans in Massachusetts Bay were more or less "narrow" than their counterparts in England. It is true that the Puritans sought to set up a society based on a rather narrow franchise, but this was common in the seventeenth-century world. The difference between England and New England was not the percentage of individuals within the society who could vote (in both societies it hovered around 15 percent) but the way in which those who could vote were chosen.[12] Whereas in New England a fundamentally spiritual criterion was utilized, in England the criterion was overtly economic. That is, in English society in the seventeenth century, voters had to possess a 40-shilling freehold. "Narrowness" can, therefore, be no more charged against the Puritans than it can against their English counterparts. Indeed, what was true in England was true in most other European countries of the day. By selecting a spiritual criterion for the franchise, the Puritans did make quite clear where their societal priorities rested. For them, fundamental values were not economic but spiritual, and this determined the tone of their entire society.

The third point has to do with the specific criterion that the Puritans utilized for membership in their churches. In addition to the normal British Puritan and continental criteria of doctrinal orthodoxy and moral life, the New England Puritans requested applicants for their churches to describe the experience they had of the grace of God. This criterion has been roundly criticized by many historians who have argued that the Puritans were guilty of the old Donatist heresy of perfectionism.

Nothing could be further from the truth. The Puritans asked candidates for membership in their churches nothing more than "a credible profession of faith" — a request made by most conservative Presbyterian bodies today.[13] That this and nothing more than this was sought by the Puritans can be confirmed quickly by even a cursory perusal of the confessions of faith of fifty persons who applied for membership in Thomas Shepard's church in Cambridge, Massachusetts, between 1638 and 1645.[14] Not only were the Puritans not Donatists, but in the matter of church membership, they were actually much closer to conservative twentieth-century American Presbyterians than other seventeenth-century British and continental Presbyterians are to the modern situation. The Puritans of New England believed in the corporate nature of God's people. They sought, both by their church membership and franchise criterion, to do all they could to achieve a holiness of the political and ecclesiastical units.

In this *corporate sense*, the New England Puritans were far more Presbyterian than Congregational, at least as those two terms are normally understood. Indeed, as one examines the way in which the Massachusetts Bay (both church and state) dealt first with Roger Williams and then with Anne Hutchinson, one is impressed with the Presbyterian character of those dealings. When, for example, the church at Salem wished to hire Williams as its teacher, it was strongly counselled not to do so by the other Massachusetts Bay churches. The church at Salem declined to follow that counsel, and the general court entered the picture to enforce the judgment of the churches.[15] In fact, the actions of both the court and the churches was so clearly "Presbyterian" that Williams himself charged the churches of Massachusetts of having given up the principle of congregational independence.[16]

Dealings with Anne Hutchinson were no less definitive. When one church (the Boston church) seemed to be moving in the direction of accepting Hutchinsonian Antinomianism, meetings and councils of the ministers were called in order to deal adequately with this threat to the doctrinal well-being of the corporate community.[17] Because they were convinced of the essential unity of the civil and ecclesiastical bodies, the Puritans could not and did not allow challenges to that unity to go unchecked. It may be that the New England Puritans acted in this manner because, as Cotton Mather remarks, more than four thousand Presbyterians entered New England prior to 1640.[18] But even more likely is the simple fact that these Puritans from the very beginning thought in corporate terms. This made them Presbyterian even if they did not realize it themselves. Once again, it is Charles Hodge who summarizes the situation most accurately.

> The influence of Presbyterian principle in New England is, however, much more satisfactorily proved by the nature of the ecclesiastical systems which were there adopted, than by any statements of isolated facts. These systems were evidently the result of compromise between two parties, and they show that the Presbyterian was much stronger than the Independent element. The two leading points of difference between Presbyterianism and Congregationalism, particularly as the latter exists at present, relate to the mode of government within the congregation, whether it should be by elders or the brotherhood, and to the authority of Synods. As to both these points the early discipline of the New England churches approached much nearer to Presbyterianism than it does at present.[19]

If all of this is true, why were there so many outspoken statements of opposition to Presbyterianism in New England in the 1630s and 1640s? Why specifically did both John Cotton and Thomas Hooker write formal treatises seeking to vindicate the Congregational system as over against the Presbyterian? To be sure, it would be inaccurate to suggest that New England Puritans actually were Presbyterians in every way. They did seek to maintain, at least in theory, a degree of congregational independence that moves away from a Presbyterian model. Nevertheless, two facts about the Presbyterianism of these New England churches should be kept clearly in mind.

First of all, their corporate sense made it impossible for them to see their churches as completely separate from one another. Each church was part of the whole, and it was in terms of the whole that each church was expected to act. Therefore, the theoretical independence of the churches was largely mitigated by the even greater emphasis upon the unity of the body.

Secondly, the reaction which we frequently see in early New England to Presbyterianism was to the Presbyterianism *of that day*. As already suggested, Hooker and Cotton and most of the other New England Puritans identified Presbyterianism with the state-church situation which, in their opinion, had proven inimical to true reformation and biblical holiness. While the state-church model might seem to be successful in Scotland, Scotland was under the political control of England. In New England minds, the Scottish church was incapable of living as fully by the Word of God as New Englanders thought was necessary. Therefore, it was the seventeenth-century version of Presbyterianism that Cotton and Hooker were rejecting, not Presbyterianism as we know it in the twentieth century. To gain a better understanding of that seventeenth-century version of Presbyterianism, at least as understood by New England, it is necessary only to reread Chapter 23 of the original version of the *Westminster Confession of Faith*. Section 3 of that original chapter reads as follows:

> The civil magistrate may not assume to himself the administration of the Word and sacriments, or the power of the keys of the kingdom of heaven: yet he hath authority, and it is his duty, to take order that unity and peace be preserved in the Church, that the truth of God be kept pure and entire, that all blasphemies and heresies be suppressed, all corruptions and abuses in worship and discipline prevented or reformed, and all the ordinances of God duly settled, administered, and observed. For the better effecting thereof, he hath power to call synods, to be present at them, and to provide that whatsoever is transacted in them be according to the mind of God.[20]

New Englanders feared this kind of arrangement and rejected such Presbyterianism.

However, when the Puritans of Massachusetts Bay came to adopt their own doctrinal statement, the *Cambridge Platform of 1648*, they not only adopted without change all of the doctrinal sections of the *Westminster Confession of Faith*, but they also created what has been astutely called "a Congregationalized Presbyterianism or a Presbyterianized Congregationalism."[21] As a result of this doctrinal stand, New England was criticized both by British Independents for exercising too tight control over individual churches and by Scottish Presbyterians for allowing too much diversity among the churches. In fact, however, the New England Congregationalism of the *Cambridge Platform* had remarkable similarities to the American Presbyterianism we know at the end of the twentieth century.

One of the most fascinating discussions of the Puritan attempt to maintain theological unity within the churches and of the degree to which this represented a form of Presbyterianism is Philip Gura's *A Glimpse of Sion's Glory: Puritan Radicalism in New England, 1620–1660*. And one of the most illuminating aspects of Gura's discussion is his consideration of the *Woburn Memorial* of 1663. In that protest, ten individuals petitioned the general court objecting to a recent order of the court in which it was stated that "no person in this jurisdiction shall undertake any constant course of public preaching without the approbation of the elders of four of the next churches, or of the county court."[22] In their memorial the petitioners "arraigned the Massachusetts General Court for encouraging both presbyterianism and Erastianism."[23] Needless to say, the petition was dismissed by the court, but the very fact of its existence seems to verify yet again the ecclesiological model that was being used.

So in the 1640s and 1650s, New England was increasingly Presbyterian in orientation. These were crucial years because it was precisely at the same time that New England Puritans began moving south into Long Island and New Jersey. Leonard Trinterud is just one of the historians who has documented this particular migration. He describes the movement of Francis Doughty, an English Puritan of decidedly Presbyterian views, from Taunton, Massachusetts, to Mespat on Long Island in 1642.[24] Hodge, Lefferts Loetscher, and William McKinney also chronicle these early years of Presbyterian settlements in the middle colonies.[25] The point is that the earliest settlement in this country which could clearly be regarded as Presbyterian was begun by New Englanders drifting down into the middle colonies and bringing with them the theological perspectives and ecclesiological models of early Massachusetts Bay. This was another important aspect in the overall transition of Presbyterianism to the New World.

At the same time, much larger numbers of Scottish Presbyterians were moving from their homeland to the four northern-most provinces of Ireland, the area known as Ulster. The history of the Presbyterian church in Ulster is a fascinating story in itself, but for our purposes that story must be passed over quickly.[26] The point is that these individuals brought to Ulster a very rigorous doctrinal form of Presbyterianism that their new circumstances caused them to clarify even more fully. It was, after all, basic biblical doctrine that separated these Presbyterians from their Roman Catholic counterparts in the southern provinces of Ireland and from the Anglicans from whom they received such persecution in the middle decades of the seventeenth century.[27] And we must remember, as Trinterud points out, "The Presbyterians of Scotish origin who came to America during the colonial period were mostly from north Ireland. Few came direct from Scotland. Scotch-Irish Presbyterianism, while transplanted originally from Scotland, had been modified in many ways by its experiences of poverty and persecution in Ireland."[28]

During the 1640s and 1650s, slow migration of these Scotch-Irish to the middle colonies of the new world was taking place. By the early 1680s, there were enough Scotch-Irish Presbyterians in the middle colonies to warrant an appeal for pastors from Northern Ireland.[29] The respondent to this appeal, which formally had gone out from Colonel William Stephens in Maryland, was Francis Makemie, often called "the father of American Presbyterianism."[30] No sooner had he arrived in Maryland than Makemie began his church planting work as he itinerated widely along the coasts of Maryland, Virginia, the Carolinas, and Barbados.[31] Makemie seems to have been the catalyst drawing together many of the incipient strands of Presbyterianism in the middle colonies. The Presbyterianism that gathered around him was a combination of two distinct strains, the New England Puritan strain and the Scotch-Irish strain. These two strains would make their own contributions to emerging American Presbyterianism.

While Makemie preached and planted churches through the middle colonies, events were transpiring in New England which would move some aspects of the Congregationalism there even more in a Presbyterian direction. On October 23, 1684, the Massachusetts Bay Puritans were notified that the King of England had annulled their charter. This crisis had been brewing for many years, but the event was nonetheless traumatic.[32] Loss of the charter meant the loss of the Puritans' ability to structure their society as they saw fit. Concomitantly, it meant a dramatic challenge to the corporate ideal of a holy commonwealth because, without the ability to restrict the franchise to church members, the Puritans now, at least in their estimate, had lost the essential means of bringing the church and state in obedience to God. Without such political means at their disposal, the Puritans, who were disinclined to abandon their corporate sense, recognized very quickly that a more formally Presbyterian arrangement was their last best option.

Consequently, Increase Mather, who was in London in 1691 seeking to negotiate the return of some charter to New England, joined with other ministers in sponsoring the *Heads of Agreement*. This plan was essentially a union of Presbyterian and Congregationalist ministers which was designed to make it possible in New England to retain some degree of spiritual hegemony in the church and state.[33] Increasing secularism, centered particularly at Harvard, made it impossible for Mather to sell his plan in Massachusetts. He was opposed by a wide variety of churchmen and the *Heads of Agreement* largely came to nought in his home state.

The concern that had been inaugurated by the loss of the charter and exacerbated by the developments at Harvard had more specific results in Connecticut. There the *Saybrook Platform* was adopted in 1708. Hodge summarizes its content.

> In giving, therefore, the exercise of discipline to the pastors and elders, and in making the determinations of councils definitive and binding, on pain of non-communion, the Saybrook Platform, unanimously approved by the Assembly which prepared it in 1708, and adopted by the legislature as the discipline of the churches established by law, comes very little short of Presbyterianism. It is very evident, as this Platform was a compromise between two parties, being less than the one, and more than the other wished to see adopted, that one party must have been thorough Presbyterians. That they were, moreover, the stronger of the two, is evident from the Platform approaching so much nearer to their system, than to that of the Independents.[34]

The loss of the charter, then, and the response to that loss in Connecticut at least, resulted in an even greater similarity between the Congregationalism of New England and modern Presbyterianism than has been indicated earlier. Furthermore, the date is crucial. While there had been continual slow migration both from New England and from Northern Ireland to the middle colonies throughout the second half of the seventeenth century, this migration from both sources increased early in the eighteenth century. Those Puritans who came to the middle colonies from southern New England were particularly amenable to the Presbyterian mindset. It was, therefore, most natural for them to join with the Scotch-Irish who were also arriving there in increased numbers.

It is clear then that a variety of circumstances, all under the sovereign control of God, contributed to making the middle colonies at the beginning of the eighteenth century particularly ripe for Presbyterian expansion. Wayland Dunaway outlines the reasons for the massive migration of Scotch-Irish Presbyterians to the middle colonies beginning early in the eighteenth century.[35] As they came, they joined with New Englanders of similar persuasion to create an American Presbyterian church.

Relations between the two groups in the new world may be seen to some degree in the origins of the first presbytery. The presbytery was set up in 1706, largely as a result of the work of Francis Makemie. As Trinterud points out, the backgrounds of the seven ministers who joined Makemie in founding the presbytery have been strongly disputed in the history of the church.[36] Trinterud's summary of their credentials is most instructive.

> Francis Makemie, the first moderator of the Presbytery, was a Scotch-Irishman, with strong ties to both England and New England. Samuel Davis, the merchant-pastor of Lewes, Delaware, probably came from Ireland. Three of the ministers in this newly founded presbytery were from New England. Jedediah Andrews, pastor of the church at Philadelphia, was the son of New England Presbyterians and a graduate of Harvard College. John Wilson, pastor at New Castle, was also from New England. Increase and Cotton Mather had been instrumental in sending him to Delaware since many New Englanders were settling there on lands purchased by Connecticut. The third pastor from New England was Nathaniel Taylor, of Patuxetent, Maryland. George McNish and John Hampton, whom the United Brethren had sent over to the colonies, were the other two charter members of the Presbytery. McNish was a Scot and Hampton was Scotch-Irish.[37]

The results of this particular mix of elements in the formation of a first presbytery of the New England and Scotch-Irish elements are noteworthy in two ways, according to Lefferts Loetscher.

> For one thing, it (the Presbytery) united in the persons of its seven ministers the two quite differing and often conflicting heritages of Puritan Presbyterianism and of Scotch and Scotch-Irish Presbyterianism, anticipating the pluralism, even at times polarity, that was to characterize American Presbyterianism. A second important feature of this first presbytery was that it was organized "from the ground up," not "from the top down," as was the Presbyterianism of Scotland which had been adopted by Parliament, and implemented by the General Assembly. In America, on the contrary, the higher judicatories, were created by the lower, establishing the more democratic nature of American Presbyterianism, and strengthening the concept that undelegated powers remain in the Presbytery, not in the higher judicatories.[38]

This combination of ingredients continued to dominate the period of transition of the Presbyterian Church. Trinterud summarizes the development of the synod in terms very similar to those that he used to describe the formation of the first presbytery.

By 1716, Presbyterian churches had so multiplied that a Synod was formed to comprise four presbyteries— Philadelphia, New Castle, Long Island, and Snow Hill — though the last named was never erected. . . . Seventeen additional ministers had joined the Church since its founding. Five had come from New England, three from Wales, six from Scotland, two from Ireland, and one was of uncertain origin. He also was probably a New Englander. Of the eight Scotish and Scotch-Irish clergymen, three had been sent out by the Presbyterian ministers of London. The total number of ministers in active service was now 25: 8 Scotsmen, 7 Scotch-Irishmen, 7 New Englanders, and 3 Welshmen.[39]

As one analyzes even more carefully the backgrounds of those individuals in early Presbyterianism who exercised the most influence on the development of the denomination, one is struck again with the degree to which New England Puritanism and Scotch-Irish Presbyterianism predominated. Surely the two most famous names in early Presbyterianism were Dickinson and Tennent. Jonathan Dickinson, a graduate of Yale, was one of those Presbyterianized Congregationalists from Connecticut who consistently represented the New England perspective within Presbyterianism. William Tennent, the father of the Log College and four famous sons, had been educated at the University of Edinburgh and ordained by the general synod of Ulster at Amtrim in Northern Ireland.[40] Together, Dickinson and Tennent provided the infant Presbyterian Church with the bulk of its theological leadership during the early days of its existence.

What did these two different traditions bring to the new mix that was forming American Presbyterianism? Generally speaking, historians have agreed that the Scotch-Irish brought to the marriage a rigorous commitment to doctrinal orthodoxy. To say this is not to suggest that New Englanders did not care about doctrinal orthodoxy. Their response to the doctrinal deviations of Roger Williams and Anne Hutchinson should leave no doubt that they were deeply concerned about major theological issues. However, the experience in Scotland and Ireland had led the Scotch-Irish to be even more rigorously concerned about the degree to which doctrinal commitments must be precise and measured. Trinterud describes the two major backgrounds of this perspective: that of the Scottish situation itself going back to the provisions of the *Solemn League and Covenant* and extending through the Marrow Controversy; and that of the situation in Ulster where the danger of Arianism had led to the development of rigorous subscriptionist standards.[41]

For their part, the New Englanders brought to the marriage a particularly strong emphasis upon experimental religion. Of course, the same disclaimer must be issued here as above — after all, it was the Tennent family which led the Great Awakening in the middle colonies. Nevertheless, arising out of their "narrative of grace" criterion for church membership, the New Englanders emphasized the degree to which a credible profession of personal faith was a vital ingredient in the qualification for church membership and for ordination to the ministry.

At its best, any marriage builds upon the strengths of both partners and this has, to a large degree, been true of American Presbyterians. Both a solid doctrinal foundation for piety and a warm, breathing orthodoxy describe what directed Presbyterianism in the transition from the old to the new world. The heritage of American Presbyterianism reminds one of two beautiful descriptions of the Christian life. William Ames begins his *Marrow of Theology* with the words "Theology is the doctrine or teaching of living to God," and Jonathan Edwards, who was probably America's greatest theologian and who began his ministerial career as a Presbyterian pastor in New York, summarizes his most important work, *Treatise on Religious Affections*, "No light in the understanding is good which does not produce holy affection in the heart."[42] These perspectives represent the best of American Presbyterianism as it arises out of the distinct strands that produced it.

At the same time, divergent strands within a marriage may also produce controversy, and this also happened in American Presbyterianism. It would not be too much to say that the subscriptionist controversy (which resulted in the Adopting Act of 1729) arose at least partially out of the clash of New England and Scotch-Irish perspectives. Furthermore, the more divisive controversy that developed during the Great Awakening and resulted in the first split in the church might be said to have its roots in the divergent backgrounds of the members of the church. While it certainly is over-simplistic to try to identify either side in either controversy with one particular group, nevertheless because the New Englanders placed greatest priority on the experience of individual conversion and because the Scotch-Irish placed greatest priority on doctrinal orthodoxy, the marriage of the two was almost certain to produce friction. That friction reappears frequently in the history of the Presbyterian Church throughout the middle part of the eighteenth century.

Two final points should be made with regard to the heritage of American Presbyterianism. First, most of the present chapter has focused upon the degree to which New England Puritanism might legitimately be said to have been Presbyterian at least in thrust. The reason for this is that frequently in Presbyterian circles the Puritan component of our heritage is neglected or relegated to secondary status. As a matter of fact, the New England Puritans were, as I have sought to demonstrate, in most ways Presbyterian in their ecclesiology just as in their theology. Furthermore, their contribution to Reformed theology in America and to the Presbyterian tradition is supremely important. In addition to all of the points made above, it should be noted that the first president of the College of New Jersey (the Presbyterians' first college in the new world) was a New Englander, Jonathan Dickinson. Furthermore, there is abundant evidence to suggest that if the Lord had spared Jonathan Edwards, who served less than three months as president of the college of New Jersey before dying of smallpox in 1758, the history of Christianity and the history of the Presbyterian Church in the United States would have been quite different. Under the extended leadership of John Witherspoon, Scottish common sense philosophy, rather than the "affectionate" piety of Edwards, came to dominate the nation's and the church's religious life. Therefore, understanding New England Puritanism particularly as it reached its zenith in Edwards might very well be a most profitable exercise for twentieth-century Presbyterians who would reclaim the best of their heritage.

Nevertheless New England Puritanism without the extraordinarily valuable Scotch-Irish contribution would not be American Presbyterianism. Confessionalism with piety, light in the understanding combined with affection in the heart — it is this combination that produced American Presbyterianism, and it is this combination that we would do well to reclaim today.

Finally, what about the *corporate sense* that was so vital to the Presbyterianized Congregationalism of New England? Have we adequately taken account of what this concept can and should mean for us as Christians, and as Presbyterians, in the twentieth century? Modern Presbyterians affirm this notion in ecclesiastical matters but tend, possibly without adequate reflection, to ignore its possible implications in civil affairs. Does the political unit of which we are a part have *any* corporate identity and responsibility before God? Or have we so thoroughly severed church from state that we no longer even ask questions about the holiness of the state of which we are part? A demonination as a whole can be more or less faithful to the Word of God. When it is more faithful it stands in a line of blessing, and when it is less faithful it stands in a line of judgment. Can the same be said in any way of political units?

The New England Puritans and their Presbyterian brothers in Scotland in the mid-seventeenth century thought it could. But the loss of the New Englanders' charter in 1684 and the emigration of the Scotch and Scotch-Irish Presbyterians to a pluralistic environment in the middle colonies led to a dramatic modification of this answer to the question. Most historians concede that such modification arose out of historical circumstances but few have adequately addressed the question of whether it was biblical. The question remains for us today, Is it possible that, at least on this issue, the Puritans of early New England were more consistent Presbyterians than we are?

NOTES

1. Charles Hodge, *The Constitutional History of the Presbyterian Church in the United States of America*, Part I (Philadelphia: Presbyterian Board of Publication, 1851), 19.

2. Ibid.

3. Leonard Trinterud, *The Forming of an American Tradition: A Re-examination of Colonial Presbyterianism* (New York: Arno Press, 1970), 16.

4. Ibid., 16–20.

5. Hodge, 21–22.

6. For details of this situation, see especially William Haller, *The Rise of Puritanism* (New York: Harper and Row, 1957).

7. Hodge, 27.

8. Haller, 182.

9. See, for example, Perry Miller, *Orthodoxy in Massachusetts, 1630–1650* (Gloucester, Massachusetts: Peter Smith, 1965) and Edmund Morgan, *Visible Saints: The History of a Puritan Idea* (Ithaca: Cornell University Press, 1963).

10. John Winthrop, "Letter to His Wife, May 15, 1629" in *The Puritans: A Sourcebook of Their Writings*, Volume Two, ed. Perry Miller and Thomas H. Johnson (New York: Harper and Row, 1963), 466–67.

11. Edmund Morgan, *The Puritan Dilemma: The Story of John Winthrop* (Boston: Little, Brown, and Co., 1958).

12. For a comparison of franchise figures in England and New England, see Williston Walker, *The Creeds and Platforms of Congregationalism* (New York: Scribner's, 1893), 165; Miller, 207; and Edmund Morgan, *American Slavery, American Freedom: The Ordeal of Colonial Virginia* (New York: Norton, 1975), 60.

13. See the Orthodox Presbyterian Church *Form of Government* XIII, 2.

14. Bruce Chapman Woolley, *Reverend Thomas Shepard's Cambridge Church Members 1636–1649: A Socio-Economic Analysis*, (unpublished Ph.D. dissertation: University of Rochester, 1973), 85–211.

15. Morgan, 125–29.

16. Ibid., 126.

17. Ibid., 134–54.

18. Cotton Mather, *Magnalia Christi Americana*, Volume I (Edinburgh: Banner of Truth, 1979), 80.

19. Hodge, 30.

20. *Westminster Confession of Faith*, Chapter 23, III (The Publications Committee of the Free Church of Scotland, 1967), 101–3.

21. Trinterud, 21.

22. Philip Gura, *A Glimpse of Sion's Glory: Puritan Radicalism in New England, 1620–1660* (Middletown, Connecticut: Wesleyan University Press, 1984), 207.

23. Ibid., 208.

24. Trinterud, 22.

25. Hodge, 35–37; Lefferts Loetscher, *A Brief History of the Presbyterians* (Philadelphia: Westminster Press, 1978), 59–60; and William McKinney, "Beginnings in the North" in *They Seek a Country: The American Presbyterians*, ed. Gaius Jackson Slosser (New York: Macmillan Co., 1955), 30–32.

26. Wayland Dunaway, *The Scotch-Irish of Colonial Pennsylvania* (Chapel Hill, North Carolina: University of North Carolina Press, 1944), 13–23.

27. Dunaway, 18–22; Loetscher, 42–45.

28. Trinterud, 15.

29. Loetscher, 60.

30. McKinney, 32.

31. Trinterud, 26–27.

32. Perry Miller, *The New England Mind: From Colony to Province* (Boston: Beacon Press, 1981). 130–46.

33. Trinterud, 20; Miller, 217–25.

34. Hodge, 34.

35. Dunaway, 28–33; McKinney, 42–43.

36. Trinterud, 31.

37. Ibid.

38. Loetscher, 61–62.

39. Trinterud, 34–35.

40. Ibid., 35.

41. Trinterud, 39–41. See also Charles Hartshorn Maxon, *The Great Awakening in the Middle Colonies* (Gloucester, Massachusetts: Peter Smith, 1958), 22–24.

42. William Ames, *The Marrow of Theology,* trans. and ed. John Eusden (Boston: Pilgrim Press, 1968), 77; and Jonathan Edwards, *Treatise on Religious Affections* in *The Works of Jonathan Edwards,* Volume I (Edinburgh: Banner of Truth Trust, 1974), 243.

James R. Payton, Jr.

9 The Background and Significance of the Adopting Act of 1729

O N SEPTEMBER 19, 1729, the fledgling Presbyterian church in the American colonies[1] staved off impending division: the Synod of Philadelphia, which had experienced a growing rift over the question of subscription to the *Westminster Confession and Catechisms*, found a *via media* in the agreement which has come to be known as the Adopting Act. Given the considerable pressures of the moment, together with the limited awareness then possible of matters of "symbolics,"[2] it is hardly surprising that the profound significance of that event went unrecognized. On the occasion of the semicentennial of the denomination that counts itself the legitimate heir of those pioneering Presbyterian fathers, it ought to be worthwhile to call attention to some aspects of that significance.[3]

The Background of the Adopting Act

The importance of a creed, not as the blasé muttering of dogmatic summaries but as the utterance of living faith, is urged already in the New Testament: the affirmation, "Jesus is Lord," in which the living faith of the heart expresses itself before men (Rom 10:9–10; cf. Matt 10:32), was a creed that marked out the members of the apostolic church for eternal life — and, from time to time, for temporal death. Other creedal formulations are to be found in the New Testament writings.[4] In the later epistolary literature we find some more explicit in detail as to what is involved in a faithful confession of Christ.

A clear example of such expansion is to be found in 1 John 4. Whatever may ultimately be made of the possible tension between the orthopraxy required in the context of 1 John 4:1–3 and the orthodoxy required in verse 2, that verse unquestionably demands a confession of faith including more than simply the assertion of Jesus' dominical dignity. Conceivably, the verbal acknowledgement of Jesus as Lord might have fallen from the lips of one of the errorists in some fashion which still allowed him reservations about Jesus' incarnation. The apostle required the further elaboration that He "has come in the flesh." For the apostle, this affirmation was doubtlessly assumed in the earlier creedal declaration (cf. the argument of 1 John 1). Subsequent historical struggle, however, necessitated an explicit amplification of the earlier creed to respond to and guard against the erroneous conceptions that had arisen to threaten the integrity of the faith. The apostolic church was called upon to recognize that necessity and to state more explicitly what the faith involved.

For our investigations, two important points arise here. First, the creed grew in history by way of further elaboration and explicit affirmation of the "faith once for all delivered unto the saints" (Jude 3); this pattern continued in the post-apostolic history of the church. Secondly, the required confession was expected of all the members of the church, not just of her ministers; this also continued to be the pattern of the post-apostolic church.

The writings of the church fathers indicate that a substantial part of the catechetical training of converts included the communication of and instruction in the ancient creed of the church. The creed would then be either personally recited or at least personally affirmed at the time of one's baptism.[5] This leaves no doubt that the ancient church saw reception into the church as intimately tied up with the personal confession of the creed with which she confessed her faith collectively. In addition, the creed continued to enlarge, becoming increasingly explicit in the face of further heterodox challenges, until it attained, throughout the whole church, a close approximation to the Apostles' Creed as we know it today.[6]

At the Council of Nicea, with Constantine's power as emperor lending political clout to ecclesiastical authority, the Nicene Creed was promulgated as the standard of orthodoxy, as over against Arianism. Again, the church's creed expanded to state, against false teaching, what is necessary to believe unto salvation. Intimately related to this purpose, the closing phrases of the original creed propounded an anathema on anyone who confessed any of several distinctively Arian tenets, without distinction being made between the holders of ecclesiastical office and laymen.[7]

The full weight of the imperial decree enforcing the creed turned itself against the Arian bishops who obstinately held to their position.[8] Indeed, the emperor's subsequent letter to the church in Alexandria, published also more widely as a general epistle, called all Constantine's subjects to the Nicene faith. Little room was left for doubt that failure to embrace it would involve unpleasant consequences.[9]

The subsequent modifications of the church's creedal stance at the Councils of Constantinople, Ephesus, and Chalcedon all moved in the same direction.[10] The culmination of this course of development in Christian antiquity can be seen in the Athanasian Creed. There one finds the crystallization of the orthodox faith over against the variety of Trinitarian and Christological errors with which the ancient church had so valiantly struggled. Clearly, much more was consciously, explicitly involved in confessing the Christian faith than the brief statement, "Jesus is Lord." The Athanasian Creed began by declaring, "Whosoever will be saved, before all things it is necessary that he hold the catholic faith; which faith except every one do keep whole and undefiled, without doubt he shall perish everlastingly" (clauses 1,2), whereupon follow forty-one clarifying clauses on Trinitarian and Christological dogma. The mind of the ancient church expressed itself on the importance of this explicit confession in the closing clause, "This is the catholic faith, which except a man believe faithfully, he cannot be saved" (clause 44). The beginning and the end of this ancient ecumenical symbol make it abundantly clear that, for all its theological rigor, this creed was intended, not just for ministers, but for the generality of the members of the church.

However disquieting the salvific restrictions may appear, and however much this creed may seem to tend in the direction of a bare intellectual assent to dogmatic definitions,[11] its approach was rooted in the constant practice of the ancient church and could claim apostolic precedent. This approach, furthermore, was not simply one option among others; it was the only symbolical tradition of the ancient ecumenical church.

During the medieval period neither the creeds nor their use experienced any significant change[12] or development.[13] With the coming of the Reformation, however, a flurry of confessional writing took place. The Protestant confessions regularly argued their continuity with the ancient creeds,[14] claiming to introduce no novelties but only further explication of the common Christian faith shared by God's people in all times and places.[15] The early simplicity of the *Augsburg Confession* of 1530 found further but still comparatively straightforward statement in subsequent confessions. Nevertheless, the "faith once for all delivered unto the saints" increasingly received, as the Reformation era wore on, detailed elucidation (although within the sixteenth century, the various Protestant confessions remained relatively simple and popularly written).

A further indication of Protestant continuity in the symbolical tradition of the ecumenical church was the universal understanding that these Protestant symbols were the confessions of the church as a whole and not just of her ministers. In Geneva, for example, Calvin produced in late 1536 a confession which was to serve as the confession of the church in that city.[16] Those unwilling to embrace the faith as thus confessed would

thereby forfeit membership in the church (and faced the political consequences attendant upon that, given the understanding of the time).[17]

Another example was the 1560 ratification of the *First Scots Confession*
by the Scottish Parliament as the confession for the whole nation. The
readiness of the Scottish people to subscribe to renewals of the covenant
as a national body, with the personal subscription to the confession entailed in the act, showed their acceptance of this position.[18] The attitude
of the church throughout her history on this point was the orientation of
the Protestants of the sixteenth century; namely, the church's confessions
were seriously embraced as the confessions of all her members.

A particularly striking instance of the seriousness with which the Protestants took their confessions occurred at the Diet of Augsburg in 1530.
With all the pressures there for a united Protestant front as over against
the emperor-supported Roman Church, the representatives of the cities
of Strasbourg, Constance, Memmingen, and Lindau were refused permission to subscribe to the *Augsburg Confession*. Although in agreement with
everything else in the confession, these representatives demurred at a
particular point in Article 10, which asserted the distinctively Lutheran
perspective on the recipients of the Lord's Supper. Their request to subscribe with a proviso was denied: subscription had to be to the confession
in toto or not at all.[19] The rigor with which this defense of an unqualified
confessional subscription was maintained in the midst of exceptionally
dangerous circumstances speaks volumes regarding the attitude of the early
Protestants toward a confession.[20]

The process of confessional amplification continued into the 1600s
under the twin impulses of struggle with a resurgent Roman Catholicism
and further intra-Protestant divergences. As a result the confessions became increasingly precise. The *Canons of Dordt* of 1619 were considerably
more specific on certain points than either the *Belgic Confession* of 1561
or the *Heidelberg Catechism* of 1563. The clinical precision of the *Westminster Confession and Catechisms*, with their abundance of subordinate
clauses and qualifications, interlaced with the subtleties of grammatical
expression of the time, presented the most detailed, theologically exacting
confession produced in the period. The pointed exactitudes of the *Helvetic
Consensus Formula* of 1675 carried the process to an extreme. Its scholastic
rigor soon lost its appeal to the church upon which it had been foisted and
the document was rejected.[21] By the end of the seventeenth century, the
bright daylight of symbolical composition in the Reformation era had
given way to a night of silence, with no confessional dawn until well into
the twentieth century.[22]

With the increasing detail of the late-Reformation confessions, a slight
modification developed in the conception of the relationship between the
church and her confession. This can be seen most readily in the structures
adopted by the Synod of Dordt. There unqualified subscription to the

Canons of Dordt, as well as to the *Belgic Confession* and the *Heidelberg Catechism*, was required of the ministers of the Dutch Reformed church.[23] For the members of the church in general, the profession of faith by which they were to be received into the Reformed church was to be a "profession of the reformed religion."[24] Clearly, this allowed for a certain disjunction between the familiarity with and comprehension of the church's confessions on the part of the ministers, on the one hand, and of the members, on the other. Just as clearly, however, the joining member had to have received instruction in[25] and himself profess acceptance of what was confessed by that church of which he then became a part. The difference thus permitted was one only of degree. The modification thereby introduced in order to accommodate the situation of a more detailed confession did not depart from the pattern sanctioned by the practice of the church universal.

The *Westminster Confession of Faith and Catechisms*, however, presented a potentially more difficult situation. Originally summoned to revise the *Thirty-Nine Articles* of the Church of England, the Westminster Assembly soon determined upon the more ambitious task of drafting an entirely new document. Much longer and more detailed than the *Thirty-Nine Articles* (and, indeed, than any other Protestant confession to that time), the *Westminster Confession and Catechisms* produced by the assembly spoke with such precision upon a host of theological topics that an unqualified subscription, such as had hitherto been the pattern in the church's history, would have been difficult to expect of every minister, to say nothing of a simple member of a church. Indeed, some of the framers of the Westminster documents opposed any such imposition of subscription. Whether that expressed the mind of the whole assembly can remain a doubtful point.[26] Political developments in England made it a moot one.[27]

Consequently, the early immigrants to the American colonies who were of Puritan outlook had not been forced to give an answer to the question of confessional subscription. Contact with their confreres in the British Isles, however, kept them abreast of developments there and the question soon received a considerable amount of attention. In the decade of the 1690s, the Presbyterian churches in Scotland, England, and Ireland had each adopted the *Westminster Confession* and come to require subscription to it. Though in differing manners, reflecting the divergent circumstances in which each church found itself, controversy over subscription ensued. Intended in each case as a bulwark against the inroads of heterodox opinion, subscription either failed of its intention or else provoked much opposition to the imposition of standards of merely human provenance. These churches in the British Isles were still embroiled in their controversies when in 1721 an overture moving in the general direction of requiring subscription to the Westminster standards came on the floor of the Synod of Philadelphia.[28]

In the opening sermon of synod the following year, Jonathan Dickinson declaimed against the idea of yielding to man-made sanctions as a reversion to the Romanism and Anglicanism against which their forebears had urged the sufficiency of the Bible as the church's rule for faith and life.[29] The issue had been firmly joined, and in ensuing years the tensions which had begun to surface between the more recently arrived Scots and Scotch-Irish immigrants and the longer established settlers of English Puritan stock increased. Generally, the Scots and Scotch-Irish favored, the New Englanders opposed, subscription.[30] Suspicions as to motives abounded, and specters of the transoceanic disputes haunted the still frail structure of American Presbyterianism.

In 1727 John Thomson introduced an overture explicitly calling for subscription to the *Westminster Confession and Catechisms* by all ministers and candidates for the ministry, urging that by this means the pernicious errors of the times could be prevented in the American Presbyterian church.[31] Dickinson again led the response, arguing that, since every Christian must defend the gospel, therefore any such subscription must be demanded of every member of the church. To his way of thinking, this would result, given the circumstances, in much confusion and considerable division in the entire body. Questioning the basic postulate that subscription was the chief means of preserving the theological purity of the church, he urged that the attitude which thus pursued subscription actually gave the honor due only to the Scriptures to a man-made document.[32]

Eventually, a compromise was reached, in the terms of what has come to be known as the Adopting Act. By virtue of its provisions, American Presbyterianism accepted a form of confessional subscription. Given the previous practice of the church in these matters, however, its provisions involved a new departure in the symbolical tradition. For the general membership of the American Presbyterian church, no commitment to the Westminster standards was demanded; rather, its membership should be as open as Christian charity could allow the gates of heaven might well be. For ministers and prospective ordinands, a qualified subscription was to be rendered, allowing for individual provisos.

The text of the Adopting Act is as follows:

Although the Synod do not claim or pretend to any authority of imposing our faith upon other men's consciences, but do profess our just dissatisfaction with, and abhorrence of such impositions, and do utterly disclaim all legislative power and authority in the Church, being willing to receive one another as Christ has received us to the glory of God, and admit to fellowship in sacred ordinances, all such as we have grounds to believe Christ will at last admit to the kingdom of heaven, yet we are undoubtedly obliged to take care that the faith once delivered to the saints be kept pure and uncorrupt among us, and so handed down to our posterity; and do therefore agree that all the ministers of this Synod, or that shall hereafter be admitted into this Synod, shall declare their agreement in, and app: bation of, the Confession of Faith, with the Larger and Shorter Catechisms of the Assembly of Divines at Westminster, as being in all the essential and necessary articles, good forms of sound words and systems of Christian doctrine, and do also adopt the said Confession and Catechisms as the confession of our faith. And we do also agree, that all the Presbyteries within our bounds shall always take care not to admit any candidate of the ministry into the exercise of the sacred function but what declares his agreement in opinion with all the essential and necessary articles of said Confession, either by subscribing the said Confession of Faith and Catechisms, or by a verbal declaration of their assent thereto, as such minister or candidate shall think best. And in case any minister of this Synod, or any candidate for the ministry, shall have any scruple with respect to any article or articles of said Confession or Catechisms, he shall at the time of his making said declaration declare his sentiments to the Presbytery or Synod, who shall, notwithstanding, admit him to the exercise of the ministry within our bounds, and to ministerial communion, if the Synod or Presbytery shall judge his scruple or mistake to be only about articles not essential and necessary in doctrine, worship, or government. But if the Synod or Presbytery shall judge such ministers or candidates erroneous in essential and necessary articles of faith, the Synod or Presbytery shall declare them uncapable of communion with them. And the Synod do solemnly agree, that none of us will traduce or use any oppobrious terms of those that differ from us in these extra-essential and not necessary points of doctrine, but treat them with the same friendship, kindness, and brotherly love, as if they had not differed from us in such sentiments.[33]

This agreement, achieved in the morning of September 19, 1729, led to the presentation that afternoon of the various scruples entertained by the several ministers, all of which were found to be acceptable within the boundaries framed in the earlier decision. With the explicit exception of certain statements regarding the relationship of the civil magistrate to the church in Chapters 20 and 23, the Synod of Philadelphia adopted the *Westminster Confession and Catechisms* as the confession of faith for the American Presbyterian church, according to the terms of the morning's decision.[34]

In 1736 the strict subscriptionists, when their numbers were in the ascendancy, made an abortive attempt to impose a "jot and tittle" subscription upon the church by declaring that this had been the synod's intent in 1729. Their subterfuge of ignoring the Adopting Act of the morning and fixing solely upon the statement which it had made possible in the afternoon convinced the Presbyterian church as a whole of nothing, except that strict subscriptionism was no adequate insurance against sub-Christian aberrations.[35]

In due course, the church returned to the stance taken in the morning of September 19, 1729.[36] The Adopting Act became, in confessional matters, the constitutional cornerstone of American Presbyterianism and, thus, a powerful determinant of the resultant structure of American Presbyterianism's history. Furthermore, as an ecclesiastical determination for a different symbolical path than had hitherto been traversed by the church universal, it raised many questions about American Presbyterianism and about the whole theologico-symbolical enterprise, questions which still await adequate answer.

The Significance of the Adopting Act

The significance of the Adopting Act for the subsequent course of American Presbyterian constitutional history and for the theologico-symbolical enterprise has been momentous. In suggesting the contours of that significance in what follows, no attempt is made to be exhaustive and no claim is advanced that the Adopting Act produced the effects in a simplistic monocausal fashion. In a manner too often unrecognized, however, the Adopting Act played an important role in each of the various developments to which attention will be drawn.

The stance toward the Westminster standards embodied in the Adopting Act was enshrined as constitutional law for the Presbyterian church by the 1788 synod. The second of the vows adopted, required of all ministerial ordinands, called for an affirmative answer to the question, "Do you sincerely receive and adopt the Confession of Faith of this Church, as containing the system of doctrine taught in the Holy Scriptures?" With the exception of the United Presbyterian Church in the United States of America after 1967, that question has continued to the present day in the American Presbyterian scene.

Although no direct quotation of the 1729 agreement appears in the 1788 question, the continuity of attitude is unmistakable. No thoroughgoing subscription is required, for it is the confession *as containing the system of doctrine* that one must "sincerely receive and adopt," not the confession in its detail. While a strict subscriptionist might assert that the system of doctrine included everything to be found in the confession, nothing in the vow necessitated such a perspective. Rather, the 1788 question in continuity with the 1729 agreement left room for an individual to demur from any number of statements, or even whole articles, in the confession which, to his mind, were inessential to the system of doctrine presented by Scripture. Neither in 1729 nor in 1788 were any limits explicitly delineated as to the *sine qua non* of an acceptable subscription to the Westminster standards. In a strict constitutional sense, each prospective ordinand, after 1788, had the freedom to determine for himself what those limits might be.[37] Each presbytery, with which the power of ministerial ordination is vested, had the duty to examine its ordinands regarding the nature and limits of their acceptance of the confession. It also had the right to determine for itself whether the relationship to the confession thus elicited impinged upon fidelity to the "essential and necessary articles," the "system of doctrine" therein presented.

This constitutional stance invited the eventual emergence among the various presbyteries of significant differences. Given the subsequent intra-denominational tensions, there developed increasing latitude in understanding the perimeters and contents of that "system of doctrine."[38] In this historical situation and because of the constitutional limitations, the Westminster standards' influence within the denomination eventually had to decrease from being (even in a limited sense) binding to the level of offering general theological guidance, at best.

From this vantage-point, the United Presbyterian Church in the United States of America's 1967 modification of the ordinand's vow to be a pledge to "perform the duties of a minister of the gospel in obedience to Jesus Christ, under the authority of the Scriptures, and *under the continuing instruction and guidance of the confessions* of this Church" (emphasis added) appears a legitimate historical development of, and not a departure from, the genius of the American Presbyterian constitutional position. Furthermore, that early constitutional history exacts the conclusion that the action of the general assembly of 1910 (repeated in 1916 and 1923) in delineating five "essential and necessary articles" was an unwarranted and illegitimate imposition. Regardless of the theological stance one takes on the controverted matters, these actions invited, from a scrupulously constitutional perspective, the negative responses of the 1924 Auburn Affirmation and the special commission report of 1925, unanimously adopted by the general assembly of 1927.[39] Finally, if one wishes to specify a point at which doctrinal latitudinarianism was fathered upon the American Presbyterian church, as has often been attempted within the Orthodox Presbyterian Church, then it would seem that the 1801 Plan of Union with the Congregationalists so often decried[40] has a less credible claim of paternity than the Adopting Act of 1729.

The theologico-symbolical significance of the Adopting Act can be best recognized by pointing to the implications of the various departures from the symbolical tradition of the universal church involved in the 1729 agreement. The above historical treatment indicates that the Adopting Act involved three such departures.

First, the provision for a qualified subscription to an ecclesiastical creed flew in the face of the perspective embraced by the church from Christian antiquity through the Reformation period. The degree to which subscription to a confession had hitherto been able to insure a modicum of doctrinal unity, a focal reason for subscription in the first place, was thereby considerably diminished. The greater freedom thus afforded to the individual minister was purchased at the expense of ecclesiastical unanimity. To be sure, this same transaction has taken place in denominations which have never officially endorsed anything resembling the Adopting Act. Nevertheless, American Presbyterianism officially anticipated subsequent theological history by providing, however unintentionally, for such a development. In this regard, the Adopting Act authorized an individualism that symbolics has not yet been and may never be able to assimilate.

A second departure involved the distinction between the knowledge of and personal commitment to the confession on the part of ordained ministers, on the one hand, and the rest of the church's membership, on the other. Does American Presbyterianism, consequently, present the face of a genuinely confessional church? It would seem that an affirmative answer to this not insignificant question must result in being impaled on one or the other of the horns of a dilemma. The one horn would necessitate a restriction of the church to her clergy, a position reminiscent of the posture of pre-Vatican II Roman Catholicism. The other horn would require a relationship on the part of the general membership to the confession — in which they need not *necessarily* be instructed prior or even subsequent to their reception into the full membership of the church— in which they embrace by an implicit faith what the church confesses. (The irony of this would be, of course, that the church's confession condemns the conception of implicit faith in Chapter 20, Paragraph 2.)

Furthermore, with the above distinction, the church's confession stands at some significant remove from the actual needs of the simple believer. However stringently he might be admonished to learn and identify with that confession, the inference that saving faith can exist for him quite apart from the conscious, intelligent embrace of the confession of the church in which he is a member would seem ineluctable. A cursory acquaintance with the religious world of the twentieth century indicates that this situation is hardly the exclusive property of American Presbyterianism. The Adopting Act, however, made the situation an authorized possibility. Consequently, it raised the question, not only for American Presbyterianism, but for all churches, what does it mean to be a confessional church in the modern world? The complexities of the question have only increased since 1729, and symbolics has yet to develop a sufficient answer.

The third departure from the symbolical tradition of the universal church was that, with the Adopting Act, a church for the first time gave official, if only implicit, acquiescence to the judgment that its confession actually stated more than was necessary for the confession of Christian faith. The positing of "essential and necessary articles" within but not necessarily coextensive with the confession invited this deduction. The ecclesiastical humility manifest in this stance casts no aspersions on the boldness with which the church had confessionally spoken in preceding generations, for previous confessions had not been nearly as detailed and exacting as the *Westminster Confession and Catechisms.*

Furthermore, the ecclesiastical charity thereby accorded to many Christians unable to endorse the Westminster standards doubtlessly reflected the realities of post-Restoration Presbyterian disappointments in England

and the encounter with other Christians who were outside the Presbyterian fold in the new world. At the same time, that ecclesiastical caution indicated a certain hesitation regarding the way of the Spirit of Truth with the church in history (cf. John 16:13). The facile conception that the development of doctrine has been constantly progressing in the direction of increasing precision and detail — a staple of many popular treatments of the history of doctrine — runs aground on the reef of the Adopting Act. There a church, for the first time in history, implied a collective doubt that the way of the Spirit could be so easily identified and that the confessions were so self-evidently the mileposts of that way.

Although unwittingly, nevertheless surely, the pioneering fathers of American Presbyterianism thus anticipated the questions regarding the nature of Christian truth, the degree to which it can be encapsulated in verbal statements, and the actual nature of the history of doctrine which are so much today at the heart, not only of symbolics, but of the whole theological enterprise. These questions have yet to receive conclusive answers which could amount to a new and unifying symbol in the twentieth century. The founders and subsequent leaders of the Orthodox Presbyterian Church, together with the generality of her membership, have struggled with these questions, questions bequeathed to them by the founding fathers of American Presbyterianism in the Adopting Act of September 19, 1729.

NOTES

1. The first presbytery on American soil, the Presbytery of Philadelphia, was erected in 1705 or 1706. (The first page of its minutes is no longer extant, so there is some dispute as to which year is the more likely. The preponderance of scholarly opinion seems to favour 1706.) While many of the immigrants of preceding generations held Presbyterian inclinations, the Puritan movement in England had not differentiated itself into its Presbyterian and Independent-Congregationalist strains prior to the founding of the New England colonies. In the course of time, as the differences which subsequently surfaced in England began to manifest themselves in America as well, the Puritans of Connecticut showed a more Presbyterian strain, and the churches there together with the New Jersey and Long Island congregations spawned by them began moving toward a self-consciously Presbyterian structure. Scotch-Irish and Scottish immigrants reinforced this direction, so that by the end of the seventeenth century, several Presbyterian congregations had been founded. By 1716 the first presbytery had so grown that it was subdivided into three presbyteries, united in the Synod of Philadelphia. For a detailed treatment, see Leonard J. Trinterud, *The Forming of an American Tradition: A Re-examination of Colonial Presbyterianism* (Philadelphia: Westminster, 1970 reprint ed.), 15–37.

2. "Symbolics" is the designation for the field of theological study concerned with the creeds and confessions of the Christian church. While the creeds had, of course, long been used in both church and theology, symbolics — as a discipline examining the history, development, and relationship of the creeds and reflecting on the significance of affirming them — did not develop into a distinct branch of theological endeavor until the early decades of the nineteenth century (cf. C. A. Briggs, *Theological Symbolics* [New York: Scribner, 1914], 3–33).

3. A full exploration of that significance is far beyond the scope of a brief essay: if the thrust of this essay is correct, such an exploration would require a full-length monograph.

4. Among these are Rom 1:3–4; 1 Cor 8:6; 15:3–5; Phil 2:5–11; 1 Tim 3:16; 1 John 2:22; 4:2,15; 5:1,5. Scholars from across the whole theological spectrum agree in finding several early creeds in the New Testament, with these passages being the most frequently mentioned. Suggested literature for exploration of this area would include Oscar Cullmann, *The Earliest Christian Confessions* (London: Lutterworth, 1949); Ralph P. Martin, *An Early Christian Confession* (London: Tyndale, 1960); Vernon H. Neufeld, *The Earliest Christian Confessions* (Leiden: E. J. Brill, 1963); and (expanding the treatment into the post-apostolic church) J. N. D. Kelly, *Early Christian Creeds* (London: Longman, 1950).

5. Irenaeus and Tertullian mention *regulae fidei* shared by the church and taught to those who joined her. During the ante-Nicene period, the creed was kept as a secret by and for the church, so its communication to catechumens came rather late in their preparations for confession of faith (cf. Philip Schaff, *Creeds of Christendom* 1:18. From the expansive *Catechetical Lectures* of Cyril of Jerusalem in the mid-fourth century, it is manifest that that detailed instruction in the creed culminated in personal affirmation of it at baptism.

For the variations in practice regarding the precise format for the profession of the creed, see the brief treatment by Williston Walker in *A History of the Christian Church*, 3d ed. (New York: Charles Scribner's Sons, 1970), 58–59.

6. Schaff, *Creeds* 1:16–20 (for a wide presentation of the sources, cf. 2:11–57).

7. What is known today as the Nicene Creed is, in fact, the creed as modified at the Council of Constantinople in 381. (Hence, it is more accurately called the "Nicaeno-Constantinopolitan Creed.") The creed propounded in 325 contained the following declaration, not retained in the later version, "But the holy catholic and apostolic Church of God anathematizes those who affirm that there was a time when the Son was not, or that he was not before he was begotten, or that he was made of things not existing: or who say, that the Son of God was of any other substance or essence, or created, or liable to change or conversion."

8. In addition to Arius, only two Arian bishops persisted in their views, Secundus of Ptolemais and Theonis of Marmorica. Constantine banished these men, now excommunicated, into exile. Not long after the close of the council, he also banished Eusebius of Nicomedia and Theognis of Nicea for continuing to have contact with some Arians from Alexandria (cf. Walker, 108–9).

9. "Let us receive, therefore, that doctrine which was delivered by the Almighty. . . . What was approved by three hundred bishops can only be considered as the pleasure of God. . . . Wherefore, let no one hesitate; let no one delay; but let all return with alacrity to the path of truth. . . . With all convenient speed, I shall visit you. . . . " (The full letter is reproduced in *Eusebius' Ecclesiastical History* [Grand Rapids: Baker, 1955], Appendix by Isaac Boyle, 50–51.)

In the following year, Constantine followed up on his initiatives against the Arians in general by excluding them from the enjoyment of the various privileges he had bestowed on the church (Philip Schaff, *History of the Christian Church* 3:140–41).

(None of the presentation on this point is intended to describe the actual success of this policy, for, as is well known, some fifty-five years of further theological wrangling ensued on related questions. The intent of this section has been to set forth the attitude toward the creed as manifest in the stance of the church and the emperor.)

10. From the outstanding resource provided by Henry R. Percival, *The Seven Ecumenical Councils of the Undivided Church* (Nicene and Post-Nicene Fathers, 2d series, Vol. 14: Grand Rapids: Eerdmans, 1974 reprint ed.), cf. the following: (1) for the Council of Constantinople (381): 164–65, 170, 172, 188–89; (2) for the Council of Ephesus (431): 194–95, 201–2, 218, 240; (3) for the Council of Chalcedon (451): 260, 262–65.

11. The creed's rigor would seem to raise serious doubt about the possibility of salvation for all those unable to penetrate the theological complexities. Schaff's suggestion, that what

is required is not such comprehension but rather a faith with the church which does thus understand, and that only those who reject the truth thus confessed are excluded by the creed (*Creeds* 1:39–40), offers an attractive (and common) interpretation of the creed, but one which moves in the direction of affirming the doctrine of "implicit faith." (In that regard it would appear that the use and practical understanding of this creed during the medieval period leading up to the Tridentine affirmation of implicit faith would offer fruitful ground for research.)

12. This is not to slight the importance of the insertion of *filioque* into the Nicene Creed during the early medieval period, an insertion which contributed to the eventual rupture between Eastern and Western Christianity that occurred in 1054 and has yet to be healed. That insertion, however, was due not to further theological dispute and deeper insight, as previous developments in the creeds had been, but to a variety of factors traceable to the limitations of education and communication between East and West in the 600 years after the Council of Chalcedon. (For a fuller treatment of the history and theology of the insertion, see my unpublished 1975 Timothy D. Knudsen Memorial Prize Essay at Westminster Theological Seminary entitled, "On the Person and Work of the Holy Spirit: The Question of the *Filioque*," and the bibliography given there.)

13. It has often been suggested that the lack of theological development during the medieval period was due to the limited familiarity with Scripture evident in the time. Without diminishing the importance of that factor, I would also point to the importance for symbolical development of an historical consciousness — a controlling awareness not only of the unique work of God in Christ in past history but also of the flux of subsequent history. The periods of symbolical dormancy have been marked by the absence of one or the other or both of these aspects of such an historical awareness; the medieval era was one of these periods.

14. Cf. the *Augsburg Confession* (1530), Art. 1; the *Gallican Confession* (1559), Art. 6; the *Belgic Confession* (1561), Art. 9; the *Thirty-Nine Articles* (1563), Art. 8. The *Second Helvetic Confession* (1566) makes the same point by the unusual device of starting with an approving quotation of an imperial edict of 380 A.D. from the Justinian Code against the ancient heresies condemned in creeds.

15. This reflected the conviction of most of the reformers that God had promised such an historical continuity and that, consequently, the legitimacy of their movement depended also on being in that continuity; for an extended treatment of this and related questions with two of the leading reformers, see my " 'Sola Scriptura' and Church History: The Views of Bucer and Melanchthon on Religious Authority in 1539" (Ph.D. diss., The University of Waterloo, 1982).

16. The full title of the confession was *Confession of Faith which all the citizens and inhabitants of Geneva and the subjects of the country must promise to keep and hold.* (The confession is printed in J. K. S. Reid, ed., *Calvin: Theological Treatises* [Philadelphia: Westminster, 1954], 26–33.)

17. Geneva's city council voted on March 13, 1537, to adopt the 1536 confession. Opposition from some citizens and periodic dissent within the council inhibited its enforcement (cf. Arthur C. Cochrane, *Reformed Confessions of the 16th Century* [Philadelphia: Westminster, 1966], 117–19; T. H. L. Parker, *John Calvin: A Biography* [Philadelphia: Westminster, 1975], 57,63–65).

18. David H. Fleming, *The Reformation in Scotland: Causes, Characteristics, Consequences* (London: Hodder and Stoughton, 1910), 244; Schaff, *Creeds* 1:680–89.

19. Cf. the treatment by Hastings Eells in his biography of one of the leading figures of the time, *Martin Bucer* (New Haven: Yale University, 1931), 99–108; in less detail, Schaff, *History* 7:718–21.

20. The matter was subsequently settled through the indefatigable labors of Martin Bucer of Strasbourg which eventuated in the *Wittenburg Concord* of 1536. That lengthy statement

offered an explanation of Article 10 acceptable to *and subscribed to* by both sides and providing, consequently, for a unified and unqualified subscription to the *Augsburg Confession*.

21. Briggs, 214; Schaff, *Creeds* 1:478,485–86; John H. Leith, ed., *Creeds of the Churches* (Garden City: Doubleday and Company, 1963), 308–9 (which is followed by the text of the formula, 309–323).

22. Throughout the period thus encompassed, the various theological parties across the whole ecclesiastical spectrum were marked by the absence of one or the other or both of the aspects of historical awareness urged above (cf. n. 13) as essential for symbolical development.

23. The apposite section of the lengthy form of subscription (*ondertekeningsformulier*) states: "We the undersigned ministers of the Word of God . . . , declare sincerely and in good conscience before the Lord by this our subscription that we are persuaded and heartily believe that all the articles and points of doctrine in this Confession and Catechism of the Reformed Dutch churches, together with the explanation about some points of the previously mentioned doctrine in the national synod held at Dordrecht in the year 1619, are in full agreement with God's Word" (translation J. R. P.; cited from F. L. Bos, *De Orde der Kerk, toegelicht met Kerkelijke besluiten uit vier eeuwen* ['s Gravenhage: Guido de Brés, 1950], 197).

24. Article 61 of the Church Order of Dordt required this *"belijdenis der gereformeerde religie"* (cited from Bos, 222). What this requirement stipulated is more precisely stated in the current Church Order of the Christian Reformed Church in North America, which requires "a public profession of Christ *according to the Reformed creeds*" (Art. 59a [emphasis added]).

25. The decisions of the Synod of Dordt relating to profession of faith required a prior process of instruction which would eventuate in a "profession of the reformed religion." Cf. the citations in Bos, 224–25.

26. Trinterud's assertion that the Westminster divines opposed any subscription (p. 50) is not warranted by the reference he cites (p. 324, n. 37). The most that can be concluded from the statement by Anthony Tuckney there adduced is that Tuckney himself opposed such subscription and that, at a vote whether subscription should be required, others voted negatively, as he did. It would appear, furthermore, that Tuckney's statement implies a preceding discussion on the merits of subscription, the resolution of which required a vote being taken. Nothing in the reference cited by Trinterud indicates that the negative votes carried the decision. A thorough study of discussions on subscription at the Westminster Assembly, and the respective views of its leading members, is a desideratum in scholarship on the Westminster standards and their symbolical significance.

27. Although parliament granted eventual approval to the *Westminster Confession and Cathechisms* in 1648, Oliver Cromwell and his army, by the end of the year in total control of England, opposed any rigorous Presbyterianism. As a result, general subscription to the Westminster standards, even if it had been proposed, would never have been enforced (cf. Walker, 413–15).

28. Trinterud, 38–43.

29. Ibid., 43–44.

30. Lefferts A. Loetscher, *The Broadening Church: A Study of Theological Issues in the Presbyterian Church since 1869* (Philadelphia: University of Pennsylvania, 1954), 1–2; Trinterud, 15,47–48.

31. Trinterud, 45–46.

32. H. Shelton Smith, Robert T. Handy, and Lefferts A. Loetscher, *American Christianity: An Historical Interpretation with Representative Documents* (New York: Scribner, 1960), 1:263–65 (the abbreviated document of Dickinson appears on 1:263–68).

33. William M. Engles, comp., *Records of the Presbyterian Church in the United States of America 1706–1788* (Philadelphia: Presbyterian Board of Publication, 1841), 94.

34. Ibid., 94–95.

35. Trinterud, 65–67. The skewed orientation of the 1736 action was nonetheless embraced by the "Old School" Presbyterians in subsequent generations and became the standard

view of the (predominantly Old School) Southern Presbyterian Church (Presbyterian Church in the United States). This pro-1736 attitude is still urged by Morton H. Smith (now Stated Clerk of the Presbyterian Church in America) in his *How is the Gold Become Dim: The Decline of the Presbyterian Church, U.S., as Reflected in its Assembly Actions,* 2d ed. (Jackson, Mississippi: Steering Committee for the Continuing Presbyterian Church, 1973), in which he, consequently, draws the untenable conclusion that the Adopting Act thus involved "an absolute and unreserved adoption" of the Westminster standards (pp. 38–39).

36. The "Old Side/New Side" breach, occasioned in part by the 1736 action and the attitude manifest in it, was healed in 1758. The agreement for reunion included a return to the qualified subscription provided in the original Adopting Act. (For a full treatment of this reunion, cf. Trinterud, 144–65.)

37. In 1728 Jonathan Dickinson had stated, "I take a Subscription to imply a solemn Declaration to the World, that we believe the Articles subscribed to be the Mind and Will of God, free of all Error and Mistake. A Subscription in any laxer sense, is to open a Door to all the Unsincerity in the World. Every one of what-ever Sentiments, may subscribe with his own Reserves; and so the Subscription instead of a Test of Orthodoxy becomes A Door to Hypocrisy" (reproduced at Smith, Handy, Loetscher 1:266). Nevertheless, Dickinson accepted precisely that kind of subscription in the Adopting Act of the following year, which in turn paved the way for the same variety of subscription in 1788.

38. It is surely significant that as learned a scholar of American Presbyterianism as Lefferts A. Loetscher entitled his treatment of American Presbyterian theological history *The Broadening Church* (cf. n. 30 above). He opened that volume with a treatment of the Adopting Act, about which he concluded, "Thus, though the theology of the Church was now formally tied to the Westminster Standards, the door was thrown open for a continually expanding breadth of interpretation" (p. 2).

39. For a fuller treatment of the history of these negative responses, cf. Loetscher, 117–18,130–34.

40. Edwin H. Rian negatively answers the question of the title of his article, "Unbelief in the Presbyterian Church in the U.S.A. — Is it Recent?" [*The Independent Board Bulletin* 2 (April 1936) 4:1–8], pointing to the 1801 Plan of Union as the launching point of doctrinal defection in presbyterian circles (p. 3). In his *Why the Orthodox Presbyterian Church?* (Philadelphia: OPC Committee on Christian Education, [1965]), John P. Galbraith urges the same point (p. 14).

Allen C. Guelzo

10 Jonathan Edwards and the New Divinity:

Change and Continuity in New England Calvinism, 1758–1858

O N JANUARY 18, 1758, Jonathan Edwards paid a last visit to Samuel Hopkins, his prize pupil and now pastor of a strife-ridden congregation in Great Barrington, Massachusetts. Trustees of the College of New Jersey at Princeton had asked Edwards to come and succeed his dead son-in-law, Aaron Burr, as president, and despite severe misgivings Edwards had agreed. He delivered to Hopkins a pile of manuscripts for safekeeping, and the next day departed, promising to return in the spring. Hopkins felt a chill of foreboding, and wrote before the day was over to Joseph Bellamy, another of Edwards's great pupils and now a pastor in Bethlehem, Connecticut. Mr. Edwards "expects not to return till next May," Hopkins explained to Bellamy. He grimly added, "Alas, his mantle has gone with him. . . . " Hopkins's forebodings were well justified. The spring came, but Edwards never returned, dying of a mishandled smallpox inoculation at Princeton in March. The American Elijah (as Gilbert Tennent eulogized him) was no more.[1]

But what of this Elijah's mantle? Later historians of New England theology proved to be only too happy to accept at face value Hopkins's comment that Edwards had taken his mantle away with him, implying that he had not bestowed it, or a double portion of his spirit, on either Hopkins or Bellamy. It has made no difference that Hopkins and Bellamy spent the next forty-odd years constructing an enormous body of Edwardsean interpretation and Calvinist divinity built upon the foundations of their mentor. To the contrary, their "New Divinity," which pervaded New England for the next century, has been dismissed as a ruse by which Edwards's theology was cleverly twisted and perverted. And almost as a punishment for having thus bit the hand that fed them, they have been virtually read out of the history of American thought. To Perry Miller, the legitimate descent of Edwards's philosophy belonged, not to the New Divinity, but to Emerson and the Transcendentalists. To many modern American Calvinists, it is rather vaguely thought that, perhaps because he died at Princeton, the real heirs of Edwards's theology are to be found in the Princeton Presbyterian tradition of Witherspoon, Alexander, and Hodge. As late as 1976, Henry F. May could marvel that Hopkins and Bellamy and all that they stood for had been "long since forgotten."[2] No other school of American, let alone Calvinist, theology has disappeared so utterly from historical attention.

But it must be questioned whether this oblivion is justified. Did Hopkins and Bellamy really sell Edwards and New England Calvinism down the Connecticut River? The answer, along with the real significance of Hopkins and Bellamy in the history of American theology, can only be determined by understanding the intellectual agenda of Jonathan Edwards.

Jonathan Edwards spent almost all of his life on or near the frontier of the British province of Massachusetts. But it would be a mistake of colossal proportions to conclude from this fact that Edwards's mind was likewise provincial. Edwards's thinking, even in his revival treatises, cannot be given any meaningful shape apart from the broader context of eighteenth-century philosophy.

The eighteenth century was not the happiest of times for Calvinist intellectuals to work. The century preceding Edwards's birth (b. 1703) had disposed of the entire apparatus of classical psychology and physics at breathtaking speed. It also came perilously close to disposing of Christian ethics and supernatural revelation. The physical universe, which had once seemed a closed system in which things *moved* by intelligent, purposeful causation (either external or internal) became a place where things *were moved*, without the nature of the *thing* in question playing any active role in its own motion. The universe was no longer an organism but a machine.

If the physical world was nothing more than a mechanism, then it was worth inquiring whether man who inhabited that world was a machine, too. In general, there were three possible answers. One of these, offered most loudly by Thomas Hobbes (and with some tactical conditions by John Locke) cheerfully embraced the notion that man was indeed only material substance, that spiritual substance was a figment of the imagination, and that the idea of a free, self-determining will was a delusion. Man, like his world, was a machine, governed by natural laws and appetites more rigid than Calvin's doctrine of decrees. The other two answers were offered by those who were staggered by the radical social and metaphysical implications of Hobbes. They attempted to find a new defense for the reality of theism and spiritual substance. On one hand, Descartes and Newton offered rival models of the physical universe that continue to allow room for material and spiritual substance to coexist. On the other hand, Fr. Nicholas Malebranche and Bp. George Berkeley rejected any such attempt at compromise and insisted that spiritual substance alone was the only reality. Without doubt, Newton's paradigm achieved the greatest popularity in the English-speaking world, especially since his theory of gravity ("attraction at a distance") seemed a handy analogue to how God could give order to his creation without, like Hobbes, subjecting the wills of his creatures to brute force. On the issue of the will, however, even Berkeley and Malebranche scrambled to find enough grounds for free will so as to avoid even the appearance of Hobbesianism.[3] Even English Calvinism rushed to escape from association with Hobbes's determinism by watering down predestination. Isaac Watts, the celebrated psalm-singer of Congregationalism, wrote a treatise awarding free will to men. One of Watts's biographers has observed that he was far from alone: "of thirty-nine Presbyterian churches surveyed in 1731, eleven were Arminian, twelve were unwilling to declare themselves, and only sixteen were orthodox Calvinists."[4]

It is fairly clear, from the manuscript notebooks which he began assembling in the 1720s, that Edwards and his New England peers had read most of this literature. It is also clear that, despite his admiration for Newton's physics and his respect for Locke's reputation, Edwards's real sympathies lay with the immaterialism of Malebranche and Berkeley, both of whom he had probably read by the time he had assumed the pastorate of his grandfather's church in Northampton, Massachusetts. When he did discuss Newtonianism (as in the essays "Of Atoms" and "Of Being"), he manipulated the new physics to serve his own immaterialist objectives. But if Edwards used Newton and Locke only to further his immaterialist ends, he did not regard the immaterialist philosophy merely as an end in itself. Unlike Malebranche and Berkeley, he felt no urge to placate the *zeitgeist* by protesting that he did not believe in determinism. Rather, Edwards maintained a deep, personal loyalty to his ancestral Calvinism, and early in life it became his "delight to approach God, and adore him as a Sovereign God, and ask sovereign mercy of him." It particularly concerned Edwards that, in their indecent haste to evade Hobbes's materialism, his fellow Calvinists were shedding their belief in God's sovereignty. They were subscribing to "Arminian doctrines" and new notions of free will in the illusory hope that these would make their defense of theism easier. To Edwards, these notions only made theism more, and not less, indefensible. "Some of the ill consequences of the Arminian doctrines," Edwards wrote, "are that it robs God of the greater part of the glory of his grace, and takes away a principal motive to love and praise him." "Free-will-ism" especially could only backfire on those who tried to turn it against Hobbes and Locke.

> The doctrine of a self-determining will, as the ground of all moral good and evil, tends to prevent any proper exercises of faith in God and Christ, in the affair of our salvation, as it tends to prevent all dependence upon them. . . . Thus our holiness is from ourselves, as its determining cause, and its original and highest source.[5]

As far as Edwards was concerned, the only way to stop materialism was a front-line defense on Calvinistic grounds, rather than fleeing to the shallow last ditch of free will.

On the other hand, Edwards was also aware that those who had been made gun-shy by Hobbes of any form of determinism (divine or otherwise) were not going to welcome a restatement of Calvinism, unless Calvinism and the Calvinists' God were made to appear eminently fair and reasonable. It became Edwards's task to show that "it belongs to God, as the Supreme ruler of the universality of things, to maintain order and decorum in his kingdom," and that God's "moral government" and "constitution," although fixed, were not arbitrary and destructive of society, as Hobbes's war-of-all-against-all determinism was. At first, when the Great Awakening came to New England in the early 1740s, Edwards thought that the revival itself would authenticate the value of New England Calvinism and force men to decide "whether any good medium can be found, where a man can rest with any stability, between owning this work and being a Deist." In 1742 he thought "[now] is a good time for Arminians to change their principles." But they did not, and the Awakening was strangled in New England by the hostility of its enemies, as well as the idiocy of some of its friends.[6]

Despite its dismal conclusion, the Awakening accomplished two things for Edwards. No matter what the Arminians thought, the revival had fully vindicated his confidence in Calvinism. Its failure to persuade others only stiffened him to the point of brittleness. In a series of sermons which he published as *The Religious Affections*, Edwards rewrote the entire psychology of New England conversion. Rather than conversion being a gradual work which involved the preparation of the intellect by catechesis and use of the "means of grace" (preaching, Bible-reading, the sacraments), Edwards now argued that intellect and will were really only two aspects of a central psychological entity which he called "the affections." To affect the intellect was to affect the will. From this it was logical to conclude that those who knew about the gospel but failed to appropriate it were obviously only pretending to know. Edwards, therefore, jettisoned preparationism and demanded that applicants for membership in the Northampton church give testimony that they had gone through what amounted to their own private revival. He denied that "God has promised his saving grace to men's sincere endeavours in praying for it, and using proper means to obtain it." He insisted that "Natural men, or those that are not savingly converted, have no degree of that principle from whence all gracious actions flow. . . . " Conversion could only be an abrupt change of the entire man from impurity to purity, "an immediate and instantaneous work like to the change made in Lazarus when Christ called him from the grave. . . . "[7] This absolutism was too demanding for the town of Northampton, and in 1750 Edwards was dismissed from his pulpit.

The other product of the Awakening was a renewal of Edwards's philosophical interests. If the revival could not justify the ways of Calvinism to men, then perhaps close reasoning would. Therefore, he turned the guns of his immaterialism directly on the materialists in order to demonstrate to the Arminians how Arminianism, not Calvinism, betrayed Christianity into the hands of atheism. To this end, he produced during the last four years of his life several short but devastating critiques of eighteenth-century ethics and two major works, which have secured his reputation permanently in American thought.

The first of these two works, *A careful and strict ENQUIRY into The modern prevailing Notions of that FREEDOM OF WILL* (1754), took as its premise that only Calvinistic determinism, not Arminian liberty, could provide a foundation for ethics. Edwards built upon this premise several interlocking ideas. First, the will is not a separate "faculty" within the self, existing apart from the mind. It is only the executor of the mind's desires. Strictly speaking, then, the will does not choose or "will," it only executes what the mind deems worth doing. The "freedom" of the will consists, not in doing "what it wills," but only in having an unobstructed path to do "as it wills." Second, Edwards had to account for what in the mind caused the will to move, if it did not move itself. This he did in two ways: first, the will is determined by whatever "motive" the mind perceives as the strongest; and second, to put more point on his insistence that mind and will are an inseparable whole, Edwards added, "the will always is as the greatest apparent good is."[8] There is thus a direct path from whatever is attractive or pleasing to a person, to his volitions. For Edwards this meant that ethical choice had more to do with one's "temper" than one's ability to exercise a discriminating intellect.

However, a will determined by anything is still a necessary will, and necessity is just what Hobbes had attributed to volition. Edwards, therefore, added as his third idea the concept of *moral necessity*. He did not disagree with the Arminians when they complained that necessity was destructive of ethical responsibility. But he agreed only because he found most Arminians thinking of necessity as an objective, compulsory force against which our wills consciously and vainly struggle. Edwards suggested that there was also a kind of "philosophical necessity" which, although it was as "full and fixed" as this other "relative" necessity, nevertheless differed from it in one crucial respect. "Relative" necessity described a relationship in which resistance could be offered, so that the real force of this kind of necessity lay in the *connection* of the terms involved. The strength of the connection determined whether one thing would succeed in determining another. Edwards defined "philosophical necessity" as a necessity which occurred, not because of the strength of the connection, but because of the nature of the terms involved. "Philosophical necessity" was really "nothing else than the full and fixed connection between the things signified by the subject and predicate of a proposition, which affirms something to be true." The genius of this sort of necessity was that it produced a necessitated result fully as much as the compulsion of "relative" necessity, and yet it did so without struggle and without any freedoms being violated. Indeed, every equation, every skein of logical demonstration employed "philosophical necessity" simply by virtue of the "full and fixed connection" implied by logically-related terms. And no Arminian had yet accused logic of exerting a force contrary to free will.

Edwards further suggested that this "philosophical necessity" embraced, not just logical terms in general but two very specific kinds of terms, *natural* and *moral*. A *natural necessity* described a relationship between two "natural" terms or causes, in which the necessity of their relationship grew out of the terms themselves rather than a force bringing them together; e.g. "All birds lay eggs," in which the natural term, "bird," necessarily implies laying eggs rather than hatching offspring alive, and all without either birds or eggs in any sense offering resistance to the process. Likewise, a *moral necessity* similarly described a relationship between two "moral" terms or causes which was necessarily implied in the definition of the terms. "By 'moral necessity,' " Edwards explained, "is meant that necessity of connection and consequence, which arises from such *moral causes*, as the strength of inclination, or motives, and the connection which there is in many cases between these, and such certain volitions and actions."[9] Hence, the drunkard who has the dram poured down his throat by a bully is the victim of a "relative" necessity (the necessity of the dram and the drunkard meeting one another was here determined by the strength of the connection, namely, the bully). A drunkard born with a dram-glass attached to his hand and with a nervous tick that compulsively raises it to his lips is the victim of a "natural" necessity (there was a necessity between this peculiar species of creature and its drinking which was inherent in its very structure). But a drunkard who finds a dram altogether too pleasing a motive to drunkenness is also operating under a necessity which is just as predictable; because it stems from a "moral" cause, it produces an act which is morally reprehensible. It was this kind of necessity, free of mechanical force, that Edwards seized on as the determinism Calvinism embodied.

The *Enquiry* only established the theoretical possibility that necessary choices can still be responsible ones. It remained for Edwards to prove that such choices actually take place. This he set out to do in *The Great Christian Doctrine of Original Sin* (1758), a gigantically tedious effort to prove from Scripture and contemporary behavior that mankind is depraved to the core. Only at the end, where he attempts to explain how Adam's sin was transmitted to his progeny, does he resort to speculation nothing short of daring. Here Edwards claimed that mankind is guilty, not because they inherit Adam's guilt, but because they committed it with him. "All dependent existence whatsoever is in constant flux," Edwards wrote, "ever passing and returning; renewed every moment. . . . " There is, in this flux, a constituted sharing of identity, so that "Adam's posterity are from him, and as it were in him, and belonging to him . . . as much as the branches of a tree are, according to a course of nature, from the tree, in the tree, and belonging to the tree." When Adam grasped the forbidden fruit, "guilt . . . and also depravity of heart, came upon [his] posterity just as they came upon him, as much as if he and they had all co-existed, like a tree with many branches."[10]

This was, to say the least, clever since it knocked the props out from under those who attacked the orthodox explanation of the imputation of original sin as "unfair." At the same time, it was too clever because it exposed the one central weakness of eighteenth-century immaterialism. Although they defended the reality of spiritual substance, neither Berkeley nor Malebranche had been able to explain how we obtain direct knowledge of spiritual substance. Edwards's argument in *Original Sin* indicated that he had no solution, either. By recasting original sin as an act which everyone committed in Adam, he was obviously dodging the need to explain how sin was transmitted through the spiritual substance of succeeding generations. Rather than explain human depravity in terms of an inherited nature, Edwards explained it as if God simply constituted, in an act of continuous creation, a shared moral identity between Adam and his posterity. "All oneness," Edwards wrote, "by virtue whereof pollution and guilt from past wickedness are derived, depends entirely on a divine establishment."

Risky as this notion was, Edwards considered that the risk was worth taking. After *Original Sin*, men could not complain that a Calvinist God made them sinners merely by inheritance. After the *Enquiry*, sinners could not complain that their wills were bound by God's decrees, since only their perception of motives and their tempers stood in the way of repentance. Edwards had, in fact, set the intellectual stage for a new Awakening that, this time, could not be gainsaid by nitpicking Arminians. Doubtless he at least once dreamt of reentering Northampton in revivalistic and philosophical triumph. But it was not to be. *Original Sin* was still at the printer when he died at Princeton.

"I like good, strong, old-fashioned doctrine," said Harriet Beecher
Stowe's indignant grandmother in Stowe's reminiscent novel, *Oldtown
Folks,* "I like such writers as Mr. Edwards and Dr. Bellamy and Dr.
Hopkins."[11] Stowe's grouping of Edwards, Bellamy, and Hopkins together
would have pleased the latter two enormously, since their lives were spent
in defending and codifying Edwards's attitudes, doctrine, and practices.
They produced what they called "Consistent Calvinism" and what their
enemies called, "New Divinity."

Primarily it was their imitation of the Edwardsean attitude that stirred
remembrances like that of Mrs. Stowe. Stiff-necked and sometimes stiff-
mannered, they gave neither themselves nor their congregations any refuge
from the rigors of Edwards's logic. Hopkins firmly told a dying parishioner
in 1755 that all of the "joy and comfort" she was deriving from "saving
discoveries of Christ" were probably "only the workings of her imagination." Nathanael Emmons, preaching his son's funeral sermon in 1820,
declared that he had seen nothing in his son's life that suggested he was
not in hell.[12] They were fully as hard on themselves as others. Like
Edwards, they were furious students. Emmons studied "for seventy-eight
years . . . from ten to sixteen hours a day," wearing four holes in the floor
where the legs of his desk-chair rubbed.[13] Like Edwards, they were indifferent to the hard consequences of preaching hard things. Hopkins so
exasperated his congregation in Great Barrington that he was forced to
obtain a dismissal from it, whereupon he went to the First Congregational
Church of Newport, Rhode Island, and there emptied the church with
his preaching against the slave trade.

If the New Divinity men mimicked some of Edwards's faults, it has to
be remembered that they also successfully reproduced many of his virtues.
Just as Edwards prepared Hopkins and Bellamy for the ministry in his own
home, they in turn created their own parlor seminaries (like Emmons)
and log colleges (like Bellamy). Bellamy trained some sixty students for
the ministry, including John Smalley, Samuel Spring, Levi Hart, and
Jonathan Edwards, Jr. They likewise trained still more: Levi Hart trained
Asa Burton (who trained another sixty ministers between 1786 and 1816)
and Smalley and Nathan Strong trained Emmons (who set the record by
training 87 students). In a very short time, the New Divinity men swamped
Connecticut and Massachusetts. From only four or five in the 1750s, New
Divinity ministers swelled to over a hundred by the 1790s. It is true that
some of them, like Hopkins, really did seem to lose touch with their
congregations. Many more, however, touched their congregations with
revival. Asa Burton preached revivals in his Thetford, Vermont, parish
in 1781, 1794, and, near the end of his life, in 1821. He was described
afterwards by an adoring student as greatly successful in "winning souls."
Emmons led revivals in Franklin, Massachesetts, in 1784, 1794–95, and

1809; his teacher, Nathan Strong, lit revival fires in Hartford in 1794, 1798–99, and 1815.[14]

Where the Edwardsean current ran most strong and plain, it was the habit of the New Divinity to ascribe, routinely and unflinchingly, all events, great and small, to the absolutely sovereign decree of God. The world of the New Divinity was, as Bellamy put it, "created for a stage"— not for men to strut their little hour, but upon which God "designed to exhibit a most exact image of himself." The proper human response was to be abased, to be filled with "earnest longings that God would glorify himself" and "a free and genuine disposition to consecrate and give up ourselves entirely to the Lord forever." According to one witness, Bellamy's preaching "made God so great— SO GREAT."[15]

When they turned from the stage of the world to the inner life of the human will, the New Divinity men reflected their Edwardsean origins even more sharply. "That we have a power of will or of determining is granted on all hands," Edwards the Younger wrote. But as Asa Burton hastened to add, "the will is only an *executive* faculty. It is no more than a servant to the heart, to execute its pleasures." It was not an independent psychological entity in men which reached out for what it pleased, since that would mean (as Edwards had foreseen in the *Enquiry*) that the will could well be pleased with something the mind loathed, or apprehend that for which the mind had no desire. The only way the will could be said to be free was if it had the liberty sufficient to execute the commands of the willing self. "*Men* are free," said John Smalley, "whenever they act their own choice: or whenever they choose to act according to their own dispositions." Liberty, as Levi Hart contended, "is frequently used to denote a power of *doing as we please*, or of executing our acts of choice; this refers principally to external action, or bodily motion."[16] Thus, as in Edwards's *Enquiry*, the utter subservience of the will to another power becomes a demonstrable psychological fact and not just a dogmatic assertion.

Still, if volition was, as Stephen West claimed, "nothing more than the mind's preferring the one to the other, by a free, *voluntary* determination," then it behooved inquirers to wonder where the mind acquired its preference. Again, the answer came directly from the *Enquiry*. "By a motive," Asa Burton explained, "I mean any thing which moves, excites, or induces an agent to act." Since that in one sweep accounted for all activity "at all times," it was safe for Bellamy to proclaim, as yet another psychological fact, that "all rational creatures, acting as such, are always influenced by motives, which appear to us as most worthy of our choice." The outlines of Edwards's old paradigm thus became clear: the will obeyed the mind, the mind perceived a desirable motive, the will apprehended the motive and did so freely because no obstacle sat in its way (and not, of course, because it independently wished to). To this, Edwards the Younger anticipated an objection, for if the mind merely acted to process desirable motives down to the will, then there was little difference between saying this, and saying as bluntly as Hobbes did, that motives always caused the will to do what it did. That smacked too much of mechanism. But Edwards the Younger had been prepared for this by his father: "I do not pretend, that motives are the *efficient* causes of volition," he protested. "All that President Edwards means by *cause* in this case, is *stated occasion* or *antecedent.*" So long as the relationship between the motive and the will was defined, in terms that Edwards had borrowed from Malebranche's occasionalism — as a "stated connection" — then the charge of mechanism fell away. Motives, as perceived by the mind, could cause the will, but "the word cause, it must be carefully remembered, implieth nothing more than an occasion of the event. . . . " So long as the notions of causality could be separated from mechanism, and dissolved into occasionalism, then the New Divinity could harmonize freedom and causality, and affirm with Stephen West, "Whoever acteth voluntarily, acteth in the view of motives."[17]

The New Divinity borrowed once more from the *Enquiry* to explain how the necessity of a "stated connection" was any different from any other brand of necessity. It was not immediately apparent how the demonstration that one's actions could be "necessary" without being mechanical made those actions any more free. However, like Edwards, the New Divinity resorted to distinguishing between a natural and a moral necessity. Generally, necessity was the product of mechanical compulsion. But a moral necessity, said Edwards the Younger, "is nothing but a previous certainty of the existence of any moral act." Hence, as Emmons put it, "if men always act under a divine operation, then they always act of *necessity*, though not of *compulsion.*" By the same token, the existence of a natural necessity implied a natural *inability* to do otherwise. This consisted in a "want of understanding, bodily strength, opportunity, or, *whatever may prevent*, our doing a thing, when we are willing. . . . " Likewise, a moral necessity implied a moral *inability* to do otherwise, consisting "only in the want of a heart, or disposition or will, to do a thing." The last deduction served the practical purpose of explaining how unregenerate sinners could be commanded to make themselves new hearts without the command in any way diminishing the sovereignty of God in salvation. Samuel Spring explained,

> As natural ability consists in having intellectual and bodily strength to perform every action required of man, it is evident that moral ability must consist in a willing mind. . . . It is, therefore, evident, that the inability of sinners to repent, is of the moral kind only. The inability of sinners to repent lies only in the aversion of their hearts and wills from repentance.[18]

It was possible, therefore, to say that though an individual suffered from a moral inability to repent (because of his wicked heart), he nevertheless had full natural ability to repent, and could be held accountable for it. From the technical point of vew, this meant that the New Divinity located depravity (or inability) *solely in the will*, and not in the "natural" faculties of the understanding or the constitution, lest they grant to sinners the excuse of a natural inability not to repent. On the other hand, this meant that now the New Divinity had achieved a near-perfect weapon for a consistently Calvinistic revivalism. So armed, they told men, with perfect sincerity, that God's decree of reprobation would never exculpate their guilt in not repenting. By juxtaposing the awful sovereignty and unchangeableness of God's decrees with the obligation that natural ability implied, the New Divinity skillfully forged a mentality of crisis suited ideally to provoking a new Great Awakening. "What do you mean by being under an absolute impossibility to believe and repent?" the 300-pound, six-foot-six Bellamy could thunder; "it is plain that there is nothing but the want of a good temper, together with the obstinate perverseness of sinners, that hinders their return to God; and that, therefore, all their pretenses of being willing to do as well as they can, are mere hypocrisy."[19]

It was this suspicion of "hypocrisy" which led the New Divinity to their most sensational assertion. If men had full natural ability to repent (regardless of the moral inability of their hearts) then there was no reason why they should not do so at once. Sinners "have no excuse for neglecting to do their first work till a more convenient season," exhorted Emmons. "God now commands," he continued, "everyone who is in the state of nature to put away his native depravity and immediately comply with the terms of mercy which he has proposed in the gospel." Bellamy, too, insisted that the sinner was able and obligated "immediately to repent of your sins and return to God through Jesus Christ, looking only to free grace through him for pardon and eternal life." So long as sinners "are under no natural impossibility of doing this," then to delay repentance could only be laid to insincerity.[20]

The call for immediacy struck, as had Edwards's own call, with particular force at the old preparationist model of New England conversion. To be sure, John Smalley recognized that "many are ready to argue that since repentance and faith are the gifts of God, and not in the power of sinners so long as they are in a state of unregeneracy; the only duty at present incumbent on them respecting these matters" is to make use "of those outward means, whereby saving grace is ordinarily communicated to the souls of men." But the New Divinity strenuously declared that the sinner *did* have natural power. Sinners, as well as saints, have wills; the essence of the will's freedom and power lies merely in the fact that *it can will*, not (as Edwards had shown) in a power to will its own willings. That the sinner always wills sinfully merely establishes that there is a moral necessity between his heart and will; that he wills at all shows that he really does have a natural power and freedom, after all. In terms of natural power, a sinner's will can as easily will good or bad. "He is under no kind of inability or difficulty that is in the way of turning to God immediately," Hopkins said. "All the difficulty lies in the corruption of his heart . . . for if they had a real desire to repent . . . they would repent; for nothing is in the way of this but opposition of heart."[21] With that, the whole preparationist system which Emmons sneered at as "unregenerate duties," which "has been built on the principle that sinners are under an ethico-physical inability," now appeared at best "to be without the least foundation in scripture or reason." At worst, claimed Nathan Strong, "it is a dangerous error to suppose the inquiring, convinced sinner is gradually becoming holy, and in a slow manner acquiring a moral conformity to God."[22]

This denunciation of "unregenerate doings" on the grounds of natural ability had three momentous corollaries for the New Divinity in both doctrine and practice.

(1) *Moral absolutism:* If it is true, in practical terms, that "sin cannot by any melioration of its nature grow into holiness," then there was no reason why, in more general theoretical terms, it shouldn't also be true that "holiness and sin are essentially opposite in their nature." Nathan Strong concluded from this that "the character and actions of sinners are wholly unholy," and "nothing, either in sentiment or practice, can be harmless, which arises from a wicked heart." This stood to reason since only utter perversion of heart could explain why a person with full natural power to repent did not actually do so. At the same time, since the measure of ability was the measure of one's natural power, the abilities of the saint to obey God stretched as far as those powers. Thus Bellamy declared that we are obligated "to love God in a measure exactly proportionable to the largeness of our natural powers." Functionally, if not intentionally, Bellamy was advocating perfectionism. Given the Edwardsean logic, there was really no avoiding this. The reality of full natural ability eliminated any need to limit oneself to "one-by-one" steps to salvation. It also implied the obligation to obey down to the last degree of that ability. All that the New Divinity did was to make explicit what had only been logically implicit in Edwards's *Enquiry.* Hopkins was only being thoroughly Edwardsean when he announced that "every voluntary exercise of the creature is either in perfect conformity to [God's law], and so is perfectly right, or, as far as it is not so, is wrong, and a violation of it. There are therefore, in truth, no exercises or conduct of the moral agent which are indifferent . . . there being no medium in the case between right and wrong, virtue and sin."[23]

(2) *Separation:* Because Puritanism was devoted to discerning purity, it had always had a strong urge to create churches only for the "pure," who had separated from the general population of England. But because the pure are always the few, New England Puritanism feared of having its churches filled with only the few. So, although New England called itself

Congregationalist, thereby implying churches based on the purity principle, it was split from the beginning between those who made no effort at separating the pure from the impure in a given town church and those who wanted the church sharply separated from the town and reserved only for the few. The Great Awakening, however, made the "pure" unmistakeably visible and in unprecedented numbers. It gave Edwards fresh incentive to try to restore separatism to Congregationalism. Northampton foiled him. The New Divinity, however, caught the separatistic urge, and their entire ideology spurred them toward furthering Edwards's plans.

Despite Alan Heimert's extravagant claims for the Revolutionary activism of the New Divinity in 1776, they desired nothing so much as to repudiate the notion of an active church-in-society. They sought to limit the church to "real Christians, who have made a profession of evangelical obedience, by repentance towards God and faith in our Lord Jesus Christ." John Smalley had little patience for elaborate distinctions between a visible church, which is compelled to tolerate wheat and tares alike, and an invisible church of the pure alone. The kingdom of God, said Smalley, most emphatically "is the invisible church of Christ here below; comprehending all true christians, and no others." In their own churches in Great Barrington and Bethlehem, Hopkins and Bellamy followed Edwards's lead in Northampton. They ended the practice of admitting to the church, on the strength of their baptisms, those who had made no profession of faith. (Bellamy coined the phrase which has been subsequently used to describe this practice— the "half-way covenant.") "Your baptism," Bellamy warned, "gives you not the least right to any one of the peculiar blessings of the covenant of grace . . . but you are now, this moment, in fact, as liable to be struck dead and sent to hell, by divine justice, as any unbaptised sinner in the land."[24]

Once again, the critics were scandalized. They wailed that, by closing off the church to all but the pure, the church was shutting out nine-tenths of the population and terminating the good influence it could exercise in society. Bellamy, however, cared only for purity, not good influences. "Were it not better," he demanded, "were it not more for the honour of Christ and Christianity, in the sight of Pagans, Jews, and Mahometans . . . and more for the good of their own souls, that nine-tenths should be shut out of the church, if need so require, than to come in by wilful lying."[25] Again, it is hard to see how, given the overall drift of New Divinity thought, he could have come to any other conclusion. A comprehensive, parish-type church made sense only if it was assumed that purity was never absolute in men and could only be cultivated in varying degrees by all who were not openly profligate. Such a church acted, not as a separatistic refuge, but as the moral sheet-anchor for the community at large— indeed, the community was itself, in a comprehensive church, a covenantal entity. But the New Divinity theology eliminated gradualism, and with it, the need to nurture gradualists. The covenantal community was replaced by individual decision, and profession of faith replaced baptism as the sacrament of initiation.

Hence, the New Divinity treated the notion of a church-in-society with profound hostility. Those who yearned, like Nathan Strong, to love God "with the whole heart" had no time for "religious civilities." Strong warned against expecting "civilization" to "alter the moral qualities of men's hearts and actions." It is "ambition, pride or avarice" which really makes ordinary people "diligent in their business, fair in their dealings, humane to their neighbors, or intrepid defenders of the public weal" — not the influence of the church. The veneer of public morality merely gives "a more specious appearance to crimes, and better accomodate[s] the principles of depravity to the taste of those who call themselves refined."

> They may often come where God hath appointed social prayer to be offered, and may sit before him as his people; but their service is more fitly to be called the civility of a christian land where providence hath placed them, than a worship of the Father in spirit and in truth. . . . Is this religion? . . . No, it is not.[26]

(3) *Atonement:* The most startling departure from Calvinist doctrine to which the New Divinity resorted was its rejection of justification by the imputation of Christ's righteousness. In its place was substituted an essentially governmental model which applied the atonement potentially to all men. Governmental images came easily to the New Divinity, since it was one of the chief philosophic objects of Edwardseanism to prove that God was a moral, not an arbitrary, Governor of creation. But if God was a governor, then the essence of sin was not so much wickedness as *lese-majeste.* Bellamy had claimed that God "appears in his public conduct, as one infinitely engaged to give everyone his due, and as one absolutely governed by a spirit of the most perfectly disinterested impartiality." Therefore, sin (in Smalley's words) "consists in the disrespect shown to the supreme Governor of the world, and the reproach cast upon his great and holy name." No government can afford to have its authority flouted openly. Would not God be thoroughly within his rights, in showing that his laws can and will be enforced, by exterminating mankind? However, God preferred not to destroy mankind. Instead, he sent his Son, who suffered the full penalty of God's anger himself — and the principal purpose served by this atonement was not to make propitiation for human sin, but to demonstrate that God was no weakling, that he hated sin, and that he had all the power he needed to punish it.

> *The pangs of our expiring Lord*
> *The honours of thy law restor'd:*
> *His sorrows made thy justice known,*
> *And paid for follies not his own.*

The atonement did not thus provide redemption for sinners: it provided "an opportunity" for God to show that he meant business about sin.[27]

Having shown that beyond all question, God could now proceed to forgive sinners and regenerate them without being accused of inconsistency with his own moral government. "By [Jesus] fulfilling all righteousness," Smalley declared, "a foundation was laid for God, to the eternal honor of his remunerative justice, to give grace and glory to all who believed in Christ and belong to him." To put it another way: Christ did not die on behalf of any individuals. His atonement was intended to justify God for forgiving sinners— not to justify men. When God forgave anyone, it was not because Christ had merited it for them personally. Christ had only "opened a way for the sinner's salvation" by making it possible for God to forgive in general. Therefore, as Smalley warned, God had sent his Son, "not to be laid under obligation in justice, to justify anyone," but only to make his justifying then "honorable." Indeed, far from God being placed under obligation, God's forgiveness was restored to being a matter of pure grace. The atonement arranged matters so that God *could* forgive; there was no guarantee that he actually *would* forgive any individual. Salvation remained an act of sovereignty. Smalley continued: "he is at full liberty to choose the subjects of his renewing mercy, as he thinks proper. Even the obedience and sufferings of Christ, do not lay God the Father under any obligation which is inconsistent with his most sovereign grace. . . . God hath left himself at liberty in his word, to regenerate or to leave in unregeneracy any impenitent sinner whom he pleases."[28]

This put an end to the received Calvinist doctrine of a limited atonement. Christ's death did not provide redemption for a particular elect band— it served rather to allow God to save any and all whom he wished. Thereby, "a way is opened," said Bellamy, for "all and every one of the human race, who shall fall in with the Gospel design." In his first major work, *True Religion Delineated* (which became one of the two major systematic expositions of the New Divinity, along with Hopkins's *System of Doctrines*), Bellamy was already declaring,

> The *obedience* of Christ has brought as much honor to God and his law, as the perfect obedience of Adam, and of all his race, would have done: the rights of the Godhead are as much asserted and maintained: So that there is nothing in the way, but that mankind may, through Christ, be received into full favor, and entitled to eternal life.[29]

This is so far from Westminster or Dordrecht Calvinism, and apparently even Edwards, that numerous commentators have seized on the New Divinity's doctrine of unlimited atonement as a prime example of their "betrayal" of Edwards. Others have hypothesized that Bellamy must have found his way to Hugo Grotius and dredged up governmentalism from there.[30] A little reflection, however, will show that the New Divinity doctrine represented hardly more than an elaboration of the foundation Edwards himself had laid. First, by abandoning the imputation of Adam's sin as the grounds of natural depravity, Edwards had already undercut any similar imputed connection between Christ and the elect. Second, and far more important, the New Divinity balked at the idea of a limited atonement because it seemed to conflict with Edwards's notion of the natural ability of all sinners to repent. Limited atonement implied that, for some, repentance was doomed to be a natural inability. As Bellamy saw it, the chief virtue of an unlimited atonement was precisely this: "it is attributed to sinners themselves that they perish at last— even to their own voluntary conduct." It is true that nothing in Edwards's published works openly embraces a governmental or unlimited atonement. But in his private notebooks — the bulk of which remain unpublished — he inclined sharply toward such ideas. And furthermore, it was Edwards who contributed the preface to *True Religion Delineated* when Bellamy published it in 1750, describing it as "a discourse wherein the proper essence and distinguishing nature of saving religion is deduced from the first principles of the oracles of God. . . . "[31]

Enough has been said about how faithfully the New Divinity reproduced and extended the fine points of Edwards's thinking. It is even more of an indicator of the depth of their loyalty to Edwards that they reproduced as well some of his vaguenesses. For example, they proved no more successful than Edwards had been in *Original Sin* in arriving at a definition of spiritual substance. The most conservative wing of the New Divinity continued to hold that there was an underlying spiritual substance in men that remained constant despite changes in personal self-consciousness and self-identity. Hopkins, especially, was distressed at "the *new* notion of no spiritual substance," while Asa Burton was absolutely insistent that there exist "properties, or faculties, antecedent to the operations of thinking, feeling, and willing, and distinct from them." Both Burton and Smalley admitted that this spiritual "nature is something beyond the direct view of men." Nevertheless to this they said, "[W]e answer, just as well might it be thus concluded, that all invisible beings and things are unrealities, or that there is no evidence of their having any existence." Neither Smalley nor Burton had any other way of accounting for why certain motives pleased the minds, and others not. Unless it was said that "depravity of nature must be antecedent to all sinful actions, and the cause of them," then the only other cause for human pleasure at evil motives would be a direct divine influence, and few of the New Divinity men wished to go that far. Whether they called it "nature" or "heart" or "taste" or "disposition," most of the New Divinity agreed with Burton that a spiritual substance underlay consciousness, and that "there is a plain distinction made [in the Bible] between the *heart,* and the *good or evil* which proceeds from it."[32]

In contrast to this "Taste Scheme," a minority party headed by Nathanael Emmons and Samuel Spring insisted that "all sin and holiness consist in positive exercises of the mind." This "Exercise Scheme" read

Edwards in a starkly Berkeleian light. (Emmons candidly confessed his fondness for Berkeley.) Contending as Berkeley did that "minds are conversant only with their own ideas," an "Exerciser" like Stephen West concluded that

> If mankind have any consciousness or immediate perception of any power of will, distinct from what they feel in the actual exercises of volition — if they are conscious of any power of action, distinct from the consciousness they have in actual voluntary exertion, and previous to it; they must nevertheless be conscious of this power as *being in exercise.*

If there was an underlying spiritual substance, they professed to know nothing of it. Man was merely a bundle of conscious moments, and terms like "habit" or "temper" indicated nothing more than "a certain fixt connection between our *present* exercises of will and future voluntary exertions of the same nature and denomination."[33]

Sin, then, does not originate in a depraved "taste." Sin is "a wrong choice," said Samuel Spring. Emmons added, "There is no morally corrupt nature distinct from free, voluntary, sinful exercises." But where does sin originate? Certainly not in the will's own choice; that would be Arminianism. "It seems necessary," concluded Emmons, grasping the nettle, "to have recourse to the divine agency, and to suppose that God wrought in Adam both to will and to do in his first transgression. . . . A divine energy took hold of his heart and led him to sin." Not surprisingly, this answer won Emmons few friends. But Emmons was not looking for friends. He was looking for consistent Calvinism. The enemies of Calvinism were only too happy to concede that he had found it.[34]

The New Divinity was an Edwardsean movement. Its theology, even in the most dire throes of the Exercise Scheme, aimed only to be a clarification and application of Edwards. Above all, the New Divinity was a prescription for Edwardsean revival, and there is no doubt that it achieved this in New England. Under the leadership of Asahel Nettleton and Bennet Tyler, "Hopkinsianism" fueled a Second Great Awakening in western New England which climaxed in the 1820s. Alas, the race is not always to the swift. By the end of the twenties theological education in America had mostly fallen into the hands of theological seminaries which were inimical to the New Divinity. At Andover and Yale, the "old Calvinism" which remained loyal to comprehensive ecclesiology and compromising philosophy occupied positions of power and legitimacy. At Princeton, Presbyterian Calvinism based on the Scottish "common sense" philosophy waged its own war to rid Presbyterianism of "Edwardsean" influence. Chained to their "parlor seminaries," the New Divinity could not compete with the numbers or the professionalism which the seminaries could produce. When Bennet Tyler died in 1858, the active tradition of New Divinity theology died with him.

But the New Divinity could not simply be suppressed. Instead, "old Calvinism" at Yale and Andover absorbed the most salient doctrines of the New Divinity and synthesized them into a "New Haven theology" in the teaching of Nathaniel W. Taylor of Yale. Embedded in this synthesis, the Edwardsean theology was given a new lease on life. Under the terms of the "Presbygational" Plan of Union of 1801, it spread the old ideas of natural ability, depravity, and unlimited atonement into the heart of Presbyterianism, where it produced the famous trials of Albert Barnes and the New School–Old School schism of 1837. This bowdlerized New Divinity found its most popular spokesman in Charles G. Finney. Much as Finney protested that his theology came direct from the Bible, his memoirs are topheavy with Hopkinsian ideas and slogans. In his methods, the demand for immediate repentance found its most dramatic form. The "call" to the "anxious bench" was only Finney's way of demonstrating the old axiom that men did indeed have the natural ability to respond to the gospel at once. Later in his career, his perfectionist theology at Oberlin was merely a realization of Bellamy's and Hopkins's demand for the full use of natural abilities.

Perhaps it is because Finney does indeed represent the ultimate version of the New Divinity that subsequent generations of Calvinists have been so eager to uncouple Hopkins and Bellamy from Edwards. Finding Finney so awful and Edwards so attractive, they have felt compelled to obliterate the ideological middle movement that links them together. Ignoring this distinction, however, only blinds us to how much in modern American Calvinism can be traced to the models of church, conversion, and society which were forged in the Great Awakening. It deflects our attention from the real legacy of Jonathan Edwards. For better or worse, the patterns of much of American evangelicalism were drawn by Edwards, and the transmission of those patterns was the work of Hopkins, Bellamy, and the New Divinity.

NOTES

1. Samuel Hopkins to Joseph Bellamy, January 19, 1758, in *Bellamy Papers*, Presbyterian Historical Society, Philadelphia, PA; Alan Heimert, *Religion and the American Mind from the Great Awakening to the Revolution* (Cambridge: Harvard University, 1966), 7.
2. Perry Miller, "From Edwards to Emerson," in *Errand Into the Wilderness* (Cambridge: Harvard University, 1956), 195, 197; Henry F. May, *The Enlightenment in America* (New York: Oxford University, 1976), 59; since May's comment, a number of new, and surprisingly sympathetic, evaluations of the New Divinity have appeared— principal among these are Joseph Conforti, *Samuel Hopkins and the New Divinity Movement* (Grand Rapids: Christian University, 1981) and Conforti's article, "Samuel Hopkins and the New Divinity: Theology, Ethics, and Society in Eighteenth-Century New England" in *The William and Mary Quarterly* 34 (October 1977): 572–89; and William K. Breitenbach, "New Divinity Theology and the Idea of Moral Accountability" (unpublished Ph.D. dissertation, Yale University, 1978) and Breitenbach's articles, "The Consistent Calvinism of the New Divinity Movement" in

WMQ 41 (April 1984): 241–64, and "Unregenerate Doings: Selflessness and Selfishness in New Divinity Theology," in *American Quarterly* 34 (1982):479–502. The standard works upon which the older, more negative view of the New Divinity was built are Frank Hugh Foster, *A Genetic History of the New England Theology* (Chicago: University of Chicago, 1907), George Nye Boardman's *A History of New England Theology* (New York: A. D. F. Randolph, 1899), and especially Joseph Haroutunian's frankly contemptuous *Piety Versus Moralism: The Passing of the New England Theology* (New York: Holt, 1932).

3. John H. Gay, "Matter and Freedom in the Thought of Samuel Clarke," *Journal of the History of Ideas* 24 (1963):98; Perry Miller, "Bentley and Newton" in *Isaac Newton's Papers and Letters on Natural Philosophy*, ed. I. Bernard Cohen (Cambridge: The University Press, 1958), 274; R. W. Church, *A Study in the Philosophy of Malebranche* (London: G. Allen & Unwin, 1931), 251–54; Anita D. Fritz, "Berkeley's Self — Its Origin in Malebranche" in *Journal of the History of Ideas* 15 (1954): 569–71.

4. Isaac Watts, "An Essay on the Freedom of Will in God and in Creatures" in *Works* (London, 1753), 6:405; Arthur P. Davis, *Isaac Watts: His Life and Works* (New York: Dryden, 1943), 40.

5. Edwards, "Of Atoms" and "Of Being" in *The Works of Jonathan Edwards: Scientific and Philosophical Writings*, ed. Wallace E. Anderson (New Haven: Yale University, 1980), 206, 215; Edwards, "Personal Narrative," in *Jonathan Edwards: Representative Selections*, eds. C. Faust and T. H. Johnson (New York: American Book, 1935, 1962), 67; Edwards, "Miscellaneous Remarks" in *The Works of Jonathan Edwards*, ed. Edward Hickman (London: Westley, 1834), 2:534; Conrad Cherry, *The Theology of Jonathan Edwards: A Reappraisal* (Gloucester, MA: Peter Smith, 1974), 188; Wallace E. Anderson, "Immaterialism in Jonathan Edwards's Early Philosophical Notes," in *Journal of the History of Ideas* 25 (1964):182–89, and Murray Murphey, "Jonathan Edwards," in E. Flower and M. Murphey, *A History of Philosophy in America* (New York: Capricorn, 1977), 1:144.

6. Edwards, "Miscellanies no. 779," in Norman Fiering, *Jonathan Edwards's Moral Thought In Its British Context* (Chapel Hill, NC: University of North Carolina, 1981), 69; Edwards, "Some Thoughts Concerning the Revival," in *WJE: The Great Awakening*, ed. C. C. Goen (New Haven: Yale University, 1972), 503.

7. Edwards, "Miscellaneous Remarks: Concerning Efficacious Grace," in *Works*, ed. Hickman, 2:545, 563; E. S. Gaustad, *The Great Awakening in New England* (New York: Harper, 1957), 106–107; Patricia Tracy, *Jonathan Edwards, Pastor: Religion and Society in Eighteenth-Century Northampton* (New York: Hill and Wang, 1979), 169–76.

8. Edwards, *WJE: Freedom of the Will*, ed. Paul Ramsey (New Haven: Yale University, 1957), 137–40.

9. Ibid., 149–62; Murphey, "Jonathan Edwards," in *Philosophy in America*, 1:168–70.

10. Edwards, *WJE: Original Sin*, ed. Clyde Holbrook (New Haven: Yale University, 1970), 385, 389, 404; Daniel T. Fiske, "New England Theology," in *Bibliotheca Sacra* 22 (July 1865): 496.

11. Stowe, "Oldtown Folks," in *Three Novels*, ed. K. K. Sklar (New York: Literary Classics of the United States, 1982), 956.

12. Edwards A. Park, "Miscellaneous Reflections of a Visiter, Upon the Character of Dr. Emmons," in *Works of Nathanael Emmons, D.D.*, ed. J. Ide (Boston: Crocker & Brewster, 1842), l:clii–cliii; Ann Douglas, *The Feminization of American Culture* (New York: Knopf, 1977), 155–56.

13. "Nathanael Emmons," in *Annals of the American Pulpit*, ed. W. B. Sprague (New York: R. Carter and Brothers, 1857), 1:701, 704.

14. Sprague, ed., *Annals*, 1:695, 2:143–44, 147, 276; Conforti, *Samuel Hopkins*, 93–94; Jacob Ide, "Memoir," in *Works of Emmons*, l:xcii; Michael P. Anderson, "The Pope of Litchfield County: An Intellectual Biography of Joseph Bellamy, 1719–1790," (unpublished Ph.D. dissertation, Claremont Graduate School, 1980), 184–190.

15. Joseph Bellamy, *True Religion Delineated* (Boston: S. Kneeland, 1750), 3–11, 20.

16. Jonathan Edwards, Jr., "Dissertation on Liberty and Necessity," in *Works*, ed. T. Edwards, (Boston: Doctrinal Tract and Book Society, 1850), 1:333; Asa Burton, *Essays on Some of the First Principles of Metaphysics* (Portland: A. Shirley, 1824), 89, 91; John Smalley, "On the Preservation and Perseverance of the Saints," in *Sermons on a Number of Connected Subjects* (Hartford: Oliver D. Cooke, 1803), 374; Levi Hart, *Liberty Described and Recommended* (Hartford: E. Watson, 1775), 9.

17. Edwards, Jr., "Dissertation," in *Works*, 1:344, 467; Burton, *Essays*, 138; Stephen West, *An Essay on Free Agency* (Salem: Thomas C. Cushing, 1794), 17, 20, 30, 66–67; Bellamy, *True Religion Delineated*, 12.

18. Edwards, Jr., "Dissertation," in *Works*, 1:312; Emmons, *Works*, 4:351; Samuel Spring, *Moral Disquisitions and Strictures* (Newburyport: John Mycall, 1789), 189.

19. Bellamy, *True Religion Delineated*, 196, 358.

20. Emmons, *Works*, 4:514; Bellamy, "The Half-Way Covenant: A Dialogue," in *Works* (New York: Stephen Dodge: 1812), 3:443; Hopkins, "The True State and Character of the Unregenerate," in *Works* (Boston: Doctrinal Tract and Book Society, 1854), 3:445.

21. Smalley, "On Repentance, Conversion and Pardon," in *Sermons*, 321; Hopkins, "The True State and Character of the Unregenerate," in *Works*, 3:296–98.

22. Nathan Strong, *Sermons on Various Subjects, Doctrinal, Experimental and Practical* (Hartford: Oliver D. & I. Cooke, 1798–1800), 1:164; Emmons, *Works*, 4:360.

23. Strong, *The Doctrine of Eternal Misery Reconcileable with the Infinite Benevolence of God* (Hartford: Hudson and Goodwin, 1796), 305, 308, 341; Strong, *Sermons*, 2:23, 185; Bellamy, *True Religion Delineated*, 93–95; Hopkins, "The Knowledge of God's Law," in *Works*, 3:521–24.

24. Strong, *Sermons*, 2:106–107; Smalley, *Sermons on Various Subjects, Doctrinal and Practical* (Middletown, CT: Hart & Lincoln, 1814), 255; Bellamy, "The Half-Way Covenant: A Dialogue," in *Works*, 3:443.

25. Although Bellamy remained within the Connecticut state establishment, he did not hesitate to throw his support behind the struggle of the Separatist Congregationalists— see Mark Noll, "Ebenezer Devotion: Religion and Society in Revolutionary Connecticut," in *Church History* 45 (September 1976):298; also, Conforti, *Samuel Hopkins*, 80, 82; Bellamy, "The Half-Way Covenant: A Dialogue," in *Works*, 3:439–40.

26. Strong, *Sermons*, 1:117, 272, 274; 2:60.

27. Bellamy, *True Religion Delineated*, 26, 30; Smalley, "On Repentance, Conversion and Pardon," in *Sermons* (1803), 308; Daniel Read, "Providence" in *The American Singing Book* (New Haven, 1787).

28. Smalley, "Two Sermons," in *The Atonement: Discourses and Treatises*, ed. Edwards A. Park (Boston: Congregational Board of Publication, 1859), 50; Smalley, *Sermons* (1814), 216; Smalley, "On the Sovereignty of God, In the Effectual Calling of Sinners," in *Sermons* (1803), 244–45.

29. Bellamy, *True Religion Delineated*, 343.

30. On the supposed Grotian connection, see Foster, *Genetic History*, 112–16, Haroutunian, *Piety Versus Moralism*, 161, and Robert L. Ferm, *A Colonial Pastor: Jonathan Edwards the Younger, 1745–1801* (Grand Rapids: Eerdmans, 1976), 114–15; on "unlimited atonement" as a departure from Edwards, see Conforti, *Samuel Hopkins*, 164–67, and Boardman, *History of New England Theology*, 153–61.

31. Bellamy, *True Religion Delineated*, 344; Edwards, "The Preface to True Religion," in *WJE: The Great Awakening*, ed. C. C. Goen, 572; Breitenbach, "Consistent Calvinism," *WMQ* 41 (April 1984):253.

32. James Hoopes, "Calvinism, Consciousness, and Personal Identity from Edwards to Taylor," unpublished manuscript, 9; Burton, *Essays*, 13, 18, 225, 227; Smalley, *Sermons* (1814), 401.

33. Gardiner Spring, *Personal Reminiscences* (New York: C. Scribner & Co., 1866), 2:142; West, *Essay*, 23, 56.

34. Spring, *Moral Disquisitions*, 20; Emmons, *Works*, 4:355–56, 490.

George M. Marsden

11 The New School Heritage and Presbyterian Fundamentalism

I N THE LORE OF CONSERVATIVE PRESBYTERIANISM, the nineteenth-century American heroes of the faith are found in the Old School Presbyterian Church and at Princeton Seminary. New School Presbyterians, on the other hand, are the culprits in the plot. They were the progenitors of modernism (theological liberalism);[1] or if not that, they certainly left ajar the door through which the intruder entered, eventually to usurp the Presbyterian birthright. Edwin H. Rian in *The Presbyterian Conflict* speaks of "Modernism" as "the child of New School theology." C. Gregg Singer asserts that the issues that from 1838 to 1869 separated the Presbyterian Church in the USA (New School) from its Old School counterpart "were never satisfactorily resolved and the division in the theology persists even until our own day."

Less conservative historians, while finding different heroes, assume similar continuities in American Presbyterian history. Elwyn A. Smith, for instance, refers in passing to the parallels between the divisions of 1741, 1838, and 1936 as common knowledge. "Open controversy in Presbyterianism," he says, "between the historic disputants (Old Side–Old School–Fundamentalist on the one hand; New Side–New School–Broad Churchmanship on the other) was quelled in the wake of the Machen dispute." Similarly, Lefferts A. Loetscher, though cautioning against "any over-simplified attempt to extend the Old School–New School line of cleavage into the new Biblical questions," argues that "broad continuities can be discerned, if the identity is not pressed too closely, between earlier New School positions and the later 'liberalism.' "[2]

Such accounts of the New School Presbyterian legacy are to some extent justified, yet insofar as they suggest that the New School was *primarily* a proto-modernist force in Presbyterian history they are misleading. Examination of the history of the New School itself reveals that it was above all an integral part of the evangelical revival of the first half of the nineteenth century, and accordingly, despite its undeniable contributions to twentieth-century theological liberalism, had at least as much affinity to twentieth-century fundamentalism.[3]

The New School and Nineteenth-Century Evangelicalism

New School Presbyterianism was a product of the resurgent international (primarily British and American) evangelical movement, which in America was marked by recurring episodes of widespread revivals between 1801 and 1858. Following the pattern established in the eighteenth century during the first Great Awakening, the majority of America's Protestants adopted revivalism as the most potent response to the threats of infidelity. Harnessing the momentum provided by the revivals, American evangelicals inaugurated a comprehensive program for Christianizing the nation and the world. During the first four decades of the nineteenth century they established a host of non-denominational societies, including the American Board of Commissioners for Foreign Missions, the American Home Missionary Society, the American Bible Society, the American Tract Society, the American Education Society, the American Sunday School Union, and numerous local equivalents. The new Awakening also inspired rigorous moral concerns, leading to the establishment of an additional large group of organizations dedicated either to benevolence or to abolishing conspicuous national sins such as slaveholding, drinking, or Sabbath-breaking. The leadership of this vigorous "Evangelical Empire" was predominantly Congregationalist and Presbyterian.

One of the earliest manifestations of evangelical cooperation was the 1801 Plan of Union between the Congregationalists and the Presbyterian Church in the USA. To meet the urgent needs of home missions more efficiently, the two denominations agreed to found together churches with mixed governments in the new settlements. As a result, large numbers of transplanted New Englanders, who had moved west, became Presbyterian. New England leaders, of whom Lyman Beecher (1775–1863) was the best known, moved into Presbyterianism as well, bringing with them both the New England version of the Reformed theological tradition and irrepressible zeal for all aspects of the evangelical Awakening. These New Englanders, though having no monopoly on such evangelical zeal, formed the nucleus for the party in the Presbyterian Church that by the late 1820s became known as the New School.

By the 1830s the clash of two traditions, that of the New Englanders on the one hand and of the more traditionalist Scottish-Irish on the other, erupted into a furious controversy and brought schism in 1837–38. Several distinct, but interrelated, types of issues defined the lines of division, and a review of these issues will provide an outline of distinctive New School positions. Probably the least significant of the contested issues was that of polity. The Old School engineered the division on the immediate grounds that the Plan of Union represented a departure from strict Presbyterian order. At the general assembly of 1837 they managed to abolish the Plan of Union retroactively, and hence to exclude four New School synods formed according to the Plan. Although it was true that the New School party with its interdenominational interests and Congregational ties had relatively less concern for strict Presbyterian church order, it was clear as well that the Old School was employing the technical issue of polity in the interest of weightier concerns.

Among the other substantial issues, the questions of participation in the non-denominational organizations of the "Evangelical Empire" and in the campaigns for social reform, particularly anti-slavery, played important though nonetheless secondary roles. The New School, reflecting more of the American activist spirit, maintained that the necessity for cooperation in the urgent task of evangelizing the nation outweighed denominational loyalties. Furthermore, in opposition to the more conservative Presbyterian tradition, they felt that the institutional church should actively promote national moral reforms such as total abstinence and abolitionism.

Revivalism, the heart of the New School program, added to the tensions. Enthusiasm for conversions had in some cases led to sensationalism. This was especially true in the overwhelmingly New School areas of western New York State, where itinerants such as Charles G. Finney and his imitators were feeding the fires of revival with "new measures" in order to create intense psychological pressures that would help lead their audiences toward immediate decisions for Christ. Even such sensationalism probably would not have brought Presbyterian division had not the preoccupation with revivalism and immediate conversion brought with it genuine theological issues. These theological issues, in turn, became the primary factors in creating the Old School alarm that led to the drastic acts of schism.

The doctrinal innovations that became identified with New School Presbyterianism had grown directly from evangelistic and apologetic concerns. Such innovations were products of the merging of the evangelical theological tradition that had developed from the first Great Awakening in New England with a moderate form of Enlightenment rationalism. The overwhelming majority of New School Presbyterians claimed to stand in the tradition of Jonathan Edwards, usually as that tradition had been modified by Edwards's more rationalistic disciples, especially Samuel Hopkins (1721–1803). "Hopkinsianism," though strictly Reformed in many respects, represented an attempt to demonstrate in terms acceptable to an enlightened era the benevolence of God in his "moral government" of the universe, and emphasized "disinterested benevolence" in describing the moral behavior of regenerate men. Although the teachings of Hopkinsians, especially on imputation and the atonement, were sometimes attacked by the most rigorous Presbyterian conservatives, more moderate Old School spokesmen such as Charles Hodge and the Princeton party considered the Hopkinsian "errors" not sufficiently great to be incompatible with sincere subscription to the standards of Westminster.

Nathaniel W. Taylor (1786–1856) of Yale, however, carried the rationalistic and moralistic tendencies of the New England theology beyond the realms of Reformed orthodoxy. Searching at once for a reasonable answer to Unitarian challenges and a rationale for more effective revival preaching, Taylor adopted the principles of Scottish common sense philosophy in his explanations of the faith. Common sense led him to the essentially Pelagian conclusion that "There can be no sin in choosing evil, unless there be power to choose good." Taylor argued therefore that unregenerate men, though sufficiently depraved so as always to choose evil, had the full ability to choose the good. Hence the evangelist could properly urge sinners to "Choose ye this day," as a moral obligation which no one could escape on the grounds of lack of ability.

By the late 1820s forms of Taylor's views were being heard within the Presbyterian Church. During the early thirties Old School Presbyterians launched a series of heresy trials, the alleged heretics including most notably Lyman Beecher (Taylor's closest friend, though somewhat more moderate theologically), Albert Barnes (subsequently a well-known biblical commentator), and George Duffield (a pastor and scholar from one of the most distinguished families of Presbyterian clergy). In each case the Old School failed. While most of the New School party did not share Taylor's views, their more tolerant attitudes toward subscription to the Westminster standards repeatedly won the day in the church's judicatories. The Old School, frustrated by such failures to combat heresy through constitutional means, at last turned to the more extreme scheme of retroactively abrogating the Plan of Union, and thereby forcing the New School party out of the denomination.

Freed from Old School influences, the Presbyterian Church in the USA (New School) might have been expected to veer toward theological radicalism. Such, however, was not the case. The New School, anxious to establish its claims to represent the true "constitutional" tradition of American Presbyterianism, became during its years as a separate denomination somewhat uncongenial to theological innovation. Without reviewing the entire history of the New School church, this point may be demonstrated with regard to the negotiations that led to the reunion of 1869. The minority in the Old School who opposed such a reunion left few theological stones unturned; yet in their efforts to defeat the proposed merger they failed to produce any real evidence of heresy within the New School group other than that alleged against the aging New School spokesmen in the debates of the 1830s. Hence it is the issues raised in that earlier era that should be considered first in determining the extent to which the New School tradition may have fostered either modernism or fundamentalism.

If New School Presbyterianism is to be categorized as "proto-modernist," the chief candidate for a liberal influence must be the "New Haven theology" of Nathaniel Taylor. Taylor's teachings represented the only distinctly New School theological views that were ever substantial points of issue with the Old School. Admittedly, the New Haven theology bore some resemblances to the later modernism, especially in its optimistic view of human nature, its emphasis on morality, and a faith in progress. Yet New Haven theology and later forms of theological liberalism grew out of quite different intellectual movements and depended on opposed philosophical assumptions. New Haven theology was a late product of the Enlightenment; it was based on the common sense philosophy, which emphasized the objectivity of man's perception and reason. The early manifestations of what later became known as modernism in America grew out of German and American "romanticism," and emphasized man's subjective religious experience. The New Haven theologians were among the firmest opponents of such romantic theology when it first appeared in the form of transcendentalism. Furthermore, any direct continuity between the New Haven views and the forms of "liberalism" that appeared after the Civil War is highly unlikely, since the New Haven views had nearly disappeared, at least in the New School, by 1865.

Indeed, there is, on the contrary, considerable similarity between the controversial New Haven views and the theology of much of fundamentalism. Each originated in opposition to more radical theological tendencies, the New School theologians vigorously opposing Unitarianism, just as fundamentalists reacted to modernism. Each tended to react on the other hand to Calvinism's low view of man and to stress instead the worth of the individual. Each emphasized revivals, the conversion experience (often with a non-Calvinist emphasis on man's ability to accept the gospel), and rigorous moral standards. A case can, in fact, be made for some direct continuity between New Haven theology and fundamentalism. As Richard Hofstadter points out, for instance, Charles Finney, who adopted many of Taylor's views, had a significant effect in setting the standards for later fundamentalist revivalists.[4] Though such continuities probably cannot be pressed on a large scale, the similarities in the outlook of the two movements are clearly present.

It might, however, still be argued that, although the New Haven theology itself had few affinities to modernism, later New School theologians hastened the rise of such liberalism by their interests in German idealist philosophy and biblical criticism. The strongest evidence for this argument is that, in the controversies over these issues that began in the 1890s, former New School areas, and especially the former New School seminaries (Union in New York, Auburn, and Lane), were centers of strength for the new more liberal views. Such continuities certainly do establish the point that the New School tradition of doctrinal tolerance contributed substantially toward allowing new views to enter the denomination. As Lefferts Loetscher points out in his fine study of this question, "the New School tradition, with its greater readiness for change, its greater emphasis on emotion and experience rather than on rational demonstration, was inherently more inclined to adjust its Biblical views than was its more rigid Old School counterpart." Yet Loetscher shows also that there were far too many exceptions to this generalization to carry the Old School–New School line of division into the later controversies.[5]

One reason for the lack of such general continuity is that, aside from its disposition toward tolerance, there was relatively little tendency in the New School denomination prior to 1869 toward the later forms of liberalism. There was, however, some such tendency. Most notable was the work of Laurens P. Hickok (1790–1888), a New School clergyman, Professor of Christian Theology at Auburn Theological Seminary from 1843 to 1852, and one of the American pioneers of German idealism. Hickok advocated a moderate form of idealism, affirming a dualism between the spirit and the flesh. Yet he insisted that "the inspired word of God" must be "the field in which the facts are to be sought" in the science of theology, and criticized the tendencies of German idealism to make "the inner law of thought" its only God — a position which Hickok warned could end only in "a transcendental pantheism."[6]

While Hickok's guarded sympathies for German thought were undeniable, even such sympathies were by no means always welcomed in the New School. Hickok, for instance, was criticized in the *Biblical Repository,* a predominantly New School journal, for "a certain air of Germanism or transcendentalism."[7] Anti-German sentiments seem in fact to have been more characteristic of the New School than pro-German sympathies. Samuel H. Cox (1793–1880), for instance, who in the 1830s was on Charles Hodge's list of most notorious New School heretics, himself a decade later was attacking scholars who had "lost the millennial arithmetic of the Holy Ghost" in Germany.[8] By the 1850s the vigilant in the New School were demonstrating considerable concern over German thought. The editorial spokesman for the *Presbyterian Quarterly Review,* the official New School theological journal, noted in 1859 that "We shall be ready to sound the alarm whenever we see real danger," adding that "if we should be disposed to indicate the direction from which it is likely to come, we should unhesitatingly point to Germany." The German speculations, he

warned, would lead to the biblical criticism of D. F. Strauss, the philosophy of Hegel, and "the practical results in Sunday balls and theatres."[9]
That such alarms had to be sounded, certainly indicates on the one hand
that some in the New School were moving in the direction of the new
theology from Germany; yet on the other hand the alarms themselves
indicate that pro-German leanings were by no means a characteristic New
School trait. In any case, the imported philosophy had apparently not yet
led to any doctrinal innovations, since the issue of German thought seems
never to have been mentioned by Old School critics during the debate on
the reunion.

Indisputably, by the time of the reunion of 1869, the most influential
New School theologian was Henry Boynton Smith (1815–1877) of Union
Seminary in New York. Smith had studied in Germany, and even acknowledged a debt to Schleiermacher to the extent that the German
theologian had suggested that the mediatorial work of Christ should be
the central organizing principle for theology. Yet Smith himself did not
carry his own Christological principles to conclusions that subverted Presbyterian orthodoxy. He explicitly repudiated Schleiermacher's low views
of the atonement, of the historicity of the facts concerning the life of
Christ, and of Scripture.[10]

While Smith's interest in German thought, including translations of
several major German works on historical theology, doubtless prepared the
way for later liberal influences, his own theological stance seemed unas-
sailable. Charles Hodge, the chief opponent of the Presbyterian reunion,
of which Smith was the chief exponent, never raised any questions concerning Smith's own orthodoxy. Hodge and Smith, in fact, shared one
major theological concern in common — their unrelenting opposition to
the New Haven theology. On this point, as one Old School observer
remarked, Union Seminary seemed to "out-Princeton Princeton itself."[11]
Smith, perhaps, got to the heart of the issue more clearly than did Hodge.
The New Haven theology, Smith pointed out, had made all other theological considerations subservient to an ethical theory based on the principle that the power of contrary choice was necessary for moral responsibility.
Such ethical concerns, he argued, were superficial compared to the central
Christian proclamation of the mediatorial work of Christ. "Nor can such
an ethical system," he concluded, "satisfy man's profoundest wants or
solve the real problem of his destiny."[12]

The crucial issue that separated Henry B. Smith from his more liberal
successors at Union Seminary was his high view of Scripture. Smith in a
careful defense of the doctrine of inspiration insisted that "the Protestant
position of the supreme authority of the Bible stands or falls with the
evidence for its infallibility."[13] Such statements seemed foreign at Union
a generation later; so much so that in the 1890s Smith's otherwise eulo-

gistic biographer felt it necessary to apologize for Smith's stand for infallibility.[14]

The difficulties with identifying the New School with later liberal tendencies in Presbyterianism are most apparent when the views of New School men toward Scripture are considered. Without exception, they expressed a high regard for the authority of Scripture. This assumption pervaded everything they wrote. One of the primary bases for their early attacks on the complex Old School theology was their claim that they desired to return to the simplicity of the biblical message. This express desire not to depart from Scripture perhaps helps explain why the New School during its denominational independence did not move toward increasingly radical theological positions, as the Old School predicted it would.

On the question of Scripture the usual interpretation of the New School as proto-liberal simply breaks down. Accepting the usual interpretation, George Duffield, Sr. (1794–1868), for instance, would have to be classed as one of the leading liberals, since he was throughout the New School's history a primary target for Old School attacks. In fact, however, Duffield was an outstanding champion of Biblical literalism and infallibility. Writing in 1863 a summary statement of the doctrines of New School Presbyterians, Duffield maintained that "faith concerns itself with matters of fact reported or made known by infallible inspiration, to be believed, simply and exclusively on the ground of God's veracious testimony."[15]

Similarly, by the usual interpretation, Albert Barnes, whose acquittals in two trials before the general assembly in the 1830s sealed Old School resolution to separate from the New School, would have to be classed as proto-liberal. On the doctrine of Scripture, however, Barnes was nothing of the sort. Writing in 1862 on certain unacceptable "readjustments of Christianity," especially higher criticism of Scripture and Darwinism, Barnes listed scriptural infallibility first among the doctrines that could not be readjusted. It is the established teaching of the church, he said,

> . . . that the Bible is a book given by supernatural inspiration of God; that is, that truths are recorded there which in fact have their origin *directly* in the mind of God, and have been imparted by him to the minds of the writers by a direct communication; that . . . they have been so guided by the Holy Spirit as to be preserved from error; that this principle applies to every part of the sacred volume; that the Bible is in fact, to all intents and purposes, *one book*, whose real author is the Spirit of God.

Barnes used the same article to ridicule Darwinism unmercifully, thus becoming one of the earliest American opponents of the new theory.[16] In a similar vein, Barnes warned in 1865 that "the friend of revelation is not at liberty to modify the system; to accommodate it to prevailing theories of philosophy; or to adjust it to new facts as they develop themselves in the progress of human affairs."[17] Barnes, whose popular biblical commentaries are still in print and in use in fundamentalist circles, was anything but progressive when the authority of the Bible came into question. If the line dividing fundamentalist from liberal is drawn on the basis of scriptural infallibility (as it was for many years during the later controversies in Presbyterianism), the affinities of Barnes and the New School were hardly liberal.

On the more positive side is the question of resemblances between the New School and fundamentalism. One aspect of New School thought that suggests such resemblances is the strong emphasis in the New School on millennialism. Almost all New School ministers, it seems, looked forward to clearly supernatural manifestations of the millennial age in this world. Most interpreted the biblical prophecies concerning the last times quite literally. Nearly all, for example, shared the belief that twelve-hundred and sixty years was the revealed lifetime of the Papacy (the Anti-Christ). The majority in the New School held post-millennial views. They were confident that the progress of the world in the spread of the gospel, the rise of moral standards, science, and knowledge was a sign of the approach of the millennial age. To the extent that such post-millennial views looked toward progress and fostered social reform they have some connections to the later modernist Social Gospel; yet the lack of the supernatural in the later movement separates it sharply from New School attitudes. One incidental characteristic of New School thought related to millennialism and suggestive of later fundamentalist characteristics, on the other hand, is extreme patriotism. New School spokesmen, more so than Old School, expected the millennium to start in America and they related such beliefs, especially during the Civil War, to extreme expressions of flag-waving nationalism.[18]

While the post-millennialism of the majority in the New School suggests only vague relationships to fundamentalism, the pre-millennialism held by a significant minority suggests some direct connections. As pre-millennial views became increasingly popular in America by about the 1840s, some New School men emerged among the leading spokesmen for the re-emphasis of such views. Samuel H. Cox and George Duffield, Sr., for instance, are listed in C. Norman Kraus's study of *Dispensationalism in America* among the leading exponents of historic pre-millennialism. Their views paved the way for the later popularity of the dispensationalism of John Nelson Darby, the Plymouth Brethren, and C. I. Scofield. Cox, though perhaps not directly influenced by the Plymouth Brethren, even developed a scheme of seven dispensations which was "in outline, though not in nomenclature, the exact parallel of Dr. Scofield's system."[19] Duffield, though not sharing the dispensational scheme, published in 1842 one of the earliest nineteenth-century American defenses of pre-millennialism.[20] One of the works which Duffield recommended was a magazine called *The Literalist*, published in Philadelphia from 1840 to 1842. This periodical may have been a source through which British premillennial views were learned in America and certainly suggests the biblical literalism that attracted many in the New School.[21]

Resemblances between New School attitudes and later fundamentalism are easier to document than are such direct lines of continuity. The heart of the difficulty is that after the reunion of 1869 Presbyterians were faced with a new set of challenges and issues, so that the lines of controversy between fundamentalists and modernists simply cannot be read back into the Old School–New School era. Nonetheless, the presence of such difficulties is compatible with the central contention of the present analysis — that, taking into account that any continuities will be blurred by the later issues, the New School contributed substantially (as, no doubt, the Old School did also) to the heritage of fundamentalism *as well as* to that of modernism.

A few suggestions of direct lines of continuity between the New School and fundamentalism may be sufficient to support this central point. The influence of Charles Finney (who was in the New School party until he left for Congregationalism in 1835) on revivalism, and the influence of Albert Barnes's commentaries on fundamentalism have already been mentioned. Also the independent evangelical agencies, such as the American Bible Society, the American Temperance Union, the American Sunday School Union, and other missionary and benevolent societies, continued to function into the fundamentalist era. Another example of some direct continuity is that Jonathan Blanchard, who founded Wheaton College in Illinois in 1859, had been a New School Presbyterian from 1838 to 1845, before moving into the ministry of the closely allied Congregationalists.

Even more direct continuity can be demonstrated by the participation of former New School men in the International Prophecy Conferences which marked the first stages of the organized movement that later became known as fundamentalism. At the first such conference, held in 1878, sixteen of the thirty-five speakers listed were Presbyterians. Of these, seven had formerly belonged to the Old School and three to the New School, while six had been neither. Considering that in 1869 the Old School had had nearly twice as many ministers as the New School, the percentage of participants is not significantly different.[22] An incidental but somewhat revealing sidelight to such connections is that the 1878 conference was held in the Episcopal church of Stephen H. Tyng. Tyng was the father of the young evangelist whose dying words in 1858 had inspired his close friend, George Duffield, Jr. (1818–1888), to write the hymn "Stand Up, Stand Up for Jesus," which may be New School Presbyterianism's most lasting contribution to the fundamentalist heritage.

At the very least even a few direct continuities such as these establish the point that the spirit of the New School movement had affinities to the spirit of fundamentalism.

The New School and Twentieth-Century Fundamentalism

Parallels between New School attitudes and those of twentieth-century fundamentalists shed additional light on the characteristics of both. One such parallel is the career of William Jennings Bryan in the Presbyterian Church in the USA. Bryan, running true to his usual political form narrowly missed election as moderator of the 1923 general assembly. At the same time he was becoming the best known spokesman for American fundamentalism. In terms of the Presbyterian tradition, however, his style and his message were closer to those of the New School than to the Old School. His campaigns against Darwinism and alcohol (an old New School cause) were conducted with the fervor and the techniques of a revivalist. His message, emphasizing simple biblical literalism more than strict confessional orthodoxy, likewise suggests affinities to the New School side of the Presbyterian heritage.

An even more striking parallel is suggested by the career of Carl McIntire, especially as he was involved in the division of the Presbyterian Church of America (Orthodox Presbyterian Church) in 1937. While the majority of the newly founded denomination, including the closest associates of J. Gresham Machen at Westminster Seminary, took clearly conservative (or Old School) positions on the divisive issues, the minority led by McIntire took positions not only more typically fundamentalistic but also remarkably similar to those taken by the New School a century earlier. The specific programs for which McIntire and his associates fought were (1) tolerance of a doctrine (dispensational pre-millennialism) which the majority in the church considered incompatible with the *Westminster Confession of Faith*; (2) continuation of the Independent Board for Presbyterian Foreign Missions, rather than forming an official denominational mission board; and (3) adoption by the general asembly of a statement that total abstinence from all that may intoxicate is "the only true principle of temperance"— precisely the statement first adopted by the New School general assembly of 1840. These programs, together with McIntire's claim to represent "American Presbyterianism" (a former New School term), his avid (anti-Communist) patriotism, his zeal for revivalism and legalistic reforms, his emphasis on interdenominational cooperation, and his lack of concern for strict Presbyterian polity[23] all suggest a continuation of distinctly New School traditions within the fundamentalist wing of Presbyterianism.

The antipathies between the Bible Presbyterian followers of McIntire and the Orthodox Presbyterian followers of Machen suggest a distinction that must be maintained if the continuities of Presbyterian history are to be understood clearly. Rather than characterizing the anti-modernist movement in Presbyterianism as simply "fundamentalist" or as simply "conservative," it should be made clear that the movement was a coalition of *both* fundamentalists and conservatives. Machen recognized the tension in his 1926 comment on fundamentalism:

> Do you suppose that I do not regret my being called, by a term that I greatly dislike, a "Fundamentalist"? Most certainly I do. But in the presence of a great common foe, I have little time to be attacking my brethren who stand with me in the defense of the Word of God. I must continue to support an unpopular cause.[24]

Machen's own plight may be better understood if the New School element in the heritage of Presbyterian fundamentalism is considered. In the early 1920s the anti-modernist coalition could still command a majority in the general assembly of the Presbyterian Church in the USA. The prominence of William Jennings Bryan in the Presbyterian struggles at that time suggests the possibility that much of that strength came from those who were more fundamentalist than conservative in their leanings. Hardly more than a decade later, however, when Machen led the formation of the Presbyterian Church of America, he was followed by only a tiny minority, most of whom could be classed as conservatives. Why did not more Presbyterians follow? One factor was that many of Presbyterian fundamentalists had their own evangelistic agenda and (like the New School, even if unconsciously) were unwilling to pursue the issues of strict Presbyterian confessionalism, especially when such a course would endanger the unity, and hence (they argued) the witness, of the church.

By tracing the roots of the conservative-fundamentalist coalition back to the Old School and New School heritage, both the twentieth-century anti-modernist movement and the nineteenth-century conflict may be understood more clearly. The New School, of course, differed in some very important respects from fundamentalism. The nineteenth-century movement stood in the mainstream of American religious, intellectual, and cultural life and was generally progressive in outlook. Fundamentalism often retreated to the cultural hinterlands, and appeared retrogressive. Yet both have been essentially evangelical, or more accurately, evangelistic, in their driving motivation. The New School, although it took a broad view of the creeds, and sometimes a lax view of traditional doctrine, did so largely because of its emphasis on the urgency of preaching the gospel. When new issues arose in a new age, it turned out that such evangelistic emphases had helped breed *both* fundamentalism and modernism. If a moral may be drawn, perhaps it is that the possibility of fostering doctrinal laxity is the risk that the evangelical almost inevitably takes when he wholeheartedly emphasizes his evangelism.

On the other hand, viewing the twentieth-century Presbyterian anti-modernist movement from the perspective of the earlier controversies, it appears that the conservatives in that movement, like their Old School predecessors, lost something of the evangelical strain when they were separated from their fundamentalist allies. In conservative Presbyterian circles, ever since the time of the controversy with the New Side in the eighteenth century, the evangelical-pietist-revivalist tradition has been accepted only uneasily, sometimes tolerated, but seldom loved. The uneasiness concerning potential or actual doctrinal latitude has often been justifiable; yet in the abandonment of the more evangelical aspects of the American Presbyterian tradition conservatives have sometimes also lost that dynamic evangelistic thrust that must always balance doctrinal orthodoxy.

NOTES

This is a slightly revised edition of an article originally published in *The Westminster Theological Journal* 32 (May 1970) 2: 129–47.

1. Although a distinction can be drawn between modernism and theological liberalism, the two terms will be used interchangeably in this essay to designate the theological movement that reached its peak in America between about 1900 and 1940.

2. Edwin H. Rian, *The Presbyterian Conflict* (Grand Rapids: Eerdmans, 1940), 23; C. Gregg Singer, *A Theological Interpretation of American History* (Philadelphia: Presbyterian and Reformed, 1964), 66; Elwyn A. Smith, *The Presbyterian Ministry in American Culture* (Philadelphia: Westminster, 1962), 264; Lefferts A. Loetscher, *The Broadening Church* (Philadelphia: University of Pennsylvania, 1967), 27, 18.

3. The analysis that follows is based on "The New School Presbyterian Mind: A Study of Theology in Mid-Nineteenth Century America," the author's Ph.D. dissertation, Yale, 1966. Some brief passages in this essay are directly from that work. Cf. the book that grew out of that work, *The Evangelical Mind and the New School Presbyterian Experience* (New Haven: Yale University, 1970). Since the point that the New School contributed to liberalism is being granted, the evidence here selected is weighted toward that which relates the New School to fundamentalism.

4. Richard Hofstadter, *Anti-Intellectualism in American Life* (New York: Alfred A. Knopf, 1962), 81–136.

5. Loetscher, *op. cit.*, 27. See pp. 9–89 for a thorough account of these later controversies with some attention to Old School–New School connections.

6. Laurens P. Hickok, "Christian Theology as a Science," *Biblical Repository*, Third Series, I, 3 (July 1845), 462; cf. p. 483; and "The Idea of Humanity in its Progress to its Consummation," (New York, 1847), 20.

7. Review of Hickok, *Rational Psychology* (Auburn, 1849), in *Biblical Repository*, Third Series, V, 18 (April 1849), 375.

8. Samuel H. Cox, "The Bright and Blessed Destination of the World," (New York, 1849), 13.

9. "Do We Need a New Doctrinal Agitation in Our Church?" *Presbyterian Quarterly Review*, VII, 4 (April 1859), 557f; cf. "Religion and Philosophy," *PQR* II, 4 (March 1854), 665ff.; and [Albert Barnes], "Readjustments of Christianity," *PQR*, XI, 1 (July 1862), 10f. for similar negative views.

10. Henry Boynton Smith, *Faith and Philosophy* (New York: A. C. Armstrong, 1877), 37f.

11. Thomas H. Skinner, Jr., quoted in Lyman Atwater, "The Late Assemblies on Reunion," *Princeton Review,* XLI, 3 (July 1869), 430.

12. Smith, *Faith and Philosophy,* 160.

13. Henry B. Smith, *"The Inspiration of Holy Scriptures,"* (New York, 1855), 3.

14. Lewis F. Stearns, *Henry Boynton Smith* (Boston: Houghton Mifflin and Co., 1892), 198f.

15. George Duffield, "Doctrines of the New School Presbyterian Church," *Bibliotheca Sacra,* XX, 70 (October 1863), 573.

16. [Albert Barnes], "Readjustments of Christianity," *Presbyterian Quarterly Review,* XI, 1 (July 1862), 32; 68–72.

17. Albert Barnes, "Christianity and the World's Progress," *American Presbyterian and Theological Review,* New Series, III, 12 (October 1865), 569.

18. For discussion of this topic see the author's The *Evangelical Mind and the New School Presbyterian Experience,* 182–211.

19. Quoted from Arnold Ehlert in C. Norman Kraus, *Dispensationalism in America* (Richmond: John Knox, 1958), 30.

20. Duffield, *Dissertations on the Prophecies, Relative to the Second Coming of Jesus Christ* (New York: Dayton and Newman, 1842). Cf. Kraus, 54.

21. Duffield, *Dissertations,* 163. Strict biblical literalism was almost always characteristic of nineteenth-century pre-millennialism. See Kraus, *op. cit.,* 57.

22. [James H. Brookes], "Conference about Christ's Coming," *The Truth: or Testimony for Christ,* IV, 9 (August 1878), 407f. On the rise of millenarianism, see Ernest R. Sandeen, *The Roots of Fundamentalism: British and American Millenarianism, 1800–1930* (Chicago: University of Chicago, 1970).

23. For a more detailed account of the 1937 controversy see the author's "Perspective on the Division of 1937," *The Presbyterian Guardian,* XXXIII, 1–4 (January to April 1964), and in this volume chapter 18.

24. Quoted in Ned B. Stonehouse, *J. Gresham Machen: A Biographical Memoir* (Grand Rapids: Eerdmans, 1954), 337f.

John R. Wiers

12 Henry B. Smith, Theologian of New School Presbyterianism

THE HISTORY OF AMERICAN PRESBYTERIANISM in the nineteenth century reveals a broad panorama of important issues and key personalities. During the century the main body of Presbyterians experienced two splits, one reunion, vigorous theological debate on a wide variety of issues, and the traumatic experience of the Civil War. Most of these were not unique to the Presbyterian church, but for it, a highly theologically conscious tradition, the discussions were intense. The Civil War years themselves played a unique role in that the events of these years actually were instrumental in bringing about the union of two of the main bodies of Presbyterians.

One of the most important, yet frequently overlooked, personalities in nineteenth-century Presbyterian history is Henry Boynton Smith. Both an active churchman and highly respected theologian, Smith has received little study, and the actual influence which he wielded over a considerable part of mid-nineteenth-century Presbyterianism is virtually unknown.[1] The focus of this study will be to examine Smith as both an important theologian and as a churchman who wielded great influence in the reunion of the Old School and the New School in 1869.

The Old School–New School split is a familiar story to students of nineteenth-century Presbyterianism, but a review of the basic details is necessary to place Smith and the events of the mid-nineteenth century in their proper context.[2] The Old School–New School conflict led to a division in 1837, which lasted until 1869. The primary issue was theological, but there were historical and sociological factors involved as well. Although the distinction was not absolute, the New School consisted primarily of New Englanders and had a more revivalistic emphasis. The Old School, on the other hand, was primarily of Scotch-Irish stock and had a much less enthusiastic attitude toward revivalism. These two streams had both come into the Presbyterian church during colonial days, but the difference of outlook became more obvious as the result of the Plan of Union of 1801. This cooperative venture lasted until 1837, when a split occurred after a series of heresy trials. The result of this split was two bodies, both claiming to be the true Presbyterian church — the New School and the Old School. Although some attempts were made at merger, the two churches essentially went their own ways until the 1860s.

Henry Boynton Smith (1815–1877) emerged as the preeminent theologian of the New School branch of the church.[3] He has been ranked among the most prominent theologians of the mid-nineteenth century by some historians.[4] Since Smith was the most notable theologian of the New School, his theology and its influence are very important in the consideration of the reunion of the two branches in 1869. His role as an active churchman is also very important in that reunion.

As a theologian Smith has been evaluated in a number of ways. Perhaps to some later confessionalists who viewed the 1869 merger as a mistake, Smith was simply a typical, compromising New School theologian. Indeed, some have seen Smith as a crypto-liberal.[5] However, many others have seen Smith as a truly orthodox theologian. This study argues that Smith was a conservative, orthodox theologian in the Edwardsean tradition and that it was his theology that allowed him to play such an important role in the reunion of the Old School and the New School.[6] Our examination of Smith's theology will focus on his anthropology because that was the most crucial issue between the two branches of the Presbyterian church.

Henry Boynton Smith was born in 1815 in Portland, Maine, into a prosperous merchant family.[7] His grandfather had been a prominent New England Congregational minister. Both his mother, who died when he was five, and his stepmother were steeped in the warm, evangelical piety of New England orthodoxy. However, they were members of the First Parish of Portland, which had come under the sway of the Unitarian theology that had begun to emerge in 1815. Young Smith became fully convinced of the theological position of his pastor at First Parish. Thus, in 1830, armed with a rationalistic Unitarian outlook, he entered Bowdoin College in Brunswick, Maine, at the age of fifteen. His biographer, Stearns, describes his student life there by saying:

> Here, as elsewhere, his personal attractions, his wit, and his fondness for society, as well as his intellectual ability, gained him many friends. . . . While he took a high rank in all departments of study, he showed an especial aptitude for philosophy.[8]

While a senior in college, Smith had an experience that would drastically change his whole career. In 1834, as a part of the revival movements that came in the aftermath of the second Great Awakening, revival visited Bowdoin College. As a result young Smith experienced a conversion from his Unitarian position to an evangelical theology and to a personal faith in Christ. His description of his conversion reveals a sin-conscious, Christ-centered piety, as well as a concern for the intellectual ramifications of Christian doctrine.[9]

In the fall following his graduation, Smith turned his attention to the study of theology and entered Andover Seminary. Besides Moses Stuart, one of the leading American biblical scholars of the time, Andover's faculty included Leonard Woods, one of the most notable defenders of the conservative New England theology. Smith was only at Andover for a few months when he experienced the first of several physical breakdowns that were to plague him throughout his life. The next fall (1835), he entered Bangor Theological Seminary in Bangor, Maine, where he studied under Enoch Pond, a student of Nathaniel Emmons. Emmons was one of the well-known earlier proponents of the so-called New Divinity which developed from the theology of Jonathan Edwards. He also studied there with Leonard Woods, Jr., from whom he probably developed his interest in German theology.[10]

Smith's formal theological training in America ended after one year and the next fall he took a position as a tutor at Bowdoin, where he perfected his German. During the year his health again deteriorated and he went to Germany to recuperate and study. There he studied for nearly two years at the universities of Halle and Berlin. Among the scholars with whom he studied were Ulrici, the philosopher at Halle; Leopold von Ranke, the historian; Trendelenburg, the post-Hegelian philosopher; Neander, the church historian; and, above all, Halle's theologian, Tholuck, who became a life-long friend of Smith's. Stoever describes Tholuck as "the leading theologian of the resurgent pietistic movement in Germany."[11] Muller says,

> From Tholuck and from the great Neander, Smith learned the criticism of rationalism on the basis of a Christocentric piety. On his return to America in 1840, Smith brought a deep respect for Germany's evangelical scholarship and he engaged almost immediately in the work of making available in English the best of German theological endeavor.[12]

After his sojourn in Germany, Smith taught for a year at Bowdoin College, served five years as the pastor of the Congregational Church at West Amesbury, Massachusetts, (during which time he was a part-time instructor at Andover Seminary) and then spent three years as Professor of Mental and Moral Philosophy at Amherst College, Amherst, Massachusetts. While at Amherst, he delivered his famous lecture, "The Relations of Faith and Philosophy," before the Porter Rhetorical Society of Andover Seminary in 1849. The speech was printed both in the United States and Scotland and "made the author's theological reputation."[13]

In 1850 his reputation as a theologian and historian led to his unanimous appointment to the chair of church history at the young Union Theological Seminary in New York. During his five years as a church historian, he emphasized historical theology in the spirit of the organic development of his mentor Neander.[14] In 1854 he transferred to the chair of systematic theology, which he served until his retirement, brought about because of health reasons in 1873. While at Union, Smith transferred his ecclesiastical connection to the New School branch of the Presbyterian church. Here he was very active as a preacher and ecclesiastical statesman.

Smith's literary output was not tremendous yet sufficiently full to see clearly how his position developed. His works include: *Faith and Philosophy* (1877), a collection of articles which he wrote for various theological journals, *Lectures on Apologetics* (1882), *Introduction to Christian Theology* (1883), and *System of Christian Theology* (1884). The last three were edited by William S. Karr of Hartford Theological Seminary, a former student of Smith's, from Smith's lecture notes and the stenographic notes of a number of students. Smith also edited a major theological journal (which went through several mergers and name changes) and translated a number of important theological works from German.[15]

From our survey of Smith's background, it is clear that Smith was a product of the New England theological tradition that caused so much concern to the Old School Presbyterians. Yet Smith was actually a product of the more conservative branch of that tradition closer to orthodox Calvinism. Space does not permit a full discussion of the history of the New England theology that had as its source the thought of Jonathan Edwards and developed into several streams.[16] However, Edwards's distinction between natural and moral ability and his concept of true virtue as "love toward being in general" were the two issues that caused the most intense discussions among the New England theologians. Shortly after Edwards, the governmental theory of the atonement became prominent with the majority of New England theologians as well.

These variations from Edwards came to be most clearly seen in the theology of N. W. Taylor of Yale, who advocated a true power of contrary choice in conversion in his development of the distinction between natural and moral ablility. Taylor also developed an essentially utilitarian concept of the nature of true virtue and denied that the death of Jesus was a satisfaction for the wrath of God. Smith in particular entered into discussion with Taylor in a manner equally as vigorous as that of the faculty at Princeton Seminary. To Smith, the New Haven theology was a betrayal of, rather than a true development of, the theological tradition stemming from Edwards.

Smith, as has been mentioned, transferred his ecclesiastical connection to the New School Presbyterian Church when he took up the position at Union Theological Seminary. He found no difficulty in making this transition. In his inaugural address on the occasion of his introduction into the chair of systematic theology, he showed his indebtedness to Edwards when he said,

> Sundry extreme positions are extracted from him by inference, not by testimony; it is what his expositors think he ought to have said, and not just what he did say. Thus fares it, for example, with the philosophemes that all that is moral is in exercises; that the power to the contrary is the radical idea of freedom; and that virtue has ultimate respect to happiness. Neither the divine efficiency, nor the human efficiency, into which the New England controversies afterward degenerated, can be justified from Edwards, any more than from our Confession of Faith.[17]

While Smith clearly saw himself as a conservative theologian, he had a methodological difference from most other contemporary Reformed theologians. In this he saw himself as progressive. He claimed to have developed a "system of theology adapted to our times . . . both conservative and progressive."[18] Smith's methodological approach was to make Christology his formative principle. As early as 1837 he wrote, "My object is to make and harmonize a system which shall make Christ the central point of all religious truth."[19]

This Christological method is evident in his main theology text, *System of Christian Theology*, which is divided into three main sections: "Antecedents of Redemption," "The Redemption Itself," and "The Kingdom of Redemption." Under these headings he discusses the traditional loci of theology. His method no doubt was influenced by his German experience, and, while disagreeing with some of the German theologians, especially Schleiermacher and Dorner, he could applaud their emphasis on Christ as the center of their theological enterprises.

Smith's German influence, however, was not alone in the formation of his methodology. In his inaugural address in 1850 as the chair of church history at Union, he appealed to the historical Christocentrism of Edwards's unfinished *A History of the Work of Redemption* as his model for teaching church history.[20] Mark Noll points out that Smith had a particular fondness for this work.[21]

Smith was never completely satisfied with the results of his methodology, but he felt that it was the most fruitful method for doing theology.[22] As will be seen in our later discussion of his critique of the New Haven theology, it was one of his key safeguards against what he saw as the main error of many of the later New England theologians, i.e., the imposition of an ethical starting point rather than a theological one.

This opposition to an ethical starting point was very important to Smith. He said,

One of the reasons— is it not so— why theology has been less fruitful, is that we study ethics and not divinity, our own words, and not the will of God and expect in psychology to find the being of God. But the registry of God's wisdom is in His own revelation.[23]

While Smith himself was a capable philosopher, holding to a modified common sense realism, he was quite critical of those who allowed philosophical reasoning to determine the shape of their theology.

As previously mentioned, one of the key issues among nineteenth-century American Congregationalists and Presbyterians was anthropology. Perhaps in no other area of his theology was it so obvious that Smith intended to follow Edwards. For example, Smith had a strong concept of the unity of the human race in the classical Augustinian and Reformed tradition. He said,

What he is as a member of race is the substratum of what he is as an individual being. The unity of the race as a whole underlies the idea of the individual. . . . The unity and solidarity of the race is at the basis of the doctrines of sin and redemption. . . . The race is an idea before the individual . . . men cannot be considered as isolated beings.[24]

This organic concept of the whole human race is one of his chief weapons in his attack upon those who would deny original sin and inherited depravity.

An area of Smith's anthropology in which his conscious connection with the Edwardsean tradition is evident is in his discussion of the nature of true virtue. Smith stated Edwards's purpose in writing his great treatise, *The Nature of True Virtue*:

The Arminians held that human nature could not be wholly depraved, inasmuch as it retains more or less commonly deemed virtues: honesty, kindness, temperance, etc. His object is to show that, although these may be virtues in a minor sphere, yet they are not true virtues, because they do not contain the essence of true virtue.[25]

Smith's discussion of true virtue was not an uncritical adoption of Edwards's position. He said Edwards's definition of true virtue as "love of being" was too abstract. He instead gave a refined definition of true virtue as "love of all intelligent and sentient beings according to their respective capacities for good, with chief and ultimate respect to the highest good, or holiness."[26] This was set in clear opposition to theories of true virtue that defined it as happiness. (He particularly criticized Taylor for making subjective happiness the highest good.)[27] Such views, in his opinion, ultimately led to self-love as the highest good and became by definition "Arminianizing" and ultimately blurred the distinction between right and wrong.[28] He appealed to Jesus' summary of the commandments as pointing to his (and Edwards's) view of true virtue, and he paraphrased his definition by saying, "The fundamental principle of true virtue would be that it consists in love to God and to all other beings in their relations to, and as part of, the divine system of things."[29] Thus, Smith saw the proper definition of true virtue as being essential to the understanding of man as he relates to both God and other men.

In his discussion of the will in particular, Smith very clearly showed the Edwardsean derivation of his thought. In true Edwardsean manner, he defined the will as simply the act of choice.

> The man choosing; the person choosing — is will. The will is not anything distinct from the person; it is the person himself considered as acting or having the power of acting in a certain way, the way of choosing. The distinctive and only function of the will is choice.[30]

He followed Edwards in rejecting what he called "the self-determining power of the will."[31]

Smith declared that it is impossible for the will to determine itself apart from the rest of the person (especially the motives). He followed the typical Edwardsean reduction of a self-determining power to be "a fiction, an absurdity, involving the contradiction that it at the same time is, and is not."[32]

Smith, like Edwards, claimed to have a true doctrine of freedom, yet it was a carefully circumscribed definition of freedom. He said freedom is an essential attribute of will.[33] His definition of freedom was that when one chooses, by definition this choice is free. "Wherever there is choice there is freedom."[34] However, he denied the Arminian definition of freedom as involving "power to the contrary" because it makes freedom reside in what one does not do, rather than what one does.[35] In this connection he also approved of Edwards's assessment of "liberty of indifference" in which the end result of all actions would be their loss of moral quality entirely.[36]

Smith's discussion of the importance of motives points out again the Edwardsean character of his anthropology. Following Edwards's *Freedom of the Will*, he laid down as an essential truth the proposition that "the man in his choice is effectually influenced by motives."[37] Smith appealed to a number of "proofs" of this truth: the fact that the whole concept of reward and punishment is an appeal to motives; that one always asks why a person did this or that action; that the appeals of the gospel presuppose the idea of motives; that for God to have an orderly, providential universe, it must be true; and that one feels he always has a reason for acting and he cannot conceive of an action without a motive.[38] Like Edwards, he appealed to the strongest motive as the determining factor in making a choice and defined the strongest motive as not necessarily that which is intrinsically the strongest but rather "that which appears most desirable at the instant preceding actual choice."[39]

Smith was a determined opponent of the Arminian conception of free will and his opposition is clearly demonstrated in his lengthy review of Methodist theologian Daniel Whedon's book on the will.[40] In this review he charged Whedon with misunderstanding Edwards's distinctions and pointed out that the position advocated by Whedon logically ended one in Pelagianism.

In his discussion of the question of sin, Smith showed his continuity with the historic Reformed tradition, especially as interpreted by Edwards. He began his discussion of the subject by quoting Question 13 of the *Westminster Shorter Catechism,* and, aside from the contemporary German work on sin by Julius Müller, he recommended further reading in Edwards on original sin and in Edwards's disciple, Samuel Hopkins.[41]

Perhaps the clearest section in which Smith not only showed his Edwardsean roots, but lined himself up with the historic Reformed tradition in general, is his lengthy discussion of the fall and original sin. On the question of the historical character of the temptation narratives, Smith clearly stood in the conservative tradition. Even though he said that there may be symbolic elements in the account found in Genesis, he believed in an historical Adam and Eve and an historical fall.[42] In his discussion of original sin in his theology text, he again began that section with an appeal to the *Westminster Shorter Catechism* and summarized:

> The emphasis here is on *mankind:* the fall affected man as man, every man as a member of the human race. The divine dealing was with Adam, not only for himself, but as "a public person." All mankind *descending from him by ordinary generation* are involved in this first act of disobedience.[43]

Smith appealed both to experience and scriptural testimony for his proof of the universal sinfulness of man and developed his position that the biblical view is that depravity affects the whole man and is native to man in his current state.[44] It is interesting to note, though, that Smith said that "the full power of sin is known only by the redeemed, to whom the law has been a schoolmaster to bring them to Christ. Grace has taught them in respect to sin."[45] It is especially informative that he quoted Thomasius, one of the influential nineteenth-century German Christocentric theologians that he admired on this point.[46] Thus, we see some small glimpses of the way in which he applied his Christological method to a traditional theological question.

In his extended discussion of inherited depravity, Smith made frequent reference to Edwards and had a very sharp critique of the work of N. W. Taylor. He was especially critical of Taylor's exegesis of Ephesians 2:3 and said that Taylor made the text read, "We were by nature such that we became through our own act the children of wrath."[47] Smith found this an unacceptable exegesis of the text. It deviated not only from the Edwardsean tradition but was not in line with the best of current exegesis.

On the question of imputation of sin, Smith advocated mediate imputation rather than the federal headship view that was held by Princeton and many other traditional Reformed theologians. In his advocacy of this position, Smith was consciously attempting to stand with the Westminster standards as well as with Edwards, whom he interpreted as teaching mediate imputation.[48] To his way of thinking the historic Augustinian and Reformed tradition emphasized as the source of depravity the natural connection which the race has with Adam.[49]

Interestingly, Mark Noll interprets both Smith and Edwards as teaching a combination of both mediate and immediate imputation.[50] Smith's editor found a note in his posthumous papers that read, "Neither Mediate nor Immediate Imputation is wholly satisfactory." There were no further comments.[51] In light of Smith's clear appeal to the Reformed tradition, the Westminster standards, and the parallels between Adam and Christ which he so strongly developed in his exegesis of Romans 5:12, it seems unreasonable to consider, as some have, Smith's doctrine of original sin to be a departure from Reformed orthodoxy.[52] This is especially true in light of his clear criticism of the New Haven theology.

To examine one more important area of Smith's theological anthropology, it is helpful to look at his discussion of natural and moral ability. He considered this a crucial theological question (as evidenced by his sharp critique of Whedon and Taylor for confusing the issues), and he again had a clear dependence on Jonathan Edwards. He set forth the position, "Man has the natural ability to repent, while he is morally unable, and the two are consistent with each other. This is the New England Statement, the position of Edwards."[53]

Smith gave definition to what he meant by natural ability and moral ability. Natural ability is "having all the faculties and powers of choice."[54] Moral inability is "such a state of the heart or will as makes continued sinful action certain, such, e.g., as makes it certain that the sinner will not repent without divine grace."[55] He explicitly criticized the later New England theology for changing the meaning of the term "natural ability" to include the power of contrary choice, which he considered to be an illegitimate definition of natural ability.[56] In his review of Daniel Whedon, he also repudiated the Wesleyan concept of a graciously restored moral ability to all men.[57] Thus, in all the discussions of this vital area of theology, Smith clearly identified himself with the Edwardsean type of Reformed theology and distanced himself from the "Arminianizing" and liberalizing tendencies in much of the contemporary New England theology.

As has been mentioned, Smith was not only a prominent theologian, but also an important churchman. Nowhere were his roles as both churchman and theologian more important than in the reunion of the Old School and New School branches of the Presbyterian church in 1869. The issues between the two churches included most predominantly that of interchurch cooperation (especially with the Congregationalists), the issue of theological differences, and differing views on slavery.[58] The isssue of inter-church cooperation among the New School had taken a different course when the Congregationalists began a new aggressive denominational emphasis of their own, especially in the area of home missions in the mid-nineteenth century. This led the New School to develop many areas of ministry through its own denominational boards and committees, thus developing a greater consciousness of denominational loyalty.[59]

In the crucial issue of slavery, the New School, with its almost exclusively northern constituency and strong New England background, took a decidedly abolitionist viewpoint. (Smith himself was typical of New School people in that he was not only pro-abolitionist, but took a radical Republican view of reconstruction after the war.)[60] The Old School, on the other hand, had a strong southern element, and even many of the northern leaders like Charles Hodge, while not pro-slavery, took a very cautious position and disliked what they saw as the extremism of the abolitionists.[61]

The Civil War played a very decisive factor in changing the relationship of the two churches. First of all, the Old School lost its southern churches when they formed the Confederate Presbyterian Church. Secondly, the Old School not only began to change its position on slavery to a closer approximation of the New School's position, but the membership was caught up in the patriotic fervor of the importance of maintaining the Union as well. The New School was also strongly in support of the federal government. Marsden says, "From the outset of the war New School Presbyterians were united in maintaining that it was the duty of Christians to help preserve the federal government."[62] Marsden demonstrates the millennial overtones of much of the patriotic fervor of the New School.[63] As the Old School progressively changed from mild opposition to slavery to a strong abolitionist attitude and imbibed the patriotic fervor of the war, the position of the two churches by 1864 became virtually indistinguishable.[64]

During most of the years of separation between the two parties, there had been a number on both sides who had advocated reunion. When the issues of ecclesiastical cooperation and attitudes toward slavery were no longer divisive, the only major problem remaining was theology. It was here that Smith played a crucial role. Not only had he taught a conservative theology at one of the leading New School seminaries, but he was highly respected by many Old School leaders. A. A. Hodge said that Smith was the "greatest theologian of the American Presbyterian Church."[65] Lyman Atwater of Princeton, at first an opponent of reunion, became an advocate of union because of his conclusion that the graduates of Union had become thoroughly imbued with the sound theology of Smith. Also, the fact that Union graduates were accepted for ordination without any objections even in Old School presbyteries impressed Atwater.[66] Charles Hodge, who opposed the reunion to the end, told Smith that if all the New School men were like him, he would have no fear of reunion.[67]

Thus, Smith's theology was seen as thoroughly orthodox and was acceptable to the Old School men. While most of them did not explain their anthropology in terms of the particular Edwardsean distinctions and would not have been satisfied with Smith's view of mediate imputation nor some aspects of his doctrine of the atonement, they did not see any serious problems. Thus, during the war, fraternal relations were established between the two churches and reunion discussions began.[68]

While Smith's theology was acceptable to Old School men, there was concern among many of them that the New Haven theology of Taylor was being tolerated by the New School. The basis of this charge was that some of the men who had been the reason for the division of 1837 had never been disciplined by the New School. In 1864 Smith had preached a sermon as moderator of the New School general assembly advocating reunion. In this discourse he made the claim that the overwhelming majority of the New School had moved away from the somewhat looser interpretation of the Westminster standards of its earlier days. "Our branch of the church is much closer to its standards, taken even in the strictest interpretation, than it was a quarter of a century ago."[69]

Smith was later called upon to defend the reunion just before it was consummated. In 1867, during the time the Old School was considering the reunion issue, Charles Hodge wrote an article critical of the reunion in the *Princeton Review* of July 1867. Hodge argued that the New School had a much more lax definition of subscription to the confession and that the Old School "would be guilty of a great moral wrong should it accept of the proposed plan."[70] Hodge's article brought a swift reply from Smith in two ways.

Smith's first reply was to publish a forty-two page article in *The American Presbyterian and Theological Review* specifically refuting Hodge's charges. He began his response by saying:

> If the New School and the Old School be here as represented, all talk about reunion is a waste of breath; for the [Princeton] *Review* knows that we deny these charges, and yet reiterates them, as if the dictum were infallible against our disclaimer.[71]

Smith argued that changes had come over both schools,[72] that he personally knew many Old School men who made the same distinction between moral and natural ability that he did and adopted mediate imputation,[73] that those who "deny these cardinal doctrines of the Reformed System" (including original sin and inability) were not admitted to the New School ministry,[74] and that Hodge's claim that the New School tolerated the anthropology of the New Haven theology was simply wrong; in fact, a document drawn up by the New School repudiated the essential features of that system.[75] Thus, Smith said that the New School was thoroughly orthodox and he gave a number of historical examples of minor differences among confessional Reformed theologians who were yet all considered a legitimate part of the orthodox Reformed tradition.[76]

However, Smith added an answer to Hodge of a different type. In November 1868, in the middle of the merger discussions between the Old School and the New School, a "Presbyterian National Union Convention" was held in Philadelphia composed of delegates from all the Presbyterian bodies in America (including, in addition to those from the Old School and the New School, delegates from the Southern Church, the United Presbyterian Church, the Reformed Presbyterian Church, the Cumberland Presbyterian Church and the Reformed Dutch Church).[77] The idea behind the convention was to explore the possibility of the union of all the churches. Smith was a delegate from the New School and when the discussion on the form of subscription was being formulated, Smith presented a motion that his biographer described as "a stroke of statesmanship which will always be memorable in the annals of Presbyterianism."[78] Smith proposed that instead of the usual subscription to the confessional statement of the church, the words be added, "It being understood that this Confession is received in its proper historical, that is, the Calvinistic or Reformed, sense."[79] This addition, which took everyone by surprise, was not adopted by the convention, and the convention did not succeed in bringing about a union between all the Presbyterians. Yet Smith's proposal showed once and for all that he wanted to go on record for himself and the church he represented as opposing any loose subscription to the confessional standards.

The reunion between the two schools was consummated in 1869. While the Hodges remained opposed to the end, they accepted the situation. They insisted that the terms of subscription had indeed been broadened.[80] While there might be some truth to those charges in light of events in the latter part of the nineteenth century, it certainly was not Smith's intent to broaden them, nor, from his perspective, was it the intent of the overwhelming majority of New School men. Going further, numerous historians have seen a direct link between the New School and the rise of later liberalism,[81] but this view must be seriously tempered by the strong connection between a significant strand of the New School tradition and the later rise of fundamentalism.[82] Also, those with Old School background often were susceptible to the lure of liberalism, as well as those whose roots were New School. The rise of biblical criticism, Darwinism, and the whole complex of issues connected with industrialization are crucial factors in the rise of liberalism, so that a simple direct line between the New School and liberalism cannot be made. Henry Boynton Smith's theology stands as a prime example of a dominant orthodox theology in the later New School tradition.

This affirmation of the orthodoxy of Smith raises the question as to why some have seen Smith as a proto-liberal. The usual reasons given are the direction taken by some of his students and his appreciation of many of the contemporary theologians. As far as his students are concerned, some of them certainly moved in a liberal direction. For example, two of his students, H. A. P. Torrey and George Sylvester Morris, became philosophy professors (at the University of Vermont and Johns Hopkins University, respectively). They departed from the theological framework taught at Union. However, in both cases there were significant other influences on them besides their time of study with Smith.[83]

One of Smith's most prominent students who became liberal, his biographer Lewis F. Stearns, professor of theology at Bangor Seminary, at times wrote almost apologetically about some of Smith's views. He distanced himself from Smith's adoption of Edwardsean anthropology,[84] and criticized him for not giving Christian experience enough of a role in his theological system.[85] Stearns admitted that on the question of the inspiration and inerrancy of Scripture, Smith took a decidedly conservative position and said that a number of his students who adopted the newer biblical criticism had debated among themselves whether or not Smith would have changed his mind if he had lived longer.[86] However, Stearns admitted that "there is not the slightest reason to believe that he would ever have changed his fundamental position respecting the divinity and authority of the Bible.[87] Thus, while Stearns was very appreciative of Smith's theology (he said it was "preeminently living"),[88] he made it clear that he had moved from some of the essential features of his mentor's system. Perhaps the best way to explain this phenomena of the liberal trend of some of Smith's students is the attitude of open inquiry which he fostered, as well as the new intellectual influences of the late nineteenth century.

One of the most recent attempts to see Smith as a proto-liberal is by William Hutchison in his study, *The Modernist Impulse in American Protestantism*. Hutchison claims that Smith adopted positions very similar to Horace Bushnell[89] and that Smith had been instrumental in introducing Schleiermacher to the American evangelicals.[90] As far as these charges are concerned, I have found no influence of Bushnell in Smith. He rarely mentioned him and his apologetic method, with its emphasis on fact, is radically different from Bushnell's fluid theory of language. Smith's view of the atonement and sin are also quite distinct from Bushnell's. Also, while he certainly mentioned Bushnell a few times, his remarks were always very cautious, praising him for his desire to be Christological, but questioning many of his results. Smith was appreciative of some German theology, but his real kinship was to the evangelical theology of men like Tholuck and Thomasius, rather than Schleiermacher. Hutchison also seems to be unfamiliar with the strong Edwardsean emphasis in Smith, which would mitigate against a liberal direction.

Thus, the question of Smith's place in the history of nineteenth-century American Presbyterian theology is raised. I have attempted to show that Smith was a thoroughly orthodox theologian who was open to insights from contemporary theology, while clearly retaining an historic Reformed theology of an Edwardsean cast. His theology deserves to be re-examined and rescued from historical neglect. Such an exercise should prove that, as important as the Princeton tradition is, it is not the only stream of Reformed orthodoxy to be found in American Presbyterianism. Certainly appreciation of the variety in the historic Reformed tradition can have an enriching effect in our attempt to formulate a Reformed theology for today.

NOTES

1. The only recent studies of Smith are the valuable chapter by George Marsden in *The Evangelical Mind and the New School Presbyterian Experience* (New Haven: Yale University, 1970) and two journal articles: Richard A. Muller, "Henry Boynton Smith: Christocentric Theologian," *Journal of Presbyterian History* 61 (1983) 4: 429–44, and William Stoever, "Henry Boynton Smith and the German Theology of History," *Union Seminary Quarterly* 24 (1968) 1:69–89. William Hutchison in his work, *The Modernist Impulse in American Protestantism* (Cambridge: Harvard University, 1976) also mentions Smith in passing, but I am convinced that Hutchison is fundamentally wrong in his assessment of Smith's significance.

2. The discussion of the New School–Old School division is found in Marsden, *Evangelical Mind and the New School Presbyterian Experience*.

3. Marsden says of him, "Smith was easily the first among New School theologians and as such deserves attention as the most influential representative of later New School thought." *The Evangelical Mind*, 156.

4. James Hastings Nichols finds Smith to be a theological equal to Charles Hodge, Horace Bushnell and Philip Schaff, all men from Smith's generation. *Romanticism in American Theology: Nevin and Schaff at Mercersburg* (Chicago: University of Chicago, 1961), 3.

5. H. Shelton Smith, Robert T. Handy, and Lefferts A. Loetscher in their volume *American Christianity: An Historical Interpretation with Representative Documents*, Vol. 2 (New York: Charles Scribner's Sons, 1960–1963), 256, place Smith in the category of "christological liberals" and William Hutchison sees Smith as having an important part in "the modernist impulse." I believe both of these assessments are inaccurate.

6. Mark Noll is one who concurs with this assessment. He argues that Smith came the closest of any nineteenth-century theologian to being a successor to Edwards. (Unpublished paper, "Jonathan Edwards and Nineteenth Century Theology," presented at conference on Jonathan Edwards, Wheaton, IL, October 1984). This paper will appear in the volume *Jonathan Edwards and the American Experience*, eds. Nathan O. Hatch and Harry S. Stout (forthcoming).

7. The major sources of information on Smith are *Henry B. Smith: His Life and Work* (New York: A. C. Armstrong and Son, 1881), a memoir edited by his wife, Katherine Smith, consisting of numerous letters connected with her editorial comments, and the short biography *Henry Boynton Smith* by Lewis R. Stearns (Boston and New York: Houghton Mifflin and Co., 1893), one of his prominent students.

8. Stearns, 8.

9. For a firsthand account of Smith's conversion, see *Smith: Life and Work*, ed. Katherine Smith, 14–15.

10. Stearns, 20.

11. Stoever, 83.

12. Muller, 432.

13. Stearns, 118.

14. Stoever, 83.

15. This information is taken from his memoirs and Stearns, as well as from the biographical sketch in G. L. Prentiss's *Fifty Years of the Union Theological Seminary* (New York: Anson Randolph and Co., 1889).

16. For the most comprehensive survey, see the dated, yet still useful work, *A Genetic History of the New England Theology* by Frank H. Foster (Chicago: University of Chicago, 1907).

17. Henry Boynton Smith, "The Idea of Christian Theology as a System" in *Faith and Philosophy*, ed. George L. Prentiss (New York: Scribner, Armstrong & Co., 1877), 159.

18. Henry Boynton Smith, *Introduction to Christian Theology*, ed. William S. Karr (New York: A. C. Armstrong, 1883), 44.

19. Muller citing Philip Schaff, *Theological Propaedeutic: A General Introduction to the Study of Theology* (New York: Charles Scribner's Sons, 1892), 398.

20. Smith, *Faith and Philosophy*, 59–60.

21. Mark Noll, "Jonathan Edwards and Nineteenth Century Theology."

22. Smith, *Introduction to Theology*, iv.

23. Ibid., vii.

24. Henry Boynton Smith, *System of Christian Theology*, 4th ed., rev., edited by William S. Karr (New York: A. C. Armstrong and Son, 1891), 162.

25. Ibid., 198.

26. Ibid., 223.

27. Ibid., 210.

28. Ibid., 211.

29. Ibid., 231.

30. Ibid., 238.

31. Ibid., 239.

32. Ibid.

33. Ibid., 242.

34. Ibid.

35. Ibid.

36. Ibid., 243.

37. Ibid., 245.

38. Ibid.

39. Ibid. 247.

40. Entitled "Whedon on the Will" and reprinted in *Faith and Philosophy*, 359ff.

41. Smith, *System*, 260.

42. Ibid., 260–61.

43. Ibid., 274.

44. Ibid., 274–77.

45. Ibid., 274.

46. He quoted Thomasius as saying "It is a striking fact in Scripture that statements of the depth and power of sin are chiefly from the regenerate," undocumented quote, *System*, 275.

47. Smith, *System*, 281.

48. The interpretation of Edwards on this issue is somewhat divided. Charles Hodge (*Systematic Theology*, Vol. II, 208) saw Edwards as teaching a form of the realistic theory. B. B. Warfield ("Edwards and the New England Theology" in *Works of Warfield*, Vol. IX, 530 –31) saw Edwards as teaching both mediate and immediate imputation. John Murray (*The Imputation of Adam's Sin*, 94) saw Edwards as eesentially in the camp of immediate imputation on the basis of an overlooked distinction between initial and confirmed corruption in Edwards. For a full discussion of Smith in relation to the rest of the Reformed tradition, see George P. Hutchinson, *The Problem of Original Sin in American Presbysterian Theology* (Nutley, NJ: Presbyterian and Reformed, 1972).

49. Smith, *System*, 287.
50. Noll, "Jonathan Edwards and Nineteenth Century Theology."
51. Smith, *System*, 285, n. 1.
52. J. Oliver Buswell, though he did not directly mention Smith, said that the only doctrine of the atonement which is compatible with mediate imputation is the moral influence theory (*A Systematic Theology of the Christian Religion*, Vol. I, 298–99). Hutchinson shows the clear lack of agreement on the question of original sin among nineteenth-century orthodox American Presbyterians.
53. Smith, *System*, 327.
54. Smith, *System*, 328.
55. Ibid.
56. Ibid.
57. Smith, *Faith and Philosophy*, 393–94.
58. For a good discussion of all the issues involved, see Marsden.
59. See Marsden's chapter, "The Triumph of Denominationalism, 1852–1861."
60. Smith, *Memoir*, 251.
61. For a complete discussion of the church's attitudes toward slavery and the Civil War, see Lewis Vander Velde, *The Presbyterian Churches and the Federal Union, 1861–1869* (Cambridge: Harvard University, 1932).
62. Marsden, 200.
63. See his chapter, "Civil War: The Flag and the Cross."
64. For complete documentation as exhibited by the preaching, writing and official pronouncements of the Old School, see Vander Velde.
65. Quoted in Vander Velde, 365.
66. Marsden, 226.
67. Quoted in *Memoir*, 281.
68. For a full discussion of these events, see Marsden, 212–230, and Vander Velde, 479–525.
69. Henry B. Smith, "Christian Union and Ecclesiastical Reunion," *Faith and Philosophy*, 282.
70. Quoted in Vander Velde, 511.
71. Henry B. Smith, "Presbyterian Reunion," *American Presbyterian and Theological Review*, new series, 5 (October 1867), 634.
72. Ibid., 635.
73. Ibid., 650.
74. Ibid., 654.
75. Ibid., 648.
76. Ibid.
77. See Vander Velde, 511–12.
78. Stearns, 300.
79. Ibid.
80. Zenos made this claim on the basis of Hodge's exposition of the terms of subscription in his classes at Princeton Seminary, ten years after the reunion. Andrew Zenos, *Presbyterianism in America* (New York: Thomas Nelson and Sons, 1937), 93.
81. For example, Edwin H. Rian, *The Presbyterian Conflict* (Grand Rapids: Eerdmans, 1940), and Lefferts A. Loetscher, *The Broadening Church: A Study of Theological Issues in the Presbyterian Church Since 1869* (Philadelphia: University of Pennsylvania, 1957).
82. See Marsden's epilogue, "The New School Presbyterian Tradition in the Twentieth Century — Fundamentalist or Liberal?" and his essay on the New School in the present volume.
83. On Torrey, see Lewis S. Feuer, "H. A. P. Torrey and John Dewey, Teacher and Pupil," *American Quarterly* 10 (Spring 1958):34–54, and George Dykhuizen, "John Dewey, the Vermont Years," *Journal of the History of Ideas* 20 (1959):515–44. On Morris, see Marc

Edward Jones, *George Sylvester Morris: His Philosophic Career and Theistic Idealism* (Philadelphia: David McKay, 1948).

84. Stearns, 208.

85. Ibid., 195.

86. Ibid., 198.

87. Ibid., 199.

88. Ibid., 187.

89. William Hutchison, *The Modernist Impulse in American Protestantism* (Cambridge: Harvard University, 1976), 45.

90. Ibid., 88.

Paul H. Heidebrecht

13 Chicago Presbyterians and the Businessman's Religion, 1900–1920

A N ANONYMOUS EDITORIAL in the August 23, 1906, *Interior,* a Chicago-based Presbyterian journal, entitled "A Lay Address to the Ministry by a Pew Occupant," voiced the concerns of one layman for a modernized brand of Christianity. "Modernity is not our fault. It is our inheritance from the ages," this individual argued, so "cease trying to adjust us to some medieval theological hypothesis of life. Help us to adjust to the present crisis. Give us Christ's simple teachings on the everyday virtues. We need this ethical preaching."[1]

The sentiments of this beleagured soul hardly represented all Presbyterian church members, but the criticism did reflect a widespread desire for a religion more suited to the urban industrial culture. Presbyterian clergy were by no means slack in providing the contemporary gospel demanded by increasing numbers of laymen, but the initiative gradually passed into the hands (and minds) of men and women who sat in the pews. The early decades of this century reveal a distinct aggressiveness on the part of leading laymen in urban churches who banded together to accomplish specific religious tasks. In the course of "making religion efficient" (a popular phrase of the period), these laymen shaped evangelical Protestantism more powerfully than most ministers and theologians of the time realized.

Historical accounts of the collapse of the Protestant consensus in America usually focus upon the theological debates between conservative and liberal ministers and seminary professors (most of which began in the 1890s and continued up through the 1920s). Frequently overlooked are the subtle and not-so-subtle adjustments made by laymen that served to undermine the Protestant ethos of the nineteenth century. Whether one calls this process the modernization, secularization, accommodation, or domestication of Protestantism, it would appear that the flock was often one step ahead of its shepherds. The unsophisticated theological constructions of these laymen deserve more attention for they clearly impact the course of Presbyterianism in this century.

This study proposes to explore this phenomenon within the framework of one presbytery and with reference to a selected group of laymen. The Chicago Presbytery is particularly suitable because during the period of 1890 to 1920, it contained clergy of both traditional and progressive orientation. As a body, the presbytery simultaneously endorsed both social gospel programs and urban revival campaigns. The laymen chosen for this study were all prominent figures from the corporate world of early-century Chicago. Not only did these individuals influence the economic life of the city, but they also played key roles in various political reform and cultural movements. Accustomed to success in their occupational pursuits, these men offered their services to the churches and religious associations that were struggling to preserve a Christian presence in Chicago.

Presbyterians had been active in Chicago since the city's earliest days, and though never the largest religious body, they were always influential. By 1900 there were over 80 congregations in Chicago and in the surrounding area of northeastern Illinois representing over 20,000 members; more than a dozen of these churches had memberships of over 500. By World War I that number had climbed to 106 churches with over 35,000 members. The increase was due partly to the addition of Cumberland Presbyterian churches as a result of the 1906 denominational merger. It also reflected a vigorous church extension program by the presbytery among the numerous immigrant communities of Chicago. Through settlement houses, missions, and foreign-language Sunday schools, the presbytery eventually established congregations among Bohemians, Poles, Italians, Mexicans, Czechs, Persians, and Asians. Several black congregations also emerged during this period.[2]

The presbytery made gallant efforts to respond to the host of urban ills resulting from the period of tumultuous population growth. Presbyterians were in the forefront of local temperance campaigns, anti-vice crusades, public school battles, and community welfare efforts. The Presbyterian Hospital was a favored charity of the social register set as was the Chicago YMCA.[3] By the end of the War the presbytery had established its own social service commission to deal with "social questions in the light of Christianity."[4] One of the commission's first studies was the 1919 race riot that rocked the city and belatedly awoke the white population to the mushrooming black communities on the south and west sides.

Spiritual concerns remained at the top of the presbytery's agenda, however. The salvation of an individual soul continued to be the only lasting solution to any social problem. Thus, traditional evangelistic approaches were rarely questioned. In fact, Presbyterian ministers were intimately involved with the Gipsey Smith campaign in 1909, the Wilbur Chapman crusade in 1910, and the Billy Sunday crusade in 1918. These urban revivals were in fact sophisticated business operations (Sunday estimated that it cost $395 to save a soul in Chicago), but they still aimed to win allegiance to Christ above all else. Those within the fold required continual spiritual nurture. To this end, the educational agencies of the presbytery poured their energies into more effective Bible instruction. A Presbyterian Training School was launched in 1908 to prepare church workers. Christian Endeavor societies, Young Men's and Young Women's Bible classes, and Presbyterian Brotherhood chapters all received strong support from ministers.

While vigorous on the home front, the presbytery maintained a cosmopolitan view of the world. Foreign missions inspired both clergy and laity; the challenge of evangelizing 100 million heathens around the world, presented eloquently by such Presbyterian national leaders as Robert Speer, a regular visitor to Chicago, enabled denominational fund-raising efforts to be rather successful. In 1911 the presbytery called the proposed general arbitration treaties the "longest step in advance of the promotion of peace since the birth of Christ."[5] Yet the presbytery ardently supported the war effort and even urged Wilson to demand nothing less than unconditional surrender from the Kaiser and his allies.[6]

Perhaps because of their penchant for doing business in an orderly (and, therefore, plodding) fashion, Presbyterians were rarely innovators. They tended to move slowly, reaching positions only after arduous deliberation. Any zealots in their ranks easily became frustrated with the inertia of the decision-making process. Nevertheless, Presbyterian doctrine had the effect of reinforcing a sense of responsibility for the larger society in which the church operated; it tended to encourage clergy and laity to enter periodically the public arena on behalf of higher values and noble ideals. Neither the ministers nor the church members in the Chicago Presbytery were to any degree isolationists. They consciously applied their faith, however that was understood, to the exigencies of their world. This can be observed in the examples of several leading Presbyterian layman.

Charles Holt, a lawyer and active member at Second Presbyterian Church until his death in 1918, exemplified a loyalty to his denomination that earned him the praise of many in the church hierarchy. Holt pioneered the Presbyterian Brotherhood, a loose national affiliation of men's societies that had begun to emerge in Presbyterian churches in the 1880s and 1890s.[7] The purpose of the Brotherhood was to promote a spirit of loyal service to the church. Holt directed several national conventions at which thousands of Presbyterian men and clergy gathered to hear well-known speakers and engage in dialog and mutual encouragement.

For Holt "the church is a worthy place for the investment of our life and influence in the service of humanity."[8] The church was especially a context for men because it appealed to their "sense of the heroic," and it was a useful "instrument for the adjustment of antagonisms." In the church, religion could be infused with the ethical and philanthropic spirit. The ideals of righteousness could be put into practice. Therefore, he pleaded for "individual loyalty to the church from the inside, and that we stop criticizing and go to work."

In 1911 the Brotherhood under Holt's leadership endorsed and actively supported the Men and Religion Forward Movement, an inter-denominational campaign to arouse men in urban churches to engage in evangelism and social service. The campaign lasted for about a year with speakers like Charles Stelzle and Raymond Robins traveling from city to city conducting rallies and advertising the ideals of Christian service. Holt noted that the dominant theme of the Forward Movement was "more men in the Church and more efficiency in the men."[9] Not only was this movement a lay phenomenon, it was a public relations campaign conducted by men who attempted to apply the best of sales technology on behalf of the church.

What attracted Holt to "men's work" in the Presbyterian Church was the experience of belonging to a powerful movement. He likened his Brotherhood to a military campaign, the goal of which was "the winning of the world, especially the men of the world, and loyalty to Jesus Christ and his Church."[10] As he saw it, "the pathetic eagerness of men to be about something in their Church life and for Jesus Christ" could only be satisfied in a broad movement that transcended theological disputes and even distinctions between clergy and laity and emphasized "the great facts of eternal destiny, of sin, of forgiveness, of the love of our Elder Brother, revealing the greater love of our Father."

Another layman of similar dedication was Henry Parsons Crowell, one of the founders and by 1901, president of Quaker Oats. Though a somewhat nominal church member in his earlier years, Crowell underwent a personal religious awakening at the age of forty-three and became an ardent church leader.[11] He served as an elder at Fourth Presbyterian Church, strongly supported the presbytery's church extension and foreign missions committees and added his name to a variety of evangelistic and municipal reform efforts. But he reserved the bulk of his energy and money for the Moody Bible Institute in Chicago over which he maintained a controlling influence for several decades.

Crowell's involvement with the institute reveals a man who combined deep piety with tough business acumen. An admirer of D. L. Moody whom he never met, Crowell joined the institute board in 1901 two years after Moody died. When he became board chairman in 1904, he engineered a change in the institute's leadership and restructured the school along corporate lines. This involved a power struggle with some of Moody's hand-picked successors but Crowell proved to be more than their match. He had long before learned how to maintain the competitive edge when he outmaneuvered opponents in the milling industry and gained control of the American Cereal Company, the holding company of Quaker Oats. Once in power, the "Godly autocrat" as his associates called him, ruled quietly but ruthlessly.

Moody's son-in-law, A. P. Fitt, became the institute's administrator as Moody had requested in his will. Fitt's ally was R. A. Torrey, another member of Moody's inner circle, who simultaneously pastored Moody's Chicago Avenue Church, functioned as institute superintendent, and conducted numerous evangelistic campaigns around the world. Both Fitt and Torrey preferred to rely upon the informal structure of the Moody subculture with its network of evangelists and pastors for support and sustenance. Their goal was quite simple: to teach lay people the Bible and equip them to be church workers.

Yet the financial pressures upon the institute allowed Crowell to steer the school's direction. He enlarged the board from seven to fifteen trustees, almost all of them businessmen and professionals. He centralized administrative control in the hands of an executive committee composed of himself, Fitt, and the man whom he wanted to lead the institute, James Gray. Crowell personally hired Gray at the rather astounding salary of $5,000. Torrey, more interested in evangelistic work, faded from the scene and by 1908, Fitt was gone as well. [12]

In the following years, Crowell and Gray guided the institute's development according to a business model. Crowell's financial stewardship program brought long-term stability though he occasionally had to underwrite losses. The curriculum, though heavily Bible-centered, became more academic in its framework. Gradually, the school carved out its own constituency and geared itself to service its needs. Theological controversies were avoided as a rule and little effort was made to engage in dialog with those who were more accepting of biblical criticism, such as Moody's own son, William.

Crowell identified himself with those Protestants who held to a strict view of biblical inerrancy, a position that was largely abandoned by leading Presbyterian clergy in the 1920s. (Ironically, Crowell did not sever his relations with the Presbyterian Church until 1943 at the age of eighty-eight, and then only in protest to the election of Henry Sloane Coffin as moderator of the general assembly.) He viewed the institute as a missionary organization that would send biblically-literate laymen into the front lines of the church's mission outposts. [13]

Probably the most prominent name among Chicago Presbyterians was McCormick. Not only was this family responsible for the presence of a major theological seminary in Chicago, but it controlled one of the larger manufacturing interests in the Midwest, International Harvester. When the patriarch and reaper inventor, Cyrus McCormick, died in 1884, his son, Cyrus, who was still a college student at Princeton at the time, took over the family firm. McCormick's wife, Nettie, who was 27 years his junior, remained an influential figure in the family business and personally directed the distribution of $8 million in philanthropic gifts (about half of it went to educational agencies).[14]

Both the young Cyrus and his mother remained loyal Presbyterians and somewhat sympathetic to McCormick's Old School convictions. The seminary continued to be a major family interest receiving sizable donations on regular occasions. The faculty hired before the 1920s tended to be pious scholars who showed a great willingness to assist the congregations in the presbytery. James G. K. McClure, who became the seminary's first president in 1905, was one who avoided "controversial theology" and who in the eyes of the trustees personified "the best of modern Christianity."[15] This posture certainly pleased the McCormicks who did not mind a dose of "enlightened theology" provided that the Presbyterian network stayed intact.

The McCormicks applied their wealth to a variety of religious causes. The salaries of world travelers, John R. Mott and Sherwood Eddy, both of whom represented the burgeoning American missionary enterprise, were heavily underwritten by the McCormicks. The International YMCA and Princeton University also received large donations and the personal interest of Cyrus and Nettie.

Another business family with firm religious convictions was the Farwells, a clan of New Englanders who became part of Chicago's early elite. John V. Farwell, Sr., established himself in the dry goods business and was a close associate of the shoe salesman-turned-evangelist, Moody. The firm was eventually absorbed into the Sears, Roebuck Company though John Farwell, Jr., formed his own company. The younger Farwell was a major figure in the Chicago YMCA as his father had been.

The most notable member of the family was Farwell's cousin, Arthur Burrage Farwell, who helped launch both the Hyde Park Protective Association and the Law and Order League.[16] The initial impetus of these pressure groups was to campaign for local option laws turning large sections of the city into prohibition districts. At the same time, there was concern to ensure the enforcement of existing regulations upon saloons. However, they were soon drawn into battles against corrupt aldermen, fraudulent voting practices, houses of prostitution, the "white slave traffic," and the intrusion of Negro populations into traditionally white neighborhoods. Arthur Farwell became a crusader for righteousness, speaking in public schools "to impress upon the mind of children everything that makes for purity, industry and integrity."[17]

John Farwell, Jr., not only participated with his cousin in the Protective Association but also served for a time on the directorate of the state Anti-Saloon League. These prohibitionists tended to link their fight against liquor with an anti-Catholic "Protestant Americanism" and a fairly overt racism.[18]

One Presbyterian businessman who published some of his religious reflections was David Forgan, a Scottish-born banker who actually gained his reputation as a champion golfer. Forgan grew up in a strict Scottish Presbyterian home and recalled attending five religious services every Sunday. But he outgrew his "child-like faith" in the simple "scheme of salvation" and preferred a religion of inspiration that protected him from "soul-shrivelling materialism."[19] By 1925 he noted, "It is years since I heard a minister in the pulpit refer to the fall of man, original sin, the pains of hell, a need of conversion in the old sense of an instantaneous change. What we get now are lectures and discussions in moral philosophy. I believe that the example and teachings of Jesus Christ applied to every experience of life is the best preaching. He taught little doctrine, except the Fatherhood of God and the brotherhood of man."

True religion for Forgan combined reverence for God with human determination, what he called "matters of Grip and Grit."[20] He elevated the "bulldog traits of human nature" which had served him well in his business career; human willpower brought into some kind of relationship with the "will of God" was the key to success. Forgan's hero, Theodore Roosevelt, stood "right with God" because he stood right with his home, his community, his country, and his world.

Forgan credited businessmen for the quality of urban life observing that "any good work, whether it is charitable, civic, religious, or anything else that is well done . . . contains a few good successful business men who are not only supplying the funds but have their hands on the management."[21] He was gratified that the press and the pulpit were showing more respect for the honorably successful businessman.

One other Chicago Presbyterian deserves mention. Howard Van Doren Shaw, a leading architect whose clients included major business figures, articulated through his work a religious orientation that suited his clients admirably. An active member of the upper-crust Second Presbyterian Church, Shaw redesigned the church nave after a fire in 1900. He introduced free-standing angels and exquisite stained-glass windows that reflected the European tastes of many Chicago elites.[22] He also designed the ornate sanctuary of Fourth Presbyterian Church and numerous homes for the newer aristocrats, like Adolphus Bartlett and Thomas Donnelley. His residential designs offered conservative appearances with gracious living space and elaborate gardens that usually required hired workers to maintain. Quite unlike his contemporary, Frank Lloyd Wright, who despised Eastern establishment standards and tried to create a Midwest prairie school of architecture, Shaw attempted no overt ideological statement through his work nor did he try to challenge the establishment in any way.[23] Shaw gave his clients what they wanted; he was a superb craftsman, but not a self-conscious intellectual. Shaw and Wright were friendly but didn't seem to understand one another. Shaw's religious inclinations moved along similar lines. A devout family man, he viewed his faith in terms of performing duties and holding positions within the corporate structure of the church.

Isolating a set of religious beliefs peculiar to these men of the business and professional community may not be possible, but one can detect certain tendencies in their religious perspectives. These tendencies proved to be critical in the formation of the self-styled modern Christianity.

One emphasis that already has been illustrated is their preference for the practical in religion rather than the esoteric. Religion of any significance had to relate to the ordinary concerns of these laymen; this usually implied the ethical dimensions of Christianity, but it also suggested a religion that worked, that produced tangible results. Speaking at a Religious Education Association convention in 1904, *Interior* editor, Nolan Best, pleaded, "Let us advocate practical things in our papers rather than retail much theory."[24] He deplored "the preponderance of the scholastic element" in the religious education field and called for "a great popular brotherhood of people loyal to the Bible and determined to exalt it as the law of mankind." He urged his fellow journalists to concentrate on reporting illustrations of how religion works.

Woodrow Wilson, who was highly regarded among Chicago Presbyterians, gave frequent expression to a this-worldly faith rooted in the moral actions of individuals. "Our Christian religion is the most independent and robust of all religions," Wilson claimed, "because it puts every man upon his own initiative and responsibility."[25] In Christianity men discovered the underlying principles of moral action and a vision of a society that could be achieved by selfless Christian leaders. Wilson often depicted himself as orthodox in his faith, though unorthodox in his understanding of the traditional doctrines of the Christian faith. He was able, like many other Presbyterian laymen, to distinguish between two modes of Christian thought, one that operated within the walls of the church (and seminary) and one that functioned outside the walls. Of course, his sympathies were with the latter.

One obvious product of this pragmatic bias was the keen desire to apply notions of business efficiency to religious activity. Nolan Best described a "Gospel of Efficiency" which attempted to employ the insights of scientific management to the church.[26] He warned that running a church on business principles was not as easy as it sounded, but it could be done if a church determined to "increase decidedly the average output from each individual worker." This would require studying each man's individual fitness, deciding what constituted a fair product to expect, and enforcing any rules and policies that would be developed. Though some churches took up this challenge, the agencies of the churches, dominated as they were by laymen, were even more inclined to apply efficiency standards. Local chapters of the Sunday School Association, the Christian Endeavor Society, and the Presbyterian Brotherhood did so with great vigor. Typically, these efficiency campaigns led to detailed statistical analyses of an agency's work and to streamlined administrative structures that centralized control in the hands of a few individuals with professional credentials.

If the laymen gravitated toward those aspects of Christian action that resembled their vocational experience, they also selected elements more suited to their identity as "men on the make" (a phrase popularized by Wilson). In other words, they tended to describe modern Christian faith as masculine rather than feminine. Ann Douglas in her *The Feminization of American Culture* argues that through the nineteenth century, Protestantism became associated with a feminine image, particularly within more liberal churches. Like their women parishioners, liberal clergy became purveyors of a sentimentalized culture. They attempted "to achieve religious ends through literary means."[27] Douglas further suggests that the old virile religion, especially of the frontier variety, gave way to dignified unassertive sentimentality that rendered ministers, if not the church itself, irrelevant to many people.

By the early twentieth century, this feminine image of religion was clearly under attack. Active laymen portrayed vital Christian faith as distinctively masculine and inherently appealing to successful men. Such a vision was the foundation of the numerous male-oriented religious movements, such as the Brotherhoods (by 1909, a dozen denominations had such associations), the Laymen's Missionary Movement, the Laymen's Evangelistic Council, the Men and Religion Forward Movement, and the increasingly popular Men's Bible classes (that often doubled as church baseball teams).[28] The concept of masculinity utilized by these groups was rarely defined; usually, it was linked with modern business practices, with hard work by dedicated men, and with militant crusading on behalf of a glorious cause.

The Chicago Presbyterian Brotherhood published its own journal, *Men At Work* for a period of years, and extolled the masculine, virile qualities of the Christian religion. The periodical beckoned Presbyterian men to respond to their "common ancestry whose heroism in service for Christ" was their glory, and with their masculine powers, to "get to work."[29] To further inspire its readers, the editor included reviews of "masculine religious books" especially written for "the life of a red-blooded, hard-headed, all-around Christian man."[30]

Evangelistic work whether overseas or locally became a domain of male lay leadership. "There is something heroic about the task of missions," wrote William Ellis, also a *Continent* editor. "It is a job for strong men. Missions thrill men, not only because of its innate heroism and chivalry, but also because they are a mighty enterprise on a sound reasonable basis."[31] Promoting the gospel required the same skills as merchandising a product. Argued Ellis, "The essential masculinity of missionary propaganda is certain to impress every man who makes a first-hand study of it in operation."

Revival campaigns such as the ones led by Wilbur Chapman and Billy Sunday were labeled as "businessmen's campaigns" because of the direct involvement of prominent figures like Crowell and the use of "businesslike methods" including precisely-timed sermons and efficiently-conducted altar calls.[32] Sunday himself did not hesitate to invoke a business image in his revivals. "I am not only a preacher but a businessman," he said. "I endeavor to bring 1. System and organization; 2. Business principles; 3. Common sense into revival work."[33]

These men hardly supplanted the hosts of women who filled the ranks of loyal church workers, but they controlled the key leadership positions of the religious agencies. While they did not all oppose women's suffrage, they continued to relegate women to other spheres of activity. "There is a womanly instinct," opined the *Continent* in 1918, "which ordinarily makes it impossible for a woman to think of a property interest before a human interest."[34] Any woman who might have possessed such a property interest certainly would have found it difficult to penetrate the exclusive men's clubs where business deals were often made.

The thrust of this emphasis on masculine Christianity tended to diminish the stature of the clergy. Though ministers participated actively in the men's organizations, they did so partly because they were men. Charles Holt viewed the Brotherhood as transcending lay-clergy distinctions. Within the church itself, ministers maintained a priestly status but they were less able to transfer their authority into other realms. Woodrow Wilson even went so far as to say that the ministry was "the only profession which consists in *being* something" as opposed to doing something.[35] Like Levites, ministers could serve in their tabernacles but laymen carried the burden of religion into the real world.

A third tendency in this businessmen's version of religion was to be inclusive rather than narrow. Both in their occupational pursuits and their civic affairs, they cooperated with laymen from other denominations and developed close working relationships. Thus, they were less inclined to press denominational distinctives. In 1918 the *Continent* took the side of John D. Rockefeller, Jr., when he was attacked by fellow Baptists for suggesting that baptism by immersion ought not to be a required belief of church members. "Everybody must be willing," editorialized the journal, "that the majority shall decide all joint practices, and that individual faith shall be governed entirely by individual conscience. A disagreement over a specific doctrine or a specific church custom requires the disagreeing elements to divide or else abase their convictions."[36]

For most Presbyterian laymen in this period, such ecumenism did rest on a commitment to Jesus Christ as the focal point of their faith. In their minds, he was still the supernatural Son of God as well as the teacher of the world's finest system of morals and the exemplar of self-sacrificing service. Some, like Holt and Crowell, spoke of maintaining personal communication with Christ; others, like Forgan, stressed the example of Jesus, even in such matters as church attendance.

The origin of these religious perspectives can be traced partly to the environment in which these laymen worked. An unusual numer of Presbyterians occupied the upper echelons of Chicago's corporate world. They belonged to the old elite (e.g., Marshall Field, George Pullman, John Farwell, Cyrus McCormick, Philip Armour) and to the new (e.g., John Shedd, Ezra Warner, David Forgan and George Reynolds).[37] These men provided the muscle for the burgeoning Chicago industrial community. Shedd and Forgan were the first and second presidents of the Chicago Association of Commerce, a powerful affiliation of merchants organized in 1905. "Our Association is not primarily a reform organization," stated Forgan. "The reforms it may attempt will be as stepping-stones to good business, and to enhance the city's standing as a market and financial center. We would seek to cultivate greater respect for law and order, whereby business may prosper."[38] According to Forgan, the most able men of the city could be found in the association. These "men of brains" as Shedd called them were responsible for the rapid growth of Chicago as "the storehouse for the nation's treasure— a center of finance, commerce and industry."[39] Their civic patriotism was to be applauded and was to serve as an inspiraton to the "men of brawn" who had not as of then been very cooperative.

Though association members were indefatigable boosters for Chicago's commercial opportunities (and sent delegations regularly to other cities and countries encouraging trade and investment), they also formed a common front against organized labor. Several Presbyterian businessmen were involved directly in efforts to crush strikes and curb union activity. The young Cyrus McCormick received a rude initiation into labor strife when many of his workers became involved in the disturbances that led up to the Haymarket Riot in 1886. Forced to acquiesce to union demands, he developed a bitter hatred for unionism and determined to resist its intrusion into his company on every occasion. This led him to experiment with various scientific management and welfare union schemes that gained him a favorable reputation among some social scientists but rarely the respect of his employees who mostly wanted higher salaries and job security, the two things over which McCormick was incalcitrant.[40]

As the vice-president of Marshall Field & Company (and president after Field's death in 1906), John Shedd fought several battles with teamster unions, most of which he won.[41] Like Field, Shedd had a strong distaste for the closed shop and helped form both the Illinois Manufacturers' Association in 1897 and the Chicago Employers' Association in 1902 to oppose it. Both employer groups did little to hide their belligerent attitude toward unions, hiring armed guards to protect plants, importing Negro strikebreakers and employing their own private police. The IMA eventually became a powerful lobby in Springfield opposing minimum hour, factory safety, and workmen's compensation legislation.[42] At times the anti-union sentiment of IMA members (Presbyterian John Wilder was one of its directors) bordered on paranoia. Its full-time director, John Glenn, adopted an "IMA — Right or Wrong" stance and at one congressional hearing noted, "I don't see how labor unions and the church can exist together. Anyone who thinks they can doesn't know who Christ expelled from the Temple."[43]

Presbyterian businessmen like Shedd and McCormick did not lack sympathy for the laboring person; they simply had their own ideas about the best interests of the worker. Shedd donated $3 million to the Park District for the construction of an aquarium and for natural history exhibits, all for the benefit of school children. McCormick's interest in the YMCA was shared by many other Presbyterians. The Art Institute, United Charities, the Presbyterian Hospital, and the American Red Cross all received the attention of Presbyterian benefactors. The philanthropy of these individuals was clearly devoted to enhancing the cultural and moral tone of the city which they believed would serve the best interests of all the citizens. However, evil forces in the city threatened the spiritual life of the city: socialists, union bosses, corrupt politicians, saloon-keepers, and prostitutes preyed upon the ordinary citizen. Proper stewardship called for the support of numerous organizations whose mission was to suppress the wicked element (the Municipal Voters' League and the Hyde Park Protective Association were just two of the structures available for this task).

More recent literature on the progressive era has shown the prominent role of business and professional leaders in various reform movements.[44] Their interests were not so much to extend democracy and overthrow vested interests which the rhetoric of the period might suggest, but rather to extend their control over the urban, industrial environment and continue to shape it according to their values. The profile of the Presbyterian businessmen in this study lends support to this conclusion.

Religion can hardly be discounted as a factor in the business leaders' motivation to engage in civic betterment. In fact, some studies have shown there is a distinctly religious side to the whole progressive movement; so intertwined was it that David Johnson claims it is "difficult to discern when progressives were using religion or when they were guided by it."[45] For some, the traditional view that until an individual became a professing Christian, he or she could not be expected to sacrifice their own interests for the societal good, continued to be a strong conviction. Others were content with preserving a Christian influence and general acceptance of Christian moral standards.

One might ask what difference it made, if any, that these men were Presbyterians. The fact that many were officers in their local congregations likely strengthened aristocratic impulses, given the fact that Presbyterianism reflected a republican form of church government by qualified leaders (theoretically, to be determined by spiritual criteria but more easily chosen by external standards of success). Majoritarian democracy was kept in check by Presbyterian structures, a condition that would have pleased these Presbyterian men if it were also true in Chicago politics.

Yet another factor about these Presbyterians was their Anglo-Saxonism. Rooted in the Scotch-Irish immigrations of the eighteenth century, the main stream of Presbyterianism had produced its share of sturdy patriots who conceived of American culture as a distinctively Christian civilization, to be cherished, protected, and expanded. "I believe that the destinies of mankind, the salvation of civilization, and the hope of permanent peace are by God's providence largely in the hands of English-speaking people," claimed Forgan, calling for the ideas of Napoleon and the Kaisers to be discarded and the teachings of Jesus Christ to be adopted.[46] Woodrow Wilson shared a similar view when he said, "The Anglo-Saxon people have undertaken to reconstruct the affairs of the world and it would be a shame upon them to withdraw their hand."[47] Few Chicago Presbyterians objected when Billy Sunday prayed publicly in his crusade, "Thank God the Huns will never see Heaven."[48] Their ministers conveyed the same message in their occasional attacks upon "German ideas and influences." Evanston minister David Hugh Jones even suggested that attending Sunday afternoon concerts was in effect to "promote German Kultur and help the German invasion of our land."[49]

Anglo-Saxonism displayed its racist edge when these Presbyterians viewed both the east European and the black populations of Chicago. Individuals from these inferior races could only achieve success by adopting the ethics of hardworking, white Protestants. That great model of manhood, Jesus Christ, was available to them, according to the *Continent* in 1911: "the negro already is beginning to recognize that color separates absolutely the two races (and) that between white and black, peace and harmony is to depend on their living together in separation but each recognizing the other's rights. In a negro decently dressed, industrious, sober, provident, law abiding and courteous, the white man will find no cause for offense."[50] A few years later the journal urged whites to call blacks "mister" and "mistress" but recognized that "racial aspiration and personal self-esteem alike conspire to make him (the progressive black man) prefer the companionship of his own people."[51] On several occasions the *Continent* protested the rash of Negro lynchings across the nation, even scoring Protestant churches in a Pennsylvania town for not intervening on behalf of a victim. Yet, at the same time, there was little evidence that Presbyterians in Chicago had much familiarity with any black Protestants in Chicago.

Another source of the religious understanding of these Presbyterian businessmen was the ministers who preached to them weekly and articulated the contents of church doctrine. The clergy in the Chicago Presbytery were a conservative group in general; only nineteen percent signed the Auburn Affirmation in 1924, indicating that even at that date a majority were reluctant to question the fundamental doctrines of Christianity.[52] Some of the seminary faculty had obtained advanced degrees in German theological schools and were exploring the implications of the higher criticism of the Bible yet without calling for any wholesale rejection of traditional beliefs (only fourteen percent of the McCormick faculty signed the Affirmation). Theologian Andrew C. Zenos in his *The Elements of Higher Criticism* claimed that it was a useful weapon to employ in Bible study, but not necessary to authenticate the Bible; "the Bible commends itself, apart from criticism or authority of the Church, as a source of religious information and inspiration."[53] Nolan Best sounded the same reassuring note when he wrote that the "true proof of inspiration is that it is profitable." He claimed, "Men obey the Bible because it imperiously calls to what is deepest in the consciousness of their souls."[54] The efficacy of the Bible did not require acceptance of an error-free text because its spiritual power lay elsewhere, in fact, in the sympathetic, but informed reading of its contents. Best urged church workers to teach with an unhostile attitude: "Teach it, teach it, whatever you believe, and just as much as you can believe."[55] (This balancing of an acceptance of biblical authority with a skepticism of the Bible's veracity became increasingly difficult. By 1920 McCormick professor Arthur Hays assigned the individual conscience the authority to determine which books of the Bible were God's revelation.)[56]

If these ministers were willing to concede some of the Bible's authority in areas of scientific and historical knowledge, they continued to campaign for its moral authority. Periodically, the presbytery called for legislation to require a portion of the Bible to be read daily in the public schools. Princeton Seminary professor, Charles Erdman, told a gathering of the Presbyterian Brotherhood, "the Bible is the very foundation of our free institutions, the palladium of our national life."[57] The study of the Bible would result in new efficiency and power for any organization. Apparently, many took that idea seriously for the support of Bible-distribution agencies, the Gideons, and the Pocket Testament League, flourished among Presbyterians.

The Chicago clergy often described religion as a spiritual force, as a dynamo at work in the church and in society as a whole. Charles Lemuel Thompson, a national Presbyterian executive who once pastored in Chicago, said, "the Church must more deeply spiritualize her life and institutions."[58] The machinery of the church was of little value without the activity of a divine spirit.

Zenos depicted the Christian life as a "spiritual movement which begins with the appearance of Christ before the soul, and the soul's acceptance of Him as the revelation of God the Father."[59] Once enlivened, the Christian was able to "infuse his own soul-force" into the affairs of society. He was able to act selflessly and in response to Christ's law of love. Samuel Dickey, another McCormick professor, wrote, "Religion was a matter of the Spirit, and the ultimate authority in morality was the voice of God in the soul."[60]

Despite the archaic vocabulary, these ministers were groping for a viable role for religion. They were convinced that religion, and in particular, the Protestant version, was essential in American society. The church, according to Hyde Park minister Joseph Vance, was a servant of the nation to stabilize society, to Americanize foreigners, and to direct the idealism that had emerged during the war years into constructive channels.[61]

"The people make our laws," argued Chicago minister Hugh Scott, "but the Churches must first make the people and fill them with high ideals of justice, truth and brotherhood before they can make laws that exalt a nation."[62] Added Scott, "Religion blesses and makes unselfish and catholic national aims and ambitions."

In the final analysis, religion became an attitude, one that was to be preferred to the prevailing materialism that was infecting even those within the church; religion meant concern for others in need, respect for moral purity, patriotic fervor, and an appreciation for the Christian heritage. Whether laymen engaged in the business of making money, or in the business of making war, their Christian motivation would in effect sanctify their activity. By focusing their attention upon these inner dynamics, Presbyterian clergy left themselves vulnerable to the further erosion of theological reflection and the decline of influence by the church upon its members.

The religious enemy for many of the clergy was still the Catholics (who monopolized the public schools, detention houses, and health stations to the chagrin of the presbytery).[63] This false religion simply did not fit into their amalgam of Protestantism, patriotism, and modern business values. Interestingly, one of the problems Presbyterians had with Catholics was what they perceived as the supposed dictatorship of priests over Catholic laymen. A *Continent* editorial wondered whether a Catholic should run for national office because he could not be counted upon to refuse the orders of his priest and "go beyond his own church with perfect patriotic fellowship."[64]

There was little hint of any trouble within the fold. Zenos spoke of "exclusionists" within the church, "well-meaning though misguided champions of the old faith."[65] He remained confident that these traditionalists would come to appreciate the modernizing that was incumbent upon the church. At the same time, he maintained close ties with those who espoused the old faith, including Billy Sunday.[66]

This essay has attempted to sketch a profile of a group of laymen and a group of clergy, both operating in a similar environment, both dependent upon each other, and both fleshing out their religious commitments. In comparing the two groups within the Chicago Presbytery, the lay leaders clearly implemented their faith with more self-confidence and optimism. They were able to modernize the faith more easily and gradually redefine the posture of Presbyterianism.

What was at stake in that period was the role of Protestantism in American culture; each denomination struggled with the challenge of modernity, the Presbyterians perhaps as intensely as any of them. In their tradition, the ambivalent relationship of a religion that claimed God's authority over all of life functioning within a nation that wanted to restrict all religion to the private sphere was most pronounced. Though mildly Calvinist, American Presbyterians still carried Puritan baggage, including the ideal of a Christian commonwealth subject to God's laws and ruled by men of spiritual stature. Their acceptance of the separation of church and state was a concession of sorts, to avoid denominational strife; it never meant the separation of God or Christianity from government or any other area. Thus, most Presbyterians never gave up the compulsion to Christianize the nation and institute a sacred covenant between God and America.

At the same time Presbyterians were tough pietists who had grudgingly accepted the fact that the nation would not always be hospitable to them. Not only were there other more powerful denominations, but there were sizable numbers of persons unwilling to affiliate with any church. One result of this acquiescence to religious pluralism was greater concentration upon the church's internal affairs, what Elwyn Smith called the "ecclesiasticizing of church life."[67] This tendency toward disengagement from the culture allowed Presbyterian clergy to focus upon refining doctrinal formulations, stimulating individual piety, and building institutional structures.

This polarity within the Presbyterian mind expressed itself in other forms as well. Allegiance to the system of truth outlined in the *Westminster Confession* had always strained against the earnest desire for genuine religious experience. The trouble arose when that experience could not be explained in the categories of the Confession. This tension had divided Presbyterians several times in the past. Within the Chicago Presbytery prior to the War, it could be felt in the occasional distinctions that emerged between the strict Calvinists associated with Princeton Seminary and the more numerous and more moderate evangelicals, who like Cleland McAfee, pastor of First Church, viewed the Confession as "a platform on which one rises to take wide views. . . . a system glorified by new challenges for these times which Christ and the Holy Spirit present to the Church."[68] The former tended to approach social issues from what they perceived as God's agenda; the latter were more inclined to begin with the human agenda and try to relate Christianity to it.[69]

For the most part the Presbyterian laymen in this study were found on the evangelical, experience-oriented side of the spectrum. Few could have been labeled confessionalists. The same could be said of their ministers, but there was a noticeable difference. The laymen were setting the terms for the church's dialog with the world. They were determining the aspects of the faith that were to be emphasized. They were in fact leading their ministers in applying an updated religion to a modern society. Such an assertion is made with some hesitation because of the limited scope of the study.

The question is not one of whom to credit (or blame) for Presbyterianism's evolution into a pluralist denomination with decidedly liberal sympathies. Rather, the issue was, and still is, one of power. In a period when the traditional authority of the Bible, refracted through the formulations of the Confession, gave way to multiple authorities, and finally to the claims of the individual conscience itself, a way was cleared for men of worldly influence to play a stronger role in shaping a modern faith.

NOTES

A condensed version of this article is to appear in a forthcoming issue of *Journal of Presbyterian History.*

1. *Interior* (Chicago), August 23, 1906.
2. Kenneth Wylie, ed., "Presbyterians in Chicago, 1833–1983" (Chicago: Presbytery of Chicago, 1983); Clifford M. Drury, *Presbyterian Panorama: 150 Years of National Missions History* (Philadelphia: Presbyterian Church of USA, 1952).
3. Joan W. Moore, "Stability and Instability in the Metropolitan Upper Class" (Ph.D. diss., University of Chicago, 1959); Emmott Dedmon, *Great Enterprises: 100 Years of the YMCA in Metropolitan Chicago* (Chicago: Rand McNally, 1957); Kathleen D. McCarthy, *Noblesse Oblige: Charity and Cultural Philanthropy in Chicago, 1849–1929* (Chicago: University of Chicago, 1982).
4. Presbytery of Chicago, Minutes of December 2, 1918.
5. Presbytery of Chicago, Minutes of October 2, 1911.
6. Presbytery of Chicago, Minutes of October 7, 1918.
7. Daniel W. Martin, "The United Presbyterian Church Policy on the Men's Movement — An Historical Survey" in *Journal of Presbyterian History* 59 (1981) 3:408–39.

8. Charles S. Holt, "The Church and the Man" in *Presbyterian Brotherhood: 1906 Convention Proceedings* (Chicago: Presbyterian Brotherhood, 1907), 71–82.

9. *Men At Work* (Chicago), October 1911.

10. Charles S. Holt, "The Scope and Significance of the Brotherhood Movement" in *Men's National Missionary Congress* (New York: Laymen's Missionary Movement, 1910), 562–65.

11. Richard E. Day, *Breakfast Table Autocrat* (Chicago: Moody Press, 1946), 155; see also Arthur Marquette, *Brands, Trademarks and Good Will: The Story of the Quaker Oats Company* (New York: McGraw-Hill, 1967).

12. James A. Mathison, "The Moody Bible Institute: A Case Study in the Dilemmas of Institutionalization" (Ph.D. diss., Northwestern, 1979).

13. Henry P. Crowell, "The Magnetic Moody" in *Commerce* (Chicago), December 1936; 28.

14. Charles O. Burgess, *Nettie Fowler McCormick: Profile of an American Philanthropist* (Madison: State Historical Society of Wisconsin, 1962); John Tebbel, *An American Dynasty: The Story of the McCormicks, Medills and Pattersons* (New York: Doubleday, 1947).

15. *James Gore King McClure* (Chicago: privately published, 1932). For related discussion on Presbyterianism in Chicago, see Lefferts A. Loetscher, *The Broadening Church* (Philadelphia: University of Pennsylvania, 1954); William T. Hanzsche, *The Presbyterians* (Philadelphia: Westminster, 1934). Also Robert H. Nichols, *Presbyterianism in New York State* (Philadelphia: Westminster, 1963).

16. John Clayton, "The Scourge of Sinners: Arthur Burrage Farwell" in *Chicago History* 3 (1974) 2:68–77.

17. Chicago Law and Order League, Report of August 28, 1919. Chicago Historical Society.

18. *Chicago Tribune*, February 17, 1912; March 15, 1912. Also William H. Anderson and Anti-Saloon League Papers, University of Chicago.

19. David R. Forgan, *Sketches and Speeches* (Chicago: privately published, 1925), 24.

20. Ibid., 99.

21. *Commerce* (Chicago), May 28, 1909.

22. Eine R. and Florence Fureh, *The Second Presbyterian Church of Chicago: Art and Architecture* (Chicago: Second Presbyterian Church, 1978).

23. Leonard Eaton, *Two Chicago Architects and Their Clients* (Boston: MIT, 1969).

24. Nolan Best, "The Relation of the Religious Press to Religious Education" in *Proceedings of Second Convention of Religious Education Association, 1904* (Chicago: Religious Education Association, 1904).

25. Quoted in John Mulder, *Woodrow Wilson: The Years of Preparation* (Princeton: Princeton University, 1978), 148.

26. *Continent* (Chicago), July 6, 1911.

27. Ann Douglas, *The Feminization of American Culture* (New York: Alfred A. Knopf, 1977), 94.

28. William B. Patterson, *Modern Church Brotherhoods* (New York: Fleming Revell, 1911). See also George A. Salstrand, *The Story of Stewardship* (Grand Rapids: Baker, 1956), 47–52; Robert Speer, *The Stuff of Manhood* (New York: Fleming Revell, 1917).

29. *Men At Work* (Chicago), May 1912.

30. *Men At Work* (Chicago), October 1911.

31. William R. Ellis, *Men and Missions* (Philadelphia: Westminster, 1910), 41, 43. See also James A. Patterson, "Robert E. Speer and the Crisis of the American Protestant Missionary Movement, 1920–1937" (Ph.D. diss., Princeton, 1980).

32. *Chicago Tribune*, October 17, 1910.

33. William McLoughlin, *Modern Revivalism from Charles G. Finney to Billy Graham* (New York: Ronald, 1959), 420.

34. *Continent* (Chicago), March 7, 1918.

35. Woodrow Wilson, *The Minister and the Community* (New York: Association, 1912). See also John Milton Cooper, Jr., *The Warrior and the Poet* (Cambridge: Belknap, 1983).

36. *Continent* (Chicago), January 3, 1918.

37. Andrew Stevenson, *Chicago, Preeminently a Presbyterian City* (Chicago, 1907).

38. *Bulletin of Chicago Association of Commerce* (Chicago), May 18, 1906.

39. John Shedd, "More Visions of Chicago Leaders" in undated *Chicago Commerce,* Chicago Historial Society.

40. Robert Ozanne, *A Century of Labor-Management Relations* (Madison: University of Wisconsin, 1972).

41. Robert W. Twyman, *History of Marshall Field & Co., 1852–1906* (Philadelphia: University of Pennsylvania, 1954), 166. See also Lloyd Wendt, *Give the Lady What She Wants* (Chicago: Rand McNally, 1952).

42. Alfred Kelly, "A History of the Illinois Manufacturing Association" (Ph.D. diss., University of Chicago, 1938); also unpublished paper, "The Illinois Manufacturing Association: A Case Study of Interest Group Politics in the Progressive Era" by Thomas R. Pegram (Fifth Annual Illinois History Symposium, Springfield, December 1984).

43. Quoted in Kelly, ibid., 75.

44. Robert H. Wiebe, *The Search for Order, 1877–1920* (New York: Hill & Wang, 1967); Michael McCarthy, "Businessmen and Professionals in Municipal Reform: The Chicago Experiment" (Ph.D. diss., Northwestern, 1970); Gabriel Kolko, *The Triumph of Conservatism* (New York: Free Press of Glencoe, 1963); Samuel Hays *The Response to Industrialism* (Chicago: University of Chicago, 1957); Frederic C. Jaher, *The Urban Establishment: Upper Strata in Boston, New York, Charleston, Chicago and Los Angeles* (Urbana: University of Illinois, 1982); Maureen Flanagan, "Charter Reform in Chicago, 1890–1915" (Ph.D. diss., Loyola, 1980).

45. David W. Johnson, "The Social Significance of Religion in the Progressive Period" (Ph.D. diss., University of Kansas, 1972); Henry May, *Protestant Churches and Industrial America* (New York: Harper, 1949).

46. David R. Forgan, 220.

47. John Mulder, 231.

48. *Chicago Tribune,* March 15, 1918.

49. David Hugh Jones, "German Kultur and American Christianity" (sermon preached at First Presbyterian, Evanston, Illinois, on May 19, 1918). Chicago Historical Society.

50. *Continent* (Chicago), July 13, 1911.

51. *Continent* (Chicago), January 21, 1915.

52. Charles Quirk, "A Statistical Analysis of the Signers of the Auburn Affirmation" in *Journal of Presbyterian History* 43 (1965) 3:182–96.

53. Andrew C. Zenos, *The Elements of Higher Criticism* (New York: Funk & Wagnalls, 1896), 46.

54. Nolan Best, *Inspiration* (Chicago: Fleming Revell, 1923), 80, 108.

55. Nolan Best, *Proceedings,* 427.

56. Arthur A. Hays, "Pilgrim: Puritan: Protestant" (Inaugural address at McCormick Seminary, Chicago, September 14, 1920).

57. Charles Erdman in *Presbyterian Men* (Chicago: Presbyterian Brotherhood, 1911), 214.

58. Charles L. Thompson, *The Soul of America* (Chicago: Fleming Revell, 1919), 234.

59. Andrew C. Zenos, *The Teaching of Jesus Concerning Christian Conduct* (New York: American Tract Society, 1905), 12, 120.

60. Samuel Dickey, *The Constructive Revolution of Jesus* (New York: George Doran, 1923), 155.

61. Joseph A. Vance, "What Does It Mean to Be a Christian?" in *The Fourth Church* 9 (July 1920).

62. Hugh M. Scott, "Religion and National Life" in *The Presbyterian and Reformed Review* XI (October 1900), 567.

63. Presbytery of Chicago, Minutes of September 10, 1917.

64. *Continent* (Chicago), January 7, 1915.

65. Andrew C. Zenos, *Vital Christianity* (Address at McCormick Seminary on September 11, 1923).

66. Presbytery of Chicago, Minutes of October 3, 1918.

67. Elwyn Smith, *The Presbyterian Ministry in American Culture* (Philadelphia: Westminster, 1962), 106.

68. Cleland B. McAfee, "The Westminster Confession of Faith and the Present Task of the Church" (Chicago: Fleming Revell, 1913), 43–44.

69. George Marsden, *Fundamentalism and American Culture* (New York: Oxford University, 1980); William R. Hutchison, *The Modernist Impulse in American Protestantism* (Cambridge: Belknap, 1976); Gary S. Smith, "Calvinism and Culture in America, 1870–1915" (Ph.D. diss., Johns Hopkins, 1980).

James T. Dennison, Jr.

14 John McNaugher and the Confessional Revision of 1925, UPCNA

A MERICAN PROTESTANTISM FOUND ITSELF in a state of flux following the peace of Appomattox Court House in 1865. The swirl of conflict which had convulsed a nation in blood produced a climate of doctrinal gradualism and progressivism that was to be enshrined in the movements for creedal revision — movements which would reach their climax in the euphoria following the Great War of the next century. With respect to the dominant Presbyterian body in America during this period, the chronicle has been appropriately captured in the title of the book, *The Broadening Church*.[1] It was not only the instinctual revulsion towards bloodshed; it was the general consensus that dogma no longer dominated American culture. Were the hermeneutics of slavery worth spilling blood for? Were there not more enlightened ways of adjusting the traditions of the past to the insights (or 'revelations') of the present? Denominational distinctives of the antebellum era were increasingly regarded as passé and irrelevant. The great port cities of New York, Boston, and Philadelphia were glutted with immigrants yearning for assimilation in the ethnic melting-pots of Pittsburgh, Cleveland, Chicago, and St. Louis. These great industrial centers were exploding with productivity under the new industrialization. And the frontier was propositioning the east with open space, fresh starts, unbounded opportunities. Pressures were being exerted — pressures which altered the course of a nation, her institutions, and her denominations.

This essay is an examination of the changes which occurred in one small Reformed denomination; changes which came as a result of cultural pressures; changes which finally altered her doctrinal stance; changes which transformed her from a distinctively Reformed church to one which was, in the main, doctrinally neutral at worst or broadly evangelical at best.

In September 1921, the Alliance of Reformed Churches met in Pittsburgh, Pennsylvania, where Dr. John McNaugher, President of Pittsburgh Theological Seminary, was elected president. Professor August Lang of Halle University was a representative from the German Reformed Churches. While appreciative of his experience in Pittsburgh, Lang lamented the lack of theological depth in the discussions and the relegation of confessional Calvinism to the background.[2] But by 1922 the distinctively Reformed emphasis was waning in the churches of the Alliance. Indeed, the worldwide mood of the times was a "broadening church." The Auburn Affirmation was only two years away. The modernist-fundamentalist rupture in establishment American Presbyterianism was imminent. And the confessional revision of the United Presbyterian Church of North America (hereafter UPCNA) was wending its way to final ratification in 1925.

Creedal revision had become a dominant item on the agenda of progressive forces within evangelicalism worldwide. From the conclusion of the Civil War in America, modernizing pressures had begun to transform the face of Protestantism. On the continent, German rationalism and liberalism made creedalism anomalous. In the British Isles, the W. Robertson Smith case rendered future confessional adherence problematic. The Briggs case in American had much the same effect — New York Presbytery, PCUSA, becoming the bastion of the *avant-garde*.

Creedal revision was but a part of tremendous shifts in evangelicalism. The American scene was aglow with revivalism, millennialism, interdenominational cooperation, social reform, and progressivism. When joined by the parallel forces of industrialization, immigration, and urbanization, the mood of late nineteenth-century America was one of boundless optimism. The impact of modernization altered secular and sacred domains alike.[3] But the ethnic and demographic alteration of American population centers brought the rush of pragmatism and utilitarianism. Traditional ecclesiastical approaches no longer 'worked.' The burgeoning frontier and the teeming metropolis demanded untrammeled methods.[4]

The optimism of the Gilded Age seeped into the church; she responded with 'possibility thinkers' of her own. D. L. Moody's increasing popularity across denominational lines and the magnetic attraction of his Northfield Conferences changed mass evangelism forever — the focus shifted to the method (pumped by business/managerial techniques) and a patently inoffensive (Moody avoided discussing God's wrath) Arminianism.[5] The millennial fervor of the Niagara and dozens of other prophetic conferences galvanized millions with a hope for the personal reign of Jesus in Jerusalem.[6] Progressive forces or liberal 'evangelicals,' finding inspiration in Social Darwinism and German idealism, began to capture the citadels of orthodoxy. When the monolith was shattered in the 1890s by the desupernaturalization of historic Christianity and the onset of the social gospel, the polarization of evangelicals became evident to all. Conservative forces reasserted the traditional othodoxy, but few were listening. By the end of the Great War, the majority of evangelical clergy had abandoned classic orthodoxy (or conservatism) in favor of a broad-based pragmatism.[7] Accommodation was evident in every evangelical establishment— the raging themes for denominational publications were: the social question and reform; interdenominational alliances; evangelization and Americanization of immigrants; moderate, scientific rationalism and a veiled form of asupernaturalism (usually evident in 'agnosticism' about the virgin birth of Christ). It was a period of acculturization with a vengeance.

The major shifts which had taken place in Protestant denominations were increasingly embodied in the creedal revisions of the late nineteenth and early twentieth centuries.[8] Not only was doctrinal accommodation evident in the ranks of the clergy, but the formal expression of this broadening church began to be incorporated in the standards. This was particularly true of the Presbyterian churches.[9] Charles Augustus Briggs put it bluntly— the dominant forces in the Presbyterian churches worldwide were abandoning incrementally the seventeenth-century formulae.[10] By 1910 none of the major Scottish Presbyterian churches was "bound in every particular by the utterances of Westminster."[11]

Even the traditional "dissenting" Presbyterian bodies began to echo with the rhetoric of progressive orthodoxy: pragmatism on the social front; administrative organization on the bureaucratic/hierarchical front; moderatism on the doctrinal front; the opiate of promotion and denominational "success." These were subtle demons and few escaped being possessed of them. The United Presbyterian Church of North America was one such church. Throughout the first half of the twentieth century, her dominant and charismatic spokesman was John McNaugher. Born and bred in the heartland of Presbyterianism, McNaugher rose with meteoric speed to become Mr. United Presbyterian.[12] He was appropriately rewarded with the presidency of the denominational seminary, an office he held for more than thirty years.[13] The bewitching power of his rhetoric left his audiences spellbound, and every UPCNA minister to graduate from Pittsburgh Seminary from 1896–1943 sat at his feet. Even now, his sermons have a dramatic ring; the literary flourish is frequently quite powerful.[14] It is easy to understand why he was dubbed "The Pope" of Pittsburgh's northside.

John McNaugher's destiny was cast in a denomination that arose from two streams— the Associate Presbyterian Church (1754–1858) and the Associate Reformed Presbyterian Church (1782–1858). On May 26,

1858, these two streams converged at Seventh and Smithfield Streets in Pittsburgh, Pennsylvania. With moderators arm-in-arm, they proceeded to old city hall (now Market Square), where the United Presbyterian Church of North America was born. A bone of contention prior to the union had been the use of a testimony to exegete the Westminster Standards. The united church adopted eighteen articles as a declaration of her place in Protestant and Reformed circles.[15] Articles III–XII were explicitly Calvinistic.

On June 2, 1925, the general assembly of the UPCNA meeting in Topeka, Kansas, adopted the Confessional Revision of 1925.[16] Following the precedent of the "Short Statement of Doctrine (1918),"[17] the Revision of 1925 modified the Calvinism of the Westminster Standards.[18] The new statement was to take priority over the seventeenth-century formulary and "wherever it deviates from the Westminster Standards its declarations are to prevail."[19] And yet, the denomination still declared its adherence to the Calvinistic system. How could a denomination jettison three of the five points of Calvinism yet still claim to be thoroughly Calvinistic? What occurred between 1858 and 1925 to bring about such confessional paradox in one of the strictest dissenting Presbyterian bodies in America?

The answer lies in the distinctive claim of the UPCNA following the turn of the century. Prior to the Civil War, UPCNA distinctives in addition to her firm Calvinism were listed in Articles XIV–XVIII of her Testimony.[20] But each of these had disappeared with the progress of modernity.[21] In truth, the distinctive of the UPCNA after the turn of the century became her progressive spirit.[22] The times had changed and Dr. John McNaugher moved to meet those times.[23]

Because of the disuse of the Westminster Standards, because of the need for a more contemporary statement of faith, because of the need for a progressive evangelical creed, McNaugher proposed revision. His language regarding the *Westminster Confession* was blunt. It was "scholastic and antique" in phraseology and long in need of "substantial revision."[24] He denominated it the "archaic Westminster Confession."[25] The Confession and Catechisms were "ultra theological."[26] In his presidential address to the Alliance of Reformed Churches at Cardiff on June 23, 1925, he described the seventeenth-century Reformed confessions as "extreme."[27] The *Westminster Confession* he regarded as holding a "one-sided emphasis on (God's) sovereignty and justice."[28] A progressive twentieth-century church could not well advertise herself by means of a seventeenth-century creed.[29]

McNaugher was himself the embodiment of an irenic and ecumenical modern Protestant spirit. From 1896 he was active in the Alliance of Reformed Churches, serving as president from 1921–25. He was a regular UPCNA delegate to this pan-presbyterian body— Liverpool, 1906; New York, 1909; Pittsburgh, 1921; Cardiff, 1925; Boston, 1929; Belfast, 1933;

and Montreal, 1937. In 1901 he was denominational representative to the Ecumenical Missionary Conference.

Always catholic and evangelical, McNaugher's sermons and books show little passion for historic Calvinism. He affirms Calvinism as his denominational tradition, but nowhere in the hundreds of pages of his sermons, addresses, and articles does he expound the famous Five Points or otherwise exegete Calvinism. His published works abound in exposition and defense of evangelical truths; i.e., virgin birth of Christ, substitutionary atonement and bodily resurrection, yet he never expounds Calvinism. In his *apologia* for revision, he cites the imperfections and inadequacies of the *Westminster Confession;* yet discussion of the confession's strengths — even its Reformed heart — is strikingly absent. McNaugher appears to have reduced Reformed theology to evangelicalism and his denominational Calvinism to mere tradition. Was McNaugher simply ambivalent about historic Calvinism; or was he redefining Calvinism in the image of the "present-day" thinking of international Presbyterianism?

If McNaugher was ambivalent (at best), W. I. Wishart was candidly hostile to seventeenth-century Calvinism. Wishart was McNaugher's great ally in the campaign for confessional revision that began in 1919. He was pastor of Eighth UPCNA, Allegheny, Pennsylvania, conveniently situated to McNaugher and Pittsburgh Seminary.[30] In his disenchantment with the *Westminster Confession,* Wishart was even more candid than McNaugher. The creeds of the seventeenth century are "antiquated," "static," and "do not reflect (the) belief of the contemporary church."[31] They should be relegated "to the museum of theological antiquities."[32] Wishart's defense of the Revision of 1925 was two-fold: on the one hand, he embraced the dream of a progressive church — one astride the mainstream of modern Protestantism;[33] on the other hand, he distanced himself from the extreme Calvinism of the *Westminster Confession* while claiming to embrace Calvinism himself.[34] Thus, he could successfully insinuate that he was a Calvinist while repudiating the (extreme) Calvinism of the Westminster Standards. In fact, the essence of Calvinism for Wishart did not require adoption of unconditional election (he favored single predestination and dropping the decree of reprobation),[35] limited atonement, or irresistible grace. Calvinism was essentially evangelical Presbyterianism — no more, no less. What familiar resonance this view would receive in American Presbyterian circles of the 1920s and 1930s!

Wishart's technique was pacesetting. In fact, one may query, "Was he McNaugher's front-man?"; i.e., saying things McNaugher believed, but dared not say? At any rate, McNaugher and Wishart were progressive, broad evangelicals — men actually more liberal than conservative, practically speaking. Yes, both defended the heart of evangelical faith — the inspiration of the Bible, the deity of Christ, the virgin birth. But neither defended *in toto* the five points of Calvinism. Since both expressed hesitation about double predestination, their doctrine of sin becomes suspect as does their concept of irresistible grace.

Many within the church and, later, many without the church became alarmed. The Westminster Standards were to be "shelved for good" as McNaugher put it.[36] That was serious enough, but to incorporate elements opposed to historic Calvinism in a confessional formula — that was betrayal.[37] Dr. James H. Grier was McNaugher's and the revision's most formidable opponent.[38] Grier argued that the revision endorsed all the doctrines eliminated from the *Westminster Confession* by the Cumberland Presbyterian Church in 1813; i.e., preterition, limited atonement, salvation of elect infants, and the saving operation of the Holy Spirit on the elect only. Thomas McKee echoed these sentiments calling the proposed revision "Arminian."[39] These same objections and more were cited later by John Murray and J. Gresham Machen.[40] History has vindicated the critics. In 1925, the UPCNA ceased to be a five-point Calvinistic denomination. The confessional revision left only total depravity and the perseverance of the saints.

With her confessional revision in place, the UPCNA had surrendered virtually every distinctive position she held. The movement for revision brought her more in line with broadening impulses in the PCUSA. By 1930 John McNaugher announced the UPCNA no longer had a *raison d'être*.[41] He suggested that the continued separate existence of the UPCNA was "schism." Although the Plan of Union was defeated, union itself was a foregone conclusion. The broadening forces knew what McNaugher knew in 1930 — the UPCNA no longer maintained any distinctives. She was in fact no different than any other broad evangelical church. Merger in 1958 was a certainty — yes, even from 1925.

John McNaugher was a man buoyed by the spirit of his age — a spirit of yearning optimism in which the kingdom of God advanced against every barrier. His vision was that of the wonder of Christ galvanizing the ministry of the church to overcome every obstacle. But in fact his agenda was a form of reductionism. His great themes were manly virtues of strength, vigor, power, and vision.[42] Unity was ever central to him — a unity built around the Christ-figure (perhaps somewhat mystical in his connotative or symbolic rôle). Christ's rôle was one of forward-looking vigor, manly triumph over dark forces of evil, sacrificial eudaemonism, servanthood in humiliation. The imitator of Christ was one moulded into manly progress, scholarly vision, and rhetorical flourish.

Much of what McNaugher wrote was striking. But it doesn't arrest; it doesn't stick. He sought the common denominator of Protestant experience. Ever avoiding the distinctives (except to score atheism and base liberalism), the pages of his books are commonplace. Unique dimensions of his own denominational tradition are never mentioned. Even the particular elements of his branch of the Reformation are absent.

McNaugher was a man for all elements — all elements of the broad, progressive mainstream of entrenched evangelicalism. He was a man of the majority spirit, an establishment arbiter. No offense would emanate from his writings or his speeches. Indeed, he was *the* embodiment of United Presbyterianism; comfortable in the mainstream; eschewing extremism to the right or left; advancing, promoting, extending the common heritage. So like his age that no differentiation obtains; so like his times that no distinction is evident. The party line of his era is now forgotten as are his books, now ignored as are his sermons, now dismissed as is his name.

The tragedy of John McNaugher is the tragedy of a denomination that had lost its place. Merger, disappearance: this was the only contribution to be made by the UPCNA. McNaugher's legacy was finally achieved in 1958; the UPCNA was swallowed up by the PCUSA. And why not? From 1925 the UPCNA had no distinctive testimony among Calvinistic churches. Her Calvinism surrendered, she had become *de facto* like the denominations around her (PCUSA, PCUS). Merger was a *fait accompli.*

NOTES

1. Lefferts A. Loetscher, *The Broadening Church* (Philadelphia: University of Pennsylvania, 1957).

2. Report: "Professor Lang on the Pittsburgh Council," *The Presbyterian*, 92 (April 20, 1922), 3.

3. Cf. James D. Hunter, *American Evangelicalism: Conservative Religion and the Quandry of Modernity* (New Brunswick, NJ: Rutgers University, 1983).

4. Notice the shift in home mission philosophy in the UPCNA for example. In 1880, the denomination abandoned its previous practice of establishing western and inner-city churches via a nucleus of UPCNA families. The pressure to evangelize resulted in relegating denominational distinctives to the background. Everywhere the emphasis was on growth and organization, not doctrine. Cf. *Our Country . . . and . . . Our Church: United Presbyterian Missions in America* (Pittsburgh: UP Board of Publication, 1906); R. W. McGranahan, *At Work in the Homeland* (Pittsburgh: UP Board of Publication, 1930). It is significant that at this time also, UPCNA distinctives were being abandoned (cf. note 21 below).

5. George Marsden, *Fundamentalism and American Culture* (New York: Oxford University, 1980), 35; James F. Findlay, Jr., *Dwight L. Moody: American Evangelist 1837–1899* (Chicago: University of Chicago, 1969), 228–29.

6. The standard work is Ernest R. Sandeen, *The Roots of Fundamentalism* (Chicago: University of Chicago, 1970).

7. The best evidence for this lies in the support of traditionally orthodox denominations for the Federal Council of Churches (1908), Men and Religion Forward Movement (1911–12), the New Era Movement, the Student Volunteer Movement, and the Interchurch World Movement 1919–20); cf. Eldon G. Ernst, "The Interchurch World Movement of North America, 1919–20" (Ph.D. dissertation, Yale University, 1968).

8. Arthur M. Schlesinger, "A Critical Period in American Religion, 1875–1900," in *Religion in American History*, ed. J. M. Mulder and J. F. Wilson (Englewood Cliffs, NJ: Prentice-Hall, 1978), 302.

9. The United Presbyterian Church of Scotland adopted a Declaratory Act in 1879 which removed one of the five points of Calvinism; i.e., limited atonement, and relegated the doctrine of preterition to an "unmentionable." The Free Church of Scotland adopted much the same sentiment in their Declaratory Act for 1892. The Church of England adopted

Twenty-four articles in 1890 which became a virtual substitute for the *Westminster Confession*. The PCUSA passed its revision of the *Westminster Confession* in 1903 (cf. the summary discussion by Gary S. Smith, *The Seeds of Secularization* [St. Paul, MN: Christian College Consortium, 1985], 23–35). In 1906 the United Free Church of Scotland determined that all subordinate standards may be revised; in theory, even those sections containing essential doctrines. In 1910 the Church of Scotland modified her subscription questions and by 1925 the United Free Church of Scotland subscribed only the substance of the *Westminster Confession*. Cf. the review in Alexander C. Cheyne, "The Place of the Confession Through Three Centuries," in *The Westminster Confession in the Church Today*, ed. A. I. C. Heron (Edinburgh: St. Andrew, 1982), 17–27, and the Documents in the Appendix, 141–49. John McNaugher understood the drift of these actions well: "nearly everyone of these Churches has been trying for years back to adjust its relation to the Westminster documents" ["The Confessional Statement and Church Relations," *United Presbyterian* (hereafter *UP*), September 20, 1923]. Would the UPCNA be left behind?!

10. Charles A. Briggs, *Theological Symbolics* (New York: C. Scribner's Sons, 1914), 411. Compare his 'prophetic' remarks in *Church Unity* (New York: Scribner, 1909), 308ff.

11. Cheyne, 19.

12. McNaugher was born Dec. 30, 1857, in Allegheny (City), Pennsylvania (now the northside of Pittsburgh).

13. He was appointed Professor of New Testament in 1886 when the seminary was called Pittsburgh Theological Seminary (merged with Xenia Seminary of St. Louis in 1930 to become Pittsburgh-Xenia). In 1909 he was chosen president. He remained active in both the previous positions until his retirement in 1943. From 1943–47, he was New Testament professor and president emeritus. His death occurred December 11, 1947.

14. In addition to his published books, which are mostly sermons, McNaugher's baccalaureate sermon to Pittsburgh Seminary graduates was printed regularly in *The United Presbyterian*. For McNaugher's magazine material, cf. citations in James T. Dennison, Jr., *An Index to the Periodicals of the Associate Presbyterian Church (1754–1858), Associate Reformed Presbyterian Church (1782–1858), and the United Presbyterian Church of North America (1858–1958), 1824–1958* (1983).

15. The text of the testimony is reproduced in R. D. Harper, *The Church Memorial* (Columbus, OH: Follett, Foster, 1858), 88–133.

16. The story of the confessional revision begins in 1918 when the general assembly adopted a Short Statement of Faith containing thirty articles; cf. *Minutes*, 1918, 471–76 [also *UP* (April 4, 1918), 10–12]. At the Monmouth (Illinois) general assembly June 3, 1919, John McNaugher issued a resolution calling for a "Revised Statement of Faith." The assembly adopted the resolution unanimously; cf. *Minutes*, 1919. A committee of nine was appointed including: Dr. Charles S. Cleland, pastor of 2nd UPCNA, Philadelphia; Dr. Jeremiah B. Work, vice-president and professor of Bible at Tarkio College (Missouri); Dr. Jesse Johnson, professor of church history and apologetics at Xenia Theological Seminary, St. Louis; Dr. Thomas H. McMichael, president of Monmouth College; Robert J. Miller, editor of the *Christian Union Herald*; Dr. John McNaugher, president of Pittsburgh Theological Seminary; Mr. John B. Eichenauer, attorney, elder at 6th UPCNA, Allegheny, PA (now Pittsburgh's northside), and chairman of the denomination's board of home missions; Hugh R. Moffett, editor of the Monmouth *Daily Review Atlas*; and Hugh T. Martin, Chicago barrister.

The Committee reported progress in 1920 and 1921. By the Cambridge (Ohio) assembly of 1922, the committee reported a statement of forty-two articles "substantially complete" to be mailed to all ministers and elders on December 1. Replies and comments were to be returned to the committee by January 15, 1923. At the Buffalo (New York) assembly of 1923, the committee reported a "most assuring" response "revealing that the statement in the main was satisfactory"; cf. *Minutes*, 1923, 866–67. A firestorm of protest was conducted in the pages of the two denominational organs: *The United Presbyterian* and *The Christian*

Union Herald; cf. the scrapbook of John McNaugher containing most of the relevant articles (the scrapbook is in the possession of Pittsburgh Theological Seminary). But by the first of the year, the protests had diminished to debate about only one point — exclusive psalmody vs. hymns. At the Richmond (Indiana) assembly (1924), a new preamble was adopted and at Topeka, Kansas, the "Revised Confessional Statement of the United Presbyterian Church of North America-(1925)" was adopted. The statement may be found in pamphlet form dating from 1925; cf. also *The Confessional Statement of the United Presbyterian Church of North America* (1956). For a further summary of the events surrounding the confessional revision, cf. Paul R. Coleman, "The Life and Works of John M. McNaugher" (Ph.D dissertation, University of Pittsburgh, 1961), 176–94.

17. McNaugher was also chairman of the Committee of Five appointed in 1914 to bring in this statement. In 1918, a fourteen-man commission was appointed to review the work of this committee and bring a recommendation to the assembly; cf. the review of this matter in Coleman, 172–75. Three of those involved in the "short statement" were to be appointed to the Committee on Confessional Revision in 1919— McNaugher, Cleland, and Eichenauer.

18. Cf. Coleman, 173–74 for the evidence regarding the Short Statement. On the revision of 1925, most admit that it removed three of the five points of Calvinism. For many like Wallace Jamison this was a bold, progressive, and much-needed step; cf. his *The United Presbyterian Story* (Pittsburgh: Geneva, 1958), 128–43 especially note 30, p. 238. Even as staunch a conservative defender of the UPCNA as Dr. John H. Gerstner, while denying that the "high Calvinism" of the Westminster Standards was abandoned in 1925, admits, *"The Confessional Statement* is less explicit than the Confession at some crucial points, is ambiguous at some others and downright inconsistent in at least one place, namely Article XIV" ["Origins and Later History of the United Presbyterian Church" (1953), typescript in the library of Pittsburgh Theological Seminary]. A different version of this paper appears as chapter four of *They Seek a Country,* ed. Gaius J. Slosser (New York: Macmillan, 1955). Slosser's editorializing has made Gerstner's statements seem more negative than he intended (from Gerstner's reply to a letter from me on this matter dated November 9, 1984). Others who admit the modifications of the Calvinism in the UPCNA include: Coleman, *op. cit.,* 182–83, 315; W. I. Wishart, *Our Calvinistic Holdings* (1928), 13, 15, 18–20; Lefferts A. Loetscher, "Some Trends and Events Since 1869," in *They Seek a Country,* ed. G. J. Slosser (1955), 261; Robert M. Karr, "The Confessional Statement," *UP* (September 10, 1956), 7.

19. "Preamble," *The Revised Confessional Statement* (1925).

20. Cf. Harper, 114–31. The articles discuss slaveholding (XIV), secret societies (XV), closed communion (XVI), public covenanting (XVII), and exclusive psalmody (XVIII).

21. In 1868 closed communion began to be modified and was eventually dropped completely (1925). Instrumental music drifted into some UPCNA sanctuaries and by 1882 instruments were approved. The strictures against secret societies were completely ignored by 1900 and removed in 1925. Exclusive psalmody also disappeared finally with the 1925 confessional statement. Cf. Jamison, 100, 113–27 and John McNaugher, "Presbyterian Union," *UP* (January 2, 1930), 10–11.

22. This was her own claim; cf. John McNaugher, "The United Presbyterian Church— Its Origin and Mission," in *Tenth Anniversary Memorial: Young People's Christian Union of the United Presbyterian and Associate Reformed Presbyterian Churches of North America, 1889 –1899* (1899), 24; Jamison, 97; W. E. McCulloch, "The Fear of Change," *UP* (October 18, 1925). It was also the assessment of others; cf. *Executive Commission of the Alliance of Reformed Churches Throughout the World Holding the Presbyterian System: Western (American) Section, Minutes February 14-15, 1933,* 17.

23. The following are a sample of numerous comments by McNaugher reflecting this sentiment: "bring the Statement into harmony with the present-day convictions . . . of the Church" ("Proposal Regarding a Revised Statement of Faith," *Minutes of the General Assembly,* June 3, 1919); "seeking such phrasing as would embody and satisfactorily express the

present-day convictions of the United Presbyterian Church" ("Report on the Revised Statement of Faith," *Minutes of the General Assembly,* 1922); "withdrawal of the adherence of the church because of changed convictions regarding Divine teaching and requirement" (*Minutes,* June 3, 1919); "It is a relentless fact that the old standards have lost their grip on both the ministry and laity, and that without cure" (McNaugher, "The Confessional Statement and the Present Standards," *UP* [September 13, 1923]); "The vast majority of our membership have lost acquaintance with it [*Westminster Confession*], so that for them it is purely nominal" (McNaugher, "The Confessional Statement — Origin and Aim," *UP* [September 6, 1923]).

24. John McNaugher, "The Overtured Confessional Statement," *UP* (June 21, 1923).

25. John McNaugher, "The Confessional Statement and Church Relations," *UP,* (September 20, 1923).

26. John McNaugher, "Proposal Concerning a Revised Statement of Faith," *Minutes of the General Assembly,* June 3, 1919.

27. John McNaugher, "Opening Address at Cardiff Council," *UP* (June 25, 1925), 18.

28. John McNaugher, "The Plan of Union: The Doctrinal Basis," *UP* (January 11, 1934), 10.

29. McNaugher also emphasized the adjustment of Calvinism in the creeds of other Reformed churches as a compelling justification for the revision; cf. "The Confessional Statement and Church Relations," *UP* (September 20, 1923) and note 9 above. McNaugher was responding to the modernizing forces abroad within and without his church. He was well aware of the changes occurring in world Presbyterianism and in American Presbyterianism. He wanted his denomination to match the "forward-looking" (his phrase) energy of these changes.

30. Wishart was the brother of Charles F. Wishart who was professor at Pittsburgh (Allegheny) Seminary from 1910 to 1914, but moved on to become the noted, progressive president of the College of Wooster, Ohio; cf. L. Gordon Tait, "Evolution: Wishart, Wooster and William Jennings Bryan," *Journal of Presbyterian History* 62 (1984), 306–21.

31. W. I. Wishart, "The Church and Present Progress," *Executive Commission of the Alliance of the Reformed Churches Throughout the World Holding the Presbyterian System: Western (American) Section—Minutes, February 14-15, 1923,* 14.

32. Ibid., 15.

33. Ibid., 10–13. Compare his articles in defense of the revision in the *UP:* "The Theology of the New Statement" (August 30, 1923), where he endorses the rejection of limited atonement (inconsistently implied by Article XIV) by repudiating the historic third point of Calvinism as grounded in "logic . . . not scriptures"; "The New Statement and the Westminster Confession" (August 23, 1923), where he suggests the revision is still too Calvinistic but rejoices that the "U.P. church has led out in this work of rewriting our Calvinism."

34. Cf. especially the article in note 30 above and his telling essay "The Doctrinal Basis for Presbyterian Church Union," *Union Seminary Review* (VA) 42 (April 1931), 267–77. Compare his pamphlet *Our Calvinistic Holdings* (1928).

35. Wishart, *Our Calvinistic Holdings,* 14–15, 18–22. McNaugher also endorsed the single predestination view applauding the omission of preterition as "better left unstated" ["The Confessional Statement and the Present Standards," *UP* (September 13, 1923)].

36. "The Confessional Statement and the Present Standards," *UP* (September 13, 1923).

37. Many members of the church argued that they were unaware that the revision proposed in 1919 was to displace the Westminster Standards; cf. J. Alvin Orr, "At the Cross Roads," *UP* (November 22, 1923); David F. Matchett, "The Confessional Statement vs. the Westminster Confession," *UP* (October 11, 1923); John Heslip, "Some Serious Defects in the New Statement," *UP* (October 4, 1923). Others rejoiced in the substitution of the Revision for the Westminster Standards as just what the church needed; cf. John G. King, "The Proposed New Confessional Statement," *UP* (September 6, 1923).

38. Cf. his three-part series "Shall We Abandon the Westminster Confession?" *UP* (July 19, July 26, and September 6, 1923). Grier was professor of Old Testament at Pittsburgh Seminary from 1922 to 1926. Coleman has some tantalizing remarks on Grier and Mc-Naugher, 130–31.

39. "The United Presbyterian Revolution," *UP* (September 20, 1923).

40. Machen and Murray became involved as a result of the PCUSA–UPCNA merger proposal of 1930. McNaugher and his counterpart at Princeton, Dr. J. Ross Stevenson, took a prominent part in promoting this merger [cf. the reports of McNaugher's vigorous defense of the 1925 confessional statement at the PCUSA general assembly in 1934; he declared the statement had been "viciously maligned" — *General Assembly Daily News* (May 26, 1934), 1; also H. McAllister Griffiths, "Man Versus Machine: the 146th General Assembly," *Christianity Today* 5 (July 1934), 41]. After several years of negotiation, the merger was defeated by the UPCNA at its assembly in 1934. Leading the opposition in the PCUSA were Machen, Murray, and Samuel Craig, editor of *Christianity Today.* Cf. John Murray, "The Confessional Statement of the United Presbyterian Church," *Christianity Today* 2 (January 1932), 7–8, 13–15; "The Proposed Doctrinal Basis of Union," ibid., 2 (February 1932), 8–10. J. Gresham Machen, "The Truth About the Presbyterian Church: The Present Situation," *Christianity Today* 2 (January 1932), 4; "Three Observations About the Assembly," ibid., 4 (June 1933), 5–6; "The Final Form of the Plan of Union," ibid., 4 (January 1934), 5–14; "Stop, Look, Listen," ibid., 4 (April 1934), 4–7.

41. John McNaugher, "Presbyterian Union," *UP* (January 2, 1930). Cf. also his "A Reply to an Intemperate Pamphlet," *UP* (September 10, 1931).

42. Frequently, his sermon to the graduates of Pittsburgh Seminary was printed in the *UP* and these qualities were uniformly emphasized. Cf. "Address to the Graduating Class . . . ," *UP* (May 18, 1916), 10–11 [same sermon as "I Am a Debtor," *UP* (May 17, 1923), 9–11]; "I Am Ready to Preach," *UP* (May 15, 1919), 10–12; "The Ministry," *UP* (May 19, 1921), 11–13; "Servants of the Message," *UP* (May 11, 1922), 13, 20–21; "God's Fellow Workers," *UP* (May 29, 1924), 17–19.

Part III

Perspectives on the Orthodox Presbyterian Church

The Second General Assembly

Mark A. Noll

15 The Spirit of Old Princeton and the Spirit of the OPC

THE FOUNDING of Westminster Theological Seminary in 1929 was the first of the three events that led to the establishment of the Orthodox Presbyterian Church. Hard upon its heels came the new Independent Board for Foreign Missions which set the stage, in turn, for judicial proceedings in the northern Presbyterian church against the officers of the mission board. The new Presbyterian denomination of 1936 was the final result. Although Westminster Seminary has never been an official agency of the Orthodox Presbyterian Church, its history is nonetheless bound tightly with the formation of the denomination and its ongoing life.

This link between Westminster and the OPC raises an important question of continuity. J. Gresham Machen and the other founders of Westminster had been long-time teachers at, graduates from, or supporters of Princeton Theological Seminary. They moved to found a new seminary only after the governing structure of Princeton was reorganized. The new Princeton Seminary, while not denying its heritage entirely, was becoming an inclusive school where the institution's historic confessional Calvinism would be but one of several options on a broader theological menu. Machen and his colleagues founded Westminster in order to preserve the old Princeton tradition. Their activities on behalf of the independent missions board, which would support only consistently Calvinistic candidates, and in beginning a new denomination, where the Westminster standards could be maintained without equivocation, grew from similar motives. The founding events of the OPC were all marked by a desire to perpetuate the sort of Calvinism for which Princeton Seminary had been the representative.

This state of affairs leads naturally to questions that are most appropriate for a semicentennial retrospective. What in fact have been the continuities between the Old Princeton theology and the new OPC? In what ways does the denomination preserve the heritage of the seminary, in what ways has it taken a different path than that which the older tradition trod? These are historical questions where evaluation plays a secondary role. But more directly evaluative inquiries are also appropriate to this subject. Where did the older theological tradition do better than the new denomination? Where has the OPC done things better than Old Princeton?

A number of factors makes it difficult to answer these questions satisfactorily. One problem is the difficulty in comparing two different institutions. Although Old Princeton was always interested in the practical life of the church and although the OPC has always possessed a lively theological concern, it is nonetheless true that a seminary is not a denomination nor vice versa.

A second problem is one of historical context. The American nineteenth century in which Old Princeton flourished was very different from the twentieth century in which the OPC made its way. Throughout the years of its greatest influence, Old Princeton was only one of several major Calvinistic voices in the land. However much the Princetonians, the New School Presbyterians, New England's "consistent Calvinists," and the German Reformed of J. W. Nevin and Philip Schaff may have quarreled among themselves, together these groups, all aspiring to speak as representatives of Calvinism, constituted a substantial collective voice in American religious life. By contrast, in the twentieth century the number of confessional Calvinists in America is much diminished. They are, moreover, dispersed in several communities — the small, conservative Presbyterian denominations, remnants in the large Presbyterian denominations, the Christian Reformed Church, scattered representatives in the institutions of American evangelicalism which have few organic connections with each other. Given this difference in historical context, it would not be surprising if Old Princeton and the OPC appear in different lights.

A final difficulty for this kind of study is the standpoint of the one who makes the comparisons. I believe I possess at least a modicum of that disinterestedness which is prerequisite for objective historical inquiry. Yet there can be no doubt that my own readings of the nineteenth century, my own theological preferences, and my own experience in the OPC color my conclusions on this subject. These major difficulties notwithstanding, this kind of essay may still have value, if only to encourage others to gather the lessons to be gleaned from the histories of Old Princeton and the OPC. Both institutions, regrettably, are regularly characterized by snap judgments. But both should, especially in comparison with each other, serve to enlighten and edify those who take the time to consider them seriously.

I would like to proceed by making four comparisons: first, where the OPC maintains a praiseworthy aspect of the Old Princeton spirit; second, where the OPC continues an unfortunate characteristic of Old Princeton; third, where the OPC has deviated from Old Princeton to its disadvantage; and fourth, where developments in the OPC represent an advance over Old Princeton. Before making these assessments, however, it would be well to sketch in brief the major themes and the major figures of the Princeton theology.

Princeton Seminary was founded in 1812 to provide Presbyterians with an educated clergy that could lead the denomination in responding to the crises of the time. Leaders like Ashbel Green, who became president of Princeton College in 1812, the same year that he assumed his position as the first president of the seminary's board of directors, had worked for more than a decade for such an institution. He and others hoped that a school especially devoted to clerical instruction would help to overcome a severe shortage of ministers, repulse the tides of secularization, shore up the learned defense of the faith, and assist the forces of civilization. Princeton was the country's second major seminary, after Andover which had been founded near Boston in 1807. As it turned out, Princeton proved to be a remarkably resilient institution. Even more important, it provided the institutional setting for a remarkably persistent theology.

Although other seminaries soon arose within the Presbyterian church, Princeton remained the largest and most influential center of training for the Presbyterian ministry. By the time of its centennial in 1912, Princeton had enrolled over 1,000 more students than had attended any other seminary in the United States. Over 6,000 students, including many mainstays of Presbyterianism and not a few leaders in other denominations, had studied with the major exponents of the Princeton theology.

That theology was a major expression of conservative Calvinism. It owed its force to the remarkable series of theologians who taught at Princeton and to the significance of that institution within the denomination and the country at large. The three most important Princeton theologians were Archibald Alexander (1772–1851), founding professor of the school; Charles Hodge (1797–1878), who taught over 3,000 students in his more than fifty years as a Princeton professor; and Benjamin Breckinridge Warfield (1851–1921), who upheld Old Princeton positions during a period of fading evangelical influence. These three were joined by a host of other important figures, including most notably Hodge's son, Archibald Alexander Hodge (1823–86), two sons of Alexander, James Waddel (1804–59) and Joseph Addison (1809–60), and the New Testament scholar and apologist, J. Gresham Machen (1881–1937), who was so important in the founding of the OPC.

The Princeton theologians upheld Reformed confessionalism, they defended high views of biblical inspiration and authority, they organized their thinking with the aid of the Scottish philosophy of common sense, and they had a surprisingly large place for the role of the Holy Spirit in religious experience. The theologians of Old Princeton were jealous guardians of Calvinistic views on the divine preeminence in salvation, the unity of the race in Adam's guilt and of the elect in the work of Christ, and the moral inablility of humans apart from God's grace. They upheld these positions against continental romanticism and rationalism, against domestic forms of subjectivity, against the excesses of enthusiastic revivalism, against all varieties of theological liberalism and against evangelical perfectionism.

One of the Reformed positions which the school held most doggedly was the infallibility of the Bible. This was a central theme in the apologetics of Alexander, it was an essential foundation for Charles Hodge's *Systematic Theology* and for the polemics which he carried on in the *Princeton Review*, and it provided Warfield with the position that he defended in countless essays toward the end of the nineteenth century. The well-known monograph on "Inspiration" in 1881 by Warfield and A. A. Hodge summed up the Princeton position: the church's historic belief in the verbal infallibility of the Bible should be maintained both because of external proofs for Scripture's divine character and because of the Bible's own testimony concerning itself.

Principles of the Scottish philosophy of common sense provided guidelines for the Princeton theologians in their organization of scriptural material and for their approach to theology. In this they reflected the teaching of two Scottish-born presidents of Princeton College, John Witherspoon (1723–94) and James McCosh (1811–94), whose work influenced all of the major Princetonians directly or indirectly. At Princeton Seminary the Scottish philosophy was not so much a guide for convictions about the native powers of the 'moral sense' as was the case among New England Calvinists. It provided rather a confidence in empirical science and simple inductive procedures by which to chart a theological course. The opening pages of Charles Hodge's *Systematic Theology* provide the clearest illustration of these procedural commitments.

But even as the Princetonians adopted the scientific standard of the Scottish philosophy, they always retained a large place for distinctly spiritual influences. The major Princeton theologians were all powerful preachers. Although they distrusted unrestrained revivalism, they worked for renewal in the church. Charles Hodge especially, in his commentaries and some of his polemics, could write as movingly about the inward effects of the Holy Spirit as any of his contemporaries.

Critics of the Princetonians accuse them of scholastic rationalism and a mechanical biblicism. While these claims are not without a particle of truth, the larger reality is that the theologians of Old Princeton were faithful representatives of historic Calvinism who energetically adopted their confessional position to the needs and opportunities of the American experience.

This sketch of the Princeton theology provides a basis for comparison with what came later in the OPC. It is to those comparisons that we now turn.

First, it is possible to say that the OPC has maintained probably the most important aspect of the Old Princeton theology. Like the nineteenth-century seminary, the twentieth-century denomination is marked by a responsible theological conservatism. Modern Christians in other traditions may question some manifestations of this conservative bent, but its general thrust — to preserve the best in the heritage of confessional Calvinism — must be respected by all who value a Reformed perspective. When much of the rest of America was exulting in human potential and trumpeting the human ability to tame frontiers, perfect society, and bring in the Kingdom, Old Princeton never deviated from its realistic view of human nature and its biblical confession concerning God's grace. In similar ways the OPC has maintained, against an even greater tide, that all humans are sinners who must perish — in spite of uplift, technique, prosperity, self-fulfillment, or whatever — if God does not intervene out of the sheer goodness of his nature.

The great institutions that embodied the Princeton theology were devoted to this kind of theological conservatism. The seminary itself was founded in 1812 in response to a feeling that America was undergoing a cultural crisis of unprecedented magnitude. The great periodical of the seminary, *The Biblical Repertory and Princeton Review,* began in 1825 in order to report on trends in biblical scholarship from overseas, but was transformed in 1829 by Charles Hodge into a watchdog guarding confessional Calvinism from depredations at home and abroad. The Princetonians were also active Old School Presbyterians who from 1837 to 1868 protested the innovations of the "progressive" New School — whether in polity, theology, or stances toward the world. Hodge's *Systematic Theology,* an institution between covers, not only summed up a lifetime of personal study, but also bequeathed in permanent form conceptions of theology and apprehensions of error that had been rooted in his own study under Archibald Alexander at the start of the nineteenth century. The lengthy tenures of the Princeton professors were themselves conservative phenomena. The combination of these inter-locking factors gave the theology of Old Princeton a stability noticeably lacking in most other forms of nineteenth-century evangelical thought.

Much the same may be said of the more recent history of the OPC. While others have chased theological fashion or bent to the winds of modernity, Orthodox Presbyterians have clung to the treasures of the past.

Again, there are aspects of this backward-looking tendency open to criticism of the most serious sort. But beyond all that might be wrong with it, this is a stance which has preserved essentials. And like Old Princeton, the OPC has enjoyed resilient institutions and the long and faithful service of distinguished mentors. Westminster Seminary with its twin commitments to confessional Calvinism and exacting intellectual activity has been the most important of these institutions. The distinguished service to the denomination of Cornelius Van Til, Paul Woolley, John Murray, Ned Stonehouse, and others of similar mettle likewise bequeathed a consistent conservatism to the denomination.

Although the conservatism of Old Princeton was most conspicuous in its own day for its defense of Calvinism, in more recent times the Princeton position on Scripture has received most attention. On this subject Old Princeton blazed a decisive trail through the underbrush of unthinking pietism and fashion-hungry modernism. From Archibald Alexander's first call for a seminary in 1808 to B. B. Warfield's last words on the subject and J. Gresham Machen's exposition in *Christianity and Liberalism* over a century later, the Princetonians propounded and defended a high view of the inspiration and authority of Scripture. Alexander felt that a genuine adherence to Scripture would fit the church for life in hard times, it would reveal the inadequacies of Roman Catholic conceptions of authority, and it would provide the boundaries for legitimate science. Charles Hodge maintained these convictions, but expounded them more carefully to show how a fidelity to Scripture contrasted with both "rationalism" (i.e., higher criticism) or "mysticism" (i.e., subjective pietism). Hodge also began the process of refining Alexander's concept of biblical authority which his son and Warfield carried further in their collaborative efforts. These two restated in more precise terms the Princeton doctrine of Scripture in their famous essay from 1881 on "Inspiration." In a series of careful essays, Warfield brought the tradition to its culmination by defining exactly what it means for Scripture to be inerrant (the Bible means exactly what its authors intended to say, no more, no less), to be both a divine and human book (the inspiration of the Holy Spirit and the normal human activity of the writers took place *concursively*), and to be the uniquely inspired norm of divine revelation (neither reason, "the best modern knowledge," nor privileged religious experiences could have the last word). The Princetonians wrote on Scripture with both reverence and intelligence. They applied the best of the learning of their day in the effort while foreswearing naturalistic speculation or fundamentalistic anti-intellectualism.

The result was a heritage largely maintained by the OPC. Whether in John Murray's examination of neo-orthodox views of the Bible during the 1930s, Ned Stonehouse's pathbreaking studies on the synoptic gospels in the 1940s and 1950s, Edmund Clowney's responsible leadership of the International Council on Biblical Inerrancy in the 1970s and 1980s, or in the host of local ministers and laymen and women who have sought to align their lives with Scripture, rather than the reverse, the OPC has lived up to the Princeton legacy on the Bible. This is perhaps the most signal instance of the denomination perpetuating, and expanding fruitfully upon, the basic conservatism of the seminary which made it such a powerful force in its own day.

There are, however, other Princeton tendencies which the OPC perpetuates to its detriment. Chief among these is the Old Princeton weakness in cultural analysis and the concomitant lack of effective Christian outreach in society. A fine recent article by William Barker ("The Social Views of Charles Hodge: A Study in 19th-Century Calvinism and Conservatism," *Presbyterion: Covenant Seminary Review* 1 [Spring 1975], 1–22) and a sturdy dissertation by David Murchie ("Morality and Social Ethics: The Thought of Charles Hodge," Drew University, 1980) have illuminated this situation. Old Princeton lacked not so much a will to do good, but a strategy for bringing it about. Even as Charles Hodge vacillated on how to approach the question of slavery, he nonetheless protested against the general evil of the system. But it took the Civil War to move him to a definite position on emancipation. And in all of this it was never entirely clear how he linked his tentative positions on this social evil to the foundations of his theology. To cite another example of the same thing, Hodge late in life wrote in the *Princeton Review* about the growing problems of the American cities ("Preaching the Gospel to the Poor" 43 [January 1871], 83–94). Hodge's heart was in the right place here, but his intellectual cupboard was relatively bare. All that he could propose as a counter to the growing problems of urbanization was higher salaries for Presbyterian ministers working in the cities as missionaries. After Hodge's time the Princeton tradition had even less to offer. Warfield was (understandably) consumed by the theological battles of his day. And if one can generalize from Stonehouse's fine memoir, J. Gresham Machen had time for only *ad hoc* forays into the realm of public morality.

Similar difficulties have attended the history of the OPC. While many in the denomination have been active in local efforts to speak for the Kingdom beyond the walls of the church, these efforts have been neither comprehensive nor particularly effective. An unthinking equation of confessional theology with conservative or libertarian politics, an inability to empathize with the disadvantaged, and a strongly self-righteous foreign policy have all too frequently characterized the OPC in its efforts to take the measure of the modern world.

In this kind of negative assessment it is important to speak carefully. The problem for Old Princeton and the OPC has not been indifference. Nor has it been an entire lack of effectiveness. (A recent book by Gary Smith shows that Calvinists at Old Princeton made a positive contribution to some aspects of Christian social witness at the end of the nineteenth century: *The Seeds of Secularization: Calvinism, Culture, and Pluralism in America, 1870–1915* [Grand Rapids: Eerdmans, 1985].) The difficulties have been, rather, a woodenness of analysis and an artificially restricted theological response. In particular, Old Princeton aligned itself with the privatistic tendency of nineteenth-century American evangelicalism, as opposed to the reformist strands which also marked the century. And the OPC has tended to stress antithethical elements of Calvinism in the twentieth century, rather than those which bespeak God's common grace and his power to transform the world.

The end result, for both Old Princeton and the OPC, has been a reluctance to bring theological resources to bear which could speak powerfully to analyze the diseases of our age — modernization, secularism, industrial and urban alienation, materialism of both the communist East and the hedonistic West, economic deprivation, and the like. We have been content, with only a few conspicuous exceptions, to regard our confessions as a barricade keeping out the world rather than as a manifesto with a message for the marketplace. The Princeton tendency to perceive service to the Kingdom in narrowly ecclesiastical and theological terms has continued in the OPC.

The passage of years as well as many differences in historical context, personalities, and crises also account for significant differences between Old Princeton and the OPC. In some ways, the narrower circumstances of the modern denomination have led it to improve upon its legacy. And in others there has been a falling away.

One of the places where this falling away has been most obvious is in the exercise of ecclesiastical skills. In this particular the OPC inherited a decline which began late in the nineteenth century. Archibald Alexander, Charles Hodge, and A. A. Hodge were all, in their distinctive ways, savvy ecclesiastics. Alexander had been an evangelist, a college president, and a pastor of rural and urban churches before he began, at age 40, to teach at the seminary. Hodge was not as active, but he was a close and discerning observer of the general assembly and an active participant in his presbytery. His son was a veteran of the mission field and the pastorate before beginning his career as a theological professor. By contrast, the last phase of Old Princeton, as well as the bulk of the OPC's history, has been dominated more thoroughly by the professorial mentality. Warfield did not aspire to participation in denominational affairs. After he died, his own brother said that Warfield was marked by "a certain intellectual austerity, a loftiness and aloofness." (Ethelbert D. Warfield, "Biographical Sketch of Benjamin Breckinridge Warfield," *Works*, 1, viii.) Francis L. Patton described him as nearly "a recluse," as "pre-eminently a scholar [who] lived among his books." ("B. B. Warfield," *Princeton Theological Review* 19 [July 1921], 371, 370.) Warfield was the mentor of Machen who, though much more active a participant than Warfield in denominational affairs, still was a man with a curious naiveté about the ways of the world. And Machen fathered the OPC.

If I may insert a personal story relevant at this point, I received a telling testimony to Machen's strengths and weaknesses during a year as a visiting professor at Juniata College in Huntingdon, Pennsylvania. Dr. Calvert Ellis, president emeritus at Juniata, spoke at length with me about his memories of Machen who had been his teacher in the late 1920s at Princeton. Ellis, who completed doctoral work at Yale and who had extensive experience with higher education of all sorts in the east, told me he was "eternally grateful" that his father had steered him to Princeton where, in his words, "I discovered the living Christ." Machen, moreover, was one of the two or three best instructors that President Ellis had ever known. Yet Dr. Ellis also wished to make clear that he considered Machen somewhat heavy-handed as an ecclesiastical politician and as someone who lacked a sense of proportion about the theological battles he was waging. This is only one man's opinion, but it is striking that Dr. Ellis, after the lapse of over fifty years, singled out Machen's Christ-centeredness, his pedagogical brilliance, and his ecclesiastical woodenness as his most memorable characteristics.

It is possible to say very many good things about the dedication of Warfield and Machen to scholarship and polemical apologetics. These good things clearly must predominate when any confessional Calvinist records their influence on the OPC. Yet for all its benefits, the style of Warfield and Machen has not left their successor denomination with an entirely well-balanced perspective. The OPC has been a body more given to denominational infighting than denominational outreach. It has prided itself more on confessional precisionism than on ecclesiastical diplomacy. Its movers and shakers, at least until very recently, have been academic theologians instead of missionaries, pastors, and evangelists. It has sometimes shown more enthusiasm for the niceties of judicial procedure than the nitty-gritty of community involvement.

The OPC, in short, has narrowed the concerns of Old Princeton. The seminary never stood for less than theological rigor, but it had often stood for more — a determined, sometimes winsome, and frankly practical concern for its denominational setting. This latter concern is by no means absent from the history of the OPC, but it also by no means is as prominent as in the early history of Old Princeton.

In at least one other area the OPC has come close to abandoning its heritage from Old Princeton. This is the analysis of its tiny size. It should be a question of continuing importance to members of the OPC why this group, possessing as we believe a singularly sound theology, remains so small. Some members of the denomination do not seem concerned about this issue, some lay all the blame on those who do not recognize our virtues, some bemoan our own sins, and some attribute it to the secret workings of God's will. All of these responses may be correct, but if we go no further, we abandon an important means of analysis from Old Princeton.

Here it is Warfield, the one who avoided practical concerns, who yet provided a clue for practical advance. His principle of *concursus* gives the OPC what it needs to face the question of its relatively small size. For Warfield the idea of *concursus* meant the simultaneous activity of divine and natural agency, neither replacing the other, neither excluding the other. Warfield himself used this idea to reconcile Scripture and evolution, by claiming that what happened in nature must in principle reflect the constant, overarching providence of God. But he made greatest use of the concept in his doctrine of Scripture. The Bible was a thoroughly divine book; the Bible was a thoroughly human book. Christians, of all people, should be eager to do the research which illuminates the natural history of the Bible, its process of human composition. In principle nothing discovered in such inquiry can negate the divine inspiration of Scripture, because that inspiration works *through* human agency, rather than as a substitute for it.

The relevance of this conception for OPC considerations of its own history is this: when we are tempted to say that our denomination has remained so small because it is the will of God, we have done no more than set out an agenda for research. Of course God wills it. God wills all that comes about. But what has God revealed through natural means (i.e., the analysis of social groups and their setting, the analysis of historical expectations and actual realities, the analysis of crucial personalities and turning points) to aid us in understanding his will? What has he revealed in Scripture, about pharisaism as well as apostasy, about decay within as well as decay without, to help us work through the question of why we are what we are? Trust in God, Warfield reminds us, should lead to careful sifting of evidence, to painstaking toil; it should not result in platitudinous piety about the work of God in the world.

Finally, it is a privilege to mention ways in which the history of the OPC improves upon the foundation provided by Old Princeton. Of all historical fallacies, that myopia is probably the worst that insists upon reading recent history as a descent from glory. In certain instances the OPC has in fact risen above Old Princeton.

The first of these ascents is the OPC openness to theological strategies that were foreign to Princeton. J. Gresham Machen seems to have acted quite self-consciously when he invited Cornelius Van Til to join the Westminster faculty. Yet this was an adventuresome move for one steeped in the verities of Old Princeton. That school was determinedly common sensical in its approach to the world; it was thoroughly evidentialist in its apologetics. Van Til, by contrast, brought with him an idealistic and presuppositional point of view with roots in the Dutch theological revival associated with the name of Abraham Kuyper. This presuppositional perspective went against the grain of over a century's teaching at Princeton where the natural moral sense, the neutral procedures of science, and the gentleman's appeal to reasonableness had all featured prominently. Yet to their credit, first Westminster, then the denomination more generally added presuppositionalism to their earlier evidentialism, or even went over wholesale to the newer point of view. The result has been a sophistication about theological method and a sensitivity to the perspectival quality of all discourse that was largely absent at Princeton.

The OPC has also risen above Old Princeton in its dogged persistence in holding to culturally unpopular truths without the benefit of powerful institutions or a numerous constituency. The genius of Old Princeton had been its embodiment of confessional Calvinism in great institutions: the school itself, the *Princeton Review*, Hodge's *Systematic Theology*, and the Old School party among the northern Presbyterians. Although these institutions were sometimes imperiled, they still received unquestioning respect. Everyone in the nineteenth century knew that the voice of Old Princeton counted. It spoke with dignity, gravity, and great seriousness. And almost everyone, even those who opposed it most violently, listened.

The contrast with the OPC could hardly be greater. The denomination's origins were not auspicious. Its institutions have never been the object of deference. Its wealth was meager. Its clout was a function of individuals rather than of heritage. Over its history the situation has changed but slightly. Whatever insiders and those close to the OPC may think of it, the religious world at large has treated it casually or, with even greater disdain, paid it no heed at all.

Still, in this situation the leaders of the OPC have spoken, as did their predecessors at Princeton, with dignity, gravity, and great seriousness. Sometimes the denomination has given way to the temptation to repay its detractors in kind, but far more often it has chosen the high road of learned discourse and careful biblical reflection.

Just as remarkable is the denomination's faithfulness to confessional Calvinism. A position that was waning in the nineteenth century has become ever more suspect in the twentieth. These cultural obstacles, this lack of respect for institutions, this perseverance in the face of great odds mark the OPC as the equal in courage, if not more, to its Princeton predecessors.

This essay has merely scratched the surface of what could be said about the spirit of Princeton in relationship to the spirit of the OPC. Enough has been written to expose my biases; enough praise has been offered, enough blame has been assigned. It remains to say that Princeton and the OPC are but institutions of dust, that they bear a full measure of human limitation and evil. Yet in spite of these frailties the two share, in their common commitment to the God of sovereign grace and the Christ of the Scriptures, a measureless inheritance. Although much else deserves to be said about both groups, that is still the most important thing.

NOTES

My evaluation of the theologians of Old Princeton in this essay draws heavily upon interpretations first set forth in the introduction to *The Princeton Theology: Scripture, Science, and Theological Method from Archibald Alexander to Benjamin Breckinridge Warfield* (Grand Rapids: Baker, 1983), and in an essay, "The Princeton Theology" for a book edited by David F. Wells, *American Reformed Traditions: Essays in its Modern Development* (Grand Rapids: Eerdmans, 1985). The anthology contains also a bibliography of works by and about the Princetonians. For my understanding of the early days of the OPC, I am heavily dependent upon Ned B. Stonehouse, *J. Gresham Machen: A Biographical Memoir* (Grand Rapids: Eerdmans, 1954). Two recent studies of the Dutch Reformed shed most interesting comparative light on the history of confessional Presbyterian Calvinism in America: Stephen R. Spencer directly in "A Comparison and Evaluation of the Old Princeton and Amsterdam Apologetics" (Th.M. thesis, Grand Rapids Baptist Seminary), and James D. Bratt indirectly through an interpretation of the various stances in the Christian Reformed Church and the western section of the Reformed Church in America, *Dutch Calvinism in Modern America* (Grand Rapids: Eerdmans, 1984).

D. Clair Davis

16 Machen and Liberalism

J GRESHAM MACHEN's life-work was clarifying and presenting the Christian faith. In his time that was bound to mean showing how the precious gospel of Christ must be distinguished from that misrepresentation of it known as Protestant liberalism. To a great extent that necessarily was true also of the two great Christian institutions he was instrumental in founding, Westminster Theological Seminary and the Orthodox Presbyterian Church. Certainly Machen believed and taught the Reformed faith in its totality and did not desire to limit the scope of his theology to a mere fundamentalist reaction to liberalism. Nevertheless he believed with Martin Luther that if you are not faithful at the precise point where the gospel is under attack, then you are not really faithful to the gospel at all.

So Machen saw clearly it was the liberalism of his own time that had to be answered, and it is not surprising that he gave so much of his life to that task. In order to understand his life and work, it is necessary then to examine the nature of the movement he opposed, particularly its religious and theological character. Obviously Machen knew of liberalism's social and political face, perhaps as important to its supporters as its theology. While some attention could be given to Machen's conservative political stance and its emphasis on limited government, predisposing him against liberalism in general, it would be a mistake to think it was all that important to Machen. Rather it is the theological issues that must be considered.

While "liberalism" can mean any repudiation of supernatural Christianity, the term has a more specific meaning for Machen. It derives from its setting within nineteenth-century romanticism. The older rationalism had explained the supernatural events recorded in the gospels as misunderstandings of unusual events, typical of the uneducated in all ages. Thus, Christ's walking on water was really his walking through the early morning mist on the shore of the lake. His resurrection could be attributed to premature burial! In this way earlier rationalism "preserved" the Christian faith for the educated man. But such "Christianity" was merely morality and Jesus was only a great teacher. The historical events surrounding him were useful only for illustration of general ethical principles.

Obviously the price for this "preservation" was much too high. All that remained was a sterile legalism, with no more appeal to the broader needs of people than mathematics, which by the way was the movement's model. Over against this barrenness it is not surprising that the nineteenth century clamored for a view of reality that would include more of the richness of human life. Ushering in this broader understanding was the philosophy of Immanuel Kant, which attempted to provide not only a justification for scientific reality but also for moral, aesthetic, and religious truth. While human freedom had been impossible within the structure of rationalist science, it now became the foundation of broader romantic reality.

Friedrich Schleiermacher introduced Kantian philosophy into the world of religion. He stressed that for life to be appreciated in all its fullness, the religious dimension must be present. This he defined as man's feeling of personal dependence. He reformulated Christian doctrine in terms of its significance for religious experience. When the doctrine of the Trinity could not be expressed in this way, it was reduced to an appendix! As Cornelius Van Til has shown, it is this "dimensionalism" that has dominated modern theology down to the present day. No longer did the opponents of the Christian faith label its foundational doctrines as false and misleading. Instead they spoke of them as having a poetic, symbolic character— or more precisely, a mythical one.

Concretely, the liberal no longer saw the resurrection as illustrating the need for a public health regulation; namely, that one should not bury the dead until their deaths have been verified. From then on its meaning was that the personality of Jesus was so powerful that the conviction of his abiding presence lived on after his physical death. Such was the heart of the romantic subjective Christianity of the early nineteenth century.

But by the middle of the century the philosopher Hegel and the theologian Ritschl had modified that outlook. They were convinced that it was necessary to add to Kantian subjectivism an appreciation of Christian community and its progression through history. Christianity for them was much more than subjective, introspective "pietism." To personal experience Ritschl added a second focus to the Christian ellipse, the perception of the coming of the Kingdom of God within society. To the psychologizing of Christianity was added communal sociologizing.

This is the theological setting within which Machen did his work. He knew he was not opposing a mere theological abstraction, but an extremely powerful and vital movement. Machen knew his own doubts concerning the Christian faith, and he saw in the theology of Wilhelm Herrmann, the great University of Marburg theologian and popularizer of Ritschlianism, at least a partial solution to those doubts.

While Herrmann is hardly thought of today, his powerful personality had a striking effect upon his generation. His students included the two great leaders of early twentieth-century theology, Karl Barth and Rudolf Bultmann. Though Herrmann produced a systematic theology, it is more helpful to consider his work from the perspective of his famous *The Communion of the Christian with God.* This book served as the basis for the lectures that Machen heard in Marburg in 1905.

Machen's letters reveal the impact Herrmann had upon him.

> Such an overpowering personality I think I almost never before encountered — overpowering in the sense of religious devotion . . . so much deeper is his devotion to Christ than anything I have known in myself during the past few years. . . . He is a Christian not because he follows Christ as a moral teacher; but because his trust in Christ is (practically, if anything even more truly than theoretically) unbounded. It is inspiring to see a man so completely centered in Christ. . . . In New England those who do not believe in the bodily Resurrection of Jesus are, generally speaking, religiously dead; in Germany, Herrmann has taught me that that is by no means the case. He believes that Jesus is the one thing in all the world that inspires *absolute* confidence, and an *absolute* joyful subjection; that through Jesus we come into communion with the living God and are made free from the world. It is the faith that is a real experience, a real revelation of God that saves us, not the faith that consists in accepting as true a lot of dogmas on the basis merely of what others have said.[1]

In reflecting on his education much later in life, Machen expressed his conviction that "In contact with any great movement, it has always seemed to me important to attend to its best, and not merely to its worst, representatives; and Herrmann certainly represented Ritschlianism at its best." Even late in life Machen can say that he was not insensible of the attractiveness of Ritschlianism's solution to religious problems; "and I am not insensible of it now," he wrote.[2] Certainly he saw in Ritschlianism no straw man to be dismissed easily and lightly, but a movement addressing significant theological issues. It is likely that his first-hand experience with the charm of liberalism had a great deal to do with his concept of proper theological training, that in the presentation of biblical content it is necessary to relate that content to modern liberal criticism.

What was so important about Ritschlianism? For Machen, it was the emphasis that Christianity could not be reduced to personal mystical experience, but must be related to the *historical* Jesus.

There is no more pivotal question in all of modern theology than how Christian faith is related to the historical knowledge we have of the life and teachings of Jesus Christ. At one time, history seemed to be a fairly objective discipline with results adequate for any reasonable purpose. But now it is seen as important to focus upon the observer of phenomena just as much as upon that which he observes. Science has taken note of the fact that the presence of the observer alters that which he is to observe. Similarly, to the historicist (one who believes that the study of history is uniquely relativistic) it seems clear that the old ideal of an objective, disinterested historian is simply not attainable nor even desirable. The historian cannot look at history from without, but is himself a part of the subject matter that he is studying. That is, he cares about the meaning history has for people today. He is obliged to take responsibility for the world around him and may not just look on passively or objectively. That briefly is the view modern theologians have toward the study of biblical history.[3]

Herrmann himself set forth virtually all of the above view, even though of course there have been technical refinements within the enterprise known as the "new hermeneutic." Also he was certain that history could yield only probable results, not the certainty necessary for faith. But he is hardly neutral concerning the biblical narratives; much of what is there is actually a hindrance to faith, he believes, since it is so opposed to what modern man believes. Nevertheless he continually emphasized that the way to faith is not through some mystical experience which has nothing to do with Jesus. That he terms Roman Catholic, the clear opposite of Protestant Lutheran faith, which sees that it is only through Jesus that we can come to the Father.

But if the biblical narratives are not reliable, what is left except some sort of mysticism? How can one come to God through an unknowable Jesus? Machen was right to be intrigued by Herrmann's forthright and impassioned statement of the great modern dilemma. But what did Herrmann have to offer? Precisely this: that one could know Jesus, not dogmas about him, through the experience of the disciples, the gospel writers. Such an approach has nothing to do with the gospel writers' infallibility. Instead, one can see in their accounts something that is totally beyond human experience and beyond the ability of any writer to imagine; i.e., the mighty personality of Jesus. This comes through regardless of difficulties one may have over the events recorded in the gospels, says Herrmann. Far from mysticism, Herrmann taught that the reality of Christianity only comes from our sharing the experience of others. Furthermore, it does not depend upon accepting unbelievable dogmas about Jesus but is a matter of receiving Jesus himself. Here is a Jesus of history, not of imagination, since it is a Jesus who commands our attention through the accounts written about him.[4]

There can be no question but that this sort of thinking is that which determined the course of Machen's scholarly life. No doubt he encountered American varieties of liberal thought as well, but at bottom the program was still the same. With this in mind, Machen's characteristic responses are almost predictable. He was certain that liberalism did not really present a third alternative after all. Specifically, its methodology does not yield any reliable knowledge about Jesus. Its theories concerning Hellenistic sources for the Christian message simply do not hold water. Machen is sure the only real alternative is the Christian faith.

But listen to Machen's own analysis of Ritchlianism:

> . . . radicals have denied its historicity; 'consistent eschatologists' have pointed out in the sources elements which contradict it at its root. The picture is faulty, moreover in itself. The Ritschlians thought that the moral life of Jesus— their Jesus, reconstructed by their particular type of naturalistic criticism of the Gospels — was capable of calling forth mankind's unbounded reverence, was capable of having for all mankind the value of God.[5]

Thus Machen points out that later radical scholarship did not discover the liberal ideal of a great personality by which others were convinced to take on Jesus' relationship to God and, thus, bring about a better world. Rather they have found in Jesus' teaching the conviction that only by God's putting an end to history and to human striving can the kingdom come. Further, the liberal understanding of Jesus himself as one who really did nothing about sin simply does not address religious need. Even if one were to attempt to base theology upon man's religious need, it must be upon his real need. "A man under real conviction of sin will never be satisfied with the Ritschlian Jesus, but will seek his way into the presence of that Jesus who redeemed us by His precious blood and is ever living to make intercession for us at the throne of God."[6]

In summary, Machen is sure that liberalism is both bad scholarship and bad Christianity because it does not do justice to what the New Testament says. In his more scholarly works this is what he sets out to demonstrate. In *The Origin of Paul's Religion* he presents the liberal arguments for Paul's receiving his religion from pagan Hellenistic sources and not from the Old Testament and from Jesus himself. He shows how liberal theories cancel each other out. He also shows how it is much more reasonable to believe that similarities between the gospels and Paul come from Paul learning from Jesus rather than from editorial revisions of the gospels that cause them to conform to Paul. Throughout he combats the liberal separation between the religion of Jesus and the religion about Jesus, maintaining the heart of what Jesus taught was his own person and work.

His other great work, *The Virgin Birth of Christ*, follows much the same structure. After investigating all the alleged parallels in Hellenism to the Virgin Birth, he then shows the great differences between them and the biblical doctrine. Again he argues that Christianity depends upon historical events for its validity, and that those events are much more than illustrations of trans-historical truths of a Hellenistic sort. Instead they form the heart of the Christian gospel.

From this background his more popular presentations, *Christianity and Liberalism* and *What is Faith?*, may be examined. In the first Machen asserted that liberalism is not another variety of Christianity but a totally different religion.

> Liberalism differs from Christianity with regard to the presuppositions of the gospel (the view of God and the view of man), with regard to the Book in which the gospel is contained, and with regard to the Person whose work the gospel sets forth. It is not surprising then that it differs from Christianity in its account of the gospel itself; it is not surprising that it presents an entirely different account of the way of salvation. Liberalism finds salvation (so far as it is willing to speak at all of 'salvation') in man; Christianity finds it in an act of God. [7]

Of course he did not claim knowledge of the hearts of those who held liberal doctrine. Yet he was convinced that Christianity may not be so defined in terms of religious experience so that commitment to the great events of the life of Christ is irrelevant. Someone who does not hold to them can hardly be considered a Christian. To be sure, there may be no one who actually holds to the entire liberal position. Nevertheless, there is a liberal system with implications for all of life even if those implications are not drawn by all.

What is Faith? continues the theme but focuses even more vividly upon the nature of salvation in Christ.

> Christ is offered to us not in general, but 'in the gospel'; but in the gospel there is included all that the heart of man can wish. We ought never, therefore, to set present communion with Christ, as so many are doing, in opposition to the gospel; we ought never to say that we are interested in what Christ does for us now, but are not so much interested in what he did long ago. Do you know what soon happens when men talk in that way? The answer is only too plain. They soon lose all contact with the real Christ; what they call 'Christ' in the soul soon comes to have little to do with the actual person, Jesus of Nazareth; their religion would really remain essentially the same if scientific history should prove that such a person as Jesus of Nazareth never lived. In other words, they soon came to substitute the imaginings of their own hearts for what God has revealed; they substitute mysticism for Christianity as the religion of their souls.
>
> That danger should be avoided by the Christian man with all his might and main. God has given us an anchor for our souls; He has anchored us to Himself by the message of the Cross. Let us never cast that anchor off; let us never weaken our connection with the events upon which our faith is based. Such dependence upon the past will never prevent us from having present communion with Christ; our communion with Him will be as inward, as intimate, as untrammelled by any barriers of sense, as the communion of which the mystics boast; but unlike the communion of the mystics it will be communion not with the imaginings of our own hearts, but with the real Saviour Jesus Christ. The gospel of redemption through the Cross and resurrection of Christ is not a

barrier between us and Christ, but it is the blessed tie, by which, with the cords of His love, He has bound us forever to Him.[8]

Here is Machen's answer to the great dilemma. For him gospel history is not an embarrassment to the Christian faith but its very foundation. Because this was so pivotal for him, it is not surprising that his outlook was to have great significance for his ecclesiastical life as well as his theological, and consequently for Westminster Theological Seminary and the Orthodox Presbyterian Church. If Christianity indeed depends upon the acceptance of the historicity of certain events, then the rejection of those events can hardly be a matter for negotiation within the Christian church. While the modernist Auburn Affirmation of the Presbyterian Church said that the issue in the church did not concern doctrines, but only differing theories of the meaning of those doctrines, Machen and those who agreed with him could hardly agree. For example, any view of the resurrection that speaks only of the ongoing force of Christ's personality but considers irrelevant the question of whether Christ was physically raised and his tomb empty, is not really a theory of the Christian view of the resurrection but simply a denial of it. Hence Machen's position that the enemies of the gospel are not only those who overtly deny the resurrection but also those who refuse to stand up for it. Theories may differ from each other only in degree, but whether or not the great gospel events have happened is the difference between Christianity and something else.

Consequently Machen could not see any value for Christ's church in a reorganized Princeton Theological Seminary where all "theories" within the church must be allowed to speak. After all it was not theories that were at stake but gospel facts. So he founded Westminster Theological Seminary to carry on the heritage that had been Princeton's. Included in the new venture to a great extent was the Princeton curriculum. Therefore Westminster stressed knowledge of the biblical languages as the foundation of scholarly study of the Scriptures and emphasized critical evaluation of non-evangelical approaches to the Bible. Supporting the curriculum was an apologetic not satisfied with examination of peripheral questions. Instead it went to the very root of questions as Machen himself had done.

Since Machen agreed that "truth is in order to goodness" (from Chapter 1 of the old Presbyterian *Form of Government*), it was to be expected that his theological approach would influence his ecclesiastical life. For example, there are many knotty issues involved in the question of who has responsibility for the doctrinal oversight of a foreign missionary. Machen, however, could not accept a situation in which the church board supported missionaries who were unsure whether the Christian faith is definitive religious truth or only one of many culturally conditioned forms of it. Just as intolerable was the fact that the Presbyterian board, in the interests of harmony on the field, was excluding candidates who shared Machen's views that some missionaries were presenting anti-Christian propaganda.

Here was the occasion for Machen's founding of the Independent Board for Presbyterian Foreign Missions, and also for his unwillingness to resign from it later at the direction of the church. He and those joined with him were convicted by the ecclesiastical courts of the Presbyterian Church USA. The consequent founding of the Orthodox Presbyterian Church seemed inevitable. Again, if the Christian faith depends upon the truth of historical events, there can hardly be compromise with those who do not agree with that fundamental premise. For the life and doctrine of J. Gresham Machen, as well as for Westminster Theological Seminary and the Orthodox Presbyterian Church, there was no more pressing issue than the nature of Protestant liberalism and how it compared to biblical Christianity.

A half-century should provide sufficient perspective upon Machen's doctrine and its practical results. Machen himself would not see any point to sentimental hagiography. Therefore, he would expect us to ask how his approach should be realistically evaluated today.

No doubt there are still those who believe it possible to enjoy a relationship with Jesus Christ without committing themselves to anything the Bible has to say about him— but that should not be charged to Machen's account. No doubt most contemporary theology does not accept biblical doctrine any more than in Machen's day — but that is not because his critique was invalid. But the important question is, does current thought agree with Machen's specific criticism of Ritschl and Herrmann? Certainly the critique offered by the history of religion theologians at the turn of the century and later by Karl Barth was directed against the confusion of culture and the gospel. Today, "civil religion" is something repudiated by almost everyone. Growing insight that there is in principle little difference between confusing Christianity and contemporary culture and confusing it with first-century Hellenistic culture has strengthened acceptance of Machen's argument.

But even more pointedly, what contribution did Machen make to the problem of Christianity and history? As has been noted already, the issue has become more subtle. What is now under discussion is the professional activity of the historian, not necessarily the reality of the events he studies. When it is said that the Christian faith is not historical, or that it is not a proper object for historical investigation, ordinarily what is intended is an affirmation that the truth of the Christian faith does not depend upon a discipline which is only useful for the analysis of broader developments and cannot determine the truth or falsity of unique, unrepeatable events. Is there in practical terms any great difference between saying there is no evidence for the resurrection and saying the historian cannot determine that evidence? Not really, if one follows the ordinary assumption that if anyone is competent to evaluate historical reality, it is the historian!

What is actually under discussion is apologetic method. Whatever convictions Machen may have developed later concerning the value of analyzing the presuppositions of Christian and non-Christian thinking (in interaction with Cornelius Van Til), they were not present in his earlier work. Machen's method was painstaking analysis of his opponents' arguments, followed by careful explanation of why those arguments were substantially less believable than his own position. It is not going too far to say that he employed the ordinary scientific argumentation of probability reasoning. Note his appreciation of the argument of Francis L. Patton, comparing faith in Christ with the choice of a ship in which to sail. The point of the argument was that even though one could not have absolute certainty in the choice of a ship, it would be foolish to use that as a reason for choosing the ship in worse condition.

> Such, said Patton in effect, is *our* conduct if we refuse to act on reasonable probability in this matter of religion. We have no choice about undertaking this business of living— and of dying. We cannot choose but make the voyage. The only question is in which ship we shall safely go. One ship presents itself with evidences of safety far superior to those of all others. It is the ship of Christianity, the way of living and dying founded upon the supernatural revelation that the Bible contains. Shall we desert that ship for one far less approved, simply because the evidence in its favor does not amount to apodictic certitude? Or, acting on the best evidence that we can obtain, shall we make the great venture of faith and launch forth into the deep at Christ's command?[9]

Obviously Machen's apologetics was in the tradition long associated with Scottish and Princeton Calvinism, that of common sense realism. This approach pointed out the futility of asking theoretical Kantian questions and instead emphasized the value of proceeding in philosophy the way one did in ordinary life. Included was making decisions on the basis of probability. It is easy to see in Machen's scholarly methodology and emphasis on the event character of Christianity his indebtedness to this method.

Does that suggest Machen's approach is no longer useful? Is it outmoded because the issues today are more subtle or because those coming after him, influenced by Cornelius Van Til, no longer feel theologically justified in using his method? Certainly there has been little interest at Westminster in showing in *detail* the fallacies in liberal argumentation. The one exception is Meredith G. Kline who provided strong evidence for an early date for Deuteronomy. But even that was a by-product of Kline's main interests. While allowing for the fact that Machen's genius is not easily duplicated, it is worth remembering that Van Til intended to make the best of the worlds of both Kuyper and Warfield. While it was not always easy to see this in Van Til because of his idealist terminology, there is more potential in his apologetic for discussion of the "facts" of Christianity than has always been seen. The application of Van Til by Robert Knudsen to the methodology of the social sciences and by John Frame to contemporary empiricism is bearing fruit that Machen would have appreciated.

But apologetics is only one element in the Machen heritage; his chair was in New Testament. It might seem ironical that the Princeton biblical scholar with the most lasting contribution to Machen's Westminster decided to remain at Princeton and not come to Westminster! It was Geerhardus Vos whose thinking is most suited for developing Machen's grand theme; namely, that the Christian faith concerns the great *objective* change that has been accomplished by the work of Christ. The newness of the age that Christ has inaugurated was at the heart of Machen's protest against the mysticism of the liberals; it is today at the heart of biblical work at Westminster.

Even a brief summary of Machen and Westminster would not be complete without mention of practical theology. Within the context of Princeton's decline it seemed to him that the ever-increasing demands of students for more practical theology posed a threat to their scholarly preparation. The combination of inadequate undergraduate preparation for seminary and increasing demands placed upon pastors is bound to lead to tension in balancing a seminary curriculum. At any rate, Machen and hence Westminster were widely thought to be interested more in the training of scholars than pastors. Doubtless it did not help that at Princeton the forces in favor of broadening the theology were the same as those that believed in greater emphasis upon the needs of the pastor. The course was charted by practical theology professors J. Ross Stevenson and Charles Erdman. Certainly liberalism, especially in the United States, was likely to find more guidance for the pastor in sociology than in Hebrew.

Granting that Machen's instincts were sound, especially in view of practical theology as he knew it, what implications do they have for the present day? For the record, Westminster's two presidents have come from practical theology, from the small minority of the faculty with significant pastoral experience! The real question is again the hermeneutical one. That is, to what extent is theology, and especially practical theology, responsible for the translation or contextualization of biblical teaching into the life situations of contemporary men and women, in the United States and in the developing churches? At stake here are two issues of vital importance to Machen. The first is that the gospel not be psychologized away into religious experience. The second is that that gospel is needed by society and culture. Presbyterian theology today is confronted with a challenge similar to the one Machen faced and must do its best to meet it.

Westminster has done much. It has set forth foundational biblical teaching for the church and its work. This was the accomplishment of R. B.

Kuiper through systematic theology and Edmund P. Clowney through biblical theology. Jay Adams has effectively applied biblical exegesis to the needs of pastoral counseling. Harvie Conn and Roger Greenway are carrying forward the work in missions contextualization. The interest of the entire faculty in biblical theology, with its inherent concern for utilizing biblical structures of thought not necessarily found in systematic theology, will be of help in this enormous task. Machen and Westminster never were committed just to perpetuation of tradition. Formulating theology for the needs of the church constitutes a challenge it cannot refuse. No doubt there is abroad confusion between contextualization and sellout to liberalism; to a great extent Westminster's ability to clarify this issue effectively will determine the extent to which she enjoys the confidence of the church.

Ecclesiastically the Machen heritage of opposition to liberalism is undergoing a complex development. Machen refused to apply the idea that there are differing theories on the same doctrines to the struggle of liberalism with traditional Presbyterianism. In this he was surely correct; liberalism did constitute a different religion. He spoke of a liberal system, present even when the individual involved disavowed his commitment to certain of its doctrines. He was opposed to the compromisers or moderates within the church who never could quite see what actions of the church implied. All this follows logically and correctly from his understanding of the nature of liberalism.

From this point has arisen the issues of secondary or tertiary separation. Are some doctrines really secondary in importance? Does subscription to the system of doctrine mean subscription to all doctrines in the standards as well as to the implications of those doctrines? Is this the Machen heritage?

Certainly, it was not the position of Hodge and Warfield. They insisted that subscription was to "generic" Calvinism. This is what Machen himself seemed to believe as he insisted that there was room for pre-millenarians in the church without the necessity for creedal reform to make that possible. But it is only fair to remember that Machen's death preceded many controversies; it would be wrong to try to psychologize him too.

Can the line still be drawn between agreement on the principles of Presbyterianism and divergent theories on those principles? Are Presbyterians to work together with fundamentalists, evangelicals, both or neither? Is union between the Orthodox Presbyterian Church and the Presbyterian Church in America desirable? The answers are still forthcoming, but it is clear that the questions have arisen because of Machen's approach to liberalism.

Machen appeared in a day of great confusion within theology and the church and did as much as any man could possibly do to dispel that confusion. Because of him the gospel is seen more clearly today than could have been expected without him. This is true also for many who have never heard his name! But as he himself would say, this is still a day where much hard work and prayer needs to be done, that God's grace may be seen ever more clearly in the midst of a dark world.

NOTES

1. Ned B. Stonehouse, *J. Gresham Machen: A Biographical Memoir* (Grand Rapids: Eerdmans, 1954), 106–7.

2. J. G. Machen, "Christianity in Conflict," from *Contemporary American Theology*, ed. Vergilius Ferm (New York: Round Table, 1932), 256.

3. Cf. Van A. Harvey, *The Historian and the Believer* (New York: Macmillan, 1969) and Friedrich Gogarten, *Demythologizing and History* (London: SCM, 1955).

4. Wilhelm Herrmann, *The Communion of the Christian with God*, trans. J. Sandys Stanyon (London: Williams and Norgate, 1895), 70–91.

5. "Conflict," *op. cit.*.

6. Ibid., 257.

7. Machen, *Christianity and Liberalism* (New York: Macmillan, 1923), 117.

8. Machen, *What Is Faith?* (New York: Macmillan, 1925), 153–54.

9. "Conflict," 262; cf. *Faith*, 90.

Greg L. Bahnsen

17 Machen, Van Til, and the Apologetical Tradition of the OPC

A POLOGETICS GAVE BIRTH to the Orthodox Presbyterian Church and continues to be its legacy and reputation.

The modernism of the early twentieth century was not simply a theological variant within historic Christianity, not merely a new version of Christian doctrine which retained at its center the *evangel*. It was, according to J. Gresham Machen's analysis in *Christianity and Liberalism*,[1] a departure from the Christian religion altogether, abandoning the proclamation of the supernaturalistic good news of redemption which had distinguished the Christian church throughout history. Liberalism was simply another religion or philosophy of man in competition with the historic biblical faith. Accordingly, the battle with modernism was more than "polemical theology" against an exegetically weak or inconsistent school of evangelical Christianity. It was *apologetics* with unbelief.[2]

Apologetics and the OPC

Machen's confrontation with modernism and broad churchmanship at Princeton Theological Seminary and within the Presbyterian Church in the USA — which in time gave rise to both Westminster Theological Seminary (1929) and the Orthodox Presbyterian Church (1936)[3] — was thus apologetical in nature. Both institutions were founded in the effort to "contend earnestly for the faith which was once for all delivered unto the saints" (Jude 3). Accordingly, the *Evangelical Dictionary of Theology* states: "evangelical Christianity in the Western world owes a large debt to Machen and to the organizations he founded for their intelligent and courageous explanation of and stand for historical Christian truth."[4]

259

Apologetics was used, then, in the providence of God to bring about the Orthodox Presbyterian Church fifty years ago. Throughout its half century the Orthodox Presbyterian Church has retained a reputation for apologetics. This reputation has been tied, not only to the interests and requirements of its ministers, evangelists, and teachers,[5] but especially to the scholarly careers of two leading professors at Westminster Theological Seminary who were Orthodox Presbyterian ministers: Machen himself (who died in 1937) and Cornelius Van Til (who retired in 1973).

It can be said without partisan prejudice that preeminence in the twentieth-century defense of biblical faith belongs to the labors of Machen and Van Til— the former in historical studies, the latter in philosophical studies, as they interfaced with Christian theology. Dr. Clarence Edward Macartney said of Machen: "he was the greatest theologian and defender of the Christian faith that the church of our day has produced."[6] About Van Til *Christianity Today* said: "Cornelius Van Til wanted to be a farmer. . . . Instead he became one of the foremost Christian apologists of our time."[7]

So then, to understand and appreciate the outlook, history, and ministry of the Orthodox Presbyterian Church— even more so than Westminster Theological Seminary[8]— one needs to be familiar (if not sympathetic) with the theological perspective, apologetical distinctives, and scholarly efforts of J. Gresham Machen and Cornelius Van Til. It has been Machen and Van Til who, as theologians and apologists, have given the denomination its early bearing and character.[9] As a social group the Orthodox Presbyterian Church has a self-conception and mindset which are rooted in, and will continue to develop in interaction with, the distinctive stances assumed by Machen and Van Til in their teaching and publishing ministries.

A House Divided?

These introductory observations bring us to an engaging question. If the intellectual identity of the Orthodox Presbyterian Church is tied up with the perspective and influence of both Machen and Van Til, is not the denomination a house philosophically divided against itself? William White honestly asks, "Did Machen understand how far from the old Princeton apologetic the new Westminster apologetic really was?"[10] Others would turn that into a *rhetorical* question. To many people, anyway, it has seemed that the apologetical approach taken by Machen was conceptually at odds with the presuppositional methodology subsequently advanced by Van Til. In the thinking of such individuals Machen's empirical tendencies do not comport readily with Van Til's philosophical peculiarities. The heritage in apologetics bequeathed by these two Christian scholars, we are told, lacks inner harmony— like a conceptual dissonant chord.

There is no doubt about this much: Machen and Van Til certainly manifested different scholarly specializations and developed different emphases in their publications. Machen labored over detailed historical challenges to the Christian faith, paramount illustrations being *The Origin of Paul's Religion*[11] and *The Virgin Birth of Christ*[12] — whereas Van Til strove to counter the broader, underlying philosophical challenges mounted against the Christian understanding of reality, knowledge, or ethics, as exemplified in his books, *A Survey of Christian Epistemology*[13] and *Christianity and Idealism*[14]. Machen waxed eloquent about the historical foundation of faith: "Christian piety must be grounded firmly in historical knowledge."[15] Van Til argued that historical knowledge has philosophical preconditions which in themselves drive one to Christian faith: "the conflict between those who believe in historic Christianity and those who do not cannot be carried by a discussion of 'facts' without at the same time discussing the philosophy of fact";[16] "one has to go back of the 'facts' of history to a discussion of the meaning of history."[17]

The intellectual temperaments, preparation, and interests of Machen and Van Til likewise led them in different directions. Machen was fascinated and absorbed with the particulars of classical philology and ancient history, while not feeling at ease in the rarified atmosphere of philosophical speculation. As a student, Machen distinguished himself in classics, but once relayed to his older brother, Arthur, an offer of "$1,000 for a satisfactory exegesis of a single page" of Kant's *Critique of Pure Reason*.[18] On the other hand, Van Til's preparation and doctoral work were devoted, not to the details of empirical science or historical study, but precisely to the broader and intellectually necessary issues of philosophy; therefore he mastered, as a candidate at Princeton University, the complete works of Plato, Aristotle, Kant, and Hegel in their original languages. He later wrote about the fact that historical investigation bolstered the work of apologetics, but added this autobiographical note: "I do not personally do a great deal of this because my colleagues in the other departments of the Seminary in which I teach are doing it better than I could do it."[19]

The critical claim goes beyond what we have recognized here, though. It maintains that Machen was a practitioner of the "Old Princeton" approach to apologetics[20] against which Van Til took a decided stand as a professor at Westminster Seminary.[21] If that premise is substantially accurate, then some of Van Til's deepest reservations and most critical comments about the traditional method of apologetics fostered at (old) Princeton Seminary would prove to be against Machen himself — creating, in perspective and procedure, a momentous parting of the ways between the two apologists. In essence, Van Til would have been correcting the methods of Machen[22] and striving to replace them with a presuppositional approach alien to Machen's thinking. Their contributions to the defense of the historical Christian faith are not simply different from each other, then, but are at diametric odds with each other. Van Til's work would not complement that of Machen, but stand in fundamental conflict with it. The "apologetic tradition" of the Orthodox Presbyterian Church would actually turn out, in that case, to be *two separate* traditions standing over against each other. Many think (at least on first appearance) that this is the actual state of affairs. I do not.[23]

It would be anachronistic and undiscerning, of course, to hold that Machen completely anticipated and clearly expressed the very same transcendental, presuppositional challenge in apologetics as did Van Til, who merely perpetuated it after Machen. Van Til's distinctive philosophical contribution and significant step forward in self-conscious, apologetical methodology cannot be trivialized. Likewise, one cannot forget the immense admiration and commitment Machen had for the grand theological reputation of Princeton Seminary, with its stalwart professors famous for their propounding and defending of Calvinism as the truth of God, the purest and best exposition of the gospel. Machen was indebted to this intellectual tradition, openly identifying himself with the outlook and scholarship of B. B. Warfield[24] and Francis L. Patton, the first professor in the chair of "the Relations of Philosophy and Science to the Christian Religion" and later seminary president, with whom Machen had a particularly close (and mutually supportive) relationship.[25] When the apologetics chair created for Patton was vacated in 1892, it was assumed by William Brenton Greene, Jr., who served both as Machen's instructor and later as his supportive colleague in the seminary and presbytery.[26] It could be expected, therefore, that the attitude, concerns, and argumentation of Machen would bear a close resemblance to that of his Princeton predecessors— making it understandable (though too simplistic) that, not only might his *theology*[27] and his *empirical* concern with evidences[28] be readily identified with theirs, but his *conception of apologetics* as well.

The situation was far more intricate than that. While not coming to a fully and systematically worked-out understanding of presuppositional epistemology— much less shifting fields from his area of historical expertise to philosophical defense of the faith (which presuppositionalism would not have required of him anyway) — Machen does seem, in a manner unlike his Princeton mentors, to have recognized and appreciated that the insights of presuppositionalism were the consistent and self-conscious end of thinking which is true to Reformed theology. Personal experience and scholarly reflection brought him to a conception of apologetics— and of his own continuing work in historical defense — which was an advance over old Princeton in various ways and a corrective to some of its weakest philosophical distinctives. His own perspective on, and pursuit of, defending the faith were much more presuppositional than we would expect from someone who conformed exactly to the old Princeton outlook.[29] In short, because Machen moved away from the old Princeton conception of apologetics in a presuppositional direction, Van Til could applaud and support his historical defense of the faith, even as Machen could appreciate and approve of the developments in methodology and philosophical defense by Van Til. Any minor incongruities between (and even within) their two scholarly efforts do not belie the basic harmony of perspective which runs through them both.

Some Relevant History

Rehearsing some history relevant to Machen and Van Til would lead us to anticipate that evaluation.[30]

Eleven years after Van Til's birth, Machen joined the faculty of Princeton Theological Seminary (1906). It was during Van Til's teenage and college years that Machen became known as someone who stood for the intelligent defense of the historic Christian faith, publishing such engaging articles (among others) as "Jesus and Paul," "Christianity and Culture," and "History and Faith."[31] The year Van Til entered Calvin Theological Seminary (1921), Machen's first major book and apologetical masterpiece, *The Origin of Paul's Religion,* came off the press, elevating Machen in the esteem of all who sought a Christianity capable of scholarly defense. Impressed with the noble faculty of Princeton Seminary (Machen, Vos, C. W. Hodge, Wilson) and the international prestige of the University (with A. A. Bowman the head of the philosophy department), Van Til transferred there the next year (1922), eventually earning the Th.M. from the seminary in 1925 and the Ph.D. from the university in 1927.

During those five intellectually intense years he came to know and respect Machen, on a personal basis especially while a seminary student, living on the same floor with Machen in Alexander Hall.[32] This time of contact between Van Til and Machen was a momentous period in the latter's career. He published two major works important to the apologetical setting of the time, *Christianity and Liberalism* in 1923 and *What is Faith?*[33] in 1925. He constantly wrote on themes of apologetical significance: "Is Christianity True?" (1923), "The God of the Early Christians" (1924), "The Modern Use of the Bible" (1925), "The Relation of Religion to Science and Philosophy" (1926), "Is the Bible Right About Jesus?" (1927)[34]. Also he often preached fervently in defense of the faith as stated supply (1923–1924) in the First Presbyterian Church of Princeton.[35] Public focus during Van Til's seminary years was on events which would embroil Machen in theological and ecclesiastical controversy; e.g., on Fosdick's notorious address, "Shall the Fundamentalists Win?" (1922), on the signing of the "Auburn Affirmation" (1923).

In light of Van Til's admiration for Machen,[36] Machen's personal proximity, and the obvious bearing of Machen's scholarship on Van Til's chosen interest in apologetics, it is unreasonable to think Van Til could be unaware of Machen's position and the details of his method of defense.

Given Van Til's brilliance, it is unreasonable to think he did not understand them.

It turns out that at the same time Van Til was making an equally strong impression on Machen. Van Til entered Princeton as a middler,[37] having already studied under W. H. Jellema and reading the Dutch works of Kuyper. Could Machen have missed this in his personal contacts and conversations with the Christian Reformed transfer student from Calvin Seminary? (After all, during Machen's own years as a seminary student, his esteemed mentor, B. B. Warfield, published a critical discussion of Kuyper's view of apologetics.)[38] Van Til's philosophical prowess became readily apparent to his Princeton professors, more particularly by his writing the prize-winning student papers for both 1923 (on evil and theodicy) and for 1924 (on the will and its theological relations), as well as by his taking simultaneous philosophy courses at the University each semester (with Machen hearing of A. A. Bowman's high praise for his competence in metaphysics).

Two months before the granting of his doctorate, Van Til published in *The Princeton Theological Review* a discussion of A. N. Whitehead's Lowell lectures for 1926, *Religion in the Making.*[39] The review clearly contained those lines of thought for which Van Til's presuppositional analysis has come to be recognized throughout the years. Van Til introduced his foil, significantly (especially in the old Princeton setting), as someone who "seeks to apply the scientific method to religion." Crucial to his own approach, Van Til laid bare his opponent's presupposition: "experience and the history of experience is his starting point." The prevailing sin of unbelieving philosophy was criticized: "the great line of distinction between God and man is effaced"; i.e., no adequate Creator/creature distinction. Van Til complained that God is, then, subjected to man's own autonomous judgment: "the Good is higher than God. . . . This accords strictly with his starting point which regards the moral consciousness as the judge of religion." But autonomous philosophy is not equal to such a task, internally suffering from its own dialectical tensions, according to Van Til. Whitehead posited process (change) as the basic feature of reality, trying "to get order and system out of this moving whole" by reference to God. This is impossible, Van Til observed, since Whitehead's philosophy already "implies that God is subject to the conditions of the world." Having offered an internal critique of the unbeliever's thought, Van Til finally pointed to the only viable alternative. The Christian philosopher does not face Whitehead's major problem because the biblical God is both transcendent and personal, "the self-sufficient creator" of the historic particulars (i.e., the source of both order and change). Van Til's conclusion rings with the kind of note which is famous in his apologetical efforts: "Theism makes God the source of possibility; only thus can the transcendence as well as the immanence of God be maintained; only thus is God qualitatively distinct from man; only thus is He personal; only thus is He God."[40] So then, from Van Til's very first published article his presuppositional direction of thought was manifest for all to see.

The following year (1928) Princeton Seminary invited Van Til to take a leave from his new pastorate and serve the seminary as an instructor in apologetics — quite an honor, making him the youngest member of the faculty. His friendly and godly hero, "Das" Machen, was pleased with the development and maintained a close personal relation with Van Til and his wife during that year.[41] These words from a letter to his mother on September 25, 1928, leave no doubt about Machen's endorsement of Van Til:

> The best piece of news for some time is that Mr. Van Til, a recent graduate of the Seminary, has, despite Dr. Stevenson's vigorous opposition, been asked by the Directors' Curriculum Committee to teach the classes in Apologetics during this year, *and has accepted.* It is the first real forward step that has been taken in some time. Van Til is excellent material from which a professor might ultimately be made.[42]

In January 1929, Van Til published a review of two books by Bavinck, insisting that we must abandon the impossible notion of a "neutral territory" of truth or study — making necessary schools which are self-consciously Christian in starting point and goal[43] — "if we would truly employ all the means given us for the propogation and defense of the faith."[44] One of the cherished assumptions and touted ideals of the old Princeton approach to apologetics could not be accepted by Van Til. That was open for all to see, and Machen had excellent perception.

In May of 1926, the board of directors for Princeton Theological Seminary had extended to Machen a call to the Stuart Professorship of Apologetics and Christian Ethics, which he accepted after some hesitation (especially over transferring from the New Testament department). In the throes of the political fight over reorganization of the seminary, though, Machen came to doubt the wisdom of his acceptance.[45] On June 20, 1928, he requested permission from the board to withdraw his previous acceptance, which it did. Who then could take Machen's place? The overwhelming approval of Van Til's work in apologetics could not have been more forcefully expressed by the board of Princeton Seminary[46] than by what it did in the spring of 1929 — electing Van Til, after but one year of teaching, to occupy the very chair of apologetics which Machen had turned down! On May 12 "Machen expressed his intense gratification at this development, speaking of Van Til's special equipment for the work and his great success with the students."[47] From this it is evident that Machen was conscious of, interested in, and personally applauded the character and quality of Van Til's apologetical teaching.

On June 14, 1929, Machen communicated his determination not to teach under the reorganized board of Princeton Seminary.[48] He was joined in this by Van Til. When plans were pursued that summer to establish Westminster Seminary, Machen had his own opportunity to seek the very kind of man in apologetics he wanted. We can be sure Machen recognized how crucial and determinative this position would be, especially in light of the "purpose and plan" for the new seminary which Machen propounded at its opening exercises: notably, "we believe that the Christian religion welcomes and is capable of scholarly defense." He considered no one else to be as suited and qualified to do the work desired than Van Til. There was no doubt in his mind about the choice. Machen was so determined to have Van Til be the apologist at Westminster that, when Van Til initially declined the invitation (even after a visit from O. T. Allis to plead the cause), in August Machen himself traveled to Spring Lake, Michigan, to use all his influence and persuasion to change Van Til's mind — like Farel pleading with Calvin to come to Geneva, Van Til recalls.[49] In September Van Til joined the faculty, being asked to teach the same course material he had advanced at Princeton earlier (including an elective in the history of metaphysics). It is manifest from what transpired, then, that neither Machen nor Van Til found irreconcilable differences with each other's own conceptions and practice of apologetics. They both made well thought out decisions to labor together.

There was plenty of opportunity over the next few years to understand even further the nature and practice of one another's apologetical scholarship. Van Til would read Machen's stirring 1932 address: "The Importance of Christian Scholarship,"[50] and hear Machen's famous radio talks in 1935 which were published as *The Christian Faith in the Modern World*[51] and *The Christian View of Man*. In 1933 Van Til developed and clearly set forth his transcendental, presuppositional apologetic in his first major syllabus at Westminster, *Metaphysics of Apologetics*.[52] The distinctive tack taken by his presuppositional apologetic finds its finest and earliest statement right here. He reflected critically on the empirical approach to religious truth in the syllabus, *Psychology of Religion*. Very importantly, Van Til produced in 1935, not only his quintessential statement of presuppositionalism which appears in the syllabus entitled *Christian Apologetics*, but also the syllabus with most direct relevance to the old Princeton method of apologetics, *Evidences*. All of these written studies, which abundantly advertised the presuppositional character and method of defending the faith, were produced and discussed in the presence of Machen, a man who was consumed with enthusiasm for Christianity's defense. He surely took note of the accomplishments and teaching of his chosen professor for apologetics. Prior to Machen's death, Van Til also published a large number of magazine pieces, including some twenty articles or reviews of important religious and philosophical books in the very periodicals which Machen himself helped to establish, finance, and edit: *Christianity Today* and the *Presbyterian Guardian*.[53] At one point Machen and Van Til enjoyed a two-day train trip together in which they talked at length with each other about apologetic method.

Therefore, Machen was hardly in the dark as to Van Til's point of view and method,[54] and Van Til could not have been ignorant of Machen's. The scholarship and argumentation of these two apologists, who had known each other for so long, could not have slipped the attention of each other. Nor can we credibly suppose that either of them lacked the requisite scholarly powers to realize what the other was contending. Given their joint and eager dedication to apologetical work, they would have been especially interested in the bearing of each other's line of thinking on their own labors. And given their none-too-shy commitment to matters of principle and importance, we cannot believe they would have swept any fundamental ideological conflict under the rug.

So then, our short rehearsal and integration of relevant details in their careers exhibits, from the very fact that Machen and Van Til chose to minister and teach together, that neither of them found in the apologetic propounded by the other any root hostility to his own. William White justly records: "It is a known fact that Machen, as far as he comprehended it, fully endorsed Van Til's thinking and gave it his hearty and unqualified backing."[55] If the two master apologists themselves did not perceive tension between their two approaches, it would seem a high-minded and precarious course for students of them to pursue some fundamental conflict between them.

The Objective Proof of Christian Theism

The temptation to suggest apologetical incompatibility between Machen and Van Til springs, it seems, from harboring misleading assumptions about Van Til's view of such tools as empirical evidence and theistic proofs in defending the faith,[56] if not from an equally misconceived notion of what Machen felt about them as well. These misrepresentations cannot be justified in light of the published works of Machen and Van Til, but arise from faulty preconceptions of what their positions must imply and from inadequate familiarity with their teaching.[57] To take just one of many available illustrations, Clark Pinnock has portrayed Van Til as maintaining that "it is not only useless, but wrong, to appeal to theistic arguments or historical vindications in defense of the Christian faith"; standing over against Van Til, he thinks, Pinnock teaches that "a philosophy of Christian evidences which employs theistic argument and historical evidence is needed, lest the gospel be discredited as a grand and unwarranted assumption."[58] Efforts must be made, then, to clarify and explain the matter,[59] looking first at the issue of theistic proofs and second at the issue of empirical evidences for Christianity.

We should begin by observing that Van Til's criticism of the "theistic proofs" has always and only been directed against the proofs as they were *traditionally* formulated, understood, and applied. Such proofs have erroneously suggested that (1) the evidence for God's existence is ambiguous (so that there is some excuse for denying it or holding that it is only probably true), (2) that there are matters which are epistemically more certain than God (from which one then moves on to prove, with less certainty, God's existence), (3) that the unbeliever's espoused presuppositions about reality and knowledge are sufficient to account for the intelligibility of his experience and reasoning (so that he has every philosophical right to question God's existence on his own terms), (4) that unregenerate men can be intellectually neutral and open-mindedly fair about this subject (rather than unrighteously and self-deceptively suppressing the truth), and (5) that the "god" which can be rationally proven may or may not be the God of the Christian Scriptures (since we deal only with isolated truth-claims, one by one, not an all-embracing worldview). In addition to the internal, philosophical flaws with the traditional formulations of a theistic proof,[60] Van Til finds these preceding assumptions to be theologically and philosophically unacceptable. Paul taught in Romans 1:18–22 that the very living and true God in all of his eternal power and divine character (contrary to 5) is so clearly and inescapably revealed in man's experience (contrary to 2) that they all know God, and there is absolutely no excuse for denying it (contrary to 1); nevertheless, all men strive to suppress the truth in unrighteousness (contrary to 4) and end up becoming vain and foolish in their reasoning (contrary to 3). For instance, they presuppose that all events are random ("chance," freedom), and then turn around and insist on rigid explanation by means of scientific laws (order, necessity); they presuppose that there is nothing but matter in motion (materialism), and then turn around and call for adherence to the (non-materialistic) laws of logic.

Van Til realizes that there is no natural *theology*, *if* we mean that according to Romans 1 the created realm simply provides *uninterpreted* raw data which merely makes *possible*, provided men rationally reflect upon it correctly, a natural knowledge of God as the eventual *conclusion* of their reasoning. From the epistemological side, there is no uninterpreted sense data ("no brute facts"); and from the metaphysical side, there is no logic free of commitment to some view of reality ("no neutrality"). Theologically, men do not naturally interpret their experience of nature in such a way as to reach and affirm correct conclusions about God. About the natural man, who "cannot know" the things of God's Spirit (1 Cor 2:14), Paul said "there is none who seeks after God" (Rom 3:11). In that case we should not really speak of natural theology, but rather of a "natural atheology." Until men are driven to abandon their intellectual autonomy and to think in terms of the truth of God as their point of reference, they will never read the evidence properly for God's existence, *but* Van Til adds, neither will they be able to make sense of *any* area of their experience. The theistic proofs should not, therefore, cater to man's pretended autonomy.[61] It is important to stress the "basic difference between a theistic proof that presupposes God and one that presupposes man as ultimate."[62]

Van Til's apologetic is based upon confidence in natural *revelation*, for Romans 1 teaches that the created order is a conduit of constant, inescapable, *pre-interpreted information* about God, so that all men already possess an *actual* knowledge of him at the very *outset* of their reasoning about anything whatsoever, a knowledge which makes possible their use of evidence and reason. Van Til asserts that "the revelation of God to man is so clear that it has absolute compelling force objectively," and from that standpoint "I do not reject 'the theistic proofs' but merely insist on formulating them in such a way as not to compromise the doctrines of Scripture."[63] Natural revelation is crucial to the formulation of proof for God's existence: "God's revelation is everywhere, and everywhere perspicuous. Hence the theistic proofs are absolutely valid. They are but the restatement of the revelation of God."[64]

Far from rejecting theistic proof, Van Til insists upon it, and in fact insists upon a very strong version thereof: "The argument for the existence of God and 'for the truth of Christianity is objectively valid. We should not tone down the validity of this argument to the probability level. . . . Christianity is the only reasonable position to hold."[65] If men will not intellectually acknowledge that they know and must presuppose God, their attempts to reason and interpret experience (on some other espoused presupposition) cannot be made intelligible. Thus Van Til states his proof quite concisely and forcefully: "The only 'proof' of the Christian position is that unless its truth is presupposed there is no possibility of 'proving' anything at all."[66] In short Van Til's approach is to challenge unbelievers in the words of Paul: "Where is the wise? where is the scribe? where is the disputer of this age? Has not God made foolish the wisdom of the world?" (1 Cor 1:20; cf. Rom 1:21).

If the debate with unbelievers comes down in principle to a conflict over ultimate presuppositions which control all other reasoning and interpretation, though, does not all use of rational argumentation cease? According to Van Til, *not at all*. This was the whole point of chapter XIV in *A Survey of Christian Epistemology.* It opened by saying "the question that comes up at once is whether it is then of any use to argue about the Christian theistic position at all with those who are of contrary convictions" (p. 183). Van Til forcefully refutes the notion that it is useless for the regenerate to reason with the unregenerate, insisting that we must. "It is exactly because of our deep conviction that God is one and truth is therefore one, that we hold that there is only one type of argument for all men" (p. 198). We must not abandon rational debate with the unbeliever: "we cannot choose epistemologies as we choose hats . . . [as if] the whole thing is but a matter of taste"; rather, those who hold antithetical presuppositions "ought to be refuted by a reasoned argument, instead of by ridicule and assumption" (pp. xiv, 23). Christian commitment is not intellectually ungrounded: "Faith is not blind faith. . . . Christianity can be shown to be, not 'just as good as' or even 'better than' the non-Christian position, but the *only* position that does not make nonsense of human experience."[67] Van Til does not permit the argument for the truth of Christianity to be washed out into subjectivism: "There is objective evidence in abundance and it is sufficiently clear. Men *ought*, if only they reasoned rightly, to come to the conclusion that God exists. That is to say, if the theistic proof is constructed as it ought to be constructed, it is objectively valid, whatever the attitude of those to whom it comes may be."[68]

Elsewhere Van Til is decidedly critical of the "fideistic attitude [which] comes to expression frequently in the statement of the experiential proof of the truth of Christianity. People will say that they know that they are saved and that Christianity is true no matter what the philosophical or scientific evidence for or against it may be. . . . But, in thus seeking to withdraw from all intellectual argument, such fideists have virtually admitted the validity of the argument against Christianity. They will have to believe in their hearts what they have virtually allowed to be intellectually indefensible."[69] His commitment to a reasoned apologetic, rather than blind authority, is manifest: "It might seem that there can be no *argument* between them. It might seem that the orthodox view of authority is to be spread only by testimony and by prayer, not by argument. But this would militate directly against the very foundation of all Christian revelation."[70] This brief discussion demonstrates how terribly misinformed is Montgomery's criticism that Van Til's apologetic "gives the unbeliever the impression that our gospel is as aprioristically, fideistically irrational as the presuppositional claims of its competitors."[71]

Since the argument with the unbeliever is finally over those presuppositions which control all other reasoning and interpretation, what kind of argument can be rationally employed? It will be an argument regarding the *preconditions* of all intelligible experience, logic, science, ethics, etc. — an argument "from the impossibility of the contrary."[72] For this one must use the *indirect* method of argument: "The method of reasoning by presupposition may be said to be indirect rather than direct. The issue between believers and non-believers in Christian theism cannot be settled by a direct appeal to 'facts' or 'laws' whose nature and significance is already agreed upon by both parties to the debate. The question is rather as to what is the final reference-point required to make the 'facts' and 'laws' intelligible."[73] To settle that question, Van Til continues, the believer and unbeliever must "for argument's sake" place themselves on each other's position to see what their respective outworkings are regarding the intelligibility of facts and laws. Van Til put it this way in his first syllabus:

> The Reformed method of argument is first constructive. It presents the biblical view positively by showing that all factual and logical discussions by men take place by virtue of the world's being what God in Christ says it is. It then proceeds negatively to show that unless all facts and all logical relations be seen in the light of the Christian framework, all human interpretation fails *instantly*. It fails instantly *in principle*. [74]

The Proper Approach to Evidences

When we turn from "theistic proof" to the subject of scientific and historical evidences for the Christian faith, we again see how far off the mark Van Til's critics have been. Montgomery misrepresents him as presenting the unbeliever "with an a priori dogmatic" instead of "the factually compelling evidence for the Christian truth-claim," and Pinnock alleges that Van Til "refuses to have anything to do with . . . rational arguments and empirical demonstrations." To hear them, one is led to believe Van Til would "recoil from" presenting verifying evidence for the faith and "dismiss [the unbeliever's] questions without a hearing." [75] The actual truth is that Van Til does not in the slightest reject the proper use of inductive reasoning and empirical evidences in apologetics.

Listen to what Van Til says about the phenomena of Scripture:

> The point is, we are told, that in an infallible Bible there should not be any discrepancies. There should be no statement of historical fact in Scripture that is contradictory to a statement of historical fact given elsewhere. Yet higher criticism has in modern times found what it thinks are facts that cannot possibly be harmonized with the idea of an infallible Bible. What shall be the attitude of the orthodox believer with respect to this? Shall he be an obscurantist and hold to the doctrine of the authority of the Scripture though he knows that it can empirically be shown to be contrary to the facts of Scripture themselves? It goes without saying that such should not be his attitude. [76]

The presuppositionalist is not allergic to employing empirical, inductive study according to the scientific method— just the opposite:

> It is quite commonly held that we cannot accept anything that is not the result of a sound scientific methodology. With this we can as Christians heartily agree. . . . The Christian position is certainly not opposed to experimentation and observation. [77]

> Depreciation of [the] sense world inevitably leads to a depreciation of many of the important facts of historic Christianity which took place in the sense world. The Bible does not rule out every form of empiricism any more than it rules out every form of *a priori* reasoning. [78]

The greater amount of detailed study and the more carefully such study is undertaken, the more truly Christian will the method be. It is important to bring out this point in order to help remove the common misunderstanding that Christianity is opposed to factual investigation. . . . The difference between the prevalent method of science and the method of Christianity is not that the former is interested in finding the facts and is ready to follow the facts wherever they may lead, while the latter is not ready to follow the facts.[79]

Such affirmations by Van Til fully comport with presuppositional thinking and method; they are not out of character or inconsistent with the system as a whole. "Evidentialist" critics might jump back with the challenge, "Why, then, does Van Til rule out the historical argument for the resurrection!" The question displays the blinding effect of preconceptions again, for just listen to Van Til's own words: "Historical apologetics is absolutely necessary and indispensable to point out that Christ rose from the grave, etc."[80] Not only is it indispensable in general, Van Til says of himself in particular: "I would therefore engage in historical apologetics."[81] The plain and simple fact is that, from the very start, Van Til's presuppositionalism has not been antagonistic to— or meant as a substitute for— evidences and empirical reasoning in support of the historic Christian faith. He has always had tremendous confidence in them: "Every bit of historical investigation, whether it be in the directly biblical field, archeology, or in general history is bound to confirm the truth of the claims of the Christian position. . . . A really fruitful historical apologetic argues that every fact *is* and *must be* such as proves the truth of the Christian theistic position."[82]

As was discussed above, Van Til lays strong emphasis upon *natural revelation* in his apologetic. Since he takes that to be a clear communication from God through the facts of nature and history, one which leaves men guilty for rebelling against God, it is altogether consistent that Van Til endorses the work of scientists and historians in offering verification for the claims of the Christian faith. It is of particular value in, first, strengthening the confidence of believers and, second, embarrassing unbelievers in their criticisms against the Bible's scientific and historical claims. Evidences offer God's children the answers *they* need so as not to be intellectually troubled when hearing the learned objections of non-Christian scholars. Evidences can also silence the futile empirical objections of unbelievers to the claims of Christianity, if not also "clearing away the mental debris" of intellectual prejudice (e.g., "only anti-scientific, emotional superstition could lead someone to believe biblical claims") so that unbelievers can better hear and consider the message of Scripture.

As indispensable and valuable as they are, though, it would be a misleading conception to think that evidences can stand on their own in Christian apologetics. This should be obvious enough from what God's word teaches us. (1) What people will think *about* the observed evidence is affected by non-observational beliefs (e.g., Matt 28:12–13,17; Luke 24:16,31; John 21:12). (2) In dealing with the claims of Christ, nobody is truly *detached* and uncommitted one way or another: "No man can serve two masters. . . . He who is not with me is against me" (Matt 6:24; 12:30). What one presupposition sees as foolish, the other sees as wisdom (1 Cor 1:18–25). (3) The non-observational commitments of the unbeliever (e.g., Ps 10:4; Rom 1:25; 3:11–12) are objectively foolish and lead to the *destruction of knowledge* (Prov 1:22,29; Rom 1:21–22; 1 Tim 6:20) because "the fear of the Lord is the beginning of knowledge" (Prov 1:7; cf. Ps 36:9). (4) All men inescapably have an *inner knowledge* of God (Gen 1:27; Rom 1:20–21; 2:15), the One whose sovereign power and plan uphold the universe *with regularity* (Gen 8:22; Jer 31:35; Heb 1:3; Ps 33:11; Acts 15:18; Dan 4:35), "working all things after the counsel of His own will" (Eph 1:11). (5) Yet unbelievers are deeply *hostile* to this knowledge and "suppress it in unrighteousness" (Rom 1:18–21), preferring to walk in the vanity of their minds and darkened understanding (Eph 4:17 –18). (6) That explains why it is that, regarding such empirical evidence as the resurrection, "If they hear not Moses and the prophets, *neither will they be persuaded though* one rise from the dead" (Luke 16:31; cf. 24:25– 26). (7) Nevertheless, the objective revelation provided by God in the evidence of history and Scripture is such that we can through the resurrection "know *for certain* that God has made this Jesus whom you crucified both Lord and Christ" (Acts 2:36; Luke 1:4 says we can "know the certainty of the things" in which we have been instructed, and cf. 1 John 2:3, "we know that we know").

To Van Til's epistemological credit, then, he has recognized throughout his scholarly career, not only the many detailed errors in the outworking of the non-presuppositional (traditional) arguments from inductive evidence (say, for the resurrection),[83] but more fundamentally the philosophical and theological truths (corresponding to the above list) that: (1) all empirical observation is inescapably *theory-laden* (there are no uninterpreted "brute facts"). (2) The acceptance and interpretation of what one takes as "factual" is not determined by sense perception *alone,* but in interaction with one's fundamental philosophical convictions (there is no presuppositionless neutrality). (3) Empirical, inductive study in itself has certain *preconditions* which can be intelligibly *accounted for* only on the presupposition of Christianity (so that scientific and historical study wittingly or unwittingly assumes what believers are defending). (4) What is assumed by the consistently non-Christian understanding of empiricism and induction[84] contradicts biblical teaching *as well as* rendering empirical, inductive reasoning impossible in philosophical principle. (5) Unbelievers (like believers) are not at all unbiased, impartial, without motive and goal, completely open-minded, and purely disinterested in where they will be led by their handling of the empirical evidence. (6) If the unbeliever's espoused presuppositions are not challenged, and if he holds tenaciously and *consistently* to them, he can for very good reason refuse to be driven from his position by consideration of empirical evidences *alone*.[85] (7) Likewise, because the believer's *intellectual basis* for certainty[86] about the claims of the Christian faith is broader than his (admittedly) limited and fallible reflections upon the (admittedly) incomplete pool of available empirical indicators alone— which would, if all by itself, require humble and mitigated conclusions— those claims (even about history and nature) should not merely be considered or presented as *probably* true.[87]

In line with these insights Van Til states: "For any fact to be a fact at all it must be a revelational fact."[88] By thus repudiating the idea of "brute fact" Van Til precludes an essential element of the traditional, non-presuppositional approach to evidentialist apologetics, which holds that the objects of perception carry no inherent meaning or interpretation and can be approached in a neutral fashion, without man's mind assuming any meaning or interpretation. In that case the "facts" could disclose nothing whatsoever. There would be nothing within the facts or within the mind of the investigator to determine objectively an order, relationship, specific quality or modality for these random sensations. If facts signify nothing in themselves, they— whatever "they" amounts to! — cannot be used to test worldviews because they would be compatible with any number of conflicting (imposed) systems of meaning or interpretation. Van Til's denial of "brute facts" and "purely observational" knowledge is in line with recent philosophical criticism of the epistemological theory of empiricism as traditionally understood (eventuating in the distinctive tenets of positivism). What complicates the apologetical situation, though, is that the non-Christian tries (unsuccessfully) to suppress completely the evidential force of the facts by choosing and thoroughly applying presuppositions which run counter to what these facts indicate; i.e., the truth (meaning) of Christianity. Apologetics is thus required to argue in such a way as to strip away the autonomous and rebellious "glasses" through which unbelievers look at the revelational facts. Accordingly Van Til's defense of the faith "argues that every fact . . . *must be* such as proves the truth of the Christian theistic position." The evidences, which are innumerable, must be presented in a manner which compels a return to their true nature as confirmatory of Christianity.

How is this done? Van Til says it is indispensable to present empirical evidences to unbelievers, but he immediately *adds:* "I would not talk endlessly about facts and more facts without ever challenging the non-believer's philosophy of fact."[89] Philosophical (presuppositional) apologetics forms the context within which the use of evidences is intelligible and forceful. Without recognizing his biblical presuppositions and their epistemological necessity, the Christian cannot make sense out of his own apologetical argumentation with unbelievers based upon empirical evidence. For instance, if he agrees to base his reasoning upon the assumption of complete contingency in history (chance), then he cannot justify inductive, empirical thinking any more than his opponent can. Moreover, his appeal to miracles is unintelligible (since there is no objective background of uniformity in terms of which an event is miraculous).[90] Furthermore, if the apologist does not challenge the unbeliever's underlying philosophy, the appeal to empirical evidences need not lead to anything like Christian conclusions. For instance, if you empirically argue with a naturalist and convince him that the body of Jesus came back to life, he should — to be philosophically consistent — conclude that there are (as yet unknown) natural factors which can biologically cause and rationally account for the resuscitation of the dead.[91] With his presuppositions, he need not at all infer that a "miracle" ocurred, that Jesus was "raised from the dead," that he must then be the "divine Son of God," or much less that he was resurrected "for our justification" and as a sign that "he will judge the world." None of these latter judgments are purely empirical in nature, and none of them follows logically (within the worldview or basic system of thought of the naturalist) from the empirical item that a dead body came back to life.[92] Consequently, Van Til has taught that "it is impossible and useless to seek to defend Christianity as an historical religion by a discussion of facts only. . . . If we would really defend Christianity as an historical religion we must at the same time defend the theism upon which Christianity is based and this involves us in philosophical discussion" — a philosophical discussion where the "fact" of the resurrection is not artificially and sharply separated from the "system of meaning" in terms of which it is inevitably understood.[93] Therefore, Van Til would not in the least "disparage the usefulness of arguments for the corroboration of the Scripture that came from archaeology" [for instance]; he would simply want to insist "that such corroboration is not of independent power."[94]

Because unbelievers self-deceptively *espouse* presuppositions contrary to those of the Christian, while *nevertheless* in actuality knowing God and inconsistently living in terms of that suppressed truth, truth which constitutes the Christian's acknowledged presuppositions,[95] they can understand the evidences presented by the the believer and do — if the Holy Spirit graciously removes their resistance to the truth — in some cases, on that basis alone, draw the correct conclusion from the evidences. "We [should] present the message and evidence for the Christian position as clearly as possible, knowing that because man is what the Christian says he is, the non-Christian will be able to understand in an intellectual sense the issues involved. In so doing, we shall, to a large extent, be telling him what he 'already knows' but seeks to suppress. This 'reminding' process provides a fertile ground for the Holy Spirit, who in sovereign grace may grant the non-Christian repentance so that he may know him who is life eternal."[96]

However, if the unbeliever stubbornly and consistently clings to his espoused presuppositions and by means of them resists the force of the evidence as confirming Christian claims, then we must of necessity (and as usual) make explicit use of presuppositional argumentation. We must discuss the foundations of empirical study and inductive method in order to show that Christianity alone saves any scientific, historical knowledge. "Christianity does not thus need to take shelter under the roof of a scientific method independent of itself. It rather offers itself as a roof to methods that would be scientific"![97] We must aim to show the unbeliever that by striving to move away from the revealed meaning indicated in the facts, he simultaneously moves away from the possibility of giving any account of the intelligibility and possibility of scientific knowledge about nature and history. "What we will have to do then is to try to reduce our opponent's position to absurdity. Nothing less will do."[98] For instance, the apologist "must challenge the legitimacy of the scientific method as based upon an assumed metaphysic of chance."[99] At the heart of it all, "the point is that the 'facts of experience' must actually be interpreted in terms of Scripture if they are to be intelligible at all."[100]

In short, Van Til contends that: "I am unable to follow [Kuyper] when from the fact of the mutually destructive character of the two principles [regenerate and unregenerate presuppositions] he concludes to the useless-ness of reasoning with the natural man. . . . Christianity is objectively defensible. And the natural man has the ability to understand intellec-tually, though not spiritually, the challenge presented to him. And [con-trary to Warfield] no challenge is presented to him unless it is shown him that on his *principle* he would destroy all truth and meaning."[101]

We are thus brought back in our "evidentialist apologetic" to the same underlying strategy which is used more generally for "theistic proof." Traditional, old Princeton apologetics separated the general defense of theism (step 1: the proofs supplied in natural theology) from the more specific defense of Christian theism (step 2: scientific and historical evi-dences). In Van Til's apologetic these find their proper, underlying unity in the presuppositional and transcendental strategy of arguing "from the impossibility of the contrary" — arguing by means of an internal critique of the unbeliever's worldview, and then presenting the only positive al-ternative, the Christian worldview, if the intelligibility of experience or any rational knowledge is not to be lost. Van Til puts it this way: "the true method for any Protestant with respect to the Scripture (Christianity) and with respect to the existence of God (theism) must be the indirect method of reasoning by presupposition. In fact it then appears that the argument for the Scripture as the infallible revelation of God is, to all intents and purposes, the same as the argument for the existence of

God."[102] Having and arguing for the right presuppositions is, therefore, the fundamental requirement in defending the faith.

Machen's Agreement in Perspective

When one thinks of the reputation and accomplishments of Machen in the area of Christian apologetics, one thinks of clear and cogent historical arguments for the truthfulness of the Christian faith. One thinks of outstanding work in apologetical *evidences.*

The preceding analysis of Van Til's conception and method of Christian apologetics as it bears on "theistic proof" and "empirical evidence" discloses that, although their personal career emphases may have been in different areas, there is nothing in Machen's apologetical use of historical evidences which, as such, stands in conflict with Van Til's approach to the defense of the faith. The main reason why some critics pit Machen's apologetic work against that of Van Til is that they, without justification, construe Van Til to be opposed to any appeal to empirical evidence and to any form of rational argumentation in apologetics. That not being the case (but a misreading on a massive scale), Machen's argumentation from historical evidences may not reasonably be taken as diametrically at odds with Van Til's method of argument. Van Til's outlook provides for (as no competing apologetical school can), encourages, and even demands the use of those very empirical evidences which Machen mastered.

So, Machen utilized historical apologetics.[103] In harmony with him, Van Til says "I would . . . engage in historical apologetics."[104] They were both committed to making use of empirical evidence, but, we might ask, did they have the same conception of what they were doing with this empirical evidence? Did they have the same intention or aim in developing arguments from nature and history? There might be an initial inclination to think that they did not. After all, Van Til's point is that the correct use and persuasiveness of such evidences requires one to have the correct — the Christian— outlook as his presupposition. Otherwise the evidences will not be accepted, not be interpreted accurately, and not even be made intelligible at all. This necessity of proper, revealed presuppositions in assessing the evidence from history explains why historical apologetics is so convincing and beneficial to the faith of the Christian, but not nearly so much so (by a wide, wide margin) with self-conscious unbelieving scholars. In some cases, to be sure, the historical argument brings unbelievers to the Christian conclusion— but not ever with a self-conscious, intellectually astute, and unceasingly determined unbeliever. At best in such cases, the historical apologetic is useful for embarrassing the arrogant claims and anti-religious hypotheses created by unbelieving scholarship.

Because of Machen's tie with old Princeton and its tradition of scholarship, one might *not expect* him to have conceived of his work in historical apologetics as requiring and resting upon Christian presuppositions, as Van Til taught. After all, Machen's great teacher, B. B. Warfield, maintained that apologetics must appeal to a notion of "right reason" which is *independent* of any commitment to belief or unbelief (neutrality), that apologetics must prove the historical trustworthiness of the New Testament *before* proving its inspiration and then presupposing it in other reasoning (autonomy), and that this kind of presuppositionally-neutral, historical apologetics is *directed particularly at unbelievers*, having a positive— indeed, the major— part to play in their *conversion*.

> It is easy, of course, to say that a Christian man must take his standpoint not *above* the Scriptures, but *in* the Scriptures. . . . But surely he must first *have* Scriptures, authenticated to him as such, before he can take his standpoint in them. . . . [Faith is not] an irrational faith, that is, a faith without grounds in right reason. . . . We are arguing that faith is . . . necessarily grounded in evidence. And we are arguing that evidence accordingly has its part to play in the conversion of the soul. . . . And we are arguing that this part is not a small part; nor is it a merely subsidiary part; nor yet a merely defensive part . . . [but] rather a primary part, and it is a conquering part. It is the distinction of Christianity that it has come into the world clothed with the mission to *reason* its way to its dominion. Other religions may . . . seek some other way to propogate themselves. Christianity makes its appeal to right reason.[105]
>
> Let it not be said that . . . we found the whole Christian system upon the doctrine of plenary inspiration. We found the whole Christian system on the doctrine of plenary inspiration as little as we found it upon the doctrine of angelic existences. Were there no such thing as inspiration, Christianity would be true, and all its essential doctrines would be credibly witnessed to us. . . . Inspiration is not the most fundamental of Christian doctrines, nor even the first thing we prove about the Scriptures. It is the last and crowning fact as to the Scriptures. These we first prove authentic, historically credible, generally trustworthy, before we prove them inspired.[106]

We might expect Machen to have the same old Princeton conception of, and goal for, his historical apologetic; namely, to reason his way to dominion, to persuade intellectually unbelievers who do not presuppose the inspiration of Scripture of the truth of Christianity by using historical evidence which is compelling in itself to the unbeliever's neutral reasoning.

However, there is a remarkable passage in Machen's works where he reflects quite self-consciously and clearly upon what he is trying to accomplish and why he engages in historical or evidential argumentation in defense of the faith. This passage appears in two places, with slight variations between them, so Machen obviously felt it bore repeating. He was quite open about his reason for engaging in apologetics, clearing delineating it and setting it before his audiences on more than one occasion. What he said moved decidedly, even if with some remnants hanging on at places, out of the Warfieldian camp and a long way toward Van Til's presuppositional conception of evidences. This becomes manifest when we compare Warfield's words above with these from Machen's addresses, "The Importance of Christian Scholarship" (1932) and "Shall We Defend the Bible?" (1935). As the dates indicate, this reflects his most mature thinking, being toward the end of his life and career.

> Sometimes, when I have tried — very imperfectly, I confess — to present arguments in defence of the resurrection of our Lord or of the truth, at this point or that, of God's Word, someone has come up to me after the lecture and has said to me very kindly: "We liked it, and we are impressed with the considerations that you have adduced in defence of the faith; but, the trouble is, we all believed in the Bible already, and the persons that really needed the lecture are not here." When someone tells me that, I am not very greatly disturbed. True, I should have liked to have just as many sceptics as possible at my lecture; but if they are not there I do not necessarily think that my efforts are all in vain. What I am trying to do by my apologetic lecture is not merely — perhaps not even primarily — to convince people who are opposed to the Christian religion. Rather I am trying to give to Christian people — Christian parents or Sunday School teachers— materials that they can use, not in dealing with avowed sceptics, whose backs are up against Christianity, but in dealing with their own children or with the pupils in their classes, who love them, and long to be Christians as they are, but are troubled by the hostile voices on every side.
>
> It is but a narrow view of Christian apologetics that regards the defence of the faith as being useful only in the immediate winning of those who are arguing vigorously on the other side. Rather is it useful most of all in producing an intellectual atmosphere in which the acceptance of the gospel will be seen to be something other than an offence against the truth.
>
> But because argument is insufficient, it does not follow that it is unnecessary. What the Holy Spirit does in the new birth is not to make a man a Christian regardless of the evidence, but on the contrary to clear away the mists from his eyes and enable him to attend to the evidence.
>
> So I believe in the reasoned defence of the inspiration of the Bible. Sometimes it is immediately useful in bringing a man to Christ. It is graciously used by the Spirit of God to that end. But its chief use is of a somewhat different kind. Its chief use is in enabling Christian people to answer the legitimate questions, not of vigorous opponents of Christianity, but of people who are seeking the truth and are troubled by the hostile voices that are heard on every hand.[107]

> Sometimes, when I have given a lecture in defence of the truth of the Bible, a lecture, for example, which has adduced considerations to show that Christ really did rise from the dead on the third day, somebody has come up to me afterwards and has said very kindly something to the following effect: "We liked your lecture all right, but the trouble is that the people who need it are not here; we who are here are all Christian people, we are all convinced already that the Bible is true, so that we are not the ones who really needed to listen to what you had to say."

When people have told me that I have not been much discouraged. . . . It does seem rather surprising that people who pride themselves on being so broadminded should take their information about what is called by its opponents "Fundamentalism" from newspaper clippings or from accounts of "Fundamentalism" written by opponents . . . instead of reading what these [conservatives] . . . have published in serious books over their own signatures, or instead of listening to what they have to say when they lecture. But although I do wish that my opponents in this debate would give me a fairer hearing, yet I am not too much discouraged when they are not present at one of my lectures. You see, what I am trying to do in such a lecture is not so much to win directly people who are opponents of the Bible as to give to Christian parents who may be present or the Christian Sunday-school teachers materials that they can use, not with those whose backs are up against Christianity, but with the children in their own homes or in their Sunday-school classes, the children who love them and want to be Christians as they are Christians, but are troubled by the voices against Christianity that are heard on every side.[108]

Many aspects of these two (similar) presentations of Machen's reflexive conception of his own work in historical apologetics are worth isolating for notice. First and foremost, Machen viewed the work of evidential, historical reasoning to be directed, quite contrary to Warfield, mainly to *believers*. Because believers come to the objections and evidences presupposing the biblically revealed perspective on knowledge and reality (the Christian worldview), the historical evidences will make a tremendous difference to them. Evidential reasoning will fortify their faith and will especially provide intellectual reassurance to those who are troubled by hearing the scholarly objections against Christianity raised all around them. That is, historical apologetics, diverging from Warfield again, is used chiefly for *defensive* purposes. Faith of a biblical sort (unlike purely emotional or volitional counterfeits) needs intelligent and detailed answers to the empirically oriented objections of critics, even when it already has the right presuppositions. It is just the discrepancy between those presuppositions and the unbeliever's claims which needs intelligent resolution.[109] By appealing to evidence for this purpose, even if the unbeliever's basic commitments prevent him from accepting it, the apologist genuinely bolsters the faith of the believer by considerations which are objectively, intellectually sound. While inductive evidences may sometimes be used directly (in themselves) to bring someone from unbelief to faith, they do not ordinarily serve that function, says Machen (unlike Warfield).

The reason for this is not hard to find. Those who have alien presuppositions (e.g., avowed sceptics) are not at all neutral or "broad-minded"; they cannot give apologetical discussions "a fair hearing." Machen says that such people rather attend to their own preconceived notions and display a mindset of having "their backs up against Christianity." They have an axe to grind and are far from being committed to what Warfield called "right reason." They cannot receive or interpret the evidences correctly because, unlike the Christian parents, Sunday school teachers, and young believers who are troubled by "hostile" objections being raised, they are "vigorous opponents of Christianity" who do not bring to the evidences a mind of faith which has submitted to God's revelation previously. As such, in their intellectual rebellion, they must have their "eyes" changed *so that* they can, at last, "attend to the evidence" properly.

Without the enabling work of the Holy Spirit in their minds, nothing like Warfield's "right reason" is at their disposal. Such an evaluation and analysis from Machen is plainly in line with Van Til's presuppositionalist understanding of the situation. One may point to places in Machen's writings where he addresses his historical apologetic or evidential considerations to the open-minded, good sense of all rational people. One would fail Machen miserably, however, if one did not also recognize that Machen did not believe that such a description actually applied to the unbeliever. In theory (and objectively) if people used good sense, the evidences would drive them to Christian conclusions— but in actual living practice (subjectively), there are no instances of such good sense and open-mindedness among the ranks of the unregenerate. Therefore, in an extremely revealing passage in *What is Faith?*, Machen forthrightly declared that a personal conviction of sin was a prerequisite to the historical argument for Christ's resurrection:

> Thus even in order to establish the fact of the resurrection, the lesson of the law must be learned. . . . Thus even in order to exhibit the truth of Christianity at the bar of reason, it is necessary to learn the lesson of the law. It is impossible to prove first that Christianity is true, and then proceed on the basis of its truth to become conscious of one's sin; for the fact of sin is itself one of the chief foundations upon which the proof is based.[110]

If Machen said (ideally) that "anyone whose mind is clear" and who will pursue "a fair scrutiny of the historical evidence" will find it "thoroughly reasonable to . . . accept the truth of Christianity," he no less clearly said *"but no one's mind is clear who denies the facts of his own soul."*[111] Unlike Warfield's conception of "right reason," Machen's conception was that regeneration "is necessary in order that [the] truly scientific attitude may be attained; it is not a substitute for the intellect, but on the contrary by it the intellect is made to be a trustworthy instrument for apprehending truth."[112] Accordingly, although in the face of Christianity's intellectual foes Machen took the bold stand that the scientific method applied to the objective evidences of history would lead to the truth of Christianity, he was equally cognizant that unbelievers cannot utilize such a method due to their suppression of the truth about God. To be rational and open-minded and scientific, so as to draw Christian conclusions from the evidence, men must acknowledge their sin and their rebellion— intellectual rebellion— against God. On the same page as the previous remark Machen thus said: "In order that Christianity may be recognized as true by men upon this earth the blinding effects of sin must be removed."

Furthermore, Machen will be found to have departed from Warfield's view in the direction of Van Til's on the issue of whether the doctrine of scriptural inspiration is the foundational conviction, or instead the crowning confession for the Christian system of thought. Warfield went to pains to make clear that he did not hold that the Christian viewpoint is based upon the doctrine of the Bible's plenary inspiration. It is, instead, based upon and supported by evidences, which in turn provide the proof or support needed for the doctrine of inspiration. Machen took the position, in contradistinction to this, that the doctrine of Scripture's plenary inspiration "is not in accordance with the wisdom of this world." Therefore, it can hardly be thought to stand acknowledged and proven according to the evidence and reasoning which are found acceptable to the worldly wise. Nevertheless, "that blessed doctrine of the inspiration of the Bible . . . belongs not to the superstructure but to the foundation. If a man really holds to it, everything else for that man is changed."[113] What Warfield tried to make the "last and crowning fact" in the Christian outlook, Machen treated in the very opposite fashion as "belonging to the foundation" as the commitment which affects every other belief for a man. In this area, again, Machen's best insights are more in accord with the contours of Van Til's thinking than with Warfield's.

The significance of this for us is that, while Machen was unquestionably concerned to propound a historical apologetic which employed evidences in support of the Christian faith, he nevertheless progressed beyond Warfield (even if not perfectly), putting inspiration in the place of a *presupposition*. Here was a final authority which is not accepted according to any more basic standard, such as human experience or the judgments of men. Machen taught that "we make the Bible, and the Bible only, the test of truth and of life. . . . But is it not a dangerous thing to reject other authorities in this fashion and submit ourselves unreservedly to the authority of this one Book? Yes, it is a very dangerous thing. It puts us sharply in conflict with the whole current of the age."[114] It is not simply in the church or within theological circles that Scripture is a standard more basic than human experience and human judgments. In the face of the whole current of modern thought Machen makes unreserved endorsement of the Bible as the final standard of thought.[115] Furthermore, our most basic (presuppositional) convictions as taken from Scripture are to be held firmly, whatever contrary voices or events challenge us: "Others may heed these voices that bid us lose confidence in the power of our God, but as for us Christians, we will say still, though ten million times ten million universes unloose against us all their mighty power, though we stand amid the clash of falling systems and contemplate a universal ruin

— we will say still" what the Bible has taught us about God and our relationship to him.[116]

Very much like Van Til, who argued that Christianity must be defended "as a unit," Machen repeatedly stressed that the various teachings of the entire Bible all hang together, so that "we ought to take it as a whole" and not separate its parts from one another in the system.[117] But this is precisely what the neutral inductive approach must do, subjecting each isolated biblical claim to independent verification by some autonomous standard. Further, Machen recognized that the Christian worldview does not epistemologically divorce scientific matters from religious matters; that would be "just about the most destructive thing that could possibly be imagined," because the Christian religion is "most emphatically dependent upon facts."[118] What the apologist defends, then, is the full and integrated system of Christian truth— a worldview. This worldview stands in sharp antithesis with that of unbelievers, being "out of accord with the main trend of opinion both outside the Church and inside of it."[119]

Machen recognized that presuppositions control the divergent implications which will be drawn from the evidence, and thus sometimes castigated opponents of Christian conclusions in the study of the New Testament precisely for their starting points in false philosophy. Neutrality from philosophical bias could not be found, he said:

> If the separation of science from religion is unwarranted, so also, it may be remarked in passing, is the separation of science from philosophy. Dr. Mullins seems . . . to be supposing that there is such a thing as a "modern scientific criticism" of the New Testament which is independent of philosophical presuppositions, and the results of which can safely be accepted by men of differing shades of philosophical and religious opinion. . . . As a matter of fact we do not think that such a neutral, purely scientific criticism exists. The study of the New Testament, even in the sphere of literary criticism, and certainly in the sphere of historical criticism, cannot get along without presuppositions.[120]

One can discern in Machen's own scholarship, precisely in his brilliant historical apologetic, that he held philosophically to a different view of history than the one which substantially prevailed among the historians of his day.[121] Unlike the conceptions of secular philosophy of history, Machen's presuppositions were absolutistic and supernaturalistic. He proceeded on the assumption that events have a fixed, inherent significance (i.e., were not "brute facts") and that "facts" (i.e., ideas about, or the meaning of, events) should be true and changeless. He still stands over against the cultural relativism and sociology of knowledge which infects the philosophy of history in our own day. Marsden perceives correctly that "Machen appeared fully to understand the tenets of modern scholarship; yet he was willing to concede nothing to its assumptions and implications."[122]

Machen also recognized that the unbeliever's presuppositions are bound up with his sinful desire to suppress God's revelation.[123] Accordingly, unlike the old Princeton tendency to minimize it, Machen spoke explicitly of "the intellectual effects of sin."[124] If the sinner clings to his *autonomy* in suppressing the revelation of God, held Machen, he will remain in darkness: "so long as we stand in our right, and have not had our eyes mysteriously opened, [we] are lost and blind in sin."[125] All unbelieving philosophies are of necessity destructive of knowledge: "we hold for our part that wherever a process in metaphysics is in antagonism to Christianity it is not rational but irrational."[126]

Over against the unbeliever's presupposed worldview which is destructive of knowledge, Machen sets the Christian position which is the key to all knowledge:

> The supernatural Jesus is thus the key to a right understanding of early Christian history. But He is also the key to far more than that. Mankind stands in the presence of more riddles than the riddle of New Testament times. All about us are riddles— the riddle of our existence, the riddle of the universe, the riddle of our misery and our sin. To all those riddles Jesus, as the New Testament presents Him, provides the key. *He is the key not to some things but to everything. Very comprehensive,* very wonderfully cumulative, very profound and very compelling is the evidence for the reality of the supernatural Christ.[127]

Such words have the distinct ring of a presuppositional challenge to unbelief, claiming that nothing about the world and human experience can make sense apart from the "key" found in Christ. It also harmonizes with the presuppositional understanding of the comprehensive breadth of the evidence for proving the Christian position.

Although our indicators from Machen have been taken from scattered portions of his presentation, and although we should recognize that he did not extensively and self-consciously develop those presuppositional elements of thought in any one place and indeed may have fallen short of these insights from time to time (with traces of old Princeton ways of expression or argumentation),[128] we still cannot help but see that his conception of the defense of the faith bore definite lines of similarity with the distinctives of presuppositional thinking. In these particular points, anyway, Machen moved away from and beyond Warfield, the representative of the old Princeton approach. When we now add this observation to the previous considerations which have been adduced regarding Machen and Van Til, we come up with a rather strong case for concluding that there was a basic unity of conception between them regarding apologetics and evidence.

So let us recapitulate the discussion of those considerations. The personal histories of Machen and Van Til, we observed, are relevant to this question of the harmony betwen the two apologists, showing that they were quite cognizant of each other's contribution to the task of apologetics. There is every reason to expect that Machen and Van Til were able to understand what the other was saying in his published apological discussions or arguments, and that they would have been interested and motivated to do so. Consequently, from the fact that both Machen and Van Til were self-consciously dedicated to working with each other, and from their own expressions of respect and gratitude for the apologetic advanced by each other, we should infer that neither one of them found overwhelming objections in the other scholar's conception of apologetics. Furthermore, once Van Til's presuppositional approach to proof and evidence is analyzed, it becomes readily apparent that his method is not only open to the use of empirical evidences in the defense of the faith, it encourages and requires it. In that light, there is no conflict between Machen's engaging of historical argument for Christianity and the presuppositional method of argument which, in addition to setting forth evidences, would challenge the unbeliever to make intelligible his use of the scientific method and his interpretation of any part of his experience whatsoever. The key factor in Van Til's own philosophy of Christian proof and evidence is the requirement of having proper presuppositions as the preconditions for empirical, inductive study — as well as to interpret the facts of nature and history in such a way as to support the claims of Christianity. Then an examination of Machen's expressed conception and aim for his work in historical apologetics revealed that it too, along with Van Til's writings, acknowledged and was formulated in terms of the necessity of Christian presuppositions in order to make a profitable use of evidences for the faith. In what he said about this matter, Machen's reflections upon his own use of evidential apologetics proved to be at odds in significant ways with the old Princeton outlook represented by B. B. Warfield. Indeed, as we have just seen, a number of scattered features in Machen's defense of the faith coordinate with characteristic presuppositional emphases. The judgment is thus warranted in terms of personal history and ideology that the apologetic of Machen and that of Van Til do not stand diametrically opposed to each other, but rather, when taken in concert, sound a strong and harmonious trumpet call to arms in defense of the historic Christian faith.

Conclusion

There are not two conflicting apologetical traditions in the Orthodox Presbyterian Church, but one unified conception with two major and complementary emphases. That conception sets forth the truth of Christianity as (1) the philosophically necessary precondition for intelligible reasoning in any area of study, as well as (2) the conclusion to which every line of competent, painstaking, and empirical scholarship leads when applied to detailed questions in history, natural science, etc. Just because of the first emphasis, the second is approached with assurance and a dedication to resolving purported conflicts between secular scholarship and faith. The second emphasis, in order to be consistent, well-grounded, and effective requires and leads inescapably to the first.

Neither emphasis survives well without the other. Given the specific character of the Christian proclamation, we cannot defend the faith apart from consideration of the facts of nature and history. But given the character of the Christian worldview proclaimed, we cannot self-consciously discuss or debate those facts or evidences without asking what philosophical presuppositions are necessary for these or any facts to be known and intelligibly interpreted.

It is a concern, not that the teachers and pastors produced by the Orthodox Presbyterian Church have completely forgotten this rich apologetical tradition of Machen and Van Til, but rather that they have failed to understand and live up to it.[129] What is taken for granted is often lost. May it not be so in the next half century of our denomination's life. God graciously grant us power to "make foolish the wisdom of the world" (1 Cor 1:20) while leading men to "know for certain" that Jesus rose from the dead as Lord and Messiah (Acts 2:36).

NOTES

1. (Grand Rapids: Eerdmans, 1923): "the great redemptive religion which has always been known as Christianity is battling against a totally diverse type of religious belief, which is only the more destructive of the Christian faith because it makes use of traditional Christian terminology. This modern non-redeptive religion is called 'modernism' or 'liberalism'. . . . The many varieties of modern liberal religion are rooted in naturalism. . . . Despite the liberal use of traditional phraseology modern liberalism not only is a different religion from Christianity but belongs in a totally different class of religions" (pp. 2, 7).

2. The same could be said, according to Cornelius Van Til, about the *new* modernism (given the misnomer of "neo-orthodoxy") of the later dialectical theologians (*The New Modernism: An Appraisal of the Theology of Barth and Brunner* [Philadelphia: Presbyterian and Reformed, 1946]): "the dialectical theology of Barth and Brunner is built on one principle and this principle is to all intents and purposes the same as that which controls Modernism. . . . The new Modernism and the old are alike destructive of historic Christian theism and with it of the significant meaning of human experience" (p. xx). As is evident here, Van Til has carried forward Machen's own battle with twentieth-century theological apostasy, even as Van Til has carried on Machen's case against the United Presbyterian Church in U.S.A. (e.g., *The Confession of 1967: Its Theological Background and Ecumenical Significance* [Philadelphia: Presbyterian and Reformed, 1967]): "the new theology . . . is an essentially humanistic theology which disguises itself as an up-to-date Christian theology"; "it is founded upon a new and relativistic view of truth" (p. 1).

3. The denomination has continued through the years to have a strong affiliation with the seminary, but the two have no legal tie or identification with each other.

4. D. F. Kelly, "Machen, John Gresham," *Evangelical Dictionary of Theology*, ed. Walter A. Elwell (Grand Rapids: Baker, 1984), 673.

5. One of the marks which distinguishes trials for ordination in the Orthodox Presbyterian Church from those in other denominations is the requirement that candidates be examined specifically in apologetics ("The Form of Government" XXIII.6, *The Standards of Government, Discipline and Worship of the Orthodox Presbyterian Church*, 1984, 57).

6. *The Presbyterian Guardian* (February 13, 1937), 189.

7. David E. Kucharsky, "At the Beginning, God: An Interview with Cornelius Van Til," *Christianity Today* 22 (December 30, 1977) 6:18. For the significance of Van Til in the history of apologetical theory, see Greg L. Bahnsen, "Socrates or Christ: The Reformation of Christian Apologetics," *Foundations of Christian Scholarship*, ed. Gary North (Vallecito, CA: Ross, 1976), 191–239.

8. In some ways the seminary has not lived up to the high principles of Machen and Van Til (e.g., political expediency, pushing "practical" theology, meager publishing), but more particularly it has steadily erased the specific legacy of these two champions, even though showing them public deference. Contrary to the spirit and convictions of Machen, the seminary has broached a more inclusivistic theological posture (de-emphasis of Reformed distinctives), catered to the vanity of a professional degree (non-academic), and advanced (through some instructors) social views at odds with Machen's clear conservatism. Obscuring Van Til's distinctive direction, the seminary appointed a president more sympathetic to Clark, granted tenure to someone in the apologetics department more sympathetic to Dooyeweerd, and now has an instructor in apologetics more sympathetic to Schaeffer.

9. The stature and influence of these two in the history of the denomination was concretely illustrated at the denomination's two most disconcerting times: Machen's during the rupture associated with Buswell-McIntire, and Van Til's during the later rupture associated with Clark.

10. *Van Til, Defender of the Faith: An Authorized Biography* (Nashville: Thomas Nelson, 1979), 99. White wonders whether the hectic events, busy agendas, and administrative burdens surrounding the transition years from Princeton to Westminster might have rendered Machen oblivious to Van Til's new apologetical direction. The question, which prima facie might be asked regarding just about anybody else, underestimates the masterful mind of Machen and his absorbing personal concern for apologetical issues.

11. The James Sprunt Lectures at Union Theological Seminary in Virginia (Grand Rapids: Eerdmans, 1925).

12. The Thomas Smyth Lectures at Columbia Theological Seminary (New York: Harper and Row, 1930).

13. Vol. II of the series "In Defense of Biblical Christianity," published by the den Dulk Christian Foundation (n.p., 1969) — originally titled as a 1932 syllabus "The Metaphysics of Apologetics." The writer deems this publication a crucial key to grasping the transcendental thrust and philosophical implications of Van Til's apologetic method.

14. (Philadelphia: Presbyterian and Reformed, 1955), a republication of a number of earlier articles from various journals.

15. *The New Testament: An Introduction to its Literature and History*, ed. W. J. Cook (Edinburgh: Banner of Truth Trust, 1976), 9.

16. *Christianity in Conflict*, vol. 1, part 1 of a mimeographed syllabus for a course at Westminster Seminary in the history of apologetics (1962), 17.

17. *The Psychology of Religion*, vol. 4 in the series "In Defense of Biblical Christianity" (n.p.: den Dulk Christian Foundation, 1971 [1935 syllabus]), 87.

18. Ned B. Stonehouse, *J. Gresham Machen: A Biographical Memoir* (Grand Rapids: Eerdmans, 1954), 73.

19. *The Defense of the Faith* (Philadelphia: Presbyterian and Reformed, 1955), 258. The first edition, though more prolix and complex, has definite advantages in understanding Van Til's presuppositionalism over the abridged second (1963) and third (1969) editions, which delete the discussion in which the above comment occurs. The quotation appears again in *A Christian Theory of Knowledge* (n.p.: Presbyterian and Reformed, 1969), 293.

20. William Masselink, "Machen as Apologist," doctoral dissertation in 1938 under V. Hepp at the Free University of Amsterdam [later published as *J. Gresham Machen: His Life and Defence of the Bible* (Grand Rapids: Zondervan, n.d.)], 139ff.; John C. Vander Stelt, *Philosophy and Scripture: A Study in Old Princeton and Westminster Theology* (Marlton, N.J.: Mack, 1978) [another dissertation, this mainly under G. C. Berkouwer, at the Free Univer-

sity of Amsterdam], 7, 201, 301. Cf. William D. Livingstone, "The Princeton Apologetic as Exemplified by the Work of Benjamin B. Warfield and J. Gresham Machen: A Study in American Theology 1880–1930" (doctoral dissertation at Yale University, 1948); R. C. Sproul, John Gerstner, and Arthur Lindsley, *Classical Apologetics: A Rational Defense of the Christian Faith and a Critique of Presuppositional Apologetics* (Grand Rapids: Zondervan, 1984), 209.

21. *The Defense of the Faith,* 1st ed., chap. 13 (chap. 11 in later editions); *A Christian Theory of Knowledge,* chap. 8–10; "My Credo" in *Jerusalem and Athens: Critical Discussions on the Theology and Apologetics of Cornelius Van Til,* ed. E. R. Geehan (n.p.: Presbyterian and Reformed, 1971), 10–11, 18–19.

22. In that vein, George M. Marsden argued at the Westminster Jubilee Conference (Aug. 31–Sept. 3, 1979) that "a Christian presuppositional approach to truth" can and should redress defects in the "Baconian inductive" approach to truth taken by Machen ("J. Gresham Machen, History, and Truth" printed in *The Westminster Theological Journal* 42 [1979] 1:157–75.

23. Vander Stelt also maintains (in *Philosophy and Scripture: a Study in Old Princeton and Westminster Theology*) that between Machen and Van Til there was a basic agreement in philosophical and theological approach — but with Van Til thought to be as essentially committed to the fundamental flaw of the *old Princeton approach* as was Machen (p. 313)! Such an innovative thesis is hard to take seriously, revealing (it would seem) much more about the mindset with which Vander Stelt approached his subject than the subject itself. He opposes any "scholastic," "intellectualistic," and "dualistic" thinking with its "static conception of truth" since it leads, as he imagines, to a "biblicism" which makes the grave error of seeing the Bible "as a rational rather than a religious revelation" (pp. 304–22). Of course, from that standpoint with its telling polarization of rational and religious, Van Til must indeed be grouped together with Machen — to the credit of both of them, I would think ("intellectualistically" and "dualistically") — along with Warfield, the Hodges, Berkhof, Bavinck, Kuyper, Edwards, Ames, Rutherford, Knox, Ursinus, Bucer, Calvin, Augustine and the host of orthodoxy throughout history. Vander Stelt's principle of differentiation offers little benefit in drawing distinctions *within* that circle.

24. See, for instance, the autobiographical note in *Contemporary American Theology,* vol. 1, ed. Vergilius Ferm (New York: Round Table, 1932), 254; cf. Machen's "Preface" to *The Christian View of Man* (New York: Macmillan, 1937), Upon the death of Warfield in 1921 Machen wrote "It seemed to me that the old Princeton — a great institution it was — died when Dr. Warfield was carried out. . . . With all his glaring faults he was the greatest man I have known" (quoted by Stonehouse, 310).

25. Stonehouse, esp. pp. 60–68, 147ff., 183ff., 410ff.

26. Stonehouse, 307, 381, 385, 390–91. Machen admired Dr. Greene as "one of the best Christians I have ever known" (p. 439).

27. Mark A. Noll calls him "the last of the major defenders of this tradition" in *The Princeton Theology: 1812–1921* (Grand Rapids: Baker, 1983), 16.

28. Marsden says Machen's view that "nothing could be held true if it did not pass the test of conformity to the rules of empirical scientific inquiry" was built on the epistemological foundation of Scottish common sense realism, "which had been the overwhelmingly prevailing philosophy at Princeton Theological Seminary" ("J. Gresham Machen, History, and Truth," 165, 167).

29. This point is similar, I take it, to that made by Marsden in the article cited above. Despite its epistemological weaknesses, claims Marsden, Machen's actual approach to truth surpassed in presuppositional characteristics the practice of others who were also committed to "Baconian induction" (pp. 174–75). It should be observed, however, that the antithesis posited by Marsden between induction and presuppositionalism (p. 173) is somewhat overgeneralized.

30. For particular historical points about the lives of Machen and Van Til, which I have interwoven below, see the respective biographies by Ned. B. Stonehouse and William White, Jr., cited earlier.

31. Respectively: *Biblical and Theological Studies* by members of the faculty of Princeton Theological Seminary (New York: Charles Scribner's Sons, 1912); *The Princeton Theological Review* 11 (January 1913) and 13 (July 1915).

32. White, chap. 7.

33. (Grand Rapids: Eerdmans, 1925), dedicated to F. L. Patton.

34. Respectively: *The Bible Today* (May 1923); *The Princeton Theological Review* 22 (October 1924), 23 (January 1925), 24 (January 1926); "The Bible League Lectures" for 1927 (reprinted in J. Gresham Machen *What is Christianity? and Other Addresses,* ed. Ned B. Stonehouse [Grand Rapids: Eerdmans, 1951]).

35. See the first eight selections in J. Gresham Machen, *God Transcendent, and Other Selected Sermons,* ed. Ned B. Stonehouse (Grand Rapids: Eerdmans, 1949).

36. That Van Til took a decided and personal interest in Machen's struggles is evident later (for instance) in his articles for *The Banner* on such things as "The Story of Westminster Theological Seminary" (vol. 65 [1930]: 657–58), "Recent Events in the Presbyterian Church" (vol. 69 [1934]: 582–83), and "A Crushing Experience" (vol. 71 [1936]: 1062–63).

37. Machen's close associate and Warfield's successor, Casper Wistar Hodge, Jr., was Van Til's advisor in the master's program.

38. "Introductory Note" to Francis R. Beattie's *Apologetics* (Richmond: Presbyterian Committee of Publication, 1903), 20–30.

39. 25 (1927) 2:336–38.

40. Van Til maintained from the start that *all* apostate philosophies fell prey to the same fundamental critique. In 1930 he wrote: "Idealism as well as Pragmatism, it seems to me, has embraced the relativity of truth and value. . . . Together they form a secret alliance against Theism. . . . The God of Idealism is not the God of Theism but is rather the God of Pragmatism" ("God and the Absolute," *The Evangelical Quarterly* 2 [1930]:358; reprinted in Van Til's *Christianity and Idealism,* chap. 1).

41. White surmises that (1) Van Til's caution and courtesy as a student and (2) the seminary's preoccupation with its own political unrest while Van Til was an instructor kept the Princetonians from seeing the implications of his views (pp. 63, 76–77). But his visibility was not really that low— not after five years of course work in the same town, prize-winning papers, graduate accomplishments, the published review of Whitehead, and being invited to teach at the very time and *in the very department* where all the concentration of controversy over Machen came to a head!

42. Quoted by Stonehouse, 437.

43. Machen himself would later write on "The Necessity of the Christian School," "The Christian School, the Hope of America" (both in the proceedings of the National Union of Christian Schools, 1933 and 1934), and "Shall We Have Christian Schools?" (*The Presbyterian Guardian* [January 9, 1937]). The first mentioned article is reprinted in *What is Christianity? and Other Addresses.*

44. *The Princeton Theological Review* 27 (1929) 1:135–36.

45. The general assembly of 1926 had postponed confirmatory action on Machen's call, using this as the occasion to erect a committee to investigate Princeton Seminary and tensions there. The investigating committee proceeded to work for the complete reorganization of the institution in such a way as to stifle its conservative theological thrust.

46. Within weeks, it turns out, this conservative board would lose its struggle to retain control of the seminary. At the very time of Van Til's call, the plan to reorganize Princeton was impending, waiting to be acted upon by the general assembly.

47. Stonehouse, 437. Despite such words, some might doubt that Machen really would have been attentive to theoretical matters (like apologetics) in the midst of the political storm over the loss of Princeton and the hurried beginning of Westminster in the spring and

summer of 1929. But Machen was an extraordinary person in this regard, maintaining his "academic" interests despite the practical turmoils of the day. During that same hectic summer in which Westminster was born, Machen did his concluding work on the manuscript for *The Virgin Birth of Christ*, one of his apologetical masterpieces! Moreover, even if his words of endorsement for Van Til were uttered in harried circumstances, Machen had been acquainted with Van Til and his work for a considerable time previous to the commendation.

48. The 1929 general assembly voted decisively for the plan of reorganization, appointed two signers of the Auburn Affirmation to the new board of control, and (illegally) invested the new board with immediate governing direction prior to necessary charter changes. Hence the seminary would no longer be under conservative control.

49. White, 89.

50. *The Bible League* (London: W.C.I); reprinted by Shelton College Press (Cape May, NJ: 1969) and in *What is Christianity? and Other Addresses*.

51. (Grand Rapids: Eerdmans, 1936).

52. Later titled *A Survey of Christian Epistemology*.

53. For a listing of these, see "Writings of Cornelius Van Til" in *Jerusalem and Athens*, 492–98.

54. Even if the exact depth of Machen's comprehension of, and ability to give philosophical enunciation to, presuppositionalism is unknown (cf. White, 99), there can be no doubt that he was cognizant of its basic features and distinctives over against traditional "evidentialism."

55. White, 99.

56. In my office the morning following a public debate over apologetic method, I read out loud to R. C. Sproul numerous quotations from Van Til on these matters to show how he had misconstrued the professor. He was shocked that such things could be found in Van Til's works. (I was shocked that he would debate against presuppositionalism without knowing about them.) Mr. Sproul has still not appreciated or understood what Van Til says here, judging from his recent book on the subject, *Classical Apologetics*, where Van Til is presented with stubborn inaccuracy in the guise of "fideism" (pp. 184–87, 307–309). One is amazed at the way the book labors to recast all the hard, contrary, empirical evidence from Van Til, Frame, Notaro, and myself so as to protect its subjectively chosen presupposition that Van Til must be *called* a "fideist." A polemic this desperate is on its last legs. [A tape of the "Sproul-Bahnsen Debate" is available from Covenant Tape Ministry, 4155 San Marcos Lane, Reno, NV 89502.]

57. To be honest, we must also admit that some who claim to follow these scholars have proven "embarrassing advocates" (as C. S. Lewis would put it), bolstering these false preconceptions in testimony and practice. Armed with a few slogans (e.g., about "autonomous man" suppressing the truth, about "presuppositions settling everything," about "reasoning in circles"), if not a bit of intellectual laziness, some ministers disdain intellectual argumentation with unbelieving challenges to the gospel. Forget detailed study and philosophical reasoning, they figure, since such can make no difference to somebody with contrary presuppositions anyway. People in different circles of thought cannot persuade each other, but only mutually loathe what each other says. Bible professors can ignore well-reasoned, detailed answers to higher critical attacks on the Bible, dismissing the critics with a simple reference to their rebellious presuppositions. And reasoning about those conflicting presuppositions themselves is (hastily) rejected as out of the question. To cite the name of Van Til in connection with such attitudes or practices brings unwarranted insult.

58. "The Philosophy of Christian Evidences," *Jerusalem and Athens*, 420, 425.

59. See, e.g., my response to Daniel Fuller and Clark Pinnock, who together painted Van Til as opposed to empirical procedures and inductive investigation ("Inductivism, Inerrancy, and Presuppositionalism," *The Journal of the Evangelical Theological Society* 20 [December 1977]: 289–305; also Thom Notaro, *Van Til and the Use of Evidence* [Phillipsburg, N.J.: Presbyterian and Reformed, 1980]).

60. E.g., does the cosmological argument fallaciously move from 'each event has a cause' to 'all events (together) have a (single, common) cause'? Is it warranted to move from a premise pertaining to natural events and relations (e.g., 'every event has a cause'— something interpreted according to, and proven from, our experience) to a conclusion which— unlike the premise — pertains to a non-natural event, relation, or object (which is beyond our experience)?

61. *The Defense of the Faith*, 1st ed., 94–95.

62. "A Letter on Common Grace" (1953), reprinted in *Common Grace and the Gospel* (n.p.: Presbyterian and Reformed, 1973), 193.

63. *The Defense of the Faith*, 1st ed., 197, 256.

64. "A Letter on Common Grace," 181.

65. *Common Grace* (Philadelphia: Presbyterian and Reformed, 1947), 62.

66. "My Credo," *Jerusalem and Athens*, 21.

67. *A Christian Theory of Knowledge*, 33, 19.

68. *Common Grace*, 49.

69. *Christian-Theistic Evidences* (syllabus at Westminster Theological Seminary, 1961 [originally 1935]), 37.

70. "Introduction" in B. B. Warfield, *The Inspiration and Authority of the Bible* (Philadelphia: Presbyterian and Reformed, 1948), 38.

71. "Once Upon an A Priori," *Jerusalem and Athens*, 391; cf. Pinnock's charge that Van Til is guilty of "irrational fideism" which holds that "truth in religion is ultimately based on faith rather than on reasoning or evidence" ("The Philosophy of Christian Evidences," 423, 425). Both Montgomery and Pinnock distort Van Til's view as being Barth's error that belief cannot argue with unbelief, a voluntaristic position which "demands the non-Christian make a total and ungrounded commitment" (391, 422–23). With bewildering inaccuracy Pinnock summarizes Van Til's approach as being the fideistic combination of "a bare authority claim [and] a bare religious experience claim" (*Biblical Revelation — The Foundation of Christianity Theology* [Chicago: Moody, 1971], 38–42). Should it not embarrass such advocates of the use of inductive evidence that, in their characterizations of Van Til, they choose to portray him according to their (false) a priori conceptions, rather than by looking at the abundant (empirical!) evidence in his writings which can be inductively ascertained? Just compare the quotations from Montgomery and Pinnock with those adduced from Van Til himself.

72. *A Survey of Christian Epistemology*, 205.

73. *The Defense of the Faith*, 1st ed., 117.

74. *A Survey of Christian Epistemology*, 225.

75. Montgomery, "Once Upon an A Priori," 392; Pinnock, "The Philosophy of Christian Evidences," 421, 424–25.

76. *A Christian Theory of Knowledge*, 35.

77. *Christian-Theistic Evidences*, ii, 62.

78. *An Introduction to Systematic Theology*, vol. 5 of the series "In Defense of Biblical Christianity" (Phillipsburg, NJ: Presbyterian and Reformed, 1974 [first edition in 1937]), 45.

79. *A Survey of Christian Epistemology*, 7, 9.

80. *Introduction to Systematic Theology*, 146.

81. *The Defense of the Faith*, 1st ed., 258; Van Til adds that the only reason he did not engage in it extensively in print is that his colleagues in other departments at Westminster Seminary were already doing it better than he thought he could.

82. Ibid.; these remarks are *repeated* in *A Christian Theory of Knowledge*, 293.

83. E.g., why should the unbeliever accept "the basic reliability" of the extant New Testament documents simply due to their (usually overstated) "early date"? If a document is full of what is taken as the most obvious absurdities and superstitions (e.g., the large number of purported "miracles"), even if we possess the autographical copy of it, the naturalistic unbeliever will not grant its "basic reliability"! Secondly, how can the naturalistic unbeliever

be expected to treat these documents simply as reliable reports of what Jesus *said* about himself? Such reports have a mere man (according to the naturalistic sceptic) claiming an incredible divine character and prerogative, as well as predicting his own resurrection. It will certainly seem more probable to the consistent use of "common sense" that the apostles misconstrued what their teacher was trying to say (a general tendency in students, as we can easily verify), exaggerated it later in veneration for him, or simply did not recall it accurately. The defense made to this by virtually every non-presuppositional evidentialist (e.g., Montgomery, Sproul) is that Christ promised the gift of the Holy Spirit to his followers to enable them to remember and interpret correctly what he taught— a defense which blatantly begs the question at hand since it assumes the very deity of Jesus which the argument was supposed to prove. Numerous, similar gaffs in the traditional evidentialist reasoning might be pursued.

84. E.g., if we rigorously reject the intrusion of arbitrary metaphysical prejudices, man's mind is taken as a "tabula rasa" in a completely contingent, "chance" universe where only "particulars" (not abstract universals) exist. In such a case, there can be no logical or natural laws, no generalization or probability, no intelligible appeal to causality; language could not be learned, radical subjectivity and the ego-centric predicament could not be avoided, and there could be no justification for maintaining the reliability or sense perception or memory.

85. That is, apart from engaging in philosophical apologetics, such as is found in the transcendental theistic proof discussed above or in considering matters such as 3 and 4 here.

86. Not simply emotional confidence, subjective assurance, volitional commitment, etc.

87. If they are, then apologists like Montgomery, Pinnock, or Sproul must (1) resort to subjective matters like "experiential proof," the "practical certainty" which compels us to take action despite risks, or the inward convicting witness of the Spirit in order to enable them to take the "*leap* of faith" up from the level of what intellectual proof honestly warrants (*no more* than probability, according to them) to the higher level of *full* belief and personal confidence, and (2) press the fallacies of overstatement and hasty generalization into service so as to maintain a public stance of being committed to "full biblical inerrancy" exclusively on the platform of evidentialism or natural theology (despite their not examining or proving Scripture's every claim, and despite the admission of unresolved empirical difficulties regarding some scriptural phenomena). From these two observations it becomes ironically evident that those who have (falsely) criticized Van Til for "fideism" are much closer to it in reality than he has ever been.

88. *Apologetics*, Westminster Seminary syllabus (1966 [original edition 1935]), 36.

89. *The Defense of the Faith*, 1st ed., 258; (repeated in *A Christian Theory of Knowledge*, 293).

90. The apologist "will throw all these facts [the resurrection and the evidences verifying it] at the unbeliever, and the unbeliever throws them over his back into the bottomless pit of Chance. . . . David Hume, the great skeptic, has effectively argued that if you allow any room for Chance in your thought, then you no longer have the right to speak of probabilities. . . . No one hypothesis would have any more relevance to facts that any other hypothesis. . . . On this basis nature and history would be no more than a series of pointer readings pointing into the blank" (Ibid., 336–37).

91. "We must allow that it is quite possible [in terms of a neutral scientific method] that at some future date all the miracles recorded in the Bible, not excluding the resurrection of Christ, may be explained by natural laws" (Van Til, *Christian-Theistic Evidences*, 65).

92. "But the completely unusual, the nearly unique, nature of such an occurrence must be appreciated," we may hear. Yes, but *exactly how* one philosophically treats the realm of "the unusual" is open to a much wider variety of intellectual options than evidentialists seem to recognize. As Van Til cryptically observes: on non-Christian assumptions, far from needing to be a matter of religious solemnity or significance, "the resurrection of Jesus would be a fine item for Ripley's *Believe It or Not*" (*The Defense of the Faith*, 1st ed., 334).

93. Ibid., 23–24, 332–33.

94. "Introduction" to Warfield, 37.

95. This is a crucial aspect of Van Til's apologetic outlook: e.g., *The Defense of the Faith,* 1st ed., 107ff., 171ff., 181ff.; *A Christian Theory of Knowledge,* 18–19, 21–24; etc.; Greg L. Bahnsen, "The Apologetic Implications of Self-Deception" (tapes #217–218 from Covenant Tape Ministry, 4155 San Marcos Lane, Reno, NV 89502).

96. Van Til, "My Credo," *Jerusalem and Athens,* 21.

97. *Christian-Theistic Evidences,* 56.

98. *Survey of Christian Epistemology,* 204.

99. *Christian-Theistic Evidences,* 63.

100. *A Christian Theory of Knowledge,* 26.

101. *The Defense of the Faith,* 1st ed., 363, 364.

102. Ibid., 125–26.

103. For an excellent illustration, see the address delivered by Machen at his inauguration as assistant professor of New Testament Literature and Exegesis at Princeton Theological Seminary: "History and Faith," *The Princeton Theological Review* 13 (1915) 3:337–51.

104. *The Defense of the Faith,* 1st ed., 258.

105. "Introduction to Francis R. Beattie's *Apologetics,*" reprinted in *Selected Shorter Writings of Benjamin B. Warfield* vol. 2, ed. John E. Meeter (Nutley, N.J.: Presbyterian and Reformed, 1973), 98–99.

106. "The Real Problem of Inspiration" reprinted in *The Inspiration and Authority of the Bible,* ed. Samuel G. Craig (Philadelphia: Presbyterian and Reformed, 1948), 210.

107. "The Importance of Christian Scholarship," Shelton College press reprint (1969), 18–19.

108. "Shall We Defend the Bible?," *The Christian Faith in the Modern World,* 63–65.

109. Machen, like Van Til, insisted that because "truth is essentially one," the Christian cannot ignore or be indifferent to objections raised against his faith ("Shall We Defend the Bible?," 61–62), Obscurantism is not any help to the cause of Christ. Accordingly, Machen also pointed out, as we have done above, that evidences can perform a kind of "debris-clearing" function in the unbeliever's thinking, disabusing him of the prejudice that Christians are anti-intellectual people, without a ghost of an idea of how to reconcile their faith with scientific criticisms: "A man hears an answer to objections raised against the truth of the Christian religion; and at the time when he hears it he is not impressed. But afterwards, perhaps many years afterwards, his heart at last is touched. . . . And when he will believe he can believe because he has been made to see that believing is not an offence against truth" ("The Importance of Christian Scholarship." 18).

110. *What is Faith?,* 133–34.

111. Ibid., 134–35, emphasis added.

112. Ibid., 135.

113. *The Christian Faith in the Modern World,* 37.

114. Ibid., 84–85; cf. 76ff.

115. Of course, since Machen deemed the churchmen and theologians whom he opposed as not holding to the Christian position, *their* opposition represented the opposition mounted by unbelief just as much as opposition voiced by those "in the world." He explicitly said that the defense of the faith "should be directed not only against the opponents outside the Church but also against the opponents within" ("The Importance of Christian Scholarship," 21). So we have good reason to say that Machen maintained that unbelief must be combatted by an unreserved commitment to Scripture as the sole, foundational, and unchallengable standard for our thoughts.

116. *The Christian Faith in the Modern World,* 109–110.

117. Ibid., 54–58, 68–69, 80, 111.

118. Ibid., 54–55.

119. Ibid., 34; cf. 37, 59; ["One thing needs always to be remembered in the Christian Church— true Christianity, now as always, is radically contrary to the natural man" ("The Importance of Christian Scholarship," 16).]

120. "The Relation of Religion to Science and Philosophy," _The Princeton Theological Review_ 24 (1926) 1:51–52.

121. See Marsden's discussion of this fine insight, "J. Gresham Machen, History, and Truth," 158–64, 169–70. My essay betrays, of course, that on some matters it seems to me Marsden forces his interpretation of Machen (e.g., regarding "common sense," "Baconian induction," "elimination of any legitimate place for [cultural] perspective").

122. Ibid., 158.

123. _The Christian Faith in the Modern World_, 21–22; e.g., 69.

124. "The Relation of Religion to Science and Philosophy," 59.

125. _The Christian Faith in the Modern World_, 22.

126. "The Relationship of Religion to Science and Philosophy," 60.

127. _The Christian Faith in the Modern World_, 70, emphasis added.

128. E.g., Machen sometimes talks as though the apologist can show an unbeliever, even before accepting inspiration, that on the same basis as one uses in evaluating any other historical book, he ought to conclude that the Bible is "substantially true" and then, from that conviction, logically go on to conclude that it is "altogether true" (Ibid., 51–52; cf. 68, 70). An earlier indication of old Princeton thinking was Machen's notion that "the historical evidence for the resurrection amounted only to probability; probability is the best that history can do" ("History and Faith," 350).

129. One cannot help but observe, with disappointment, the way so few candidates for the OPC ministry actually grasp and can intelligently put into practice the presuppositional method in philosophical apologetics (as expounded for so many years by Van Til), as well as the sparse number of masterful publications of empirical scholarship produced by our ministers in answer to modern challenges (on the order of Machen's contributions).

George M. Marsden

18 Perspective on the Division of 1937

M ACHEN WROTE, "We became members, at last, of a true Presbyterian Church. What a joyous moment it was. . . . "[1]

American Presbyterianism

The formation of the Presbyterian Church of America (PCA) on the
afternoon of June 11, 1936, was certainly a moment of deep satisfaction
for Dr. Machen. The organization of the new church was a tribute to the
faith which he loved, and the enthusiastic unanimity of the assembly in
electing him to be its first moderator was a tribute to his leadership in the
fight to preserve historic Presbyterianism within the Presbyterian Church
in the USA (PCUSA).

Yet the emotion of the eminent leader of the new denomination could
not have been only joy that afternoon. The formation of the PCA marked
the last entrenchments in a war that had been all but lost. Machen
recognized that the events of the last decade had "been a triumph of
unbelief and sin in the Presbyterian Church in the USA."[2] The sorrow
of continued defeats was tempered only by the joy of Christian fellowship
and the hope for the future of a strong and united truly Presbyterian
church. The members of the newly-constituted assembly appeared to be
united if not strong. They were united in their opposition to modernism,
and they were united in their expression of loyalty to "historic
Presbyterianism."

A year later, in June of 1937, the PCA was divided. Immediately
following its Third General Assembly a minority of its ministers and elders
withdrew to form the Bible Presbyterian Synod. This new denomination

295

was organized, its founders stated, "because of the departure of the Presbyterian Church of America from the historic position of American Presbyterianism."[3] The *Presbyterian Guardian*, speaking unofficially for the majority who had remained in the PCA took an opposite view. "The Presbyterian Church of America," it wrote, "has shown once again that it is determined to go forward in the historic channels of Presbyterianism regardless of cost."[4] Within less than a year the men who had united with Machen in forming "a true Presbyterian Church" were divided into two denominations, each of which claimed to represent the tradition of "historic (American) Presbyterianism." That each side should make such an appeal to the history of Presbyterianism in America suggests that the issues which divided the PCA were not entirely new, but that they reflected two distinct traditions within American Presbyterianism.

The Third General Assembly of the Presbyterian Church of America which met in Philadelphia on June 1, 1937, found its delegates sharply divided into two parties. Their differences focused on three distinct issues. The first was a doctrinal issue, concerning the attitude of the church toward the dispensational form of premillennialism. The second was a moral issue, centering on the question of whether the church should officially recommend to its members total abstinence from alcoholic beverages. The third was a matter of polity, concerning the question of whether the church should continue to conduct its foreign missions through an independent agency in cooperation with non-Presbyterians.

History generally does not repeat itself in one-hundred-year cycles. Yet the commissioners to the Third General Assembly of the PCA may well have felt at home had they been able to attend the Presbyterian general assembly which had met in Philadelphia just one century earlier. In 1837 the PCUSA was similarly divided between two parties, the "Old School" and the "New School." In that year the disagreement between the two parties had focused on three major issues. The first was a doctrinal issue, concerning the attitude of the church toward the "New Theology" which was being imported into the New School from New England. The second was a moral issue, centering on the question of whether the church should officially condemn certain practices, most notably Negro slavery and the beverage use of alcohol. The third issue was a matter of polity, concerning the question of continued cooperation with Congregationalists in the Plan of Union of 1801 and with non-Presbyterians in independent agencies for missions, Christian education, and moral reform.[4a]

This striking parallel between the issues which divided the New School from the Old School in 1837 and those which divided the Bible Presbyterians from the PCA in 1937 hardly can be entirely coincidence. Although the details on which the controversies focused were quite different, the essential lines of division were nearly identical. In both cases we find one party (the Old School and the majority in the PCA) insisting on a strict interpretation of the Presbyterian standards, and a second party (the New School and the minority) maintaining that subscription to the the standards should not preclude a certain latitude of interpretation in doctrine and in ethics and cooperation with non-Presbyterian agencies. The cleavage between the two schools in 1837, like the cleavage within the PCA in 1937, reflected the conflict of two traditions which have survived within American Presbyterianism since its beginnings. In the eighteenth century this conflict had first developed in the debate over subscription to the Westminster Standards and then in the controversy of the "Old Side" and the "New Side" over revivalism which resulted in a division of the church from 1741–1758.

The character of these two traditions within American Presbyterianism has been admirably summarized by Smith, Handy, and Loetscher in *American Christianity:*

> Presbyterians of English Puritan or New England Puritan background tended toward a "low church" or more subjective, less authoritarian conception of Presbyterianism, which in the eighteenth century was called New Side and in the nineteenth century New School; while Presbyterians of Scottish and Scotch-Irish background tended toward a "high church" or more objective and authoritarian conception of the heritage, known in the eighteenth century as Old Side and in the nineteenth as Old School. In a sense the history, especially the theological history of American Presbyterianism has revolved around these two poles.[5]

In general it has been assumed that after the reunion of the Old School and the New School in 1869 the conflict between these two traditions re-emerged in the conservative-modernist controversy which culminated in the formation of the PCA in 1936.[6] But it is only partially true to say that there is a continuity between the New School and modernism. Certainly there was an element of continuity in their common opposition to the strict subscription of the Old School and to the theology taught at Princeton Seminary. And certainly the New School attitude of tolerance of doctrinal innovation may have helped to open the door which let theological liberalism into the church. But it would be misleading to imply that there was any considerable direct continuity between the *theology* of the New School and modernism. The theology of the New School had been born in New England and grew out of a strict Reformed tradition. As it developed in the New School it never strayed very far from that tradition.[7]

A certain continuity between the New School and modernism might be suggested in the areas of ethics and polity. The modernists had an interest in social reform and favored cooperation with non-Presbyterianism. On the other hand, it was the liberal wing which favored strong central control of the PCUSA in the early decades of the twentieth century.

Whatever we might conclude about the possible continuity between the New School and modernism, we can find clear evidence that the two traditions of American Presbyterianism survived into the twentieth century within the conservative camp itself. While they were allied against the common enemy of modernism the conflict of the two traditions was not always obvious. But once the conservatives who left the PCUSA in 1936 found themselves united in the PCA the old lines of controversy re-emerged almost immediately.

That each side in the Presbyterian Church of America could present itself as the legitimate heir to a major tradition within American Presbyterianism may be seen from an examination of the background of each of the three major issues which divided the young church.

We turn first to dispensational premillennialism. Dispensationalism in its modern form originated in the nineteenth century. It grew largely out of the work of John Nelson Darby (1800–1882) and his followers, particularly the Plymouth Brethren.[8] In the second half of the nineteenth century dispensational schemes of biblical interpretation became widely popular in America and became closely associated with premillennial eschatology.[9] The influence of the new methods of Bible study was never confined to any one denomination of American Protestantism. The most notable manifestations of the movement were the International Bible and Prophecy Conferences held in New York State from 1878–1897. These conferences were closely associated with the popular revival movements of the late nineteenth century, and like the revival movements were interdenominational.[10]

The interdenominational character of the movements associated with dispensationalism was natural to the dispensational scheme of things. The dispensationalists' doctrine of the church emphasized the spiritual quality of the church's life, often to the point of denying the reality of its organizational structure or earthly boundaries.[11] Despite the interdenominational character of the movement, dispensationalism initially had its greatest appeal among Protestants of Calvinistic background, who already had acquaintance with covenantal schemes. According to Norman Kraus, "the basic theological affinities of dispensationalism are Calvinistic."[12] Because of these affinities, it was natural that the new emphases should develop strong roots within the PCUSA.

The question relevant to our study is: how did dispensationalism relate to the two major traditions in American Presbyterianism? Since dispensationalism did not become a major force in the religious life of America until after the time of the reunion of the Old School and the New School in 1869, it is impossible to make any positive identification of dispensational tendencies in either of the two Presbyterian schools. Yet dispensationalism did become a considerable factor in American Presbyterianism very shortly after the reunion. So we may look for affinities between dispensational interpretations and the traditions of the two schools.

Factors which would lead us to expect dispensationalism to appeal to the New School tradition include the following: both were closely associated with revivalism,[13] both favored interdenominational cooperation and work through independent agencies; both tended to favor a less authoritarian role of the visible church; and the tendency of the New School to emphasize a simple Christianity, as opposed to intellectualism, would tend to make the New School more susceptible to the simple literalism of dispensational exegesis. More positive continuity of the two movements is suggested by the fact that dispensationalism seems to have flourished in the same areas that the New School flourished— upstate New York and the midwest. There is also at least some identity of personnel between the two movements.[14] The least we can say is that there is some continuity in their common opposition to the traditionalism of the Old School– Princeton theology.[15]

Nevertheless, at the time when biblical Christianity was challenged by modernism in the PCUSA, the dispensationalists were firmly allied with the conservative camp. Dispensationalists claim first of all to be biblicists,[16] and their emphasis on literal interpretation of Scripture suggests a thoroughgoing reaction to all tendencies which might suggest the methods of liberal exegesis. Such strict views on Scripture make them natural, though sometimes uneasy, allies of the Presbyterians who championed the Old School heritage. In the PCUSA during the 1920s, the crucial decade in the battle against modernism, there seems to have been no question of any rift within the conservative camp. As long as conservatives were confronted with the presence of modernists within their own institutions, and as long as there was real hope of retrieving control of the church, there was little time for disputes on fine points. The militant defense of the authority of the entire Bible itself was the crying need of the hour.

Turning to the issue of total abstinence, questions of moral reform have long been debated by American Presbyterians. The two sides of the debate represent roughly the two major traditions in Presbyterianism. On the one hand is the tradition associated with English Puritanism, New England Puritanism, New School Presbyterianism and revivalism, which stresses the obligation of the church to take a strong official stand with regard to all sorts of moral and social problems that are not explicitly condemned or condoned in Scripture. On the other hand is the tradition associated with Scottish and Continental Presbyterianism, the Old School, and Princeton Seminary, which has maintained that the individual should be allowed the liberty to judge for himself on such matters.

In 1818, at the time when the PCUSA was cooperating closely with the Congregationalists under the Plan of Union of 1801, the Presbyterian general assembly first recommended that the officers and members of the church, "abstain even from the common use of ardent spirits."[17] The assemblies of 1829 and 1830, controlled by a New School majority, adopted similar resolutions and recommended the formation of temperance societies.[18] The Old School party opposed such recommendations and at the time of the division of 1837 rejected any official stand on moral reforms.

After the division the New School took a strong stand for total abstinence, declaring in 1840 that total abstinence from everything that may intoxicate is "the only true principle of temperance."[19] In direct reference to such a statement, Charles Hodge, the most distinguished representative of the Old School position, wrote in 1843:

> This declaration of the immorality of the manufacture, sale and use of all intoxicating drinks as a beverage . . . is a declaration that their sale and use are, and always have been sinful. . . . It has led to a disregard of the authority of the Word of God, to a shameful perversion of its meaning, to shocking irreverence in the manner of speaking of our blessed Redeemer.[20]

The Old School general assemblies maintained their silence on this subject until 1865, when, just after the Civil War and when there was much talk of reunion with the New School, they did recommend that their ministers enjoin their young men to practice total abstinence.[21] After the reunion of the two schools the general assembly of 1877 reconfirmed the New School resolution of 1840. In the years following the First World War and prohibition the PCUSA reaffirmed its official stand in favor of total abstinence, declaring in 1934 and 1936 that total abstinence was the "Christian ideal."[22] In the twentieth century many of the defenders of total abstinence were found within the conservative camp of the Presbyterian Church and were the most enthusiastic supporters of the fundamentalist movement. But not all conservatives were in favor of total abstinence. They were allied with the fundamentalists in their fight against modernism, but did not share the ethical views of their reform-minded brethren.

The final issue was independency. In the early nineteenth century, prior to the founding of official denominational mission boards, the PCUSA had cooperated with non-Presbyterians in various independent agencies such as the American Board of Commissioners for Foreign Missions. At the time of the division of 1837 the Old School opposed cooperation with independent agencies because these agencies helped to spread a theology which was not distinctly Presbyterian. Accordingly, the Old School conducted its mission work through its own denominational agencies. The New School, on the other hand, favored interdenominational cooperation and continued to conduct its missions through independent agencies for a time. Eventually, however, the New School was forced to end its close cooperation with other denominations and to establish denominational mission boards. After the reunion of 1869 the PCUSA continued to conduct all its missions through denominational boards.

In 1933 this pattern was broken when J. Gresham Machen and his associates established the Independent Board for Presbyterian Foreign Missions. In support of an independent mission board its founders appealed both to the constitution of the church and to the precedents in Presbyterian history. But in the last analysis the board was founded and maintained, not because of the inherent virtues of independent missions agencies, but because its founders were convinced that it was the only means through which they could conduct truly Presbyterian mission work free from the influence of modernism.

In establishing the Independent Board Machen and his associates at Westminster Seminary were breaking with their own tradition which favored a strong and unified system of church government. Dr. Ned B. Stonehouse recognized this in his biographical memoir of Machen when he wrote:

> It must be admitted that there was an element of abnormality about the formation of an Independent Board since under ordinary circumstances the missions program would be conducted by official agencies of the Church. But these were abnormal times, and the bold and explosive action of the organizers of this Board, if it is to be fairly evaluated, must be understood in the context of the historical situation.[23]

Not everyone associated with the Independent Board shared these sentiments. As in the PCA, both of the Presbyterian traditions were represented on the board. Certain of its members maintained that the practice of independency was not incompatible with Presbyterian missions, and they favored some cooperation with sympathetic non-Presbyterians. Nevertheless, every effort was made to insure that the board would be as distinctly Presbyterian as possible. With this interest the charter of the board explicitly stated that it would support only those missions which were consistent with the Westminster Standards and the "fundamental principles of Presbyterian Church government."[24]

Clash of Two Traditions

The men who met together in the First General Assembly of the PCA were well aware that they were not of one mind on every detail of doctrine and practice. Yet, from all appearances, they had reason to believe that their essential agreement in their common faith would far outweigh their differences as to detail. All agreed that the Scriptures were the infallible Word of God, that the Westminster Standards contained the system of doctrine taught in the Holy Scriptures, and that the principles of Presbyterian church government were founded upon the Word of God.[25] Yet almost as soon as the business of the First Assembly commenced it became evident that it would be the differences in detail which would be accentuated. Each delegate had a vision of this "true Presbyterian Church." It was to represent the true succession of "historic Presbyterianism." But already there were two opinions as to the precise course which the achievement of such an ideal would require.

The emerging discord centered first on the adoption of the constitution. A committee on the constitution was appointed and authorized to recommend the adoption of the Westminster Standards at the Second General Assembly. They were given power to recommend no changes except the possible elimination of the changes in the standards which had been made by the PCUSA in 1903.[26] This action was favored by the majority of the assembly, but opposed informally by a minority who claimed that the standards should be adopted intact in the interest of maintaining the direct spiritual succession of the PCUSA.[27] Although the issue of the exclusion of the 1903 amendments from the constitution was not ultimately one of the major factors in the division of the denomination, the lines drawn in this debate were essentially the same as would develop over the other issues.[28]

Whatever notes of discord there were at that First General Assembly seem to have been swallowed up by the dominant theme of harmony and of hope. "There were sometimes vigorous exchanges of opinion," commented the *Guardian*. "But always there was the unity of the spirit in the bond of peace."[29] When the First General Assembly adjourned there were only intimations of anything but concord among its members. But by the time the Second General Assembly met, five months later, the lines of division between the two parties in the church had already been sharply drawn.

The first major theological issue on which the PCA was forced to take a stand was that of eschatology. By the time the new church was organized the questions involved had already been well developed in a debate which centered around Westminster Seminary. When the seminary was founded in 1929 its position on eschatology was not altogether clear. The faculty was primarily concerned with continuing the battle against modernism. Since Westminster had grown directly out of Princeton Seminary it tended toward the Old School Presbyterian tradition. This tendency was accentuated by the presence on the early faculty of representatives of the Dutch and Scottish traditions. Nevertheless, in the early years the faculty did include at least one representative of the opposing tradition, Allan A. MacRae of the department of Old Testament.[29a]

Dispensational premillennialists associated with the seminary claimed that beginning in about 1933 the emphasis of Westminster began to include an attack on their position. Several of the members of the faculty began to present strong criticisms of "Modern Dispensationalism," particularly in the form which was taught in the notes of the Scofield Reference Bible.[30]

In the spring of 1936 firm evidence of Westminster's position on dispensationalism and premillennialism appeared in the pages of the *Presbyterian Guardian*.[31] John Murray of the department of systematic theology was writing an extended series of articles on "The Reformed Faith and Modern Substitutes." In the February 3 issue it was announced that "Modern Dispensationalism" would appear in a later issue as one of the "modern substitutes." But the *Guardian* wanted to make it abundantly clear that Mr. Murray's articles were not intended in any way to exclude *premillennialists* from Reformed fellowship. The editor of the *Guardian*, H. McAllister Griffiths, who was himself a premillennialist, stressed in the May 4 issue that neither the *Guardian* nor the Presbyterian Constitutional Covenant Union (which it then repesented) were opposed to premillennialism as such. Concerning the position of the Reformed faith on the return of Christ, the editorial stated: "Differences over the *mode* in which that return will take place, whether according to the pre-, post-, or a-millennial view, have certainly been historically regarded as being within the area of permitted liberty."[32] "The series of articles by Mr. John Murray appearing in the *Guardian*," the editorial went on, "is emphatically not to be interpreted as an effort to read premillenarians out of the communion of the church."[33] Murray himself stated that the articles would deal only with that form of dispensationalism "which discovers in the several dispensations of God's redemptive revelation distinct and even contrary principles of divine procedure and thus destroys the unity of God's dealings with fallen mankind."[34]

When Murray's article appeared in the next issue, the author confined himself to this position, which he characterized as "Modern Dispensationalism." His attack was centered on the dispensational scheme present in the popular Scofield Reference Bible, and on the interpretations of dispensationalism presented by Lewis Sperry Chafer in *The Kingdom in History and Prophecy* and by Charles Feinberg in *Pre-millennialism or Amillennialism?*. Murray's thesis was that Modern Dispensationalism "contradicts the teaching of the standards of the Reformed Faith."[35] After contrasting the statements of the dispensationalists and of the *Westminster Confession of Faith*, Murray concluded: "Herein consists the real seriousness of the dispensationalist scheme. It undermines what is basic and central in Biblical revelation; it destroys the unity of the covenant of grace."[36]

The force of Murray's argument was to demonstrate that dispensationalism teaches that radically opposite, mutually exclusive and destructive principles prevail in the differing dispensations concerned. In the dispensation of law and kingdom the administration of law prevails. In the church age, or the dispensation of grace, it is grace which prevails. And, according to the statement of Feinberg, "God does not have two mutually exclusive principles as law and grace operative in one period."[37] The

Westminster Confession, on the other hand, teaches that the covenant of grace became operative as a result of the fall, and that it is this same one unified covenant which is administered in the time of the law as well as in the time of the gospel.[38] Hence, Murray argued, the dispensational teaching must be inconsistent with the Reformed standards. Murray admitted that dispensationalists might attempt to reconcile their teachings with the Reformed standards by saying that all men in all times were saved by the blood of Christ. But such a position, he maintained, is impossible for the dispensationalist to hold unless he contradicts himself. The Westminster Standards are explicit that the Mosaic dispensation was an administration of the covenant of grace. "The contrast between the two positions is absolute."[39]

It is certainly striking that this explicit and uncompromising attack upon "Modern Dispensationalism" should appear in the *Guardian* at such a critical moment in the struggle against modernism in the PCUSA. Within less than a month the general assembly of that church was to meet and there was little doubt that the necessary sequel to decisions of that assembly would be the dissolution of the Presbyterian Constitutional Covenant Union and the formation of a new Presbyterian denomination. Yet at this moment of decision the *Guardian,* the voice of the Covenant Union, was speaking out against those who might have been the most numerous of their potential allies! Certainly many dispensationalists who may have been sympathetic with the Covenant Union's fight against modernism must have been disillusioned by the exclusivism of the new group.

Yet the strong stand against dispensationalism had an important effect upon the character of the new denomination. The PCA was to be explicitly Reformed and to tolerate no doctrines which were considered inconsistent with its standards. It was clear that the doctrinal position of the church was to be dominated by the strict constitutionalism characteristic of the majority of the faculty of Westminster Seminary. On the other hand, the new denomination included within its ranks a minority of premillennialists who feared the implications of such a thoroughgoing attack upon dispensationalism.

The test case came almost as soon as the denomination was organized. The expressly premillennial Duryea (Pennsylvania) Presbyterian Church applied for membership in the Philadelphia Presbytery, which was the center of the amillennialists' strength. The Duryea Church requested that "Full eschatological liberty be granted by the Presbyterian Church of America."[40] After an extended debate the Duryea church was finally received into the presbytery at its October meeting. At the same time the presbytery passed a resolution which stated:

The question whether or not our Lord's bodily return is held to precede the "thousand years" referred to in Revelation 20 is in our opinion, despite its importance, not to be regarded as a test whether a man does or does not adhere to the system of doctrine contained in the Westminster Confession of Faith and Catechism.[41]

Despite this satisfactory resolution of the Duryea case, the debate over eschatological liberty was beginning to leave its scars. A premillennialist minority felt that the majority's concessions of "eschatological freedom" were not consistent with their uncompromising and continued attacks upon "Modern Dispensationalism." The breach became public in the October 1 issue of the Rev. Carl McIntire's paper, the *Christian Beacon*. The editorial on "Premillennialism" in that issue revealed that the editor disagreed with the policies of the church in the strongest terms. "Why is it necessary even to talk about 'eschatological liberty'?" asked McIntire,

Such liberty has been recognized. The answer, we believe, is that the a-millennialists have been attacking more strenuously the premillennialists. The premillennialist position has been quite generally accepted by Christian people, and the a-millennialists have launched their attack upon it.[42]

McIntire's reaction was directed partially toward Murray's series on "Modern Dispensationalism," but primarily toward a statement made by R. B. Kuiper, professor of practical theology at Westminster Seminary. Writing in the *Banner* for a Christian Reformed audience, Kuiper had said in reference to the examination of ministerial candidates in the PCA:

It would have warmed the cockles of the heart of any Christian Reformed minister to hear how closely they were questioned about the two errors which are extremely prevalent among American fundamentalists, Arminianism and the Dispensationalism of the Scofield Bible. The Assembly wanted to make sure that these prospective candidates were not tainted with such anti-reformed heresies.[43]

Kuiper's article, which was republished in the *Guardian*, hardly warmed the cockles of the heart of the editor of the *Beacon*. To him a characterization of the dispensationalism of the Scofield Bible as an "anti-reformed heresy" amounted to an attack on all premillennialists. "The remark in regard to the 'Dispensationalism of the Scofield Bible'," he wrote, "is an attack upon the premillennialists as heretics."[44]

Here was the clearest expression of the difference between the two positions. The Westminster Seminary and *Presbyterian Guardian*[45] group said clearly and repeatedly that their criticism of "Modern Dispensationalism" had nothing to do with premillennialists who did not adopt Scofield's schemes. The *Beacon* group, on the other hand, felt that such criticism constituted an attack on their own position.

The premillennialists in the PCA never claimed to be "Modern Dispensationalist," and no one ever charged them with being such. They never claimed to hold, nor were they charged with holding, the entire dispensational scheme of the Scofield Bible. Yet they were convinced that their premillennialism involved a form of dispensationalism. H. Mc-Allister Griffiths wrote a year later:

> It is true that there is a bare form of premillennialism in which it is possible to think of the coming of Christ as being prior to the millennium, and to hold that view unrelated to the bulk of the prophecies of the Bible. But I do not know one premillennialist in a hundred who holds such a restricted view. The real premillennialist views the events revealed of the end-time in proportion and perspective, as part of a great, unified unfolding of the various dispensations of God's providence to man.[46]

McIntire viewed the identification of the two positions as even more extensive. With reference to Kuiper's statement he wrote: "His generalized condemnation of the Scofield references leaves no room for the premillenarian to join with Scofield in believing that the millennium is a dispensation. . . . We are unable to see in our own thinking how the amillennials can say they grant liberty to the Premillenarians and then turn in such a manner as this and condemn them as heretics."[47] But if Mr. McIntire could not understand the amillennialist's position, the amillennialists were mystified by his line of reasoning. R. B. Kuiper expressed this bewilderment in a lengthy letter to the *Beacon* in which he stated: "It is a matter of common knowledge that there is ever so much more to the Dispensationalism of the Scofield Bible than the mere teaching of Premillennialism. Nor do the two stand or fall together."[48]

The debate on dispensationalism and premillennialism was reaching crisis proportions as the time approached for the Second General Assembly. The Presbytery of California addressed to the assembly a resolution and an overture which expressed complete agreement with the sentiments of McIntire's editorial of October 1. Referring directly to Kuiper's statement, the presbytery resolved that the *Presbyterian Guardian* be requested to cease printing attacks upon dispensationalism or to make it clear that such statements in no way represented the position of the church. On the same grounds the overture requested ". . . that definite, emphatic, and unambiguous eschatological liberty be written into the constitution of our beloved church."[49]

In response to the imminent crisis the issue of the *Guardian* which appeared just prior to the assembly dealt with the millennial question at great length. The leading editorial by Machen set forth clearly the position of the *Guardian* and of the majority of the faculty of Westminster. Machen was sharply critical of McIntire's editorial of October first, which he termed as "misrepresentation."[50] Further, Machen continued, the refusal of the editor of the *Christian Beacon* to publish Kuiper's reply, despite the insistence of both Kuiper and Machen, has served to create "a rising tide of suspicion and injustice."[51] This new and dangerous attitude could be seen in the overture of the California presbytery.[52] Having said this, Machen presented a definition of his own and his associates' position. He stated that they were opposed to anyone who accepts *all* that is taught in the Scofield references, but that it is possible to use some of the notes and still be perfectly Reformed. With regard to premillennialism, he reiterated that he knew of no one of his associates who asserted that premillennialism was incompatible with maintenance of the Reformed system of doctrine.[53]

Machen saw that the great danger to the church was misunderstanding and consequent misrepresentation. In the interest of relieving this misunderstanding, the *Guardian* published in the same issue an article entitled "A Premillennialist's View" by J. Oliver Buswell, the president of Wheaton College and the best known representative of premillennialism in the church. Buswell's article contributed much toward defining the differences between the two views. He acknowledged that the *Guardian* had never objected to premillennialism as such. Rather, Buswell wrote: "We believe that what is objected to is a denial of the unity of the covenant of grace. . . . I do not believe that there are any in the Presbyterian Church of America or in our true constituency who really deny the unity of God's redemptive plan. . . . "[54]

Turning to the question of the Scofield references, Buswell indicated his personal feeling, "that the general 'system of doctrine' underlying the dispensationalism of the Scofield Reference Edition of the Bible does not deny the unity of the covenant of grace any more than Hodge denies it."[55] But Buswell went on to make it clear that he did not agree with everything taught in the notes: "The Scofield notes do teach that the Mosaic order was fundamentally legalistic. This teaching I reject, but I do not believe that those of my friends who regard the Mosaic system as purely a legalistic system are necessarily heretical."[56] On this point Buswell disagreed expressly with Murray. Murray, he said, was criticizing only the extreme statements of dispensationalists who were so inconsistent as to hold a view that denied the unity of the covenant of grace. Buswell agreed with such a criticism. But he did not feel that it was warranted to use such criticisms of extreme dispensationalists to condemn the moderate form of dispensationalism which holds that law and grace are supplementary. In this connection Buswell argued vigorously that in the administration of God's grace in the Old Testament and in the New Testament age there was "a difference of economy but no difference in principle."[57]

With the appearance of Buswell's article, together with Machen's editorial in the November 14 issue of the *Guardian*, a large step was taken toward an understanding and a truce on the millennium question. Yet at the same time there was already evidence of the emergence of the two other divisive issues. Prior to the Second General Assembly the issue of Christian liberty had not been raised publicly within the PCA. But as early as September 1936 there was evidence of a sharp difference of opinion. As with the issue of premillennialism, the question was raised by the Rev. Carl McIntire in connection with the policies of Westminster Seminary. Westminster Seminary did not have any legislation concerning the use of alcoholic beverages by its students or faculty. Mr. McIntire felt that all consistently Christian institutions should take a strong official stand on this issue. With this concern, and "because of conditions which prevailed and rumors which existed throughout Philadelphia in regard to the Seminary," stated McIntire, he "felt led of God to write to the registrar of the seminary about this matter."[58] In reply the registrar, Mr. Paul Woolley, observed, "I doubt whether the teaching of the Bible contemplates that there should be enforcement by regulation of this matter in specific cases. Is it not left to each Christian to judge what is temptation to his brother and how he can best avoid putting such in his way?"[59] For the time being the matter was left to stand at that point. But already the most emotionally charged of the issues had been raised.

Not as emotionally charged but just as volatile was the issue of the Independent Board for Presbyterian Foreign Missions. When the PCA was founded it established no foreign mission board but continued to support the work of the Independent Board. Prior to the meeting of the Second General Assembly nothing was said publicly within the PCA that would suggest any dissatisfaction with the work of the board. But already there was general dissatisfaction that was suddenly to develop into an important change in the leadership of the board.

Again it was Carl McIntire who, in the pages of the *Christian Beacon*, first expressed the unrest. And again it was Machen and his associates at Westminster whom he criticized. In this case the criticism was most direct. It appeared in the November 5 *Beacon* in the form of an editorial entitled "A Machine." The editorial observed that there was a "machine" controlling the PCUSA and suggested that the members of the PCA were determined "that no such unpresbyterian and unprotestant thing as a machine should ever develop."[60] McIntire proceeded to define the characteristics of "machines." These characteristics included such developments as: "A little group of men set themselves up to rule the Church. . . . They develop a complex in which they feel that their actions are right and that everyone who differs with them should not be in the Church."[61] The editorial gave no indication that anyone thought that there was such a "machine" in the PCA. But subsequent developments soon made it clear just what was McIntire's concern. The PCA, Westminster Theological Seminary, and the Independent Board were all controlled by the same small group. Machen was the acknowledged leader of each of the three organizations, and Machen and his associates controlled the policies of each. In each of the three organizations the premillennialists and the advocates of moral reform were in a minority and had little hope of official sanction for their distinctive opinions. The best the minority could hope for was toleration. And often they felt that it was toleration without respect.

When the Second General Assembly met on November 14, 1936, talk about a "machine" appeared to be little more than vague complaint. Everyone knew there were in the church two groups, resembling parties, which were clearly divided over several distinct issues. But most evident at the assembly were the efforts at reconciliation and the attempts to reestablish mutual understanding and confidence. The election of the new moderator marked the high point in the display of renewed harmony. As soon as the nominations were opened Dr. Cornelius Van Til of Westminster Seminary rose to his feet and nominated the most prominent member of the opposing party, Dr. J. Oliver Buswell. The nomination was seconded by Carl McIntire, and Buswell easily carried the day.[62]

But the true test of the unity of the new denomination came with the question of adopting the constitution. Two major issues were involved in this question. The first issue was that of the 1903 amendments. The committee on the constitution, headed by Ned B. Stonehouse of Westminster, advised that the amendments were Arminian in character and should be eliminated. McIntire, again the principal spokesman for the opposition, admitted that the 1903 revisions were "weak" in themselves, but that the 1936 version of the constitution of the PCUSA should be adopted in the interest of claiming "direct succession" in the civil suits for church property.[63] At the time McIntire himself was engaged in a struggle to retain the valuable church property in Collingswood, New Jersey, and there is no evidence that he or his followers wanted to keep the 1903 amendments for their doctrinal merits.[64]

After a lively discussion, the proposal to include the 1903 amendments was lost and the center of attention turned to the more explosive issue of premillennialism. In this case the specific question was the overture of the Presbytery of California that "eschatological liberty" be written into the constitution. In response to the efforts at mediation in the November 14 issue of the *Guardian*, the Presbytery of California had addressed a conciliatory letter to the assembly clarifying its position. In this letter they apologized for having "pierced to the heart some brethren" and acknowledged with thankfulness that their interpretation of Professor Kuiper's words had been a misrepresentation.[65]

A series of proposals for amendments to the report of the committee on the constitution followed. An overture from the Presbytery of New Jersey had asked merely for a resolution (which would have no constitutional standing) stating that there should be absolute liberty in the church regarding the millennium. Also, the Rev. Milo Jamison of the Presbytery of California proposed that this liberty should be expressed in a declaratory statement. Both the moderator, J. Oliver Buswell, and the former moderator, J. Gresham Machen, spoke against all such proposals. Buswell declared that the standards of the church should stand by themselves and that no resolution should be adopted which would make it appear that the premillennialists belonged to the outer court of the church.[66] Machen argued that the church should "start absolutely clean" by adopting the best form of the Westminster Standards and nothing more.[67] After prolonged debate the report of the committee on the constitution was adopted with no amendments, and two proposals for resolutions on eschatological liberty were withdrawn.[68]

Not all were by any means satisfied with the outcome of the debate. The Presbytery of California protested the assembly's action because of "the wide-spread and well-founded fears which are abroad that Premillennialists are not welcome in the Presbyterian Church of America."[69] Machen's estimate of the Second General Assembly, expressed editorially in the next issue of the *Guardian*, claimed confidence that the church would weather the storm. Machen praised the work of the assembly and went out of his way to commend the work of the moderator. Machen, however, did criticize the attitude of some of the opposition: "In their reaction against letting a 'machine' do everything, it did seem as though they were inclined to be unwilling to let anybody do anything." "But . . . in general," Machen added, "the faults of this Assembly were youthful faults."[70]

But while the activities of the anti-"machine" elements appeared harmless enough within the church itself, Machen had already discovered that his leadership was being challenged in another sphere. Immediately following the Second General Assembly the Independent Board met for the election of officers and the anti-"machine" group took the opportunity to assert their power on a new front.

Machen had been president of the board since its inception in 1933, and at the board meeting in November 1936 his name was again placed in nomination. But the opposition was no longer content to have the same man, or group of men, controlling every organization. With this interest they nominated Harold S. Laird, pastor of the First Independent Church of Wilmington, Delaware, in opposition to Machen. After hours of debate Laird was elected. At the same time Merril T. MacPherson, also an independent, was reelected vice-president, leaving the eight-man executive committee of the board evenly divided between members and nonmembers of the PCA.[71]

Machen is reported to have been deeply concerned by this action. The Rev. Charles J. Woodbridge, the general secretary of the board, stated that Dr. Machen had said to him on the evening of the board elections, "If it were not for our missionaries I would at once resign from the Board."[72] The Rev. Samuel J. Allen reported that shortly before his death Machen had told him, "There is nothing now that we can do but organize a board in our own church, if true Presbyterian missionaries are to be sent out and Reformed doctrine propagated."[73] How Machen would have handled the delicate relations between the Independent Board and the PCA must remain in the realm of speculation. Machen was a remarkable diplomat as well as a highly respected leader, and it is conceivable that he could have used his prestige to heal the breach. With the absence of Machen's leadership such programs of mediation were to prove impossible. As the year ended he lay dying in a North Dakota hospital.

The Year of Division

The magnitude of the crisis created in the Presbyterian Church of America by the death of J. Gresham Machen on the first day of 1937 is difficult to estimate. No one approached him in prestige or influence in the three institutions which were associated with his name.

Without Machen there was first of all a crisis in leadership. The majority of the men who had associated with Machen were younger men— mostly in their thirties. None had the stature or respect required to assume anything approaching Machen's position of leadership. The controversies which developed during 1936 had already divided his followers. His towering influence was a major force in maintaining the unity of the movement. Without him there was no one person who could effectively check the divisive influences. The magnitude of the crisis can be seen best in the speed of developments within each of the three institutions after Machen's death. In the space of six months all three institutions— the Presbyterian Church of America, Westminster Seminary, and the Independent Board— would be divided and in the sole possession of one or the other of the parties which had followed Machen.

A period of relative calm followed the shock of Machen's death. Time was needed to grasp the implications of the new situation and to determine how to proceed. But a storm had been developing in the midst of the calm. Early in 1937 J. Oliver Buswell had published two volumes in his "Lamb of God" series. Volume four of the series dealt with *The Christian Life*, and Volume five was entitled *Unfulfilled Prophecies*. In these works Buswell discussed at some length both the question of the millennium in relation to dispensationalism and the question of Christian liberty. In its February 27 issue the *Presbyterian Guardian* challenged him on both points.

The editor of the *Guardian*, Ned B. Stonehouse, addressed himself to the question of "Godliness and Christian Liberty." Stonehouse first appealed to the tradition of Presbyterianism as regards total abstinence from the use of tobacco and wine. "Among Presbyterians," he wrote, ". . . there has been a free recognition of the rights of other Christians to follow the dictates of their own consciences in matters where the Bible has not pronounced judgment."[73a] After appealing to Scripture in defense of his position, Stonehouse turned his attack toward Buswell's book. Citing the fact that Jesus produced large quantities of wine at Cana, Stonehouse observed: "Consequently, it is a serious reflection on our Lord to hold that moderate drinking inevitably leads men into a life of drunkenness, as Dr. Buswell seems to do in his recent book on *The Christian Life*, p. 88."[74]

Buswell's argument in *The Christian Life* had been that: although "the Bible does not explicitly teach total abstinence;" and although it might be proper to use alcohol "in a settled civilization where moderation had forcefully been taught for many years and where the customs of the people were relatively stable;" we in our modern "speed-machine world" where we have no well-established social inhibitions should practice total abstinence.[75] Today, he argued, many men can avoid drunkenness only through total abstinence.[76] Hence Christians should not even drink in moderation lest they lead young people into drunkenness. Buswell concluded his argument with this warning: "You, my friend, whoever you are, even with your emphasis upon orthodoxy, are guilty of the blood and souls of young men and women if by your advocacy and example of moderate drinking you lead them, as you are leading them, into a life of drunkenness."[77]

In response to this argument Stonehouse observed that the Bible very seriously condemned drunkenness. It did this, he argued, because "*the Bible was written in a time when men were wont to go to excess as well as today.*"[78] The Christian, Stonehouse said, must be very careful not to lead anyone into the sin of drunkenness. But although the Bible urges us to give up our liberty in the interest of the weaker brother at some times, "Paul does not *in every instance* call upon Christians to sacrifice their liberty."[79] Hence, he concluded, "The use which a Christian makes of his right belongs not to the church or to any other person, but only to himself."[80]

Coordinated with this strong criticism of Dr. Buswell's views on "the separated life," the *Guardian* published an equally critical evaluation of his eschatology. The attack was no longer directed toward "Modern Dispensationalism," which Buswell repudiated; but now it was directed explicitly against his *defense of premillennialism*. The criticism, entitled "Dr. Buswell's Premillennialism," by John Murray, took the form of a review of *Unfulfilled Prophecies*. This book was itself polemic in character. In this short study Buswell defended premillennialism; but he did it largely through a criticism of the eschatological views of prominent defenders of amillennialism and postmillennialism, specifically Geerhardus Vos and B. B. Warfield. Buswell noted in his Preface that he stood ready to be thoroughly corrected in his criticism of such distinguished scholars.[81] But he could hardly have been ready for the thorough censure which appeared in Murray's review.

After some preliminary remarks commending certain characteristics of Buswell's premillennial position, Murray proceeded to expound the main thesis of his review: that "Dr. Buswell grossly misrepresents both Dr. Warfield and Dr. Vos, but particularly the latter."[82] Pointing out several instances in *Unfulfilled Prophecies* where he believed this to be the case, Murray commented: "We do not accuse Dr. Buswell of deliberate distortion. He has, however, shown himself seriously incompetent to deal carefully and fairly with his opponent."[83] The effect of Murray's analysis was to say that he had very little respect for Dr. Buswell as an exegete. At one point he even accused Buswell of falling into an "unscholarly error" by using an English concordance in an argument where a Greek concordance was required. In conclusion Murray admitted: "Dr. Buswell's eschatological position is much saner and therefore more defensible than that of many premillenarians."[84] But, he said, he found the book "exceedingly disappointing. It is characterized by gross unfairness and misrepresentation, and his exegetical argumentation is frequently inconsequential."[85]

Buswell was highly disturbed by the *Guardian*'s two-pronged attack upon his distinctive views. In response Buswell addressed two communications to the *Guardian* which appeared in the April 10 issue. The first was a brief communication protesting that his argument for total abstinence in *The Christian Life* was based solely upon the biblical principle of inexpediency found in 1 Corinthians 6:12 and 10:23.[86] The second was an extended reply to Murray's review. Buswell stated that the differences between him and Murray were "within the bounds of Christian comity." Nevertheless, he said, "My whole point is that even such orthodox scholars, including Mr. Murray, do not argue against the millennium without involving themselves in contradictions and inconsistencies."[87] Buswell proceeded to make a point-by-point defense of his statements which Murray had criticized, including the observation that he had a large Greek concordance at his elbow in his study. In the most part Buswell's defense was careful and scholarly. But it concluded with four brief paragraphs which the editors of the *Guardian* refused to publish since they felt that they would impugn the motive of the receiver and were misleading in certain respects.[88]

In the same issue the editors printed Murray's reply to this communication. In this reply Murray reiterated and clarified some of his criticisms. He concluded with some observations regarding Dr. Buswell's personal feelings:

> He may have thought I was indulging in a personal attack and so may some readers. May I disabuse all concerned of such a notion. I am not without admiration for many excellent qualities in Dr. Buswell. . . . It is surely by forthright criticism, where such is necessary, that the cause of truth is to be advanced.[89]

While the young faculty members of Westminster were debating with Dr. Buswell concerning his recently published views, the old issue of toleration of dispensationalism was raised from outside the new denomination. *The Sunday School Times* of February 20, 1937, revived the charge that the leaders of the PCA were hostile to premillennial views.[90] In response to this charge, the editor of the *Guardian* stated once again that the attack upon "Modern Dispensationalism" did not constitute a criticism of premillennialism. In order to clarify the amillennial position of Westminster Seminary, the *Guardian* promised a study of that subject in an early issue.[91]

The *Guardian* of March 27, 1937, fulfilled this promise by publishing an article by John Murray entitled "What is Amillennialism?" This article had nothing of a polemic character but was a careful and patient explanation of the amillennial position directed toward a premillennialist audience. The intent of the article was to encourage the premillennialist readers to at least understand the amillennialist's position, even if they could not accept his conclusions.[92]

By mid-April 1937 the divisive issues were clearly defined and before the public. None of these issues involved a disagreement on a central point of Christian doctrine. But the extent of the disagreement on these various subjects had created parties in the church and in its associated institutions. Even in 1936 the two parties had been attempting to consolidate their power and to gain leadership. In 1937, with the death of Machen, this question of leadership was magnified. The result was a struggle for control in each of the three institutions— the seminary, the Independent Board, and the denomination. In each the pattern of the struggle was the same: the minority became acutely dissatisfied with their lack of influence; they appealed to the majority for a reform — or more correctly, a concession to their position; the appeal was rejected; the minority withdrew and formed a rival institution.

Ever since the formation of the PCA the minority in the church had been dissatisfied with the policies of Westminster Seminary. In the fall of 1936 J. Oliver Buswell had submitted to Machen an extensive critique of Westminster, which Machen had never found opportunity to answer.[93] With the death of Machen the dissatisfaction with Westminster increased rapidly.

In April of 1937 Carl McIntire took matters into his own hands and approached the faculty of Westminster personally on the matter of the use of alcoholic beverages. At the faculty meeting of April 24 McIntire appealed to the faculty that they should counsel their brethren in the matter of total abstinence. As he may well have expected, the faculty maintained its position that this was a matter of personal liberty both for themselves and for their brethren.[94]

The minority also made an attempt to reform the eschatological position of the seminary, suggesting that it add three faculty members and ten trustees all of whom were premillennialists, so as to achieve a balance of power. This suggestion too was discarded by the majority, who maintained that such was not an adequate basis for the selection of the faculty or of trustees.[95]

Two days later the division of the seminary became a reality with the resignation of the professor of Old Testament, Allan A. MacRae. In his letter of resignation MacRae explained that he was compelled to take this step because: "Control of the faculty had passed into the hands of a small alien group without American Presbyterian background."[96] "The major emphasis of the teaching of the Seminary," he continued . . . has now shifted so that it is no longer primarily against Modernism, but against Fundamentalism, so called."[97] In support of this contention, MacRae cited the two issues of a sustained attack on premillennialism in the seminary, and the vigorous defense of their right to use intoxicating liquors on the part of almost every member of the faculty.[98] Two of the members of the board of trustees, Harold S. Laird and Roy Talmage Brumbaugh, resigned at the same time as MacRae, offering much the same reasons for their action.[99]

The *Beacon* commented on the division in an editorial entitled "Liquor." "We are very very sorry that the attack of Westminster Seminary has shifted to the Fundamentalists," wrote McIntire.[100] McIntire viewed the matter of Christian liberty to be the major issue in the division; but he also saw the position of the seminary on this matter as an excuse for an attack upon fundamentalism in general. Thus he wrote: "Because this matter has been injected into this movement at this time, together with other matters which are minor in comparison to the great issue of the day, we see the utter folly of the seminary leadership. It has lost its effective leadership."[101]

The faculty at Westminster felt that the charge that the seminary had ceased firing upon modernism to turn its guns against fundamentalism was "preposterous."[102] Rather, they maintained, they were devoted solely to the Reformed faith, reiterating their position on the issues of premillennialism and Christian liberty.[103] Nevertheless, the unity of the seminary had been shattered. No realistic proposals for compromise had been offered on either side. Not that the issues involved were essential to the central message of the institution; the seminary had been divided into parties, and one of the parties had gained complete control. The minority, whose position was not represented in the official statements of the seminary, withdrew with the intention of forming a rival seminary which represented their own views.

And what about the Independent Board? Ever since the defeat of Machen in his bid for reelection to the presidency of the Independent Board, the Westminster group had been concerned about their loss of leadership in that organization. With the death of Machen they became a minority on the executive committee as well as on the board itself. Their fear was that the opposition would use their power on the board to substitute new policies, such as taking an official stand in favor of premillennialism or total abstinence.

The men at Westminster had already seen that such a development was a real possibility. Merril T. MacPherson, the vice-president of the Independent Board, was also the president of an organization known as the Philadelphia Fundamentalists. Meeting on February 4, 1937, the Philadelphia Fundamentalists amended their constitution to include a definite premillennial statement which excluded non-premillennialists from its membership. In response to this action, Mr. Paul Woolley of Westminster Seminary, an historic premillennialist, withdrew from the organization.[104]

The presence of MacPherson on the Independent Board was disturbing to the Westminster group. His ardent premillennialism was based on a form of dispensationalism. Presumably they could have challenged his orthodoxy in an attempt to remove him from the board. But the Westminster group employed a different tack in approaching the problem. MacPherson, as well as several other members of the board, including its president, were independents. The constitution of the board was clearly Presbyterian in character. They therefore decided to challenge the legality of having independents on a board for Presbyterian foreign missions. To do this they had to insert a new issue into the controversy — that of independency.

The issue of independency was raised in the May 15, 1937, issue of the *Guardian*. Ned B. Stonehouse, the editor, wrote:

> Presbyterianism is distinguished from Independentism in that it maintains, to use the word of Charles Hodge, "the unity of the church, in such sense, that a small part is subject to a larger, and a larger to the whole" (*Church Polity*, p. 119). . . . . Apart from the interdependence of the churches, which the New Testament everywhere recognizes, the task of the church, which is to proclaim the Word of God, cannot be carried out, nor can the purity of the church be maintained in any adequate fashion.[105]

When the Independent Board met on May 31, just prior to the Third General Assembly, the minority presented a resolution to the board disapproving of independency of church government and calling upon the independents to bring their practice into accord with the charter.[106] The charter of the Independent Board stated that its purpose was to promote mission work "which is true to the Bible and the system of doctrine contained in the Westminster Confession of Faith and to the fundamental principles of Presbyterian church government."[107] The charter of the board did not state explicitly that its members had to be Presbyterians or even subscribe directly to the fundamental principles of Presbyterian church government. However, it did state that its members had to pledge approval of the charter of the board.[108] The authors of the resolution argued that by making such a pledge the board member was "indicating his approval of the foregoing provisions of the charter."[109] Appended to this resolution was formal notice that if the resolution were passed its signers would undertake an investigation of the doctrinal soundness of certain members.[110]

A stormy session followed the introduction of this resolution. The emotion generated by the disruption of the institution which Machen had founded and strenuously defended was intense. Carl McIntire claimed that at one point in the meeting one of the women associated with the Westminster group "turned to the majority of the Board and declared, 'The death of Dr. Machen is on your hands.' The Westminster group and other women nodded assent," added McIntire.[111]

When the resolutions failed, eight of the board members, including four connected with Westminster Seminary, resigned on the grounds "that the usefulness of the Independent Board as an agency to promote the object for which it was founded, the conduct of truly Presbyterian foreign missions, is at an end."[112] At the same time six of the missionaries under appointment by the board requested cancellation of their appointments.[113] Also, the Rev. Charles J. Woodbridge resigned as the general secretary of the board. In defense of his action Woodbridge explained that the board was no longer true to its charter and that the executive committee which appointed the missionaries was controlled by three independents and one elder in the PCUSA. Woodbridge noted that, "It has been widely rumored that the issue throughout has been one of Premillennialism *versus* Amillennialism."[114]. But this could not be the case, he argued, because at least three of the members of the board who had resigned (including himself) were premillennialists. Independency and its implications for the future work of the board were the only issues.[115]

The majority on the board insisted that the action of the minority was merely an excuse to divide the board so that the PCA would be free to establish its own mission board, controlled by the Westminster interests. "It seems that the men were looking for an excuse on which to base their action," wrote McIntire in the *Beacon*, "and the best excuse they could get, and without doubt one of the most flimsy, was the fact that the Board was in favor of Independency."[116] The charge that the board favored independency was simply not true, argued McIntire. As evidence of this he noted: first, the board did pass a resolution in which it fully reaffirmed its adherence to its charter and to Presbyterian doctrine and polity; second, the new members which were elected to the board were all Presbyterians; third, the board simply tabled the motion of the minority, which did not in any way constitute approval of independency.[117]

Harold S. Laird, the president of the board, added several arguments in support of the majority's contention. First, he pointed out that no charge was made that the board intended to send out missionaries who were untrue to Scripture, and no specific case of doctrinal irregularities was cited. The only charge was that three members were practicing independency. Second, Laird stated that the three members in question were wholeheartedly devoted to Presbyterian doctrine and to the fundamental principles of Presbyterian church government, and that they were independents only because they could not conscientiously join any existing denomination. Third, he pointed out that in 1935 the Rev. Milo F. Jamison, who was then an independent, was unanimously elected to the board, and no question was raised by anyone as to his ability to take the pledge in all sincerity.[118]

Regardless of any evaluation of the motives of the minority or the strength of their contention, their action certainly had something to do with their conviction that it was necessary to create a denominational mission board. Close cooperation between those who controlled the church and those who controlled the Independent Board was no longer feasible. Under any circumstances they would have had to withdraw from the Independent Board before they established their own agency.

The pattern in the division of the Independent Board was essentially the same as that in the division of Westminster Seminary. The minority felt that a new institution was necessary if they were to propagate effectively their distinctive views. They proposed a reform which they knew the majority would not accept. (The minority on the board could hardly have expected the majority to pass a resolution which would have required the independents of their number to affiliate with a Presbyterian denomination.) When their proposal was rejected the minority withdrew.

With the withdrawal of the Westminster group from the Independent Board, the division of the PCA at its Third General Assembly seemed inevitable. The minority could hardly remain in a denomination which conducted missions in competition with the board they supported. Here again the pattern of division would be essentially the same. The minority recognized that their situation was hopeless and that a new institution was necessary if they were to have an effective voice in governing their denomination. The issue on which they could urge reform was that of total abstinence. Several overtures on this subject had already been made to the assembly. The majority was almost certain to reject such overtures; and this together with the other divisive factors would be sufficient to divide the denomination.

That a division of the church was imminent became apparent early in the first session of the assembly. At that time, according to the *Guardian*'s report, "Dr. Buswell openly declared his intention to withdraw . . . if the Assembly did not take what he considered to be the only proper action on the overtures involving the question of total abstinence."[119] But the first major item of business was the report of the committee on Foreign Missions, and the question of the church's relation to the Independent Board. The report recommended that, since the Independent Board was no longer true to its charter, it had now become necessary for the PCA to establish its own foreign missionary agency.[120]

In reply Carl McIntire presented an extensive minority report recommending that the church not change its mission program. McIntire reviewed in detail the charges against the board and the defense of the majority. The majority on the Independent Board, his report stated, still belonged to the PCA. Furthermore, "It should be remembered that the Presbyterian Church in the U.S.A. functioned for forty-nine years without any Board of its own, but authorized the sending of its gifts even to an agency which was congregational, the American Board of Foreign Missions. . . ."[121]

The debate on the reports was lengthy and sometimes heated. Speaking against the motion, J. Oliver Buswell protested, "These men who are attacked in the majority report were good enough for the Board till other matters came up."[122] He insisted that neither the question of independency nor eschatology entered into the matter at all. Rather, he asserted, the two issues were a "little clique" that wanted to run everything and opposition to total abstinence.[123] After several speeches by members of the majority, McIntire in a final speech again alleged that it was a "little clique" which was causing all the trouble.[124]

At last the assembly rejected the minority report by a vote of 75 to 19.[125] The defeated minority filed a protest to this action, reaffirming their defense of the Independent Board. In answer to this protest the majority stated that the assembly had based its action directly on the voted action of the Independent Board in refusing to adopt the resolution condemning independency. The action of the general assembly was, therefore, based solely on the fact that the board was no longer true to its charter, and reflected no adverse judgment on the merits of the work of the board or the integrity of its members.[126]

The intensity of the debate increased as the attention of the assembly was turned from foreign missions to the subject of Christian liberty. The issue before the assembly was also before the public in the simplest terms. The daily newspapers had already printed Buswell's statement that the PCA was a "wet" church.[127] Some declaration had to be made by the general assembly to clarify the stand of the church on this controversial issue.

Three overtures urged that the church either recommend or resolve that its members practice total abstinence. One overture, from the Presbytery of Philadelphia, resolved that only the relevant statement of the *Westminster Catechisms* be brought to the attention of the members of the church. The debate on the floor centered on two proposals. The minority chose to defend the overture of the Presbytery of the Chicago Area recommending total abstinence; while the majority united behind a substitute which expanded the Philadelphia overture.

The overture from the Presbytery of the Chicago Area was an extended appeal to "historic American Presbyterianism." Within the text of the overture were quoted seven recommendations for total abstinence which had been adopted by the PCUSA in the nineteenth century.[127a] The overture resolved that the PCA adopt the declaration which had been first adopted by the New School assembly in 1840 and reconfirmed by the reunited assemblies in 1877. It also recommended to all the members of the church ". . . unvarying exemplification of the only true principle of temperance — total abstinence from anything that will intoxicate."[128]

The substitute to the Philadelphia overture proposed the opposite extreme — that the assembly do nothing more than affirm its belief in the statements of its standards. It stated:

> We believe that the Westminster standards speak with adequacy and with force on these subjects, in the Confession of Faith XX; Larger Catechism, Questions 122–148; and Shorter Catechism, Questions 63–81. . . . We do not feel that any situation has actually arisen within the Presbyterian Church of America which calls for any further statement.[129]

Each side had chosen to defend the most extreme statement of their position. In the lengthy debate which followed there was little concord. Each side appealed to Scripture, the tradition of American Presbyterianism, the practice or convictions of J. Gresham Machen, and to the situation at Westminster Seminary. At the end of the debate the resolution for total abstinence was lost and the substitute to the Philadelphia overture was carried by a large majority. With the loss of their motion, Milo F. Jamison and J. Oliver Buswell expressed their intention to leave the denomination.[130]

Immediately following the Third General Assembly fourteen ministers and three elders withdrew from the church and announced their intention to form the Bible Presbyterian Synod. In the subsequent months the various presbyteries and individual churches who had represented the minority allied themselves with the new organization.

Although the division was generally considered tragic because of the effects it might have upon the witness of the movement, many of the participants agreed that the dissension had reached the point where division was the best solution. Edwin H. Rian of the majority stated, "Their exodus is a happy solution."[131] Carl McIntire commented, "We are thankful to God that He made it so clear in such a short time the real position of the men who are now in Westminster Seminary."[132] The statement most often used in defense of the division expressed far more than the reiteration of the divisive issues themselves. The statement came from Amos 3:3 — "Can two walk together except they be agreed?"

With their independence established, the members of the Bible Presbyterian Synod proceeded to enact the policies which had been denied them in the PCA. They already had control of the Independent Board, which they continued to support in its foreign mission program. In the fall of 1937 they opened Faith Theological Seminary to represent their distinctive views. Finally, at the first meeting of the Bible Presbyterian Synod in 1938 the new denomination took an official stand on eschatology and on total abstinence. On eschatology, the new synod adopted the Westminster Standards without the revisions of 1903 but with an explicit statement of a premillennialist position. At the same time they passed a resolution which allowed eschatological liberty within the denomination.[133] On abstinence, the synod adopted a relatively mild statement, declaring "that we deem it wise to pursue a course of total abstinence."[134]

Conclusions

In evaluating the causes of the division of the Presbyterian Church of America in 1937 two explanations are most often given. The first is that it was caused by differences over the theological issues involved. The second is that it was a matter of politics and personalities.

If we were to adopt the first of these explanations — that the division was caused by differences on eschatology, Christian liberty, and church polity — we would have to answer the question: was any one of these issues sufficient to divide the church? And if so, which one? Certainly the differences on eschatology could hardly be considered sufficient cause for the division. Neither the premillennialists nor the amillennialists ever claimed that the other position should not be tolerated within the church. The closely related issue of modern dispensationalism might have been considered a sufficient cause for division. But that issue was never officially raised within the denomination.

Likewise, the issue of church polity could not be a sufficient cause for the division. No one who joined a Presbyterian denomination could be charged with practicing independency; and so the question of independency as such was never raised within the church. Nor could the question of denominational support of the Independent Board be considered primarily a matter of principle. No one ever claimed that denominational missions were wrong. And certainly no one who had followed Machen out of the PCUSA claimed that Christians did not have a right to conduct non-denominational missions.

This leaves only the issue of Christian liberty— specifically the question of whether the church should officially recommend total abstinence from alcoholic beverages. J. Oliver Buswell and others maintained that the failure to take an explicit stand on this question was sufficient cause to leave the denomination. The merits of this position are a matter of continuing debate. But if this were the sole and sufficient cause for the division, it would seem necessary to establish either that a church which fails to take an official stand on this question can no longer be a true church of Christ, or that members have the right to leave a denomination over an issue less that that of apostasy.

The second explanation of the division is that it was not caused primarily by the differences on theological issues, but that it was the result of a contest for ecclesiastical power and the clash of personalities. On the one hand, it has been claimed that a "machine" dominated by Westminster Seminary was trying to seize control of everything connected with the denomination. On the other hand, it is often observed that subsequent history has indicated that Carl McIntire has never been content in any organization which he did not control, with the implication that it would have been nearly impossible for the majority in the church to continue cooperation with McIntire and his programs.

Certainly there is an element of truth in each of these claims. The policies of the PCA were controlled by a relatively small group of men closely associated with Westminster Seminary. And Carl McIntire objected vigorously to the extent of that control. The result was a contest for leadership, which centered in the struggle to control the Independent Board. That this contest was largely political in character can be seen by a consideration of the major move made by each side. On the one hand, no one has ever claimed that Laird was elected to replace Machen as president of the Independent Board because he would be superior to Machen as a leader or administrator. Rather, he was elected as the representative of a party. On the other hand, one can hardly imagine that the issue of the independency of certain members of the board would have been pressed as it was, if the question of control of the board had not been involved. From a practical point of view this contest for control of the Independent Board was the single most important factor in dividing the church.

But once it is conceded that there was a major political factor involved, it does not necessarily follow that the division was caused solely by political considerations or by personal antagonisms. Certainly the strained personal and political relationships could have been vastly improved if either side had been willing to be tolerant on the *principles* involved.

These two explanations of the division, if taken together, are helpful, but not entirely satisfactory. They become more satisfactory if they are viewed in the light of a third consideration— that the division represented a conflict of the two major traditions in American Presbyterianism. This third explanation was intimated at the time of the division in the claims of each side that the other had departed from "historic Presbyterianism." On the one side this division was sometimes represented as a conflict between "historic Presbyterianism" and "fundamentalism"; while on the other side it was termed "historic American Presbyterianism" *versus* a non-American (Dutch and Scottish) Reformed tradition. Neither of these representations is totally accurate; but they do support the contention of the present study that the division reflected a conflict of two traditions within conservative Presbyterianism in America.

This explanation in itself is not sufficient to explain the division. If it were, it would have to be established that the two traditions within American Presbyterianism were incompatible. This would be difficult to establish in the light of the facts that both of the two previous divisions (Old Side–New Side in 1741 and Old School–New School in 1837) were resolved within a generation (1758 and 1869); and that from 1869 to 1936 the two sides cooperated closely within the PCUSA. Nevertheless, the observation that the division reflected a conflict between two American Presbyterian traditions is extremely useful in broadening our perspective on the events of 1937.

The two traditions do not represent two incompatible theological traditions. Rather, they represent two approaches to the same tradition. One is the more subjective, less authoritarian conception of Presbyterianism, closely associated with nineteenth-century revivalism and twentieth-century "fundamentalism" with their strong emphases on the visible signs of faith, especially a conversion "experience" and a "separated life." The other is the more objective and authoritarian conception, closely associated with the European Reformed tradition with its strong emphasis on the place of the objective standards and often associated with exacting scholarship. Each of these traditions has always included many of the traits more strongly characteristic of the other.

These two emphases were both found within the PCA and corresponded closely to the two sides of the division of 1937. One observer characterized this difference as being similar to the difference between the sales and the research departments of a modern industry. The sales department is anxious to get the product on the market even if the product is not yet in its most perfect state; while the research department insists that caution should be taken not to present a shoddy product. Often one side has a difficult time understanding the emphasis of the other, even though each one has a legitimate function.[135]

The analogy is useful because it helps to explain the apparent breakdown of communications in the early months of 1937. Each side had a vision of what the new church should be like. The minority saw a Bible-believing church witnessing to the world both in the preaching of the Word and the "separated life." The majority saw an orthodox church whose witness would reflect an informed study of the scriptural principles of the church and its work. The two visions are not incompatible. But in a time when their differences rather than their similarities are emphasized it becomes difficult for one to sympathize with the emphases of the other.

Both visions have a legitimate place in the Christian church. But the balance between them is always precarious. In the spring of 1937, with the crisis of leadership which followed Machen's death, the scales were tipped and the balance lost.

NOTES

This is a slightly revised edition of articles that appeared in the *Presbyterian Guardian* 30, 1–4 (January to April 1964).

1. J. Gresham Machen, "A True Presbyterian Church at Last," *Presbyterian Guardian* 2 (June 22, 1936), 110.

2. Ibid.

3. "Act of Association of the Bible Presbyterian Synod," quoted in *Christian Beacon* 2 (June 10, 1937), 1.

4. *Presbyterian Guardian* 4 (June 26, 1937), 1.

4a. Cf. Lefferts A. Loetscher, *The Broadening Church* (Philadelphia: University of Pennsylvania, 1957), 5.

5. H. Shelton Smith, Robert T. Handy, and Lefferts A. Loetscher, *American Christianity*, Vol. I, 1607–1820, (New York: Charles Scribner's Sons, 1960), 262.

6. For example, Lefferts A. Loetscher, *The Broadening Church*, p. 18 states: "But, of course, as the present study maintains throughout, broad continuities can be discerned, if the identity is not pressed too closely, between earlier New School positions and later 'liberalism.' "

Compare Edwin H. Rian in *The Presbyterian Conflict* (Grand Rapids: Eerdmans, 1940), Chapter I, where he maintains that "the child of New School theology" is modernism, p. 23.

7. Cf. A. A. Hodge, *The Life of Charles Hodge* (New York: Charles Scribner's Sons, 1880), 289. "The subsequent course of the New School, as a separate denomination, clearly proves that in all essentials the majority of them were sound Presbyterians, alike in principles of order and in doctrine. . . . "

8. Norman Kraus, *Dispensationalism in America* (Richmond: John Knox Press, 1956), Chapters 1 and 2. Cf. George Eldon Ladd, *The Blessed Hope* (Grand Rapids: Eerdmans, 1956); and William H. Rutgers, *Premillennialism in America* (Goes, Holland: Oosterbaan and Le Cointre, 1930).

9. Premillennialism, of course, need not be associated with modern dispensationalism.

10. Kraus, Chapters 1–3.

11. Ibid., 134.

12. Ibid., 59.

13. New School revivalism, particularly in the western territories, had been one of the important sources of tension with the Old School.

14. Among the precursors of the dispensational movement is the famous New School leader and moderator, George Duffield (Kraus, 54). Another New School leader, Samuel H. Cox (Moderator of the New School assembly in 1846), is noted for a dispensational scheme which was in outline "the exact parallel of Scofield's system." (Ibid., 30).

On the other hand, James Hall Brookes and Nathaniel West, two of the most active leaders in the International Prophecy Conferences, were former members of the Old School Presbyterian Church. Nevertheless, both men worked in the midwest where Old School emphases were less distinct.

15. However, we should not press this continuity too closely. Dispensationalism was a new— and in many ways unique— development in American theology and therefore cannot be identified exactly with any of the theological or ecclesiastical developments which preceded it.

16. Kraus, 57.

17. *Minutes of the General Assembly of the Presbyterian Church in the U.S.A.*, 1818, 689 –90. From *Digest of the Acts and Deliverances of the General Assembly of the Presbyterian Church in the United States of America* (Philadelphia: Presbyterian Board of Publication, 1923), Vol. I, 468.

18. *Minutes*, 1829, 298. From *Digest*, 469.

19. *Minutes* (New School), 1840, 15. From *Digest,* 469.

20. Charles Hodge, *Discussions in Church Polity* (New York: Charles Scribner's Sons, 1878), 224–25.

21. *Minutes* (Old School), 1865, 570. From *Digest,* 469–70.

22. *Minutes,* 1934, 198; 1936, 156. From *The Presbyterian Constitution and Digest* (Philadelphia: The United Presbyterian Church U.S.A., 1956), A710.

23. Ned B. Stonehouse, *J. Gresham Machen: A Biographical Memoir* (Grand Rapids: Eerdmans, 1954), 498.

24. "The Charter of the Independent Board for Presbyterian Foreign Missions," in the *Presbyterian Guardian* 4 (June 6, 1937), 79.

25. *Minutes of the First General Assembly of the Presbyterian Church of America,* 4.

26. Ibid., 7–8.

27. Robert S. Marsden, ed., *The First Ten Years,* (Philadelphia: The Orthodox Presbyterian Church, 1946), 5; Stonehouse, *Machen,* 503.

28. Marsden, 5.

29. *Presbyterian Guardian* 2 (June 22, 1936), 111.

29a. The faculty also included one "historic premillennialist," Mr. Paul Woolley, who aligned himself with the "Old School" tradition.

30. H. McAllister Griffiths, "The Character and Leadership of Dr. Machen," *Christian Beacon* 2 (September 2, 1937), 2. Cf. letter from W. Lyall Detlor, *Christian Beacon* 2 (May 20, 1937), 2.

31. In January of 1936 Oswald T. Allis, professor of Old Testament at Westminster Seminary, published a similar attack upon modern dispensationalism in *The Evangelical Quarterly.* See "Modern Dispensationalism and the Doctrine of the Unity of Scripture," reprinted by James Clarke & Co., London, 1936.

32. *Guardian* 2 (May 4, 1936), 44.

33. Ibid.

34. Ibid.

35. John Murray, "The Reformed Faith and Modern Substitutes," Part VI "Modern Dispensationalism," *Guardian* 2 (May 18, 1936), 77.

36. Ibid., 79.

37. Quoted from Feinberg, Ibid., 79.

38. Ibid.

39. Ibid.

40. *Christian Beacon* 1 (August 20, 1936), 8.

41. Resolution of the Philadelphia Presbytery, October 13, 1936; *Guardian* 2 (October 24, 1936), 203.

42. *Beacon* 1 (October 1, 1936), 4.

43. R. B. Kuiper, "Why Separation Was Necessary," *Guardian* 2 (September 12, 1936), 227.

44. *Beacon* 1 (October 1, 1936), 4.

45. As of September 12, 1936, the editorship of the *Guardian* passed from H. McAllister Griffiths to J. Gresham Machen and Ned B. Stonehouse.

46. H. McAllister Griffiths, "The Character and Leadership of Dr. Machen," *Beacon* 2 (September 2, 1937), 2.

47. *Beacon* 1 (October 1, 1936), 4.

48. Instead of publishing Kuiper's letter in the *Beacon,* McIntire printed a "Correction" in which he apologized for the fact that Kuiper felt misrepresented, saying that the misrepresentation was entirely unintentional, but reaffirming that he still believed that the term "dispensationalism of the Scofield Bible," did include what he said. *Beacon* 1 (October 29, 1936), 4.

49. *Guardian* 3 (November 14, 1937), 55.

50. Ibid., 1.

51. Ibid., 4.
52. Ibid.
53. Ibid.
54. J. Oliver Buswell, "A Premillennialist's View," Ibid., 46.
55. Ibid.
56. Ibid., 47.
57. Ibid. Buswell's emphasis on the continuity of law and grace throughout both the Testaments was consistent with his strict moral position. As he pointed out, a dispensationalism carried to its logical extremes would lead to a denial of the place of the law in the New Testament age: "I feel that to regard the moral law in the Old Testament as in any sense more rigid or binding upon God's people than it is in the New Testament, opens the way for antinomianism, which view I have found at least as prevalent among amillenarians as among premillenarians." (Ibid.)
58. *Beacon* 2 (June 24, 1937), 2.
59. Ibid., 7.
60. *Beacon* 1 (November 5, 1936), 4.
61. Ibid.
62. "The Second General Assembly," *Guardian* 3 (November 28, 1936), 78–79.
63. Ibid., 82.
64. As evidence that he favored the eventual elimination of the revisions by constitutional amendment procedure, McIntire noted later that the Bible Presbyterian Synod eliminated these revisions from its constitution. *Beacon* 20 (March 10, 1955), 2.
65. *Minutes of the Second General Assembly of the Presbyterian Church of America,* 16–17.
66. *Beacon* 1 (November 26, 1936), 5.
67. *Guardian* 3 (November 28, 1936), 82.
68. Ibid.
69. *Minutes of the Second General Assembly,* 26–27.
70. *Guardian* 3 (November 28, 1936), 70–71.
71. *Guardian* 3 (November 14, 1936), 71.
72. Charles J. Woodbridge, "Why I have Resigned as General Secretary of the Independent Board," *Guardian* 4 (June 12, 1937), 69.
73. "Foreign Missions Forge Ahead in the Presbyterian Church of America," Ibid., (supplement).
73a. *Guardian* 3 (February 27, 1937), 201.
74. Ibid.
75. J. Oliver Buswell, Jr., *The Christian Life* (Grand Rapids: Zondervan, 1937), 86.
76. Ibid., 87.
77. Ibid., 88.
78. *Guardian* 3 (February 27, 1937), 202.
79. Ibid., 203.
80. Ibid., 204.
81. Buswell, *Unfulfilled Prophecies* (Grand Rapids: Zondervan, 1937), Preface.
82. Murray, "Dr. Buswell's Premillennialism," *Guardian* 3 (February 27, 1937), 206.
83. Ibid., 207.
84. Ibid., 209.
85. Ibid.
86. Letter from Buswell, *Guardian* 4 (April 10, 1937), 12.
87. Buswell's reply to Murray, Ibid., 13.
88. Ibid., 12.
89. Murray's reply to Buswell, Ibid., 16.
90. *The Sunday School Times,* Vol. 79, No. 8, pp. 130–32.
91. *Guardian* 3 (March 13, 1937), 217–21.

92. John Murray, "What is Amillennialism?" *Guardian* 3 (March 27, 1937), 242–45.

93. Stonehouse, *Machen,* 504.

94. *Beacon* 2 (June 24, 1937), 2. Cf. letter from Paul Woolley, *Beacon* 2 (July 1, 1937), 2.

95. Statement of R. B. Kuiper, chairman of the faculty, *Guardian* 4 (May 15, 1937), 39.

96. Allan A. MacRae, Letter of Resignation from Westminster Seminary, April 26, 1937; Ibid., 50.

97. Ibid.

98. Ibid.

99. *Beacon* 2 (April 29, 1937), 1–2.

100. Ibid., 4.

101. Ibid. It should be observed that McIntire himself had a considerable role in raising the issue of drinking at Westminster.

102. *Guardian* 4 (May 15, 1937), 37.

103. Ibid., 37–40.

104. *Guardian* 3 (February 27, 1937), 214.

105. *Guardian* 4 (May 15, 1937), 39.

106. *Guardian* 4 (June 6, 1937), 79.

107. The Charter of the Independent Board for Presbyterian Foreign Missions; Ibid., 79.

108. Ibid., 80.

109. Resolution to the Independent Board, Ibid.

110. Ibid.

111. *Beacon* 2 (June 3, 1937), 5.

112. Letter of Resignation; *Guardian* 4 (June 6, 1937), 80.

113. Ibid.

114. Woodbridge, "Why I have Resigned . . ." Ibid., 69.

115. Ibid., 70.

116. *Beacon* 2 (June 3, 1937), 4.

117. Ibid.

118. Harold S. Laird, "The Independent Board Carries on Despite New Attacks," *The Independent Board Bulletin* 3 (June 1937), 3–10.

119. *Guardian* 4 (June 26, 1937), 88.

120. "Report of the Foreign Mission Committee," *Minutes of the Third General Assembly of the Presbyterian Church of America,* 16.

121. "Minority Report," Ibid., 15. Here McIntire was appealing to the same practice which the New School had defended in 1837.

122. *Guardian* 4 (June 26, 1937), 89.

123. Ibid.

124. Ibid., 91.

125. Ibid., 89–91.

126. "Report of the Committee Appointed to Answer the Protests," *Minutes of the Third General Assembly,* 24–25.

127. *Guardian* 4 (June 26, 1937), 94.

127a. *Guardian* 33 (January 1964), 7–8.

128. "Overture #2, Presbytery of the Chicago Area," *Minutes of the Third General Assembly,* 5–7.

129. *Minutes,* 22.

130. *Guardian* 4 (June 26, 1937), 94.

131. *Beacon* 2 (June 10, 1937), 8.

132. Ibid., 4.
133. *Beacon* 3 (September 15, 1938), 1.
134. *Beacon* 3 (September 8, 1938), 4.
135. George S. Christian, "Let's Not Talk about a Split in the Bible Presbyterian Church," (By the author, 1955), 1.

Michael A. Hakkenberg

19 The Battle over the Ordination of Gordon H. Clark, 1943–1948

FUNDAMENTAL to the Orthodox Presbyterian Church throughout its history has been a commitment to doctrinal purity. It is a denomination which, in large measure, is defined by its unwillingness to compromise on its standards of conservative Reformed orthodoxy. Already at its birth in 1936 it saw itself as a church which would stand firmly for the traditional teachings of the historic Christian faith.

In breaking with the Presbyterian Church in the USA the leaders of the OPC believed that they had done so because of the older denomination's departure from orthodox Christian doctrine. Edwin H. Rian writes,

> This conflict which resulted in the formation of . . . The Orthodox Presbyterian Church, was not a controversy over some trivial matter or a difference between certain individuals but the culmination of many years of doctrinal defection. The real basic issue was a clash between divergent points of view in doctrine, one conservative or orthodox and the other liberal or modern.[1]

After its birth the OPC understood itself to be the true representative of Presbyterianism in America; to keep this status required adherence to right doctrine as defined in the *Westminster Confession of Faith* and taught at Princeton Seminary prior to its reorganization in 1929.[2] Although not officially tied to the OPC, the new Westminster Theological Seminary was to continue in the tradition of Old Princeton and provide for a scholarly defense of the faith.[3] Both Westminster and the OPC were committed to teach and defend the Christian faith against modernism. The crucial issue before the church, as its founders saw it, was the battle against modernism.

329

In the early history of the OPC, commitment to doctrinal purity remained strong. During the years 1943 to 1948, it was this devotion to doctrinal purity that led to dispute and disagreement over Gordon H. Clark's ordination in the OPC. Clark's views on certain theological matters were challenged by Cornelius Van Til, professor of apologetics at Westminster Theological Seminary, and this conflict has often been referred to as the "Clark-Van Til" controversy. However, it would be misleading to suppose that strictly doctrinal issues were involved. The crucial non-doctrinal issue that came into focus during this controversy concerned the direction and character of the OPC as a denomination: would it be distinctively Reformed and Calvinistic in its perspective, or would it become a more evangelical denomination within the mainstream of the larger American evangelical community.

It is impossible to understand the Clark case without viewing the doctrinal issues in the broader context of the question concerning the direction of the church. Therefore, in order to best explain the complexity and scope of the "Clark-Van Til" controversy, I will first state the rather narrow theological issues; then I will consider the non-doctrinal and broader issue of the character of the OPC itself. After this discussion it will be possible to understand why Clark and a number of other ministers left the OPC over seemingly non-fundamental and highly technical doctrinal matters, since on the surface it seems as though the theological issues involved should not have warranted such an extreme action.

The Doctrinal Issues

What then were the doctrinal issues that caused Clark's ordination to be challenged? They mainly centered on his understanding of the doctrine of the incomprehensibility of God and on the effect of regeneration on the intellect. Clark's views on the relationship between God's sovereignty and man's responsibility, and the well-meant offer of the gospel were also questioned, but these matters soon assumed a secondary role in the controversy.

To examine the issues I will make use of two of the earliest documents of the controversy: *The Complaint* — which initially challenged Clark's theological opinions and questioned his fitness for ordination in the OPC; and *The Answer*, written primarily by Clark, in response to *The Complaint*.[4] These two documents set the tone for much of the debate at the general assemblies in the years 1944–48.

The challenge to Clark's position on the incomprehensibility of God focused on the relationship of man's knowledge to God's knowledge. The essential objection was that Clark did not maintain a qualitative difference between God's knowledge and man's knowledge and therefore broke down the distinction between God as Creator and man as creature. The complainants consistently argue in *The Complaint* for a qualitative distinction between God's knowledge and man's knowledge— this tenet, they claim, is central to the doctrine of God's incomprehensibility. However, they also want to make it clear that they are not advocating a skepticism or agnosticism with regards to knowledge of God and his world; they recognize that "skepticism and agnosticism are thoroughly anti-Christian."[5] Man must be capable of knowing about God if the Christian faith is to be meaningful. Therefore, a distinction must be made between the knowability of God and his incomprehensibility. The Christian's claim is that God is both knowable and incomprehensible, and that his knowability does not diminish or compromise his incomprehensibility.

The complainants state their position as follows:

> In avoiding skepticism and agnosticism . . . Christianity has been insistent that the knowledge of God which is possible for men, possible because of the fact of divine revelation, is not and can never become comprehension of God. The doctrine of the incomprehensibility of God is as ultimate and foundational as the doctrine of his knowability. . . . Because of his very nature as infinite and absolute the knowledge which God possesses of himself and of all things must remain a mystery which the finite mind of man cannot penetrate. The divine knowledge as divine transcends human knowledge as human, even when that human knowledge is a knowledge communicated by God. Man may possess true knowledge as he thinks God's thoughts after him. But because God is God, the Creator, and man is man, the creature, the difference between the divine knowledge and the knowledge possible to man may never be conceived of merely in quantitative terms, as a difference in degree rather than a difference in kind. Otherwise, the Creator-creature relationship is broken down at a most crucial point, and there is an assault upon the majesty of God.[6]

A problem arises in an effort to understand the complainants' position because of their insistence upon a "difference in kind," or qualitative difference, between man's knowledge and God's knowledge. *The Complaint* speaks of "the gulf which separates the divine knowledge from human knowledge" and "of the exceeding greatness of God and of his knowledge which man as a creature cannot know in any adequate way."[7] But what constitutes man's inadequate knowledge? The basic position is that God's knowledge has a different content than man's knowledge. It is not that man's knowledge is incomplete, but rather that the content of a proposition is different for God and for man.

In rejecting Clark's position on the relationship between God's knowledge and man's knowledge the complainants explain,

> While we appreciate the effort to arrive at certainty with reference to man's knowledge of God, in our judgment this is done at too great a cost. It is done at the sacrifice of the transcendence of God's knowledge. . . . If we are not to bring the divine knowledge of his thoughts and ways down to human knowledge, or our human knowledge up to his divine knowledge, we dare not maintain that his knowledge and our knowledge coincide at any single point. Our knowledge

of any proposition must always remain the knowledge of the creature. As true knowledge, that knowledge must be analogical to the knowledge which God possesses, but it can never be identified with the knowledge which the infinite and absolute Creator possesses of the same proposition.[8]

According to *The Complaint* Clark fails "to distinguish with respect to content between the Creator's knowledge of any thing and creaturely knowledge of any thing."[9] Clark is in error for failing to recognize the difference in content between man's knowledge and God's knowledge of the same proposition. But if the content is different, does not man know one proposition and God another? How can there be knowledge of the same proposition as the complainants want to maintain? From their viewpoint the correct stance recognizes man's knowledge as analogical to God's knowledge: man's knowledge is qualitatively different from God's knowledge, but it is true because it is derived from, related to, and dependent on God's knowledge.

On the other hand, Clark's position destroys the Creator-creature distinction by recognizing only a quantitative difference between God's knowledge and man's knowledge.

> Dr. Clark denied that there is any qualitative distinction between the contents of the knowledge of God and the contents of the knowledge possible to man, but rather in so far as there is any distinction between these two the distinction is merely quantitative. . . . Dr. Clark holds that man's knowledge of any proposition, if it is really knowledge, is identical with God's knowledge of the same proposition. . . . And since Dr. Clark holds that no limitation may be placed upon God's power to reveal propositions one at a time to men, there is no single item of knowledge in God's mind which may not be shared by the human mind.[10]

On Clark's view it is not that the content of a proposition is somehow different for God and man, but rather that God knows infinitely more propositions than man and knows them intuitively rather than discursively. The failure of Clark's position, the complainants believe, lies in the fact that it "does not rise above a quantitative distinction between the content of the knowledge which man may possess"[11] and the content of the knowledge which God has. For Clark "propositions have the same content, mean the same, to God and man."[12] The complainants summarize Clark's claims about knowledge as follows:

> It would seem here that Dr. Clark is seeking to work out a theory of knowledge which, over against agnosticism and skepticism, will assure man of actual and certain knowledge. By appealing to the power of God to reveal knowledge, and by resolving knowledge into detached items, he argues that man may be assured of true knowledge since his knowledge corresponds wholly with the divine knowledge of the same propositions.[13]

However, in defending knowledge against skepticism, Clark has erred by identifying man's knowledge with God's knowledge.

Another objection raised in *The Complaint* is that Clark ascribes a primacy to the intellect which does not give proper recognition to volition and emotion in the act of faith. This position, in conjunction with his view of knowledge, leads him "to conceive of man's religion as nothing greater than knowing propositions. . . . "[14] In contrast, the complainants assert that all of man's faculties— the will, the intellect, and the emotion — are involved in man's religious experience. They believe that "pure and genuine religion is not, then, merely the intellectual apprehension of propositional truths. . . . To ascribe a primacy to the intellect is unbiblical."[15]

Finally, the complainants lay this charge against Clark:

> Dr. Clark does not deny the necessity or fact of regeneration but he makes no absolute qualitative distinction between the knowledge of the unregenerate man and the regenerate man. With the same ease, the same "common sense," the unregenerate and the regenerate man can understand propositions revealed to man.[16]

The example cited most often as evidence for this charge is that Clark believes that the proposition *Christ died for sinners* has the same meaning for both the regenerate and the unregenerate man. The complainants find this view unacceptable. They claim that it "bears all the earmarks of rationalism, humanistic intellectualism. . . . It is the product of a rationalistic dialectic."[17] In fact, the complainants consistently argue that Clark's approach to theology is rationalistic; his theology is faulty because it is "built up from certain principles derived from reason."[18] Unfortunately, *The Complaint* does not carefully explain the exact nature of this criticism. Without question, the assertion that Clark begins with reason rather than Scripture must amount to more than an *accusation.* However, at this point the complainants do little more than accuse.

In response to the complainants Clark attempts to answer the many questions that have been raised about his theology, and in the process he further clarifies his own theological views. He clearly wants to repudiate a doctrine of incomprehensibility which implies that man's knowledge is qualitatively different from God's knowledge. An analogical theory of knowledge, Clark claims, results in skepticism. He states his own position as follows:

> The doctrine of the incomprehensibility of God as set forth in Scripture and in the Confession of Faith includes the following points: 1. The essence of God's being is incomprehensible to man except as God reveals truths concerning his own nature; 2. The manner of God's knowing, an eternal intuition, is impossible for man; 3. Man can never know exhaustively and completely God's knowledge of any truth in all its relationships and implications; because every truth has an infinite number of relationships and implications and since each of these implications in turn has other infinite implications, these must ever, even in heaven, remain inexhaustible for man; 4. But the doctrine of the incomprehensibility of God does not mean that a proposition, e.g., two times

two are four, has one meaning for man and a qualitatively different meaning for God, or that some truth is conceptual and other truth is non-conceptual in nature.[19]

For God and man there is no qualitative difference in the content of a proposition. Clark explains "that God can reveal any item of knowledge in propositional form . . . and that such a revealed proposition has the same meaning for God and for man when . . . man understands it."[20] An individual may not understand every truth that God has chosen to reveal to man, but if he does understand a certain truth, then the meaning of it is identical for God and for man. God's knowledge and man's knowledge of that revealed truth would then coincide.[21] If they did not coincide, man could know nothing about God and the world because coincidence with God's knowledge, with the truth, guarantees true knowledge for man.

Clark also does not believe that his formulation of the doctrine of God's incomprehensibility shatters the Creator-creature distinction. He maintains that the difference remains.

> Man's knowledge would always be temporal, and could never include either the immediate intuitive knowledge of God or the knowledge of all the relationships and implications of any and all propositions. The necessary content of omniscience includes knowledge of what is to man the infinite future, the past in all its content, and all the infinite relationships and implications of all items of knowledge, past, present, and future, as well as the infinite self-consciousness of God, both of his own Triune nature and of the manner in which he knows the universe, including the knowledge that God has of what is possible for him to do but which he will never do. Man can never become omniscient by adding one item of knowledge to another throughout eternity.[22]

God is omniscient and man is not. God knows intuitively and man knows discursively. God knows the relationships and implications of all propositions and man does not. The fundamental distinction between God as Creator and man as creature has not been altered. Clark also asserts that the Scriptures warrant his position; they do not support a qualitative distinction between man's knowledge and God's knowledge as defined in *The Complaint*.

Furthermore, *The Answer* charges that the position of the complainants leads to skepticism:

> The Complaint definitely states that man's knowledge and God's knowledge do not "coincide at any single point." . . . The Complaint teaches that any given proposition does not mean the same thing for God as it means for man. "Two times two are four" is a given proposition; therefore it means one thing for man; and something qualitatively different for God. The truth "Christ died for our sins," does not have the same meaning for man and for God. May it mean for God that Christ did not die for our sins? The complainants of course

would deny that it could quite mean that. But does their philosophy give them reasons for making such a denial?

The Complaint teaches that the truth man may have is an analogy of the truth God has; i.e., man may have a resemblance of the truth God has; but he cannot have God's truth itself. He has only an analogy of it. . . . On the complainants' theory there is no way of ever crossing over from an analogy of truth to the truth itself. All our thinking is shut up in analogies and resemblances and cannot coincide with God's truth at even a single point. This position really cuts all connection between God's knowledge and man's knowledge and plunges us into unmitigated skepticism.[23]

Clark believes that unless one holds that man and God both know the same truth, that a proposition has the same content for God and man, the result is skepticism. Man could never be sure of his salvation because, for example, the proposition *God loves sinners* would have one meaning for man and another for God. And this, Clark proclaims, is a heterodox position.

Clark in his *Answer* also responds to the other issues which are raised in *The Complaint*. He defends, for instance, a propositional view of truth, arguing that

the Bible is logical; its teaching is propositional; and in view of the fact that God chooses words and propositions for his revelation, in view of the fact that God did not choose some non-propositional form of revelation, one should be cautious of disparaging propositions. There is therefore Scriptural support, even if not exegetical support, for a propositional view of truth.[24]

This position is in direct contrast to the position of the complainants — and particularly Van Til — who emphasize that truth is holistic in nature and that some truth is completely non-propositional in character. They believe that some truth cannot be expressed in a propositional form.

The Answer also clarifies Clark's view on the effect that regeneration has on knowledge.

Both the regenerate and the unregenerate can with the same ease understand the proposition, "Christ died for sinners." Regeneration, in spite of the theory of the Complaint, is not a change in the understanding of these words. The difference between the regenerate and the unregenerate lies in the fact that the former believes the proposition and the latter does not. . . . An unregenerate man may understand the proposition "Christ died for sinners," but far from knowing it to be true, he thinks it to be false. Strictly speaking he knows only that "the Scriptures teach Christ died for sinners." When he is regenerated, his understanding of the proposition may undergo no change at all; what happens is that he now accepts as true what previously he merely understood. He no longer knows merely "the Scriptures teach Christ died for sinners"; he now knows "Christ died for sinners."[25]

Clark does believe that a change occurs through regeneration, but it is not a change in the understanding of a certain proposition. Rather, it is that the regenerate man now accepts the proposition *Christ died for sinners* as true and believes that Christ died for his sins. He no longer refuses to acknowledge the truth of the biblical message of salvation.

Lastly, Clark explains his position in response to the repeated charge of rationalism. For one thing he claims that an appeal to reason in a theological method is not inconsistent with the Presbyterian tradition:

> If the complainants object to . . . [my] method as unsound, they must also repudiate the methods of old Princeton as "out of harmony with orthodox Presbyterianism." The Presbytery does not assert that the Confession requires adherence to everything in the Princeton apologetic. Other forms of apologetics may also be permitted. But without specifically amending our standards any attempt to exalt one method as alone orthodox and to repudiate all appeal to the *a-priori* truths of reason is intolerable.[26]

Prior to the controversy Van Til had developed at Westminster an apologetic— called presuppositionalism— in which he rejected "all appeal to the *a-priori* truths of reason." He did, in fact, want to establish a new apologetic— outside of the old Princeton tradition— as orthodox. Clark, in contrast, is simply suggesting that his appeal to reason as an apologetic tool is not out of line with the Presbyterian and Princeton traditions. Therefore it cannot be construed as unorthodox.

Clark also explains that he does not believe that the attempt to solve apparent paradoxes in the Bible is wrong, or that it results from a faulty methodology which overemphasizes the power of reason. In seeking to better understand the Scriptures, apparent paradoxes may be resolved. One should not just suppose that God has revealed something "non-understandable" to man and then claim that it is a paradox. Instead one must think hard about so-called paradoxes and work toward a resolution.[27] It is a mistake to assume that man may never come to understand certain biblical teachings such as that about the relationship between divine sovereignty and human responsibility. The Bible may contain mysteries, but man should not immediately assume that what he does not understand is a mystery. This approach to paradoxes does not result from a rationalism but rather from a desire to understand the Scriptures. The charge of rationalism, Clark maintains, is wholly without warrant.

I have now outlined the major differences between Clark and the complainants, or Clark and Van Til. Clearly, the issues involved in this controversy are highly abstract ones. The OPC is to be commended for its careful study of these matters. In the final action taken by the general assembly in 1948 Clark's theological opinions are neither accepted nor rejected. However, because of the constant and often bitter opposition to his ordination Clark left the denomination that same year.

The Character of the OPC

The question that remains is why a split occurred in the OPC over these difficult theological and epistemological issues. The answer lies in the fact that the controversy involved much more than these limited theological concerns. Those on both sides of the issue — Clark and his supporters versus Van Til and his — had a different vision for what kind of church the OPC should be. This difference then came to expression most definitively in the controversy over Clark's ordination.

Clark and particularly his supporters had a vision for the OPC in which the battle against modernism should be the main concern of the denomination. To this end they favored cooperation with fundamentalists and a more evangelical direction for the church, in keeping with conservative American Presbyterianism. In large part, such Presbyterianism defined itself in terms of the famous five-point statement of 1910. A commitment to biblical inerrancy, the virgin birth, the satisfaction theory of the atonement, the bodily resurrection of Jesus, and the historicity of miracles was essential.[28] A Reformed theology, although important to this group, was not crucial in the battle against modernism.

In contrast to the emphases of the Clark group, Van Til and his followers thought that the church should be a distinctively Reformed denomination, one that possibly stood closer to the Dutch Calvinist tradition. The OPC had already established itself as a Reformed denomination and set itself off from American fundamentalism by its rejection of dispensationalism and premillennialism in 1937. As a result of the premillennial controversy, Carl McIntire and thirteen other ministers left in order to start the Bible Presbyterian Church and Faith Theological Seminary.[29] To be consistently Reformed, many believed, the OPC could not cooperate with fundamentalist churches. To do so would weaken its Reformed character.

Thus both groups in the controversy wanted the OPC to be a certain kind of denomination. The specific theological debate reflected the fundamentally different perspectives of these groups. Clark's willingness to cooperate with the fundamentalists in the battle against modernism suggested to Van Til and others that Clark's theology was suspect: not Reformed enough and perhaps Arminian. And the main characteristic of Arminianism, according to Van Til, was its failure to recognize the sovereignty of God and the essential distinction between the Creator and the creature that a proper understanding of God's sovereignty entailed. One of the crucial charges brought against Clark, as we have seen, was his failure to maintain the Creator-creature distinction in his doctrine of the incomprehensibility of God. Over and over Van Til maintained that his formulation of the doctrine of incomprehensibility gave full recognition to God's sovereignty. Thus the question was raised if Clark's theology — which stood in contrast to Van Til's — could be truly Reformed.

Van Til believed that if Clark's understanding of incomprehensibility was not rejected the OPC would not be a consistently Reformed denomination. Obviously, much more was at stake in this conflict than a particular individual and his view of God's incomprehensibility: it was a controversy about the character and direction of the OPC. Was the OPC to be an evangelical denomination which sought to cooperate with other churches in the battle against modernism, or was it to be, as some charged, a narrow denomination within the Reformed tradition as defined by Van Til and the Westminster faculty?

To understand fully the complexity of this controversy it is necessary to consider Clark's background prior to his attempt to gain ordination in the OPC. After receiving his Ph.D. in philosophy from the University of Pennsylvania and teaching there for a few years, Clark accepted the position of associate professor of philosophy at Wheaton College in Illinois in 1936. However, his Calvinist viewpoint on predestination soon made him the source of controversy. Many of the faculty, as well as the president, V. R. Edman, believed that Clark's position was deterministic and counterproductive to the missionary emphasis at Wheaton. Clark himself believed that he was simply explicating the Reformed doctrine of God's sovereignty. Soon the differences between Calvinism and Arminianism became more pronounced at Wheaton, and because Clark continued to teach the doctrines of Calvinism, he was forced to resign from the faculty in 1943.[30]

Clark's resignation was a topic of considerable interest in the *Presbyterian Guardian*. At this time Clark was a member of the Redeemer OPC in Philadelphia, a ruling elder in the denomination, and a frequent contributor to the *Guardian*. Early in 1943 Clark's letter of resignation was published in the *Guardian*; and in a later issue Edwin H. Rian, president of the board of trustees of Westminster Seminary, wrote an article in which he explained and defended Clark's position on foreordination, election, and reprobation.[31] In forcing Clark to leave, Rian believed that Wheaton College "set itself against practically every Reformed and Presbyterian church body in the world, for all of the Calvinistic confessions contain similar teachings."[32] Rian viewed Clark's position as consistent with the *Westminster Confession of Faith* and historic Calvinism. In subsequent years, throughout the controversy, Clark's commitment to Calvinism was called into question. However, in 1943 Clark was known as a Calvinist philosopher; it is for this reason that he was forced to resign from Wheaton.

After leaving Wheaton, Clark decided to seek ordination as a minister in the OPC so that he would be eligible to serve as a pastor. At this point the OPC became embroiled in the controversy described above. A brief review of the chronology — an extremely complicated one — of the controversy will suggest the importance that this issue had in the OPC.

In 1943 Clark "requested that the Presbytery of Philadelphia ordain him to the gospel ministry."[33] At the March 20, 1944, meeting of the presbytery the committee on candidates and credentials reported that Clark was enrolled as a candidate for the ministry and had requested that the requirements of two years of study in a seminary and knowledge of Hebrew be waived. Clark had never received any formal training in theology. The committee then recommended that Clark be examined in theology by the presbytery, and that special attention be given to his view of miracles and the doctrine of God. After the examination fifteen members voted that Clark be sustained, but thirteen did not. According to the church's Form of Government another examination would have to be held because a three-fourths majority did not vote to sustain.[34] At this time the presbytery decided to "refer the matter of the licensure of Dr. Clark to the General Assembly for advice."[35] (The OPC requires that advice be sought from the general assembly when a candidate requests that certain requirements for ordination be waived.) Thus the issue concerning Clark's ordination, when it came before the Eleventh General Assembly in 1944, was not a doctrinal one; it was a matter of requirements for ordination. After considerable discussion the assembly voted to advise the Presbytery of Philadelphia that the requirement of seminary study be waived.[36]

At a special meeting of the presbytery on July 7, 1944, Clark was sustained in exam by a three-fourths majority vote, and the requirement for formal theological training was waived. His knowledge of Hebrew was also ruled sufficient. Clark was then licensed to preach, and shortly after this he was ordained.[37] In the minutes of the 1944 general assembly Clark is listed as a minister in the OPC, and his status remained unchanged until he left the denomination in 1948. However, in 1945, as the controversy over his ordination became increasingly complicated, he accepted the position of professor of philosophy at Butler University in Indianapolis.[38]

On October 6, 1944, the Presbytery of Philadelphia received a complaint (the text of which is *The Complaint* referred to above) by thirteen members of the presbytery against the presbytery's action "in the matter of the licensure and ordination of the Rev. Gordon H. Clark, Ph.D."[39] The complaint was heard at the November 20 meeting of the presbytery. It stated that

> in the opinion of the complainants the [July 7, 1944] meeting itself was illegal and . . . the theological views of Dr. Clark as indicated in his examination were of such a character as not to warrant presbytery in proceeding to his licensure and ordination.[40]

The complainants, as already stated, questioned Clark's views on the incomprehensibility of God, the effect of regeneration on the intellect, the relationship of the intellect to the other faculties of the soul, the relationship of divine sovereignty and human responsibility, and the well-meant offer of the gospel. A committee, of which Clark became a member, was then elected by the presbytery to prepare a response to the complaint. After a number of meetings in March 1945, in which both the complaint and the reply (the document referred to as *The Answer* above) to the complaint were discussed, the presbytery defeated a motion which would have recognized the legitimacy of the complaint and the error of the presbytery in proceeding to license and ordain Clark.[41]

In May of 1945 the complaint came before the general assembly by way of a letter from the complainants. Since the complainants believed that the presbytery had erred in ordaining Clark, and that the doctrinal matters involved were very important, they considered it necessary to bring the complaint before the general assembly. The assembly recongized the legality of the meeting of the presbytery on July 7, 1944, and then appointed a committee to study the doctrinal portion of the complaint to determine whether or not the "presbytery erred in its decision to proceed to licensure and ordination" of Dr. Clark.[42] Later a protest was made against the Twelfth General Assembly in its action that declared the proceedings of the July 7, 1944, meeting of the Presbytery of Philadelphia to be legal.[43]

At the Thirteenth General Assembly the committee on the doctrinal portion of the complaint presented both a majority and a minority report. The majority believed that the allegations were not warranted on the basis of the evidence cited from Clark's examination before the presbytery. The minority believed that adequate answers to certain doctrinal matters had not been obtained in the examination, and that the presbytery should not have proceeded to licensure.[44] The assembly then "defeated the motion to find ground for complaint in the actions of sustaining Dr. Clark's examination in theology, and proceeding to license him. . . ."[45] However, it did pass a motion which stated that the Presbytery of Philadelphia had violated the church's Form of Government by not allowing for a sufficient time period between Clark's licensure and his ordination; the presbytery had erred in its decision for constitutional, not doctrinal, reasons.[46]

At this assembly another protest was registered "against the failure of this General Assembly to find that there was ground for complaint against the Presbytery of Philadelphia."[47] The protest charged that, in fact, there were significant questions expressed in the complaint concerning Clark's theology, and that these questions should have been answered before Clark was licensed. Another committee was then appointed to study all the doctrinal issues involved "for the purpose of clarifying these matters."[48] This committee was to report to the Fourteenth General Assembly.

In May 1947, at the Fourteenth General Assembly, the Presbytery of Philadelphia admitted in a letter that it had violated the Form of Government of the OPC in proceeding immediately from the licensure to the ordination of Clark, and in so doing had "thereby contributed to the disturbance of the peace of the church."[49] However, in another letter to the assembly certain members of the presbytery claimed that the matter of the time period between licensure and ordination was not the cause of the failure "to preserve the peace of the church." They state, "the truth is that the issue before the church has been from the beginning doctrinal through and through. . . ."[50] But at this assembly serious discussion of the committee report on the doctrinal issues of the complaint never occurred. The committee had studied only the doctrine of the incomprehensibility of God, one member had an extended illness, and the assembly found itself short of time for discussion. Therefore, the assembly voted to reconstitute the committee which was then to report to the Fifteenth General Assembly.[51]

Finally in 1948 the committee presented its report. Because of a lack of consensus among the committee members over the doctrines studied, both a majority and a minority report were submitted. After much discussion the assembly did not adopt either report but instead recommended that they be sent to the presbyteries of the church for further study.[52] This was the last action that the assembly took in relationship to the Clark case. However, by 1948 it had become clear that many leaders of the OPC — largely the faculty at Westminster — could not tolerate Clark because of his doctrinal positions.

In 1949 Clark is no longer listed as a minister in the OPC. An issue of the *Guardian* states that

> Word has been received, without further details, that at a meeting of the Presbytery of Ohio of the Orthodox Presbyterian Church . . . the Rev. Dr. Gordon H. Clark, a minister of the church and professor of philosophy at Butler University, was dismissed to the Presbytery of Indiana of the United Presbyterian Church.[53]

With Clark's leaving the denomination, the case was decided.

From this chronology of events it is possible to see the complexity of the case. The controversy over Clark's ordination was plainly a divisive one. Both sides produced much literature in support of their respective positions, and important theological and doctrinal questions were raised and debated throughout the controversy. However, underlying all of this debate was the question of the character of the OPC. Was it to be a church that stood in the original conservative American Presbyterian tradition and supported cooperation with evangelical denominations in the battle against modernism, or was it to be a Reformed Calvinist church, especially as defined by the faculty at Westminster? The signers of the complaint included R. B. Kuiper, John Murray, Ned B. Stonehouse, Cornelius Van Til, Paul Woolley, and Edward Young, all faculty members at Westminster.[54] Only John H. Skilton did not sign because he was absent.

Initially the complexion of the issue might seem odd because Clark saw himself as a Calvinist firmly within the Reformed tradition — for this reason he had to leave Wheaton. But the emphasis of Clark and his supporters was on the battle against modernism, and therefore they were willing to cooperate with those fundamentalist churches that agreed to the five-point statement of 1910. The faculty at Westminster saw this as a compromise and repudiation of the Reformed tradition. The OPC, if it was to remain Reformed, could not cooperate with fundamentalists who were Arminian in their theology.

Early in its history Rian characterized the OPC as a Reformed denomination within the Presbyterian tradition:

> The Orthodox Presbyterian Church is what its name implies, truly Presbyterian. Its doctrinal standards, the Westminster Confession of Faith and the Larger and Shorter Catechisms are in practically the same form as they were when written by the Westminster Divines nearly three hundred years ago. All compromise with Modernism has been eliminated and strict adherence to the Presbyterian and Reformed traditions characterizes the testimony of the Church.[55]

The OPC, Rian proclaimed, "is true to the great Presbyterian heritage handed down by the church fathers of American Presbyterianism."[56] This theological lineage is borne out by the fact that J. Gresham Machen — one of the greatest representatives of American Presbyterianism — was a founding father of both the OPC and Westminster Seminary. However, after Machen's death in 1937 the intellectual leadership of the seminary shifted to Van Til and Murray. It was especially Van Til who began to promote the Dutch Calvinist tradition in Reformed theology and particularly to challenge the Old Princeton apologetic, a central component of American Presbyterianism. Thus, shortly after the OPC's birth, the *precise nature* of the denomination's commitment to the Reformed tradition was less than clear. To further complicate the issue, many of the early leaders of the church saw their main objective not to be that of promoting the Reformed tradition — either Dutch or American — but rather to be one of defending orthodox Christian doctrine against modernism. Clark clearly saw the latter as his primary role.

In 1943 Clark wrote an article in the *Guardian* entitled "An Appeal to Fundamentalists," in which, after briefly outlining the history of fundamentalism in America, he states, "In very plain words, we invite you [the fundamentalists] to unite with us, The Orthodox Presbyterian Church."[57] Together they could oppose modernism. In this article Clark recognizes the importance of holding to a Reformed theology, but his emphasis is on the need for churches to unite to fight a common enemy. In 1943 Clark also served on a committee of the general assembly to determine whether the OPC should join the American Council of Christian Churches, of which McIntire was the leader. Although in the minority, Clark endorsed membership in this council.[58] Cooperation with other orthodox churches was essential in the battle against modernism.

Support for Clark's ordination was also part of a "program for action" by certain ministers and leaders in the OPC — including Rian and the Rev. Richard W. Gray— who wanted the church to be a more evangelical denomination. Edward Heerema, a minister in the OPC and correspondent for *The Calvin Forum*, makes reference in this periodical to the "program for action" and its relationship to Clark's ordination: "Documentary evidence exists to show that a small but determined group had decided on a 'program for action' in the church, and the first [of] four 'Specific Objectives' to be sought after was the ordination of Dr. Clark."[59]

In a later issue of *The Calvin Forum* Heerema, who consistently supported the Westminster faculty in its opposition to Clark, offers his perspective on the controversy in the OPC:

> Let us begin with the latest center of trouble — the "Clark case." . . . It is accurate to think of the Clark affair as the spearhead of an all-out offensive aimed at gaining control of the O.P.C. and of all important agencies within it or associated with it. That is why the struggle centering in the ordination of Dr. Clark has been fought so intensely. . . . Now we move onward to ask this question. What are the views of these men who are seeking to win control of the O.P.C., or Westminster Seminary and related enterprises? Obviously when men put on such a determined campaign to wrest the control of the church from those who may in a word be described as suporting the clearcut Reformed stand of Westminster Seminary, it must be because there is some rather basic difference of viewpoint.[60]

This basic difference, Heerema believes, centers on their attitude toward Arminianism as expressed by a willingness to cooperate with fundamentalists. The supporters of Clark believe that "Arminianism is not 'another gospel,' but rather it is an inconsistent statement of the true gospel." Arminianism must not be opposed in the same way as modernism. The former preaches an " 'inconsistent view of the cross;' " the latter denies the cross. Furthermore, although differences do exist between an Arminian and a Reformed theology, one must not claim that Arminianism represents a rejection of the gospel of grace.[61]

Heerema goes on to explain that, in contrast to the Clark group, the faculty at Westminster opposes Arminianism because they believe it is contradictory to the gospel of grace. To hold a position contrary to the one of Westminster is inconsistent with "historical Calvinism." Arminianism cannot be reconciled with the gospel of grace, and cooperation with churches that accept an Arminian theology must be avoided.[62] Heerema also elaborates on the relationship between Clark's ordination and the efforts of Clark's supporters to gain control of Westminster and the OPC:

> It is deeply saddening to see one's fellow ministers . . . waging a determined offensive to win control of these Calvinistic institutions, an offensive in which

the ordination of a man to the sacred ministry has played an important part. These brethren have not been the least bit deterred by the fact that the entire faculty of Westminster Seminary contests the accuracy of Dr. Clark's views. Rather, it has become apparent that this group would win a major battle in their offensive if they can discredit the seminary in the disposition of the theological matters that have come to the fore in the "Clark case." Such a victory would amount to strong endorsement of their demands for change in policy and control at the seminary.[63]

In response to Heerema's account and interpretation of the Clark controversy, Floyd E. Hamilton, a supporter of Clark, provided *The Calvin Forum* with the text of the "program of action." The program itself emphasizes that the OPC needs to return to its original ideals: "to be a spiritual succession to the Presbyterian church in the USA, actively to combat Modernism, and to engage in a program of aggressive evangelism. . . . " The program also states that "the ordination of Gordon H. Clark" was its first specific objective.[64] Hamilton then goes on to explain what he sees as the real issues in the Clark controversy. He claims that "there is a difference regarding the attitude to be taken toward . . . other evangelical denominations." Those who support Clark believe that there must be a "readiness to cooperate" with Christians in other evangelical churches. The OPC should be characterized by "warm evangelical zeal. . . . Instead of fighting . . . over extra-confessional points of doctrine . . . [its] energies should be spent fighting Modernism and unbelief in the world at large."[65] Finally, Hamilton states,

> The group opposed to Mr. Heerema believes that the Orthodox Presbyterian Church should follow the American tradition in Presbyterianism, rather than the traditions of churches holding to the Reformed Faith in other lands, unless the American tradition has clearly departed from the express teaching of the Word of God.[66]

From Hamilton's own words one can see that the issues surrounding the Clark case result from more than doctrinal differences, although the divergent opinions of the two groups are reflected in their theological positions. The supporters of Clark believed that their position reflected a " 'historical, ecumenical' Calvinism, as opposed to . . . the 'narrow, personal' Calvinism of the faculty of Westminster Seminary."[67] This 'ecumenical' Calvinism would, of course, allow the OPC to pursue aggressively cooperation with other evangelical churches in order to fight modernism.

Throughout the controversy over Clark's ordination the *Guardian* took a stand which became increasingly hostile to the views of Clark and his supporters. Many of the *Guardian* editorials were written by Ned B. Stonehouse and John Murray, both of Westminster; they consistently opposed Clark's ordination as well as the position of his supporters. In an editorial Paul Woolley, professor of church history at Westminster, claimed that there was discontent in the church which centered around this question:

> Does the OPC want to have a growing revival of the preaching, teaching and application of the biblical and Reformed Faith in these United States. . . . Or does The Orthodox Presbyterian Church want to have many members and much money and read about itself in the newspapers? It can have either one, but it cannot have both.[68]

Responding to this editorial, Hamilton stated that

> The Orthodox Presbyterian Church is standing at a fork of the road. Is our beloved church to remain a small, circumscribed, obscure group, or is it to grow into a thriving, vigorous, militant, Bible-believing denomination that will play a definite part in arousing our nation to its deadly peril as a nation that has departed from God? Are we to become a narrow, peculiar, in-growing sect . . . or are we to become a church that is a rallying point for all believers in the absolute sovereignty of almighty God?[69]

Those who opposed Hamilton's position consistently viewed it as one that was willing to compromise with Arminianism because it advocated cooperation with other American evangelical churches; Hamilton and the others who supported the "program for action" were consistently accused of "doctrinal indifference," of the failure to uphold the Reformed faith. In the case of Clark it was thought that "the doctrine of God as it has been held in the Reformed theology is undermined."[70] The response of Clark's supporters to this charge was that the Westminster group was sectarian and had defined the Reformed faith in a very narrow way.

In another *Guardian* article, published in 1945, Clark himself, in a review of the early history of the OPC, claimed that the "emphasis and direction" of the church had changed. At one time "we were indeed consciously Presbyterians. But our chief emphasis was on the Scriptures, the Atonement, and the Resurrection; and our chief activity was our opposition to soul-destroying Modernism."[71] Even though the OPC disagreed with fundamentalists on points of doctrine "we held them to be brethren . . . and looked on their churches as sister churches."[72] However, the church has now shifted away from its opposition to modernism:

> The emphasis is no longer there. We are no longer fighting shoulder to shoulder with other Bible-believing Christians. . . . We have changed. . . . The customs, procedures, and temperament of American Presbyterianism are in certain quarters matters of disparagement. . . . Instead of leading the Christian forces of our country, we have assumed the position of an isolationist porcupine.[73]

In an editorial response to Clark's article John P. Clelland claims that the emphasis of the OPC has not changed. Clark represents the position of a few. Clelland further states that "The Orthodox Presbyterian Church has not ceased to fight Modernism,"[74] and also argues that

> it would appear that there is a feeling abroad that while in the old days we were primarily evangelicals we are now primarily Calvinists. We hold that we did not just begin to talk about Calvinism sometime after 1936 but have been doing

it from the beginning of the controversy that led to the formation of The Orthodox Presbyterian Church.[75]

The emphasis on a Calvinist witness is not something new. It has been present in the church from the start.

A two-part article which discusses cooperation with other evangelical churches also appeared in the *Guardian* in 1945. In the first part the author, John W. Betzold, asks rhetorically,

> If we in The Orthodox Presbyterian Church believe that her system of doctrine is Scriptural, especially as that system so eminently relates itself to the plan of salvation disclosed in the Scriptures, and if without exception all American evangelical churches which are not Reformed or Calvinistic in their creeds are therefore Arminian, how is cooperation possible between churches holding such divergent principles . . . ?[76]

The Reformed witness of the OPC would be impoverished through co-operation with other evangelical churches; compromise with Arminianism would be the result. Furthermore, in a 1946 editorial the *Guardian* proclaimed that "We stand or fall with that [Reformed] faith. . . . The entire church goes forward, then, only as it is an informed and indoctrinated church, only as it is more and more consciously Reformed."[77]

Although numerous other examples of the differences between the two groups could be cited, the main contours of the controversy are sufficiently clear. On the one side, the supporters of Clark believed that the church should be an evangelical denomination but instead was becoming a sectarian church, defined by the Reformed faith as taught at Westminster. Narrow doctrinal disputes over extra-confessional matters now characterized the OPC instead of a fight against modernism. The opposing group, represented largely by the Westminster faculty, claimed that the OPC had always been Reformed and Calvinistic and that this Reformed emphasis had not changed. They encouraged a closer alignment with other Reformed denominations but held that cooperation with evangelical churches resulted in the endorsement of an Arminian theology. They charged the Clark group with doctrinal indifference, with a lack of commitment to the Reformed faith. The Westminster group believed that if the OPC was to remain genuinely Reformed, careful scrutiny of theological and doctrinal issues was required. Such doctrinal issues, they believed, had arisen in the Clark case.

The differences between these positions did not surface only in the conflict over Clark's ordination. For example, in 1946 Rian, a strong supporter of Clark, failed to win reelection as president of the board of trustees of Westminster Seminary.[78] As might be expected, Rian and the faculty had disagreed for a number of years about the Reformed character of the seminary. Similar differences arose among the leaders of the Christian University movement. Rian, who served as general secretary for the

Christian University Association, believed that the university should be an evangelical one, characterized by a " 'historical, ecumenical' " Calvinism. He claimed that others wanted a university formed on the basis of a " 'personal and narrow' " Calvinism. Division between Rian and the board of the association resulted over this matter, and Rian was dismissed as general secretary in 1946. The following year he left the OPC and returned to the Presbyterian Church in the USA.[79]

The differences within the church were also behind both the debate at the 1947 general assembly over the composition of the committee on foreign missions and the failure of this committee to recommend Floyd E. Hamilton as a missionary for the Korean mission field.[80] Hamilton, as demonstrated, supported Clark and desired a more evangelical direction for the church.

After the 1947 general assembly the evangelical group realized that it could no longer achieve a dominant position in the church. Opposition to Clark's theology and to his ordination was strong, and it was also clear that the OPC was unwilling to cooperate with other evangelical denominations. As a result a number of ministers left. Besides Clark and Rian, Robert Strong, William Young, and Richard Gray also left. With their departure the character of the OPC was essentially decided: it was to be a Reformed — as interpreted by the Westminster faculty — rather than an evangelical denomination.

In the end then much more was at issue in the Clark controversy than certain of Gordon Clark's theological opinions. Writing a few years after the controversy, Arthur Kuschke, the librarian of Westminster Seminary, expresses well the breadth and significance of the Clark case:

> In fact the May, 1944 "program for action" . . . which may be said to have been the instigation of the whole affair, indicates that Dr. Strong and his friends regarded the Clark case as merely a means to an end, viz., the making over of the OPC along what I would call semi-fundamentalist lines. They may not have had any idea that the Clark case would assume the principle role in the struggle. . . . Their actual goal was the control of the OPC in order to direct it along a general evangelical line, rather than a specifically Reformed line. Accordingly, all of this point of view who finally left did so not because of the failure to establish Dr. Clark's views as orthodox but because they could see their attempt to control the OPC had failed.[81]

Kuschke himself opposed Clark's ordination throughout the controversy, and, although perhaps not wholly objective, his account makes it plain that this controversy was one of great importance for the future direction and character of the Orthodox Presbyterian Church.

NOTES

1. *The Presbyterian Conflict* (Grand Rapids: Eerdmans, 1940), 13.
2. Ibid., 234–35.

3. Ibid., 93.

4. The full titles of these two documents are *The Text of a Complaint Against Actions of the Presbytery of Philadelphia in the Matter of the Licensure and Ordination of Dr. Gordon H. Clark* (published in 1944), and *The Answer to a Complaint Against Several Actions and Decisions of the Presbytery of Philadelphia Taken in a Special Meeting Held on July 7, 1944* (published in 1944).

5. *Complaint*, 2.

6. Ibid., 2–3.

7. Ibid., 4.

8. Ibid., 5.

9. Ibid., 15.

10. Ibid., 5.

11. Ibid., 15.

12. Ibid., 7.

13. Ibid., 5.

14. Ibid., 7.

15. Ibid., 10.

16. Ibid.

17. Ibid.

18. Ibid., 6.

19. *Answer*, 9–10.

20. Ibid., 10.

21. Ibid., 11.

22. Ibid., 13.

23. Ibid., 21–22.

24. Ibid., 17.

25. Ibid., 32–33.

26. Ibid., 19.

27. Ibid., 35–36.

28. Sydney E. Ahlstrom, *A Religious History of the American People*, II (Garden City, N.Y.: Image Books, 1975), 285.

29. *Conflict*, 103, 243.

30. Carl F. Henry, "A Wide and Deep Swath," in *The Philosophy of Gordon H. Clark: A Festschrift*, ed. Ronald H. Nash (Philadelphia: Presbyterian and Reformed, 1968), 14–16.

31. Edwin H. Rian, "Wheaton College Today," *Presbyterian Guardian* 12 (April 25, 1943), 115–16.

32. Ibid., 116.

33. Thomas R. Birch, "The Eleventh General Assembly," *Presbyterian Guardian* 13 (June 10, 1944), 171. Taken from the request of the Presbytery of Philadelphia.

34. Ibid. (From the request.)

35. Ibid. (From the request.)

36. Ibid., 173.

37. "Dr. Clark is Licensed by Philadelphia Presbytery," *Presbyterian Guardian* 13 (July 25, 1944), 225.

38. Henry, "A Wide and Deep Swath," 18.

39. "Phila. Presbytery Hears Complaint in Clark Case," *Presbyterian Guardian* 13 (December 10, 1944), 354.

40. Ibid.

41. Thomas R. Birch, "More Deliberations on the Clark Case," *Presbyterian Guardian* 14 (April 25, 1945), 128.

42. *Minutes of the Twelfth General Assembly of the Orthodox Presbyterian Church.* Held at Westminster Theological Seminary, Chestnut Hill, Philadelphia, Pennsylvania, May 17–

23, 1945 (published by the OPC), 5. This committee was composed of Edmund P. Clowney, Lawrence B. Gilmore, Burton L. Goddard, Richard W. Gray, and John Murray.

43. Ibid., 107–108. This protest was submitted by John J. De Waard, R. B. Kuiper, and Cornelius Van Til.

44. Edmund P. Clowney, "The Thirteenth General Assembly," *Presbyterian Guardian* 15 (June 10, 1946), 171.

45. Ibid.

46. Ibid.

47. *Minutes of the Thirteenth General Assembly of the Orthodox Presbyterian Church.* Held at Westminster Theological Seminary, Chestnut Hill, Philadelphia, Pennsylvania, May 21 –28, 1946 (published by the OPC), 88–89. This protest was submitted by 43 commissioners to the general assembly.

48. Ibid., 112. This committee was composed of Edmund P. Clowney, John Murray, Richard Gray, Ned B. Stonehouse, and William Young.

49. *Minutes of the Fourteenth General Assembly of the Orthodox Presbyterian Church.* Held in Cedar Grove, Wisconsin, May 22–28, 1947 (published by the OPC), 9.

50. Ibid., 10–11.

51. Leslie W. Sloat, "General Assembly Report," *Presbyterian Guardian* 16 (June 25, 1947), 181. This committee was composed of Edmund P. Clowney, Floyd E. Hamilton, Arthur W. Kuschke, John Murray, Ned B. Stonehouse, and William Young.

52. *Minutes of the Fifteenth General Assembly of the Orthodox Presbyterian Church.* Held in Wildwood, N.J., May 13–18, 1948 (published by the OPC), 18.

53. "Dr. Clark Dismissed to U.P. Church," *Presbyterian Guardian* 17 (November 1948), 260.

54. Ned B. Stonehouse and Paul Woolley, eds. *The Infallible Word* (Philadelphia: The Presbyterian Guardian, 1946), contents page.

55. *Conflict,* 246.

56. Ibid.

57. *Presbyterian Guardian* 12 (March 10, 1943), 67.

58. *Minutes of the Twelfth General Assembly,* 63. Samuel G. Allen joined Clark in submitting a minority report.

59. "The Orthodox Presbyterian Church," *The Calvin Forum* 12 (August–September 1946), 26.

60. "The Controversy in the OPC," *The Calvin Forum* 12 (April 1947), 196.

61. Ibid., 197. Heerema here is summarizing and quoting from an article written by Richard W. Gray, "Is Arminianism Another Gospel?," *Presbyterian Guardian* 14 (January 25, 1945).

62. "The Controversy in the OPC," 197–98.

63. Ibid.

64. Floyd E. Hamilton, "The Other Side of the OPC Controversy," *The Calvin Forum* 12 (May 1947), 220. I quote here from the "program of action," the text of which is as follows:

Program for Action

1. Preservation of the ideals that characterized our Church when it was formed in 1936, — namely, to be a spiritual succession to the Presbyterian Church in the U.S.A., actively to combat Modernism, and to engage in a program of aggressive evangelism; opposition to efforts working against these ideals, for example, agitation for exclusive use of Psalms, for use of fermented wine in the Communion, for restricted or "closed" Communion, for subscription to the whole Confession of Faith by the laity as a condition of Church membership.

2. Appreciation of other Christian groups which stand for the Word of God, and readiness to cooperate with them in things of coinciding interest and concern.

3. A keeping alive of the Scriptural principles affirmed by the Rochester General Assembly (1942) in its statement on the expedient use of Christian Liberty.

4. Recognition of the principle that the Church is of first consideration, and that organizations and agencies vitally and directly contributing to its life and work should be subordinated to it and supervised by it.

Our Church in instance after instance has been led away from these objectives, and it is high time the Church reset her course.

Specific Objectives (In timely application of the above:)

1. The ordination of Dr. Gordon H. Clark
2. Affiliation with the American Council of Christian Churches
3. An official effort or deliverance against the Liquor Traffic today.
4. Seek for Church supervision over Westminster Seminary and the *Presbyterian Guardian.*

65. Ibid., 221.

66. Ibid.

67. Heerema, "The Controversy in the OPC," 187. Heerema is making reference to certain remarks of Edwin H. Rian.

68. Paul Woolley, "Discontent!," *Presbyterian Guardian* 13 (July 25, 1944), 214.

69. "Whither the Orthodox Presbyterian Church?," *Presbyterian Guardian* 13 (August 15, 1944), 231.

70. "Issues and Convictions," *Presbyterian Guardian* 13 (December 10, 1944), 349.

71. Gordon H. Clark, "Blest River of Salvation" *Presbyterian Guardian* 14 (January 10, 1945), 10.

72. Ibid., 16.

73. Ibid.

74. "Have We Changed?," *Presbyterian Guardian* 14 (January 10, 1945), 8.

75. Ibid.

76. "The Orthodox Presbyterian Church and the Evangelical Churches," *Presbyterian Guardian* 14 (July 25, 1945), 214.

77. "The Future of the OPC," *Presbyterian Guardian* 15 (May 10, 1946), 135.

78. Heerema, "The Orthodox Presbyterian Church," 26–27.

79. See the letter by Ned B. Stonehouse, president, board of trustees of the Christian University Association in "Christian University Board Holds Fall Meeting," *Presbyterian Guardian* 15 (October 10, 1946), 282–83. See also Edward Heerema, "The OPC and the University Project," *The Calvin Forum* 12 (November 1946), 71–72; "Rian Returns to USA Church," *Presbyterian Guardian* 16 (June 25, 1947), 190; and "Grist for the Modernist Mill," *Presbyterian Guardian* 16 (July 25, 1947), 215–16.

80. Leslie W. Sloat, "General Assembly Report," *Presbyterian Guardian* 16 (June 10, 1947), 164–68. See also Sloat, "Fifteenth General Assembly of the Orthodox Presbyterian Church," *Presbyterian Guardian* 17 (June 1948), 160–61.

81. In a letter to Fred H. Klooster. Dated November 16, 1951.

Thomas M. Gregory

20 Apologetics before and after Butler: A Tribute to Van Til

FIFTY YEARS AGO Cornelius Van Til asserted, "Butler has virtually controlled the method of Evidences in orthodox circles for two hundred years."[1] This statement was not intended as a fawning accolade to Bishop Butler, nor as a prefatory expression of Van Til's own purpose as a Christian apologist to emulate others who had simply refined and updated the Bishop's methodology. Neither was it a denial that many sincere Reformed thinkers had used (and continue to use) Butler's type of apologetics in defense of the faith.[2] Dr. Van Til's assertion was an introduction to his conviction that Bishop Butler did not provide the best apologetic for the Reformed community. He felt Butler's work led to "a Christianity neatly trimmed down to the needs of a method that was based upon non-Christian assumptions."[3] Van Til was also voicing his opinion that it would be difficult to displace this "traditional method" as providing the guideline for work in Christian evidences, but that the effort, nevertheless, should be made by anyone interested in Calvinism, for the "Classical Apologetics" of Butler and Paley seemed logically to entail Arminianism.

The basis for Van Til's conclusions are found in the first three chapters of his syllabus *Christian-Theistic Evidences*. The first chapter, entitled "The History of Evidences," is a detailed study of the use of empirical philosophy in framing probability judgments as seen in Butler's *Analogy of the Christian Religion*. There, Van Til found that when "we seek to defend the Christian Religion by an 'appeal to the facts of experience' in accord with the current scientific method we shall have to adulterate Christianity beyond recognition."[4]

In the second chapter Van Til analyzes Butler's *Analogy* from the viewpoint of David Hume. As Van Til shows, Hume the skeptic recognized Butler as the most gifted of those who sought to defend Christianity and gave careful attention to Butler's thought. Hume did this in his *Dialogues On Natural Religion* which he constantly revised and polished until his death. Van Til's assessment of these *Dialogues*, echoing the conclusion of Hume, is that "the upshot of the whole dialogue is, therefore, that the representative of Butler's type of thought virtually admits defeat. He will not give up his mode of appeal to facts. Yet he realizes that with this mode of appeal to facts he cannot prove anything more than a finite god."[5] If it be granted that Hume has provided a complete refutation of Butler, then it would follow that those types of apologetics which use Butler's method are either ignorant of Hume's work or, if not ignorant, are willing to settle for a view of God that is less than that called for in the Bible.

In the third chapter of Van Til's work the arguments for this "weakened" view of God are explored. Tracing these arguments through their various Kantian formulations to their conclusions, Van Til believes that the result in each case is a rehabilitated Christianity that is often adulterated beyond recognition.

If the assessment of Butler by Van Til is essentially correct in its general conclusions, then Butler's work, while remaining an important watershed in apologetics, is of questionable worth for the Reformed apologist. Other thinkers corroborate the views of Van Til. In his *Reason and Nature in 18th Century Thought*, R. W. Harris suggests that the very title of Butler's chief work, *The Analogy of Religion, Natural and Revealed, To the Constitution and Course of Nature*, indicated a profound change which had come over theologians since the seventeenth century. As Harris puts it, "A century before, a theologian would have started on the firm basis of the certainty of the God of the Scriptures and of tradition and would have interpreted nature in the light of that certainty. Now however the order is reversed. Butler accepts as certain and undisputed the laws of nature and the constitution of the universe, and he seeks to show that the fundamentals of Christianity are entirely compatible with them."[6] The profound change that Harris refers to can be seen as being the distinction between a Reformed method of apologetics stressing the primacy of the Scriptures, with reason being an aid to understanding special revelation, and the "traditional method" rooted in the system and achievements of empiricism, with reason regulating and judging all input in religion, whether counted as revelation or not.

This article will examine Butler's work as a watershed in the field of apologetics. It will first seek to provide a somewhat circumscribed survey of the history of apologetics before the time of Butler in order to ascertain the veracity of the claims set forth in the above paragraph. Next, the reasoning of Butler's *Analogy* will be presented, independently of Van Til's analysis, in order to understand how Butler's thought was an innovation in the method of apologetics. Finally, some of the uses that were made of Butler's work will be offered in support of the view that Butler's work was marvelously rich but sufficiently vague to allow a variety of apologetical applications, which have not always been helpful in defending orthodox Christianity.

Christianity has been assailed in every age by what Schleiermacher calls its "cultured despisers." The occasion for much of this opposition is found in the distinctive teaching of Christianity as providing a system of redemption and an authoritative revelation, which form the basis for the right to guide human thought and action. Adam Farrar, in his Bampton Lecture for 1862 at Oxford University,[7] points out that there have been four epochs in history during which the struggle of human reason against the authority of the Christian religion has been especially manifested. Farrar's epochs of course do not include the present age with its own unique criticism of Christianity, and nothing shall be said about this.

In the first epoch, stretching from the second to the fourth century, Christianity is seen contending with various forms of Greek philosophy. The attempt of the Alexandrian school of theology to adjust the mysteries of Christianity to the speculative thought of Plato and Aristotle, by a well-meant but extravagant use of allegorical interpretation, is evidence of the presence and pressure of opposing thought. Similarly, the Gnostics, the rationalists of the early church, summoned Christianity to the bar of philosophy and forced the church to give explicit expression to its belief. To our benefit, the conflict resulted in the careful balance and precise statement of the classical creeds, and the formulation of an authoritative canon of Christian writings from which these creeds were derived.

The revived study of Greek philosophers, particularly Aristotle, with the consequent rise of the scholastic philosophy of the twelfth and thirteenth centuries, furnished the materials for a renewal of the struggle of reason against authority, a second crisis period in the history of the church. The challenge to faith by a man like Abelard, for example, represented the critical action of free thought. Apologetical reaction to the intellectual ferment caused by the Abelards of that time can be seen in the work of someone like Aquinas. Using Scripture, though in an Aristotelian mode, he developed "scientific" definitions of the immemorial doctrines of the church that satisfied the intellectual need of that time for new formulations.

In both of these periods the philosophy of the opposition was used in the defense of the faith and in the production of a restatement of the faith that satisfied believers, without being a diminution of the faith or a capitulation to unbelievers. Augustine, followed by Anselm, had assuaged the Greek-thinking people who assumed the truth of Platonic doctrines with the argument that God existed since he was the most universal of all things and encompassed all being. Aquinas, in an age which accepted different assumptions about the nature of reality, satisfied the Aristotelianism of his time by showing that God was the prime particular of all the particulars of experience. While successful in a practical sense, these abstract formulations used in defining God did not do justice to the full personality of God, but at least did not directly subordinate special revelation to reason and allowed for the continuance of the authority of Scripture.

In the fifteenth and sixteenth centuries, the crisis confronting faith was different from the earlier threats, since philosophy had gradually succeeded in emancipating itself from theology, refusing to act anymore as a handmaiden to it. Furthermore, during the Renaissance a large body of heathen thought was introduced into the current of European life. Thus philosophy could not be used, without excessive qualification, to reconstruct a new, acceptable version of Christian doctrine; the Bible itself had to be set over against the body of non-Christian literature and culture.

Two solutions were offered to the perceived conflict between the new, secular knowledge and traditional faith.[8] One solution was to accept the new discoveries and relate them to ancient wisdom which could then be used as justification for adherence to past tradition. The second expressed a similar admiration for the new science and the ancient thought but strove not merely to comprehend the new results but also to emulate the new methods used to obtain these conclusions. The first, containing the germ of a fruitful approach to Christian tradition, was used by Calvin and the Christian humanists, while the second, with its seed of a radical reconstruction of Christian methodology, was followed by Arminians and Socinians. The second attitude became standard procedure for the evidentialists of the eighteenth century in Bishop Butler's time. The Reformation apologetic on the other hand stressed the necessity, the authority, the clarity, and the sufficiency of the Scriptures as the purveyor of a comprehensive life and world view that was able to nurture and accommodate scientific investigation without being shaped by it.

The seventeenth and the eighteenth centuries were the fourth of the epochs in which a crisis developed in the history of human thought. Farrar saw that changes in the methods used to formulate scientific law created as great a revolution in knowledge as the Renaissance had produced in literature, or the Reformation in religion. New opinions were presented on the basis of which philosophers ventured to criticize the Bible and the traditional teachings of theology. In this age Bacon and Descartes were leaders in constructing new methods for obtaining knowledge. Each man found in human consciousness the origins of knowledge. For Bacon, and later for Locke, the contents which we reflect upon in our consciousness in order to produce true propositions arise out of sense perceptions, while for Descartes they were believed to originate in the intellectual activity of thought itself. Each philosopher stressed a different strand of consciousness in the mind. What they reflected upon brought into prominence their distinctive methods for obtaining knowledge. Yet they had much in common: an analytical investigation of consciousness, a general method for investigating given spheres of inquiry, an opposition to dogmatic assumptions of former systems, a rigorous attempt to reduce a subject to its parts, and a careful assessment of how these elements are related to the whole. Such an outlook was denominated as rationalism,

This new perspective which stressed the primacy of thinking as a form of conscious activity, most commonly expressed by Descartes as "I think therefore I am," was not new in the history of thought. Augustine had used it, but with a radically different intent. He used it for deeply religious purposes. It was a way of exploring the spiritual depths of the self. Such an approach had resulted in two startling discoveries: the mind, which could have come only from God, and secondly, the ability of the mind to intuitively grasp God. Descartes, like others of the seventeenth and eighteenth centuries, contrariwise, was more of a surface psychologist. A modern commentator suggests, "The agonizing introspectiveness of St. Augustine was now lost in the analytic cataloguing of the functions of the mind."[9] When the religious contents of the mind were dissected and classified in accordance with the methods of rationalism, there resulted a consolidation of Christian principles into just a few statements that could pass muster at the bar of reason. Much of the older theological opinion was eliminated as speculative and as lacking in the universality that reason demanded. In the new theology, greater emphasis was placed upon moral activity with predictable consequences than upon abstract theological doctrine. Known as deism, this new method of doing theology was seen by many to pose a serious threat to the accustomed way of thinking about Christianity, though many were probably more disturbed by its critique of the church as an organized power structure in the society of that day.

Lord Herbert (1583–1648) of Cherbury, the elder brother of the saintly poet, is looked upon as the father of deism. For his service as a diplomat representing England at the French court he was knighted. Probably during this period of his life he came under the same intellectual influences which had shaped the thought of Descartes. Like Descartes, Herbert surveys the power of the human mind to produce truth. Universal natural instincts function as axiomatic beliefs and become the source of truth. The true religion must therefore be universal; its evidence, common consent. Herbert finds five such universal, innate principles: (1) The existence of one supreme God; (2) The duty of worship; (3) piety and virtue as the chief means of worship; (4) The efficacy of repentance for the removal of sin; (5) The existence of rewards and punishments both here and hereafter.

The writings of Lord Herbert were received with various degrees of acclaim. Some felt that his work was a helpful way of eliminating "heathen" practices and "superstitious" doctrines that had crept into the Christian church. Deists who felt this way, for the most part, worked within the church and insisted that they had the best interests of the church at heart in simplifying and liberalizing its theological beliefs. Others were attracted by the hope of universal consent that this pruning use of reason in religion promised. Here was a work that was in tune with the growing rationalism of the age. A third group of thinkers felt uneasy with Herbert's work. According to them, it implied a deep-seated dissatisfaction with the supernatural claims of the Christian religion and, moreover, was a veiled threat to the authority of the church.

Butler was in some degree sympathetic with all of these attitudes. As the son of a Presbyterian elder and a graduate of the dissenter academy at Tewkesbury, Butler would have had no difficulty in understanding the criticism of Herbert advanced by two Reformed thinkers. The second-generation Puritan thinker, Richard Baxter (1615–1691), perceived that Herbert's position would undermine the need of special revelation. Inconsistently, however, Baxter's use of reason, to show the *necessity* of special revelation, made it a form of the same logical elevation of reason above revelation that characterized Butler's approach to deism. Thomas Halyburton (1674–1712), Scottish Presbyterian professor at Aberdeen University, also recognized that the whole tenor of Herbert's writings was that the innate principles of natural religion made special revelation unnecessary. His work, *Natural Religion Insufficient*, appearing in 1712, addressed this issue. Halyburton saw that the main point at issue was one of the proper methodology to be used when speaking about the knowledge of God. He proposed a method which avoided subordinating Christian expression to reason or to natural revelation. Instead, the Christian revelation itself, as contained in the Bible, was seen as an axiomatic or self-authenticating set of principles.[10] Thus it was recognized that reason was not a method or power for producing truth but was a grammar useful in communicating information. This Reformed apologetic is in sharp contrast to what Butler proposed later in the eighteenth century. The model that Butler eventually followed was set forth in a more famous reply to deism by John Locke.

In his work, *The Reasonableness of Christianity*, Locke seemingly argued vigorously for special revelation but really was more concerned to attack Herbert's use of the innateness principle as the main tenet of reason. In its place he put empiricism's stress on the senses as the rational source of the components in our intellectual activity. Locke's work was not intended to provide succor to the deists, but merely to persuade them that there was a case for the rationality of a revealed religion. Locke did not convince the deists of the value of revealed religion, but he was more than successful in persuading all disputants of the superiority of empirical epistemology. The conclusion that the average reader drew from Locke's philosophy was that revelation must be sharply trimmed back to satisfy the condition imposed by empirical philosophy, now the dominating view in Britain; more astute readers saw that without Halyburton's more circumspect view of the function of reason, deism's claim remained unrefuted.

Locke held that God's existence could be proved by reason. From the existence of God, revelation can indeed be seen as rationally plausible, given the proper view of God. Yet if revelation is always rational, there are strong grounds for claiming as the deists did that reason itself could have given the same information. With these developments it was inevitable, as G. R. Craig points out, ". . . that the part played by reason should gradually eclipse the place given to revelation."[11] For the deists this process was already at work, and Locke himself inadvertently was partially responsible for obscuring the role he had assigned to revelation. For his own faith he saw little need for Christian belief to include anything more than a simple faith in Jesus as the Messiah. Such a belief was best inculcated by the Gospels. This meant they possessed more authority than Paul or other parts of the Bible. To give substance to this watered-down version of Christianity, Locke stressed the necessity of right conduct, and sought to develop persuasive reasons for believing that rewards for such would be forthcoming in this world from the authorities in power, and in the next from God.[12]

Baxter and Halyburton had stressed the primacy of special revelation. For them, natural revelation added little to special revelation that was of any significance for knowing God. A much larger group of thinkers was more impressed by what reason could supply for religion and sought a mediating position that attempted to do justice to both faith as traditionally conceived and the value of reason as it had been expounded by Locke. People like Sir Thomas Browne (1605–1682) and Archbishop Tillotson (1630–1694) were prominent expositors of this way of thinking. Browne had much in common with the deists but differed from them in that he did not discard faith for reason, but sought in a mystical fashion to retain both by keeping them in separate compartments. Tillotson was more in harmony with the spirit of the age in his popular sermons which are said to have favored a type of faith which "stressed practice, minimized theology, and leaned heavily on reason."[13] Tillotson was not a deist, though deists looked upon him as somewhat of a kindred spirit. Anthony Collins (1676–1729), one of the leading deists, spoke of him as "that religious and free-thinking prelate" and "the most pious and rational of all priests."[14] It became common for churchmen of the age who were deist in everything but name, to write their books developing a truncated version of Christianity from the rationalistic consideration of nature and then to add an appendix to the book setting forth a statement of faith derived from the Bible.[15] It began to appear that the prevailing sentiment in the Church of England as the eighteenth century unfolded, was a cold, rationalistic deism which was concerned only with prosperous living and a preaching of morals in order to keep order in the nation. In many ways, Butler represented this group when he wrote his *Analogy* more than those few in the Anglican communion of the eighteenth century who would have stressed the superiority of special revelation over natural revelation.[16]

Those who were most impressed by Herbert of Cherbury's works were, of course, the avowed deists like Toland (1670–1722), Shaftesbury (1671–1713), Collins, Woolston (1669–1731), and finally Tindal. Toland carried Herbert's principles to their logical conclusion and asserted the supremacy of reason to interpret all mysteries. Shaftesbury advocated a natural ethics that did not require any religious input. Collins critiqued the prophecies of the Old Testament and Woolston the miracles of the New.

Of all the deists of England, Matthew Tindal (1657–1733) probably best represented the movement. In his old age, after a lifetime of needling the church with various anti-clerical writings, he published the one book on which rests his claim to fame. It carried the title: *Christianity as Old as Creation; Or the Gospel a Republication of the Religion of Nature* (1730). This was the most important work that deism produced and bore the marks of a careful study of the chief contemporary arguments, Christian as well as deist. It called forth one hundred fifty replies and became the high-water mark of excitement in England over deism. More than any other book, it stimulated Joseph Butler, now an Anglican priest, to write *The Analogy of the Christian Religion* which, in turn, became the most enduring apologetic work produced against deism.

Tindal's main line of argument is developed from his conception of God. God is perfect, therefore any religion he gives to man must be perfect and incapable of improvement. From this he concluded that no later revelation such as the Bible could improve upon the religion given man at creation. God is immutable, thus he cannot be conceived as changing or as adding to the religion first given, and since he is also impartial he would not have given any special information to the Jews, nor even have a chosen people. At best, then, any religion claiming to have special revelation from God can only really have a "republication" of the original natural revelation; anything beyond natural revelation is therefore really superfluous.

With Tindal's work, the logic of the conflict which had been bothering the church for nearly a century was now exposed. The deist's position called for the sufficiency of natural revelation and the denial of any need for special revelation even as a supplement to natural revelation. There was no value in the Scriptures since they are, to use Mossner's phrase, an "inglorious facsimile" of natural religion, and present a petty and arbitrary God who cannot be reconciled with the impartial and magnanimous God of Natural Religion. If one was to be a Christian at all, he must be a deist.

This was a serious challenge. The "orthodox" dared not let Tindal's claims pass without an answer. For them the Bible was both necessary and sufficient as a revelation from God. Its revelation of religious principles did not require augmentation by principles derived from natural revelation, and the moral prescriptions it enjoined produced results of greater value than the "objective" moral code of deism. The entire nature of Christianity would be radically altered if Tindal's claim stood. Butler took up the challenge.

Butler saw that representatives of each side in this long-ranging conflict had said all that could rationally be said in defense of their position and likewise all that could be argued as a refutation of the other side. In spite of all this no universality of conviction appeared. The copious appeals to reason did not lead rational men to agreement. In a rationalistic age the first suspicion that crosses the mind in such a situation is that the arguments are logically defective. As a remedy, more argumentation is spawned, which then only increases the confusion. The second suspicion, a much more brilliant insight, is that reason is defective as an input for contents. As a Presbyterian student at the dissenter Academy at Tewkesbury, Butler had studied Samuel Clarke's celebrated argument for God's existence. He had discovered defects in the argument and found that neither he nor Clarke could remedy these defects. Yet he continued to believe in the existence of God. This was the dawning of a conviction that reason did not have to produce airtight demonstrations in order for one to believe in God and to act accordingly. Perhaps each side had over-stated its claim and there was really only some truth as well as much uncertainty in both sets of arguments. It followed then, that belief and a given course of activity could be rationally justified with even only a presumption of truth.

Throughout his entire life Butler was concerned with the pursuit of truth. To his famous correspondent Samuel Clarke, the leading Cartesian philosopher in England, he confided "As I design the search after truth as the business of my life, I shall not be ashamed to learn from any person."[17] Butler's Presbyterian mentors at Tewkesbury Academy were immersed as much in the rationalism of the age as anyone and like others thought of truth as the search for the proper method of obtaining certainty. Once that method was ascertained it would be applied indiscriminately to biblical content, theology, or science. Butler did not find much to encourage him in the a priori method of the Presbyterian leaders or even in the expert use of that method by Samuel Clarke. He turned instead to an empirical methodology and learned from the celebrated John Locke.

Instead of complete refutation and airtight demonstrations, Butler's empirical reasoning was used to obviate objection and to discover probabilities, or hypotheses which are sufficiently persuasive for a reasonable man to decide that he should act as if Christianity were true. The *Analogy* is designed, as Butler says, to lead the reader to "the practice of Christianity." Butler's method for achieving his objective is set forth in the preface of his work. An experimental method similar to that used by Newton in science can be applied to the facts of human life and of nature as they really are, and give rise to confident expression of order. As Hume expresses it in a similar investigative situation, "none but a fool or madman will ever pretend to dispute the authority of experience, or to reject that great guide of human life."[18] Butler observed that deists and Christians alike confirmed their religious convictions by the observed results of human moral behavior. He reasoned that the use of analogous methods in the confirmation of religious beliefs is an indicator that the disputed religious beliefs in question are probably in harmony with each other, and are not contradictories as both Christians and deists often seemed to indicate in their debate. His apologetic for Christianity is really to argue that deism and Christianity are alike since they are only at different places on a continuum of probabilities. Hence a deist ought to be willing to embrace Christianity.

The beliefs of Christians and deists, regardless of how they are originally obtained, were conceived of by Butler as probabilities which can be confirmed in the investigation of human experience, and in the observation of nature, in a manner analogous to the way in which Newton, Boyle, or other scientists confirmed scientific hypotheses. These probabilities of belief were law-like in character without being firm deductions. They could be seen as functional guides of human behavior and aspiration. That which was new and different in Butler's work was his careful, imaginative endeavor to draw analogies between the confessed convictions of people, Christian or deist, and the actual behavior of man in society or the observed operation of nature. No longer concerned to prove the truth of Christian claims, this new perspective in Christian evidences provided instead a prudential reason for belief. It was the concern to discover practical reasons for believing Christianity, Van Til claims, that led Butler to seek a common method and a common meeting ground with his opponents. Such a course of thought could lead to more of an erosion of Christian principles than a defense of them.

Butler held the view that natural religion consists of such religious theories as we can accept in principle without the aid of revelation, but that these beliefs are also to be found within the Christian revelation. Most Christians and deists of that time had no problem in accepting natural religion. Deists, however, rejected a revealed religion, since it was a useless excrescence. Butler's aim was to convince the deists that natural religion, properly understood, was the same in character as revealed religion, and that both were developed in a manner analogous to the way in which scientific ideas are established. Beginning with a careful study of natural religion, since this was what deism accepted, Butler sought to show that it was never fully perfected in character and, therefore, it was rational to think that it could be improved. This is where revelation might be helpful. Thus religious ideas, natural or revealed, are characterized by a development that is analogous to the way in which scientific views of human life and society have evolved. Once a deist accepted such an explanation, even as a possibility with limited probability, he should as a reasonable person be willing to look into the claims of special revelation since it, too, was a matter of development in the overall economy of God. Indifference where there was a probability, however small, was unworthy of a reasonable man.

When a reasonable man looked into the teachings of revealed religion he would discover here, just as in natural religion, that the doctrines of revelation, of God working through a mediator, of the atonement, of the vicarious suffering of Christ, of the revelation coming through a chosen people, the Christian doctrines most doubted by the deists, are best under-stood by various analogies that could be drawn from nature or society. If the teaching of both revealed revelation and natural revelation are found to be grasped equally well by references to analogical empirical phenom-ena, no one could deny that they must be intrinsically related. Similarly, where there are difficulties in understanding either the principle of re-vealed religion or of natural religion through the media of empirical experience there is no need to jettison either approach. In both instances the problem is the same; the degree of certitude in determining duty or belief. Thus revelation and natural theology are best seen to be in tandem to each other, each supplementing the other but neither in control; reason rather than truth provides the motivational spark through probabilities resulting from creative analogies.

Once the arguments from analogies are recognized as viable, the view Butler wanted the deists to accept becomes highly probable; namely, that special revelation is rationally acceptable. If deists still objected, as good rationalists, against special revelation coming from God, Butler's reply might be, "Every objection against revelation, on account of things dark and inexplicable, is equally valid against nature," for, as Origen says, "he who believes the Scriptures to have proceeded from Him who is the Author of Nature may well expect to find the same sort of difficulties in it as are found in the constitution of nature."[19]

The point that Butler wanted to make is more subtle and more basic than our analysis of the general analogy argument indicates, for in all his argumentation there is an assumed premise which he does not seek to establish since he believes that all thinkers in his time would readily accept it. Every system has its own presuppositions. The premise is, simply, "The course of nature originates in God,"[20] which provided the univocal point so necessary in any use of analogy. It is clear that he presupposed the existence of God, but more important that he had a certain view of God.

Hence all the details of argument are not simply to prove that there is a future life, that God rewards and punishes after death, and that Christianity in general is true. The scope of the work is more sharply focused. Butler is trying to get deists to understand that the acceptance of Christian truths is not at all unreasonable unless the deists were prepared to say "that their own beliefs about the system and course of nature are unreasonable." Butler and the deists both have a similar presupposition which functions as a mediating point of contact. We cannot demand that all difficulties and obscurities should first be cleared up before believing, for the very complexity and opaqueness of both special revelation and natural revelation, which reflect the universe created in accordance with God's intention, make it impossible to believe that either can ever comprehend all of his purposes.

Butler has a special view of nature that is sometimes called teleological. Such a view implies that there is intention behind the regularities of nature and that its laws are in some way prescriptive, like the laws made by men. The universe is a vast teleological system set up by God. This belief clearly remained from Butler's Calvinistic background. It provided a basis for optimism in a secular age ruled by the goddess of reason that was beginning to show rips in its fabric. Butler felt that a loss of vision here was the cause of the weakness and indifference in the church and was destructive of morality. He appealed to the deists to help overcome these tendencies, for, "from our original constitution and that of the world which we inhabit, we are naturally trusted with ourselves; with our own conduct and our own interest."[21] More significant than clearing up all difficulties and justifying divine providence, is the moral sense of direction, that which we ought to do. The temptation is to join in with the normal course of things which obscures our vision and forfeits interest in the moral to such an extent that we run ourselves into misery and ruin. As Butler summarizes these thoughts, "The proper *motives* to religion are the proper *proofs* of it, from our moral nature, from the presages of conscience, and our natural apprehension of God under the character of a righteous Governor and Judge: a nature, and conscience, and apprehension, given us by him."[22] All this, we can be assured, is of sufficiently high probability to accept.

Butler undoubtedly believed that his *Analogy* provided a workable set of rational reasons for embracing revealed Christianity. When the Scriptures alluded to principles that seemed to transcend understanding, he could argue that it is not against reason to accept that of which we are ignorant so long as it was not contradictory to the general order of reality. Furthermore, analogies between the natural and the spiritual could be constructed in justification of belief. However, not all were convinced. The force of the analogies depended upon accepting a natural order flowing from God, which, to the rationally minded suggested either circularity or special pleading. Thus the future course of evidentialism was set: when we act as if something is true, then it will follow that it is true. Some of this logical ambiguity in Butler's thought is reflected in the diversity of opinion about his method in the next century.

In 1833, nearly a hundred years after it was written, Butler's *Analogy* became a classic; it was made a required text at Oxford University. For the next thirty-three years it was a part of the standard degree examination for all undergraduates. The acceptance of Butler's book in the major British universities testifies to its significance as a philosophical and a theological text. The mark of a great work is the richness and ambiguity of the suggestions it provides for new directions in thought when a prevailing trend is wearing out. Butler's century, and the following one, exhibited an increasing uneasiness with rationalism, the need of refinement in the methods of empiricism and science, and the decline of biblical and religious authority coupled with a rise in moral sensitivity. Butler's work had the merit of providing a judiciously formulated store of prudential arguments from which competing interests could draw without wrestling with the knotty problems of the philosophy of fact or of law. It provided optimism where there was no certainty.

One group at Oxford thought of Butler as a way of retaining the vested interests of the school in the classics. A tutor is reported to have said that Butler was a painless way of conveying Aristotle to Greekless undergraduates, and an interesting assessment of Butler was that he is "Aristotle clad in a diaphanous mantle of Christianity."[23] Butler would have hoped that Christianity had more substance than that, but in his general use of analogy as an argument for the faith, he displayed what seemed to some, a good degree of mitigated skepticism about Christianity that had a family resemblance to the dogmatic skepticism of Hume. Logically, using the method of empiricism, the outcome of Butler's thought should have been similar to that of Hume's, as Van Til has clearly shown. However, as we indicated, a presupposition of a created order in nature and an analogous order in human faculties preserved Butler's system from Hume's negative conclusions and provided a source of optimism for nineteenth-century religious thinkers. A recent doctoral dissertation has shown some of this bifurcation in Butler's thought by examining the places where Hume gave respectful consideration to Butler's structures.[24] In its conclusions, however, that dissertation felt that Butler's fideistic appeal to brute facts, as Van Til puts it, would not support the optimism that Butler seemed to generate in nineteenth-century thinkers.

The Scottish realists considered Butler an ally and thought his method of analogous reasoning provided support for their development of induction as a logical structure for scientific investigation. They had a considerable following at Oxford. In 1827 Renn Hampden gave the Bampton

Lecture entitled *Essay on the Philosophical Evidence of Christianity*. It was avowedly based on Butler and examined theological thought in the light of the inductive method developed by Scottish realism. Hampden had much to do with the official adoption of the *Analogy* at Oxford.

A further reason for Butler's popularity at Oxford, a hundred years after his death, is that it was thought his writing would be an effective counter to the spread of secular utilitarianism. The situation is ironical. It was Butler's stress on nature as exhibiting God's purposes which had stimulated the most popular religious book of the day, namely William Paley's *View of the Evidences of Christianity*. Paley sought to broaden the basis of Christian ethics by introducing a cautious theological utilitarianism whereby an action, whether called for in the Scriptures or not, was judged to be good and acceptable to God if it brought the greatest amount of happiness to the greatest number of people. This view was taken by Bentham and developed into an ethical system that did not require reference to God. The Victorians resurrected Butler's ethics with its stress upon a God-given conscience as the antidote to the secular theories of consequence ethics. Butler's view, coupled with the whispers of a rational defense of moral imperativity found in the writings of Kant, combined to justify the stress on duty, in a society where religious foundations were shaking. It was not recognized that behind Butler's ethics was a view of the universe based upon probabilities which used practical consequences as one of its criteria for truth. Butler's philosophy provided aid against secularization, but not without some accommodation to it.

A strategy Butler frequently used against the deists in his *Analogy* was an appeal to ignorance. If one, for example, is ignorant of how or why God is motivated to judge mankind, it cannot be argued that he does not judge mankind. This was an honest recognition of the limits of rational understanding in an age which had recklessly made reason capable of comprehending everything in heaven and earth. But the appeal to ignorance was a double-edged sword. The Tractarians at Oxford made use of this argument to justify their position, much of which Butler would have rejected. For them, the failure of reason to justify completely a belief or action did not imply that we should be content with analogies from nature or society that would warrant the acceptance of a probability as a provisional hypothesis. Instead, it was thought by Newman and others in the Oxford movement, that Butler's argument implied the "necessity of some foothold of faith other than an inconsequential rest in tradition" — it demanded a positive faith sustained by the authority of the Catholic church.[25] Similarly, using a highly refined version of Butler's argument from ignorance, Henry Mansel argued a decade later that Scripture should be that authority since reason produces antinomies when it attempts to justify the conclusions of speculative theology. As a child of the age of reason, Butler could not have accepted either of these applications of his thought, though they seem amply justified as proper implications of his method and illustrate further the essential ambiguity built into his system.

When the popularity of the church began to wane in the 1870s under the increasing power of naturalism, new insights, often contradictory, were dredged from Butler's *Analogy* to meet the challenge of unbelief. One such discovery was that Butler had supposedly used the strategy of threatening prospective deists with social and religious ostracism if they did not conform to the teachings of Christianity. A late nineteenth-century churchman who perhaps wanted to use Butler this way in his own age said that the Bishop's main effort was to make "the old and fashionable half-way house of Deism untenable, consistent with its own assumptions; and so he drove it out of fashion and out of countenance by compelling the rejecters of Christianity to move forward logically and irresistibly to sheer Atheism or universal skepticism, with no intermediate halting place."[26] In contrast to this alleged purpose of purging the church of free thinkers, an American commentator suggests that *The Analogy* furthered the strategy of inclusivism. Thus *The Analogy* is not an attack upon deism from outside but an effective and subversive reorientation of it from within. Butler was himself fundamentally a deist, it is suggested, and was "engaged in winning, to a form of Deism acceptable to the Anglican community, men who would otherwise have been orthodox deists."[27]

These two evaluations are not only contrary to each other but also to the tone of Butler's carefully wrought apologetic and do not adequately reflect his sincerity of character and genuine concern for the deists as persons. His work was a rational, an intellectual, an empirical offering of the only kind of religious truth left for an inquiring mind short of acknowledging and being informed by a written revelation from God. Hoping to illumine Christian truths, the effect of Butler's work was often to obscure.

Butler told his contemporaries that his calling was to search after truth. The meaning of Butler's statement is open to several interpretations. Is he stressing the possession of truth as the highest blessing of man, the quest for truth as the most rewarding objective for man, or is being possessed by truth the highest felicity for man? For the pious rationalists and deists of Butler's day, Butler's contention seemed to be that truth can be attained by the superior methods of reason and its possession would bring blessedness. Thus natural revelation is sufficient in itself and did not require any supplementation by special revelation. This interpretation would not have satisfied Butler. He argued that truth was not fully attained either by the a priori or the empirical methods and therefore felt that the deists had a false felicity. On the other hand, Butler did not side with orthodox Christians who maintained the sufficiency of special revelation. They were also deceived. Their grounds for accepting the truth of Scripture were subject to the same tests to which natural revelation submitted. In either case no final versions of truth can result. Natural revelation and special revelation thus can best be seen as supplemental to each other but never as the validation of each other. Butler's felicitation of truth must therefore be seen as a directive to engage in the unending quest for truth. Could such a search ever eventuate in comprehending any truth, or must the effort go on indefinitely?

If Butler had allowed his hidden presupposition of a God-created purpose in nature to function clearly in his analysis, leading him to accept the primacy of special revelation, he could have given an optimistic response to this question. But then it would have been the younger Presbyterian student speaking and not the Bishop. An important contribution that Van Til has made to apologetics in the last fifty years is to make it clear that the "classical apologetics" emanating from Butler, which has controlled the methods of evidences in orthodox circles for over two hundred years, can only give as an answer to the above questions the vague pious advice: "keep on striving for truth — this is what it means to be possessed by truth."

NOTES

1. Cornelius Van Til, *Christian-Theistic Evidences* (Philadelphia: Westminster Theological Seminary, 1944), 1.

2. See R. C. Sproul, John Gerstner, Arthur Lindsley, *Classical Apologetics* (Grand Rapids: Zondervan, 1984). For a critical assessment of this modern form of Butler's apologetics see reviews by Gordon H. Clark and John W. Robbins in *The Trinity Review* 45 (September/October 1985), and John M. Frame in *The Westminster Theological Journal* 48 (1985) 2:279 –99.

3. Van Til, 48.

4. Ibid.

5. Ibid., 31.

6. R. W. Harris, *Reason and Nature in 18th Century Thought* (London: Blandford Press, 1968), 184.

7. Adam Farrar, *History of Free Thought* (New York: Appleton and Co., 1879).

8. Olive M. Griffith, *Religion and Learning: A Study in Early Presbyterian Thought from the Bartholomew Ejection (1662) to the Foundation of the Unitarian Movement* (Cambridge: University Press, 1935), 164ff.

9. H. Girvetz, G. Geiger, H. Hantz and B. Morris, *Science, Folklore and Philosophy* (New York: Harper and Row, 1966), 191.

10. See Halyburton's "An Essay Concerning the Nature of Faith" which is contained in his *Natural Religion Insufficient* (Philadelphia: Hogan and M'Elroy, 1798). Propositions 1–12 (pp. 325–50) set forth the classical Calvinistic understanding of the grounds upon which faith assents to Scripture in contrast to rationalistic methods proposed by Halyburton's contemporaries.

11. G. R. Cragg, *From Puritans to the Age of Reason* (Cambridge: University Press, 1950), 124.

12. Ibid., 124ff.

13. G. R. Cragg, *The Church and the Age of Reason, 1648–1789* (Grand Rapids: Eerdmans, 1964), 77.

14. Anthony Collins, *A Discourse of Free Thinking*, (1713), 53, 69.

15. G. R. Cragg, *Reason and Authority in the 18th Century* (Cambridge: University Press, 1964), passim.

16. See Stuart M. Brown, ed., *Five Sermons Preached at Rolls Chapel by Bishop Butler* (New York: Liberal Arts, 1950), Preface viii.

17. Quoted from the "Butler-Clarke correspondence" in Ernest C. Mossner, *Bishop Butler and the Age of Reason* (New York: Macmillan, 1936), 1.

18. David Hume, *Inquiry Concerning Human Understanding,* IV, 36.

19. Cited by F. Copleston, *History of Philosophy,* Vol. 5, Pt. 1 (Garden City, NY: Doubleday and Co., 1964), 177.

20. The proposition is a summary of Part I, ch. VIII of *The Analogy* by Joseph Butler.

21. Joseph Butler, *The Analogy of the Christian Religion,* ed. Howard Malcom (Philadelphia: J. B. Lippincott and Co., 1871), 183.

22. Ibid., 185.

23. Elmer Sprague, "Joseph Butler," *The Encyclopedia of Philosophy,* Vol. 1 (New York: Macmillan, 1967), 433.

24. See Anders Jeffner, *Butler and Hume on Religion: A Comparative Study* (Stockholm: Tryckmans, 1966).

25. Ernest C. Mossner, *Bishop Butler,* 211.

26. A. H. Drysdale, *History of Presbyterianism in England* (London: Presbyterian Publication Society, 1889), 534.

27. Stuart M. Brown, Preface ix.

David W. Kiester

21 The Life and Death
of a Dakota Church

THE UNSEASONABLY WARM Dakota winter air made visible the breath of the mourners as the distinct cadence of the preacher's monotone recited the familiar funeral liturgy. The not particularly uncomfortable crowd had come to pay final respects to "Aunt Jean" Emch, who had lived into her nineties and had fought off death for almost exactly a year. A few yards away, two young women, granddaughters to Aunt Jean, wandered off to view again the graves of their father, mother, and sister, all killed in the tragic accident they themselves had survived some fifteen years previously. The sight brought them a grief more than that felt by those assembled for the funeral. It exceeded mere relief that Aunt Jean's battle against infirmity and senility was over. On the eastern horizon stood the pale yellow shell of the building that had been church to Jean Emch. It had been closed almost ten years earlier, yet it seemed that the service on this fifth day of January 1983 was really its funeral.

The dreary, desolate day provided an appropriate and fitting conclusion to the story of her church. The matriarch was being laid to rest. A remarried widow who had raised her children, his children, and their children, she had made the names of Emch and First Orthodox Presbyterian Church of Leith, North Dakota, almost synonymous. Her church had struggled for existence through pioneer homesteading days and the great depression, had flourished for a time, and then declined when the community declined.

Other symbols of the church's decline were visible. The preacher that winter's day was the Rev. Roswell Kamrath. He had farmed west of town until his children were raised and had been an ordained elder in the church.

When he left the farm to enter the ministry, he proved irreplaceable. Also, earlier in the day the actual service for Aunt Jean had been conducted seven miles away, in the Bethel Orthodox Presbyterian Church of Carson, of which she was technically a member at the time of her death.

Homesteading and the Birth of a Church

The community of Leith, North Dakota, is located in the central portion of present-day Grant County, about sixty-five miles southwest of Bismarck, three miles south of state highway 21, and on the north side of the old Chicago, Milwaukee, St. Paul, and Pacific Railroad tracks. When Leith and the surrounding area were opened for homesteading in about 1905, it was the southern part of Morton County, whose present county seat is Mandan, and whose earlier population was concentrated along the Northern Pacific's main line. The population and development of the previously unsettled southern portion of Morton County led to the organization of Grant County in 1917.[1]

The churches in present-day Grant County predate the establishment of towns. The Presbytery of Bismarck of the Presbyterian Church in the United States of America (PCUSA) determined to conduct mission work in the newly-opened area. Two individuals stand out in the establishment of Presbyterian churches in Grant County, the Rev. Robert H. Meyers and the Rev. John R. Hughes, although only Mr. Meyers played a role in the establishment of the church at Leith.[2] Meyers served the presbytery as a pastor-evangelist, whose work consisted of visiting homesteaders, and encouraging the initiation of church services and the formal organization of churches. Hughes was a Sunday school missionary. He organized Sunday schools apparently without regard for whether establishment of a church would follow at any particular location. Both he and Meyers were present in the newly-opened territory almost from the time the first homesteaders arrived.

In 1906 several families from the area around Carroll, Nebraska, decided to establish homesteads in a newly-opened area of North Dakota. The natural leader among them was Nicholas C. Emch. As the families prepared to depart, their Christian friends made a farewell promise to them. Should they succeed in establishing a church when they reached their new home, they would be given a bell for it, the bell which had been brought to Carroll by pioneers from Ohio many years before. That promise coincided with the Carroll Methodist Church building itself a new building. Upon their arrival in North Dakota, the homesteaders learned of the plans of Presbyterians to organize churches there and applied to Robert Meyers for help. A Sunday school was organized in the Carter store in Old Carson in April 1906.[3] This Sunday school serves as the roots of both the Leith and Carson churches.

The church in Leith resulted from a community effort nearer the town. Church services began in the barn of J. W. Evans, with Evans and N. C. Emch serving as elders. Those were tentative days. The railroads, essential to the survival of townsites, had not yet been built. The population had not oriented itself yet, and the churches were strictly neighborhood projects served erratically by missionaries and Sunday school organizers.

The railroads came in 1909 and 1910. Two branch lines were constructed, the Northern Pacific (now Burlington Northern) and the Milwaukee line. Both ran east and west, and neither connected with any other railroad at their western ends. In the western part of Grant County, they ran almost perfectly parallel through New Leipzig and Elgin, with the Milwaukee line the more southerly of the two. By the eastern end of Grant County, they separated, the Milwaukee line swerving south to connect with the main line at McLaughlin, South Dakota, and the Northern Pacific turning north to connect with its main line at Mandan. The town of Old Carson moved two miles north to its present site along the Northern Pacific line, and the Carter's store building was abandoned.[4] The town of Leith was organized on the Milwaukee line, approximately four miles west and slightly south of the old Carter's store. At that time, its Sunday school was divided, some going to Carson and some to Leith.

On August 21, 1910, the First Presbyterian Church in Leith was reorganized by Mr. Meyers. It was constituted with forty-one charter members, and combined folks from the Carter's store Sunday school, the Evans barn church, and those involved in another Sunday school in the township hall southwest of Leith.[5] For a building, they first moved the township hall into Leith;[6] and later, in 1912, they moved into the community's church building. That house of worship was a community effort,[7] built in a determination to become a normal town as quickly as possible. Because the Presbyterians had first seized the opportunity, they were allowed to use the building. Later, in 1915, a parsonage was constructed,[8] with assistance from the denominational board of national missions. Thus, the congregation's building indebtedness was on the parsonage and not on the church building. At the inaugural service, N. C. Emch and J. P. Cowan were elected elders, Evans having gone with the Carson work.

From 1910 until 1922 the Carson and Leith churches were served by the same preacher. [Pastors who served in Leith during this time, with the date of the beginning of their service (the dates of the conclusion of their service being unavailable) were Benj. Iorns (April 6, 1913), J. H. Humphrey (March 10, 1915), C. M. Haas (June 13, 1917), J. P. Harley (July 17, 1921), and Rev. Mr. Ax (July 26, 1922).][9] The Presbyterian mission plan appears to have been to utilize student pastors and intinerant preachers working under Messrs. Meyers and Hughes, while special revival and evangelistic services were held as the means of gaining new members and adherents. The first recorded revival service at Leith was conducted in

December 1913 by a non-resident preacher.[10] Membership, and therefore financial support for the pastors, were fluctuating propositions. A fitting salary was hard to raise.[11] It also appears that there were gaps between ministries and that it was difficult to obtain pulpit supplies. For these reasons the presbytery arranged in 1922 to have the churches in Carson, Leith, Lark, and Raleigh served by the same pastor.[12] By that time, Frank Emch and H. W. Gibson had been added to the session in Leith, and another successful revival campaign had been completed.[13]

Daniel K. Ford, who had been a lay member of the Leith congregation for a brief period before his ordination to the ministry, moved into the area from Steele, North Dakota, to pastor the four churches. He remained until 1927, when he was succeeded by the Rev. E. W. Corbit, who served until 1931.[14] The new plan of organization succeeded only partially. While average pastoral tenure doubled, and membership in the church apparently stabilized, the old problems of inadequate pay and pulpit supplies continued. After Mr. Corbit left, the next pastor, E. E. Matteson, identified himself as an itinerant.[15] He was listed only as a stated supply preacher. He departed in 1932 for McLean County, North Dakota, and more itinerant preaching work.

Sam Allen and Church's Stabilization

The year 1932 marks a transitional year for the church. The Rev. Samuel J. Allen, formerly pastor of a Presbyterian church in Jordan, Montana, accepted a call to serve as pastor. On October 2 of that year, he had been presented a call to serve as stated supply for one year.[16] Three weeks later, however, the churches were informed that presbytery desired that each "group" of churches have an installed pastor. "Groups of churches" in this context meant the churches in Carson, Leith, Lark, and Raleigh, and coincided with the abandonment of hope that other works in Grant County would grow to become churches.

The church at Leith was, from this point, considered fully a church, as opposed to a mission or preaching station. Until now, the church had been built by special revivals, with short-term pulpit supplies providing follow-up services. Hereafter, revivals would give way to a permanent ministry. Additions to the church would now depend on the labors of the resident pastor.

Shortly after Mr. Allen's arrival, Charles Brown, who farmed two miles east of Leith on the north side of the Milwaukee Line tracks, was elected elder; he was ordained and installed on April 23, 1933.[17] This was an important milestone for the church. All previous elders disappeared from the scene within a seven-year span. H. W. Gibson died on February 17, 1930,[18] and Nicholas C. Emch died in August of that same year.[19] F. P. Emch had ceased to function as an elder at some point after September 4, 1927, the date of his last recorded presence at a session meeting. J. B.

Cowan moved to California. He was noted as residing in California in the October 6, 1935, minutes and was dismissed to a church in Pasadena in July 1936.[20] Thus, Charles Brown was left as the church's only ruling elder, an arrangement which lasted until 1954. Mr. Brown was to prove very active in affairs of both the local church and the presbytery, and his influence during the controversies of the late 1930s can hardly be overestimated.

By this time, depression and dust-bowl conditions were already serious. In spite of a parsonage in Leith, the Allens, except for one year, lived in Carson while the Leith parsonage was rented out. This provided a small economic advantage for the churches. Furthermore, the Allens by living in Carson were centrally located among the churches.[21]

Sam Allen's significance, however, had to do with more than financial and geographical matters. He was a graduate of Westminster Theological Seminary in Philadelphia and a member of that institution's first graduating class in 1930. He had transferred the previous year from Princeton Seminary.[22]

Westminster Theological Seminary was founded in the fall of 1929 under the leadership of the Rev. Dr. J. Gresham Machen as a reaction against the revision of the board of trustees of Princeton Seminary, and the inclusion on that board of men of modernistic persuasion. The founding of the seminary brought out into the open a battle between confessionalists (those desiring a strict construction judicially on the *Westminster Confession of Faith*) and modernists (whose liberal leanings brought them into conflict with the text of the Confession). As modernism came more and more to dominate the affairs of the church, Dr. Machen sought ways to protect conservative, evangelical, and confessionalist interests. In 1933 he founded the Independent Board for Presbyterian Foreign Missions in order to counter what he believed to be unconscionable practices of the denominational board.[23] For this act of insurrection, he was brought to trial and on June 1, 1936, defrocked from the ministry. By June 11, 1936, a meeting was called in Philadelphia, and a new denomination,[24] eventually called the Orthodox Presbyterian Church, was formed.[25]

Among the actions of the First General Assembly of the new church was the division of the U.S. map into presbyteries. This was followed by the appointment of convenors for the inaugural meetings of those presbyteries. Mr. Allen, as a loyal student of Dr. Machen's, and the Rev. D. K. Myers of Perkins County, South Dakota, attended that First General Assembly. A Presbytery of the Dakotas was formed, and Sam Allen was appointed convenor.

Mr. Allen did not move immediately to break with the PCUSA, preferring to visit each church family and present his case in person. Selling his position took six weeks, hindered somewhat because there were only two telephones in all of Carson.[26] Action was taken in the four churches on August 2, 1936. The Leith and Lark churches voted unanimously to withdraw from the PCUSA. The Raleigh church did not withdraw and soon folded. Those present at the meeting in Carson voted to withdraw. Some members who did not attend that meeting later claimed the church property and continued a PCUSA congregation there; to this day there are both Presbyterian and Orthodox Presbyterian churches in Carson.

The resolution by which the Leith congregation repudiated the jurisdiction of the PCUSA cites nine grounds for withdrawal. None of the nine expresses any local problem with the PCUSA's Presbytery of Bismarck.[27] All are concerned with denominational issues and are derived from the battle of Machen and his allies against denominational modernism. A similarly worded statement was entered into the record of the first meeting of the OPC's Presbytery of the Dakotas, which met in Bismarck on September 30, 1936.[28] At that meeting, three founding ministers were present: Allen, D. K. Myers, and E. E. Matteson. Undoubtedly, there were other Presbyterian ministers in North Dakota who were of conservative and evangelical stripe and might have been prospects for the new denomination. Lack of specific problems with the Presbytery of Bismarck (PCUSA) is the best explanation of why so few came out.

In the hope of strengthening the local churches and of encouraging other Presbyterians in the region to re-affiliate with the Orthodox Presbyterian Church (hereafter OPC), Allen invited Dr. Machen to conduct a speaking tour in North Dakota over the seminary's Christmas vacation of that year. As founder of the seminary with teaching and administrative loads to bear, and as founder of the new denomination, perpetually in demand for aid and advice, Dr. Machen was pressed for time and was without adequate rest. He was counseled by friends not to make the North Dakota trip. Disregarding this wisdom he arrived in North Dakota after Christmas with a cold and in weather estimated at twenty degrees below zero.[29] He spoke in Leith during a morning or early afternoon rally and then became very ill. Allen hurriedly drove him to Bismarck, where he was examined by a doctor. Again disregarding advice Dr. Machen spoke at a public rally that same evening. Afterwards he collapsed. He was admitted to the St. Alexius Hospital, where his cold degenerated into pneumonia. On January 1, 1937, he passed away. Thus the last pulpit used by Dr. Machen was the pulpit of the First Orthodox Presbyterian Church of Leith.

Without Machen's steady hand at the helm, the new denomination headed for difficulty. The members had been united in their opposition to modernism in the PCUSA. Now they discovered that they were not united among themselves. Two camps were perceivable, the confessionalists and those more broadly evangelical whose views were in line with the general milieu of evangelicalism of the 1930s. The former, because of their strong adherence to the Confession, were unashamedly Calvinistic, taught the doctrine of Christian liberty, and allowed restricted latitude in acceptable views of the second coming of Christ. The latter were less outspoken about Calvinism, opposed beverage alcohol as prohibitionists, and allowed a wider range of views of the second coming, tolerating certain premillennial strains that the former did not. Across the new denomination, a split occurred in the spring of 1937.[30] The confessionalists generally remained as the OPC. Those who left would soon organize the Bible Presbyterian Synod.

The division cut across the new Presbytery of the Dakotas, although it was delayed for one year. The immediate cause of disunion was the question of distilled spirits. The division was generally along geographical lines, with the Missouri River as the boundary. The west side of the river had been homesteaded a minimum of one generation later. The difference between 1906 homesteading and 1937 church politics was only one generation. Western Dakotas churches still faced an open-saloon frontier environment which eastern Dakotas churches had already brought under control. It would have been culturally suicidal for a professed evangelical church in western Dakota in the 1930s to decline to voice continuing support for prohibition.

Pastors Myers and Matteson appeared at the fall 1937 and spring 1938 presbytery meetings determined to commit the OPC to a teetotal position. They were thwarted by a block of eastern South Dakota churches which, by then, had affiliated with the presbytery. When Myers and Matteson failed in their efforts, they left the OPC. No church east of the Missouri went with them. Among west side churches, only the Hamill, South Dakota, church and Allen's three remaining congregations stayed in the OPC.

Allen and Charles Brown, the elder from Leith, stood strongly for the OPC's position. It must be stressed that both Pastor Allen and Elder Brown were avowed teetotalers.[31] The disagreement to them was not over practice but theory. The issue, as they saw it, was whether the church could make a rule that the Bible did not.[32] When the dust from the division had settled, the Leith church (along with Carson and Lark) found themselves in isolation, 350 miles from the nearest Orthodox Presbyterian Church (save for the unsuccessful efforts of the Rev. Curtis A. Balcom to establish churches in Burleigh and McLean Counties, North Dakota — efforts which ceased in 1947).

Years later the cost of this stand was made clear. When Charles Brown retired from the active eldership, and still later, when he died, memorial minutes printed in the presbytery record show that extreme pressure was put on him to join with the Bible Presbyterians.[33] Implicitly, the pressure came from his old friend, E. E. Matteson, who had been his pastor immediately before his election to the eldership, and under whose preaching his daughter had been converted.[34] Brown's resistance did much to keep the Leith church in the OPC. However there was also a cost in public relations. Here was a professed evangelical church in a religious, anti-saloon tradition taking a public stand against prohibition. This would not be the last time the church would break out of the evangelical mold.

Sam Allen moved on in 1940, accepting a call to a church in Philadelphia. His stay in North Dakota was twice as long as any previous pastor's. He left behind an organized parish and the flagship church of the new denomination in the state of North Dakota. His successor was the Rev. John Gray, a recent Westminster Seminary graduate. Gray's time in North Dakota was short and hard. The effects of the dust bowl had hit the area in the late 1930s. Mrs. Allen, for example, recalls one summer in which her vegetable garden was completely destroyed by a hot wind.[35] The congregations had not totally recovered from the dual blows of families leaving the area for economic reasons and the economic distress in the families remaining. Lark was down from its thirteen charter members to three by 1946, and the church was saved from extinction only by merger with a Christian Reformed congregation.[36] Gray found it necessary to take extra-long summer vacations for the purpose of supplementing his income by working in war factories.[37] He departed for a church in West Amwell Township, New Jersey, in the summer of 1944.

Walter Magee and the Church in Crisis

Toward the end of World War II, virtually every congregation in the Presbytery of the Dakotas experienced pastoral moves and had difficulty in securing new ministers. For the Leith church, a long pastoral vacancy was endured as calls to the Rev. Glen A. Williams and to the Rev. Louis Knowles were declined. Seminarian Delbert Schowalter filled the pulpit for a few months during the summer of 1945. Finally, in April of 1946, the Rev. Walter J. Magee accepted a call and moved into the parsonage in Leith. He both began and ended his ministry amid controversy.

By the time Magee had moved to North Dakota, the Leith congregation was having its title to its property contested.[38] As noted previously, the church building in Leith had originally been erected by the community. At some subsequent point, when it became apparent that the permanent tenant would be the Presbyterians, the PCUSA's Board of Domestic Missions purchased the building from the community for the First Presbyterian Church of Leith.

The establishment of the Orthodox Presbyterian Church in 1936 touched off property controversies across the nation. Briefly stated, the PCUSA attempted to prevent congregations from affiliating with the new OPC by invoking (or creating) a doctrine which stated that the property of the local church is held in trust for the presbytery.[39] Under that doctrine, presbyteries of the PCUSA went to civil courts to claim the property of congregations that withdrew. The property of the church in Carson was taken from them and a PCUSA congregation re-established in it. The property of the church in Lark was not challenged, owing to the size of the town and the congregation.

Across the whole of the new church, only two congregations whose claims were contested retained their buildings, the church in Portland, Maine, and the church at Leith. The church in Portland retained its property through an amazing oversight. They had formerly been Congregationalist, and had never formally discharged the parish officers, allowing them to function as trustees. In their case, their local technicalities established a clear-cut claim that the property of that church belonged to the parish officers. To this day, that congregation is known as Second Parish OPC.[40]

The church at Leith had retained its property and the claim of the Presbytery of Bismarck (PCUSA) was disallowed in district court on the grounds that the vote to withdraw from the old denomination was unanimous and that there was no local appeal for a continuing PCUSA in Leith.[41] When that decision was handed down, the Presbyterian Board of National Mission informed the church that the mortgage was due, and a payment schedule was arranged directly between the church and board. At that point, through an oversight, the attorney for the Leith church neglected to close the case officially. Ten years later, in late 1945, when there was only about $100 left to pay on the mortgage, the Presbytery of Bismarck, claiming to be no party to the church-board negotiations, reopened the property case and appealed it to the North Dakota Supreme Court.[42] No sooner was Walter Magee on the field than the court ruled in favor of the PCUSA and awarded them the church's property. It should be obvious that the PCUSA had little use for a church building in Leith. Making the doctrine of the presbytery's claim to local property ironclad for future purposes is a more satisfactory explanation. It then became necessary for the "squatter" congregation to reobtain their property, just shortly after their previous pastor had been forced to earn outside income due to lack of local resources. A settlement was finally reached for the purchase of the property from the Presbytery of Bismarck on December 18, 1949.[43] In essence, the congregation purchased its property twice, once from the denominational board and once from the old denomination's presbytery.

While the property controversy was winding down, another controversy broke out, this one between pastor and church. Background on the pastor is necessary to understand the sharpness of the clash. Magee had been ordained at the first meeting of the Presbytery of the Dakotas, OPC, in September 1936 and had pastored the church in Hamill, South Dakota, until 1939. He had moved to the OPC in Bridgewater, South Dakota, and from there had gone to take up labors in the Aurora, Nebraska, OPC in 1945. In each of the three, he had experienced a wide gap between official denominational theory and local church practice. The situation in

Aurora was particularly distressing. There were Arminians on the session,[44] although the church was alleged to be exclusively Calvinistic. Magee had been there only fourteen months, and apparently violated some principles of polity in his zeal to depart.[45] The Aurora church would never again have an OPC pastor, and after nine years of dialogue, left the denomination.

Now again in Leith, Magee found discrepancies between denominational policy and local practice. The issue in Leith was Sabbath observance. The custom developed by pastors of the Carson, Lark, and Leith parish was that the Lark church would have the earliest Sunday service, Carson next, and Leith the late morning service. This was convenient because the pastor, a resident in Leith, could begin his Sunday preaching furthest from home at Lark, stop in Carson on the way home, and finish his morning by preaching at Leith and walking to his residence. Unfortunately, the late morning service in Leith at times conflicted with the town softball team's schedule.[46] With deep convictions about the sanctity of the Sabbath Day, Magee sought the advice of presbytery as to how far he could proceed with disciplinary action against the Sabbath-breakers. He also sought a declaratory statement from presbytery about Sabbath observance.[47] At the same time, he appears to have pursued the issue within the congregation with a zeal some found offensive. By November 1950 the presbytery had sent a visitation committee to Leith to counsel with church and session about the problem. Presbytery's final advice to the church consisted of a mild reaffirmation of traditional Presbyterian views on the Sabbath. Furthermore, Magee was advised that he was free to pursue disciplinary action against Sabbath-breakers. However no statement was given about the extent to which presbytery would back him.[48]

Some of the tension of this controversy was broken by the sale of the parsonage in Leith and Magee's relocation in Carson during 1949.[49] Most likely, the Leith parsonage was sold to help in the settlement of debts with the Presbytery of Bismarck (PCUSA). The Carson, Lark, and Leith churches took action to work in partnership to secure a new parsonage, and manse trustees from each church functioned jointly to maintain the new property.

It is difficult to overestimate the significance of this controversy. More than Sabbath observance was at stake. The real controversy was over the identity of the church, whether it would be the servant of the community or the servant of the denomination. This is no small matter, considering the non-Presbyterian origin of the founders and the fact that the community constructed the church building. In rural North Dakota, the sense of community is of utmost importance, and attacks on elements of the community originating outside the community tend to be viewed with extreme disdain. The town's softball schedule ranks much higher on "the scale of being" than the OPC's Confession of Faith. In that sense, what

Magee accomplished by his crusade against Sabbath-breaking was to prevent the church from becoming so identified with the community that denominational issues would become irrelevant. He had determined that the church would be a Presbyterian church; for this he paid a heavy price in community relations. But his effort was not in vain. Because he made this stand, subsequent pastors inherited a tradition in which those loyal to the church understood later fights for denominational principles.

Henry Tavares and the Zenith Years

Following Magee's resignation the congregations extended a call to the Rev. Henry P. Tavares. Tavares served from 1952 through the fall of 1957. His years could fairly be called the high-water mark of the church. This was the time after Magee had confronted the community with denominational distinctives and before the area entered into economic decline.

Tavares continued the trend toward enforcement of denominational distinctives, or at least policies not originating in the will of the local populace. His first project was to oversee the revision of the church rolls, something not done since the first dozen years of the church's existence. Certain baptized children, thirty-five in all, were dropped on the ground that they resided out-of-state.[50] Also twenty-three adults were dropped— those now in membership or regular attendance in other churches and those disinterested in the life of the Leith church.

Nor could this process be considered a periodic purge. Concern developed over Franklin Emch who married a Roman Catholic woman. He apparently conceded family life to the church of Rome at the time of the ceremony.[51] After initial success in reclaiming him from Roman Catholicism, he was removed from the roll for raising his children in the church of Rome and for his indifference to the affairs of the congregation.[52] A pastoral effort, therefore, was made to reclaim wandering members. Only when it was not possible to reclaim them were they dropped.

As a result of the review, the remaining fifty adult members[53] could be defined in terms of active participation in the life of the church. Such would be the practice until the end.

Another evidence of the strenth of denominational commitment came on April 24, 1955, when Mr. and Mrs. Richard Pagel of Leith appeared before the session to apply for membership in the church. Following their examination, they were respectfully denied membership ("at this time") because they were not able to affirm belief in the doctrine of the resurrection of the body. They were encouraged to study the issue further.[54] Here again was a first— the denial of membership to a prospective addition to the church on doctrinal grounds. This takes on added significance when one speculates as to the reason for Mr. and Mrs. Pagel's denial of the resurrection. A doctrinal aberration known as neo-Kohlbrüggianism had swept through the remnants of the German Reformed denomination (hereafter RCUS). One feature of the disciples of Kohlbrügge was the notion of the absolute destruction of the sinful flesh for the purpose of preserving the immortal soul. It is likely that neo-Kohlbrüggianism existed in the RCUS congregation at Heil, North Dakota, the next town west of Carson on the Northern Pacific.[55] Thus, a position held by the OPC's closest ecclesiastical ally in Grant County was condemned.

Strictly positive developments took place as well. On March 23, 1954, after three years of training, Roswell Kamrath was examined and approved as a ruling elder candidate.[56] After his ordination on April 4, 1954, the church had a second ruling elder for the first time in almost twenty years. Mr. Kamrath would render valuable leadership for the next dozen years, after which he departed the farm at approximately age 50 to enter the pastoral ministry.

During Tavares' time as pastor, there were at least fifteen additions to the church's roll of communicant members. Most were the result of the children of the church making profession of faith, mostly Emchs, or the addition of the newlywed spouses of some of the same individuals. While the addition of fifteen members in five years does not sound impressive, it was growth unparalleled since the revivals of the early 1920s for the Leith church.

Another accomplishment for Tavares might have been an inadvertent one. A regular feature of his agenda in all of his pastorates was the organization and performance of Christmas and Easter cantatas.[57] While a case could be made that by having a cantata in Leith, Tavares was simply being Tavares, the cantatas played a major role in balancing the denominational church vs. community church issue. Such cantatas made a cultural contribution to the community; they rendered a community service that did not go unnoticed. Because of these cantatas, whatever raw nerves that might have been touched by denominational distinctives could be much more easily forgiven.

By the end of his pastorate, Henry Tavares had seen restoration of the balance between denomination and community and had left an orderly church roll and a stronger session.

Nineteen Fifty-seven and the Beginning of Decline

The year 1957 marks the next major transition in the life of the church. From this point the church entered a period of decline. There are two factors which contributed to this. The lesser cause was the departure of Henry Tavares for a church in Ft. Lauderdale, Florida. Tavares had succeeded in the delicate balancing act of both preserving denominational distinctives while not antagonizing the culture. Without describing the terms of the next two pastors as failures, there does appear to be a disturbance in the balance on both sides of the ledger. V. Robert Nilson came to serve from 1957 through 1964, and Robert Dodds occupied the parsonage from 1964 until 1967.

A much greater cause for decline was the falling of a number of economic dominoes. Of Grant County's two railroads, the Milwaukee road was by far the least profitable. By 1957 it was bankrupt. The tracks were removed in the early 1980s as a testimony to population patterns long established. Towns built on the Northern Pacific branch line in Grant County tended to retain their population, as evidenced by the following census figures: Carson, on the Northern Pacific, 1950, 493; 1960, 501; 1970, 466; 1980, 469; Elgin on the Northern Pacific, 1950, 882; 1960, 944; 1970, 839; 1980, 930; Brisbane on the Milwaukee road, 1950, 35, townsite abandoned 1956; Leith on the Milwaukee road, 1950, 160; 1960, 100; 1970, 92; 1980, 59. The economic axiom follows: the smaller the town, the fewer the businesses in the town, the fewer the visits to that town, the fewer the people culturally identified with the town. So when in 1957 Grant County paved its first roads, the east-west road along the Burlington Northern line (successor to Northern Pacific), Route 21, was surfaced. The east-west road along the Milwaukee line, through Leith, was not. In making the decision as to which roads to pave, the State Highway Department guaranteed that there would be greater access for the town of Carson; they literally decreed that Carson would economically survive and that Leith would economically die. In fairness, the problems of the Milwaukee road made that choice the only logical one, and the resulting decline of Leith was not caused by the decision, only hastened.

With these economic blows, the handwriting was on the wall, and the institutions of Leith began to collapse. The first and most important casualty was the public school. With the virtual guarantee of further, irreplaceable decline in enrollment, Leith High School graduated its last class in 1958.[58] The loss of the high school meant empty homes in Leith where teachers had lived. Fewer residences and less traffic into Leith for school-related functions meant less patronizing of Leith businesses. The closing of some of those businesses meant even more out-migration from the community.

For the First Orthodox Presbyterian Church of Leith, all these factors added up to a decline in membership as teachers and merchants moved away. Church membership figures show a downhill trend from 1958 until dissolution. Further, these factors meant the loss of opportunity for finding replacement families. Newcomers to town had represented the most fertile mission field. Now there were no more. The surrounding agricultural population was very stable and religiously settled. What few new farmers would enter the area would identify with Carson for the sake of the school and businesses there. The pastor who would try to reach them also lived in Carson and could as easily invite them to that church. With the lack of the possibility of adding members, the congregation was stricken by death and old age.

In spite of everything, the congregation on Sunday, August 21, 1960, celebrated its golden anniversary.[59] Guest minister for both morning and evening services was the Rev. W. Benson Male of Denver, Colorado, a patriarch among ministers in the Presbytery of the Dakotas and a kindred spirit with Pastor Nilson in several presbytery causes. His sermon topics, described as anniversary messages in the bulletin, were "Wrought of God" in the morning, and "Pressing On" in the evening. A supplement in the bulletin for that Sunday indicated that at that point there were seven charter members of the original forty-one still active in the church, Mrs. J. H. Emch, F. P. Emch, Mr. and Mrs. William Kamrath, Mrs. Ethel Mossman, Mrs. Tim Weatherly, and Mrs. Edw. Heaps.

The celebration could not reverse the trend. The 1960s would witness the demise of the local eldership. Charles Brown passed away on July 29, 1962,[60] following a lingering illness. His death brought to an end a long and profitable tenure in office. He was remembered by a memorial minute in the presbytery record,[61] a tribute not uniformly given to deceased elders. Responding to the need for other elders, brothers Duane and James Emch and Lester Teker were nominated for office on February 1, 1961. The brothers were ordained on March 26, 1961, while Mr. Teker declined with a request for more instruction.[62] These, however, did not provide a long-range solution. On January 31, 1966, both Emches were placed on the roll of inactive elders[63] after they relocated, Duane in Saskatchewan and James in Bismarck. In November 1965 Roswell Kamrath was asked if he would not also accept inactive status,[64] since he was by that time in Grand Rapids, Michigan, preparing for the ministry. James Emch was the only one of the three in any position to help the church in any capacity. Within two years, he was dead, killed tragically along with his wife and one daughter in a car-train accident while returning from vacation in Canada on August 21, 1967.[65] Lester Teker never was ordained and was transferred to the Orthodox Presbyterian Church of Puget Sound when he moved to Seattle in 1967.[66] There would not be another elder from among the membership of the Leith church.

At approximately the end of Mr. Nilson's term, discussions were held with the German Reformed Church at Heil, North Dakota, about the possibility of adding the German church to the parish, or at least having the OPC pastor also serve that congregation.[67] These discussions, however, came to nothing, and hopes of financial relief faded.

There is one other indication of the decline of the church during Nilson's term. He introduced a change of policy which stipulated joint session meetings, one meeting to do the business for Carson, Lark, and Leith. On October 15, 1959, the first of these meetings was held,[68] and it was determined to hold such meetings quarterly. Later on, when the

Leith church ceased to have its own elders, Richard Vandenburg of Lark was appointed to represent Leith at the fall 1966 presbytery meeting. Meanwhile Dwight Kamrath, a Leith trustee, was attending joint session meetings and signed the Leith copy of the minutes as an "observer" for the Leith congregation. The arrangement was as pragmatic as it was constitutionally suspect.

Naturally, hindsight has the luxury of the second guess. Nevertheless, the new policy did appear convenient. Convenience, however, could not obviate the problems. First, the arrangement was a violation of Presbyterian polity. An elder from one church cannot exercise original jurisdiction over members of another congregation without that congregation's consent. There is no record of the church at Leith voting on the matter. But, it could be claimed, such arrangements were not unknown in the region. The Orthodox Presbyterian Churches at Bancroft, Manchester, and Yale, South Dakota, did the same. They were not challenged until 1981.

The second problem was possibly the more serious. There is a significant difference between viewing the congregation on the one hand as the OP church at Leith and on the other as the church of Leith affiliated with the OPC. The latter provides a much stronger community identity. Did the joint session arrangement, however, connote the former, and disrupt the cultural balance Tavares had achieved during his ministry? Did it communicate the message that the OPC had given up on Leith?

But could another course have saved the day? We can only speculate. As we do, however, we cannot help but note the survival of totally rural and ghost-town Lutheran churches in southwestern Grant County. These community churches exist in the midst of economic decline. What gives them their staying power? Is it their ethnicity? an "unholy" alliance with the culture? And what about the OPC hinders it in functioning as a community church? Does this question involve serious theological issues? Here is a weighty matter for reflection not simply by declining Dakota churches but OP congregations everywhere.

The Death of a Church

From this point, the road to dissolution was a sure and steady one. Robert Dodds broached the subject of saving expenses by closing the Leith building during the winter months and worshiping jointly with the church in Carson. Thus, no services were held in Leith over the winter of 1966 –67.[69] What further plans Mr. Dodds may have had for the Leith church would shortly become irrelevant. He had served in another denomination before accepting the call to North Dakota. After a third failure to pass the examinations necessary to be received into presbytery in early 1967, he was requested to leave the field so that an installable pastor could be secured. The record is not clear whether services were held in the Leith building during 1967. The usual experience of the churches was that during pastoral vacancies there were often joint services.

The Rev. Jack J. Peterson accepted a call as the new pastor in late 1967 and was on the field by January 1968. At the congregational meeting in 1968, there was apparently a last-ditch effort to revive the Leith church, in that the Carson church was invited to worship at Leith from May through November.[70] Over the winter of 1970–71, the Leith congregation again worshiped at Carson, and this time the joint worship service arrangement became permanent. Separate rolls were maintained until 1973. On January 29, 1973, Roy Lehman and Marcia Johnson were appointed a committee to dispose of Leith church properties, building and contents.[71] By session action, on April 9, 1973, the remaining active sixteen adults and three children in the church were transferred onto the rolls of the Carson church and the remainder erased.[72] Those sixteen were constituted trustees to dispose of the remaining church properties. The church was officially dissolved in 1974 when the building was sold. The immediate cause of the death of the congregation was insufficient funds availiable to maintain the building and pay winter utilities.

The postscripts to the story are numerous, and three should be mentioned. The empty church building was purchased by the town butcher, Gottlieb Zeller, who was neither a Presbyterian nor even a regular church attender. He was, however, a shameless lover of the community of Leith. The only other church in Leith, an American Lutheran congregation, had by this time already disbanded. Its building had been removed to Elgin, where it serves as the museum of the Grant County Historical Society.[73] With the last church in town now dissolved, Zeller moved to purchase its building to prevent its removal or destruction, so that the town of Leith would still have a church building in it, a reminder of the community spirit that had built the building in pioneer days. The building stands to this day, preserved in its church-like appearance, and used for storage.

Among the redistributed contents of the building was the pulpit, which was placed in the Carson church building and continues in use to this day. Because my research had indicated that it was the last pulpit used by denominational founder J. Gresham Machen, I sought a way to memorialize it. Believing that a donor in New Jersey was soon to provide funds for a memorial plaque, I arranged at the fall 1980 presbytery meeting, held at Carson, to have the Rev. W. Benson Male, who twenty years earlier had preached at the Leith church's fiftieth anniversary service, deliver a sermon of dedication. The service was held on September 24, 1980.[74] Unfortunately, the potential donor in New Jersey died before the funds were secured, and the proposed plaque was never affixed to the pulpit.

However, there does exist a lasting memorial to the Leith church. When the building was sold, its bell, the one originally brought from Carroll, Nebraska, by N. C. Emch, was removed and stored in a quonset on the farm of Howard Johnson, one of the last sixteen members. It remained there until 1982, with the hope that a fitting memorial could some day be constructed. During 1981 it was learned that when the Leith church was dissolved, its trustees had never released its memorial funds (monies given to the church in memory of recently deceased members) to the Carson church's treasurer. As former Leith members died, funds in the Leith memorial account continued to accumulate, to the chagrin of long time members in Carson.

As pastor, I moved to find an occasion to drain the fund, and the Leith bell provided an excellent excuse. After numerous delays, a carpenter was employed to brick in a sign in front of the Carson church building and to mount the bell on top of it. A plaque on the brick reads, "This bell was brought to Leith, North Dakota, in 1912 by pioneers from Carroll, Nebr. a gift to the families of N. C. Emch. The bell was part of the Presby. Church in Leith until its closing in 1973 when the members transferred to Carson." The place of the congregation in history was thereby secured.

NOTES

1. Quentin T. Michelson and Carrie Weinhandl, *Prairie Pioneers of Grant County, N.D.* (Elgin, N.D.: Grant County Historical Society, 1976), 3.

2. "Presbyterian Church Notes," *Carson Press,* February 4, 1982 (reprint), 2.

3. First Orthodox Presbyterian Church of Leith, N.D., "Session Minutes," 1:163 (hereafter, Session Minutes).

4. Michelson and Weinhandl, *Prairie Pioneers,* 59.

5. *Carson Press,* Ibid.

6. Session Minutes, 1:163.

7. Marcia Johnson to David W. Kiester, January 30, 1985 (in possession of author).

8. *Carson Press,* Ibid.

9. Session Minutes, 1:161.

10. Session Minutes, 1:4.

11. *Carson Press* Ibid.

12. Ibid.

13. Session Minutes, 1:12.

14. Ibid., 1:161.

15. Interview by telephone with Mrs. Mildred Allen Vanderveer of Selma, Alabama, January 19, 1985 (notes in possession of author).

16. Session Minutes, 1:26.

17. Ibid., 1:27.

18. Ibid., 1:session register, 2.

19. Marcia Johnson to David W. Kiester, February 20, 1985 (in possession of author).

20. Session Minutes, 1:40.

21. Interview with Mrs. Mildred Allen Vanderveer.

22. *The First Ten Years,* (Philadelphia: Committee on Home Missions and Church Extension, 1946), 75.

23. Ned B. Stonehouse, *J. Gresham Machen: A Biographical Memoir* (Grand Rapids: Eerdmans, 1955), 482.

24. *The First Ten Years*, 3.

25. The new denomination was not officially named Orthodox Presbyterian Church until 1939. Nevertheless, this name is affixed to its pre-1939 history for simplicity.

26. Interview with Mrs. Mildred Allen Vanderveer.

27. Session Minutes, 1:41.

28. Presbytery of the Dakotas, Orthodox Presbyterian Church, "Presbytery Minutes," 1:3 (hereafter, Presbytery Minutes).

29. Stonehouse, *Machen*, 506.

30. *The First Ten Years*, 6.

31. The sources for these affirmations are notes from pastoral visits with John Wagner of Carson, N.D., and Miss Elsie Brown of Leith, N.D. The notes are in the author's personal file of North Dakota church material.

32. Presbytery Minutes, 1:34.

33. Presbytery Minutes, 2:136, 161.

34. The source of this affirmation is a note from a pastoral visit with Miss Elsie Brown of Leith, N.D. The note is in the author's personal file of North Dakota church material.

35. Interview with Mrs. Mildred Allen Vanderveer.

36. *The First Ten Years*, 44.

37. Session Minutes, 1:63. The cause of Mr. Gray's extended absence is confirmed by a note from a pastoral visit with Chester Brown of Leith, N.D. The note is in the author's personal file of North Dakota church material.

38. *The First Ten Years*, 42.

39. Ibid., 12.

40. Edwin H. Rian, *The Presbyterian Conflict* (Grand Rapids: Eerdmans, 1940), 255.

41. *The First Ten Years*, 42.

42. Ibid.

43. Session Minutes, 1:73.

44. The source of this affirmation is a paper now in the possession of the Orthodox Presbyterian Church's general assembly historian.

45. Presbytery Minutes, 1:174.

46. Mrs. Erma Magee to David W. Kiester, January 17, 1985 (in possession of author).

47. Presbytery Minutes, 1:232.

48. Ibid., 1:238.

49. Mrs. Erma Magee to David W. Kiester.

50. Session Minutes, 1:97.

51. Ibid., 1:126.

52. Ibid., 1:142.

53. Ibid., 1:102. A document with this figure on it has not been seen by the author. The figure results from a compilation of gains and losses for the church.

54. Ibid., 1:119.

55. The source of this affirmation is several conversations with the Rev. Roger L. Gibbons, currently of Bethany, Oklahoma, who formerly pastored the Reformed Church in the U.S. flagship congregation at Eureka, S.D.

56. Session Minutes, 1:106.

57. This affirmation is based on the author's observation of similar cantatas performed at the Covenant Orthodox Presbyterian Church of Grove City, PA., Mr. Tavares' last pastorate.

58. Marcia Johnson to David W. Kiester, February 20, 1985.

59. Session Minutes, 1:162–63.

60. Session Minutes, 1:session register, 2.

61. Presbytery Minutes, 2:161.

62. Session Minutes, 1:158.

63. Ibid., 2:25.

64. Ibid., 2:33.

65. Marcia Johnson to David W. Kiester, February 20, 1985.
66. Session Minutes, 2:53.
67. Ibid., 2:14–15.
68. Ibid., 1:155.
69. Ibid., 2:40.
70. Ibid., 2:56.
71. Ibid., 2:116.
72. Ibid., 2:119.
73. Michelson and Weinhandl, *Prairie Pioneers*, 392.
74. Presbytery Minutes, 3:363.

Part IV

The Mission of the Orthodox Presbyterian Church

Symbol of the Great Commission

Laurence N. Vail

22 Current Issues in Missions

A NUMBER OF CRUCIAL QUESTIONS now confront the church with the necessity for reexamining its missionary principles and practices. During the last two decades issues ranging from a serious debate on the definition of evangelism to angry cries of "missionary, go home" challenge us to take another look at our own understanding and conduct of missions.

Proclamation or Dialogue?

A recent *Mission Bulletin* of the Reformed Ecumenical Synod (September 1982) debates the question "proclamation or dialogue?" The discussion is concerned with the proper way for a missionary to approach people who hold to non-Christian religions such as Buddhism, Hinduism, and Taoism. Should the missionary confront such people with the biblical teaching on God, man, sin, and salvation, calling upon them to repent and be converted? Or should he take the position that there is some truth in all religions and enter into an open discussion with the idea that each can teach and also learn and both may arrive at new truth? Or is there another approach that neither compromises the gospel nor countermands the Great Commission but nevertheless enables the missionary to communicate the gospel with humility and also show genuine respect for people of other faiths?

One evangelical missions professor, after presenting a paper on interreligious dialogue in which he advocated participation by evangelicals in some forms of dialogue, remarked that his audience's lack of enthusiasm for his suggestion was understandable. Suspicion of dialogue as a usable method of missionary communication is aroused by its advocates and by ideas associated with it. The World Council of Church's Commission on

391

World Mission and Evangelism persuaded a majority at the Mexico City 1963 Conference to favor dialogue. Conciliar ecumenists have continued to promote it through commission reports and world conferences as the only proper way to encounter those of other faiths.

What causes this zeal for dialogue? For one thing, many World Council member churches believe that the conquest of other faiths by Christianity is neither possible nor desirable. Instead, the people of all faiths need to learn to respect each other, develop harmonious relationships, and together pursue the common task of humanization. Many proponents of dialogue believe that all religions are valid expressions of the revelation of God. They even find "Christ" present in all developments of history, in all social revolutionary movements, and in all human religious ideas and quests. Therefore, interreligious dialogue is the path to truth about God and the discovery of Christ.

In opposition, evangelicals affirm the exclusiveness of the Christian faith, the supreme authority of the Bible in religious matters, and the universal Lordship of Christ over all other lords. Convinced that Christ has commanded his church to evangelize those of other faiths or none, evangelicals proclaim the gospel of Christ as the only way of salvation. Supporting this conviction is the belief that adherents of non-Christian religions are without God and without hope.

Where then do non-Christian religions come from? Are they merely demonic in origin and totally false? In his excellent study, *A Christian Introduction to Religions of the World*, Johannes Vos summarizes the Bible's teaching concerning the origin and development of the true religion and of false religions. He shows from Romans 1 and 2 that the revelation of the true God in creation was distorted by sinful men resulting in idolatry and false religions. But because of the operation of common grace, elements of truth have been preserved in them even though as systems they are false.

In his book, *An Introduction to the Science of Missions*, J. H. Bavinck develops an approach to non-Christian religions which seeks to unmask all false religions as sin against God and to call upon idolators to acknowledge the only true God. However, when personal contact is made with the adherents of other religions, it is with people and not religious systems that we are dealing. Such contacts must be loving and made in reliance on the Holy Spirit.

In establishing such contacts, evangelical leaders such as John Stott and Waldron Scott see a place for dialogue. However it must be of a certain kind and with the right goal in view. It is certainly proper to sit down with another person, ask sincere questions about his faith, and listen patiently to his answers. To be a good witness for Christ requires of us to respond to the questions and objections of unbelievers with honest answers. There is no place for pride or arrogance, or for a sense of personal superiority when presenting the gospel. "We do not preach ourselves, but Jesus Christ as Lord, and ourselves as servants for Jesus' sake" (2 Cor 4:5).

Salvation or Liberation?

Section 5 of the Covenant signed by many participants at the International Congress on World Evangelization held at Lausanne, Switzerland, in July of 1974, says in part, "We affirm that God is both the Creator and the Judge of all men. We therefore should share his concern for justice and reconciliation throughout human society and for the liberation of men from every kind of oppression. . . . The message of salvation implies also a message of judgment upon every form of alienation, oppression, and discrimination, and we should not be afraid to denounce evil and injustice wherever they exist." The same statement also carefully denied that political liberation is salvation.

What was it that impelled the framers of the Lausanne Covenant to speak out in this way about the liberation of men from oppression? Why did "Liberation Theology" become a dominant theme in western theological thought between 1970 and 1975? How does this emphasis on liberation from oppression affect our understanding of missions? Latin America supplies some of the answers.

Although the book *Mission Trends No. 4: Liberation Theologies* contains contributions from the black, feminist, native American, Asian American, and Chicano liberation movements, nevertheless, Orlando Costas is correct in identifying liberation theology as first and foremost a Latin American development. In its earlier stages (1968) it was mainly associated with Roman Catholic reflection groups that grew out of the stimulus of the Latin America Bishops Congress in Medellin, Columbia. It has since widened its scope to include the thinking of the Latin America Church and Society movement which has a Protestant origin and such Protestant theologians as Jose Miguez Bonino, Luis Rivera Pagan, Julio de Santa Ana, and Emilio Castro. But the Roman Catholic theologians Gustavo Gutierrez, Rubem Alves, and Hugo Assman have made the most significant and influential contributions to the movement.

Unlike the majority of theologies from the North Atlantic which begin with such categories as God, Scripture, and church, the theologians of liberation start from the poverty-stricken, oppressive, and dominated reality of Latin America. In this context theology is conceived of not simply as spiritual or rational knowledge of the faith, but as a critical reflection on the intense interaction of faith with the actual historical situation. Basic to this approach is the use of the social sciences to analyze the historical situation, and this is often done from a Marxist or socialist perspective. Oppressive social and economic structures are usually identified with North American capitalism represented by multinational corporations.

Using social analysis as a starting point, liberation theology arrives at radically new definitions of salvation, the church, and the future. Salvation is redefined in terms of the quality of life in the world: redemption (liberation) from economic, political, and social bondage (oppression). The Old Testament exodus of God's people from bondage in Egypt is regarded as the model for modern missions. Therefore the mission of the church is to enter the struggle on the side of the oppressed and strive (even with violence) for their liberation and for the establishment of a society where liberty and justice prevail. It is only as the church participates in its mission that it is able to interpret Scripture correctly.

Of course we could easily point out the errors of such a movement and set forth over against such errors the biblical teaching concerning salvation and missions. Writers like John Stott have done this. However, for the discerning Reformed readers of this essay, such an exposition should not really be necessary. On the other hand, we may well ask whether the liberation movement can supply a needed correction to our own understanding and practice of missions. Have we really listened to what the Holy Spirit says in Scripture about the poor, the afflicted, and the meaning of righteousness? Do we properly evaluate and seek to emulate the ministry of our Lord and his apostles? Do we hear with compassion the cries of those who suffer — and respond appropriately? Have we really given the full weight to the mission of Christ who came to fulfill the Scripture, "The Spirit of the Lord is on me: therefore he has anointed me to preach good news to the poor. . . . to proclaim freedom for the prisoners and recovery of sight for the blind, to release the oppressed, to proclaim the year of the Lord's favor" (Luke 4:18–19)? Godliness certainly has relevance for this life as well as the life to come.

Mission or Missions?

In April 1969 the quarterly publication of the Commission on World Mission and Evangelism of the World Council of Churches became the *International Review of Mission* when it dropped the "s" from missions. Commenting on the change, the editor pointed out that by it the IRM title was brought into line with the broad consensus of missionary thinking of most of the member churches of the World Council. Realizing that the way we use words eventually shapes the way we act, we need to ask "What lies behind this change in terminology? How does it affect our understanding and conduct of the work?"

The 1963 Mexico City meeting of the Commission on World Mission and Evangelism gave wide currency to the concept of mission in six continents. Commission members rejoiced that the task of missions had succeeded. The church now flourished on all six continents. But they were uncomfortable at the thought that missions in the plural reminded the Asian, African, and Latin American members of an era in which their continents were the only targets of the thrust of one-way missions from north to south, and an era in which missions was primarily the business of professional, dedicated, expatriated Christians from the north rather than the primary business of all Christians in every country in every continent.

However, the concern expressed by the change in name was not only geographical. There was also the concensus that instead of missions being a task or function of the church, the church is mission. It exists by mission as fire exists by burning. Therefore, everything the church does is mission also, whether it is preaching, teaching, serving, witnessing, or fellowshiping. Instead of sending missionaries, the church in its totality is sent in mission. Missionaries became "fraternal workers" placed at the disposal of the needy churches along with the resources formerly committed to extending the gospel and building the church at the frontiers.

The effects of the change in direction are visible. If everything is mission, nothing is mission. The word mission was so broad that it became meaningless. The absorption of missionary work into the general ministry of the church obscured the priority of evangelism. Missionaries from the mainline denominations decreased in numbers (forty percent in some places), while the number of missionaries sent by evangelical agencies which put a priority on evangelism have increased ninety-five percent. Where there is a vision, the work grows; where there is no vision, the people perish.

Church or Parachurch?

Which is the proper agency for carrying out the missions mandate? The rapid proliferation of mission agencies — 362 new ones listed in North America since 1950 with a growing proportion of them independent of any church — raises concern over unnecessary duplication of structures and the consequent drain on qualified personnel. It appears that parachurch agencies do a commendable and legitimate work in Bible translation, production and distribution, and other specialized ministries that assist and support the church in its mission function. But what about the task of church planting? May this be done properly and effectively by an organization that is structured alongside of, and independent of, the church?

The Orthodox Presbyterian Church struggled with this problem when it first became a separated church. In November of 1936 the Second General Assembly of the Presbyterian Church of America (which became the Orthodox Presbyterian Church) noted the existence of the Independent Board for Presbyterian Foreign Missions and decided to commend it to the church for support rather than to establish a denominational missions agency.

However, the Third General Assembly meeting in June 1937 judged that the Independent Board was moving in the direction of independency rather than Presbyterianism in church government, and decided to establish a denominational agency to carry out the church's work of foreign missions.

The structure assumed by missions agencies has a definite bearing on the work they do, especially if their primary function is church planting. Because the personnel of such agencies have a strong commitment to missions, they often adopt an organizational structure modeled on business and geared for efficiency. This promises accomplishment of established goals; but it also brings problems.

An obvious difficulty is teaching biblical church government while modeling a nonbiblical organizational structure. In addition, wrong structures contribute to church-mission tensions on the field as well as at home. Such tensions are usually and correctly blamed on wrong attitudes — especially on the part of missionaries. But bad structures foster wrong relationships. The biblical principles of oversight by elders chosen by the body of believers and the parity of eldership may not be violated without paying a price.

At issue really is the biblical doctrine of the church. Christ, the Lord of the church, has given the Spirit to form, indwell, and equip his church, which is the Body, to be his fulness. It is through the church that God makes known everywhere his manifold wisdom in the uniting of people from all races and languages into one Body. Through the Spirit Christ endows his church with life, power, and gifts to fulfill his calling and commanded function. The risen Lord also orders his church through the gifts and callings he has ordained. Elders are given the oversight. Missionary society or field missions structured on a business model distort the fellowship of the Spirit and disturb the unity of the Body.

It is imperative for us to follow the Lord's teaching on the true nature of the church, its characteristics, government, and function. When the church itself is doing the work of missions, organized according to the biblical norms and recognizing the true unity of the church through the Spirit, then the dominance/dependence syndrome will be terminated. No artificial distinction will be raised between churches and sending agencies. The church in every area will have the recognized responsibility to be a missionary church, a sending agency, with the gifts and callings of Christ to fulfill the mandate for missions. Proper relationships and right attitudes will flourish in the fellowship of the Spirit. All Christians, at home and abroad, will be accepted as members of the one church, each serving in his particular place by the appointment of the Head of the church for the sake of the growth of the one church, which is his Body.

NOTE

The material for this article appeared in the December 1982/March 1983 *New Horizons in the Orthodox Presbyterian Church.*

Lendall H. Smith

23 Taiwan and the Cross-Cultural Challenge

A S CHILDREN GROWING UP on the east coast of the United States it was brought to our attention (just how I don't seem to recall!) as we dug holes in the dirt that we could eventually tunnel all the way through the earth and come out on the other side in China! Initially such information was received with the appropriate incredulity, but upon being reassured of its accuracy there followed a spate of enthusiastic and intense digging. Although the hope of tunneling through to China dissipated rather rapidly (maybe within five minutes?) for obvious reasons, the image of life on the other side of the world did not vanish from our imaginations so quickly. It was difficult to conceive what life must be like on the other side of the world. This was a topic of lively conversation on the playground. Did people on the other side of the world live upside down? If so, how did they walk, eat or sleep?

As I recall, our curiosity in those childhood days never prompted us to investigate the matter of cultural differences. It just seemed common sense that life on the other side of the globe must somehow be radically different from what we were familiar with. Never did it enter my wildest imagination that approximately a third of a century later I would be on a plane on my way to live in the Orient! I was about to discover firsthand that our childhood suspicions of life on the other side of the earth were not totally inaccurate.

Of course, in the interim we were able to acquire additional knowledge about life on our planet and had become pretty well convinced that the people in the Far East didn't walk on their hands or upside down! As we began to make specific preparations for going to the mission field, we read

books on Chinese culture and received some introductory linguistic training. These were efforts to minimize the initial shock one often experiences
as he steps into a new culture. That initial feeling of helplessness can be
as devastating as having your legs unexpectedly pulled out from under you.
Yet, in our experience it was not the immediate shock that has proven to
be the most difficult. Instead, it has been a kind of cultural radiation
emanating from a radically different approach to living which has challenged almost everything we took for granted in our own culture.

These cultural contrasts are evident in simple gestures. As Americans
we used our index finger to motion for someone to come. The palm of the
hand is up and the index finger is first straightened and then curled up in
beckoning someone to come to us. We used that gesture once to urge some
children to come to us only to watch them flee in horror. It was much
later we discovered that they probably did not flee out of fear of us as
foreigners or because of a natural shyness but partially because the gesture
is used here to symbolize someone who has died or is about to! The gesture
used to motion someone to come is an extended arm and a waving of the
hand with the palm of the hand toward the ground. It is an action very
similar to that used by a young child in the States waving good-bye. At
least that is how it appeared to us on a couple of occasions when some
friends "waved" to us. We simply waved back and continued merrily on
our way.

A reverse order is also manifested in the writing of names, addresses,
and dates. In America the given name comes before the family name, but
in China it is just the reverse. My name in Chinese became Smith Lendall
Mr. Once on a trip in the Orient I called to reconfirm my return flight to
Taiwan. The clerk informed me that she had no reservation for an L.
Smith. Momentarily, I panicked and registered my disbelief with the clerk.
Evidently, having faced this sitation before she asked me to read the name
as it appeared on the ticket. It read Lendall S. The matter was quickly
resolved as the reservation was listed under Lendall. Just recently this
inversion of names was impressed upon us again when we were discussing
with a couple of newly arrived young people from the States the possibility
of visiting the Chiang Kai Shek memorial. One of them said he would
like very much to see Mr. Shek's memorial (read Mr. Chiang's memorial).
It sounds funny to us now, but it reminded us how opposite things can be.

Addresses are likewise written just inversely from the American style of
writing the house number, street, city, state, and country. When we
received letters from the States at our first address, the envelopes always
had been written on by someone in the post office in rearranging the
numbers to assist the mailman in delivering the mail to the right address.
In the same way dates are written beginning with the year, then the month,
and ending with the day. The system is simple. It begins with the largest

unit and works down to the smallest. It just happens to be opposite the system in the west!

In the mundane affairs of living one encounters many antipodal practices. For example, umbrellas are used here as much in the sunshine as they are used in the rain. The reason is that white complexion is beautiful and a tan is not. On a couple of occasions my colleagues, the Marshalls, have been scolded roundly for exposing the delicate skin of their fair-haired daughters to the hot rays of the sun by letting them go swimming in the middle of the day. Basically, people (especially young ladies) make sure they cover up well to protect themselves from the rays of the sun and keep their skin from getting any darker.

There are numerous traffic patterns which vary radically from what we are used to even though driving is on the right side of the road as in the west. My colleague, Steve Hake, has likened the use of the horn here to a kind of radar enabling the driver to weave through the traffic and arrive at his destination. A "right-of-way" concept in driving is practically nonexistent. The size of the vehicle usually determines who has the right of way, especially in making left-hand turns across the flow of traffic!

In the home the wife is expected to go to the market and wash the family clothes every day. To buy extra groceries and store them in the refrigerator to cook another day shows the wife is lazy and thoughtless of her family by serving them "stale" vegetables. Even what you buy to serve your family reflects contrasting cultural values. The best parts of the chicken are thought to be the legs, neck, and wings. Chicken breasts are regarded as the inferior meat. Although Chinese cuisine is touted as being the world's most popular, what is eaten for breakfast is usually excepted. Bean-curd milk, or rice gruel with pickled cabbage, dried shredded pork, and peanuts hardly qualifies as a breakfast menu in our minds.

In the area of special ceremonies we also find opposite tendencies. In the first place special ceremonies almost always are planned according to the lunar calendar. On one occasion a fellow with whom I had become acquainted invited me to a feast to celebrate his moving into his new house. We never could come to a common understanding on the date as I basically use the solar calendar and didn't consciously keep up with the lunar calendar. He had no idea what day it was according to the solar calendar. We resolved it by figuring out the feast would be held on a Thursday two weeks from that day.

Another major difference about ceremonies such as weddings or funerals is the atmosphere of these events. My experiences in the States have been that a spirit of solemnity and quiet was expected to give dignity and respect to these occasions. However, expectations here are quite the opposite. Unless the event is "hot and noisy" it is not very significant. My wife and I were hurrying to make it to the chapel on time to perform a wedding ceremony. We were already ten minutes late. We rushed into the chapel only to find it empty except for some young people (dressed in jeans) practicing a song they were going to sing in the wedding ceremony a few minutes later. Only when the bride makes her entrance do the majority of the guests come in and sit down. In this case as the bride was about to come down the short aisle there was a general hubbub at the front of the auditorium in trying to make sure the groom's relatives were seated in the proper places! Non-Christian weddings do not have any kind of service so that the significant part of the wedding is a "hot and noisy" feast. Also, in China all the wedding expenses are paid for by the bridegroom's family!

Funeral ceremonies are likewise starkly different. Ordinary funeral services here are carried out by amplified incantations accompanied by the blaring of horns, beating of drums, and the wailing of paid mourners over a period of a couple of days. A professional clown troupe is invited to perform for the family to take their mind off their grief. Unless a funeral is "hot and noisy" the family has not really been filial to the deceased.

Other ceremonies are likewise evaluated. A few years ago my neighbor was traveling in Australia during the Christmas season. Upon his return to Taiwan I asked him how his trip was. His first comment was that he felt Christmas was not very significant because it was not very "hot and noisy." He concluded that Christianity could not be as important as Taiwan's religions since their religious festivals were much more "hot and noisy" than the celebration of Christmas.

In the field of language one also encounters many opposite tendencies. In the first place, the language itself is non-phonetic and the system of writing is from left to right and vertical. Books open at the back and end at the front. But it is in the use of language that one runs into communication problems. Consider the following simple dialogue in which an observation is made followed by a question expecting a negative response:

"I don't think you understood what I said, did you?"

"Yes."

"Oh! You did?"

"No!"

"Then, why did you say yes?"

"I said, Yes, because I agreed with you. I didn't understand what you said."

"Oh! I understand."

In the use of polite forms of expression one encounters vast differences. Consider this Christian wedding scene in which the ceremony is coming to a conclusion and the bride's father, according to the local custom, is about to make a few appropriate remarks on this auspicious occasion. Robert Bolton in his book, *Treasure Island*, translates the father's remarks:

It is little brother's great happiness today to have this fine, strong, healthy and intelligent young man from such an illustrious family as the bridegroom to my lazy, good-for-nothing, dumb-as-a-cow daughter . . . (p. 2)

In my own experience I have tried to express my thanks to a family for a delicious feast only to be told by the wife she doesn't know how to cook and apologized for such a poor meal. On another occasion a comment was made on the comeliness of a family's little daughter only to have the mother respond that she was ugly and dumb.

All of these responses differ radically from what we would normally anticipate in our culture, but they are common examples of Taiwanese politeness. It has been suggested that a long-standing fear of flattery, which the Taiwanese call a "smiling tiger," partially accounts for this tendency to respond in a self-deprecating way. When I asked people about this matter, one person suggested that to say 'thank you' implies you agree with the compliment given and is an expression of conceit. So the traditional Chinese way to be polite is to respond in the negative. If someone comes to your house and you ask him if he would like some tea, he will likely say, "That's not necessary." As Daniel Hung, a pastor friend in Taiwan, has pointed out, "He means yes." In respect to courtesy it should also be noted that whereas in the west it has customarily been "ladies first" in the Orient the order is definitely reversed!

In this enumeration of cultural differences we haven't even begun to scratch the tip of the proverbial iceberg. Indeed the examples given are superficial and are only meant to give a sample of antipodal cultural experiences a western missionary faces as he lives in an oriental culture. Yet, it is obvious that there is a veritable collision of cultures in almost every aspect of life. At a retreat for missionaries and national pastors the participants gather for a group picture. The photographer (usually it is the missionary who has the camera!) calls on every one to smile because it will make the picture more attractive and meaningful. But the local workers remain sober knowing that a photo of people with silly grins plastered on their faces is frivolous and unbecoming.

When cultural collisions take place they can produce various results. Sometimes, as I have already suggested in the examples given, they are funny and lead to a good laugh. (A sense of humor is a necessary qualification for all cross-cultural workers.) At other times they become for the foreigner a source of irritation, such as traffic patterns or procedures of resolving difficulties, all which can produce a feeling of frustration and anger. Many times misinterpreted cultural differences, such as the tendency of Chinese to smile or laugh at a near tragedy, creates annoyances.

As these cultural confrontations take place the missionary realizes how much he is a servant to his own cultural background. I had real difficulty just learning to like the water (tea) served at room temperature which

most Chinese give their guests. In the first place I had a biblical aversion
to lukewarm water. It should normally be spit out of the mouth (Rev
3:16). More than that it was my custom to quench my thirst with ice
water, even though our Taiwanese helper in the home reminded me it
would be better for me to drink tepid or hot water. I have gradually learned
to adjust, but at the same time more and more people here are drinking
cold drinks so that there has been a pleasant resolution of my dilemma.

A missionary must constantly evaluate his own lifestyle and practices to
determine what he needs to (wants to?) preserve and what he should
change. Decorating a tree and the house for celebrating Christmas brings
about a variety of interesting responses. Some have said, "Beautiful!" (We
thought it looked quite nice ourselves.) Others have said, "Strange!"
(Objectively, I did have to admit that a tree with lights, colored bulbs,
and tinsel on it in the middle of the living room didn't make a lot of sense
and was more cultural than Christian. My one consolation was that it
wasn't a *plastic* tree and we could make good use of the tree later on in the
year to beautify our yard!) Perhaps the classic response was the little boy
who, upon seeing the Hakes' Christmas tree, said, "Next year, my Mom
said, we would have a bigger tree than that!" (A revealing cultural comment, especially so, as Steve went on to explain that the family was
planning to put up the tree for the Chinese New Year!)

Living in another culture presents a multi-faceted challenge. First, an
individual is confronted by a whole different way of thinking and doing
things. As I have tried to illustrate very simply, many things are directly
opposite from the way we have learned them in our own culture. My wife
went to the farmer to buy strawberries, and he quoted her a price for a
kilogram of hulled berries. Remembering our past days in New Jersey
when we could pick our own berries much cheaper than buying them from
the stand she asked how much a kilogram of berries would be if she picked
them herself. The price was fifty percent more than the berries already
picked and hulled! The farmer could hire pickers and make more money
than by allowing people to pick their own and ruin his fields in the process.
What a difference the context makes!

In the second place, the foreigner realizes how much he has been molded
by his own culture and often finds it difficult to accept and adjust to the
different cultural practices that confront him each day. Frankly, I still find
it irritating to be asked by nearly everyone how much I had to pay for
everything even though I know it serves a practical social need and is
based upon a totally different concept of privacy.

The missionary realizes he cannot divorce himself from his own cultural
background, but at the same time is aware that his purpose and goals do
not allow him to ignore his cultural context. Effective communication of
the gospel is hindered if the missionary's evangelism remains enshrouded
in an alien western style. That is the ultimate challenge: the effective

cross-cultural communication of the good news of God's salvation in Christ. The messenger of the gospel is concerned that his life be a reflection of the gospel he has come to proclaim. He must be flexible and adopt many new patterns in his life. He is aware that sin has not only affected western culture but Chinese culture, too. The gospel changes both and he needs to live in such a way that it will be fleshed out in his life. This is important because the context out of which a missionary speaks makes a difference in the way he is heard.

In our present world there continues to be a growing interaction of cultures. In many cases, our cities and communities have become increasingly international. As the church seeks to carry out our Lord's mandate all of us may be forced to examine critically our cultural backgrounds and look for effective ways to communicate the gospel cross-culturally. It takes humility, sensitivity, and patience to cross cultural boundaries. Yet, in spite of cross-cultural differences and conflicts we will increasingly be able to discern the purpose of the living God in bringing our lives more and more into conformity with his will revealed through Christ his Son and be more effective in proclaiming his glory among all the nations.

Victor B. Atallah

24 Where Are We Going in Missions?

THE ORTHODOX PRESBYTERIAN CHURCH began as a result of concern for foreign missions. It was the faithful stand of Machen and his colleagues in the Presbyterian Church (USA) against the indiscriminate support of unbelieving missionaries which ultimately led to censure, rejection, and consequently the establishing of the new church. The issue was Christ's uniqueness, finality, and authority as the only Savior and hope for mankind. The mother church sent out (and still does) missionaries who were enchanted by "attractive" elements in the religions and cultures of the people to whom they were to proclaim the gospel of God's saving grace. Some even publicly denied the need for Christian faith among the people of the world. They had come to the conclusion that other faiths were of equal value and that the Christ of the Bible was not the only savior.

Machen and his followers chose to stand for the finality and sufficiency of Christ at all costs. They wrote and spoke against the unbelieving trends in the church and the lack of discipline on the mission field. Commitment to the church's standards seemed even less an obligation for missionaries who were far away and usually under serious pressures to compromise. As Machen saw things, nothing less than the integrity of the gospel was at stake. His zeal for the biblical Christ and his love for the lost led him to stand for truth and the purity of the church. The OPC was established when the mother church decided to discipline not unbelievers but believers, not those that betrayed Christ but those that stood for him and with him.

Where Have We Been?

The vitality and strength of a church can be measured by its commitment to and zeal for the proclamation of the "whole counsel of God."

From the very beginning the OPC has been missions oriented. Even when its congregations were very small and struggling and many of its pastors had to find extra work to support their families, the OPC sacrificially called and sent out missionaries to proclaim the gospel and plant faithful churches in other lands. There are at least three major facts we can observe about OPC foreign missions involvement.

First, the OPC contribution in the area of foreign missions far exceeded its size. Just as in the area of biblical and theological scholarship, the OPC was a giant in its foreign missions impact. The relatively young, small, and often struggling denomination played a major and sometimes amazing role in founding solid, indigenous Reformed churches in various parts of the world. A case in point is Korea. One frequently meets Korean believers who quickly point to their original OP missions roots. In fact, the Korean church has become much larger than the OPC itself. There are also significant fruits for OP endeavors in Japan, Taiwan, Eritrea, Ethiopia, Kenya, Lebanon, and Egypt. Because of the OPC, the faith is being proclaimed throughout the world!

Second, we notice that OPC foreign missions have been characterized by biblical devotion. In this connection one notes in praise to God's grace the consistency and fervent commitment to the historic faith of the Scriptures among OP missionaries. Implementing God-centered evangelism, building healthy Reformed churches, providing solid biblical training, and arousing zeal for the gospel has been the agenda. These fundamental elements coupled with the strategy of indigenization formed the basis for effectiveness on the different fields.

Of course, one ought to keep in mind the fact that quality missions cannot be detached from quality missionaries. Some of our early pioneer missionaries are counted among the most outstanding. Their devotion to the Lord, high regard for his inerrant Word, and godly living serve as models of true service to Christ. Their humble and sacrificial service demonstrated remarkable love for sinners and the warmest compassion for the the lost.

Indeed, their effectiveness discredits the claims and theories of the modern contextualizers and missiologists. Their reliance was on God's sure promises and their confidence was in the power of the Holy Spirit; they did not desire to put their trust in man or seek men by means of "tricks or gimmicks." They overcame "because of the blood of the lamb and because of the word of their testimony." Surely, here is the quality of missions and missionaries Machen fought to preserve.

Third, OP foreign missions have been truly ecumenical. Significantly, OP missionaries have not sought to establish carbon-copy Orthodox Presbyterian churches. This fact directly challenges the accusations that the church is rigid and narrow. In mission work the OPC has demonstrated a marvelous farsighted vision of the catholicity of the believing church.

The indigenous churches were encouraged to chart their own course by applying the guiding principles of Scripture. This should never be understood as compromise or weakness; rather it manifests maturity and strength.

If true ecumenicity were to mean organizational unity, it would be nothing more than a wishful thought. Instead, it means spiritual oneness: unity of commitment to the truth, unity in bringing glory and honor to the Triune God, unity in carrying out his commission to the rest of the world. This unity is guaranteed by the fact that "the gospel is the power of God unto salvation to everyone who believes," regardless of race, language, and culture.

Furthermore, this kind of ecumenism has not been limited to relationships with churches OP missionaries planted. It extends the hand of cooperation to all who are committed to the Reformed faith. This spirit of cooperation and openness explains why OP foreign missions receive such enthusiastic support from outside the denomination.

Where Are We Going?

The last few years have brought about significant challenges and changes on the missionary scene. The socio-political events following the Second World War have slowly yet steadily given rise to new and deep concerns, different from those that confronted our predecessors. These concerns have forced the Christian church to reexamine its strategy in order to seek new answers for new questions. The evangelicals were generally caught unprepared for this situation. Superficial and other-worldly easy-believism gave birth to radicalism. Consequently, zeal to bring the gospel to the lost gradually gave in to an activism that capitalized on such matters as the desire to feed the poor and proclaim human rights. The gospel of God's grace was reinterpreted in socio-economic and political terms.

Ironically the diminishing number of career missionaries and mission endeavors accompanies the growth and strength of the new "this-worldly" mission. Still, even more ironical is the decline of interest in theological and biblical scholarship and the growing enthusiasm for "pop" theology and the trendy theories of the missiologists.

Is the OPC immune to these dangers? Hardly! In the first place, in recent years the OPC has become more and more attracted to the broadly evangelical movement. Indicative of this direction is the "evangelicalization" of Westminster Seminary, a drift that began in the mid-sixties and gained strength in the seventies. More and more of its graduates, coming into the OPC, enter from the ranks of the evangelicals who have only Calvinistic interests.

As a result, Reformed distinctives have grown less and less popular, so much so that I have encountered sneers and ridicule regarding those distinctives. Some who hold firmly to the Reformed faith have been labeled "hard-liners," negative, and unevangelistic. I am aware of cases where men have been by-passed for pastoral opportunities, from what I can tell, because of the strength of their Reformed commitment. Also there is a creeping tendency to equate activism and participation in the new "church-growth" agenda with being evangelistic and effective, regardless of the theology and consequences of this approach. Naturally the closer we are to the evangelical camp, the more attractive its concerns, especially when such concerns sound global and all-encompassing. This can be called "the evangelical panorama factor."

In the second place, the OPC has been haunted by a reputation for rigidity, nit-picking, and narrowness of vision. The careful and cautious posture the OPC enjoyed in dealing with important issues of doctrine and practice was often viewed negatively by a few within and many outside the church, especially in evangelical circles. This reputation was there from the start, when both liberals and evangelicals in the mother church labeled the new church "separatist," "divisive," "narrow-minded," etc. This can be called "the intimidation factor"!

In the third place, the OPC has always had difficulty explaining its small size. We might call this the "size inferiority complex," productive of a "size paranoia." A commonly repeated quote from an assembly of a sister church illustrates the condition: the OPC is called "the little sister with a big mouth." This description has been used repeatedly within the denomination to silence discussion of problems in other churches. Conversely, the idea of the new church-growth movement can be increasingly applauded. So much then for the "size-paranoia" factor!

How does all of this relate to OP foreign missions? From my point of view, the answer is crystal clear. The evangelical panorama factor, together with the intimidation and size-paranoia factors have brought the neo-evangelical missiology perspective of world evangelization onto our doorsteps. In fact, in my opinion, it has already entered through the door. The new queen of sciences, i.e. missiology, looks like the light at the end of the tunnel. She brings with her all the methods, means, ideas, and dreams of growing beyond our size, our negative reputation, and our narrow identity as those committed to a fossilized form of the faith! Yes, we are told that we need to broaden our horizons and shake loose our ancient shells in order to get on the mythological boat of world evangelization.

Fashion has changed: theology is out, contextualization is in. We must feel guilty about past and present successes since we did little more than bring a decadent western Calvinistic theology to the unreached. But now we know better. Those to be reached can do their own theologizing! We ought to help them and encourage them to "do theology" which fits their own sacred cultures! All theology past and present, especially that found in the confession, must be dumped since it is western and therefore suspect. All cultures are beautiful and sacred except "damned" and horrible western culture. It seems that to dismiss any theological concept as irrelevant it is sufficient to label it "western." Every group must have its own theology. The new loci boast a "theology of the poor" and even a "theology of the rich," etc.

Part and parcel of this evangel is an emphasis on "cross-cultural" communication. Biblical understanding is conditioned by cultural awareness and sensitivity. Furthermore, missiology (or cultural anthropology), this new queen of the sciences, governs all other biblical and theological studies. Of course, it is a matter of degrees, but the further one "missiologizes" the higher he is lifted and elevated above the Scriptures. So, if we "missiologize" enough we can graduate to the level where the soteriological nature of the work of Christ is "hopelessly" Pauline and Jewish and consequently without universal value; it too is "culturally conditioned." The conclusion is plain: Machen and his fellow servants of Christ were wrong in objecting to the form of the gospel carried by unbelieving missionaries. The new prophets, i.e., the missiologists, have determined Scripture's meaning and tell us of its culturally conditioned limits.

For us who hold so dear those precious doctrines of grace, our response is clear: there is one gospel, there is one Bible, there is one Savior, there is one fallen race and there is one body of believers elect from every nation, tongue, and kindred. Therefore, it is humble commitment to the Word of God and fervent zeal to proclaim Christ who alone is the Savior and hope of all nations that constitutes the foundation of missions. Theories and missiological fantasies have at best distracted people from the glorious Savior and produced a shallow form of faith. If missiology is a mere exercise in speculation about cultural anthropology, if it becomes our *guide*, it is no more than a mythology at variance with a true missiology that always generates more love of the Bible and zeal to bring the gospel to the lost.

Let us carry on our foreign mission endeavors in the spirit of Machen, holding fast to the truth which transcends all time and culture.

John P. Galbraith

25 The Ecumenical Vision of the Orthodox Presbyterian Church

WITHIN HOURS OF ITS BIRTH on June 11, 1936, the eyes of the Orthodox Presbyterian Church were lifted from the level of its own existence, and the potential of an introverted life, by telegrams of greeting from the Synod of the Christian Reformed Church and the Reformed Episcopal Church (*Minutes*, First General Assembly, p. 15).

It would be hoped that in the course of time our Reformed view of the world and of Christ's church would have prevented us from developing our own provincial little world. But the God who had led us into a separate existence saw to it that we should be reminded without delay that we are not to be alone, and that we are not the sole repository of truth. Not only would he be with us, but so would his people who are outside our own denomination; not only are we one with him, but also we are one with his people wherever they are: "Ye are all one in Christ Jesus" (Gal 3:28).

Further, such a vision is not only promise, but responsibility, since Jesus prayed for the perfecting of what was not yet perfect: "that they all may be one, as thou, Father, art in me, and I in thee" (John 17:21), and since 1 Cor 12:12 instructs us, that "the body is one, and has many members, and all the members of that body, being many, are one body." No member of the body is sufficient unto himself, but "the members should have the same care one for another"(1 Cor 12:25). The "ecumenical vision" is a vision of the unity of the church in the true Christian faith. It has been one of the prominent visions of the Orthodox Presbyterian Church throughout its history. Those who have labeled us "isolationist" or "sectarian," as some have, simply do not know our history.

411

All of this was brought before us by the telegrams to our First General Assembly, especially by that of the Christian Reformed Church, which invited us to send a fraternal delegate to their synod. But in a very real way their initiative in extending their greetings and invitation was also a response. They had followed the struggle of J. Gresham Machen and others in the Presbyterian Church (USA) during the "fundamentalist/ modernist" controversies of the late twenties and the early thirties, and they had invited Dr. Machen to speak to them on various occasions. But perhaps more importantly, when Westminster Theological Seminary was being formed no less than three men ultimately came to its faculty from the bosom of the Christian Reformed Church— R. B. Kuiper, Cornelius Van Til, and Ned B. Stonehouse. Even before the OPC was born God was preparing to teach us the oneness of his church throughout the world.

However, if we were born to a heritage that held to the worldwide ("ecumenical") oneness of Christ's body, we were also born into an environment in which, for many evangelical Christians, "ecumenical" had become a bad word. As so frequently happens, liberals had taken a perfectly good word with an authentic biblical denotation, and had so abused and distorted the use that its connotation was completely changed. For the liberals "ecumenical" literally meant worldwide, and there were few and not very obvious theological requirements on fellowship in the movement. Fundamentalists rightly rejected such fellowship, but with it, the word that had come to describe it. To them "ecumenical" meant National Council of Churches (and later World Council of Churches) and liberal theology.

This put our new church in a difficult position. We were in disfavor with the ecumenists: they regarded us as schismatics since we refused to have fellowship with some churches that regarded themselves as Christian. At the same time, if we had expressed our convictions on interchurch fellowship in terms of "ecumenicity," we would have been misunderstood by our fundamentalist brothers and sisters. Given the new distorted meaning of the term, one could hardly have blamed them. At any rate, our new church avoided the word until 1946 when it sent Ned B. Stonehouse as an observer to the founding meeting of the Reformed Ecumenical Synod. Note that even then "ecumenical" was limited by *Reformed*. But in 1949 the general assembly established a Committee on Ecumenicity without any limiting adjective; the present Committee on Ecumenicity and Interchurch Relations is the successor to that committee. Since that time we have sought, admittedly less strenuously than the task requires, but with as much as we could give it, to restore the biblical meaning to the use of that word.

Our church was born into another environmental hazard. It was a day when, due to the growth of liberalism in large and older Protestant denominations, independency began to flower. A spirit of anti-denomina-

tionalism— the very opposite of the concept of the oneness of the body
— was abroad. People from the denominations that were defecting from
the gospel were defecting from those denominations to form congregations
independent of any denominational affiliation or responsibility. Others,
remaining in the denominations began forming with the independents,
non-denominational (sometimes mistakenly labeled "interdenominational") societies especially for sending out foreign missionaries whose faith
they could trust. Today such societies are called "para-church." To such
people a new denomination was suspect simply because it was a denomination.

Thus the environment of our birthday was one of contradictions or, at
least, of opposite-pulling tensions. On the one hand were the liberals who,
in the name of the unity or oneness of the church, were willing to bring
together churches that called themselves Christian, regardless of their
attitude toward the gospel. On the other hand were those for whom no
church was good enough, no denomination could be trusted, and for whom
a vision of the oneness of Christ's body was almost totally lacking. There
was also a peculiar irony: whereas liberal churches retained their creeds
but ignored them wholesale with the motto "no creed but Christ," many
independent fundamentalists, also rejecting creeds — though for very
different reasons— were saying the same thing.

Here then came the upstart new church in disfavor with both the
extreme left and extreme right. It held vigorously to a creed as the summary
of the teaching of the Word of God. It held also to the oneness of the
church. Both of these propositions were being denied by the independents.
The liberals denied the first and refused to define the second biblically.
The OPC could not but be aware of such judgments and sought to face
up to them and evaluate them in the light of the Word of God. [If there
is one thing that has characterized the Orthodox Presbyterian Church
throughout its history it is its commitment, even its compulsion, to deal
with all our problems by seeking first the will of God in his Word. If one
is looking for ironies he might say that we see the weakness of all traditions,
but we find strength in our tradition of searching the Scriptures to prove
all things. However, it must be recognized that, in the last analysis, that
"tradition" is not a tradition but a requirement of Scripture itself— "Study
. . .", 2 Tim 2:15; "Search . . .", John 5:39.]

At the time of the First General Assembly, obviously no extensive study
had been made on the principles of church *unity*. Our focus in the years
prior to the founding of our church had been on *separateness*, albeit in the
interest of establishing the biblical principle that true Christian unity lies
in a relationship of living branches to the true Vine, which is Christ. But
the obligation of Christian unity was so apparent at that first assembly
that it quickly decided not only to respond to the Christian Reformed
Synod's invitation to send a fraternal delegate to them (Dr. Cornelius Van
Til) but also to "initiate and conduct . . . correspondence with other

churches throughout the world holding the Reformed system" (*Minutes*, p. 20).

In the years that have passed, various brief statements relating to the unity of the church and interchurch relations have appeared, always in connection with relationships with specific ecumenical situations. The first arose in the Twelfth (1945) General Assembly, occasioned by an invitation to join the American Council of Christian Churches. The second came in the Twenty-eighth General Assembly in 1961, brought about by discussions with the Christian Reformed Church. Consonant with usual practice neither statement was formally adopted by the assembly. They have, however, served as *de facto* guidelines for our ecumenical relations until the present time. Because of their importance they appear as appendixes at the end of this article. Another committee, the Committee on Ecumenicity and Interchurch Relations, now, after exactly 25 years, is preparing a supplement to those principles for the Fifty-third (1986) General Assembly as part of its report concerning an invitation to join the Presbyterian Church in America.

It would be fair to say, as one looks over the entire history of our relationship with other churches, including the time before the 1961 statement, that we have endeavored to walk the fine line between indiscriminate ecumenism and indiscriminate sectarianism. The pursuit of this endeavor has taken us into fruitful relationships outside our own church. Some have been with individual churches and others have been in interdenominational bodies. As would be expected, the principles also kept us out of some relationships, but also we have not sought to establish relationships that the principles require us to seek.

Basically, those principles enunciate as a goal the union of churches of like faith insofar as possible— with language and the other difficulties of communication being regarded as the chief obstacles to union with churches of other nations. So, direct relationships with individual churches and membership in interdenominational bodies are an effort to resolve differences and thereby open the way to union where the conditions of communication make that practicable. Those principles may be said to lead to the conclusion that ideally, just as all of the true believers throughout the world are the true body, the one body, of Christ, that oneness should be manifested in the fullest possible way. That goal is no small thing in the mind of God. Jesus not only prayed that the church's oneness become more perfect, but he also gives reasons (John 17:23): "that they may be made perfect in one, and that the world may know that thou has sent me, and hast loved them, as thou hast loved me." We know that all believers are one in Christ, but the *world* does not, and we should make the body more perfect so that the world, seeing the whole body of Christ, may glorify the one who loved and redeemed them. The ideal, the clearest manifestation of oneness, would be one church, worldwide, in which all members are in subjection to each other (Phil 2:1–3).

As indicated above, there are very real obstacles that lie in the way of that ideal, which no one has yet been able to remove completely. There are also obstacles that lie in the sinful human heart, such as an impaired vision of what God truly wants, such as willfulness, pride, hardness of heart, little love. So, over the years of our church's life we have asked God to improve our vision, to increase our understanding of his Word, and in a little measure we have responded to opportunities for fellowship and have sought to nurture opportunities. Different means have been explored and various means have been attempted to climb over the obstacles, with a variety of results.

The least structured, and therefore the easiest, step toward churches expressing oneness in the body of Christ has been sending fraternal delegates to each other's assemblies. These delegates have conveyed the greetings and Christian interest of one church to another and observed the concerns the other has as it seeks to perform its task for Christ in the world. In this way we have learned from each other. The fraternal delegate system ideally is supposed to enable us also to seek and to give advice. The human heart being what it is, however, we have not found it easy either to seek or to receive advice. The mechanics of the system — how to go about sharing the views between churches that function differently and meet at different times — have been a hindrance. It is better, indeed, to have this system than nothing, but it needs considerable improvement.

Through the years our church has had, and in most cases still has, such a relationship with churches (1) in the United States: the Associate Reformed Presbyterian Church, the Christian Reformed Church, the Korean American Presbyterian Church, the Presbyterian Church in America, the Reformed Presbyterian Church of North America, and the Reformed Church in the United States, and (2) in other countries: the Canadian Reformed Churches, two Presbyterian Churches of Korea (Kosin and Hap Dong), the Reformed Church in Japan, the Reformed Churches of Australia, and the Reformed Churches of New Zealand.

For a period of twenty years, 1954–1973, another degree of relationship was held with the Gereformeerde Kerken in Nederland (GKN). It was a "sister church" relationship, which indicated full communion between the churches— approval of one another's membership, officers, and discipline — implying that if the churches were in one country they would become one church. It is the closest relationship between churches yet devised, implying full trust in one another, short of full union. However, over the course of those years the GKN became an entirely different church from what it had been. Doors in the GKN were opened to theological heresy of the most basic kind, relating even to Scripture and the atonement. They also entered fully into the mixed fellowship of the World Council

of Churches, and various sorts of immoral conduct came to be first tolerated, then openly approved. Our church's trust in the GKN was gradually
eroded and ultimately destroyed. Our church sought, through correspondence— the only avenue open to us— to admonish and persuade the GKN
concerning what we regarded as grievous sin, but to no avail. This experience brought us to realize that however close, formally, a relationship
may be it cannot be fruitful unless the partners have hearts willing to listen
and heed.

Within a church, when defections from truth or right occur, and instruction has no effect, the church has authority to effect discipline, even to
the final extreme of excommunication. But interchurch relationships —
relationships *between* churches — do not permit that. The only recourse
that the offended church has is to terminate the relationship and leave
the other church to go its own way. It was that course that our church
finally followed, after long and patient dealings, in 1974. The lesson was
driven home that although there are imperfections in each church, the
perfecting of the church must include a unity where we are subject to the
care and authority of one another.

Previously (1942–43) an endeavor at unity with less commitment than
was made with the GKN, had been made. On the background of, on the
one hand, the rightness of union between like churches and, on the other
hand, the practical difficulties of mergers, the Ninth (1942) General
Assembly decided to explore the avenue of a "federation" of churches,
but it would have churches work together in areas of common interest as
they might be willing. At the same time, each church would retain its
own autonomy and authority.

Although this was a step toward greater unity it had certain weaknesses.
Among these was the fact that while the federation would make everyone
responsible for the work that was done, it could neither require anyone to
participate nor enforce correcting measures where correction was required.
To accomplish those ends each church would have to relinquish some of
its autonomy, which was asking a great deal at that stage of ecumenical
thinking. Leaving the federation would be a church's only solution to
serious problems.

A committee of that Ninth Assembly then met with representatives of
three other churches: Christian Reformed; Reformed Presbyterian, General Synod; and Reformed Presbyterian of North America. These representatives agreed that although they were "in favor of" a federation of
Presbyterian and Reformed denominations "it was not practicable at present" (*Minutes,* Tenth General Assembly, pp. 19–20). There was no suggestion that efforts be made to overcome the obstacles. In the "sister
church" relationship a language-culture-distance problem had been a crucial factor in preventing subjection to one another. In the proposed fed-

eration of strictly American churches there was an unwillingness to try to apply principles that were regarded as valid.

Throughout church history achievement of unity in the church has been an elusive treasure. Failures have been far more common than successes. That has proved to be no less true for the OPC. If the "federation" concept was not attainable, neither were efforts at full union. At different times union with four different churches has been under consideration.

After the failure of the federation in 1943 our church, continuing to recognize its responsibility of unity, moved in 1945 to consult with the Reformed Presbyterian Church, General Synod, about possible union (that church is to be distinguished from the Reformed Presbyterian Church of North America, popularly known as the "Covenanters"). In 1947 this effort also came to an end. Again, not because of principles, but because it was "impractical." That church, however, was able to consummate a union with the Evangelical Presbyterian Church in 1965, forming the Reformed Presbyterian Church, Evangelical Synod.

In 1955 the Christian Reformed Church invited us to confer with them regarding "our ecclesiastical relationship" and in 1959 expressed a desire that "the way may be paved to possible eventual union." It was in the course of these discussions that the 1961 statement on church unity was developed. As the committees continued to meet over the next few years changes were noted in the Christian Reformed Church that our church came to view as increasing obstacles to union. At one time, earlier, differences of polity were judged to be the greatest obstacle; later it became doctrine. Finally, in 1973, the union aspect of our discussions was dropped and the special meetings were discontinued.

Continuing to seek the ultimate in unity our Thirty-second (1965) General Assembly, even while consultations were being held with the Christian Reformed Church, initiated discussions with the new Reformed Presbyterian Church, looking toward union. A plan of union, presented in 1975, was accepted by our general assembly, but rejected by the Reformed Presbyterian Synod. This did not terminate relations between the two churches, and another plan to unite was prepared. But in 1979 the two churches agreed to include the new Presbyterian Church in America (founded in 1973) in consultations, and consideration of the two-way plan was dropped. Subsequently the Presbyterian Church in America at its 1980 general assembly voted to propose to their presbyteries that both the Orthodox Presbyterian Church and the Reformed Presbyterian Church, Evangelical Synod, be invited to join the PCA. The presbyteries approved the proposal for the RPCES, but not for the OPC, and the RPCES accepted the invitation. They formally joined the PCA in 1982. (The 1981 OPC General Assembly voted to propose acceptance of the invitation by the presbyteries but, when the PCA presbyteries did not approve the invitation, the OPC presbyteries did not vote.) In 1983 the joined church voted — general assembly and presbyteries — to invite the OPC to join it. The invitation was presented to our 1984 general assembly and the 1986 assembly is scheduled to vote on it.

Other possible ecumenical ties, on a broader basis, have not eventuated. In 1942 the assembly received an invitation to join a recently-formed American Council of Christian Churches. This was to be a generally evangelical body rather than Reformed. As a result of this invitation the first statement of ecumenical principles by a committee of our church was formulated (see Appendix 1). This organization did seem to be a council of *churches* and that was a favorable aspect, but other considerations outweighed that one characteristic, and we did not join (further information on this matter, for which there is not space here, may be found in *Minutes* of the Ninth through the Seventeenth General Assemblies).

The International Council of Christian Churches also invited the OPC to join it, which we did, on a contingency basis in 1949. The contingencies related to certain constitutional provisions which the assembly regarded as principial and, when the council refused to make the changes, our 1952 general assembly withdrew the OPC from the council.

Another ecumenical organization, the National Association of Evangelicals, received little consideration as a vehicle for a church because, among other things, it was something other than an organization of churches.

Among all of these negatives, however, our persistent search for positives has had two significant rewards which have, in turn, led to others. First, in 1949 our church was received into the membership of the Reformed Ecumenical Synod (RES), which had been founded three years earlier by three churches committed to profess and maintain the Reformed faith, each from a different continent: the Christian Reformed Church (North America), the Reformed Churches in the Netherlands (Europe), and the Reformed Church in South Africa (Africa). Through the subsequent years the RES has demonstrated how far around the world the Reformed faith has reached; it has enabled churches, now in all the world's continents, to express unity in the faith. It has also been a source of enrichment to the member churches as they have shared their spiritual wealth with one another. In recent years the RES is being tested to see if it will continue, as it was designed to do, to profess and maintain the Reformed faith. Whatever the future may hold, the past cannot be taken from it or its churches.

A second positive interchurch relationship is that offered by the North American Presbyterian and Reformed Council (NAPARC), formed in 1976 with our church as a charter member. As a forum for joint study and action it has promoted among Reformed churches of North America both an awareness of each other and a sense of our need for one another. It is the latter that advances the reality of unity in the church and contains hope for further perfecting of that unity in days ahead.

Earlier we said that our statements of biblical principles of church unity set a "goal of union with churches of like faith." The emphasis here is on *union.* It should not go unnoticed, however, that those principles also express oneness, unity, with the *whole* body of Christ. It would indeed be a crippled "unity" if it cut off parts of the body. Our statements of principle thus far have not developed this aspect of unity adequately, and that awaits further exposition. It can be said here only that Jesus' word "one" does not mean "two," nor worse, hundreds. There is one church. All of God's elect trusting in Christ as their one and only Savior are members of that church. As such they should show it in fellowship and mutual care.

Therefore, the fact that one is "Reformed," and others are, say, "Arminian," does not mean that they are not members with us of the one body which is Christ and, thus, of one another. As members of that body with us we have responsibilities to them. They are two-fold: to express our common membership in Christ and our family love for them in every way we can, and to instruct and learn from one another to the end that we may supply to each other what each is lacking in love, faith, knowledge, and obedience.

This much is quite clear so long as we confine our thinking to the relationship between individual Christians. However, we are concerned with the relationships of *churches,* and churches are, as the *Westminster Confession of Faith* says, "more or less pure, according as the doctrine of the Gospel is taught and embraced, ordinances administered, and public worship performed more or less purely within them" (XXV,4). That concept, with which our church has heartily concurred, makes clear that a church's life, just as that of an individual, may not be all that it professes to be. It may, in fact, while still professing to believe, have so departed from purity of faith as to have become "a synagogue of Satan." Obviously no church that wishes to honor Christ may seek fellowship with a "church" that has become Satanic, because no fellowship exists between Christ and Satan.

But which "churches" are synagogues of Satan? and what degrees are there between the pure and the apostate? and how do those degrees regulate our relationships to those churches? We come back to the other two extremes that we posed previously: fellowship with all or with none, no discrimination or sectarian isolation. If both of the latter extremes are contrary to Scripture— as our Church has long accepted— where do we draw the line and how do we decide where to draw it? Difficulty in answering these questions produces a variety of responses. There is no mathematical or contrived formula. Scripture is our formula; we must therefore factor in all the elements that we know to be pertinent, and make a decision that we conscientiously believe to be the biblical formula for each situation.

The principle that perhaps more than any other has guided our inter-church fellowships is taken from the 1945 statement: "In no case may the Orthodox Presbyterian Church in its cooperation with other churches sacrifice, or even compromise, its distinctiveness. Its distinctiveness is its reason for existence." If we believe a thing to be true or right we cannot teach or do what is contrary to it. That is a hard line to follow. But so is Scripture's admonition that we not do evil that good may come. So, in the great variety of relationships that we have sought or been engaged in — federation, organic union, interdenominational bodies, sister relation-ships, or mere fraternal relationships — as well as those from which we have turned away, we have sought to extend our fellowship to the outer-most limits of our commitments of doctrine and life. We have asked ourselves, "May we enter into this fellowship? is it in accord with what we believe Scripture to teach?" If the answer is affirmative, just one response is permissible: we *must* enter this fellowship. The oneness of Christ's body requires it.

The 1961 statement (see Appendix 2), however, while reaffirming the need to retain the distinctiveness of our Reformed character, gave empha-sis to the fact of diversity in the church. After saying that differences between denominations "often manifest a diversity" that should exist in the church for the "enrichment of (its) total witness," and saying that it is possible for a union to impair diversity and impoverish the witness, the statement warns that to avoid union simply because of different historical backgrounds is so contrary "to the biblical evidence in support of union . . . however plausible, (it) must be false."

Throughout our history there has been hardly a year that we have not been dealing with such questions. Some have felt that we have leaned too far on the restrictive side. Yet, if the record is examined carefully, it will be seen that more often than not we have been the ones who would have sought to carry fellowship further in accordance with Scripture. To sum it all up we may say that our ecumenical vision has required us to seek a balance between two poles of duty: to endeavor to effect the unity of the true body of Christ, and to do so without compromising the biblical system of truth which we believe is the faith that we confess.

No doubt, the whole picture is brought together best in Ephesians 4. There we are reminded that there is "one body" (v 2) to which God gives certain ministries (v 11) for the building up of the body of Christ (v 12) until we *attain to unity of the faith* and *knowledge* of the Son of God (v 13). Which is simply to say that yes, there is only one body, one church, but it is not yet perfect; so we search the Scriptures together and as we do so our growing faith and knowledge lead us into more perfect unity. The message is clear: exhibit every last bit of unity with our brothers and sisters that we can find, and strive with all that is in us to make our unity perfect with all of the body "unto the stature of the fulness of Christ" (v 13).

Appendix 1

STATEMENT TO THE TWELFTH GENERAL ASSEMBLY, 1945

Although "the purest churches under heaven are subject both to mixture and error" (Westminster Confession of Faith, XXV,V), the distinction between true churches and false churches is valid, and no cooperation of a true church with a false church in matters of religion is permissible. Just when a given church ceases to be a true church and becomes a synagogue of Satan is sometimes difficult to say, but it can safely be asserted that a church which has officially denied such cardinal truths, to name but a few, as the Holy Trinity, the Deity of Christ, His virgin birth and bodily resurrection, or His headship over the church, has forfeited every claim to the name of a church of Christ. That all cooperation of a truly Christian church with such a church in matters of religion should be entirely out of the question is the plain and emphatic teaching of II Cor. 6:14–18 — "Be ye not unequally yoked together with unbelievers: for what fellowship hath righteousness with unrighteousness? and what communion hath light with darkness? and what concord hath Christ with Belial? or what part hath he that believeth with an infidel? and what agreement hath the temple of God with idols? For ye are the temple of the living God; as God hath said, I will dwell in them, and walk in them; and I will be their God, and they shall be my people. Wherefore come out from among them, and be ye separate, saith the Lord, and touch not the unclean thing; and I will receive you, and will be a Father unto you, and ye shall be my sons and daughters, saith the Lord Almighty."

That this passage does not forbid all association of believers with unbelievers is clear from 1 Cor. 5:9,10 — "I wrote unto you in an epistle not to company with fornicators; yet not altogether with the fornicators of this world, or with the covetous, or extortioners, or with idolaters; for then must ye needs go out of the world." It is just as clear that it is permissible in some instances for believers to be members of the same organization with unbelievers. Abraham entered into a confederacy with Aner, Eshcol and Memre, Canaanite chieftains (Gen. 14:13). And the fact that God himself in his providence brings believers and unbelievers together as citizens of one nation was recognized by the apostle Paul when he made use of his rights as a Roman citizen (e.g., Acts 25:10,11). But the passage II Cor. 6:14–18 does teach unequivocally that believers may not be yoked together with unbelievers in one *religious* organization and may not engage in united *worship* with them. "What agreement hath the temple of God with idols?" We may take it for granted that in The Orthodox Presbyterian Church this principle is regarded as excluding both cooperation with such a church as The Presbyterian Church in the U. S. A. and membership in The Federal Council of the Churches of Christ in America.

On the other hand, cooperation of The Orthodox Presbyterian Church with other truly Reformed churches is not only possible but obligatory. The reference here is to churches which not merely have Reformed standards, but also strive zealously to adhere to these standards. The principle that the visible church and the invisible church are not two churches, but that the former is a manifestation of the latter, and that the visible church must manifest in particular the unity of the invisible church, makes cooperation among truly Reformed churches a solemn duty.

That the principle just named is taught in Scripture permits of no doubt. The very fact that the writers of the New Testament did not take pains to distinguish sharply between the visible church and the invisible, but ordinarily subsumed both under the one term "church" is significant. According to the New Testament the visible church and the invisible are not two distinct entities. On the contrary, there is but one church, and visibility, and invisibility are two aspects of the one church. Therefore what is predicated of the one can frequently be predicated of the other also. The most significant difference between the two is that the one is pure, while the other has an admixture of impurity. But even that difference is an abnormality. Ideally conceived the two are identical. For that reason the visible church must manifest all the attributes of the invisible. The fact that in this dispensation it never does so to the point of perfection does not detract one iota from this obligation. Now one of the most outstanding attributes of the invisible church is its oneness. It is the body of Christ, and that He has but one body goes altogether without saying. Of the many passages of Scripture that teach the oneness of the church we refer only to Rom. 12:5, which describes the church as "one body"; Eph. 1:22, which states that it has "one head"; Eph. 4:5, which ascribes to it "one faith"; and I Cor. 12:13, which teaches that "by one Spirit are we all baptized into one body, whether we be Jews or Gentiles, whether we be bond or free; and have all been made to drink into one Spirit." The evident truth that unity not only does characterize the invisible church, but also must characterize the visible church is taught specifically in such a passage as Eph. 4:1–6— "I, therefore, the prisoner of the Lord, beseech you that ye walk worthy of the vocation wherewith ye are called, with all lowliness and meekness, with long-suffering, forbearing one another in love; endeavoring to keep the unity of the Spirit in the bond of peace. There is one body, and one Spirit, even as ye are called in one hope of your calling; one Lord, one faith, one baptism, one God and Father of all, who is above all, and through all, and in you all." Two whole chapters in the New Testament that may be said to place tremendous emphasis on the necessary manifestation of the unity of Christ's body are Romans 12 and I Corinthians 12. The same teaching is explicit in Christ's prayer "that they all may be one" (John 17:21). This petition can hardly request the spiritual unity of believers, for it is an existing reality. What it asks is that believers may become fully conscious of their spiritual unity and may fully manifest it. Hence Christ adds the words: "That the world may believe that thou hast sent me." Dean Alford comments that the "effects" of this unity "are to be real and visible, such that the world may see them."

From the Scriptural principle just stated an important deduction must be made regarding the extent to which a church which esteems certain other churches equally pure as itself must cooperate with these churches. It is no exaggeration to say that it is in sacred duty bound to seek organic union with these churches. Thus the principle of the oneness of Christ's church makes it obligatory for the truly Reformed churches in any one country— to say nothing of other countries— not only to explore the possibilities of organic union with one another, but to bend their efforts definitely to that end. The fact that in the course of history and under the guidance of divine providence they were founded amid different circumstances as distinct denominations does not warrant the continuance of their separate existence. Nor may complete unanimity on every detail of doctrine and practice be made a prerequisite for union. Nor again may differences of mere tradition keep them from merging. The church of Jesus Christ must be controlled, not by traditions of men, but by the Word of God. To be sure, before organic union could be effected much preliminary work would have to be done, and one of the most difficult aspects of this work would likely be to distinguish between human traditions and Scriptural beliefs and practices; but the path of duty is clear.

The question remains whether The Orthodox Presbyterian Church should cooperate with churches which do not fall within the two categories already discussed; that is, with churches that have not denied Christianity but are less pure in our estimation than is our own church. The circumstances that led to the election of the committee which is now reporting make it seem likely that this question was uppermost in the minds of the commissioners to the Eleventh General Assembly when they resolved that this study be made.

Here must be considered the so-called pluriformity of the Christian church. Historic Presbyterianism has recognized this pluriformity. That is to say, Presbyterianism has acknowledged as Christian churches other than Reformed communions; for example, Lutheran, Methodist and Baptist communions. It is of utmost importance to note that, in doing so, Presbyterianism was not motivated by doctrinal indifference, but by Christian love and forbearance. Presbyterianism has historically insisted on its being the most consistent manifestation of Christ's body. Therefore it could not grant that other churches are equally pure. On the contrary, it has held that other than Reformed communions are guilty of doctrinal and governmental aberrations from Scripture. But in spite of their errors it has regarded these communions as churches of Christ. In recent years the validity of this recognition of the pluriformity of the Christian church has been called into question by certain able Reformed theologians who seem to take the view that only a truly Reformed church deserves to be denominated a church and that other communions are more accurately described as sects. While it is possible that coming decades will bring much discussion of this matter, it is obviously the part of wisdom at this time for The Orthodox Presbyterian Church to adhere to the historic Presbyterian position and to permit that position to determine its policy with reference to cooperation with other than Reformed churches. Now if that be done, the conclusion is warranted that a measure of cooperation of The Orthodox Presbyterian Church with other than Reformed churches is not out of the question. The question may even be asked whether the principle that the unity of Christ's church must be manifested as fully as possible does not render our cooperation with such churches desirable and even obligatory. Your committee would answer that question in the affirmative.

At this point an important reservation must be made. In no case may The Orthodox Presbyterian Church in its cooperation with other churches sacrifice, or even compromise, its distinctiveness. The distinctiveness of our church is its very reason for existence. If it has no decidedly worth-while distinctiveness, it has no right to exist as a denomination, and its continued existence constitutes sinful schism. It must be assumed that The Orthodox Presbyterian Church is convinced that its principles and practices are more Scriptural than are the principles and practices of such churches as are not Reformed or Presbyterian. To these Scriptural principles and practices it must adhere as unswervingly in its cooperative activities as in its individual testimony. For that reason organic union of The Orthodox Presbyterian Church with a church not itself Reformed in its theology nor Presbyterian in its policy is entirely out of the question. Either such a union would be a union only in appearance, not in reality, and therefore a sham; or such a union would be effected at the expense of truth and principle. And the latter of these evils is the very thing that curses almost every present-day movement aiming at church union. It also follows that an important element in whatever cooperation The Orthodox Presbyterian Church may enter upon with churches that are not Reformed will have to consist in its calling the attention of these churches to their errors and seeking in the spirit of love and humility to dissuade them from these errors.

Appendix 2

STATEMENT TO THE TWENTY-EIGHTH GENERAL ASSEMBLY 1961

Biblical Basis for Ecclesiastical Union

In ecclesiastical union two denominations join in submitting to one common form of government. Since ecclesiastical jurisdiction includes the maintenance of spiritual discipline, unity in polity requires agreement in the standards of faith and worship which such discipline maintains. Hence unification in polity, when properly sought and achieved, involves also unity in faith, discipline and worship.

As we take account of the diversity that exists between denominations arising from differences of ethnic identity, cultural background, and historical circumstance the most conclusive evidence derived from Scripture is required to support the position that the obliteration of denominational separateness is an obligation resting upon these Churches of Christ. The differences that exist often manifest the diversity which the church of Christ ought to exemplify and make for the enrichment of the church's total witness. If ecclesiastical union impairs this diversity, then it may be achieved at too great an expense and tends to an impoverishment inconsistent with the witness to Christ which the church must bear.

Though the diversity which manifests itself in differentiating historical development might appear to make ecclesiastical union inadvisable or even perilous in certain cases, yet the biblical evidence in support of union is so plain that any argument to the contrary, however plausible, must be false.

I THE ETHNIC UNIVERSALISM OF THE GOSPEL

In Christ Jesus there is now no longer Jew nor Gentile, barbarian, Scythian, bond nor free (cf. Gal. 3:28; Col. 3:11). The New Testament does not suppose that the differences natural to individuals nor those arising from ethnic identity, cultural background, and historical circumstance are to be obliterated by the gospel. But it does mean that the unity in Christ transcends all diversity arising from language, race, culture, history. What is more, this unity embraces and utilizes all the diversity that is proper and that is created by God's providence. If we should maintain that the diversity is in any way incompatible with the unity of which the church is the expression, then we should be denying *that* unity which the ethnic universalism of the gospel implies. Implicit in the universalism of the gospel is the same kind of universalism in that which the gospel designs, the building up of Christ's church.

II THE UNIVERSALISM OF THE APOSTOLIC CHURCH

The church of the apostolic days embraces all nations, and kindreds, and peoples, and tongues. There is no evidence in the New Testament for the diversification of distinct denominations and anything tending to such diversification was condemned (cf. 1 Cor. 1:10–13). The emphasis falls upon the oneness of faith (cf. Eph. 4:5) and the oneness of the fellowship of the saints (cf. Eph. 4:2–4,11–16; Phil. 2:2–3; 4:2).

III JESUS' PRAYER FOR UNITY (John 17:20–21)

It is a travesty of this text, as of all others bearing upon the unity of the church, to think of the unity for which Christ prayed apart from the unity of faith in the bond of truth. Verse 21 must not be dissociated from verse 20. To divorce the unity for which Christ prayed from all that is involved in believing upon him through the apostolic witness is to sunder what Christ placed together. Furthermore, the pattern Jesus provided in this prayer— "as thou, Father, art in me and I in thee"— makes mockery of the application of the text when unity is divorced from the characterization which finds its analogy in trinitarian unity and harmony.

But while these and other distortions of this text are to be shunned, the prayer of Jesus does bear upon our question in two respects.

(1) The fragmentation and consequent lack of fellowship, harmony, and cooperation which appear on the ecclesiastical scene are a patent contradiction of the unity exemplified in that to which Jesus referred when he said, "as thou, Father, art in me and I in thee."

(2) The purpose stated in Jesus' prayer— "that the world may believe that thou hast sent me"— implies a manifestation observable by the world. Jesus prays for a visible unity that will bear witness to the world. The mysterious unity of believers with one another must come to visible expression so as to be instrumental in bringing conviction to the world.

IV THE UNITY OF THE BODY OF CHRIST

The church is the body of Christ and there is no schism in the body (cf. 1 Cor. 12:25). As in the human body, there is diversity in unity and unity in diversity (cf. 1 Cor. 12). The point to be stressed, however, is the unity. If there is unity it follows that this unity must express itself in all the functions which belong to the church. Since government in the church is an institution of Christ (cf. Rom. 12:8; 1 Cor. 12:28; 1 Tim. 5:17; Heb. 13:7; 1 Pet. 5:1–2), this unity must be expressed in government. The necessary inference to be drawn is that the government should manifest the unity and be as embracive in respect of its functioning as the unit of which it is an expression. A concrete illustration of this principle is the decree of the Jerusalem council (Acts 15:28–29; 16:4).

V THE KINGDOM OF CHRIST, etc.

Christ is the head of the church. So ultimately there is the most concentrated unity of government in the church of Christ. He alone is King. Any infringement upon this sovereignty belonging to Christ is a violation of what is basic and central in the government of the church. It follows that all government in the church must adhere to the pattern of a cone which has its apex in Christ.

Christ also instituted the apostolate with authority delegated from him (Matt. 16:18–19; cf. John 20:21,23; Eph. 2:19–22). This apostolic authority is exercised now only through the inscripturated Word. But in the sphere of delegated authority the apostolate is supreme and will continue to be so to the end of time. This is the way the Holy Spirit, as the vicar of Christ abiding in and with the church, exercises his function in accordance with Christ's promise. He seals the apostolic witness by his own testimony and illumines the people of God in the interpretation and application of the same.

Subordinately, however, in terms of Matt. 16:19, the hegemony of the apostolate is undeniable and it exemplifies the descending hierarchy which Christ has established.

There is also in the New Testament institution the delegated authority of the presbyterate, always subject to the apostolic institution, to the Holy Spirit who inspired the apostles (John 16:13; 20:22), and ultimately to Christ as King and Head of the church, but nevertheless supreme in this sphere of government.

Since all office in the church of Christ can be filled only by the gifts of the Spirit, this structural subordination of the government of the church to the rule of Christ functions in living reality as a fellowship of the one Spirit. Everyone who has the Spirit of Christ is thereby called as a good steward of the manifold grace of God to minister his spiritual gifts to all the saints, so far as he is given opportunity. In particular, those whose gifts are for rule in the church must exercise such gifts in the communion of Christ and his church.

When these principles of gradation and communion are appreciated and when coordinated with other considerations already established, especially that of the unity of the body of Christ, we appear to be provided with a pattern that points to the necessity of making the presbyterate as inclusive as is consistent with loyalty to Christ and the faith of the gospel. In a word, we are pointed to the necessity of unity in government, a unity that is violated when Churches of Christ adhering to the faith in its purity and integrity are not thus united.

Leonard J. Coppes

26 The Discussion of the Theology of the Diaconate

THE THEOLOGY OF THE DIACONATE has been debated in the Orthodox Presbyterian Church for a long time. The Committee on General Benevolence (which in 1973 was renamed the Committee on Diaconal Ministries) was established in 1947 in response to an overture to the Fourteenth General Assembly from the Presbytery of Philadelphia. Its purposes were "to study the needs of Christians who would not normally come under the purview of the deacons of the local churches" and "to solicit funds for and distribute gifts to those needy Christians."[1] In 1960 the Committee described itself as "an instrument of the *whole* church in ministering to the broader areas of human need, poverty, and suffering which are the responsibility of the whole church."

The reports of the committee evidence a focus and emphasis on ministering to Christians and primarily to Christians who were not members of the Orthodox Presbyterian Church. Gifts and other forms of aid were, for the most part, administered by, and probably resulted from requests by Orthodox Presbyterian missionaries, pastors, and courts. The exceptions to this manner of administering aid (beginning as early as 1949) appear frequently and as normal administration policies of the committee. Also, aid was not confined to those identified as Christians. As early as 1953 the Committee on General Benevolence reported it had sent gifts to Korea to help in retirement homes, orphanages, lepersariums, and disaster cases. Therefore, the 1960 statement expresses a policy which had long been in operation.

In 1970 the committee was instructed "to examine ways to expand their ministry in cooperation with local congregations and presbyteries to reach

out to the needs of the poor and distressed in the church and the world."
This resulted in the adoption (1973) of a report identifying non-Christians
as proper objects of the church's diaconal aid.[2] The report argued that
"Christ's own are the *primary* objects of this (benevolence) ministry." It
added: "we have a prior commitment to those of the faith in our own
locale and then an ever decreasing, but never-ending, responsibility as we
move outward from our locale and from the church, giving of ourselves as
the opportunity and the means are provided by the Lord." The assembly
then adopted the following:

> The primary duty of the Church is to witness to the gospel, to celebrate the
> sacraments, to seek man's sanctification, and above all, to seek God's glory. To
> this end, Elders were appointed and ordained. The Office of Deacon was
> established to relieve the Elders of certain time and energy-consuming tasks in
> order that the Elders might devote themselves more fully to prayer and the
> ministry of the word. As part of the diaconal ministry, the Church has asked
> the Deacons to oversee the work of God's people as they provide fully, with
> love; first for their fellow Christians' needs, and afterwards to the needs of the
> world. We have an obligation to provide for the poor both within and without
> the Church; but the primary concern must be for those within the Church.
>
> The principle to be observed is that general benevolent operations to all men
> should not be allowed to dilute significantly the primary benevolent concern
> for fellow Christians. Most certainly, benevolence in any form should not be
> allowed to dilute significantly the preaching and prayer ministry. Proper inter-
> pretation of this statement requires that we remember always that God is
> properly glorified only when we freely minister to the needs of the poor (Refer
> to and read Mark 7:10–13 on "corban," Mark 12:28–34 on interpreting the
> law, and Matthew 25:31–46 on the criterion of final judgment).
>
> We cannot say "be filled with the Spirit" to a man whose stomach is empty
> when our pockets are full. Neither can we "hide our light under a bushel" while
> we go about feeding the poor in the humanistic fashion so popular today and
> neglecting to give to them the Bread of Life. A proper motive will cause us to
> make a proper allocation of our strength and our fortunes to each ministry in
> its proper order of primacy— always to God's glory.

The focus of the debate in the church was on the concept, "are non-
Christians proper objects of Christian benevolence?" The majority report
(which was rejected) responded "no." They argued that "proper objects"
meant those who have an inherent right to Christian benevolence by
virtue of their membership in the Christian church. The majority unsuccessfully argued that Gal 6:10 and other such passages were addressed to
the individual and not to the church as church. They urged that in the
Bible Christian benevolence is designed to serve the needs of the church.
It may be extended to non-Christians but only by way of exception and
only under unusual circumstances. The minority responded "yes." They
argued that "proper objects" meant those who have a right to Christian
benevolence by virtue of the fact that Christians are commanded to give

to non-Christians in the Bible. They queried, how can it be improper to give to those to whom God commands us to give? Their primary proof text was Gal 6:10.

The years since this theological statement was adopted have been occupied with intense debate and study attempting to further define the Committee on Diaconal Ministry's responsibility toward the Christian and non-Christian worlds. In 1975 the committee submitted an interpretation of the position set forth in 1972 and adopted in 1973. It was intended to expand and clarify the previously adopted statement. Much of the 1975 report consists of statements from and comments on the 1972 statement.

This interpretation explains the three priorities of the 1972 report. First, "the priority of the gospel" bears two implications for the committee's work:

> (1) Deacons are presumed to have as their reason for existence the prevention of the dilution and distraction of the elders from their primary responsibility.
> (2) Funds gathered for diaconal work must never siphon money from the cause of gospel proclamation.

Secondly, there is the "priority of opportunity" defined as "what God lays before us by His providence," and:

> When in the course of pursuing obedience to the Great Commission, the church encounters benevolent needs, she ministers to these needs in the name of her compassionate Lord. . . . This priority means that we do not do as the humanists do, turn over every stone, searching for needy people. We do not advertise for benevolent work. Benevolence is simply the necessary fruit in the lives of the people (corporately as well as individually) who are obeying the Great Commission.

Thirdly, "the priority of the household of faith" is explained as follows:

> If the church is busy obeying the Great Commission, the providence of God will no doubt dictate that the majority of cases which are brought to us by opportunity will also be those of the Christian community simply because this is the community in which we live. This receiving aid in the name of Christ is accompanied by the preaching of the gospel. This latter is also made on the assumption that the church continues to be busy obeying the Great Commission.

Furthermore, it is remarked that:

> Deacons are officers in the church of Jesus Christ. As such they bear no responsibility to the world by virtue of their office; their responsibility is within the church.

In 1978 the committee (upon the instruction of the general assembly) responded to a request from the Reformed Ecumenical Synod with a paper entitled "The Theology of Diaconal World Involvement." This paper was recommitted to the committee which was now augmented by two advisors (Dr. Edmund P. Clowney and the Rev. James Petty) who were elected by the assembly to assist in revising the paper. The result was a longer, more detailed paper submitted to the general assembly in 1980. This paper and its predecessor were committed to a special committee which was in-structed to draft a paper setting forth "positive principles on which the church may base its diaconal ministry." The special committee presented its report in 1983 but the debate was postponed until 1984 due to the lack of sufficient time to handle the matter at the 1983 assembly.

The special committee submitted majority and minority papers. In the view of this writer the central agreements of the two position are as follows: (1) The church may minister to the world of non-Christians; (2) the distribution of diaconal monies and aid should always be accompanied by the preaching of the gospel; (3) priority should be given to Christians in the distribution of available funds; (4) the members of the Orthodox Presbyterian Church should be urged to give liberally and joyfully to those in need; (5) diaconal aid should not be given in such a way as to support known sin. The major differences are: (1) whether or not Gal 6:10 teaches that opportunity (the knowledge of needs plus the resources available to meet those needs) obligates the church to proceed to alleviate or even remove the cause and effects of those needs, (2) whether or not our particular church is commanded and/or responsible to meet the needs of all Christians; i.e., all members of true Churches, (3) whether or not the two preceding mandates if answered affirmatively should be as aggressively pursued as meeting the needs within our own denomination.

The remainder of this article shall focus on the minority report. This report answered the disagreements (1) and (2) negatively. Yet it did agree that the Orthodox Presbyterian Church could properly help Christians (and Christian denominations) as well as non-Christians. It answered (3) negatively, although recognizing those needs within our own ranks (family) should be sought out and met.

In summary, the minority report supported those conclusions with the following argumentation:

> This report sets forth the diaconal task as one side of biblical salvation. The states of Eden and heaven are seen as models governing all human history with reference to the enjoyment of full-orbed salvation (Gen. 1–2; Deut. 7:12–16; 12:9; 15:11; Isa. 32:1–8; Ezek. 36:30; Heb. 4; Rev. 22:1–5). Hence, since the blessings of salvation fall to those under the covenant, or in the kingdom, diaconal aid is essentially and primarily covenantal aid, i.e., aid to covenantal members. This means that diaconal aid is to be covenantally contextualized and disciplined (Deut. 7:12–16; 2 Thess. 3:6–15; 1 Tim. 5:9–16).
>
> The care of the poor and needy falls upon the family and the individual (Deut. 21:17; Luke 12:33; Matt. 6:1–4; 1 Tim. 5:9–16), the state (Ps. 72:1–2; Ezek. 16:49; Dan. 4:26; Prov. 28:15; 29:14; 31:9; Deut. 16:9; Ruth 4:1–2; Prov. 31:23), and the church (Matt. 12:48ff.; 16:18–19; Acts 6:1–2; 11:28–29) respectively, though the order of responsiblilty does not necessarily proceed

in a direct line. Responsibility falls upon the group with which the object of aid is in covenant (the state being conceived as a covenantal bond).

The Lord requires families and churches to aid the brother in good standing if at all possible (Matt. 25:31–46; Acts 2:45; 2 Cor. 8:4,13–14; 9:12; 1 John 3:17). The governing rule is the basic Old Testament economic structure as it is restated, assumed, and/or developed in the New Testament. This rule entails the assumption of private ownership, the possibility of amassing wealth, the obligation and privilege of rendering the tithe, and the call to presenting sacrifices to the Lord (Exod. 25:1–9; Deut. 14:22; Neh. 13:10; Mal. 3:8–10; Matt. 23:23; Heb. 7:1–10; 1 Cor. 9:12–13; 16:2). One should give cheerfully and liberally, for the Lord loves a cheerful giver (2 Cor. 9:7).

We recognize that the Bible focuses benevolence (diaconal aid) on church/covenant members with whom we are in public covenantal relationship both in the sense that our aid goes to them first and in the sense that our responsibility is more comprehensive and pressing toward them (e.g., we should carry insurance and retirement policies on Orthodox Presbyterian ministers but not on all men, and we should redeem an Orthodox Presbyterian from losing his home but not all men). We also recognize a special responsibility toward others in public covenant with God (i.e., other churches).

On the other hand, we recognize that God commands us to help non-covenantal persons under many circumstances (Matt. 5:38–48; 8:28–34; Mark 7:26; Luke 10:30–37; Gal. 6:10; cf., Lev. 19:18). Special emphasis is given in the Scripture to helping the non-covenantal person with whom one is in physical contact and whose needs are of emergency proportions (Lev. 19:18; Luke 10:30–37). The practice of God in the Old Testament and of his Son in the New Testament comprise the model for such aid. Although the extending of such aid may be an effective evangelistic tool and may legitimately be used as such (Matt. 11:23), the church should be cautious of using it as a major evangelistic tool inasmuch as neither Jesus nor the early church did so (Mark 1:37–38; John 5:3; 1 Cor. 1:22).

The above statement seeks to build a theology of the diaconate so as to conform the design (practice) of the diaconate to its nature. Is the diaconate fundamentally in the area of common grace or special grace? Is it a product of God's common blessings upon all men or a product of his special blessing upon his elect? The above statement maintains that the diaconate is in the area of special grace, that it is covenantal and a product of God's blessing upon his people. This conclusion is supported by the extensive Old Testament instruction on helping the poor and needy (diaconate), by the way God himself administered blessings and the promise of blessings, by the way Jesus administered blessings and the promise of blessings, and by the way the New Testament recounts the activity of the early church in this area.

When it is said that the diaconate is covenantal we mean that it is defined and delimited by the covenant. That is, the biblical material recorded in God's special covenants with his elect people define and delimit the scope and practice of the diaconate.

The above statement assumes the unity of the covenant. That is, it assumes that what is recorded in the Bible constitutes a single covenant. It also assumes that the material revealed in the several expressions of the covenant (viz. the Adamic, Noahic, Mosaic, Davidic, and Christologic covenants) constitute an organic whole. Consequently, the principles introduced at an earlier stage or revelation (in an earlier covenant) are assumed or repeated in subsequent revelation unless, of course, they are changed or set aside in that later revelation.

Furthermore, this statement assumes that the covenant is now redemptive in nature. By "redemptive" we mean that the covenant is intended to communicate (tell about) salvation. The salvation, furthermore, is a salvation worked on the whole man, both his spirit or soul and his body. "Diaconal" refers to the application of covenantal blessings to the material side of life. In Eden God provided a place of total blessing for man, i.e., a place where he received what was good for him both with respect to the non-material (soul) and material sides of life. This same kind of provision is promised in the land of promise (i.e., what man needs for a happy life both spiritually and materially). As in the Garden of Eden the covenantal blessings of Palestine were conditioned on man's obedience. Thus, the principle introduced in the Edenic revelation was continued under the Mosaic covenant (material blessings are contingent on man's obedience to God's declared will). Thus, these (diaconal) blessings are placed in the realm of special grace and not in the realm of common grace.

Furthermore, the above statement of principles argues that covenantal blessings are to be disciplined covenantally, i.e., in accordance with what God sets forth in the covenant. The terms of the covenant are divinely imposed to be sure. Man cannot and does not dictate to God or even share in the formation of the terms of the covenant. Rather, as man, he receives the declaration from God. The enjoyment of some of the blessings of the covenant are unconditional, e.g., eternal life. On the other hand, the enjoyment of other blessings are conditional, e.g., the fellowship of covenantal members with one another, and diaconal blessings.

There is a side of the covenant that requires of men responsible response. Although divinely demanded submission to many elements is not divinely forced, man must accept and practice the terms or stipulations of the covenant.

One aspect of the covenant is the responsibility of men to join together organizationally. This was set forth in the Old Testament where in order to enjoy the blessings of the covenant fully one had to be circumcised and become a member of the visible church. Those who were not members of the visible church did not enjoy certain (diaconal) blessings. In this statement the bond uniting people together and by which they unite themselves together is called a public covenant.

Since diaconal aid is by nature covenantal blessing the distribution of diaconal aid should be administered accordingly. It should be covenantally administered, i.e., administered in the way the Bible sets forth. Now it should be obvious that the way the Bible sets forth the distribution should not, in principle, violate the nature of covenantal blessings. We should not conclude that diaconal aid should be given to all men regardless of their relationship to the covenant (i.e., whether or not they are members of the visible church).

In today's world where the true church is seriously divided we are faced with the difficult problem of the reasons for this division. The above statement assumes that the reason is ultimately sin (either the sin of the Orthodox Presbyterian Church or the sin of others).

In determining what this means for the diaconate it might be helpful to consider what this means for other areas of the church's labors. In spiritual matters, the OPC does not equally distribute its wealth. We do not seek to support the missionary enterprises of other true churches. It seems to this writer that we make this decision on two grounds. First, we do not support other missionary enterprises because we believe that given the knowledge of God's revelation we enjoy it would be sin for us not to put his money into preaching the gospel in the purest form possible. We are not willing to say ours is the only pure form of the message, nor are we willing to say our understanding of the gospel is without error. Yet to the best of our knowledge ours is the purest form of preaching we know. Secondly, we do not support other missionary enterprises because we cannot afford to do so. After we have gathered all our funds we find there is not enough to do all we would like to do for the Lord. The limitation of funds prohibits us from helping enterprises we might help, in principle, were there more funds (i.e., the ministry of churches who preach the gospel in a very pure form). Let us suggest that it is the concept "public covenant" that guides and determines our thinking. We give (in missionary enterprises) to the cause of that group with which we are in public covenant, to the cause of that group with which we have agreed to serve the Lord, to the cause of that group with which we share a common discipline.

The position represented in the minority report contends that the blessings of the covenant (spiritual and material) are of the same nature. The principles that guide us in the missionary enterprise are applicable to the diaconal enterprise. Within the visible church we determine the recipients of our funds by the principle of the "public covenant." Our available funds go first to those with whom we are in public covenant. Then available funds are to be distributed throughout the visible church with recipients being determined by the nature of their need and their theological purity (or the theological purity of the group with which they are in public covenant). Sometimes crucial need might set aside theological considerations. And sometimes theological considerations might set aside determined need. The conditions and circumstances of the interplay between these considerations are set forth in Scripture.

The position summarized by the minority statement would also take into consideration certain exceptions to some of the above set of principles. Namely, there are times and conditions when the church should, even must, give aid to those outside the covenant.

Thus, we have seen that the discussion of the theology of the diaconate has a long history in the Orthodox Presbyterian Church. The issues have been complex and the debate intense (at times emotional). It is the hope of this writer that the above material will help to show that there has been progress. The future may hold still further development. Perhaps this article will help to give those involved some perspective.

NOTES

1. These and other citations are from the GA Minutes of the years indicated.
2. This report may be found on pp. 128–29 of the Thirty-ninth GA Minutes.

Lawrence Eyres

27 Reflections on Professor John Murray

THE BIOGRAPHY OF JOHN MURRAY has been written.[1] Though there will be biographical elements in this essay, no effort will be made to write a "life." Material will be drawn from reflections from my student years at Westminster Theological Seminary (1935–1938), my association with Mr. Murray as a fellow-member of the Presbytery of New York and New England (1938–1943), and from less frequent contacts with him from 1943 to his last general assembly of the Orthodox Presbyterian Church in 1966.

I enjoyed special advantages in those earlier years. I served as a student trainee under the Committee for the Propagation of the Reformed Faith in New England[2] during the summers of 1936 and 1937. It was through Professor Murray's leadership of that committee that I was introduced to my first pastorate in the Deerfield Community Church, Deerfield, New Hampshire.[3] During those years (1938–1943) John Murray was our house guest on several occasions.

The prime opportunity for closeness came in my senior year at Westminster. That was the first year on the present campus, away from downtown Philadelphia where Murray, an inveterate walker, could walk to the seminary, restaurants, and to worship on the Lord's Day at New Covenant Orthodox Presbyterian Church where his friend, the late David Freeman, was then pastor. But Chestnut Hill was too far for walking and Murray would not ride a public conveyance on the Sabbath — a matter of conscience with him. So he bought a used automobile, which he could not drive. David Freeman and I shared the honors as his teacher during most of that academic year. I was supplying the pulpit of the small Atonement

435

OPC in southwest Philadelphia that year. Early Sunday mornings he and I would drive together to David Freeman's home on Carpenter Lane in the Germantown area. From there I would take surface cars to the bank building where my congregation worshiped. After evening service the procedure was reversed. We followed the same routine on Wednesday evenings. These were enjoyable times of fellowship, especially those times in the Freeman home after the evening services.

The Professor

As a beginning student at Westminster, my first impression of John Murray was not outstanding. He taught no first-year classes during my year, so all I had to go on was his casual appearances which struck me as austere and uncommunicative. He then held the rank of instructor. His reason for not moving up to the rank of assistant professor, I was told, was his inability to sign the *Westminster Confession of Faith* as adopted by the Presbyterian Church in the USA because of inclusion of the "iniquitous" chapter on "The Love of God and Missions" which had been added in 1903. When the OPC came into being, this bar was removed. He proceeded to full professorship in due time.

As a second-year student, it took some time to get used to Murray's lecture method. One had to write furiously to keep up. But it paid off inasmuch as his lecture notes became all the systematic text I could afford in those early depression years. Noteworthy was his outline method of lecturing. It was in great contrast with that of R. B. Kuiper. Kuiper's outlines were works of art in their balance. It seems that "the ideal homily" carried right into R. B.'s classroom lectures. Not so with Murray. What demanded careful exegesis and comparison consumed pages of notes. But if Hodge had already said it well enough so that Murray could not improve on it, we were told to "read Hodge." Also there were no questions; whatever portion of the theological catalogue happened to be before us got its full due without interruption from the class.

I well remember one high point in his lectures in eschatology. Referring to those unable to see the implications of the overwhelming biblical evidence for a general judgment and a general resurrection, he dubbed their ignorance "the quintessence of obtuseness." He had a way with words. In fact, I was impressed early, even in his lectures, that there was always that right word. No searching for it, out it came even if we didn't know what it meant. There was always the dictionary.

Most impressive of all was his devotion in handling the Word. From the opening prayers (always by him) to the end of the hour, he was transparently in the presence of God. He would begin each lecture in a low tone, almost inaudible. Before long his voice would rise in pitch and volume with unction in every word. Scripture for him was not the stuff of dry exegesis, but matter for reverence and worship even in his most thorough delvings. Nothing offended him more than to hear the words of Scripture perverted or lightly regarded.

Through my many out-of-class associations with my beloved professor I had opportunity to know him as a friend. Not that I ever regarded myself as his equal, for I was ever in awe of him. In conversation he was never "John" but always "Mr. Murray" or "Professor Murray." Just the same, I felt my friendship returned. In fact, I believe that those who came to know him could not help loving him. And he was vigorous in returning affection. This was more than the customary warm handshake. John Murray was known for the lateral squeeze of affection long before that sort of thing became fashionable. He loved children that way, too. Small children, my daughter among them, were a bit afraid of his hugs because of their bone-crushing intensity!

Dissent from his cherished convictions (e.g., exclusive psalmody or certain strict Sabbath practices) never affected his friendship. I felt free to draw him out on his views, but never argued with him even though I never became even a near convert.

However, I became much wiser through our frequent automobile trips, walks together, and his visits in our home. I'd ask a question on some point of exegesis or application. If walking, he'd be silent for what seemed a long time. Assuming he was going to pass on that one, I'd open a new topic only to be restrained. Then out of his mouth would flow a well-reasoned, carefully expounded answer to my question, many of which have stood by me to this day.

He loved jokes, especially on the Scots. I remember one I had heard from a Scottish missionary who had visited our Deerfield church. Next time I saw Murray I passed it on to him. He was convulsed for minutes on end. He made it his own and told it again and again in my hearing.

He was always at home in the homes of his friends. Once while visiting us in our New Hampshire home, our black cat, "Dusty," caught a bird. My wife scolded him mercilessly. Mr. Murray responded, "Gerry, don't you know that he is only acting according to his nature?" Another time when he was preparing for bed he took out his glass eye and washed it. He said, "Lawrence, this is something you can't do." During my seminary days I was apt at times to take off for a certain town in Maine (as the saying goes, "the course of true love never runs smooth"). Later, after our marriage, he said to my wife with a twinkle in his good eye, "Gerry, if I could have got to you in those days I'd have spanked you!" It was always a joy to be in his company. He was a true friend.

The Presbyter and Commissioner

I was ordained in November 1938 by the Presbytery of New York and New England. John Murray was a member of that presbytery almost from its inception till his death in 1975. Like so many in those early days, I was licensed one day and examined for ordination the next, then ordained a few days later. Professor Murray participated in my oral examinations, all of which took place on the floor of presbytery. I remember his examining me in church history. He asked me to name the Reformed creeds. I had spent most of the night before "boning up" on church history especially. I was able not only to name them, but in their right order and with their dates. He rose to his feet and squealed with glee at my answer. I had no trouble at all with my theology exam. How could I with such a teacher?

One incident sticks in my mind. Presbytery met in the home of John J. de Waard, pastor of Memorial OPC in Rochester, New York. Between business sessions we were sitting in the de Waard living room enjoying the fellowship — all but John Murray. I asked de Waard where he might be (he was a guest in their home). I was informed that the professor was in his room reading the Word and praying. He, too, was enjoying fellowship, but on an infinitely higher level!

Murray's impact on the OPC as a commissioner to its general assemblies was inestimable. He made a major contribution in dealing with the controversy surrounding the licensure and ordination of Dr. Gordon H. Clark by the Presbytery of Philadelphia in 1944. That action was complained against by five members of the faculty of Westminster Seminary joined by seven other ministers and one elder. Not being himself a complainant, the Twelfth General Assembly (1945) elected him to a committee of five to study the doctrinal portions of the complaint. The committee reported lengthily to the Thirteenth General Assembly (1946) recommending that the complaint be denied. But Murray wrote a minority report upholding the complaint in its basic contention.[4] Floor debate on the committee and minority reports stretched from Wednesday noon till near midnight Friday. In the end the complaint was substantially denied,[5] but Murray's contribution influenced the outcome of the larger controversy in the general assembly of 1947.

It was at this Fourteenth General Assembly that the action of the Committee on Foreign Missions denying the request of the Korea Theological Seminary, Pusan, Korea, to send Dr. Floyd E. Hamilton to teach theology in this fledgling seminary became the center of debate.[6] Murray was a member of the committee and his term was to expire with that assembly. The supporters of Hamilton (a strong defender of Dr. Clark) had determined to replace the former members with a slate sympathetic to them. Consequently all five incumbents were renominated along with five others.[7] It should be noted that there was no question in the minds of the majority of the committee as to Hamilton's fitness for missionary work in Korea. Only the possibility of his teaching theology in a seminary gave some pause, and that because of views that came to light in the controversy over Dr. Clark's ordination.[8]

Speeches for and against the two slates continued through the greater part of a whole day (an election unique in the history of the OPC). When the vote finally was taken, all but one of the original committee members were returned — and that by a majority of one![9] John Murray was among those reelected. The importance of this election cannot be overestimated. It was at this point that the supporters of Dr. Clark gave up the battle. Within the year following that general assembly most of his leading supporters, including Clark himself, had transferred out of the OPC. John Murray's contribution to the outcome of the struggle, however evaluated, was considerable.

Murray was for many years involved in the process of revision of the Form of Government of the OPC. He was a member of the committee which formulated the first major addition to the original Form of Government. He had a major part in framing an overture from his presbytery to the Eighth General Assembly (1941) seeking clarification of the work of the evangelist and the whole subject of OPC ministers serving non-OPC congregations.[10] The result was chapters XVIII and XIX, "Of the Work of the Evangelist" and "Of Ministers Laboring in Other Churches."[11] These chapters reflect the work of the major composer of the overture. He also served on the special Committee on Revisions of the Form of Government from its erection in 1948 till his retirement in 1966.

Another labor of love was his work on perfecting the text and proof texts of the *Westminster Confession of Faith*. He was appointed to the original committee in 1940, which committee was later dissolved. Then he was elected to the Committee on Accuracy of the Text and Proof Texts of the Confession of Faith by the Twenty-first GA (1954). The final adoption of the official OPC text of the Confession with proof texts took place at the Twenty-third Assembly in 1956. The personnel of the latter committee changed in the course of the years, but Murray chaired both committees and did the lion's share of the research.

Murray can also be credited with launching the OPC on the course of producing the Great Commissions Sunday school curriculum. It all began with the report of the Committee on Christian Education to the Twenty-second GA (1955). The committee announced the termination of the working arrangement with the Sunday school committee of the Christian Reformed Church in producing a new Sunday school curriculum suitable to the needs of the OPC. It further announced that it had no further plans to produce Sunday school materials.[12] It was John Murray, as I remember, who took the floor to propose what came out as the following action: "On amended motion it was determined that the Committee on Christian Education be directed to proceed as soon as possible to the preparation and publication of Sabbath School materials."[13] The use of the word *Sabbath* confirms my recollection. That was his word. I never heard him refer to the first day of the week in any other way. On hindsight, this bold action may be questioned as to its wisdom. In taking this step the OPC took a bear by the tail. It required the eventual help of the Presbyterian Church in America to get us out of the woods. But, for John Murray, a thing that was right must be done, no matter what the cost!

Murray's strong commitment to exclusive psalmody may not be overlooked. When the *Trinity Hymnal* was in course of preparation, it was he, with the help of David Freeman, G. I. Williamson and William Young, who made their opposition felt to the use of uninspired hymns in public worship. Being realistic, he knew he had no hope of "reforming" the church on this issue. But raise his voice he must as a matter of conscience. He presented his protests and registered his dissent for the record. Nevertheless, he did not use his parliamentary privilege to introduce delaying actions and other maneuverings. And when he'd had his say and suffered defeat, he showed no bitterness.

The Scholar

John Murray was, above all, a life-long student of the Scriptures. His thorough grasp of theology, his reverent handling of the great truths of revelation and his refusal to fit slavishly into any traditional mold— these marked him as belonging to a breed apart. He was unswerving in the areas where the Scriptures speak with clarity and cautious where they do not. Above all, he was a master of the exegetical method.

I remember attending a Christian Reformed Ministers' *Inter Nos* meeting in Chicago during the fifties. The late Peter Eldersveld was there. Speaking of the OPC and Westminster Seminary, he said that John Murray was a superb "exegetical dogmatician." That says it. And where did he get his theological learning? I asked him once. He response came quickly this time. He didn't mention Caspar Wistar Hodge, B. B. Warfield or Geerhardus Vos. These certainly left their imprint on him, and I'm sure he'd have been the first to acknowledge it. But he said he got his theological learning from his father — a Scottish elder whose worldly occupation was road building! With such a home base, refined and extended under those old Princeton greats, he became the Christian scholar *par excellence*.

John Murray did not seem to have a flair for the philosophical, though his minority report on incomprehensibility indicates that he could handle philosophical concepts. He seemed somewhat impatient with philosophizing when it came to exegetical matters. I recall the fifties, at the time that Cornelius Van Til's apologetic approach was under fire from James Daane. I had just read Van Til's book *Common Grace*.[14] I asked him what he thought of Van Til's thesis that reprobates in this life could still enjoy God's common love because they were as yet "undifferentiated." He seemed mystified by the whole idea, not that he had any problems with common grace, but such reasoning just wasn't his cup of tea.

He didn't write many books. This was most likely because of his perfectionist temperament. His earlier books on *Divorce* and *Christian Baptism* have experienced a continuing influence. But, in my judgment, *Principles of Conduct* and his commentary on *The Epistle to the Romans* are his greatest. The former is unsurpassed in its treatment of the institutions of marriage and the family, of labor and the Sabbath rest, of the dynamic of the Christian life, and of the old man/new man dichotomy. His exegetical support of the contention that there is no "old man" in the believer[15] is for me a liberating truth. His thinking on this subject and on definitive sanctification[16] seem to have been later developments. I don't recall his having dealt with these in his seminary lectures.

But his commentary on *The Epistle to the Romans*[17] was his *magnum opus*. One needs to learn to think along with him to get the full grasp of his Latinized expressions. But there is no other commentary on Romans which grapples with Paul's great epistle with such clarity and finality. Here one finds Christian scholarship at its best! *Redemption Accomplished and Applied* also deserves mention. In the sentences of this small book I can still hear his voice in the very language of the classroom, and that after a half century. The power in this book, as in many of his *Collected Writings* is the power of a brilliant mind steeped in the language and thought forms of the Bible.

The Impact of His Life and Teaching

When turning to the impact of his life and teaching, first and foremost was his influence upon the lives of his students. Somewhere I heard it said that students came to Westminster Seminary to study under Van Til and stayed to study under Murray. While I doubt that many were disappointed with Van Til, yet Murray, at least in his earlier years, had to be discovered. His writings were few and slow in coming, and he never promoted his own work. No doubt there were a few who didn't appreciate him, but those future pastors and teachers who sat at his feet determined to learn received the lifelong imprint of his thinking and belief. They could never again be the same. The Word of God could never be to them a flat collection of proof texts supporting a preconceived system. Rather, they saw God's self-revelation unfold in the history of revelation and redemption which culminated in the appearing of the Word made flesh. One not only learned this but felt it. I believe it was in my class of 1938 that biblical theology first became a required course in Westminster's curriculum. Murray leaned heavily on Geerhardus Vos, but the biblical theological method was part and parcel of his thinking from the very beginning.

As for systematic theology, his students were given to see the scripturalness of the theological catalogue as set forth in the *Confession of Faith and Catechism*, not in a dry, dull fashion, but as a living body of truth. In my ministry of forty-six years this impression is as fresh as it was in my student days. It is therefore sad to think that, through no fault of their own, there has come into our pulpits a generation of young ministers who knew not Murray!

Mention has already been made of John Murray's various contributions to the life and development of the OPC. But thus far mention has not been made as to how this has affected the complexion of his church. In its inception in 1936, the OPC was definitely an American phenomenon. Among those who stood with J. Gresham Machen as contenders for the faith were men of diverse theological stripe. Some had dispensational leanings, others were unclear as to "the doctrines of grace" and the covenant. The presence and impact of Murray who was of the Scottish tradition, together with R. B. Kuiper, Ned B. Stonehouse, and Cornelius Van Til of the Dutch tradition, had a profound effect toward making the OPC what it has become through its past crises and controversies, beginning with the division of 1937. There may be those who regret the path which our church has taken in its first half century, but none can doubt that the impact of the Scottish and Dutch influence permanently affected its course. The OPC is not the Presbyterian church in the "American" tradition that it seemed determined to be in 1936!

Something needs to be said about Murray's retirement years after 1966. I had the privilege of sitting by him at supper the last evening of the general assembly of 1966 (in Oostburg, Wisconsin). I never saw him again, but I did keep abreast of his activities. He didn't retire into seclusion. Returning to his native Scotland, he married and commenced a family. He was able to preach and lecture in many parts of the British Isles. But most happily he formed a connection with the Banner of Truth Trust and became an active trustee of the Trust till his death in 1975. He contributed to *The Banner of Truth* magazine and participated in many of their conferences with vigor. That one I loved so dearly fell in with the Banner people pleased me inasmuch as I am grateful for the service the Trust has rendered to me and many others in the OPC. Most of all, I thank God for the labor of love on the part of the Trust and its editor, Iain Murray, in assembling and publishing the four volumes on *The Collected Writings of John Murray*.

Surely a great man of God has, for a time, lived among us. That he was not longer spared to bless the church universal is cause for sorrow. But God is wise and gracious in that he gave to his church a humble servant who served him well in his own generation. No doubt the church could have survived had John Murray never been born. But it would have been a different church. The cause of Christ has been made richer by his gift to us of his worthy servant, John Murray.

NOTES

1. Iain Murray, ed., *Collected Writings of John Murray*, Vol. 3 (Edinburgh: Banner of Truth, 1982), 1–158.

2. The committee consisted of John Murray (chairman), David Freeman, John H. Skilton, and William P. Green. The committee sent and supported Westminster students and graduates to preach in closed church buildings throughout northern New England, chiefly from 1936 to 1938. It ceased its labors upon the initiation of home missionary work by the Presbytery of New York and New England.

3. The Deerfield church was a federation of Congregational and Baptist congregations.

4. *Minutes of the Twelfth GA*, 5–31. The principal contention of the complaint was that Dr. Clark's concept of the incomprehensibility of God was not in accord with the primary and secondary standards of the OPC. The complaint saw the transcript of Clark's theology examination as affirming that God's knowledge, while infinite, was capable of being stated in an infinite number of propositions, each of which if expressed could be comprehended by the mind of man. Thus, God's knowledge is incomprehensible only in that it contains an infinite number of truths capable of propositional statement. The complaint contended that God's knowledge qualitatively was incomprehensible at every point, and therefore Clark should not have been licensed and ordained. See also Murray's minority report, *Minutes of the Thirteenth GA*, 68–81.

5. The assembly did uphold the contention of the complaint that the presbytery acted improperly in judging the examination for licensure sufficient also for ordination. Nevertheless, it did not question the legality of the ordination on that account. Ibid., 84–85.

6. *Minutes of the Fourteenth GA*, 16–17. A secondary reason for the committee's unwillingness had to do with passports. Only one passport could be secured at that time, and the committee thought it more important to send Bruce Hunt than Hamilton.

7. Ibid., 22–23.

8. Ibid., 16–17.

9. Cyrus B. Ferguson, of the session of Kirkwood, Pa., OPC, was flown in on time to participate in the voting.

10. *Minutes of the Eighth GA*, 5–7.

11. *Minutes of the Thirteenth GA*, 86–88; *Standards of Government, Discipline, and Worship of the OPC*, 32–36.

12. *Minutes of the Twenty-second GA*, 27.

13. Ibid., 30.

14. Cornelius Van Til, *Common Grace* (Philadelphia: Presbyterian and Reformed, 1947), 47ff.

15. John Murray, *Principles of Conduct* (Grand Rapids: Eerdmans, 1957), 211–19.

16. Iain Murray, Vol. 2, 277.

17. John Murray, *The Epistle to the Romans*, Vols. 1 and 2 (Grand Rapids: Eerdmans, 1959, 1965).

Edward L. Kellogg

28 Wheaton College and the Orthodox Presbyterian Church

Edward L. Kellogg is the great grandson of Jonathan Blanchard, founder of Wheaton College in 1860. Born and raised in Wheaton, Mr. Kellogg graduated from the college in 1934. He then studied at Westminster Seminary and after graduation was ordained into the newly organized Presbyterian Church of America on May 23, 1937.

He is representative of many of the early leaders of the OPC. His background was in the strong evangelical tradition of the nineteenth and early twentieth centuries. Wheaton College was as much at the center of that tradition as any institution. It supplied a large number of students to Princeton Seminary when that school was known for its stand against modernism. Many Wheaton graduates also followed Machen to Westminster as controversy heated up.

Although the number of Wheaton men at Westminster eventually diminished, many who had studied there were deeply affected by its Reformed testimony. Some, like Mr. Kellogg, played an important part in the development of the OPC. In this brief reflection, he comments on the Wheaton/OPC connection. — Editors

WHEN THE PRESBYTERIAN CHURCH OF AMERICA, later known as the Orthodox Presbyterian Church, came into being in June of 1936, it was announced as the true successor of American Presbyterianism. The Presbyterian Church in the USA had been increasingly infiltrated with modernism and finally had subjected to discipline Dr. Machen and others with him who were seeking to reform the church and bring it back to a consistent biblical position. When the general assembly confirmed and finalized the discipline involving the defrocking of Dr. Machen, many regarded the action as indicative of an apostate condition and decided the one option was to establish a new Presbyterian church that would adhere to Scripture and to the subordinate Westminster standards.

The new church, though strongly influenced by the conservative element in the Presbyterian Church in the USA, was not to be a carbon copy of that element. Other influences would play a significant role. Part of the conflict in the early months while the new church was being formed was whether it would adhere as closely as possible to the form and characteristics of the conservative element of the Presbyterian Church in the USA or whether it would conform as closely as possible to the Scripture and the subordinate standards.

When Dr. Machen and those associated with him sought to establish a strong faculty for Westminster Seminary, they found a paucity of good men in the American tradition and turned to men from the Dutch and Scottish traditions. Thus Dr. Ned B. Stonehouse, Dr. Cornelius Van Til and Dr. R. B. Kuiper were drawn from the largely Dutch Christian Reformed Church and professor John Murray from the Free Church of Scotland. These men were to have a profound influence on the theological convictions of early graduates of Westminster and also on the Presbyterianism embraced by the OPC.

In addition to the influence of men from the Dutch and Scottish traditions, there was also a certain indirect influence from Wheaton College. A sizable percentage of the student body in the early years of Westminster consisted of students who came from Wheaton. The strong proponent of the seminary on the Wheaton campus was president J. Oliver Buswell. Dr. Buswell had a very high regard for Dr. Machen. He admired both his scholarship and his stand for biblical Christianity as opposed to modernism. Machen was invited to the campus to address the student body and certain student organizations. At the beginning of each semester a series of evangelistic services was held and at one of these Dr. Van Til was the speaker. However Dr. Buswell also welcomed to campus men like James M. Gray of Moody Bible Institute and Lewis Sperry Chafer of Dallas Theological Seminary.

It wasn't that Wheaton was strongly dispensational. Preceding Buswell in the office of president were Jonathan Blanchard and his son Charles. Jonathan was a postmillennialist in his convictions and though Charles swung from his father's postmillennialism to a premillennial view, yet both he and his father were strong Sabbatarians and proclaimed the Ten Commandments as the rule of life for Christians.

In the early 1920s a pastor was called to the College Church who was a dispensationalist. He, together with Buswell and others, sought to draw that church out of the Congregational denomination. In the conflict the church was divided and an independent church was formed, later known as the Wheaton Bible Church. Dispensational teaching was given in this new church. Dr. Buswell attended, though he could hardly be described as an ardent dispensationalist.

Only a small percentage of the Wheaton faculty and student body during this era were Reformed in conviction. Those who attended Westminster Seminary struggled with the Calvinism taught there. In the providence of God most of these young men embraced the Reformed faith with enthusiasm before they had completed their seminary training. Many of them were among the first ministers in the OPC.

There was a strong evangelistic emphasis on the Wheaton campus. Numerous organizations sprang up to engage in evangelistic work. The Scripture Distribution Society was one and through its efforts thousands of gospels were distributed at professional football and baseball games. Groups of Sunday school and Bible club workers were organized to go into the Chicago ghettos and to a large orphanage. Street meetings and jail services were also common. Back of these efforts was the weekly student prayer meeting where often several hundred students gathered to pray.

This influence appeared especially in the early years of the OPC when many churches held weeks of evangelistic meetings or participated in street meetings and jail services. This evangelistic emphasis which was prominent in the formative years of the denomination can be largely traced to the Wheaton College influence. Through the years Wheaton students have continued to go to Westminster for their theological training. Now the influence of Westminster and of the Orthodox Presbyterian Church has been felt at Wheaton where heads of several departments as well as many other teachers and students are active in the Wheaton congregation of the OPC. These maintain a testimony to the Reformed faith on the Wheaton campus.

James D. Phillips

29 The Church and the Harvest

A S I WRITE THIS, I am sitting in the dining room of a condominium looking out at the Smokey Mountains of North Carolina. The weather is cool, the sky is clear, the view is beautiful. Most of the tourists have gone. It is very peaceful, and yet an air of impending change is evident. Leaves are beginning to fall, winter is approaching. Workers are hastening to complete some buildings nearby. Farmers in the area are bringing in their crops. It is time to harvest the fruit of their summer labors.

It is also an appropriate place and time for reflection — reflection on my personal life, reflection on the church of which I am a part, and reflection on the spiritual harvest of Christ's church.

As I think back on the influence of the Orthodox Presbyterian Church in my personal life, I must say that it has been very positive. From a church-going Methodist background, I became a Christian at age twenty-one through the witness of a young woman and an Inter-Varsity Bible study group and finally through the invitation of a Baptist minister. After marriage to this same young woman, we began worshiping in Orlando with a small group of believers who later became the Lake Sherwood Orthodox Presbyterian Church.

Increasing responsibilities in this local church greatly stimulated my personal spiritual growth. Attendance at our local presbytery meetings was an introduction to the broader church. Taking on some committee responsibilities at the presbytery level helped me to see the biblical relationship local churches should have towards one another. Reading general assembly minutes gave an even broader view of the denomination as a whole. Visiting ministers, missionaries and professors who stayed in our home gave different positive views into the various aspects of the Lord's work in the Orthodox Presbyterian Church.

Through all these experiences I have been impressed by the Orthodox Presbyterian Church's commitment to presenting and living by the "whole counsel of God." There has been a consistent appeal to Scripture for directions in all areas of life. This has been a welcome solid rock in the midst of the constantly shifting philosophies evident in our society today. There has been a willingness to examine *all* the Bible, from cover to cover, not shying away from the areas that are difficult to understand.

As I reflect on what the Lord has done in Orlando, I am very thankful for and very impressed by the wide-open door that confronts us. From a small beginning in the early sixties — a few families meeting in homes, schoolrooms, and a woman's club — the church grew by 1970 to a total membership of seventy-four, with ten acres of land on the edge of Orlando and a building seating 125 people. By 1984 the membership has grown to 149, facilities have been expanded to seat 240, new homes are going up all around us and Orange County's population has passed 500,000.

In the midst of these positive observations, I must confess to the increasing conviction that there is one thing we lack, and it is this subject I would like to address.

Why are we here? Why the long struggle? Is it simply to preach the truths of Scripture to a small, slowly growing family of believers, strengthening the faith and lives of a few? It seems to me, upon this reflection, that God has put us in a field that is increasingly "white unto harvest." This would apply to our local church and the OPC as a whole, and this brings me to my main point: I believe God intends for his church not only to plant and to water and to nurture but also (and with equal emphasis) to *harvest*. Herein, I feel, lies a significant lack among us. We are so often content to minister to the Christians the Lord sends our way, and not willing to be harvesters. We work hard — counseling, preaching, helping, loving one another in the "household of faith" — but we do not reach out often enough to the unsaved.

In my vocation, citrus-growing, we spend a lot of time in planting young trees, then watering, cultivating, spraying, and fertilizing them. But through all this, the eventual end in view is regular bountiful harvests of fruit. In fact, in our company, about a third of our capital and manpower is invested in the area of harvesting. We would soon be out of business if we did not harvest the fruits of our labors.

In the citrus world, fruit comes in many varieties — oranges, grapefruit, tangerines, and the like. Similarly, in the spiritual realm, fruit may be viewed in various ways, as in the fruit of the Spirit. But I believe the type of harvest in view in the "field white unto harvest" is new-born Christians, and I believe we all need to be *more* willing to be used of God as harvesters of his fruit — perhaps fruit that someone else has planted and watered.

An example of this is a recent visit by an Evangelism Explosion team of two men and a woman from our church to the home of a child who had attended our vacation Bible school. In the midst of numerous distractions, the gospel was presented. The mother was evidently moved and accepted the free offer of salvation. The father did not. It seems apparent that the mother's heart was prepared. Someone else had planted a seed there and God used our willingness to go out as harvesters to be the final instrument in her entry into his family, as she placed her trust in the work and person of Jesus Christ.

In central Florida, we are experiencing explosive physical growth. Economic opportunities and favorable climate are drawing many people into our area. Numerous churches that are for the most part true to the Scriptures are reaping bountiful harvests of souls. In our local church we are beginning to respond to this "open door" with an increasing emphasis on personal, scriptural evangelism and discipleship, as we prayerfully seek to be used by God in the growth of his church. Further reflections on this situation have led to the observation that we (locally, and the OPC as a whole) have almost all the tools a good harvester needs. We have a knowledge of the Scripture and an awareness of God's primary role in salvation. Often lacking seems to be a basic expectation that God will use *us* as the final link in the chain of events that lead to a person's salvation.

I think that from time to time many of our people feel bad about not witnessing to others concerning faith in Christ. A pattern often emerges: in an outburst of enthusiasm a series of studies on evangelism is begun — attempts are made to witness verbally to others — there is little apparent fruit. Then comes frustration and a gradual cooling off. The basic driving motivation to continue, to hang in there, seems to be lacking. We feel guilty about the situation but become increasingly convinced we just can't successfully lead others to Christ.

Similarly, in citrus harvesting, often beginners come to the grove at 7 a.m., smiling and eager, only to leave at 5 p.m., tired, dirty, sore, with barely minimum wage earned. Some quit, never to return. Some come back, work the kinks out of their muscles, gradually acquiring the skills and strength necessary to pick oranges efficiently and quickly. Successful pickers go through a rigorous period of on-the-job training — watching experienced pickers, making mistakes, and learning as they work. These are soon able to earn the wages necessary to provide for their families. They are almost invariably motivated by *need*— they *need* to be successful in order to put bread on the table. For these people, it's a matter of survival — a necessity. It's not an optional endeavor, to be abandoned when the going gets hard.

I think we in the Orthodox Presbyterian Church often lack the basic motivation to be successful evangelists. We see it as an optional activity. We say, in effect, "If I have a special gift for talking to others, well, that's fine. If not, that's O.K. — someone else will do the job of evangelizing." We, for the most part, don't seem to see the *need* to take the time and expend the energy to acquire the skills that the Lord seems to use in personal evangelism. We often don't see the *need* for on-the-job training, memorizing Scripture, suffering embarrassment, and spending hours getting to know strangers. We don't see the *need* to confront personally unsaved people with the necessity of trusting Christ as the only way to salvation. Personal evangelism just doesn't seem to be a necessary activity — by our attitudes and actions, we silently say it's optional. Somehow God will do it with someone else, and it's sufficient if we minister to those already saved.

In the incident cited earlier, that of the young woman's conversion, the young man who led the presentation was a new Christian himself and had just completed sixteen weeks of on-the-job training in how to present the gospel effectively. He had seen the need to equip himself with additional knowledge and skills in the area of personal evangelism. God honored this commitment and used him to lead someone to salvation.

In our part of Florida this winter there will be only half or less of a normal crop of citrus, due to tree damage from the recent freeze. Our harvesting will be greatly curtailed due to lack of fruit to harvest. We have the tools needed to bring in a bountiful harvest — trucks, trailers, tubs, ladders, bags, manpower — but these tools will not be completely utilized this year. We are motivated to pick fruit, but the fruit is not here to be picked.

In contrast, God has set before our local church and our denomination a plentiful harvest of souls for his kingdom. We must add motivation, hard work, and skill in witness to the knowledge and faith we already have to enable us to be used by God in this harvest. It can be done. God seems to honor consistently a person's commitment and willingness to be used in this area. On-the-job training methods that are readily available seem to be the most effective means to success, if we prayerfully and earnestly see personal evangelism as a necessary part of our Christian walk.

How is it with you? Is there not also a plentiful harvest before you?

My prayer is that God will increasingly awaken us all to the *need* to *practice* his *whole* counsel, and to stop explaining away our lack of evangelism. May we be more and more committed to being used by him in the numerical growth as well as the spiritual nurture of his church. God has blessed us in so many ways. May we respond in gratitude and willingness to obey him more completely, especially in the area of harvesting.

David L. Neilands

30 A Backward Look
with a Forward Perspective

J OSHUA 4:6 READS, "What mean ye by these stones?" At the Lord's
command Joshua had twelve stones carried out of the midst of Jordan
and set up in the promised land. These stones were a memorial for the
benefit of future generations. They pointed to the mighty works of God
on behalf of his church. Furthermore, the stones testified that God was
fulfilling his covenant promises given to Abraham in Genesis, chapter 17.

Although I have served the OPC from its beginning I have not been
prone to look back but always forward. The future of the church has always
been my concern. However, the Lord's commandment to establish a
memorial is I believe a biblical warrant to look back and see what God
has done.

A False Prediction

It was but a few weeks after the establishment of the new church in
1936. As I passed by the First Presbyterian Church of Oakland I was met
by the executive secretary of the San Francisco Presbytery. He assured me
that the new church would not last six months but break up from internal
dissension.

The ways of the Lord are beyond our comprehension. Here was the
man who had been instrumental in my becoming an elder in the old
Presbyterian Church. On that occasion he promised to send me to the
general assembly someday. However, when I was nominated as an elder-
commissioner in 1936 he remained silent. I was not chosen as a delegate.

Thanks be to God, his prophetic words proved to be false. We still exist
and have celebrated the fiftieth anniversary of the founding of the Ortho-

453

dox Presbyterian Church. Not only do we exist but we have grown and established a testimony that is being heard throughout the world.

However, this does not mean that the OPC has had smooth sailing for its first half-century of existence. It became apparent that there was a strong division among the brethren even as early as the Second General Assembly held in November of 1936. The division came to its climax following the Third General Assembly in June of the following year when fourteen ministers and three ruling elders withdrew from the church to organize the "Bible Presbyterian Synod." The three issues that caused the separation centered on independency, especially as it related to the Independent Board for Presbyterian Foreign Missions, the Christian life, and premillennialism.

The departure of these brethren was a severe blow. But the church held true to the *Westminster Confession of Faith* which it believed summarized its doctrine and life as taught by the Scriptures.

A Second Dispute

It seems to me as I reflect upon the history of the church that the second great disruption came in what was referred to as "The Clark Case." The case revolved around Dr. Gordon H. Clark and was related to his licensure and ordination by the Presbytery of Philadelphia. His views became the rallying point for a group of ministers and elders in the church. The conflict extended over a period of time stretching from 1944 to 1949. No doubt the inordinate amount of time spent on this debate was because of the philosophical and theological questions involved: the free offer of the gospel, the effect of regeneration upon the intellect, and the doctrine of God's incomprehensibility as it related to man's knowledge. Also involved were the provisions of the Form of Government. For example, shouldn't there be both an examination for licensure and a further examination required for ordination with a period of time between the two?

Although these issues agitated the church for several years and although Dr. Clark's views were never decisively rejected, the church did not uphold his views. The minutes of the Sixteenth General Assembly show that several churches and ministers who had supported Dr. Clark left the church. Dr. Clark transferred to the United Presbyterian Church on October 14, 1948. The loss of these brethren was great, but I believe that once again the church had remained true to the Scriptures and to its Confession of Faith.

In Hopes of a Profitable Future

Throughout its history the OPC has had to face issues and problems like those above. But while it remains the church on earth it must ever be the church militant. Constant diligence is required of every minister and elder. We have taken a solemn vow "to seek the purity, the peace and the unity of the church." These three aims are of equal importance.

Our name, The Orthodox Presbyterian Church, is a constant reminder of the necessity of maintaining the truth. That name should be a constant witness to every minister and elder that we must be diligent in maintaining the purity of the faith as well as of life. I'm mindful that some dislike our name, but I would remind you that God in his wise providence provided it.

It is no secret that my hopes, prayers, and activities are to the effect that the OPC live on in history for many years to come and that it be faithful in the propagation of the Reformed faith. To this end, I believe there is nothing more important for us than a sound doctrine of the covenant.

The Rev. Robert K. Churchill was our first pastor in the OP church at Berkeley. Shortly after his coming in 1937 he took me to visit a family in another Reformed church. I have never forgotten the impression that visit made upon me. The man in that family freely discussed theological problems, the Reformed faith, and the covenant of grace. To my great surprise he was at that time reading Calvin's *Institutes.* Imagine my greater surprise when I learned that he was a longshoreman! Hardly the type of individual that you would expect to find reading Calvin's *Institutes.*

In my continued contacts with this man and his church I was impressed by their clear and positive witness to the Reformed faith. His church held firmly to the doctrine of the covenant of grace. This doctrine directed and motivated the denomination's life and that of its people. Here, I thought, was the ideal. My hope was that someday the OPC would be like that.

I must confess that I do not think that we have reached the heights of that church at that time. Why? There may be contributing factors, but I am firmly persuaded that it is because we have never given the doctrine of the covenant the important place it ought to have in our lives. Because of this we have lacked the unity to our Calvinism that we knew it ought to have. We concentrated on the five points of Calvinism. Here was our concern: to get the people to know, to believe, and to understand those five points. We related the five points to the sovereignty of God and personal salvation but not to the covenant of grace and history. This has had a negative effect upon our church and its witness.

First, we have made the mistake of thinking of the covenant of grace as a purely academic matter; something for theological students. We have not seen the covenant as something that affects the life and testimony of the church. But an inability to see the covenant as something that affects our thinking and living, has left us unable to see the covenant aright.

Secondly, we forget that Jehovah established his covenant of grace with Abraham to be his God and to be the God of his *seed.* Jehovah reaffirmed his covenant promises to Isaac and Jacob thereby establishing continuity in the *covenant family*.

In light of this, the Christian home under God is a covenant home. When Christians marry they should understand that in obedience to God they are establishing covenant homes. In these homes the parents and the children belong to God. It is God's law that is to be learned and obeyed by all the family members. Nothing else is the standard of truth, righteousness, and holiness. It is the Word of God that binds the family together. If only this view prevailed there would be far fewer unhappy and broken homes and stronger families, yes, even in the OPC.

Next we must remember that these families make up the church, the covenant community. The covenant family had grown into a nation while in Egyptian bondage. But here was no ordinary nation since it belonged to Jehovah. As his covenantally-gathered assembly it was his church. It cried and groaned for deliverance. We learn from Exod 2:24 "God heard their groaning, and God remembered His covenant with Abraham, Isaac and Jacob." It was to his redeemed church that Jehovah gave his covenant promise in Lev 26:12: "I will walk among you, and will be your God, and ye shall be my people."

When we join the church, we should understand that we are covenant individuals who are members of covenant families who are joining a covenant community. God has promised to dwell with us in this community.

But how well do we maintain our awareness of church and covenant? Alas, I fear not very well at all! I believe that if only we had been a covenant-conscious church with an understanding of covenant administration we might have escaped some of our trials. This would be equally true for the future.

If we need proof, we find it in church history. There is a tragic sequel in the story of that glorious Reformed church to which I previously referred. It is no longer a covenant-conscious church. Its great heritage is now lost. It has slowly moved away from its Reformed commitment. Significant to me is the fact that with its departure from the faith it has encountered distress and divisions of a magnitude unprecedented in its prior history. If we are slipping we need to grasp hold of the covenant before we slip further. If we never had a grip, it's time we did.

In the fourth place, we do well to remember that history is covenant history. We divide history into sacred and secular events but our God does not. The Scriptures teach us that all the events of history are moving toward God's predetermined goal. That goal is nothing less than the conquest of the nations, bringing them into subjection to the Lord Jesus Christ the Redeemer-King.

And what of the distinctiveness of the covenant people? The Old Testament prophets recorded history as a continuous, totally integrated succession of events. The history of the pagan nations is related to the nation of Israel, God's covenant people. Nations rise and fall but in the midst of history God establishes his own messianic kingdom, an eternal kingdom with the crucified Lord of glory as its King. History ceases when Christ returns to judge the pagan nations and when He gathers his covenant people of all ages into the church triumphant. In that day Christ will prevail. He will have subdued all his and our enemies.

Believe me, as covenant people we need nothing less than this historical perspective of the covenant to keep us from sinking into the attitude of defeat and despair.

"What mean ye by these stones?" It was the determined purpose of the founders of the OPC to establish a church that was in every respect true to the Scriptures. It was to be a memorial and a witness to God's sovereign grace in the redemption of his people. It was to be a church that proclaimed the gospel of Christ as understood and taught by our *Westminster Confession of Faith*.

I believe that as we are looking back on our history we must stop and give thanks to God for watching over and preserving the witness of this church during all these years. Many have been the hidden rocks and shoals as we sailed in this uncharted sea. It is certain that without God's preserving care and guidance we would not have come this far.

But now we must again look forward. We cannot live on past experiences. Let us, by God's grace, rededicate ourselves to the further building up of the church mindful of the covenant and our high calling. Let us press on to the fulfillment of the high hopes and aspirations that were ours at the foundation of the church in 1936. I would remind you that in that day men dedicated their lives and their fortunes so that a church might be established where the gospel would be proclaimed without fear or favor of men and without compromise with liberalism and its false message.

Let us, by God's grace and power, resolve to follow in their train. Let us further resolve to endeavor to be a church that is covenant-conscious and faithful in teaching, preaching, and living the glorious gospel of our Lord Jesus Christ as revealed in Scripture and summarized in our Confession.

Part V

The Writings of
J. Gresham Machen
1881–1937

J. Gresham Machen circa 1920

James T. Dennison, Jr., & Grace Mullen

31 A Bibliography of the Writings of J. Gresham Machen, 1881–1937

THE AUTHORS have undertaken a two-part bibliography of J. Gresham Machen, the initial phase of which is before you. Since Miss Mullen had organized the Machen archive at Westminster Theological Seminary in Philadelphia, we decided to identify all possible materials written by Machen using his papers as a check. The second phase of this project will seek to compile materials about Machen. In time, we hope to publish both parts as a single volume.

ABBREVIATIONS

CB	*Christian Beacon*
CT	*Christianity Today* (1930–1949)
EQ	*Evangelical Quarterly*
IBB	*Independent Board Bulletin*
NYT	*New York Times*
P	*Presbyterian*
PG	*Presbyterian Guardian*
PJ	*Presbyterian Journal*
PTR	*Princeton Theological Review*
SST	*Sunday School Times*

1905
"The New Testament Account of the Birth of Jesus" (first article). *PTR* 3:641–70.

1906
"The New Testament Account of the Birth of Jesus" (second article). *PTR* 4:37–81.
"Die Universitaten der Vereinigten Staaten." *Der Schwarzburgbund* 16 (December 1906):42–44.

1907
"Die Universitaten der Vereinigten Staaten." *Der Schwarzburgbund* 16 (January 1907):59–60.
"Die Universitaten der Vereinigten Staaten." *Der Schwarzburgbund* 16 (February 1907):73.
Review: *The Birth and Infancy of Jesus Christ According to the Gospel Narratives* (Louis Matthews Sweet). *PTR* 5: 315–16.

1908
Review: *Der Zeugniszweck des Evangelisten Johannes nach seinen eigenen Angaben dargestellt* (Konrad Meyer). *PTR* 6:142–43.
Review: *Des Paulus Brief an die Romer fur hohere Schulen* (Rudolf Niemann). *PTR* 6:144.
Review: *Des Paulus Epistel an die Romer: Abdruck der revidierten Ubersetzung Luthers und Auslegung fur Gymnasialprima* (Rudolf Niemann). *PTR* 6:144.
Review: *The Virgin Birth of Christ* (James Orr). *PTR* 6:505–8.

1909
Translation: "The Reformation and Natural Law" (August Lang), *PTR* 7:177–218, and in *Calvin and the Reformation*, ed. by William P. Armstrong. New York: Fleming H. Revell Co., pp. 56–98.
Review: *St. Paul's Epistles to the Thessalonians* (George Milligan). *PTR* 7:126–31.
Review: *Interpretation of the Bible: A Short History* (George Holley Gilbert). *PTR* 7:348–51.
Review: *PROS ROMAIOUS: Die Epistel Pauli an die Romer* (G. Richter). *PTR* 7:351.
Review: *A Short Grammar of the Greek New Testament for Students Familiar with the Elements of Greek* (A. T. Robertson). *PTR* 7:491–93.
Review: *The Johannine Writings* (Paul W. Schmiedel). *PTR* 7:670–74.

1910
Review: *The Irenaeus Testimony to the Fourth Gospel: Its Extent, Meaning and Value* (Frank Grant Lewis). *PTR* 8:137–39.

Review: *Der Leserkreis des Galaterbriefes: ein Beitrag zur urchristlichen Missionsgeschichte* (Alphons Steinmann). *PTR* 8:299–300.

Review: *The Pauline Epistles: A Critical Study* (Robert Scott). *PTR* 8:300 –301.

Review: *Commentar uber den Brief Pauli an die Romer* (G. Stockhardt). *PTR* 8:490–91.

1911

Review: *Selections from the Greek Papyri* (George Milligan, ed.). *PTR* 9:327–28.

Review: *The Bible for Home and School: Commentary on the Epistle of Paul to the Galatians* (Benjamin W. Bacon). *PTR* 9:495–98.

Review: *The Childhood of Jesus Christ According to the Canonical Gospels* (A. Durand). *PTR* 9:672–73.

1912

"Jesus and Paul," in *Biblical and Theological Studies*. New York: Charles Scribner's Sons, pp. 545–78.

"The Hymns of the First Chapter of Luke." *PTR* 10:1–38.

"The Origin of the First Two Chapters of Luke." *PTR* 10:212–77.

"The Virgin Birth in the Second Century." *PTR* 10:529–80.

Review: *Christ and His Critics: Studies in the Person and Problems of Jesus* (F. R. Montgomery Hitchcock). *PTR* 10:334–35.

1913

"Christianity and Culture." *PTR* 11:1–15.

Review: *Kurzgefasste Grammatik des Neutestamentlichen Griechisch mit Berucksichtigung der Ergebnisse der vergleichenden Sprachwissenschaft und der KOINH-Forschung* (A. T. Robertson). *PTR* 11:129–30.

Review: *St. Paul's Epistle to the Galatians* (Cyril W. Emmet). *PTR* 11:320 –22.

Review: *Die Geisteskultur von Tarsos im augusteischen Zeitalter: Mit Berucksichtigung der paulinischen Schriften* (Hans Bohlig). *PTR* 11:518–21.

Review: *Elchasai: Ein Religionsstifter und sein Werk. Beitrage zur judischen christlichen und allgemeinen Religionsgeschichte* (Wilhelm Brandt). *PTR* 11:524–25.

Review: *The New Testament Documents: Their Origin and Early History* (George Milligan). *PTR* 11:672–73.

1914

A RAPID SURVEY OF THE LITERATURE AND HISTORY OF THE NEW TESTAMENT TIMES — Student's text book, Part 1. Philadelphia: Presbyterian Board of Christian Education.

A RAPID SURVEY OF THE LITERATURE AND HISTORY OF NEW TESTAMENT TIMES — Teacher's manual, Part 1. Philadelphia: Presbyterian Board of Christian Education.

A RAPID SURVEY OF THE LITERATURE AND HISTORY OF NEW TESTAMENT TIMES — Student's text book, Part 2. Philadelphia: Board of Christian Education of the Presbyterian Church in the U.S.A.

A RAPID SURVEY OF THE LITERATURE AND HISTORY OF NEW TESTAMENT TIMES — Teacher's manual, Part 2. Philadelphia: Board of Christian Education of the Presbyterian Church in the U.S.A.

Review: *A Critical and Exegetical Commentary on the Epistles of St. Paul to the Thessalonians* (James Everett Frame). *PTR* 12:150–51.

1915

THE LITERATURE AND HISTORY OF NEW TESTAMENT TIMES. Philadelphia: The Presbyterian Board of Publication and Sabbath School Work.

A RAPID SURVEY OF THE LITERATURE AND HISTORY OF NEW TESTAMENT TIMES — Student's text book, Part 3. Philadelphia: Board of Christian Education of the Presbyterian Church in the U.S.A.

A RAPID SURVEY OF THE LITERATURE AND HISTORY OF NEW TESTAMENT TIMES — Teacher's manual, Part 3. Philadelphia: Board of Christian Education of the Presbyterian Church in the U.S.A.

A RAPID SURVEY OF THE LITERATURE AND HISTORY OF NEW TESTAMENT TIMES — Student's text book, Part 4. Philadelphia: Presbyterian Board of Christian Education.

A RAPID SURVEY OF THE LITERATURE AND HISTORY OF NEW TESTAMENT TIMES — Teacher's manual, Part 4. Philadelphia: Presbyterian Board of Christian Education.

"Matthew 1:16 and the Virgin Birth." *P* 85 (Mar. 18, 1915): 8–11.

"History and Faith." *PTR* 13:337–51. Inaugural Address — Assistant Professor of New Testament Literature and Exegesis, Princeton Theological Seminary, May 3, 1915.

Review: *Die Apostelgeschichte* (Hans Hinrich Wendt). *PTR* 13:292–95.

Review: *Kommentar uber den Ersten Brief Petri* (G. Stockhardt). *PTR* 13:298–99.

Review: *A Grammar of the Greek New Testament in the Light of Historical Research* (A. T. Robertson). *PTR* 13:482–83.

Review: *Friedrich Blass' Grammatik des neutestamentlichen Griechisch* (Albert Debrunner). *PTR* 13:483.

1917

Review: *A Pocket Lexicon to the Greek New Testament* (Alexander Souter). *PTR* 15:179–80.

1918

Against Woman Suffrage (letter to Representative John R. Ramsey). *Congressional Record,* Jan. 10, 1918.

"The Minister and his Greek Testament." *P* 88 (Feb. 7, 1918):8–9. Reprinted in the *Banner of Truth* (April 1972):21–23 and *The New Testament Student,* I (1974), pp. 152–55.

1919

"The Church in the War." *P* 89 (May 29, 1919):10–11.

"Recent Criticism of the Book of Acts." *PTR* 17:585–608.

Review: *The Acts of the Apostles: The Greek Text Edited with Introduction and Notes for the Use of Schools.* (W. F. Burnside). *PTR* 17:151–52.

Review: *The Virgin Birth of Jesus: A Critical Examination of the Gospel Narratives of the Nativity, and Other New Testament and Early Christian Evidence, and the Alleged Influence of Heathen Ideas* (G. H. Box). *PTR* 17:152–53.

Review: *The Synoptic Gospels and the Book of Acts* (D. A. Hayes). *PTR* 17:675–77.

1920

"The Proposed Plan of Union." *P* 90 (June 10, 1920):8–9.

Review: *Christianity According to St. Luke* (S. C. Carpenter). *PTR* 18:518–19.

Review: *The Rival Philosophies of Jesus and Paul: Being an Explanation of the Failures of Organized Christianity and a Vindicaton of the Teachings of Jesus which are Shown to Contain a Religion for All Men and for All Time* (Ignatius Singer). *PTR* 18:519–20.

1921

THE ORIGIN OF PAUL'S RELIGION. New York: Macmillan Co. Reprinted by Eerdmans, 1965.

"The Life of Christ and the Development of the Church in Apostolic and Post Apostolic Times," in *Teaching the Teacher: A First Book in Teacher Training,* ed. by James Oscar Boyd. Philadelphia: Westminster Press, pp. 53–144.

"For Christ or Against Him." *P* 91 (Jan. 20, 1921):8–9.

"The Second Declaration of the Council on Organic Union." *P* 91 (Mar. 17, 1921):8,26.

Review: *Jesus and Paul* (Benjamin W. Bacon). *PTR* 19:684–87.

1922

A BRIEF BIBLE HISTORY: A SURVEY OF THE OLD AND NEW TESTAMENTS. Philadelphia: Westminster Press.

"Liberalism or Christianity?" *PTR* 20:93–117.

Review: *A Critical and Exegetical Commentary on the Epistle to the Galatians* (Ernest De Witt Burton). *PTR* 20:142–48.

Review: *Is Mark a Roman Gospel?* (Benjamin W. Bacon). *PTR* 20:326–27.

Review: *Mensch und Gott: Betrachtungen uber Religion und Christentum* (Houston Stewart Chamberlain). *PTR* 20:327–29.

Review: *The Style and Literary Method of Luke* (Henry J. Cadbury). *PTR* 20:329–30.

Review: *The New Testament Today* (Ernest Findlay Scott). *PTR* 20:330–33.

Review: *The Variants in the Gospel Reports* (T. H. Weir). *PTR* 20:333–34.

Review: *The Sayings of Jesus from Oxyrhynchus* (Hugh G. Evelyn White, ed.). *PTR* 20:334–36.

Review: *Dictionary of the Vulgate New Testament* (J. M. Harden). *PTR* 20:336.

Review: *The Pastoral Epistles* (R. St. John Parry). *PTR* 20:490–93.

Review: *The Four Gospels: Their Literary History and Their Special Characteristics* (Maurice Jones). *PTR* 20:493–95.

Review: *The Temptation of Jesus* (W. J. Foxell). *PTR* 20:495–97.

1923

CHRISTIANITY AND LIBERALISM. New York: Macmillan Co. Reprinted by Eerdmans, 1946.

NEW TESTAMENT GREEK FOR BEGINNERS. New York: Macmillan Co.

Nebraska's Language Law (letter to editor). *New York Herald Tribune* (Feb. 26 (?), 1923).

Urging Repeal of Lusk Anti-Sedition Laws (letter to editor). *NYT* (Feb. 27, 1923):18, col. 8.

"Christianity vs. Modern Liberalism." *Moody Monthly* 23:349–52.

Lusk Law Boatrockers (letter to editor). *New York Herald Tribune* (Apr. 12 (?), 1923).

"Religious Work Program of the Y.M.C.A." Paper presented at the Fifty-fourth State Convention of the Young Men's Christian Associations of Pennsylvania, April 14, 1923.

"Is Christianity True?" *The Bible To-day* 17:197–99.

"The Source of Paul's Missionary Zeal." *The Westminster Teacher* 51:647–48.

Sermon on the Present Issue in the Church Preached in the First Presbyterian Church of Princeton, December 30, 1923. Philadelphia: The Presbyterian [1924]. Reprint from P 94 (Jan. 24, 1924):16–18.

Review: *Apology and Polemic in the New Testament* (Andrew D. Heffern). P 93 (Sept. 13, 1923):10–11.

Review: *The Psychic Health of Jesus* (Walter E. Bundy). PTR 21:310–13.

Review: *The Apostle Paul and the Modern World: An Examination of the Teaching of Paul in its Relation to Some of the Religious Problems of Modern Life* (Francis Greenwood Peabody). PTR 21:480–82.

Review: *Christian Ways of Salvation* (George W. Richards). PTR 21:482–86.

Review: *He Opened to Us the Scriptures: A Study of Christ's Better Way in the Use of Scripture* (Benjamin W. Bacon). PTR 21:640–42.

Review: *The Constructive Revolution of Jesus: A Study of Some of His Social Attitudes* (Samuel Dickey). PTR 21:642–45.

Review: *The Acts of the Apostles* (A. W. F. Blunt). PTR 21:645–46.

Review: *The Second Epistle of Paul to the Corinthians* (Wilfred H. Isaacs). PTR 21:646–48.

Review: *Here and There Among the Papyri* (George Milligan). PTR 21:648–49.

Review: *Life of Christ* (Giovanni Papini). PTR 21:649–51.

Review: *The Apostolic Age: A Study of the Early Church and its Achievements* (William Bancroft Hill). PTR 21:651–54.

Review: *Inspiration: A Study of Divine Influence and Authority in the Holy Scripture* (Nolan R. Best). PTR 21:672–79.

1924

The Parting of the Ways. Reprint (with slight changes) from P 94 (Apr. 17, 1924):7–9; (Apr. 24, 1924):6–7.

"Sermon on the Present Issue in the Church Preached in the First Presbyterian Church of Princeton." P 94 (Jan. 24, 1924):16–18.

"Dr. Merrill in the World's Work." P 94 (Feb. 7, 1924):6–7.

"Honesty and Freedom in the Christian Ministry." *Moody Bible Institute Monthly* 24:355–57.

"An Earnest Plea for Christian Freedom — and Honesty!" *The Lookout: Magazine of Christian Education* 36 (Mar. 2, 1924):6.

"Religion and Fact." *The Real Issue* 1 (Apr. 15, 1924):3–4.

"The Parting of the Ways— Part I." P 94 (Apr. 17, 1924):7–9.

"The Parting of the Ways— Part II." P 94 (Apr. 24, 1924):6–7.

"Dr. Zenos on the Present Issue in the Church." P 94 (May 22, 1924):7–8.

Acceptance of Challenge to Cite Where Harry Emerson Fosdick Denies Divinity of Christ (letter to editor). *New Brunswick Daily Home News*, June (?), 1924.

"Does Fundamentalism Obstruct Social Progress? The Negative." *The Survey Graphic* 5 (July 1924):391–92, 426–27.

"Faith and Knowledge." *Fourth Biennial Meeting of the Conference of Theological Seminaries and Colleges in the United States and Canada: Bulletin* 4 (August):12–23.

Modernism and the Faith (letter to editor). *The British Weekly* 77 (Sept. 11, 1924):501,509.

"A Rejection of Truth." *The Herald and Presbyter* 95 (Oct. 15, 1924):6.

"Dr. Fosdick's Letter." *P* 94 (Oct. 23, 1924):6.

"Rupert Hughes and the Christian Religion: Why His Attack on the Bible is Representative of the Intellectual and Moral Decadence Widely Prevalent Today." *SST* 66:671.

Child Labor Referendum — Massachusetts Vote (letter to editor). *NYT* (Nov. 18, 1924):24.

Child Labor Referendum — Massachusetts Vote (letter to editor). *New York Herald Tribune* (Nov. 19, 1924):18, col. 7.

"The Biblical Teacher and Biblical Facts." *Christian Education* 8:98–107. Reprinted in *SST* 66:803–804 with the title "The Bible Teacher and Biblical Facts."

"The Central Period of Christ's Ministry." *The Westminster Teacher* 52:655–56.

"The Virgin Birth." *The Bible To-day* 19:75–79.

"Too Park-Like" (letter to editor). *New York Herald Tribune* (Dec. 10, 1924):26, col. 6.

"A Debate: Is the Teaching of Dr. Harry Emerson Fosdick Opposed to the Christian Religion? Yes." *The Christian Work* 117:686–88.

"The Bible Teacher and Biblical Facts." *SST* 66:803–804. Reprinted from *Christian Education* 8:98–107. Reprinted in German in *Kirchenzeitung* 18 (May 5, 1925).

Child Labor and Liberty (letter to editor). *The New Republic* 41 (Dec. 31, 1924):145.

Dr. Abbe Replies to Mr. Machen (letter to editor). *Bar Harbor Times* 10 (Dec. 31, 1924):1. Reprinted from *New York Herald Tribune* (Dec. 10, 1924):26, col. 6.

Review: "Christian Fellowship and the World-Wide Conflict" (Review of Emile Doumergue, *Le Christianisme est-il Chretien?*). *P* 94 (Nov. 20, 1924):6–7

Review: *The God of the Early Christians* (Arthur Cushman McGiffert). *PTR* 22:544–88.

Review: *Jesus of Nazareth: A Biography* (George A. Barton). *PTR* 22:665–67.

Review: *The Character of Paul* (Charles Edward Jefferson). *PTR* 22:667–70.

1925

WHAT IS FAITH? New York: Macmillan Co. Reprinted by Eerdmans, 1946.

"The Virgin Birth." *The Bible To-day* 19:111–15.

"The So-Called Child Labor Amendment." *P* 95 (Jan. 22, 1925): 6–7.

Child Labor Amendment (letter to editor). *Trenton Sunday Times-Advertiser* (Jan. 25, 1925).

"Dr. Machen Replies to Dr. Erdman." *P* 95 (Feb. 5, 1925):20–21.

The Beauty of the Forest (letter to editor). *NYT* (Feb. 18, 1925):18:7.

"Child Labor and Liberty" (from a letter to *The New Republic*). *The Woman Patriot* 9 (Mar. 1, 1925):39.

"Shall the General Assembly Represent the Church?" *P* 95 (Mar. 5, 1925):6–8.

The Separateness of the Church. Philadelphia: The Presbyterian Press Association. Reprinted in *PG* 42 (October 1973):116–19; *CB* 30 (June 10, 1965):2–3, 33 (Mar. 28, 1968):7–8, 35 (Apr. 2, 1970):5,7.

"The Resurrection." *The Bible To-day* 19:223–27, 265–68.

"The Presbytery of New Brunswick." *P* 95 (Apr. 23, 1925):21.

"Der Lehrer der Bibel und die biblischen Tatsachen." *Kirchenzeitung* 18 (May 5, 1925):3–6. Reprinted from *SST* 66:803–4.

"The Present Situation in the Presbyterian Church." *P* 95 (May 14, 1925):6–8. Also in *Christian Work* 118 (May 16, 1925):626–28 with the title "The Issues at Columbus: The Conservative View."

"What Fundamentalism Stands for Now, Defined by a Leading Exponent of Conservative Reading of the Bible as the Word of God." *NYT* (June 21, 1925):9:1, col. 1.

Against Phi Beta Kappa Resolution on Free Speech in Colleges (letter to editor). *NYT* (Sept. 18, 1925):C:22, col. 7.

"The Real Issue Stated: What Evangelical Christians Stand For." *The Bible for China* 22 (October 1925):11–17. Cover Title: "The Real Issue Stated: the Factual Basis of Our Faith."

"What Fundamentalism Stands For." *The Bible Champion* 31:489–92.

"The Conversion of Paul." *The Westminster Teacher* 53:594–95.

"My Idea of God." *Woman's Home Companion* 52 (December 1925):15, 124. Also printed in *The Globe* (Toronto) (Nov. 21, 1925) and *Morning Chronicle* (Halifax, NS) (Nov. 28, 1925). Reprinted in *The Bulletin of Westminster Theological Seminary* (PA) 20:3 (Summer 1981):1–3.

Against Alien Enrollment (letter to editor). *New York Herald Tribune* (Dec. 7, 1925):14.

Review: *The Modern Use of the Bible* (Harry Emerson Fosdick). *PTR* 23:66–81.

Review: *Jesus and the Greeks* (William Fairweather). *PTR* 23:672–75.

Review: *Light from Ancient Letters: Private Correspondence in the Non-literary Papyri of Oxyrhynchus of the First Four Centuries and its Bearing on New Testament Language and Thought* (Henry G. Meecham). *PTR* 23:675.

1926

"My Idea of God," in *My Idea of God*, ed. by Joseph Fort Newton. Boston: Little, Brown and Co., pp. 37–50.

"Prophets False and True," in *Best Sermons, 1926*, ed. by Joseph Fort Newton. New York: Harcourt, Brace and Co., pp. 115–23.

Statement by J. Gresham Machen [on the Eighteenth Amendment]. Princeton: Unpublished.

Italy in the Tyrol (letter to editor). *New York City Tribune* (Feb. 13, 1926).

"Shall We Have a Federal Department of Education?" (an Address Delivered . . . before the Sentinels of the Republic, Washington, D.C., January 12, 1926). *The Woman Patriot* 10:25–29.

Statement of Dr. J. Gresham Machen on the Proposed Department of Education (Joint Hearings before the Committee on Education and Labor, United States Senate, and the Committee on Education, House of Representatives, . . . Feb. 24, 25 and 26, 1926). Washington: Government Printing Office, pp. 95–108.

"The Mission of the Church." *P* 96 (Apr. 8, 1926):8–11.

"Dr. Machen Finds God in Creation and Revelation." *Morning Star* (Vancouver) (Apr. 10, 1926). Reprinted from *Woman's Home Companion* 52 (December 1925).

Vestal Copyright Bill (letter to editor). *New York Herald Tribune* (Apr. 19, 1926).

"Educators Discuss New Education Bill — Con." *Congressional Digest* 5:157–59.

"Faith and Knowledge." *The College Record, Review Supplement* (Goshen College, IN) 27 (May–June):8–19. Reprint of Chapter 1 of *What Is Faith?* (1925).

"Dr. Machen's Acknowledgement" (for a series of articles dealing with *What Is Faith?*) (letter to Dr. Hutton). *The British Weekly* 80 (Sept. 23, 1926):517.

Documents Appended to a Statement by J. Gresham Machen Submitted to the Committee Appointed by Action of the General Assembly of 1926 "to make a sympathetic study of conditions affecting the welfare of Princeton Seminary . . ." Printed: Not Published.

Statement by J. Gresham Machen Submitted to the Committee Appointed by Action of the General Assembly of 1926 "to make a sympathetic study of conditions affecting the welfare of Princeton Seminary, and to co-operate in striving to adjust differences and to report to the next Assembly". Printed: Not Published.

Additional Statement Concerning the Personal Relations Between the Rev. Professor Charles R. Erdman, D.D., LL.D., and J. Gresham Machen. Printed: Not Published.

"The Relation of Religion to Science and Philosophy" (Review of *Christianity at the Cross Roads*, by E. Y. Mullins). *PTR* 24:38–66.

Review: *The Approach to Christianity* (Edward Gordon Selwyn). *New York Evening Post Literary Review* (Jan. 9, 1926). Also *Public Ledger* (Philadelphia, PA) (Jan. 16, 1926):15.

Review: *The Reasonableness of Christianity* (Douglas Clyde Macintosh). *New York Evening Post Literary Review* (Jan. 30, 1926):5.

Review: *Christian Beginnings* (F. C. Burkitt). *PTR* 24:132–34

Review: *The Credibility of the Virgin Birth* (Orville E. Crain). *PTR* 24:134–36.

1927

"The Integrity of the Lucan Narrative of the Annunciation." *PTR* 25:529–86.

"What Is the Gospel?" *Union Seminary Review* (Richmond) 38:158–70.

"Criticism and Comments on Prof. Cole's Article." *Religious Education* 22:118–20.

"The Claims of Love." *Brooklyn Eagle* (Mar. 7, 1927).

"A Symposium Review of *My Idea of God.*" *Unity* 99:4 (Mar. 28, 1927):64–65.

Is the Bible Right About Jesus? London: Bible League. Also published in Philadelphia: Committee on Christian Education of the Orthodox Presbyterian Church, n.d.

"Christianity vs. Modern Liberalism." *Southern Churchman* 92 (June 11, 1927):7–8.

"Christianity vs. Modern Liberalism, II." *Southern Churchman* 92 (June 18, 1927):7–8.

"Christianity vs. Modern Liberalism, III." *Southern Churchman* 92 (June 25, 1927):9–10.

"Dr. Machen Declines the Presidency of Bryan University." *P* 97 (July 7, 1927):8–9. Reprinted in *Moody Bible Institute Monthly* 28 (September 1927):16.

"Statement on Proposed Reorganization of Princeton Seminary." *New York Evening Post* (Sept. 29, 1927).

The Attack Upon Princeton Seminary: A Plea for Fair Play. Princeton: J. Gresham Machen.

1928

"Dr. Machen's Pamphlet." *Presbyterian Banner* 114 (Jan. 19, 1928):5–6.

"The Virgin Birth, the Auburn Affirmation, and the Presbyterian Advance." *P* 98 (Feb. 9, 1928):12. A letter refused by the *Presbyterian Advance.*

Princeton Seminary Control (letter to editor). *New York Herald Tribune* (Feb. 12, 1928):8, col. 7.

"The Action of the Presbytery of New Brunswick." *P* 98 (Mar. 1, 1928):13–15,16.

"The Gist of the Princeton Question." *P* 98 (May 17, 1928):16.

"Forty Years of New Testament Research." *Union Seminary Review* (Richmond) 40:1–12.

"Is the Bible Right About Jesus? I. What the Bible Teaches About Jesus." *The Evangelical Student* 3 (October 1928):4–11.

"What Is Christianity?" *The Gospel Witness* 7:521. (Address given at Des Moines University, December 10, 1928.)

"Why Overture C Should Be Rejected by the Presbyteries." *P* 98 (Dec. 27, 1928):8–9.

Review: *Paul the Man: His Life, His Message, and His Ministry* (Clarence Edward Macartney). *PTR* 26:471–72.

1929

WHAT IS FAITH? (Korean), trans. by Floyd E. Hamilton. The Christian Literature Society of Korea.

"Is the Bible Right About Jesus? II. The Witness of Paul." *The Evangelical Student* 3 (January 1929):7–15.

"The Good Fight of Faith." *P* 99 (Mar. 28, 1929):6–10. Reprinted in *The Fundamentalist Journal* 2:3 (March 1983):34–36,45.

The Good Fight of Faith: A Sermon. Reprinted from *P* 99 (Mar. 28, 1929):6–10.

"Is the Bible Right About Jesus? III. The Witness of the Gospels." *The Evangelical Student* 3 (April 1929):11–20.

"Ministers & Modernism: Pacifists and Protagonists." *The Standard Bearer* (Belfast, Ireland) 5 (May 1929):53. Excerpts from "The Good Fight of Faith." *P* 99 (Mar. 28, 1929):6–10.

"Fight the Good Fight of Faith" (a sermon preached in the Chapel of Princeton Theological Seminary on Sunday morning, March 10, 1929, a stenographic report). *Presbyterian Standard* 70 (May 1, 1929):4,12–13.

"Dr. Machen's Protest." *P* 99 (June 6, 1929):29.

"Speech of J. Gresham Machen at the 141st General Assembly in the Debate Concerning Princeton Seminary." *P* 99 (June 13, 1929):13.

Westminster Theological Seminary: Its Purpose and Plan. Print off from *P* 99 (Oct. 10, 1929):6–9.

"Westminster Theological Seminary: Its Purpose and Plan." *P* 99 (Oct. 10, 1929):6–9.

1930

THE VIRGIN BIRTH OF CHRIST. New York: Harper. (Also London: Marshall, Morgan & Scott). Reprinted by Attic Press, 1958 and Baker Book House, 1967.

"A Future for Calvinism in the Presbyterian Church?" *The Banner* 65:320,333.

"The Present Situation in the Presbyterian Church." *CT* 1 (May 1930):5–7.

Copyright Bill (letter to editor). *New York Herald Tribune* (Dec. 28, 1930):28, cols. 4–5.

"Dr. Machen Surveys Dr. Speer's New Book" (Review of Robert E. Speer, *Some Living Issues*). *CT* 1 (October 1930):9–11,15.

1931

"Notes on Biblical Exposition; I. A Man Who Could Say 'No'." *CT* 1 (January 1931):9–11.

"Comment on the Question 'Has Inspiration Ceased?' " *SST* 73 (Jan. 24, 1931):40.

"Notes on Biblical Exposition; II. The Witness of Paul." *CT* 1 (February 1931):10–11,15.

"The Character of Mary, the Mother of Our Lord." *The Bible To-day* (March 1931):125–37. (Selections from *The Virgin Birth.*)

"Christianity and Liberty: A Challenge to the 'Modern Mind'." *Forum and Century* 85:162–66.

"Notes on Biblical Exposition; III. Plain Speaking in a Time of Peril." *CT* 1 (March 1931):12–14.

"Notes on Biblical Exposition; IV. The Freedom of the Christian Man." *CT* 1 (April 1931):8–9,18.

"Notes on Biblical Exposition; V. The Gospel of Christ." *CT* 2 (May 1931):6–9,17.

"Notes on Biblical Exposition; VI. The Message and the Messenger." *CT* 2 (June 1931):8–10,12.

"Notes on Biblical Exposition; VII. How Paul Received the Gospel." *CT* 2 (July 1931):5–7.

"Notes on Biblical Exposition; VIII. The Call of God." *CT* 2 (August 1931):6–8.

"Notes on Biblical Exposition; IX. After the Conversion." *CT* 2 (September 1931):4–6.

"Notes on Biblical Exposition; X. Paul and the Jerusalem Church." *CT* 2 (October 1931):12–14,18.

"Facing the Facts Before God." *The Evangelical Student* 6 (October 1931):6-10.

"Skyscrapers and Cathedrals." *McCalls* 59 (October 1931):23,118.

"Notes on Biblical Exposition; XI. Harmony of Acts and Galatians." *CT* 2 (November 1931):9-11.

"The Truth About the Presbyterian Church: I. Modernism in the Judicial Commission." *CT* 2 (November 1931):5-6.

"Notes on Biblical Exposition; XII. Paul at Jerusalem." *CT* 2 (December 1931):15-17.

"The Truth About the Presbyterian Church: II. Secrecy in Councils and Courts." *CT* 2 (December 1931):6-9.

"The Virgin Birth of Our Lord." *Revelation* 1:399.

Review: *The Historic Jesus*. (James Mackinnon). *EQ* 3:312-21.

Review: *Die Synoptischen Evangelien* (H. J. Holtzmann). *EQ* 3:312-21.

Review: *Lexicon Novi Testamenti* (Francisco Zorell). *American Journal of Philology* 52:383-86.

1932

THE VIRGIN BIRTH OF CHRIST (2nd ed.). New York: Harper & Brothers.

"Christianity in Conflict," in *Contemporary American Theology*, Vol. I, ed. by Vergilius Ferm. New York: Round Table Press, pp. 245-74. Reprinted with parts omitted in *PG* 3 (1937):165-68.

"Notes on Biblical Exposition; XIII. False Brethren and a True Gospel." *CT* 2 (January 1932):9-11.

"The Truth About the Presbyterian Church; III. The Present Situation." *CT* 2 (January 1932):4-6,12-13.

"The Truth About the Presbyterian Church." *Christian Fundamentalist* 5 (January 1932):257-59.

"Notes on Biblical Exposition; XIV. Paul's Commission and Its Importance to Us." *CT* 2 (February 1932):11-14.

"Notes on Biblical Exposition; XV. 'The Apostolic Decree'." *CT* 2 (March 1932):6-9,19.

"Notes on Biblical Exposition; XVI. The Right Hand of Fellowship." *CT* 2 (April 1932):12-14.

"Notes on Biblical Exposition; XVII. Consequences Versus Truth." *CT* 3 (May 1932):10-12.

"Notes on Biblical Exposition; XVIII. The Power of Example." *CT* 3 (June 1932):8-9.

The Importance of Christian Scholarship. London: The Bible League. Reprinted in *CB* 34 (July 3, 1964):5,7; (July 10):3,8; (July 17):3; (July 24):3,7.

"Notes on Biblical Exposition; XIX. Justification by Faith." *CT* 3 (July 1932):8-9

"Notes on Biblical Exposition; XX. The Peril of Inconsistency." *CT* 3 (August 1932):10–12.
"Notes on Biblical Exposition; XXI. The New Life." *CT* 3 (September 1932):8–10.
"Notes on Biblical Exposition; XXII. The Cross of Christ." *CT* 3 (October 1932):6–7.
"The Importance of Christian Scholarship for Evangelism: An Address Delivered in London Before the Bible League, June 17, 1932." *CT* 3 (November 1932):8–10.
"Notes on Biblical Exposition; XXIII. The Spirit of God." *CT* 3 (December 1932):12–13,17.

1933

"The Responsibility of the Church in Our New Age." *Annals of the American Academy of Political and Social Science* 165:38–47. Reprinted as a pamphlet— Philadelphia: American Academy of Political and Social Science. Also reprinted *PG* 36:3–5,10–13; 45 (January 1976):3,10–12; (February 1976):5,13–14.
"Notes on Biblical Exposition; XXIV. The Authority of the Bible." *CT* 3 (January 1933):10–11.
"Notes on Biblical Exposition; XXV. The Atonement." *CT* 3 (February 1933):7–8.
"What Is the League of Evangelical Students?" *Moody Bible Institute Monthly* 53 (March 1933):308–9.
Modernism and the Board of Foreign Missions of the Presbyterian Church in the U.S.A.; Argument of J. Gresham Machen in Support of an Overture Introduced in the Presbytery of New Brunswick at Its Meeting on January 24, 1933, and Made the Order of the Day for the Meeting April 11, 1933. Philadelphia: J. Gresham Machen.
What Bible-Believing Christians Should do at the General Assembly of 1933: Informal Memorandum. Philadelphia: Unpublished, May 19, 1933.
"The Christian View of Missions." *Revelation* 3:203–4,227.
"Three Observations About the Assembly." *CT* 4 (June 1933):5–7.
Boycotting by the N.R.A. (letter to editor). *New York Herald Tribune* (Aug. 25, 1933):12.
"New Light on the Bible: Important Discoveries of Biblical Manuscripts." *CT* 4 (September 1933):4–5,12–13.
Against Fingerprinting (letter to editor). *NYT* (Sept. 6, 1933):20.
Compulsory Registration (letter to editor). *NYT* (Sept. 13, 1933):18.
"The Necessity of the Christian School," in *Forward in Faith* (Convention Book, Year Book). Chicago: National Union of Christian Schools, pp. 5–30. Reprinted as a pamphlet— Chicago, 1934. (Excerpted in *Renewal* 8 [March 17, 1982]:4–5.)

"Freedom in the Presbyterian Church: Dr. Machen's Protest in the Pres-bytery of New Brunswick." CT 4 (October 1933):5,8.

Opposing the Child Labor Amendment (letter to editor). Public Ledger (Philadelphia, PA) (Nov. 4, 1933):10.

"The New Presbyterian Hymnal." CT 4 (December 1933):5-6,8-9.

"Why We Believe in the Virgin Birth." SST 75:775-76.

Against the Child Labor Amendment (letter to editor). Public Ledger (Philadelphia, PA) (Dec. 14, 1933):14.

Review: "Dr. Robert Speer and His Latest Book" (Review of The Finality of Jesus Christ). CT 4 (May 1933):15-16,22-26.

Review: Scientific Theory and Religion: The World Described by Science and Its Spiritual Interpretation (Ernest William Barnes). The Evening Sun (Baltimore, MD) (July 29, 1933):4.

1934

"The Christian School the Hope of America," in The Christian School the Out-Flowering of Faith (Convention Papers). Chicago: National Union of Christian Schools, pp. 1-19. Reprinted as a pamphlet— Chicago, 1934.

"The Final Form of the Plan of Union." CT 4 (January 1934):5,14.

"The Resurrection and the Modern Church." Boston Evening Transcript, March 31, 1934:(Part 4),1-2.

"Stop, Look, Listen: Why the Plan of Organic Union Should Be Op-posed." CT 4 (April 1934):4-7.

"Servants of God or Servants of Men: Address to the Graduating Class at the Commencement of Westminster Theological Seminary, Phil-adelphia, Tuesday Evening, May 8, 1934." CT 5 (May 1934):9-10.

"Mountains and Why We Love Them." CT 5 (August 1934):66-69. Reprinted as a pamphlet.

"Impressions of West Pittston." CT 5:149-50.

"Westminster Seminary Begins Sixth Year: Dr. Machen's Address to New Students." CT 5:148.

1935

"Designation of Gifts — A Snare to Christian People." IBB 1 (January 1935):5-7.

"A Debate About the Child Labor Amendment." The Banner 70 (Jan. 4, 1935):15-17.

"Sham Orthodoxy Versus Real Orthodoxy: The Present Conflict in the Presbyterian Church in the U.S.A." IBB 1 (February 1935):11-13.

"Dr. Machen's Statement." IBB 1 (March 1935):5.

Statement to the Special Committee of the Presbytery of New Brunswick in the Presbyterian Church in the U.S.A. which was Appointed by the Presbytery . . . to Confer Further with Dr. Machen with Respect to His

Relationship with the Independent Board for Presbyterian Foreign Missions . . . Philadelphia: By the Author.

Letter on the Address of Charles G. Trumbull, "Betrayal of the Faith, in Our Foreign Mission Board and in the Field" (*SST* 77:195–99). *SST* 77:179.

"Dr. Machen's Profession of Faith." *IBB* 1 (April 1935):5.

"What May Be Learned from the 1935 General Assembly of the Presbyterian Church in the U.S.A." *IBB* 1 (June 1935):5–10.

"Darkness and Light." *IBB* 1 (September 1935):7–9.

"Introduction" [to the *PG*]. *PG* 1:4. Reprinted in *PG* 14:274,285; excerpted in *PG* 39:61.

"What Should Be Done by Christian People Who Are in a Modernist Church?" *PG* 1:22.

"A Cincinnati Broadcast: Excerpts from a Broadcast over Station WLW, Cincinnati, Ohio, Sunday, May 26, 1935." *IBB* 1 (November 1935): 7–10.

"What is 'Orthodoxy'?" *PG* 1:38. Reprinted in *PG* 28:82.

"The Purpose of the Covenant Union." *PG* 1:54.

"The Second Part of the Ordination Pledge." *PG* 1:70.

"The League of Evangelical Students." *PG* 1:86.

1936

THE CHRISTIAN FAITH IN THE MODERN WORLD. New York: Macmillan Co. (Also London: Hodder and Stoughton.) Reprinted by Eerdmans, 1947.

"Dr. Barnhouse on Foreign Missions." *IBB* 2 (January 1936):7–10.

"What Is Wrong with 'Teacher-Oath' Bills?" *PG* 1:106.

"A Precious Fragment of the Gospel According to John." *PG* 1:122. Reprinted in *The Evangelical Student* 11 (April 1936):6–7.

"What Shall We Think of Kagawa?" *PG* 1:138.

"More About Kagawa." *PG* 1:158.

"Can Christian Men Enter the Ministry in the Presbyterian Church in the U.S.A.?" *PG* 1:174.

"Secrecy and Misrepresentation in a General Assembly's Commission and in Philadelphia Presbytery." *PG* 1:194. Reprinted as a pamphlet by the Presbyterian Guardian.

"The Press Shall be Asked to Cooperate." *PG* 2:2.

"Dr. Machen Replies" [to a letter of Warren R. Ward]. *PG* 2:15–16. Reprinted as a pamphlet by the Presbyterian Guardian.

"Are We Schismatics?" *PG* 2:22.

"An Apostate Church?" *PG* 2:42.

"Will Christianity Survive?" *PG* 2:66.

"What Should True Presbyterians Do at the 1936 General Assembly?" *PG* 2:68–72.

"The Need of Regeneration." *PG* 2:90.

"The Church of God": A Sermon Preached at the Concluding Service of the First General Assembly of the Presbyterian Church of America . . . Philadelphia: Presbyterian Guardian Co.

"A True Presbyterian Church At Last." *PG* 2:110. Reprinted in *PG* 15:168–69 and 45 (June 1976):2.

"Evangelism." *PG* 2:146.

"The Church of God." *PG* 2:152–56.

"The Christian Reformed Church." *PG* 2:170.

"The Benefits of Walking." *PG* 2:190.

"Biblical Examples, Good and Bad." *PG* 2:206.

"A Man for the Hour." *PG* 2:221–22.

"Why the Presbyterian Guardian?" *PG* 2:245–46. Reprinted in *PG* 14:274,285.

"A Step to Avoid." *PG* 3:1–2.

"A Hard Church to Get Out Of." *PG* 3:2.

"Premillennialism." *PG* 3:21.

Constraining Love. Philadelphia: The Presbyterian Guardian Publishing Co.

"The Second General Assembly of the Presbyterian Church of America." *PG* 3:41–45,69–71.

"The Presbytery of California and the 'Christian Beacon'." *PG* 3:71.

"The Need of Edification." *PG* 3:93–94. Reprinted as pamphlet with the title *A Message from Dr. J. Gresham Machen.* Committee on Christian Education of the Orthodox Presbyterian Church, n.d.

"Constraining Love: A Sermon Preached on the Opening Day of the Second General Assembly of the Presbyterian Church of America . . ." *PG* 3:98–102.

"The So-Called 'Child Labor Amendment'." *PG* 3:113–14.

1937

THE CHRISTIAN VIEW OF MAN. New York: Macmillan Co. Reprinted by Eerdmans, 1947 and Banner of Truth Trust, 1965.

"Machen's Reasons for 'Disobedience'." *CB* 1 (Jan. 7, 1937):1–2. Reprinted in *CB* 9 (Apr. 6, 1944):5.

"Shall We Have Christian Schools?" *PG* 3:133–34. Reprinted in *PG* 41:50–51.

"Christianity in Conflict: Machen Autobiography." *CB* 1 (Jan. 21, 1937):1–2,4–5,8; (Jan. 28, 1937):1–2,4,8; (Feb. 4, 1937):1–2,4,6,8. Reprinted from *Contemporary American Theology,* Vol. I. New York: Round Table Press, 1932, pp. 245–74.

"An Interview with Dr. Machen on the National Preaching Mission." *PG* 3:171–72.

"Christianity in Conflict." *PG* 3:165–68. Reprinted with parts omitted from *Contemporary American Theology*, Vol. I. New York: Round Table Press, 1932, pp. 245–74.

"The Separateness of the Church." *The Evangelical Student* 12 (April 1937):6–12.

1939

A Message from Dr. J. Gresham Machen. Philadelphia: Committee on Christian Education of the Orthodox Presbyterian Church [1939–40]. Reprinted from *PG* 3 (1936):93–94.

1940

"The Progress of Christian Doctrine." *PG* 7:1–2,8–9.

"The Creeds and Doctrinal Advance." *PG* 7:35–38. Reprinted in *PG* 34:60–63.

"God, Man and Salvation." *PG* 7:67–69.

"Christ as Prophet, Priest and King." *PG* 7:104–6.

"What Is a Prophet?" *PG* 7:131–33.

"Prophecy and the Gospel." *PG* 7:165–67.

"The Teaching of Jesus." *PG* 8:1–2,10–12.

"Prophet and Priest." *PG* 8:37–39.

"Christ Our Redeemer." *PG* 8:67–69.

"The Doctrine of the Atonement." *PG* 8:102–4.

"The Active Obedience of Christ." *PG* 8:131–33.

"The Issue in the Church." *PG* 8:161–62,168–69.

1942

Is the Bible Right About Jesus? Philadelphia: Committee on Christian Education, The Orthodox Presbyterian Church [1942–43].

1943

"Jesus Only!" *PG* 12:337–38,349–52.

1945

"The Bible's View of the Atonement." *PG* 14:3–5.

"God Transcendent." *PG* 14:51–52.

"The Living Saviour." *PG* 14:83–84,95–96.

"The Fear of God." *PG* 14:200–201.

"Why the Presbyterian Guardian?" *PG* 14:274,285.

"Sin's Wages and God's Gift." *PG* 14:295–96.

"Isaiah's Scorn of Idolatry." *PG* 14:357–58.

1946
CHRISTIANITY AND LIBERALISM. Grand Rapids: Eerdmans.
WHAT IS FAITH? Grand Rapids: Eerdmans.
"A True Presbyterian Church at Last." *PG* 15:168–69.

1947
THE CHRISTIAN FAITH IN THE MODERN WORLD. Grand Rapids: Eerdmans.
THE CHRISTIAN VIEW OF MAN. Grand Rapids: Eerdmans.
"Machen's Explanation of His Position" (Explanation of My Position Why I Cannot Obey Order of G.A.). *CB* 12 (Oct. 23, 1947):2–3.

1949
GOD TRANSCENDENT, AND OTHER SERMONS, ed. Ned B. Stonehouse. Grand Rapids: Eerdmans. Reprinted by Banner of Truth Trust, 1982.

1950
CHRISTIANITY AND LIBERALISM (Chinese), trans. by Samuel E. Boyle, Charles Chao and Ka Lai Chao. Hong Kong: The Reformation Translation Fellowship.

1951
WHAT IS CHRISTIANITY? AND OTHER ADDRESSES, ed. by Ned B. Stonehouse. Grand Rapids: Eerdmans.

1955
CHRISTIANITY AND LIBERALISM (Korean), trans. by Cho Dong Jin. Seoul: Un Chong Mun Wha Hyup Hoe.
"The Importance of Christian Scholarship." *Blue Banner Faith and Life* 10 (January–March 1955):11–14,60–65,110–13.

1958
THE ORIGIN OF PAUL'S RELIGION (Japanese). Sendai: Seisho Tosho Kankokai.
THE VIRGIN BIRTH OF CHRIST. Greenwood, SC: Attic Press. Reprint of 1930 edition.
"Dr. Machen's Profession of Faith." *Biblical Missions* 24:2,34. Reprinted from *IBB* 1 (April 1935):5.

1959
NEW TESTAMENT GREEK FOR BEGINNERS (Chinese), trans. by Jonathan J. H. Lu and Alice E. Taylor. Kaohsiung, Taiwan: Holy Light Bible Seminary.
"What Is Orthodoxy?" *PG* 28:82. Reprinted from *PG* 1:38.

1960

A *Study Guide to the Epistle of Paul to the Galatians 1:1 to 4:4*. Philadelphia.

1961

"The Good Fight of Faith," in *Valiant for the Truth*, ed. by David Otis Fuller. Philadelphia and New York: J. B. Lippincott, pp. 448–55.

1962

NEW TESTAMENT GREEK: A TRANSLATION AND ADAPTATION OF J. G. MACHEN'S NEW TESTAMENT GREEK FOR BEGINNERS (Korean), by Chang Whan Park. Seoul: Christian Literature Society of Korea.

Letter to Clarence E. Macartney, May 9, 1936 in Article, "Macartney on Machen," by Ned B. Stonehouse. *PG* 31:4–5.

1964

"History and Faith." *Christianity Today* 8 (Sept. 11, 1964): 1109–13.

"Christian Faith in the Modern World." *Christianity Today* 9 (Dec. 4, 1964):243. Excerpted from *Christian Faith in the Modern World*.

"How May God Be Known?" *Christianity Today* 9 (Dec. 18, 1964):295. Excerpted from *Christian Faith in the Modern World*.

1965

THE CHRISTIAN VIEW OF MAN. London: The Banner of Truth Trust. Reprint of 1937 edition.

THE ORIGIN OF PAUL'S RELIGION. Grand Rapids: Eerdmans.

"Has God Spoken?" *Christianity Today* 9 (Jan. 1, 1965):343. Excerpted from *Christian Faith in the Modern World*.

"God, the Creator." *Christianity Today* 9 (Jan. 15, 1965):393. Excerpted from *Christian Faith in the Modern World*.

"The Triune God." *Christianity Today* 9 (Jan. 29, 1965):452. Excerpted from *Christian Faith in the Modern World*.

"The Deity of Christ." *Christianity Today* 9 (Feb. 12, 1965):512. Excerpted from *Christian Faith in the Modern World*.

"The Supernatural Christ." *Christianity Today* 9 (Feb. 26, 1965):567. Excerpted from *Christian Faith in the Modern World*.

"The Holy Spirit." *Christianity Today* 9 (Mar. 12, 1965):623. Excerpted from *Christian Faith in the Modern World*.

"Is the Bible the Word of God?" *Christianity Today* 9 (Mar. 25, 1965):675. Excerpted from *Christian Faith in the Modern World*.

"The Creeds and Doctrinal Advance." *PG* 34:60–63.

"Did Christ Rise from the Dead?" *Christianity Today* 9 (Apr. 9, 1965):727. Excerpted from *Christian Faith in the Modern World*.

"The Separateness of the Church." *CB* 30 (June 10, 1965):2–3.

"A Plea for Honesty." *PJ* 24 (Sept. 8, 1965):11,19. Reprinted from *PG* 8 (Dec. 10, 1940):161–62,168–69.
"No Room for Despair." *The Banner of Truth*   39 (November 1965):24.

1966
"Creeds Old and New." *PJ* 24 (Feb. 9, 1966):13,24.

1967
THE VIRGIN BIRTH OF CHRIST. Grand Rapids: Baker Books.
"Machen's Challenge to Prospective Ministers." *Torch and Trumpet* 17 (January 1967):10.
"The Responsibility of the Church in Our New Age." *PG* 36:3–5, 10–13.
"Not an Easy Life." *PJ* 25 (Jan. 18, 1967):13,19. Reprinted in *PJ* 36 (May 4, 1977):12.

1968
"The Separateness of the Church." *CB* 33 (Mar. 28, 1968):7–8.

1969
Christianity and Culture. London: Banner of Truth Trust (Foreword by Francis A. Schaeffer). Reprinted from *The Banner of Truth*   69 (June 1969):15–24. Originally published in *PTR* 11 (January 1913):1–15.
El hombre: la enseñanza Bíblica sobre el hombre. Lima, Peru: El Estandarte de la Verdad.
"History and Faith," in *Issues in American Protestantism: A Documentary History from the Puritans to the Present,* comp. by Robert L. Ferm. Garden City, NY: Anchor Books, pp. 262–76. Reprinted by Peter Smith, 1976. Originally printed in *PTR* 13 (1915):337–51.
"For Whom Christ Died." *Torch and Trumpet* 19 (March 1969):5–6. Excerpted from the sermon "Constraining Love," *PG* 3 (1936):98–102.
"The Importance of Christian Scholarship" [Part 1]. *CB* 34 (July 3, 1969):5,7.
"The Importance of Christian Scholarship" [Part 2]. *CB* 34 (July 10, 1969):3,8.
"The Importance of Christian Scholarship" [Part 3]. *CB* 34 (July 17, 1969):3.
"The Importance of Christian Scholarship" [Part 4]. *CB* 34 (July 24, 1969):3,7.

1970
"The Separateness of the Church." *CB* 35 (Apr. 12, 1970):5,7.
"Christian View of Missions." *The Banner of Truth*   84 (September 1970):1–5.

"The Creeds and Doctrinal Advance." *The Banner of Truth* 86 (November 1970):22. Reprinted from *God Transcendent and Other Sermons* (1949).

1972
MACHEN'S NOTES ON GALATIANS, AND OTHER AIDS TO THE INTERPRETATION OF THE EPISTLE TO THE GALATIANS, FROM THE WRITINGS OF J. GRESHAM MACHEN, ed. by John H. Skilton. Philadelphia: Presbyterian and Reformed.
"The Minister and His Greek Testament." *The Banner of Truth* 103 (April 1972):21–23.
"Shall We Have Christian Schools?" PG 41:50–51.

1973
"The Creeds and Doctrinal Advance," in *Scripture and Confession: A Book About Confessions Old and New,* ed. by John H. Skilton. Nutley, NJ: Presbyterian and Reformed, pp. 149–57. Reprinted from *God Transcendent and Other Selected Sermons* (1949).
"The Separateness of the Church." PG 42:116–19.

1974
"The Minister and His Greek Testament," in *Studying the New Testament Today (The New Testament Student, 1),* ed. by John H. Skilton. Phillipsburg, NJ: Presbyterian and Reformed, pp. 152–55. Reprinted from *P* 88 (Feb. 7, 1918).
"Westminster Theological Seminary: Its Purpose and Plan," in *Studying the New Testament Today (New Testament Student, 1),* ed. by John H. Skilton. Phillipsburg, NJ: Presbyterian and Reformed, pp. 161–69. Address given at the opening of Westminster Theological Seminary, Sept. 25, 1929.
"Did Christ Rise from the Dead?" *Decision* 15 (April 1973):3. Excerpted from *Christian Faith in the Modern World.*

1975
"The Virgin Birth of Christ," in *The New Testament Student at Work (New Testament Student, 2),* ed. by John H. Skilton. Phillipsburg, NJ: Presbyterian and Reformed, pp. 76–97. Originally published in *The Bible To-day* 19 (1924–25):75–79,111–15; reprinted in *What is Christianity? and Other Addresses* (1951).

1976
THE NEW TESTAMENT: AN INTRODUCTION TO ITS LITERATURE AND HISTORY, ed. by W. John Cook. Edinburgh: Banner of Truth Trust.

"History and Faith," in *Issues in American Protestantism: A Documentary History from the Puritans to the Present*, comp. by Robert L. Ferm. Gloucester, MA: Peter Smith, pp. 262–76.

"The Resurrection of Christ," in *New Testament Student and Theology (New Testament Student, 3)*, ed. by John H. Skilton. Phillipsburg, NJ: Presbyterian and Reformed, pp. 87–101. Reprinted from *What is Christianity?* (1951).

"The Responsibility of the Church in Our New Age." PG 45 (January 1976):3,10–12; (February 1976):5,13–14.

"A True Presbyterian Church at Last." PG 45 (June 1976):2.

"The Cross and the Resurrection as the Foundation of Apostolic Preaching." *The Banner of Truth* 159 (November 1976):24–28. Reprinted from *The New Testament: An Introduction to Its Literature and History* (1976).

1977

"Not an Easy Life." PJ 36 (May 4, 1977):12. Reprinted from PJ 25 (Jan. 18, 1967):13,19. Also printed in *Outlook* 27 (July 1977):4–5.

"Apostolic Preaching." PJ 36 (Sept. 14, 1977):7–9. Excerpted from *The New Testament: An Introduction to Its Literature and History* (1976).

"The Importance of Christian Scholarship." CB 42 (Nov. 24, 1977):3,7; (Dec. 22, 1977):3,7; (Dec. 29, 1977):3,7.

1978

"Is the Bible the Word of God?" in *The New Testament Student and Bible Translation (New Testament Student, 4)*, ed. by John H. Skilton. Phillipsburg, NJ: Presbyterian and Reformed, pp. 59–67. Reprinted from *Christian Faith in the Modern World*.

1981

"My Idea of God." *The Bulletin of Westminster Theological Seminary* (PA) 20:3 (Summer 1981):1–3. Reprinted from *Woman's Home Companion* 52 (December 1925):15,124.

"Has God Spoken?" in *Masterpieces from World Literature* Vol. 2, ed. by Jan Anderson. Pensacola, FL: A Beka Book Publication, pp. 456–59. Excerpted from *Christian Faith in the Modern World*.

"The Present Emergency." PJ 40 (Nov. 11, 1981):9–11. Reprinted from *Christian Faith in the Modern World*.

1982

GOD TRANSCENDENT, ed. by Ned B. Stonehouse. Edinburgh: Banner of Truth Trust.

"All Nature Sings," in *Speech Resource Book*, ed. by Charlene Monk. Pensacola, FL: A Beka Book Publication, p. 99. Excerpted from *Christian Faith in the Modern World*.

"The Necessity of the Christian School." *Renewal* 8 (Mar. 17, 1982):4–5. Excerpted from "The Necessity of the Christian School." Convention Papers of the National Union of Christian Schools, 1933.

1983

"The Fear of God." *The Banner of Truth* 232 (January 1983):21–24. Excerpted from *God Transcendent* (1982).

"The Good Fight of Faith." *Fundamentalist Journal* 2:34–36,45. Reprinted from *P* 99 (Mar. 28, 1929):6–10.

"The Importance of Christian Scholarship." *Bible League Quarterly* 335:183–86.

1984

"The Importance of Christian Scholarship (2)." *Bible League Quarterly* 337:218–23.

"The Importance of Christian Scholarship (3)." *Bible League Quarterly* 338:246–50.

Contributors

VICTOR B. ATALLAH is an Orthodox Presbyterian minister and missionary in the Middle East.

GREG L. BAHNSEN, Ph.D., is an Orthodox Presbyterian pastor in Placentia, California.

EDMUND P. CLOWNEY, S.T.M., is a Presbyterian Church in America minister and teacher-in-residence at Trinity PCA, Charlottesville, Virginia.

LEONARD J. COPPES, Th.D., is an Orthodox Presbyterian pastor in Denver, Colorado.

D. CLAIR DAVIS, Dr. Theol., is professor of church history at Westminster Theological Seminary, Philadelphia, Pennsylvania, and an Orthodox Presbyterian pastor.

CHARLES G. DENNISON, M.A., is an Orthodox Presbyterian pastor in Sewickley, Pennsylvania, and historian of the Orthodox Presbyterian Church.

JAMES T. DENNISON, JR., Th.M., is a minister in the Presbyterian Church in America and librarian at Westminster Theological Seminary, Escondido, California.

LAWRENCE EYRES is an Orthodox Presbyterian pastor in Winner, South Dakota.

RICHARD B. GAFFIN, JR., Th.D., is professor of New Testament at Westminster Theological Seminary, Philadelphia, Pennsylvania, and an Orthodox Presbyterian minister.

JOHN P. GALBRAITH is an Orthodox Presbyterian minister and chairman of the Orthodox Presbyterian Committee on Ecumenicity and Interchurch Relations.

RICHARD C. GAMBLE, Dr. Theol., is associate professor of church history at Westminster Theological Seminary, Philadelphia, Pennsylvania, and a minister in the Orthodox Presbyterian Church.

487

THOMAS M. GREGORY, Ph.D., is professor of philosophy at West-minster College, New Wilmington, Pennsylvania, and a Presbyterian Church in America minister.

ALLEN C. GUELZO, Ph.D., is assistant professor of church history at Reformed Episcopal Seminary, Philadelphia, Pennsylvania, and a Reformed Episcopal minister.

MICHAEL A. HAKKENBERG is a member of the Christian Reformed Church and a Ph.D. candidate at the University of California at Berkeley.

PAUL H. HEIDEBRECHT is an Orthodox Presbyterian elder in Whea-ton, Illinois, and a Ph.D. candidate at the University of Chicago.

EDWARD L. KELLOGG is a retired Orthodox Presbyterian minister living in Leesburg, Virginia.

DAVID W. KIESTER is an Orthodox Presbyterian minister in Edinburg, Pennsylvania.

GEORGE W. KNIGHT, III, Th.D., is professor of New Testament at Covenant Theological Seminary, St. Louis, Missouri, and a minister in the Presbyterian Church in America.

PETER A. LILLBACK, Ph.D., is an Orthodox Presbyterian pastor in Oxford, Pennsylvania.

SAMUEL T. LOGAN, JR., Ph.D., is professor of church history at Westminster Theological Seminary, Philadelphia, Pennsylvania, and an Orthodox Presbyterian minister.

GEORGE M. MARSDEN, Ph.D., is professor of history at Calvin Col-lege, Grand Rapids, Michigan, and a member of the Christian Re-formed Church.

GRACE MULLEN, M.S., is a member of the Orthodox Presbyterian Church and archivist in the library at Westminster Theological Sem-inary, Philadelphia, Pennsylvania.

DAVID L. NEILANDS is an Orthodox Presbyterian elder in Berkeley, California.

MARK A. NOLL, Ph.D., is professor of history at Wheaton College, Wheaton, Illinois, and an Orthodox Presbyterian elder.

JAMES R. PAYTON, JR., Ph.D., is academic dean at Redeemer College, Hamilton, Ontario, and a member of the Christian Reformed Church.

JAMES D. PHILLIPS is an Orthodox Presbyterian elder in Orlando, Florida.

LENDALL H. SMITH is an Orthodox Presbyterian minister and missionary in Taiwan.

WAYNE R. SPEAR, Ph.D., is professor of systematic theology at Reformed Presbyterian Seminary, Pittsburgh, Pennsylvania, and a minister in the Reformed Presbyterian Church of North America.

LAURENCE N. VAIL, Th.M., is an Orthodox Presbyterian pastor in Vineland, New Jersey, and former general secretary of the Orthodox Presbyterian Committee on Foreign Missions.

JOHN R. WIERS is an Orthodox Presbyterian minister and a Ph.D. candidate at the University of Iowa.